PLANNING AND SCHEDULING

USING

MICROSOFT® PROJECT 2010

BY

PAUL EASTWOOD HARRIS

DISCLAIMER

The information contained in this book is, to the best of the author's knowledge, true and correct. The author has made every effort to ensure accuracy of this publication, but cannot be held responsible for any loss or damage arising from any information in this book.

AUTHOR AND PUBLISHER

Paul E Harris
Eastwood Harris Pty Ltd
PO Box 4032
Doncaster Heights 3109
Victoria
Australia
harrispe@eh.com.au
http://www.eh.com.au
Tel: +61 (0)4 1118 7701
Fax: +61 (0)3 9846 7700

Please send any comments on this publication to the author.

ISBN 978-1-921059-35-3 B5 Paperback
ISBN 978-1-921059-36-0 A4 Spiral Bound
ISBN 978-1-921059-48-3 A4 eBook

1 January 2010

SUMMARY

The book was written so it may be used as:

- A training manual for a two-day training course, or
- A self-teach book, or
- A reference manual.

The screen shots for the book are mainly taken from Microsoft Project Professional 2010 but the book may also be used to learn Microsoft Office Project Standard 2010.

The book has been written to be used as the basis of a two-day training course and includes exercises for the students to complete at the end of each chapter. Unlike many training publications, this course book may then be used by the students as a reference book.

This publication is ideal for people who would like to quickly gain an understanding of how the software operates and how the software differs from Oracle Primavera Project Manager, P3, SureTrak and Asta Powerproject thus making it ideal for people who wish to convert from these products.

CUSTOMIZATION FOR TRAINING COURSES

Training organizations or companies that wish to conduct their own training may have the book tailored to suit their requirements. This may be achieved by removing, reordering or adding content to the book and by writing their own exercises. This book is available in both A4 spiral bound, which lies flat on the desk for training and/or self–teaching, and in B5 paperback as a reference manual. Please contact the author to discuss this service.

AUTHOR'S COMMENT

As a professional project planner and scheduler I have used a number of planning and scheduling software packages for the management of a range of project types and sizes.

The first books I published were user guides/training manuals for Primavera SureTrak and P3 users. These were well received by professional project managers and schedulers, so I decided to turn my attention to Microsoft Project 2000, 2002, 2003, 2007 and now Microsoft Office Project 2010. This book follows the same proven layout of my previous books. I trust this book will assist you in understanding how to use Microsoft Project on your projects. Please contact me if you have any comments on this book.

SPECIAL THANKS

I would like to thank Martin Vaughn for reviewing my draft book and making valuable comments that I have used to improve the quality of this publication.

CURRENT BOOKS PUBLISHED BY EASTWOOD HARRIS

Project Planning & Control Using Primavera® P6™
For all industries including Versions 4 to 7
ISBN 978-1-921059-33-9 - B5 – Perfect, ISBN 978-1-921059-34-6 - A4 - Spiral

Planning & Control Using Microsoft® Project and PRINCE2 ™
Updated for PRINCE2 ™ 2009 and Microsoft® Office Project 2010
ISBN 1-921059-37-0 - B5 - Perfect, ISBN 1-921059-38-9- A4 - Spiral

Planning and Control Using Microsoft® Project 2010 and *PMBOK® Guide* Fourth Edition
ISBN 1-921059-39-7 - B5 – Perfect, ISBN 1-921059-40-0 - A4 - Spiral

99 Tricks and Traps for Microsoft® Office Project 2010
ISBN 978-1-921059-41-4 - 8" x 6" - Perfect

Planning & Control Using Microsoft® Project and PRINCE2™
Updated for PRINCE2 ™ 2009 and Microsoft® Office Project 2007
ISBN 978-1-921059-29-2 - B5 - Perfect, ISBN 978-1-921059-30-8 - A4 - Spiral

Planning and Control Using Microsoft® Project and *PMBOK® Guide* Fourth Edition
Including Microsoft Project 2000 to 2007
ISBN 978-1-921059-31-5 - B5 – Perfect, ISBN 978-1-921059-32-2- A4 - Spiral

99 Tricks and Traps for Microsoft® Office Project
Including Microsoft® Project 2000 to 2007
ISBN 978-1-921059-19-3 - A5 - Paperback

Project Planning and Scheduling Using Primavera® Contractor Version 6.1
Including Versions 4.1, 5.0 and 6.1
ISBN 978-1-921059-25-4 - A4 Paperback, ISBN 978-1-921059-26-1 A4 Spiral Bound

SUPERSEDED BOOKS BY THE AUTHOR

Planning and Scheduling Using Microsoft® Project 2000
Planning and Scheduling Using Microsoft® Project 2002
Planning and Scheduling Using Microsoft® Project 2003
Planning and Scheduling Using Microsoft Office Project 2007
PRINCE2™ Planning and Control Using Microsoft® Project
Planning and Control Using Microsoft® Project and *PMBOK® Guide* Third Edition
Project Planning and Scheduling Using Primavera Enterprise® - Team Play Version 3.5
Project Planning and Scheduling Using Primavera Enterprise® - P3e & P3e/c Version 3.5
Project Planning and Scheduling Using Primavera® Version 4.1 for IT Project
Project Planning and Scheduling Using Primavera® Version 4.1 or E&C
Planning and Scheduling Using Primavera® Version 5.0 - For IT Project Office
Planning and Scheduling Using Primavera® Version 5.0 - For Engineering & Construction
Project Planning & Control Using Primavera® P6 – Updated for Version 6.2
Planning Using Primavera Project Planner P3® Version 2.0
Planning Using Primavera Project Planner P3® Version 3.0
Planning Using Primavera Project Planner P3® Version 3.1
Project Planning Using SureTrak® for Windows Version 2.0
Planning Using Primavera SureTrak® Project Manager Version 3.0

1 INTRODUCTION

1.1 Purpose

The purpose of this book is to provide you with a method for planning and controlling projects using Microsoft Office Project Professional 2010 or Microsoft Office Project Standard 2010 in a single project environment up to an intermediate level. This book also highlights the important differences between Microsoft Office Project 2010 and earlier versions but it is not intended to be used for learning these earlier versions.

The screen shots in this book were captured using Microsoft Office Project Standard and Professional 2010, Windows 7 and Windows XP. Readers using Microsoft Project Professional 2010 will have more menu options than those using Microsoft Project Standard 2010. These additional menu options will operate when a project is saved to a Microsoft Project Server. Microsoft Office Project Standard 2010 will not operate with Microsoft Project Server and has fewer functions than Microsoft Project Office Professional 2010 operating with Microsoft Project Server.

At the end of this book, you should be able to:

- Understand the steps required to create a project plan
- Set up the software
- Define calendars
- Add tasks and organize tasks
- Format the display
- Add logic and constraints
- Use Tables, Views and Filters
- Print reports
- Record and track progress
- Create and assign resources and understand the impact of task types and effort-driven tasks
- Analyze resource requirements and level a schedule
- Update resourced projects
- Customize the project options
- Understand the different techniques for scheduling.

The book does not cover every aspect of Microsoft Project, but it does cover the main features required to create and update an un-resourced and resourced project schedule. There are some chapters at the end of the book covering some more advanced features of the software. It should provide you with a solid grounding, which will enable you to learn the other features of the software by experimenting with the software, using the Help files and reviewing other literature and forums.

This book has been written to minimize superfluous text, allowing the user to locate and understand the information contained in the book as quickly as possible. It does NOT cover functions of little value to common project scheduling requirements. If at any time you are unable to understand a topic in this book, it is suggested that you use the Microsoft Project Help menu to gain a further understanding of the subject.

The term button is use for an object on the screen that may be clicked with the mouse to access a software function and icon for something that conveys information.

1.2 Required Background Knowledge

The book is intended to teach you how to use Microsoft Project in a project environment. Therefore, to be able to follow this book you should have the following background knowledge:

- The ability to use a personal computer and understand the fundamentals of the operating system,
- Experience using application software such as Microsoft Office which would have given you exposure to the Windows menu systems and typical Windows functions such as copy and paste, and
- An understanding of how projects are managed, such as the processes that take place over the lifetime of a project.

1.3 Purpose of Planning

The ultimate purpose of planning is to build a model that allows you to predict which tasks and resources are critical to the timely completion of the project. Strategies may then be implemented to ensure that these tasks and resources are managed properly, thus ensuring that the project will be delivered both **On Time** and **Within Budget**.

Planning aims to:

- Identify the total scope of the project and plan to deliver it
- Evaluate different project delivery methods
- Identify products/deliverables required to deliver a project under a logical breakdown of the project
- Identify and optimize the use of resources and evaluate if target dates may be met
- Identify risks, plan to minimize them and set priorities
- Provide a baseline plan against which progress is measured
- Assist in stakeholders' communication, identifying what is to be done, when and by whom
- Assist management to think ahead and make informed decisions.

Planning helps to avoid or assists in evaluating:

- Increased project costs or reduction in scope and/or quality
- Additional project testing and handover costs
- Extensions of time claims
- Loss of your client's revenue
- Resolving contractual disputes with subcontractors and suppliers
- The loss of reputation of those involved in a project
- Loss of a facility or asset in the event of a total project failure.

1.4 Project Planning Metrics

Components normally measured and controlled using planning and scheduling software are:

- Scope
- Time
- Effort (resources)
- Cost.

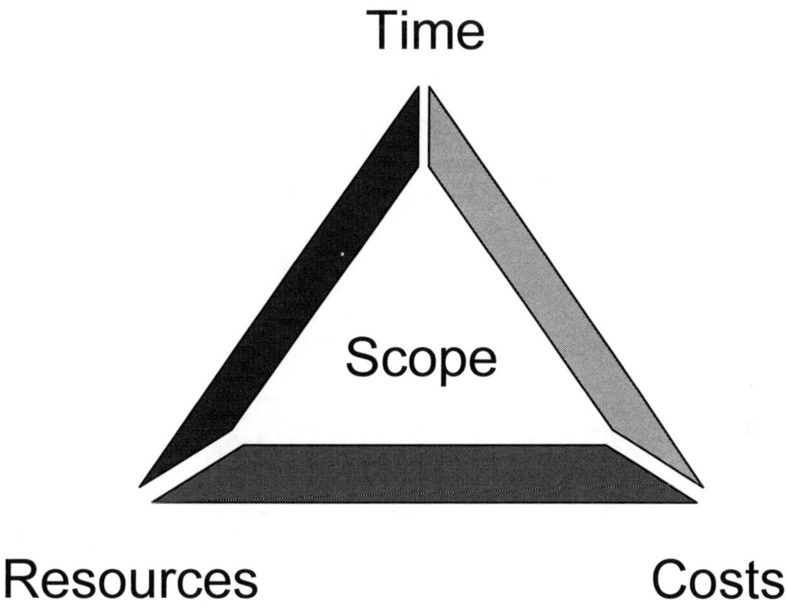

A change in any one of these components normally results in a change in one or more of the others.

Other project management functions that are not traditionally managed with planning and scheduling software, but may have components reflected in the schedule, includes:

- Document Management and Control
- Quality Management
- Contract Management
- Issue Management
- Risk Management
- Industrial Relations
- Accounting.

The development of Enterprise Project Management systems has resulted in the inclusion of more of these functions in project planning and scheduling software.

1.5 Planning Cycle

The planning cycle is an integral part of managing a project. A software package such as Microsoft Project makes this task much easier.

When the original plan is agreed to, the **Baseline** or **Target** is set. The **Baseline** is a record of the original plan. The **Baseline** dates may be recorded in Microsoft Project in data fields titled **Baseline Start** and **Baseline Finish**.

After project planning has ended and project execution has begun, the actual progress is monitored, recorded in the software and compared to the **Baseline**.

The plan may be changed by adding or deleting tasks and adjusting Remaining Durations or Resources.

A revised plan is then published as progress continues.

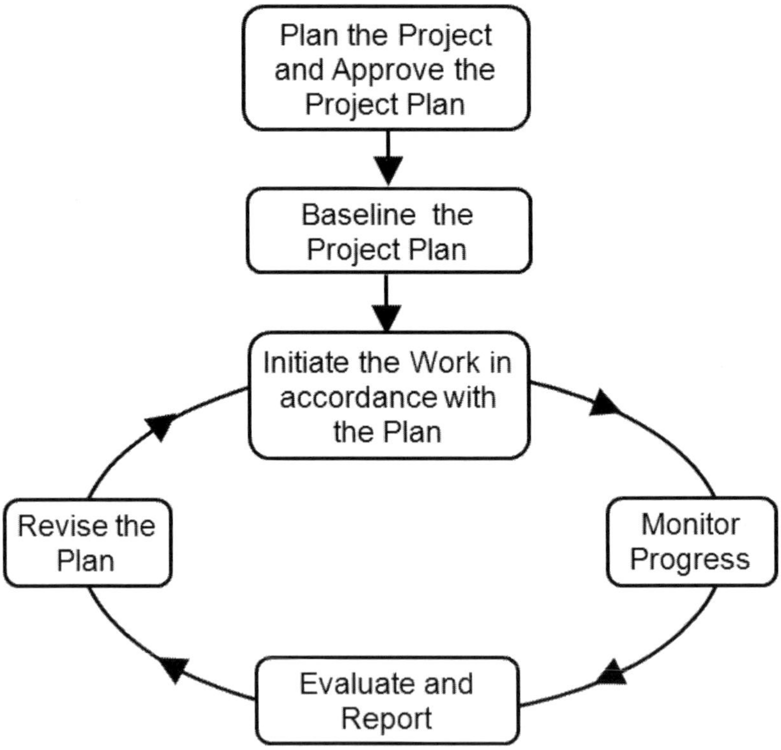

Updating a schedule assists in the management of a project by recording and displaying:

- Progress and the impact of project scope changes and delays as the project progresses,
- The revised completion date and final forecast of costs for the project,
- Historical data that may be used to support extension of time claims and dispute resolution, and
- Historical data that may be used in future projects of a similar nature.

1.6 Levels of Planning

Projects are often planned at a summary level and then detailed out in the schedule before the work is commenced. Smaller projects may be detailed out during project planning but other large or complex projects may require several levels before the project plan is fully detailed out.

The main reason for not detailing out a project early is that there may not be enough information at that stage and time would be wasted in preparing detailed schedules that will be made redundant by unforeseen changes. The following planning techniques may be considered:

***The PMBOK® Guide Fourth Edition* discusses the following techniques:**

- The **Rolling Wave**. This technique involves adding more detail to the schedule as the work approaches. This is often possible, as more information is known about the scope of the project as work is executed. The initial planning could be completed at a high level in the **Work Breakdown Structure** (**WBS**). As the work approaches the planning may be completed in more detail at a lower level such as **WBS Component** and then to a **Work Package** level for detailed planning.
- The use of **Sub-projects**. These are useful in larger projects where more than one person is working on the project schedule. This situation may exist when portions of projects are contracted out. A sub-project may be detailed out when the work is awarded to a contractor.
- The use of **Phases**. A Phase is different from a PRINCE2 Stage as Phases may overlap in time and Stages do not. Phases may be defined, for example, as Design, Procure and Install. These Phases may overlap, as Procurement may commence before Design is complete. The Phase development of a schedule involves the detailing out of all the associated WBS elements prior to the commencement of that Phase.
- The *PMBOK® Guide* does not have strict definitions for levels of plans but assumes that this process is planned when decomposing the **Work Breakdown Structure** (**WBS**). There are some other models available that may be used as guidelines, such as the PMI "Practice Standard for Work Breakdown Structures."
- Projects subject to many changes may require the work to be granulated out into more tasks immediately prior to the work starting. For example, at the end of every week the next two weeks' work (that will have had been planned at a summary level) would be planned out in detail. This is a type of **Rolling Wave** development of the project. This is often found in a software-testing phase, where the next portion of work is dependent on what has passed and what has failed testing in the previous portion of work.

PRINCE2 Level of Plans

Stages in PRINCE2 are defined as time-bound periods of a project, which do not overlap in time and are referred to as Management Stages. Under PRINCE2, a Project Plan is divided into Stages and a Stage plan is detailed out prior to the commencement of a Stage. PRINCE2 defines the following levels of plans:

- **Programme Plan** – which may include Project Plans or one or more portfolios of multiple projects,
- **Project Plan** – this is mandatory and is updated through the duration of a project,
- **Stage Plan** – there is a minimum of two Stage Plans, an **Initiation Stage Plan** and **First Stage Plan**. There would usually be one Stage Plan for each Stage.
- **Exception Plan** – which is at the same level and detail as a Stage Plan and replaces a Stage Plan at the request of a Project Board when a Stage is forecast to exceed tolerances (contingent time), and
- **Team Plan** – which is optional and would be used on larger projects where Teams are used for delivering Products that require detailed planning. A typical example is a contractor's plan, which would be submitted during the bid process.

Jelen's Cost and Optimization Engineering

This book defines the following levels of plans:

- Level 0: This is the total project and is, in effect, a single bar spanning the time from start to finish.
- Level 1: This schedules the project by its major components. For example, a level 1 schedule for a process plant may be broken into process area, storage and handling area, site and services, and utilities. It is shown in bar chart format.
- Level 2: Each of the level 1 components is further subdivided. For example, utility systems are broken into water, electrical, gas, sanitary, etc. In most cases this schedule level can only be shown in bar chart format although a bar chart with key constraints may be possible.
- Level 3: The subdivision continues. This is probably the first level that a meaningful Critical Path network can be drawn. It is also a good level for the project's overall control schedule since it is neither too summarized nor too detailed.
- Levels 4-?: The subdivision continues to whatever level of detail is needed by the user. When operating at these more detailed levels, the planners generally work with less than the total schedule. In most cases these "look-ahead" schedules span periods of 30–180 days. The user may utilize either bar chart or CPM format for these schedules.

This paragraph was reproduced from Jelen's Cost and Optimization Engineering, *author F. Jelen, copyright 1983, ISBN 0-07-053646-5, with the written permission from the publisher McGraw-Hill.*

1.7 Monitoring and Controlling a Project

After a plan has been produced, it should be followed and the work authorized in accordance with the plan. If there is to be a change in the plan, then the plan should be formally changed. If necessary, the client should be informed and if required by the contract, approval for the change should be sought. If the plan is not followed, then it may be difficult to obtain approval for extension of time claims and will make dispute resolution more difficult.

Monitoring a project ensures the project provides management with historical data, trends and deviations from plan allowing them to make decisions and control the project It should record the:

- Dates that work was started and completed
- Hours and cost required to complete the work
- Deliverables/products produced

Monitoring would also:

- Confirm the required quality is being met
- Provide trends that may be used for forecasting the remainder of the project
- Record historical data for use in assisting in planning future projects
- Obtain data required for preparing extension of time claims and for dispute resolution.

Controlling is the next level of management, analyzing the progress to date and trends to:

- Ensure that the project is being executed according to the plan
- Compare the project's progress with the original plan
- Review options in the case of deviations
- Forecast problems as early as possible, which enables corrective action to be taken as early as possible.

2 CREATING A PROJECT SCHEDULE

The aim of this chapter is to give you an understanding of what a plan is and some practical guidance on how your schedule may be created and updated as part of a project.

2.1 Understanding Planning and Scheduling Software

The project is essentially a set of operations or tasks required to be completed in a logical order to provide one or more deliverables or products. A schedule is an attempt to model these operations and their relationships. These operations take time to accomplish and may employ resources that have limited availability.

Planning and scheduling software allows the user to:

- Enter the hierarchical structure of the project deliverables or products into the software. This is often called a Work Breakdown Structure (WBS) or Product Breakdown Structure (PBS),
- Break a project down into tasks required to create the deliverables. These are entered into the software as **Tasks** under the appropriate WBS,
- Assign durations, constraints, predecessors and successors of the tasks and then calculate the start and finish date of all the tasks,
- Assign resources and/or costs, which represent people, equipment or materials, to the tasks and calculate the project resource requirements and/or cash flow,
- Optimize the project plan,
- Set Baseline Dates and Budgets to compare progress against,
- The plan should be used to approve the commencement of work,
- Record the actual progress of tasks against the original plan and amend the plan when required allowing for scope changes etc.,
- Record the consumption of resources and/or costs and re-estimate the resources and/or costs required to finish the project, and
- Produce management reports.

There are four modes or levels in which planning and scheduling software may be used.

	Planning	**Tracking**
Without Resources	**LEVEL 1** Planning without Resources	**LEVEL 2** Tracking progress without Resources
With Resources and/or Costs	**LEVEL 3** Planning with Resources	**LEVEL 4** Tracking progress with Resources

As the level increases, the amount of information required to maintain the schedule will increase and, more importantly, your skill and knowledge in using the software will also have to increase. This book is designed to take you from Level 1 to Level 4.

2.2 *Understanding Your Project*

Before you start the process of creating a project plan, it is important to have an understanding of the project and how it is to be executed. On large complex projects, this information is usually available from the following types of documents:

- Project charter or business case
- Project scope
- Functional specification
- Requirements baseline
- Contract documentation
- Plans and drawings
- Project execution plan
- Contracting and purchasing plan
- Equipment lists
- Installation and testing plan
- Historical data.

Many project managers conduct a **Stakeholder Analysis** at the start of a project. This process lists all the people and organizations with an interest in the project and their interests.

- Key project success factors may be identified from the interests of the most influential stakeholders.
- It is important to use the stakeholder analysis to identify all the stakeholders' tasks. These must be included in the schedule.

It is important to gain a good understanding of how the project is to be executed before entering any data into the software. It is considered good practice to plan a project before creating a schedule in any planning and scheduling software. These documents are referred to by many terms such as Project Execution Plan and Project Methodology Statement. You should also understand what level of reporting is required by the project team, as providing either too little or too much detail will often lead to the schedule being discarded.

The following processes are required to create or maintain a plan:

- Collecting the relevant project data,
- Entering and manipulating the data in software,
- Reviewing, revising and distributing, the plan.

The ability to collect the data is as important as the ability to enter and manipulate the information into the software. On larger projects it may be necessary to write policies and procedures to ensure accurate collection of data from the various departments and sites.

The structure, level of detail in a schedule and how resources are created and assigned depends on the schedule purpose. Types of schedule include tender, forecasting cash flows, Critical Path contract master schedule, two week look-ahead for tasking people. They will all have a different structure, level of detail and resourcing philosophy.

2.3 Level 1 – Planning without Resources

This is the simplest mode of planning, but this has limitations and may create an unachievable schedule as resources will not be considered.

2.3.1 Creating Projects

To create the project you will require the following information:

- Project Name,
- Client Name,
- Other information such as Location
- The Start Date (or perhaps the Finish Date).

2.3.2 Defining Calendars

Before you start entering tasks into your schedule it is advisable to set up the calendars. They are used to model the working time for each task in the project. For example, a 6-day per week calendar is created for those tasks that will be worked for 6 days a week. The calendars should include any public holidays and any other exceptions to available working days such as Rostered Days Off (RDO).

The finish date and time of a task (when there are no resources using a resource calendar assigned to a task) is calculated from the start date and time plus the task duration over the calendar assigned to the task.

The pictures below show the effect of nonwork days on the finish date of a 13-day duration task assigned a 5-day working week. The elapsed duration is 19 days due to the three weekends when work does not take place.

2.3.3 Defining the Project WBS Using Outlining

A WBS may be defined as a hierarchical breakdown of all the project deliverables or products. The sum of all the WBS Components (Nodes) should encompass the total project scope.

The principal method of assigning a WBS to a project with Microsoft Project is using a function entitled **Outlining**, which creates a hierarchy of summary tasks. The picture below shows a simple project where the total project duration and three WBS Nodes are represented by summary tasks and bars:

	Task Name	Duration	Start	Finish
1	⊟ **Project Summary Task**	**57 days**	**2 Apr**	**19 Jun**
2	Start Milestone	0 days	2 Apr	2 Apr
3	Finish Milestone	0 days	19 Jun	19 Jun
4	⊟ **WBS Node 1**	**20 days**	**2 Apr**	**27 Apr**
5	Task 1	5 days	2 Apr	6 Apr
6	Task 2	8 days	9 Apr	18 Apr
7	Task 3	7 days	19 Apr	27 Apr
8	⊟ **WBS Node 2**	**30 days**	**19 Apr**	**30 May**
9	Task 4	3 days	19 Apr	23 Apr
10	Task 5	19 days	30 Apr	24 May
11	Task 6	4 days	25 May	30 May
12	⊟ **WBS Node 3**	**41 days**	**24 Apr**	**19 Jun**
13	Task 7	4 days	24 Apr	27 Apr
14	Task 8	6 days	31 May	7 Jun
15	Task 9	8 days	8 Jun	19 Jun

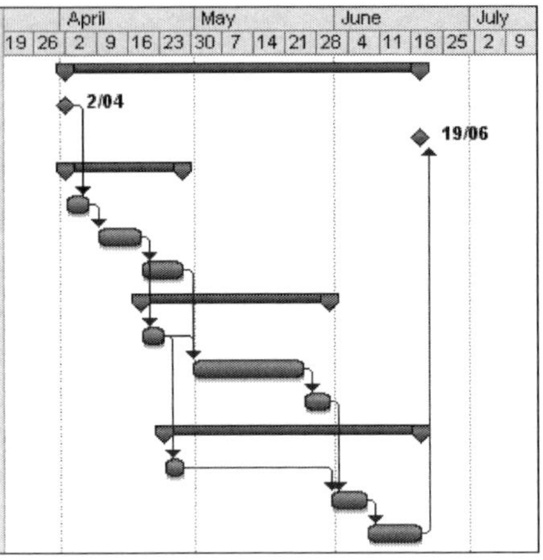

The project schedule may be rolled up using these summary tasks:

	Task Name	Duration	Start	Finish
1	⊟ **Project Summary Task**	**57 days**	**2 Apr**	**19 Jun**
2	Start Milestone	0 days	2 Apr	2 Apr
3	Finish Milestone	0 days	19 Jun	19 Jun
4	⊞ **WBS Node 1**	**20 days**	**2 Apr**	**27 Apr**
8	⊞ **WBS Node 2**	**30 days**	**19 Apr**	**30 May**
12	⊞ **WBS Node 3**	**41 days**	**24 Apr**	**19 Jun**

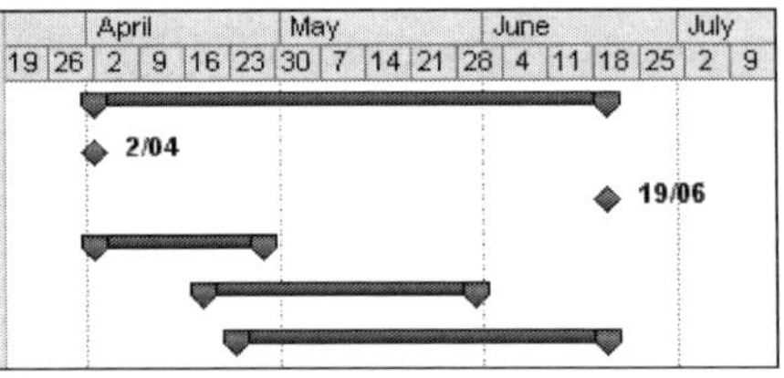

Microsoft Project also has customizable fields that may be used to assign codes and descriptions to tasks. The customizable fields may be used to sort, select, summarize and group tasks under codes and identify the project breakdown structure, thus providing a lot more flexibility than the Outlining function for developing and reporting a project schedule.

Before creating a WBS the following questions should be considered:

- What are the deliverables of the project, what is to be handed to the client/customer?
- What needs to be created to enable the final deliverable to be handed over to the client/customer?
- How many phases are there? (e.g., Design, Procure, Install and Test)
- How many disciplines are there? (e.g., Civil, Mechanical and Electrical)
- Which departments are involved in the project? (e.g., Sales, Procurement and Installation)
- How many locations, buildings or floors are involved in the project?
- What work is expected to be contracted?
- How many sites or areas are there in the project?

Use the responses to these questions to create the WBS dictionaries.

As the project progresses it may be necessary to add more detail to the project and additional WBS Nodes may be added as the scope develops or more detail is added to the schedule.

2.3.4 Defining, Adding and Organizing Tasks

Tasks must be defined before they are entered into the schedule. It is important that you carefully consider:

- The scope of the task
- How long the task is going to take
- Who is going to do it
- What the deliverable is for each task.

The project estimate is usually a good place to start looking for a breakdown of the project into tasks, resources and costs. It may even give an indication of how long the work will take and the labor hours (work) for each resource type

Usually project reports are created on a regular basis, such as every week, or fortnight, or every month. "Good Practice" says that a task should not span more than two reporting periods. That way the tasks should only be "In-Progress" for one period. If a task is "In-Progress" for more than two periods then it has slipped.

It is also good practice to have a measurable finish point for each group of tasks. The issue of documentation to mark the end of one task and the starting point of another adds to the clarity of a schedule. Examples of document issues are:

- Issue of a Drawing Package
- Completion of a Specification
- Placing of an Order
- Delivery Dockets
- Testing Certificates for Equipment.

The tasks are then added to the schedule and assigned their WBS so that they may be sorted and grouped.

2.3.5 Adding the Logic Links

The logic is added to the schedule to provide the order in which the tasks must be undertaken. The logic is designated by indicating the predecessors to, and the successors from, each task. There are two methods that software uses to sequence tasks:

- Precedence Diagram Method (PDM), where the node is the task and the arrow is the relationship, and
- Arrow Diagram (ADM), where the node is the relationship and the arrow is the task.

Most current project planning and scheduling software uses PDM, including Microsoft Project. A PDM diagram may be created using the Network Diagram view.

There are several types of dependencies that may be used:

- **Mandatory dependencies**, also known as **Hard Logic**, are relationships between tasks that may not be broken. For example, a hole has to be dug before it is filled with concrete or a computer delivered before software is installed onto it.
- **Discretionary dependencies**, also known as **Sequencing Logic** or **Soft Logic**, are relationships between tasks that may be changed when the plan is changed. For example, if there are five holes to be excavated and only one machine available, or five computers to be assembled and one person available to work on them, then the order of these tasks could be set with sequencing logic but changed at a later date.

Both **Mandatory dependencies** and **Discretionary dependencies** are entered into Microsoft Project as task relationships or logic links. The software does not provide a method of identifying the type of relationship because notes or codes may not be attached to relationships. A **Note** may be added to either the predecessor or successor task to explain the relationship.

External dependencies are usually events outside the control of the project team that impact on the schedule. An example would be the availability of a site to start work. This is usually represented in Microsoft Project by a Milestone which has a constraint applied to it. This topic is discussed in more detail in the next section.

The software will calculate the start and finish dates for each task. The end date of the project is calculated from the start date of the project, the logic among the tasks, any **Leads** (often referred to as **Negative Lag**) or **Lags** applied to the logic and durations of the tasks. The pictures below show the effect of a lag and a lead on the start of a successor task:

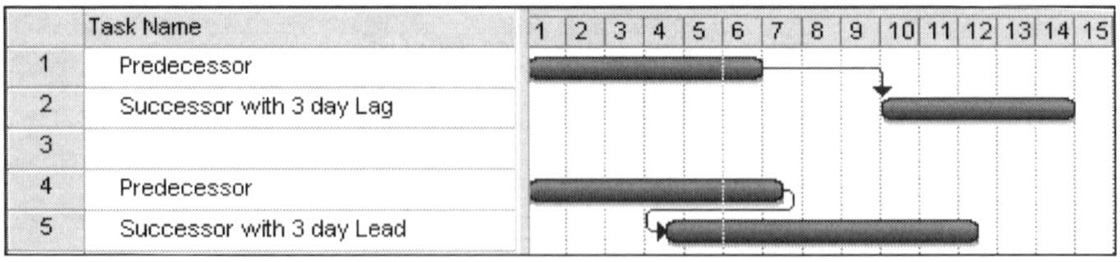

It is good practice to create a **Closed Network** with the logic. A **Closed Network** is created when all tasks have one or more start predecessors and one or more finish successors, except:

- One or more project start milestones or incoming External Dependencies which have no predecessors, and
- One or more finish milestones or outgoing External Dependencies which have no successors.

The project's logic must not loop back on itself. Looping would occur if the logic stated that A preceded B, B preceded C, and C preceded A. That's not a logical project situation and will cause an error comment to be generated by the software during network calculations.

Thus, when the logic is correctly applied, a delay to a task will delay all its successor tasks and delay the project end date when there is insufficient slippage time to accommodate the delay. This spare time is usually called **Float** (but Microsoft Project uses the term **Slack**).

2.3.6 Constraints

External dependencies are applied to a schedule using **Constraints** and these may model the impact of events outside the logical sequence of tasks. A constraint would be imposed to specific dates such as the availability of a facility to start work or the required completion date of a project. Constraints should be cross-referenced to the supporting documentation such as Milestone Dates from contract documentation using the **Notes** function. Typical examples of constraints would be:

- **Start No Earlier Than** for the availability of a site to commence work, and
- **Finish No Later Than** for the date that a total project must be delivered by or handed over to a client.

2.3.7 Risk Analysis

The process of planning a project may identify risks and a formal risk analysis should be considered. A risk analysis may identify risk mitigation tasks that should be added to the schedule before it is submitted for approval.

2.3.8 Contingent Time

The addition of contingent time should be considered when submitting a schedule for approval. Estimates usually have contingency and if this money is to be expended then an allowance for time to spend the contingent funds needs to be made. Contingent time may be assigned to a schedule in number of ways including:

- One or more contingent time tasks could be inserted in the project. These would be adjusted in length as the project progresses to maintain the planned end date.
- Work days in the calendar could be assigned as nonwork days. For example a building project could be scheduled on a 5-day per week basis, knowing that work will be undertaken on the Saturday.
- Increasing the task durations by a factor.
- Positive lags could be assigned between tasks, but this is not recommended by the author.

A lack of contingency should be identified as a Risk.

2.3.9 Scheduling the Project and Understanding Float (Slack)

The software will calculate the shortest time in which the project may be completed.

It will also identify the **Critical Path(s)**. The Critical Path is the chain(s) of tasks that takes the longest time to accomplish. This will define the Earliest Finish date of the project. The calculated completion date depends on the critical tasks starting and finishing on time – if they are delayed, the whole project will be delayed.

Thus, when the logic is correctly applied to both relationships and constraints, a delay to a task will delay all successor tasks, and, in turn, postpone the project end date. When there is insufficient spare time or **Float** to accommodate the delay. Tasks that may be delayed without affecting the project end date have **Float**.

Float is the term that is in common use and one that most textbooks refer to. Microsoft Project uses the term Slack and not Float. Either term may be used.

Total Float is the amount of time a task may be delayed without delaying the project end date. The project in the picture below is on a 5-day per week calendar, thus there is no work over the weekends. Task 4 and Task 5 both have Total Float. The delay of a task with Total Float may delay other tasks with Total Float. Task 4 would have to delay Task 5 before a delay to Task 4 would delay the project Finish Milestone.

	Task Name	Duration	Start	Finish	Total Slack
1	Start Milestone	0 days	5 Feb	5 Feb	0 days
2	Task 1	5 days	5 Feb	9 Feb	0 days
3	Task 2	5 days	12 Feb	16 Feb	0 days
4	Task 3	5 days	19 Feb	23 Feb	0 days
5	Task 4	2 days	5 Feb	6 Feb	11 days
6	Task5	2 days	12 Feb	13 Feb	8 days
7	Finish Milestone	0 days	23 Feb	23 Feb	0 days

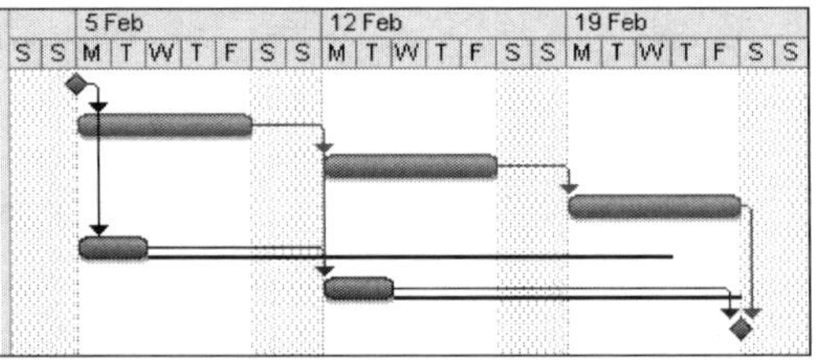

Free Float is the amount of time a task may be delayed without delaying the start date of another task. Task 4 has only 3 days' Free Float because once it has been delayed 3 days it will delay Task 5.

	Task Name	Duration	Start	Finish	Free Slack
1	Start Milestone	0 days	5 Feb	5 Feb	0 days
2	Task 1	5 days	5 Feb	9 Feb	0 days
3	Task 2	5 days	12 Feb	16 Feb	0 days
4	Task 3	5 days	19 Feb	23 Feb	0 days
5	Task 4	2 days	5 Feb	6 Feb	3 days
6	Task5	2 days	12 Feb	13 Feb	8 days
7	Finish Milestone	0 days	23 Feb	23 Feb	0 days

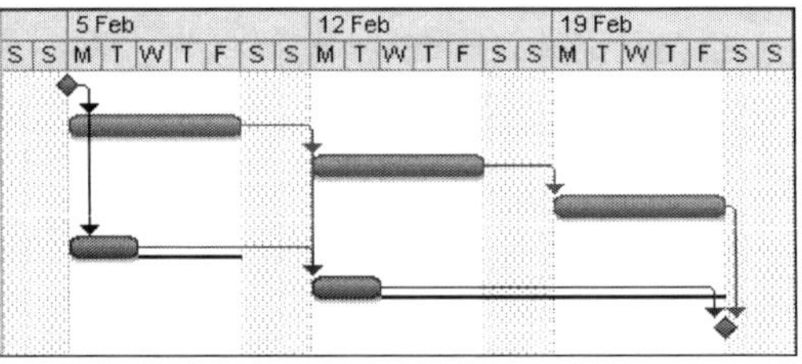

2.3.10 Formatting the Display – Filters and Views

Now it is time to present the schedule for approval. There are tools to manipulate and display the tasks to suit the project reporting requirements:

- **Filters** reduce the number of tasks that are displayed
- **Tables** display the data in columns, and
- **Views** allow the presentation of the columns of data and bars to be tailored.

2.3.11 Printing and Reports and Issuing the Plan

There are features that allow you to present the information in a clear and concise manner to communicate the requirements to all project members.

All members of the project team should review the project plan in an attempt to optimize the process and methods employed.

Printouts and reports should be used to communicate what is expected of team members while providing each with the opportunity to further improve the outcome.

2.4 Level 2 – Tracking Progress without Resources

2.4.1 Setting the Baseline Schedule

The optimized and agreed-upon plan is used as a baseline for future comparisons. The software can record the original plan dates, which are often called Baseline dates, for comparing the actual progress to the plan over the life of the project. These planned dates are stored in the **Baseline Date** fields and displayed as the upper bars in the picture below, which demonstrates that there has been a delay in the start of the project:

	Task Name	Duration	Start	Baseline Start	Finish	Baseline Finish
1	Start Milestone	0 days	7 Feb	5 Feb	7 Feb	5 Feb
2	Task 1	5 days	7 Feb	5 Feb	13 Feb	9 Feb
3	Task 2	5 days	14 Feb	12 Feb	20 Feb	16 Feb
4	Task 3	5 days	21 Feb	19 Feb	27 Feb	23 Feb
5	Task 4	2 days	7 Feb	5 Feb	8 Feb	6 Feb
6	Task5	2 days	14 Feb	12 Feb	15 Feb	13 Feb
7	Finish Milestone	0 days	27 Feb	23 Feb	27 Feb	23 Feb

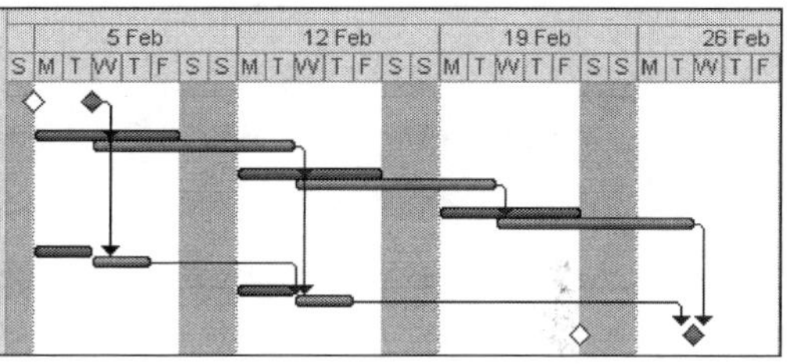

2.4.2 Tracking Progress

The schedule should be **Updated** (or progressed) on a regular basis and progress recorded at that point. The date on which progress is reported is known by a number of different terms such as **Data Date**, **Update Date**, **Time Now**, **Report Date** and **Status Date**. The Status Date is the field used in Microsoft Project to record this date. Whatever the frequency chosen for updating, you will have to collect the following task information in order to update a schedule:

- Completed tasks
  - Actual Start date and
  - Actual Finish dates.

- In-progress tasks
  - ➢ The Actual Start Date
  - ➢ Percentage Completed
  - ➢ The Remaining Duration from the Status Date or Expected Finish Date of the Task
  - ➢ Changes to logic.
- Un-started work
  - ➢ Any revisions to tasks that have not started
  - ➢ New tasks representing scope changes
  - ➢ Forecast start date for tasks due to start in the near term
  - ➢ Revisions to logic that represent changes to the plan.

The schedule may be updated after this information has been collected. The recorded progress is compared to the **Target** dates, either graphically or by using columns of data such as the **Finish Variance** column:

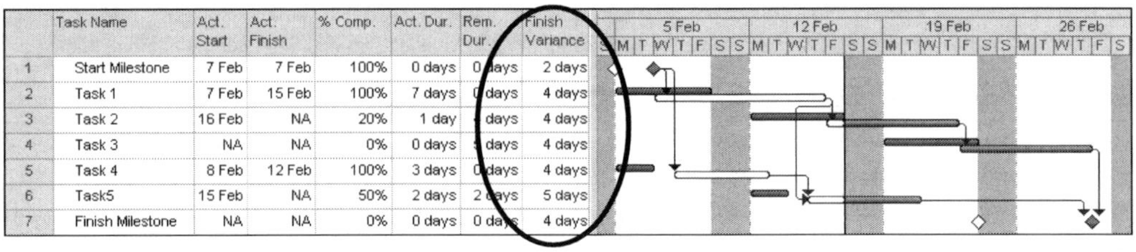

	Task Name	Act. Start	Act. Finish	% Comp.	Act. Dur.	Rem. Dur.	Finish Variance
1	Start Milestone	7 Feb	7 Feb	100%	0 days	0 days	2 days
2	Task 1	7 Feb	15 Feb	100%	7 days	0 days	4 days
3	Task 2	16 Feb	NA	20%	1 day	[illegible] days	4 days
4	Task 3	NA	NA	0%	0 days	5 days	4 days
5	Task 4	8 Feb	12 Feb	100%	3 days	0 days	4 days
6	Task5	15 Feb	NA	50%	2 days	2 days	5 days
7	Finish Milestone	NA	NA	0%	0 days	0 days	4 days

2.4.3 Corrective Action

At this point it may be necessary to further optimize the schedule to bring the project back on track. Possible options include:

- Reduce the contingent time allowance.
- Assign a negative lag on a Finish-to-Start relationship allowing a successor to commence before a predecessor is completed.
- Change relationships to Start-to-Start allowing tasks to be executed in parallel.
- Reduce the durations of tasks. In a resourced schedule this could be achieved by increasing the number of resources assigned to a task.
- Work longer hours per day or days per week by editing the calendars, or
- Reduce the scope and delete tasks.

2.5 Level 3 – Planning with Resources and /or Costs

2.5.1 Estimating or Planning for Control

There are two modes that the software may be used at Level 3.

- **Estimating**. In this mode the objective is to create a schedule with costs that are being used as an estimate so the schedule will never be updated. Tasks may have many resources assigned to them to develop an accurate cost estimate and include many items that would never be updated in the process of updating a schedule.

- **Planning for Control**. In this mode the intention is to assign resource actual units (hours) and costs, then calculate units and costs to completion. It may also be intended to conduct an Earned Value analysis. In this situation it is important to ensure the minimum number of resources are assigned to tasks, and preferably only one resource assigned to each task. The process of updating a schedule becomes extremely difficult and time consuming when a resourced schedule has many resources per task. The scheduler is then in danger of becoming a timekeeper and may lose sight of other important functions, such as calculating the forecast to complete and the project finish date.

2.5.2 The Balance Between the Number of Tasks and Resources

When planning for control a large or complex project, it is important to maintain a balance between the number of tasks and the number of resources that are planned and tracked. As a general rule, the more tasks a schedule has, the fewer resources should be created and assigned to tasks.

When there is a schedule with a large number of tasks and a large number of resources assigned to each task, the schedule may end up in a situation where no members of the project team are able to understand the schedule and the scheduler is unable to maintain it.

Instead of assigning individual resources such as people by name, consider using generic "Skills" or "Trades," and on very large projects use "Crews" or "Teams."

Therefore it is more important to minimize the number of resources in large schedules that will be updated regularly, since updating every resource assigned to each task at each schedule update is very time consuming.

2.5.3 Creating and Using Resources

A resource pool is established by entering the project resources and their unit rates into the software. Entering a cost rate for each resource enables cost analysis such as comparing the cost of supplementing overloaded resources against the cost of extending the project deadline.

Resources are then assigned to tasks and the time-phased resource requirements, cash flows and budgets may be automatically produced from this resource/cost data.

2.5.4 Resource Calendars, Task Types and Driving Resources

These are additional features that enable the user to more accurately model real-life situations. These features add a level of complexity that should be used only when the environment demands their use and should be avoided by inexperienced schedulers.

2.5.5 Resource Graphs and Usage Tables

These features allow the display and analysis of project resource requirements in both tables and graphs.

The data may be exported to Excel for further analysis and presentation.

2.5.6 Resource Optimization

The schedule may now have to be resource optimized to:

- Reduce peaks and smooth the resource requirements, or
- Reduce resource demand to the available number of resources, or
- Reduce demand to an available cash flow when a project is being financed on a customer's income, or
- Efficiently utilize resources.

The process of leveling is defined as delaying tasks until resources become available. There are several methods of delaying tasks and thus leveling a schedule, which are outlined in the **RESOURCE OPTIMIZATION** chapter.

2.6 Level 4 – Tracking Progress of a Resourced Schedule

2.6.1 Updating Projects with Resources

When you update a project with resources you will need to collect some additional information that may include:

- The quantities or hours and/or costs spent to date per task for each resource, and
- The quantities or hours and/or costs required per resource to complete each task.

You may then update a resourced schedule with this data.

Once the schedule has been updated then a review of the future resource requirements, project end date and cash flows may be made.

Updating a resourced project is time consuming and requires experience and a good understanding of how the software calculates. It should ideally be attempted by experienced schedulers or under the guidance of an experienced scheduler.

3 NAVIGATION AND SETTING THE OPTIONS

3.1 Identify the Parts of the Project Screen

After starting Microsoft Project a project will be created titles **Project1** and the default Microsoft Project 2010 screen will look like this:

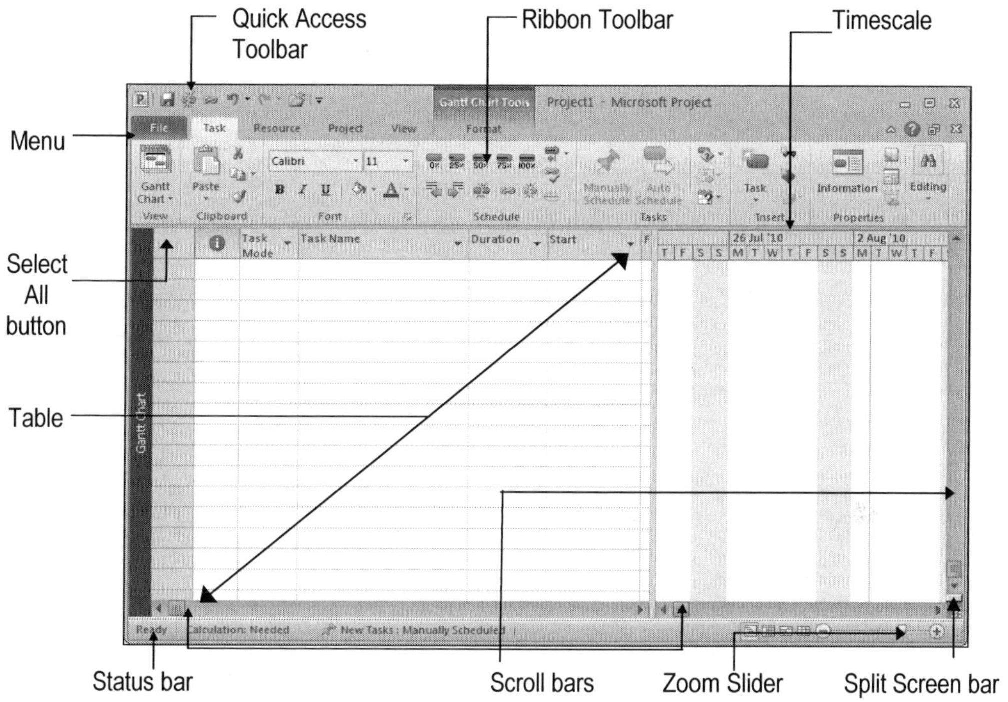

Microsoft Project has the **Ribbon** style menu system with a typical Windows look-and-feel.

- The **Ribbon** works in a similar way to the Microsoft Office products with a Ribbon.
- The project name is displayed before **Microsoft Project** at the top left-hand side of the screen.
- The **Ribbon** by default is displayed below the **Quick Access Toolbar**. This is a combination of both the traditional menu and toolbar buttons.
- The main display has the **Bar Chart** or **Gantt Chart** on the right-hand side, the **Timescale** above, and the **Table** of Data Columns on the left-hand side with their titles above them. The divider between the two areas may be dragged from side to side by holding down the left mouse button.
- The horizontal **Scroll Bars** are at the bottom of the screen and the **Status Bar** is below the **Scroll Bars**. The vertical **Scroll Bar** is at the right-hand side of the screen.
- The new **Zoom Slider** which is used for scaling the timescale is displayed in the bottom right-hand side of the screen in the **Status Bar**.

The grouping of the Ribbon commands is by software functions such as Project, Task etc and not by scheduling function such as creating or updating. Users therefore continually swap from one **Ribbon** menu to another while operating the software. You should therefore consider hiding the **Ribbon** and building your own **Quick Access Toolbar** below the **Ribbon** with the commands in logical groupings.

3.2 Customizing the Screen

The screen may be customized in a number of ways to suit your preferences. With the implementation of the Ribbon Toolbar introduced in Microsoft Project 2010 users migrating from earlier versions of Microsoft Project will have to learn the new location of all the commands.

3.2.1 Ribbon Toolbar

The toolbars will not be covered in detail in this book as they operate the same way as all other Microsoft products but the key issues will be outlined.

The Ribbon Toolbar has **Tabs** along the top and **Ribbon Groups**, which are groups of **Command Buttons**, below the Ribbon Tabs. These Ribbon Groups were either menu items or toolbars in earlier versions of Microsoft Project.

The Ribbon Format tab Groups of buttons will change as different Views are opened. Two examples of different Formats Groups of buttons are displayed below:

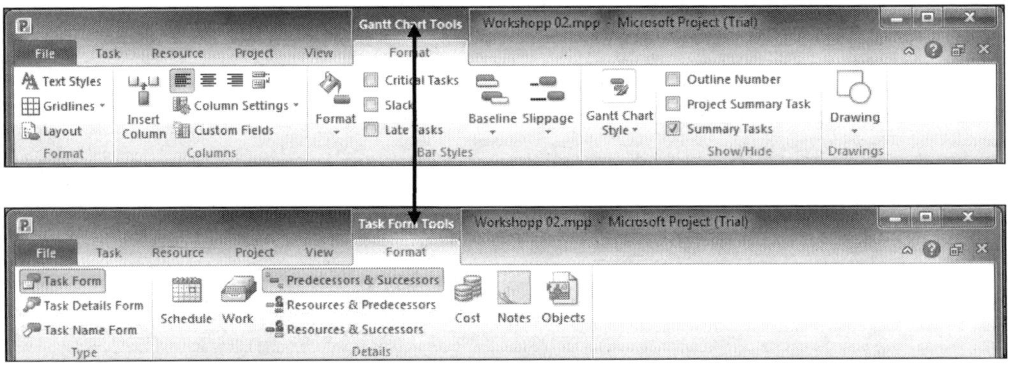

Significant productivity improvements may be made by ensuring that frequently used functions are made available on the Quick Access Toolbar and that the Ribbon Toolbar is optimized by adding and removing buttons. Right-clicking in the Ribbon will display the Ribbon menu, see the picture below:

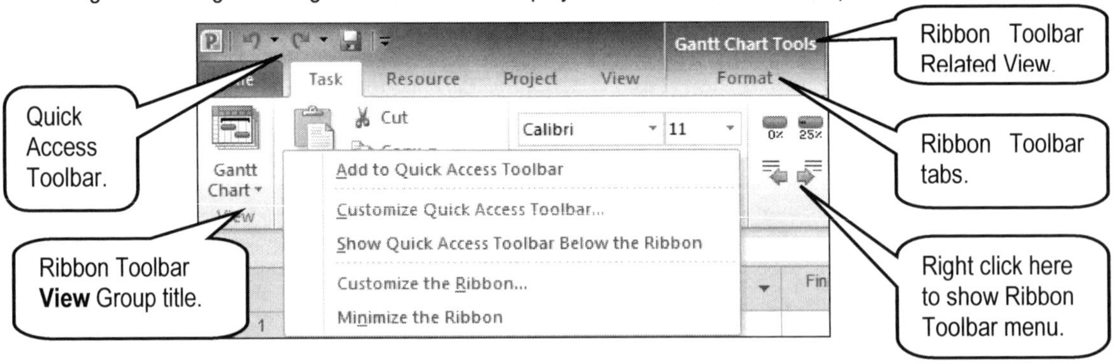

- The **Add to Quick Access Toolbar** will add a selected Ribbon Toolbar button to the Quick Access Toolbar. By default the Quick Access Toolbar is positioned at the top right-hand side of the screen and is always displayed.
- The **Customize Quick Access Toolbar...** opens the **Project Options** form **Quick Access Toolbar** tab where buttons may be added to or removed from the Quick Access Toolbar.

- Quick Access Toolbar may be moved below the Ribbon Toolbar by clicking on the **Show Quick Access Toolbar Below the Ribbon**. It is recommended that you select this option and move the Quick Access Toolbar below the Ribbon Toolbar as more buttons may then be displayed and the bar is not truncated by the Project Name at the top of the screen.
- **Customize the Ribbon...** opens the **Project Options** form, **Customize Ribbon** tab where buttons may be added to or removed from the Ribbon Toolbar.
- **Minimize the Ribbon** hides the Ribbon Toolbar and just leaves the menu displayed at the top. Clicking on one of the menu items will display the Ribbon Toolbar. This is a recommended setting. The Ribbon Toolbar may also be minimized by clicking on the and buttons in the top right-hand corner of the screen.

Ribbon Tabs, **Groups** of command buttons and individual **Command Buttons** may be added to or removed from the **Ribbon** by selecting **File**, **Options** and selecting the **Customize Ribbon** tab.

Some Ribbon tabs will change their contents to suit the view that has been selected and is active, this is covered further in the next paragraphs.

3.2.2 Quick Access Toolbar

In the picture below the:

- Quick Access Toolbar may be moved below the Ribbon bar by clicking on the **Show Quick Access Toolbar Below the Ribbon**.
- The Ribbon Toolbar has been hidden using **Minimize the Ribbon.**

Click on the button on the **Quick Access Toolbar** to display the Quick Access Toolbar menu:

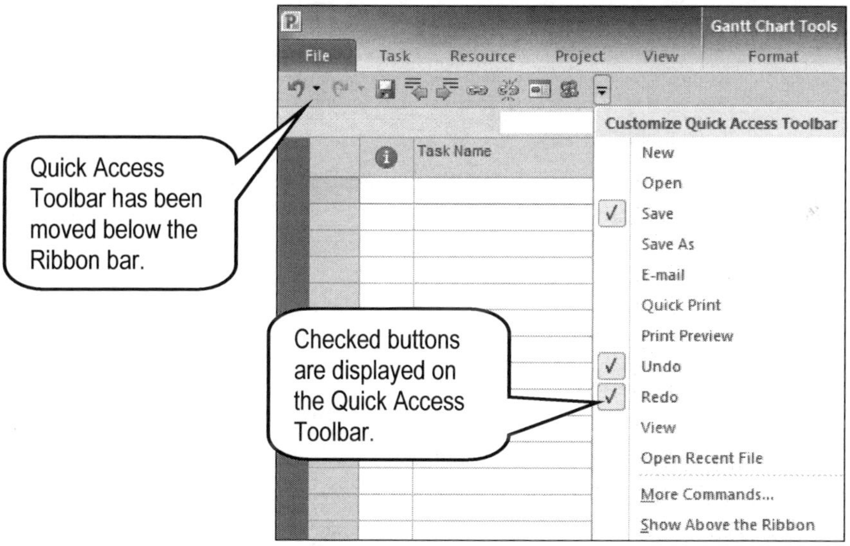

- The buttons that are checked are displayed in the Quick Access Toolbar.
- Buttons left unchecked will be displayed in the drop-down menu by clicking on the **Customize Quick Access Toolbar** button.
- **More Commands...** opens the **Project Options** form, **Quick Access Toolbar** tab where buttons may be added to or removed from the Ribbon Toolbar.

3.3 Microsoft Project 2010 Windows

3.3.1 Understanding Windows in Microsoft Project 2010

In Microsoft Project 2010 multiple projects may be opened and multiple windows for each project may also be opened at the same time. Each window may be assigned a different View. This is similar to the way Asta Powerproject operates.

The picture below shows three views of the same project have been opened at the same time, with the Gantt Chart view on the left being split:

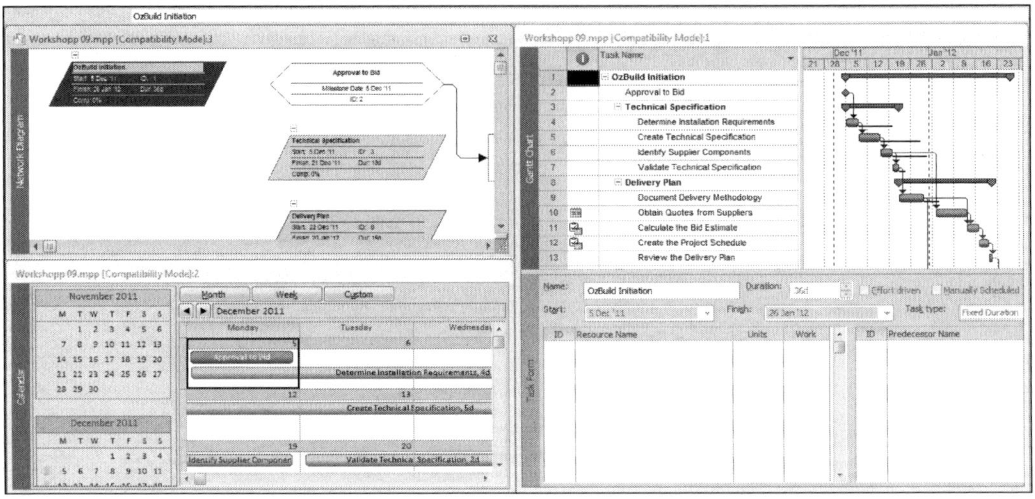

3.3.2 Creating a New Window

As each project is opened it is displayed with the Gantt Chart View. Additional windows may be created by:

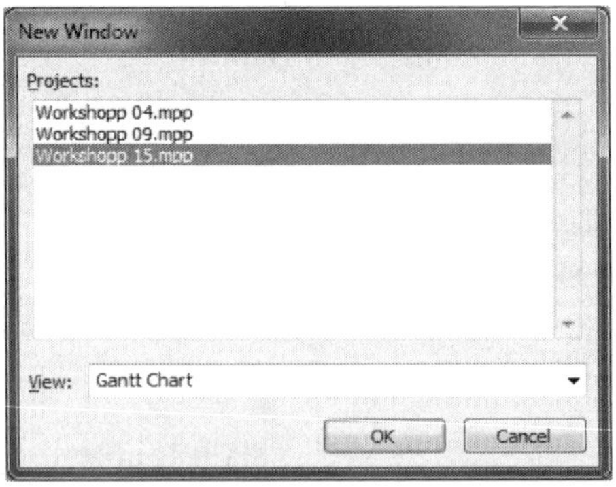

- Selecting **View**, **Window** group, **New Window**
- Select the project that requires the new window from the **New Window** form,
- The new window may be formatted using the **Ribbon**, **View** tab. This topic is covered in later chapters.

3.3.3 Managing Windows

The **Ribbon**, **View** tab, **Window** group has the following **Command Buttons**:

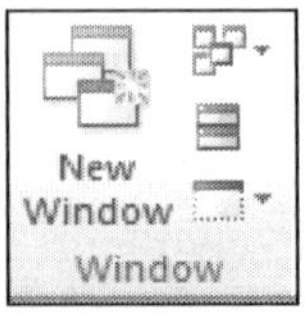

- **Switch Windows**  – allowing another window to be selected,
- **Arrange All**  – arranging the windows as per the picture above
- **Hide Window**  – which will hide a window from view, the window will not be displayed using the **Arrange All** function and the **Hide Window** command has to be used to display the window again.

3.3.4 Resizing Windows

A window may be:

- Resized by dragging with the mouse, or
- Maximized using the **Maximize** button at the top right-hand corner of each window.

3.3.5 Splitting Views

A window may be split horizontally into two panes. A different **View** may be displayed in each pane. This is termed **Dual-Pane view**. To open or close the dual-pane view:

- Select **View**, **Split View** group **Details** check box to split or uncheck to remove the split, or
- Grab the horizontal dividing bar at the bottom of the screen (see the picture in section 4.1) by holding down the left mouse button and dragging the line to resize the panes.
- Right-click in the right-hand side of the top pane and you will, in most views, be able to display a menu with a check box to **Show Split**.
- Double-click the dividing line or drag it to also remove or open the split window.

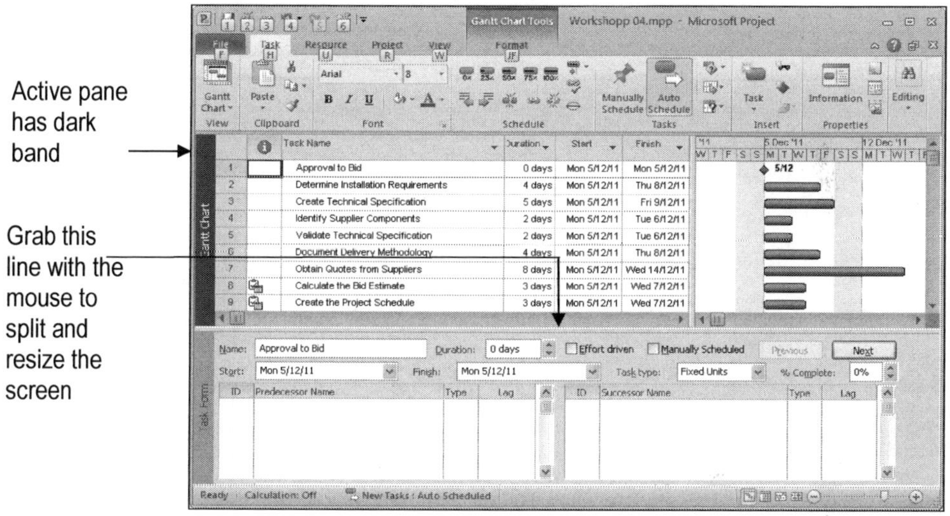

A pane needs to be **Active** before menu items pertaining to that pane become available. A dark band on the left-hand side is displayed in the **Active Pane**.

The **Ribbon**, **View** tab options will often change when different **Views** are selected in a pane.

A **Pane** is made **Active** just by:

- Clicking anywhere in the pane, or
- Pressing **F6** to swap active panes.

Only the **Active Pane** may be printed at a time. Thus it is not possible to create a printout with a Gantt Chart and a Resource Sheet (Table) or Graphs (Histograms) with Microsoft Project. Oracle Primavera P6 allows two panes to be printed at a time, a Gantt Chart from the top pane and a histogram in the bottom pane. Asta Powerproject allows a Gantt Chart plus multiple Histograms to be printed at one time.

3.3.6 Managing Details Forms

Some **Views** displayed in **Panes** have further options for displaying data. These are titled **Details** forms. The **Details** forms may be selected, when available, by:

- Making the pane active, then
- Right-click in the right-hand side of the screen and clicking the required form, see the example to the left of this menu:

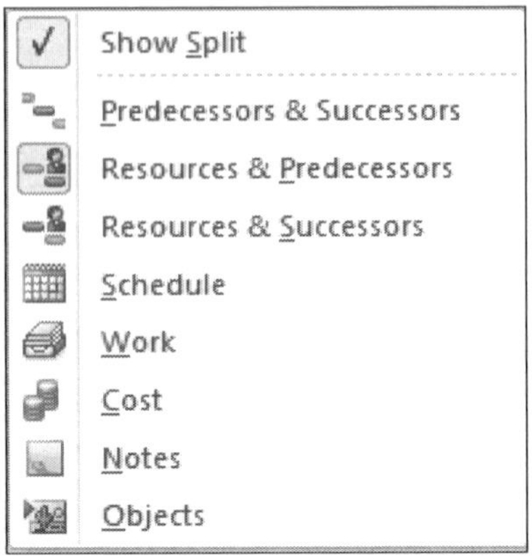

3.4 Status Bar

The **Status Bar**, located at the bottom of the screen, may be formatted by right-clicking on it:

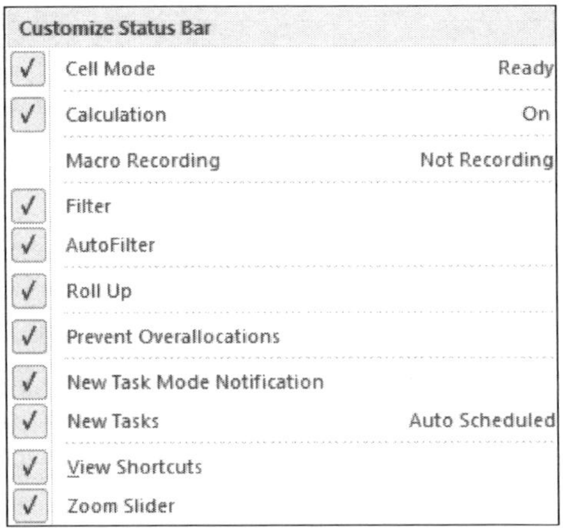

3.5 Forms Available from the Ribbon Groups

Some Ribbon groups have a little arrow in the bottom right-hand corner of the Group box. Clicking on the arrow will open up a form:

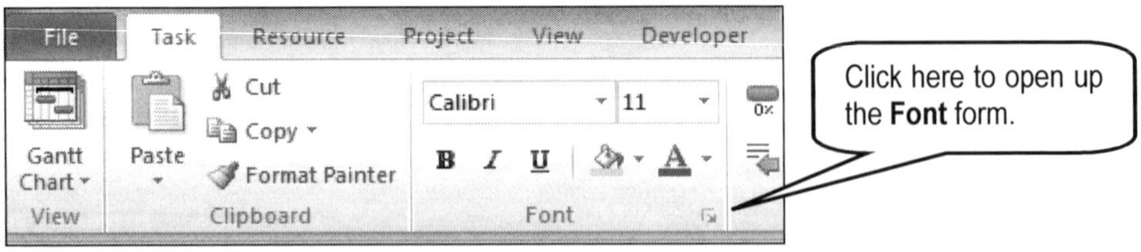

3.6 Right-clicking with the Mouse

It is very important that you become familiar with using the right-click function of the mouse as this is often a quicker way of operating the software than using the menus.

The right-click will normally display a menu, which is often different depending on the displayed View and Active Pane. It is advised that you experiment with each view to become familiar with the menus.

3.7 *Finding the Task Bars in the Gantt Chart*

When there are no bars displayed it is sometimes difficult to find them.

To find a task bar:

- Select a task that you wish to find the corresponding bar,
- Select the **Task**, **Editing** group, **Scroll to Task** button,
- This will move the Gantt Chart Timescale to display the task bar.

3.8 *Setting up the Options*

The basic parameters of the software must be configured so it will operate the way you desire. In order for the software to operate and/or calculate the way you want, some of the defaults must be turned on, or off, or changed. These configuration items may be found under **File**, **Options**.

This book assumes you have a standard install of Microsoft Project 2010, either Standard or Professional versions, and the Options and Global template have not been edited. We will discuss some of the more important Options now. All the Options are discussed in detail in the **OPTIONS** chapter. If you have a non standard install of Microsoft Project 2010 you may need to read the **OPTIONS** chapter to check and understand how your software is set up.

3.8.1 General Tab

Select **File**, **Options** to display the **Options** form and select the **General** tab:

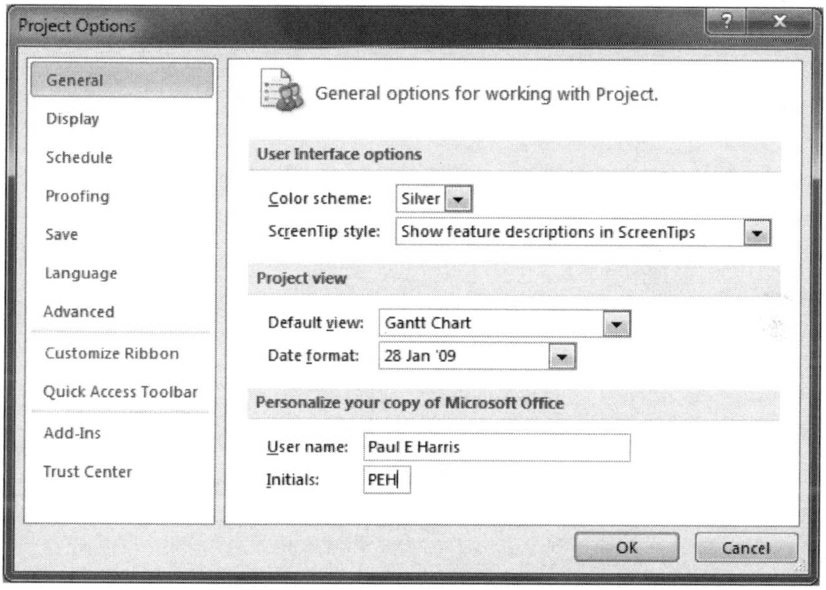

- **Default view:** is the view that is applied to any project when it is opened. It is recommended to set this to **Gantt Chart**.
- **Date format:** is used to select the display style of the dates for all projects. The date format will be displayed according to a combination of your system default settings and the Microsoft Project Options settings. You may adjust your date format under the system Control Panel, Regional and Language Options and the Microsoft Project settings in the Options form, which are covered in the **OPTIONS** chapter.

There is often confusion on international projects between the numerical US date style, mmddyy and the numerical European date style, ddmmyy. For example, in the United States 020712 is read as 07 Feb 12 and in many other countries as 02 Jul 12. You should consider adopting either the ddmmmyy style, **06 Jan '12** or mmmddyy style, **Jan 06 '12** for all your plans to avoid these misunderstandings especially when the project involves parties from within and outside the US on one project.

3.8.2 Schedule Tab – Scheduling options for this project:

Many of the default Microsoft Project Schedule options make the software operate at a more complex level making the software difficult for all users. It is suggested that the settings discussed below are considered as a starting point for all projects.

Select the **Schedule** tab and scroll down to the **Scheduling options for this project:**:

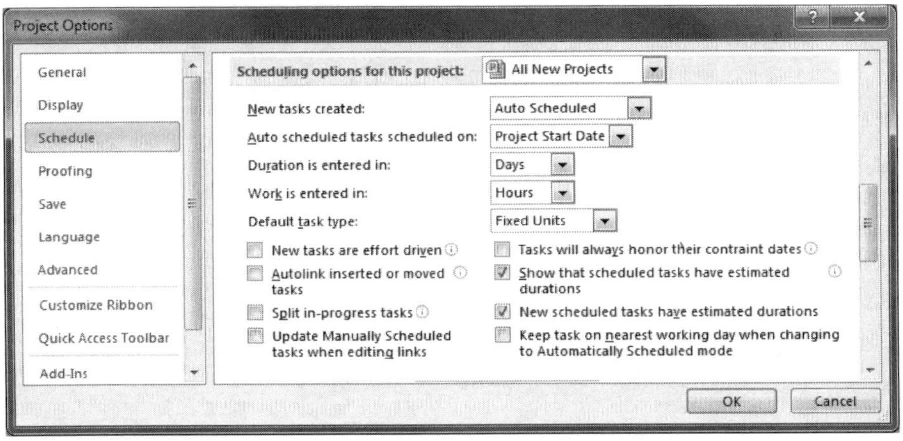

- **Scheduling options for this project**: allows the selection of **All New Projects** or any project that is currently open from the drop-down box.
  - When **All New Projects** is selected then the defaults selected in this form are applied to any new project when it is created from the **Blank project** option. These options are **NOT** used when a project is created from a template because the template options are adopted for new projects created from a template.
  - When an open project is selected then the options for that project may be edited.
- **New tasks created:** allows the selection of **Manually Scheduled** or **Auto Scheduled**.
  - It is normally considered good scheduling to select **Auto Scheduled** so tasks will acknowledge the relationships and constraints.
  - As discussed in the previous paragraph the **Manually Scheduled** option (new to Microsoft Project 2010) overrides the schedule calculations for tasks marked as **Manually scheduled**, allowing the software to be used like a white board for the selected tasks. This feature is covered in detail in the **ADDING TASKS** chapter.
- **Auto scheduled tasks scheduled on:** – When the option of **Start on Current Date** is selected new tasks are assigned an Early Start constraint as they are added to the schedule.

  It is not desirable to have tasks assigned constraints as they are created in a Critical Path schedule as this affects how the dates and float are calculated. Therefore **Start On Project Start Date** should always be selected when creating a Critical Path schedule.

- **Duration is entered in:** – This option specifies the format in which durations are entered via the keyboard. If **Day** is selected as the default, then a duration of 2 days is entered as 2 (without the d). If **Hours** is selected as the default, then a 2-day duration should be entered as 2d. Normally **days** are selected here unless your project is a very short duration and you wish to display the durations in hours.
- **Default task type:** – This option becomes active when resources are assigned and should be set to either **Fixed Duration** when the user does not want the duration of tasks to change as resources are modified or **Fixed Units** when the user prefers the estimate at completion not to change as task durations are edited. This topic is covered in more detail in the **OPTIONS** and **RESOURCES** chapters.
- **New tasks are effort driven** – This option becomes active when resources are assigned to tasks and the author recommends this should be unchecked. The reasons are covered in detail in the **OPTIONS** and **RESOURCES** chapters. If this is left checked and more than one resource is assigned to a task then either the Duration or resource Units per Time Period will change which may become confusing for new users.
- **Autolink inserted or moved tasks** option will result in relationships being changed when tasks are dragged to another position. This should **NOT** normally be checked.
- **Split in-progress tasks** will make some tasks split when they actually start before their predecessors. This can get confusing for new users when tasks generate splits. This function also creates a more conservative schedule normally taking longer to complete the tasks. The author suggests that new users turn this option off until they have some experience with the software.
- **Update Manually Scheduled tasks when editing links** makes **Manually Scheduled** tasks acknowledge their relationships when they are assigned a predecessor. A **Manually Scheduled** task will not move in time if the option is checked or not when it does not have a predecessor.
- **Tasks will always honor their constraint dates** results in the possibility of tasks being scheduled earlier than it is technically possible. This should **NOT** ever be checked.
- **Estimated Durations** – These two options do not affect the calculation of projects. When checked a new task is assigned an estimated duration and has a "**?**" after the duration. Once a duration is manually entered, the "**?**" is removed. The **General** tab on the **Task** form has a check box which establishes when a task has an estimated duration.
  - **Show that scheduled tasks have estimated durations** – A task with an estimated duration is flagged with a "**?**" after the duration in the data columns when this option is checked.
  - **New tasks have estimated durations:** – When a task is added, it will have the estimated check box checked.

Before entering a Duration

Task Name	Duration
New Task	1 day?

and after entering a Duration:

Task Name	Duration
New Task	6 days

NOTE: Summary tasks are marked as estimated when one or more **detail tasks** associated with it are marked as Estimated.

- **Keep task on nearest working day when changing to Automatically Scheduled mode** assigns a constraint to a task when it is changed from **Auto scheduled** to **Manually scheduled**. Therefore an **Auto scheduled** task does not move to the **Project Start Date** when converted to **Manually scheduled**. Constraints should be set by the user. It is bad practice to allow the software to set constraints for the user and it is recommended this option is turned off.

3.9 *Mouse Pointers*

There are a number of mouse pointers and this table will outline the important ones:

Mouse Pointers when hovering over a table:

Select cell

Adjusts width of a row

Select row

Select column

Drag one or more rows or columns to move them to a new location

Drag Cell

↔ Displayed when hovering over the Task name and used for indenting and outdenting tasks

Mouse Pointers when hovering over a bar in the Gantt Chart:

Increase or decrease task duration

Select task, before linking or dragging a task

After selecting a task, dragging left or right will move the task and set a constraint

After selecting a task, dragging up or down will add a Finish-to-Start relationship

When dragged right will assign an Actual Start and adjust the % Complete

Other Pointers:

Adjusts the width of tables in forms such as the width of columns in the Task Form

Moves the divider between the Table and Gantt chart

Moves the divider between the Upper and Lower Pane

Normal mouse pointer used to grab or click

3.10 Workshop 1 – Navigation and Setting Your Project Options

Background

In this workshop you will also practice navigating around the screen, set the options to allow durations to be entered in days, ensure that a useful date format is displayed and ensure other options are set so the software operates in a simpler mode than the standard defaults.

Navigation Practice

1. Click on the Ribbon Toolbar menu at the top of the screen, work your way through the tabs and observe what commands are located on each tab:

2. Right-click on the Ribbon Toolbar and display the Ribbon Toolbar Menu:

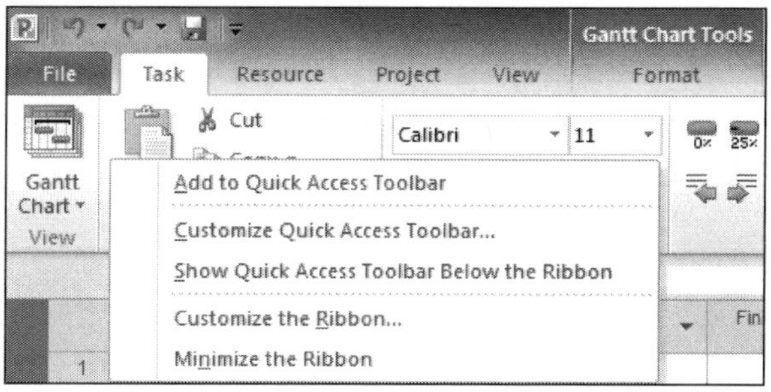

3. To allow more buttons to be displayed on the Quick Access Toolbar, click on the **Show Quick Access Toolbar Below the Ribbon** to move the Quick Access Toolbar below the Ribbon Toolbar.
4. Click on the **Customize Quick Access Toolbar...** to open the **Project Options** form. Explore the tabs on the left-hand side.
5. From the **Quick Access Toolbar** tab in the **File**, **Project Options** form, add the following frequently used buttons to the Quick Access Toolbar, if not already displayed:

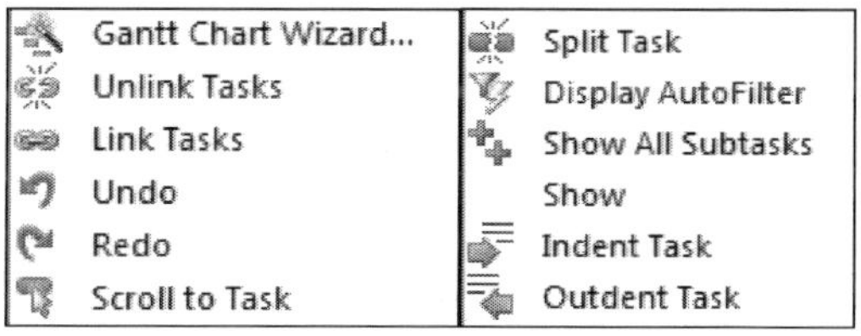

6. Click on the **Customize Ribbon** tab in the **File**, **Options** to open the **Project options** form, ensure that **Developer tab** is displayed on the **Ribbon** in order to access the **Organizer** form easily, and then close the form.
7. Right-click on the Ribbon Toolbar and display the Ribbon Toolbar Menu. Click on **Minimize the Ribbon** to hide the Ribbon Toolbar.

Continued...

8. Click on some Ribbon Toolbar menu headings to display the Ribbon Groups. When you click in the Gantt Chart area the Ribbon will minimize and more work area will be available allowing you to see more tasks.
9. Right-click in the Gantt Chart, select **Show Split** to split the window and this will show the **Task** form in the bottom window.
10. Make the bottom window active by clicking in it.
11. Note the dark bar on the left-hand side of the screen has moved from the top pane to the bottom pane.
12. Right-click in the bottom pane and select the different options to see how **Task Details** form changes with the different options. Leave this form with the **Predecessors and Successors** option displayed.
13. Activate the upper pane, by clicking in it.
14. Resize the panes by dragging the Split screen bar.
15. Close the Split screen by double-clicking on the horizontal dividing line.
16. Split the screen by double-clicking on the small bar in the bottom right-hand corner of the screen.

Assignment

1. Close you project by selecting **File**, **Close** and do not save any changes.
2. Select **File**, **Options** to open the **Project Options** form.
3. Set the **Default View** to **Gantt Chart**.
4. Select **General** tab and set the **Date format:** to either:
   - "**ddmmmyy**" i.e., 28 Jan '09, or
   - "**mmmddyy**" i.e., Jan 28 '09.

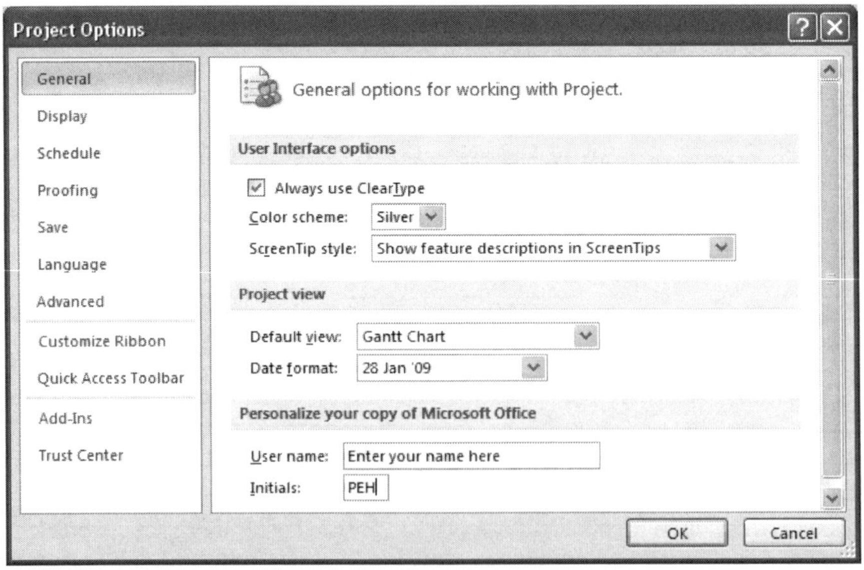

NOTE: The available date format will depend on your system settings set in the system Control Panel, Regional and Language Options.

5. Enter your name and initials.
6. Select the **Display** tab and check that all check boxes are checked.
7. Select the **Schedule** tab and set the Schedule Options for your project as per the picture below:

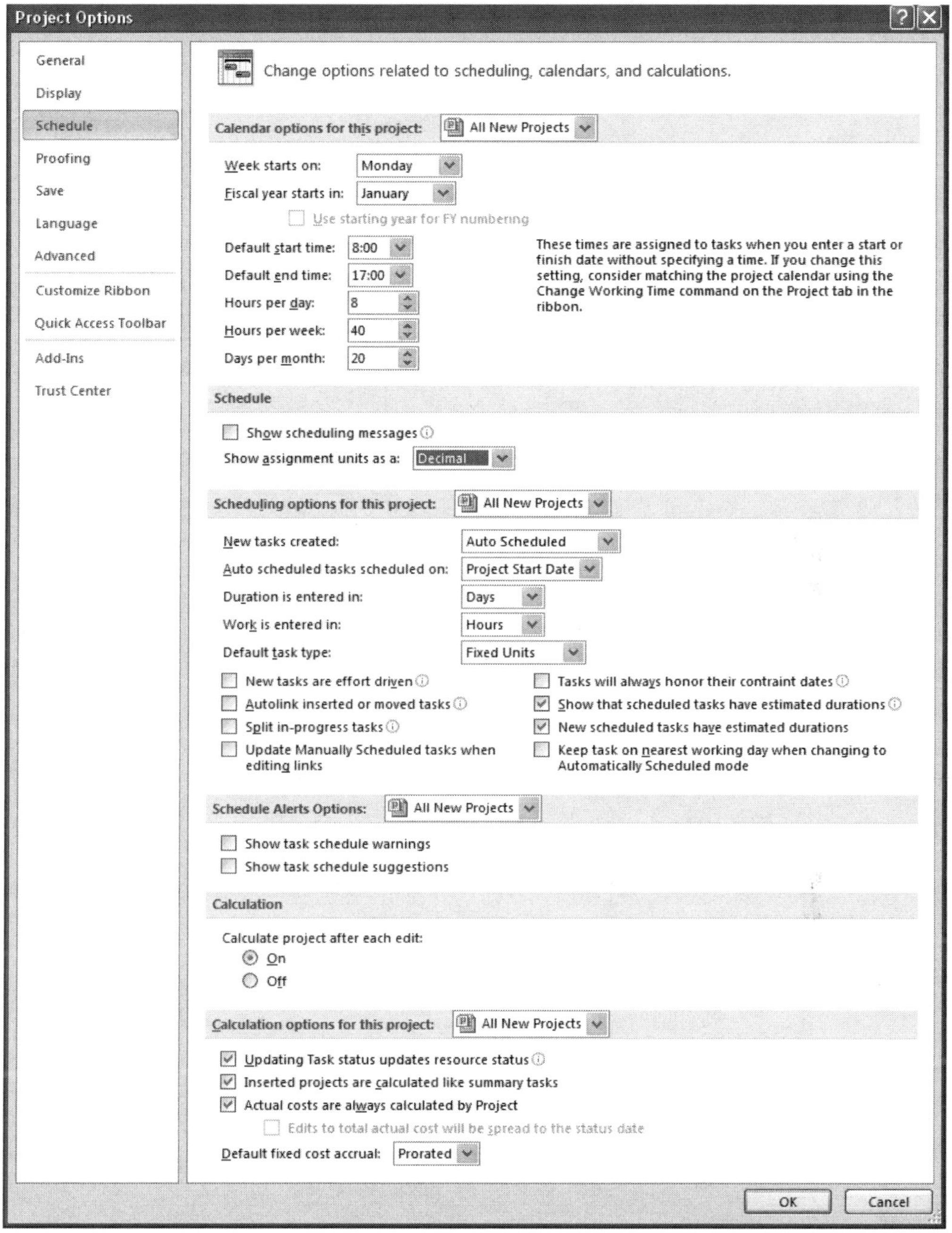

8. More details about these settings are available in the **OPTIONS** chapter.

9. Select 

to close the **Project Options** form.

10. Select **File**, **Options** to open the **Project Options** form and set the options as per below:

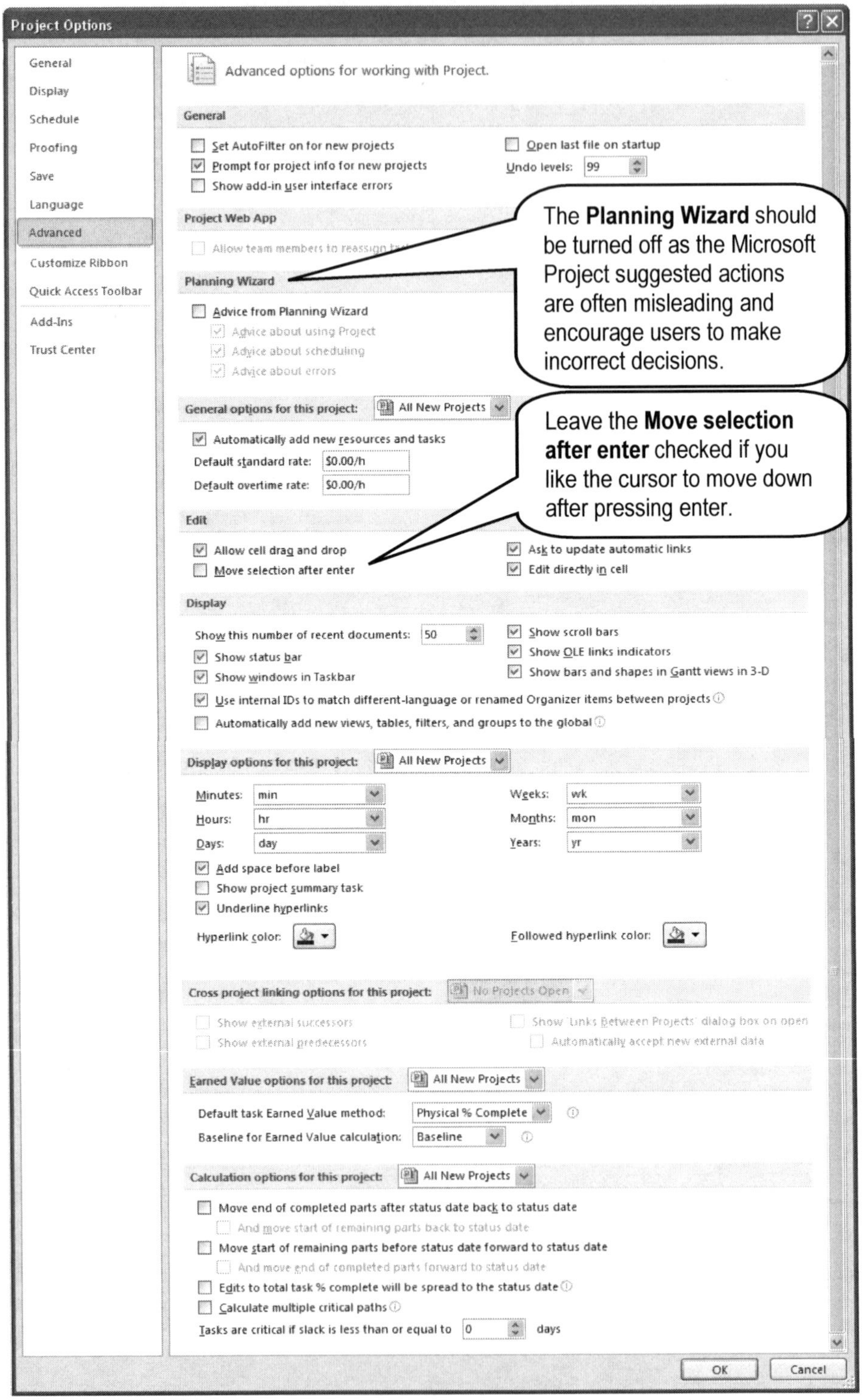

11. Select OK to close the **Project Options** form.

4 CREATING PROJECTS AND TEMPLATES

Ensure you have Automatic Updates switched on, this is part of Microsoft office, as the product is often improved over time and bugs removed.

There are three principal methods of creating a new project:

- Start with a blank project, or
- Use a template that contains default data and formats, or
- Open an old project and save it with a new file name.

4.1 Starting Microsoft Project 2010

When opening Microsoft Project 2010, you will be presented with a blank project, named Project1, which you may start working with immediately.

4.2 Creating a Blank Project

A blank project may be created from the **New Project** pane, which is displayed by:

- Keying in **Ctrl+N**, or
- Selecting **File**, **New**
- Then clicking on **Blank Project**

A new project will be displayed and the project name is shown at the top center of the screen.

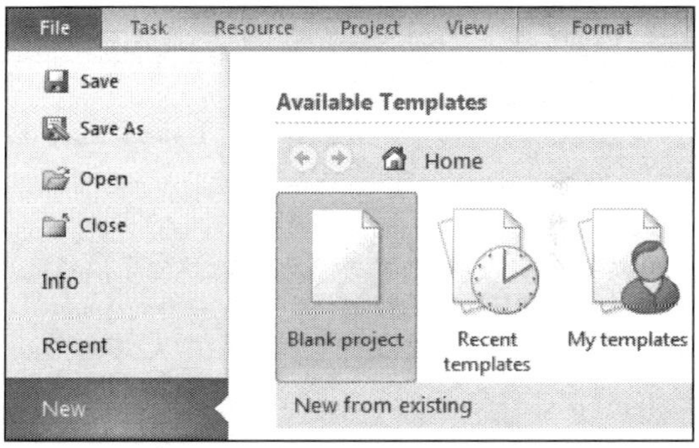

At this point the **Project Start date** is normally set in the **Project Information** form. Select **Project**, **Properties** group, **Project Information** to open this form and the time if not displayed, is set by default at 08:00hrs or 08:00pm:

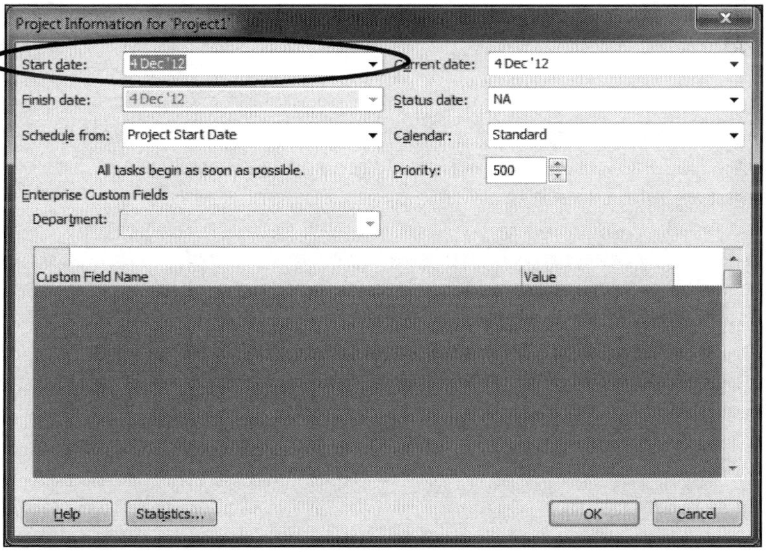

- When **Schedule from:** is set to the **Project Start Date**, which is the usual method of scheduling projects:
  - Enter the **Start date:** – This is the date before which no task will be scheduled to start.
  - The **Finish date:** – This is a calculated date and is the date of the completion of all tasks.
- When **Schedule from:** is set to the **Project Finish Date**:
  - All new tasks are set with a constraint of **As Late As Possible**,
  - Summary Tasks are set to **As Late As Possible**, and
  - Therefore, all new tasks are scheduled before the **Project Finish Date** and not after the start date which is now calculated by the software.

This option is not recommended as the schedule calculation gives some results that are difficult to understand and are covered in paragraph 22.6.5.

- **Current Date:** – This field defaults to **today's date**; it represents the date today and may be changed at any time. This date has no effect on most calculations and reverts back to the system date each time a schedule is opened. The time is by default set to 8:00am or 08:00hrs.

The **Current Date** is set to the system date each time a schedule is opened. It is recommended that this date not be used for identifying the **Data Date**. The **Status Date** does not change and this date should always be used for identifying the **Data Date**.

- **Status Date:** – This is an optional field used when updating a project. This topic is covered in the **TRACKING PROGRESS** chapter. After this date has been set, it may be displayed as a gridline. You may remove the date by typing **NA** into the field.
- **Calendar:** – This is the project **Base** calendar that is used to calculate the durations of all tasks unless they have:
  - A resource with an edited resource calendar, or
  - A different task calendar assigned.
- **Priority:** – This is the project priority when sharing resources over a number of projects. The high priority is 1000 is and the lowest is 0.
- Click on the Statistics... button to open the **Project Statistics** form, which outlines statistical information about the project.

A new blank project copies default values such as the Standard calendar from the **Global.mpt** file. The **Global.mpt** file is a template on your computer used to create blank project and this may be edited using the **File**, **Info**, **Organizer** utility.

The default Microsoft Project 2010 blank project has a Standard calendar based on 5 days per week without any holidays, which will not suit many projects. It is recommended that the **Global.mpt** Standard calendar be replaced with a project calendar that has been edited to represent your local public holidays using the **File**, **Info**, **Organizer** utility or consider using Templates to create new projects which have had the calendar edited to suit your organization's work periods.

4.3 Opening an Existing Project

Another method of creating a new project is to open an existing project, save it with a new name and then modify it. To open an existing project display the **Open** form by selecting:

- **File**, **Open**, or
- **Ctl+O**

Then select the file you want to open from the **Open** form.

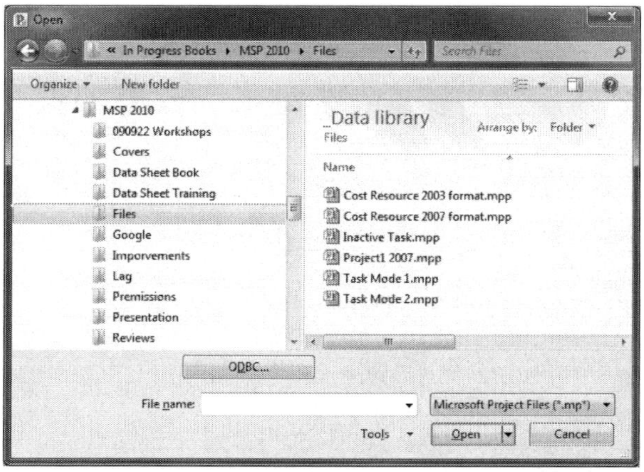

The **New Project from existing** form may be used to open an existing project:

- Select **File**, **New**, **New from existing project**,
- Then select the file you want to open from the **Open** form,
- Then use **File**, **Save As** to save the file under a different name,
  - ➢ Enter a new **Project Name**,
  - ➢ Select in which **Current Folder** you want to save the project, and
  - ➢ Click on Save to save the new project.

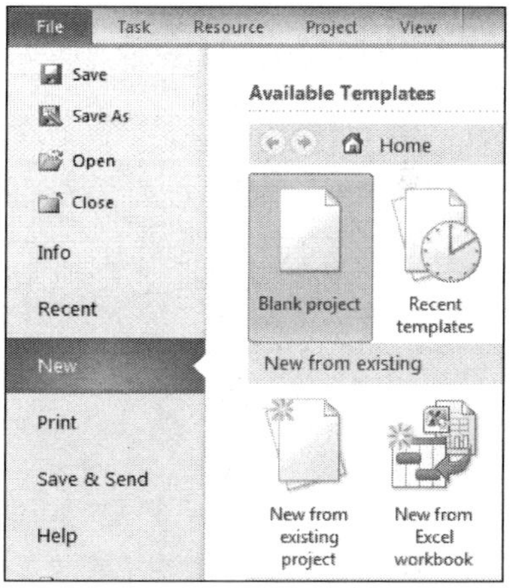

You may now alter the contents of this existing plan to reflect the scope of your new project.

4.4 Re-opening a Project

Selecting **File**, **Recent** will show a list of recently opened project files:

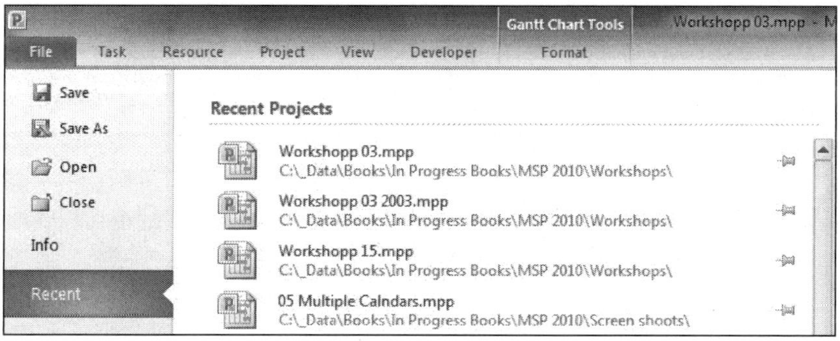

4.5 Creating a Project Template

Project templates allow organizations to create standard project models containing default information applicable to the organization. In particular, a calendar with the local public holidays should be created along with Views with redefined headers and footers to suit your organization. Therefore to save time when you create a new project, you should generate your own templates to suit the different types of projects your organization undertakes.

- Create a template by saving a project, with or without tasks, in **Template (*.mpt)** format. This template will be available when you select **File**, **New**, **My templates**.
- This directory where user templates are saved may be changed by selecting the **File**, **Options**, **Save** tab.
- Templates may be deleted by selecting the template in the **New** (project) form, right-clicking to open a menu and selecting Delete.

4.6 Creating a New Project from a Template

To create a new project from a template:

- Select **File**, **New** and there are template location options:
  - ➢ **My templates** allows you to open templates on your computer and is covered in the next paragraph.
  - ➢ **Recent templates** takes you to your recently used templates.
  - ➢ **Office.com Templates**, this will allow you to access Microsoft's templates.
- Click on the **My templates** item under the **My templates** heading to open the **Templates** form to select a Microsoft template. After you have created your own templates these will be available from the **Personal Templates** tab.

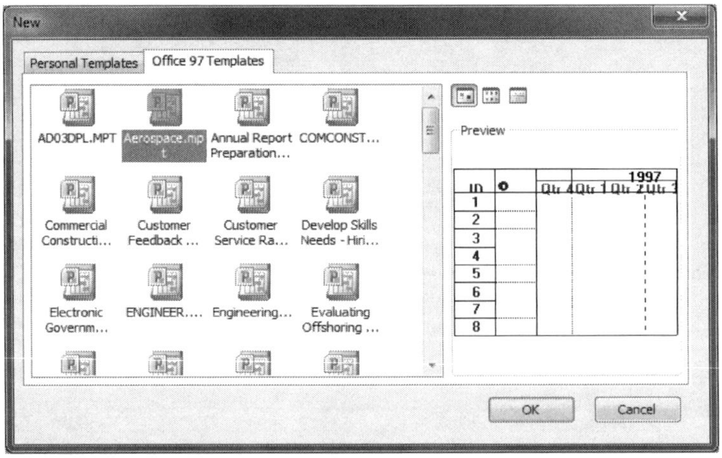

- Select the required template from the form by double-clicking on the template button or selecting the template by clicking on it and then clicking on the  button.

At this point you would normally set the **Project Start date** in the **Project Information** form. Select **Project**, **Properties** group, **Project Information** to open this form.

4.7 Saving Additional Project Information

Often additional information about a project is required to be saved with the project such as location, client and type of project. This data may be saved in the **File**, **Info**, **Project Information**, **Advanced Properties** form and these fields may be inserted into reports:

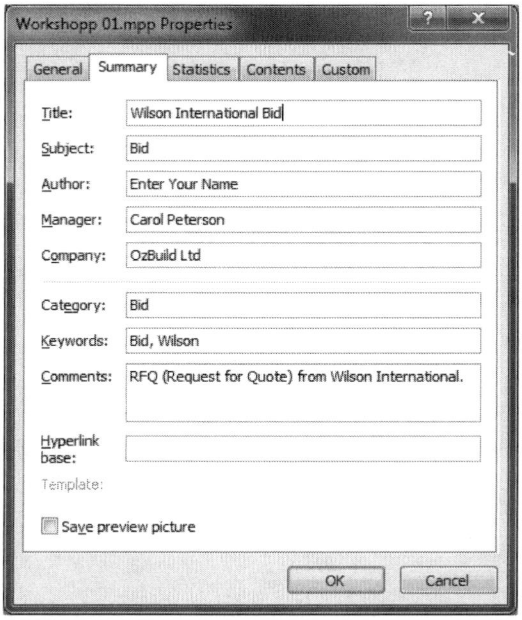

- **Hyperlink base:** This allows you to enter the path to a file or web page.
- **Save preview picture**. This saves a thumbnail sketch, which may be seen when viewing files in Windows Explorer.

4.8 Using the Alt Key and Keystrokes to Access Commands

Microsoft Project 2010 has introduced a function that displays the keystroke commands when the **Alt** key is pressed. The picture below shows the keystroke commands after pressing and holding down the **Alt** key; then, for example, pressing the **F** key will open the **File** menu:

4.9 Saving a Project

When you save a project you should consider using a file naming convention that simply allows the identification of the project name or number, the **Status Date** of the file, the type of schedule and version. Many schedulers use the international standard date format of yyyymmdd as the first 8 characters of the file name as this format sorts the files in date order in the directory they have been saved into.

To save a project file use the **File**, **Save** and **File**, **Save As** commands.

A suggested file format would be:

yyyymmyy_"Project Number"_"Revision Number"_"Schedule Type"

yyyymmdd would be in numbers which allows the files to be sorted in date order in Explorer, thus 20120911 would be 9th September 2012.

4.10 Closing Microsoft Project

If you have made changes to a project you will be asked on closing if you wish to save the project.

To close a project:

- Select **File**, **Close**,
- Click on the **Close Window** button and when the last window of a project is being closed you will be asked if you wish to save any changes
- Click on the **Close** button to close all projects and close Microsoft Project.

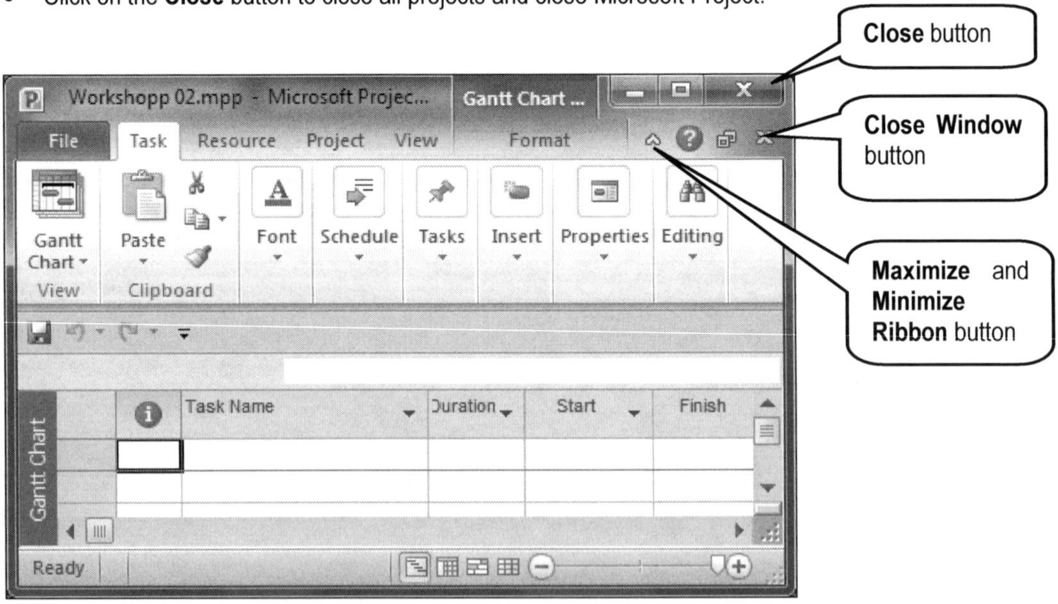

4.11 Workshop 2 - Creating a Project

Background

You are an employee of OzBuild Ltd and are responsible for planning the bid preparation required to ensure that a response to an RFQ (Request For Quote) from Wilson International is submitted on time.

Your company has completed the Startup Phase of the project, the Bid Strategy has been developed and approval to bid for this project has been given.

The Work Breakdown Structure (WBS) for the project was created with a planning product called ChangeAide and displayed below:

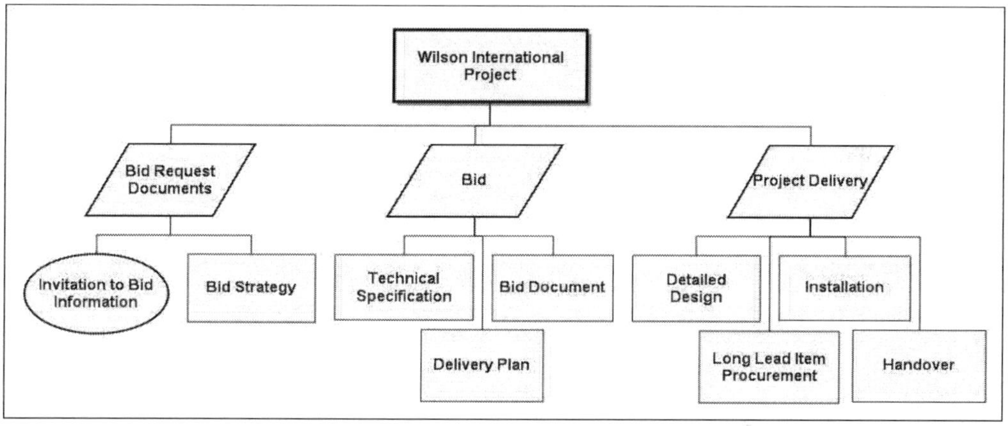

You have been requested to plan the project Initiation Phase, where the Bid will be produced, which comprises of the following deliverables/products:

- Technical Specification
- Delivery Plan
- Bid Document.

You have been advised that the RFQ will not be available until the 5 December 2011

These workshops will take you through the process of creating the Initiating Phase Plan for the development of the Bid to be submitted in response to the RFQ.

Assignment

1. Create a new project by selecting **File**, **New**.
2. Set the **Start date:** to **Mon 05 Dec 11** using the **Project**, **Properties** group, **Project Information** form but do not edit the **Current date:**. Press the OK button to save the input data.

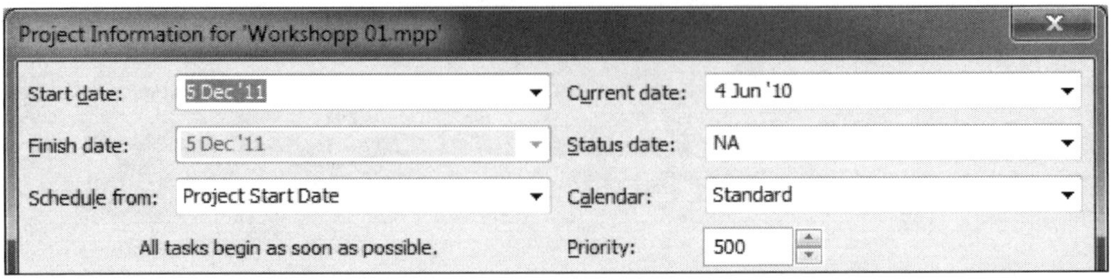

NOTE: The date format will be displayed according to a combination of the Microsoft Project Options settings and you computer system default settings. You may adjust your date format so you are able to see the day month and year using the **File**, **Options**, **General**. The order of the day, month and year is set in the system Control Panel, Regional and Language Options.

2. Add the following project information in the **File**, **Info**, **Project Information**, **Advanced Properties** form.

3. **Save** your project as **OzBuild Bid** in a location of your choice, such as the desktop.

NOTE: Completed workshops and PowerPoint Instructors slide presentations may be downloaded from the Eastwood Harris web site at www.eh.com.au.

5 DEFINING CALENDARS

The finish date (and time) of a task is calculated from the start date (and time) plus the duration over the calendar associated with the task. Therefore, a five-day duration task that starts at the start of the work day on a Wednesday, and is associated with a five-day workweek calendar (with Saturday and Sunday as nonwork days) will finish at the end of the workday on the following Tuesday.

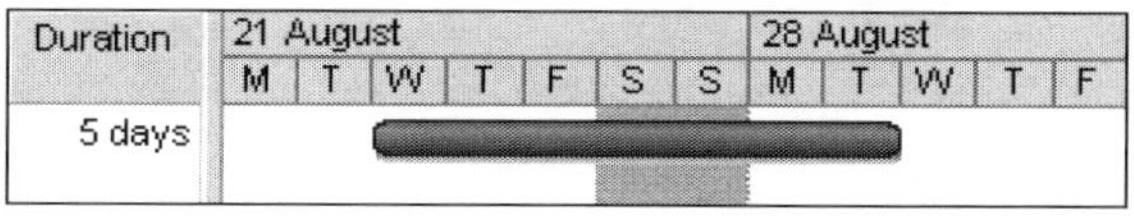

Microsoft Project is supplied with three calendars, which are termed **Base Calendars**:

- **Standard** – This calendar is 5 days per week, 8 hours per day.
- **24 Hour** – This calendar is 7 days per week and 24 hours per day.
- **Night shift** – This calendar is 7 days per week and 8 hours per day during the night.

You may create new or edit existing Base Calendars to reflect your project requirements, such as adding holidays or additional work days or adjusting work times. For example, some tasks may have a 5-day per week calendar and some may have a 7-day per week calendar.

A **Base Calendar** is assigned to each project. Microsoft Project uses the term **Project Calendar** to describe this calendar. By default all un-resourced tasks use the **Project Calendar** to calculate the end date of the task. Any un-resourced task may be assigned a different calendar and the end date will be calculated using the assigned calendar.

This chapter will cover some of the following topics, those with an * are covered in the **MORE ADVANCED SCHEDULING** chapter.

Topic	Menu Command
• Assigning a base calendar to a project	**Project**, **Properties** group, **Project Information**
• Editing a calendar's working days	**Project**, **Properties** group, **Change Working Time**
• Creating a new calendar	**Project**, **Properties** group, **Change Working Time**, **Create New Calendar...**
• *Renaming an existing calendar	**Developer**, **Organizer** group, **Calendars** tab, **Rename...**
• *Deleting a calendar	**Developer**, **Organizer** group,, **Calendars** tab, **Delete**
• *Copying a calendar to Global.mpt for use in future projects	**Developer**, **Organizer** group,, **Calendars** tab, **Copy >>**
• *Copying calendars between projects	**Developer**, **Organizer** group,, **Calendars** tab, **Copy >>**

Microsoft Project 2007 introduced significant changes in the way calendars are created and edited and which now allows for each non-work day or period to have a name or note explaining the purpose of the non-default work period. These non-work days or periods could be due to holidays or changes to working hours for a planned shutdown or system upgrade requiring people to work different or longer hours.

5.1 Editing Calendars

5.1.1 Editing Working Days to Create Holidays

To edit a calendar, select **Project**, **Properties** group, **Change Working Time** to open the **Change Working Time** form:

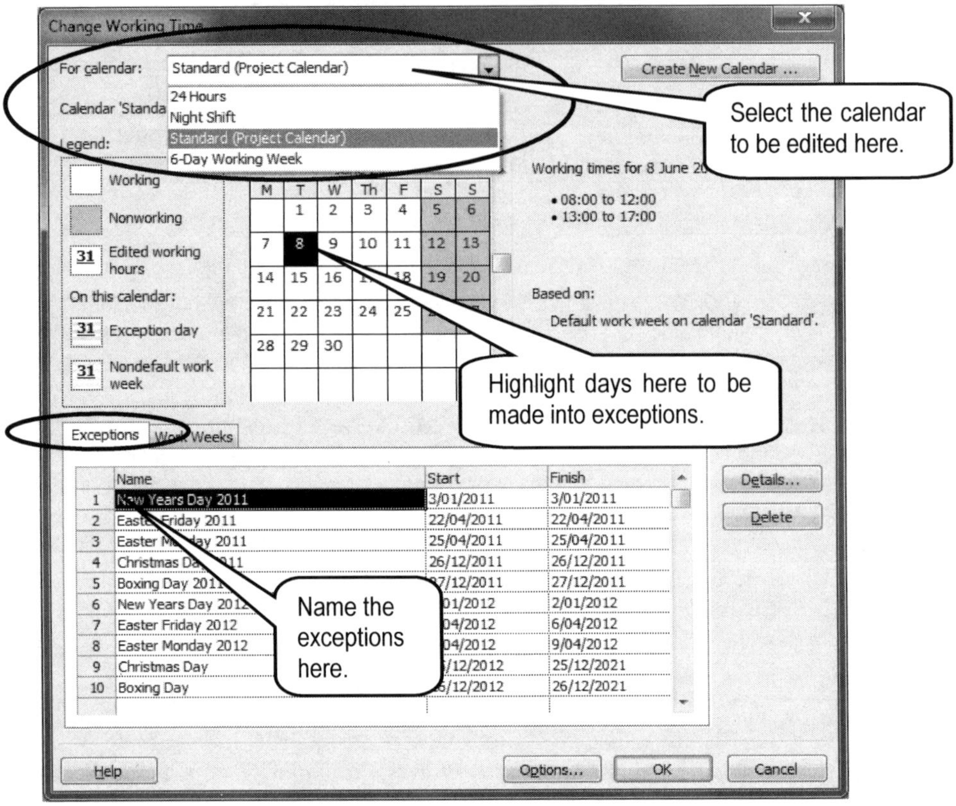

- The **Project Calendar** is also identified in the **Change Working Time** form as the calendar with **(Project Calendar)** written after the calendar name.
- Select the calendar to be edited from the **For calendar:** drop-down list at the top of the form,
- Click on the **Exceptions** tab,
- Highlight the days to be made nonwork days in the calendar,
- To make **Work Days** into **Nonwork Days**, add the following information in the first blank line in the lower half of the form:
  - Name of the Nonwork Day,
  - The Start Date, and
  - The Finish Date

  NOTE: The Start and Finish Dates of a one-day holiday are identical.

- When the holiday is recurring, such as the annual Christmas Day and New Year's Day, these days may be made recurring by clicking on the Details... button to open the calendar **Details:**
  - In the **Recurrence pattern** set the occurrence of the holiday to use the Daily, Weekly, Monthly or Yearly options. The options are displayed below:

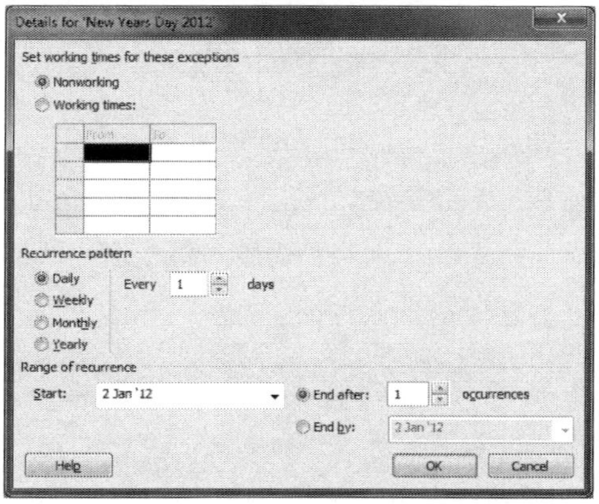

Daily

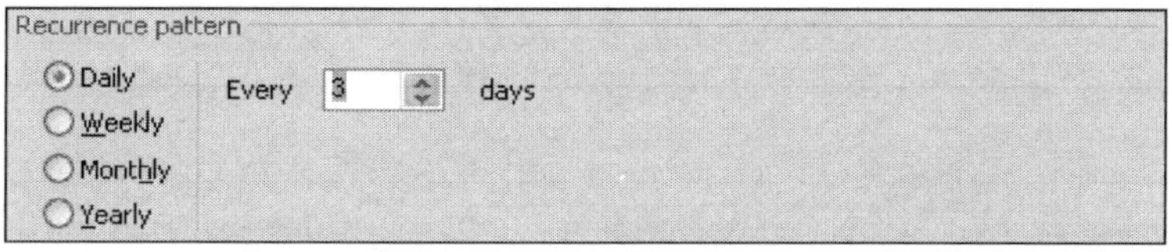

Weekly

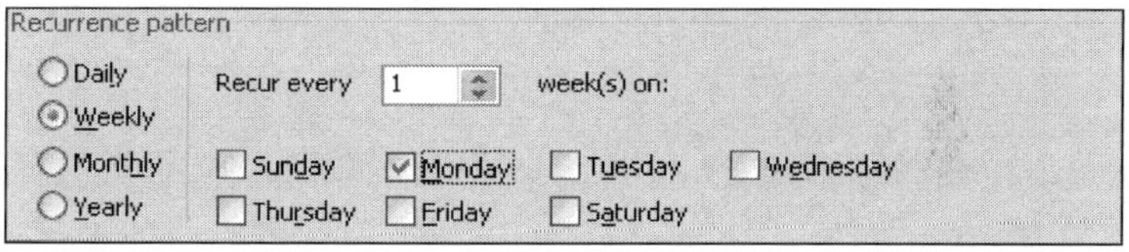

Monthly

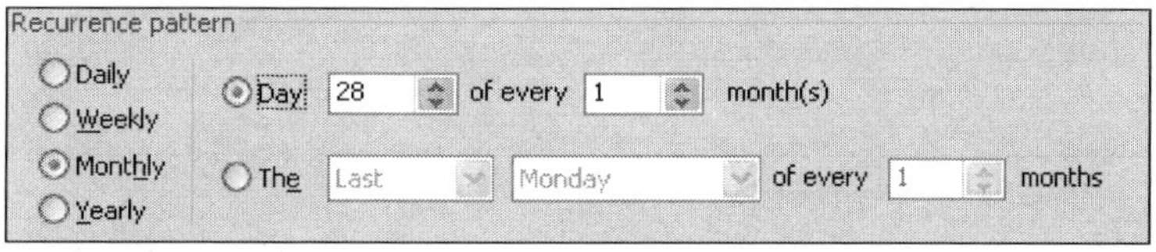

Yearly

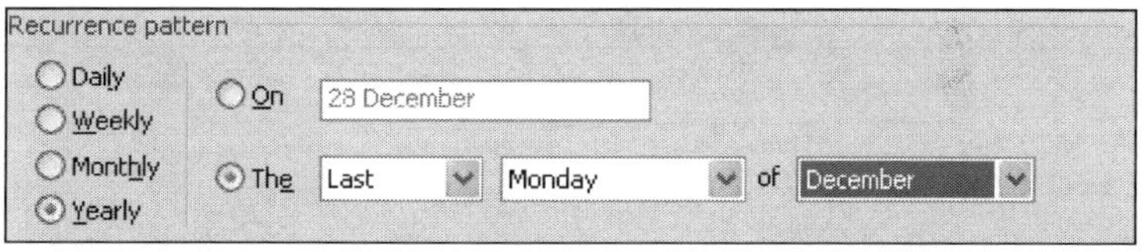

  - The **Range of recurrence** options allows the specification of the number of times the holiday occurs. The picture below shows Christmas Day is scheduled for the next 20 years.

Daily

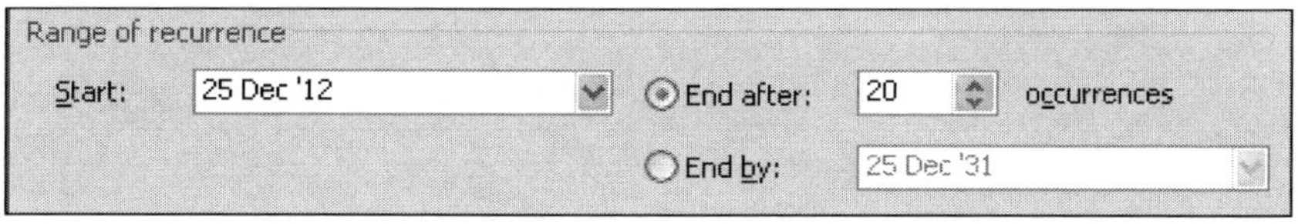

The author found by experimentation that only single day nonwork periods could be made repeating.

5.1.2 Editing a Calendar to Create an Exception

When it is desired to make a non-work day into a workday, say to make a Saturday a workday in a 5-day per week calendar:

- Open the **Change Working** form,
- Select the Calendar in the **For calendar:** drop down box,
- Select the day to be a non-workday,
- Enter the workday description a blank line in the **Exception** tab,

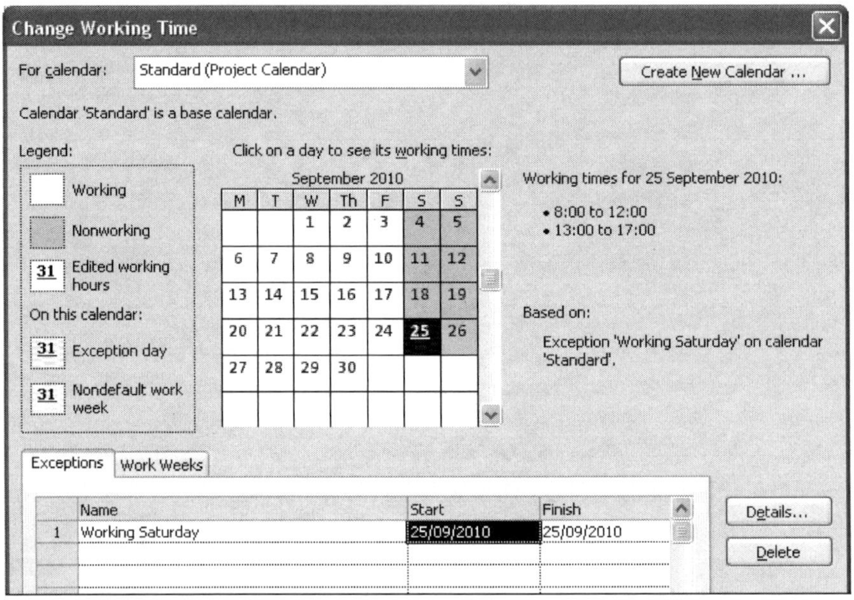

- Click on the Details... button to open the **Details** form,
- Click on the **Working times:** radio button and close the form.

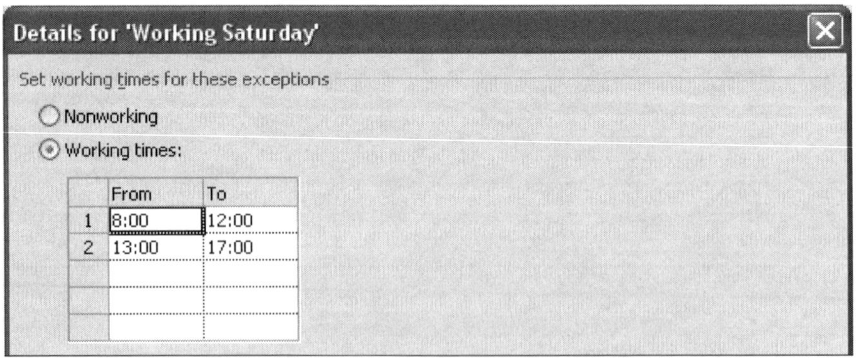

5.2 Creating a New Calendar

Select **Project**, **Properties** group, **Change Working Time** button and click on the [Create New Calendar ...] to open the **Create New Base Calendar** form:

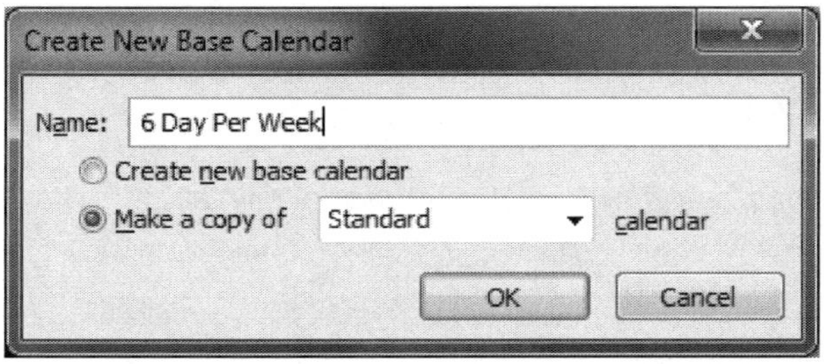

- To create a new calendar which is a copy of the Standard calendar, just type in the new calendar name in the **Name:** box and click on the [OK] button to create it, or
- To copy an existing calendar, click on the **Make a copy of** radio button and select the calendar you want to copy from the drop-down box and type in the new calendar name.

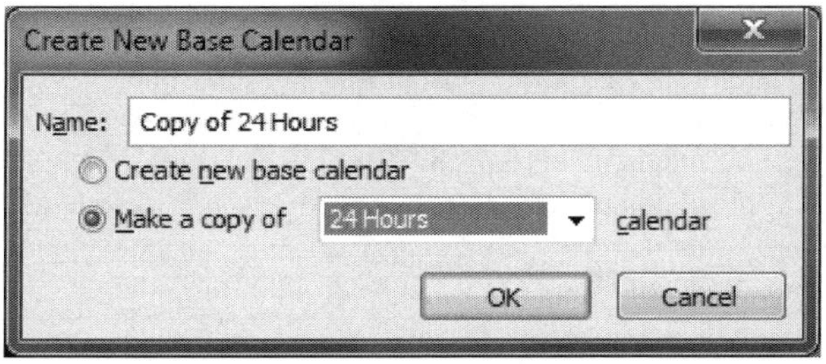

To save time when multiple calendars have the same nonwork periods, such as religious holidays, one calendar should be created and all of its nonwork periods entered. Then copy this calendar to create new calendars showing the same nonwork days.

5.3 Assigning a Calendar to a Project

In all versions of Microsoft Project a new blank project is assigned the **Standard** calendar as the **Project Calendar** when the project file is created. The **Project Calendar** is changed using the **Project Information** form by:

- Selecting **Project**, **Properties** group, **Project Information**, and
- Selecting the alternative calendar from the **Calendar:** drop-down box:

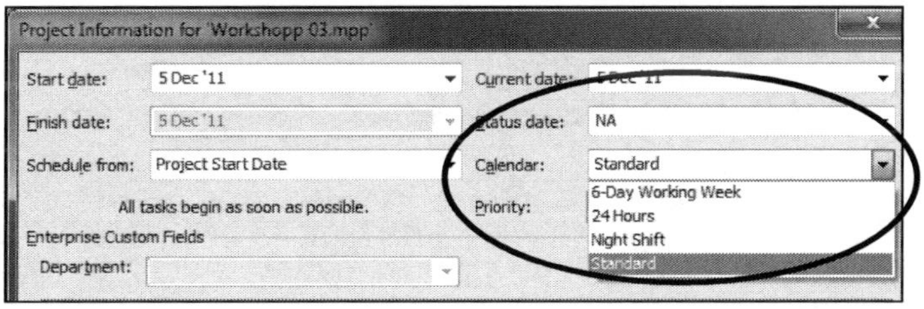

When a **Project Calendar** is changed or edited, the end date of all tasks assigned with the **Project Calendar** will be recalculated based on the new calendar. This may make a considerable difference to your project schedule dates. All new resources are assigned the **Project Base Calendar**.

5.4 Calculation of Durations in Days

Microsoft Project effectively calculates in hours and the value of the duration in days is calculated using the parameter entered in the **Hours per day:** field in the **File**, **Options**, **Schedule** tab, **Calendar options for this project:** section. It is **VERY IMPORTANT** that all users understand that the durations in days are calculated using **ONLY** the one parameter and this parameter is used with **EVERY** calendar. This makes Microsoft Project difficult to use when calendars with a different number of hours per day are being used.

For example, the **Options** form below shows the **Hours per day:** as "8". Therefore, when tasks are:

- Assigned an 8-hours per day calendar then the durations in days will be correct, and
- Assigned a 24-hours per day calendar the durations of tasks in days will be misleading.

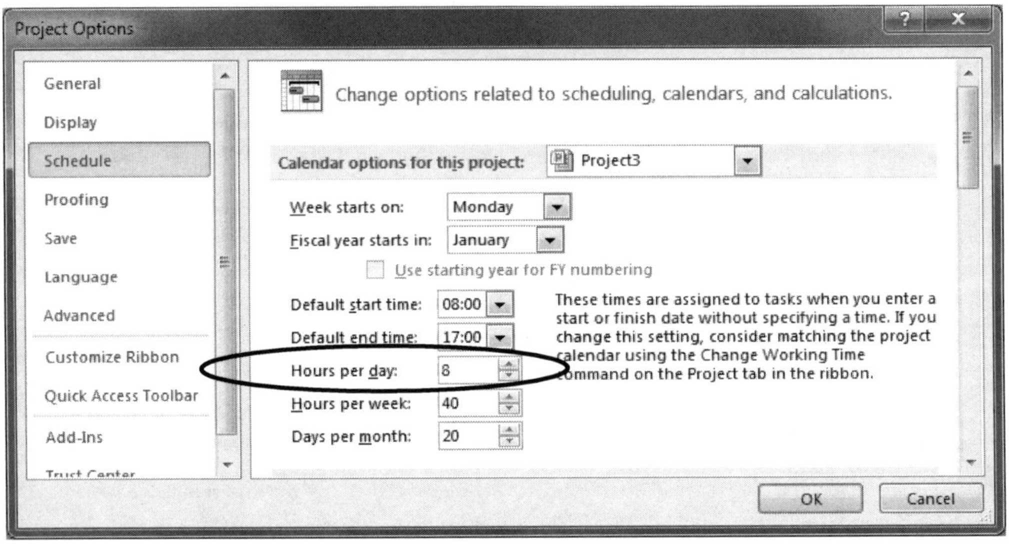

The picture below shows:

- Task 1 has the correct duration in days.
- Task 2 shows a duration that is clearly misleading.
- Task 4 and 5 display the duration in hours and are not misleading when the calendar column is also displayed.

	Task Calendar	Duration	Start	Finish
1	8 Hours per Day	5 days	Mon 8:00 AM	Fri 5:00 PM
2	24 Hours per Day	5 days	Mon 8:00 AM	Wed 12:00 AM
3				
4	8 Hours per Day	40 hrs	Mon 8:00 AM	Fri 5:00 PM
5	24 Hours per Day	40 hrs	Mon 8:00 AM	Wed 12:00 AM

The **Calendar options for this project** is covered in more detail in the **OPTIONS** chapter.

It is **STRONGLY RECOMMENDED** that inexperienced users avoid changing calendar start and finish times or assigning calendars with different numbers of hours per day whenever possible.

To display the duration in hours:

- The **Duration is entered in:** field in the **File**, **Options**, **Schedule** tab, **Schedule** heading should be set to **Hours**, and then
- Existing durations in days are changed to hours by overtyping the original durations.

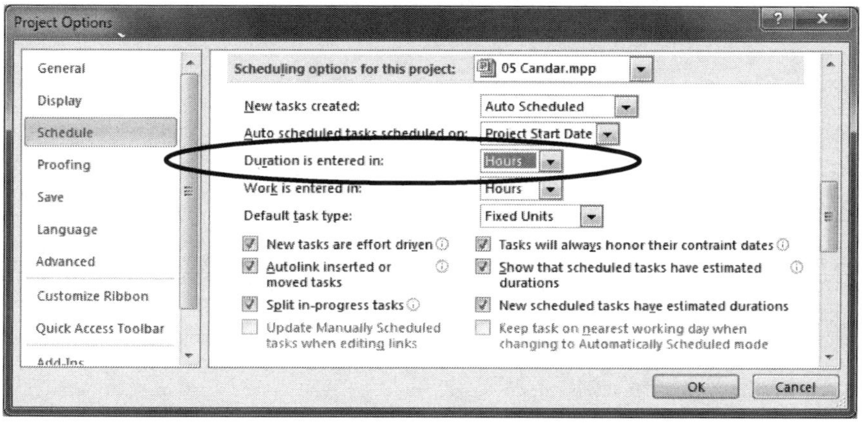

5.5 *Effect on 2007 Calendars When Saving to 2000 – 2003*

When a project file is saved from Microsoft Project 2010 or 2007 format to 2000 – 2003 format all the calendar notes are lost and each repeating nonwork period becomes an individual nonwork period without the note. The pictures below show the effect before and after saving to 2000 – 2003 format and then reopening with 2010 or 2007:

Before saving to 2000 – 2003 format

	Name	Start	Finish
1	New Years Day 2011	3/01/2011	3/01/2011
2	Easter 2011	22/04/2011	25/04/2011
3	Christmas & Boxing Day 2011	26/12/2011	27/12/2011
4	New Years Day 2012	2/01/2012	2/01/2012
5	Easter 2012	6/04/2012	9/04/2012
6	Christmas	25/12/2012	25/12/2031
7	Boxing Day	26/12/2012	26/12/2031

After saving to 2000 – 2003 format

	Name	Start	Finish
1	[Unnamed]	3/01/2011	3/01/2011
2	[Unnamed]	22/04/2011	25/04/2011
3	[Unnamed]	26/12/2011	27/12/2011
4	[Unnamed]	2/01/2012	2/01/2012
5	[Unnamed]	6/04/2012	9/04/2012
6	[Unnamed]	25/12/2012	25/12/2012
7	[Unnamed]	26/12/2012	26/12/2012
8	[Unnamed]	25/12/2013	25/12/2013

5.6 *Selecting Dates*

With the introduction of Microsoft Project 2007 there was a slight loss of functionality in selecting dates by the removal of the drop-down box that allowed the selection of months and the ability to scroll by year.

A calendar form is displayed by clicking on a date cell with the mouse pointer:

- The month may be scrolled forward or backward by clicking on the blue arrows,
- A date is selected by clicking on it, and
- When a date is selected an Early Start Constraint will be set.

5.7 Workshop 3 Maintaining the Calendars

Background

The normal working week at OzBuild Ltd is Monday to Friday, 8 hours per day excluding Public Holidays. The installation staff works Monday to Saturday, 8 hours per day.

Assignment

The company observes the following holidays:

	2011	2012	2013	2014
New Year's Day	3 January	2 January	1 January	1 January
Good Friday	22 April	6 April	29 March	18 April
Easter Monday	25 April	9 April	1 April	21 April
Christmas Day	26 December	25 December	25 December	25 December
Boxing Day	27 December*	26 December	26 December	26 December

* These holidays occur on a weekend and the dates in the table above have been moved to the next weekday.

NOTE: Boxing Day, the day after Christmas, is a holiday celebrated in many countries.

Assignment

1. Edit the **Standard Calendar** to ensure that only the holidays above in 2011 and 2012 are present by selecting **Project**, **Properties** group, **Change Working Time**, see pictures over the page.
2. You may wish to make the following annual holidays repeating, say for 10 years when you set the holidays in 2012:
   - Christmas Day 25 Dec
   - Boxing Day 26 Dec
3. Exit the **Calendar** form to save the calendar edits.
4. Create a new calendar titled **6-Day Working Week** for the 6-day week by:
   - Copying the **Standard (Project Calendar)** then
   - Select the **Work Weeks** tab, click on the [Details...] tab and make Saturdays work days with the same working hours as the other working days, see the picture over the page.
5. Save your **OzBuild Bid** project.

Answers over the page......

Answers to Workshop 3

In the edited **Standard (Project Calendar)** of the **Change Working Time** form below, the dates are displayed in the ROW (Rest of World) date format of dd/mm/yyyy. Computers configured with the US date format will see the dates in the mm/dd/yyyy format.

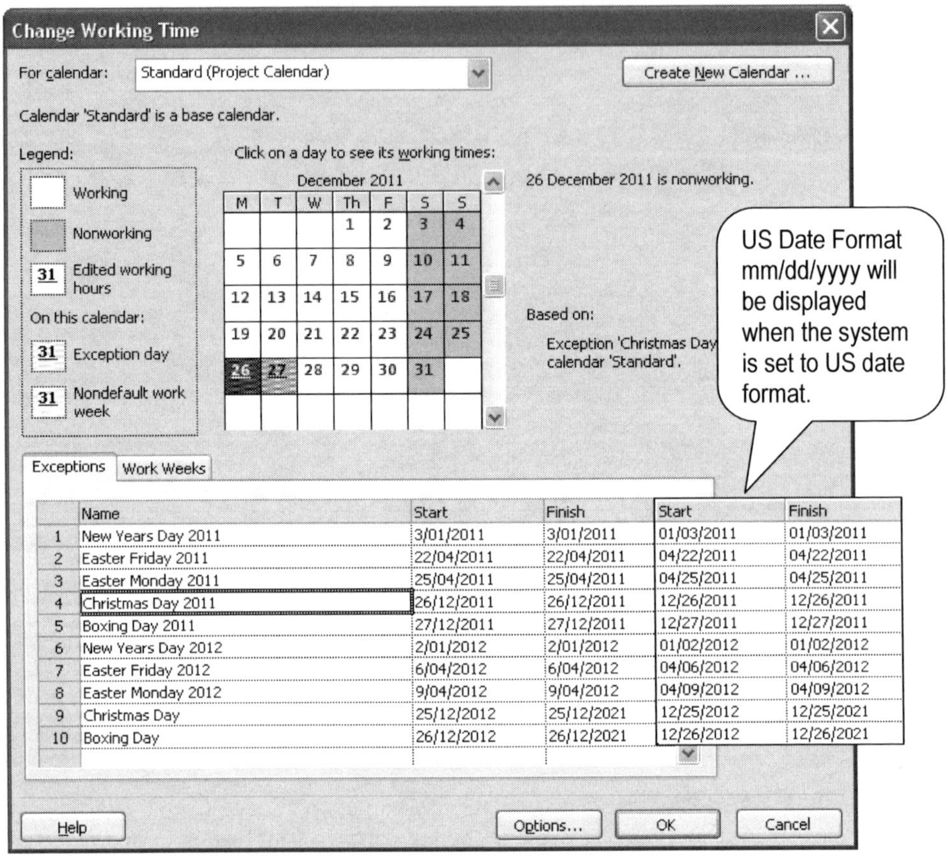

An example of setting Christmas Day as recurring:

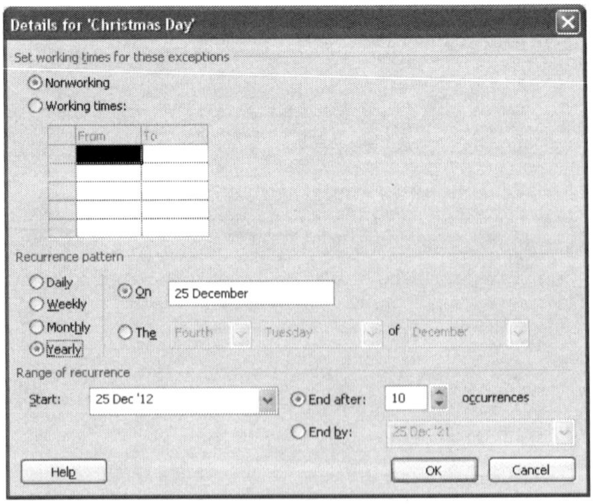

6 ADDING TASKS

Tasks, or tasks, should be well-defined, measurable pieces of work with a measurable outcome. Task descriptions containing only nouns such as "Specification" have confusing meanings. Does this mean Draft, Review, Approve, Issue, or all of these?

Adequate task descriptions always have a verb-noun structure to them. A more appropriate task description would be "Specification Approved" or "Specification Issued." The limit for task names is 254 characters, but try to keep task descriptions meaningful yet short and concise so they are easier to print.

It is considered good practice to first develop a WBS and then develop the tasks required to create the deliverables identified in the WBS.

The creation and sequencing of Detail and summary tasks are discussed in the following chapters:

- Creating **Detail tasks** in this chapter,
- Creating **Summary** tasks, which may represent the WBS Nodes, in the **ORGANIZING TASKS USING OUTLINING** chapter, and
- Adding the logic in the **ADDING THE DEPENDENCIES** chapter.

This chapter will cover the following topics:

Topic	Menu Command
• **Manually Scheduled or Auto Scheduled**	• **File**, **Options**, **Schedule** tab, **Scheduling options for this project:** section, **New tasks created:**:
• **Adding New Tasks**	• Select a line in the schedule and strike the **Ins** (**Insert Key**), or • Click on a blank line and type in a cell, or • Select **Task**, **Insert** group, **Task** button and there are three options for creating a task, 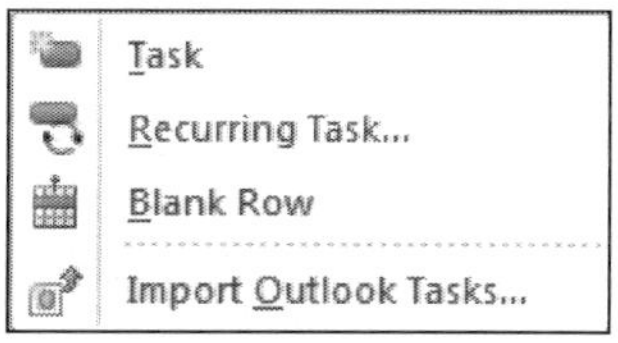
• **Reordering** tasks	• Select and drag the task(s) or cut and paste in the required location, or • Select **View**, **Data** group, **Sort** to open a menu.
• **Copying** tasks in Microsoft Project	Select the tasks and copy and paste to the required location.
• **Copying** tasks from other programs	Display the required columns and paste the data.
• **Elapsed** duration tasks	Type "e" after the duration and before the Units, e.g. 5 edays.

Topic	Menu Command
• **Milestones**	Assign a zero duration, or Check the **Mark task as milestone** box on the **Advanced** tab of the **Task Information** form.
• **Inactive Task**	A task is marked **Inactive** by checking the option in the **Task Information** form **General** tab.
• **Task Information** form	Double-click anywhere on the task line, or Highlight the task line click on the button on the **Task**, **Properties** group **Task Information** button.
• Assigning **Calendars** to tasks	• Set a task calendar in the **Advanced** tab in the **Task Information** form, or • Display the **Task Calendar** column.

6.1 Adding New Tasks

Manually Scheduled tasks will not be covered in detail in this book, we will concentrate on the aspects required to produce a **Critical Path** schedule assuming all tasks are Auto Scheduled.

6.1.1 Adding a Task Under an Existing Task

The first and easiest is to:

- Click on the first blank line under the title **Task Name** and type the task description.
- The duration of the new task is assigned a default duration of 1 day and may have a "**?**" after the duration to indicate it has been assigned an **Estimated Duration**. Overtyping the default duration with the required duration task will remove the "**?**".
- The option of assigning and/or displaying a new task with an **Estimated Duration** is controlled in the **File**, **Options**, **Schedule** tab, **Scheduling options for this project:** section, by checking or un-checking **New scheduled tasks have estimated durations**.

Summary tasks are marked as estimated when one or more **Detailed tasks** associated with it are marked as Estimated.

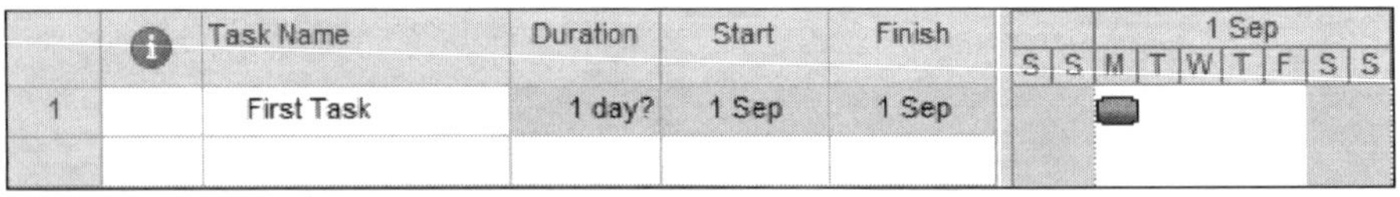

- Click into the second row and enter a second Task Name. A sequential **Task Number** starting from "**1**" will be created in the column to the left of the **Task Name**.

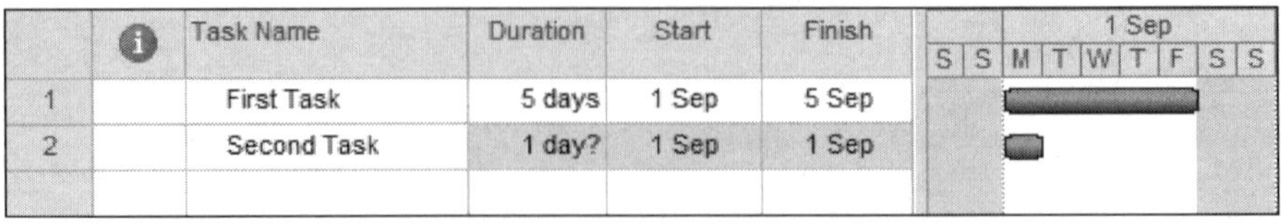

The task **Start** and **Finish** dates will be calculated from the **Project Start Date** and the task duration. This information is displayed in the **Start** and **Finish** columns.

6.1.2 Inserting a Task Between Existing Tasks

The second method of adding a task, which is used for inserting a task between two other tasks, is to highlight a task where you want to insert a new task. The highlighted task will be moved down one line after the new task is inserted. Inserting may be achieved by:

- Press the **Insert Key** on the keyboard, or
- Highlight the entire task row by clicking on the Task ID or a cell in a task, then right-click and select **Insert task** from the sub-menu.

Then enter the Task Name, Duration and other scheduling information as required.

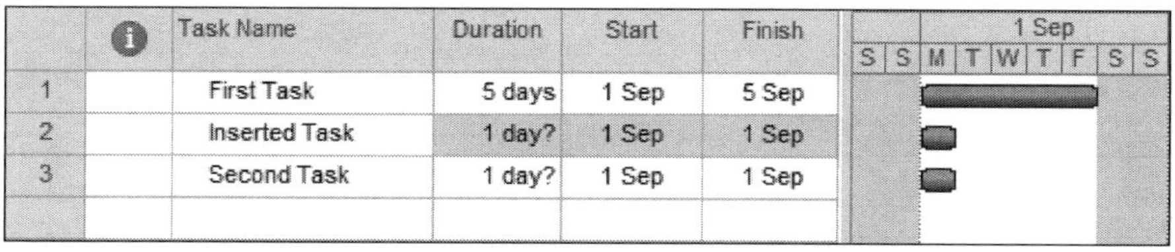

Do not type in a Start or Finish date into the **Start** or **Finish** column unless you want to set a constraint, which may override the logic.

6.2 Understanding Change Highlight

The Inserted Task in the picture above has the Start and Finish dates highlighted. This is due to the new Microsoft Project 2007 feature titled **Change Highlighting** that highlights any changed dates and durations as a result of an edit, addition or deletion of another task. This function highlights all date and duration fields that have been changed as a result of a change in a Task's dates or duration.

- Remove the highlighting produced by the last change by:
  - Pressing the **F9** key which will also recalculate the project, or
  - Saving the project, or
  - Entering a value into a changed cell twice.
- To change the color of the highlighting select **Format**, **Format** group, **Text Styles** and select **Changed Cells** from the **Item to change** list.
- Add the **Display Change Highlighting** button (there is no **Change Highlighting** button) to the **Ribbon** (if it does not exit) or add one to the **Quick Access Toolbar** to hide/display the highlighting.

This is a very useful feature as it highlights changes in all related date and duration fields as a result of a change made to a single task, thus making it simpler to see what tasks have moved as a result of the change.

6.3 Copying and Pasting Tasks

Tasks may also be copied from another project or copied from within the same project using the normal Windows commands such as **right-click Copy** and **Paste** or **Ctrl+C** and **Ctrl+V**.

You may also copy one or more adjacent tasks by using the **Ctrl Key** and dragging as follows:

- Select the whole task or tasks, not just a cell using the Task ID,
- Hold down the **Ctrl Key**, and
- Drag the tasks to the location you want to insert them. This will create a copy of the original tasks.

6.4 Milestones

A Milestone normally has a zero duration and is used to mark the start or finish of a major event. A Milestone is a Start Milestone when it has no predecessors and is scheduled at the start of a work day, and a Finish Milestone when it has predecessors and is scheduled at the end of a work day. Other products allow the user to choose if a Milestone is a **Start** or **Finish Milestone** but Microsoft Project does allow this option.

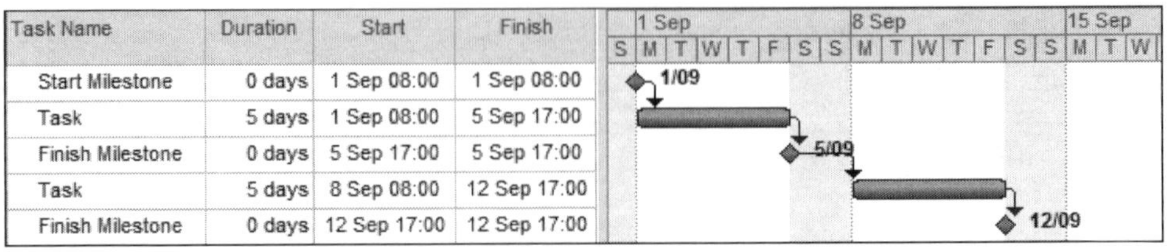

Task Name	Duration	Start	Finish
Start Milestone	0 days	1 Sep 08:00	1 Sep 08:00
Task	5 days	1 Sep 08:00	5 Sep 17:00
Finish Milestone	0 days	5 Sep 17:00	5 Sep 17:00
Task	5 days	8 Sep 08:00	12 Sep 17:00
Finish Milestone	0 days	12 Sep 17:00	12 Sep 17:00

To create a Milestone either:

- Assign a task a zero duration, or
- Click on the **Task**, **Insert** group, **Insert Milestone** button .

Milestones are normally displayed in the bar chart by a ◆.

6.5 Reordering Tasks by Dragging

You may move one or more tasks up or down the schedule by:

- Highlighting any one or more adjacent tasks by using the Task ID column; this will ensure you have selected the whole task and not just cells of the task,
- Moving the cursor to the top line of the selected tasks until it changes to an button,
- Then left-clicking and holding down the mouse to drag the row up or down. A gray line will indicate where the tasks will be inserted:

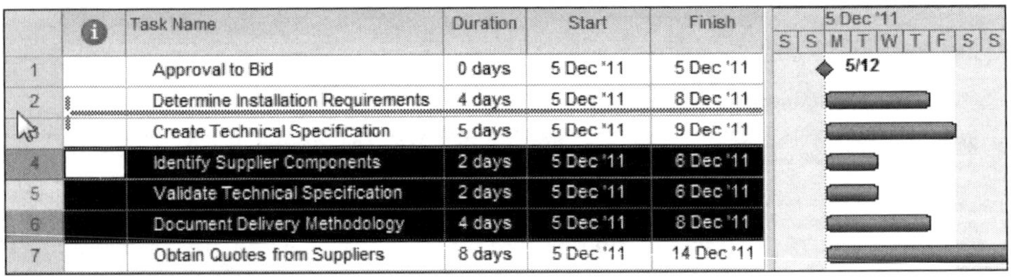

		Task Name	Duration	Start	Finish
1		Approval to Bid	0 days	5 Dec '11	5 Dec '11
2		Determine Installation Requirements	4 days	5 Dec '11	8 Dec '11
3		Create Technical Specification	5 days	5 Dec '11	9 Dec '11
4		Identify Supplier Components	2 days	5 Dec '11	6 Dec '11
5		Validate Technical Specification	2 days	5 Dec '11	6 Dec '11
6		Document Delivery Methodology	4 days	5 Dec '11	8 Dec '11
7		Obtain Quotes from Suppliers	8 days	5 Dec '11	14 Dec '11

The tasks will be renumbered when in their new location.

6.6 Sorting Tasks

Sorting tasks using fields such as Task name will not renumber them and the sort order may be restored by sorting on the Task ID.

To sort a schedule select **View**, **Data** group, **Sort** to open a menu and select an option.

> Sorting by some fields, such as Task Name, is undertaken within each Outline Level and by Outline Level. Thus the project will become jumbled up and as sorting is not allowed within an Outline Level or by selected tasks. Thus this may result in an undesirable order of the summary task.

6.7 Task Information Form

The Task Information form may be opened many ways including:

- Double-clicking on a task line, or
- Clicking on the **Task**, **Properties** group **Task Information** button when the task is highlighted, or
- Right-clicking, or
- Shift+F2.

You are able to make changes to a number of task parameters from this form. Once the form is open, it is not possible to move to another task without closing the form.

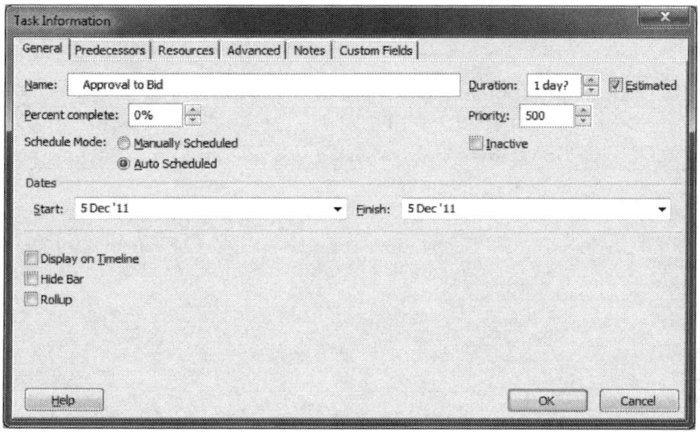

There are several tabs on the form:

- **General** – This form contains the basic information about a task:
  - ➢ The **Estimated** check box is used to indicate the task has an **Estimated Duration**. The task duration will be displayed with a "**?**" which disappears when a duration is entered against a task.
  - ➢ **Priority** is used in resource leveling. The highest is 1000 and the lowest is 0.
  - ➢ **Inactive** – when a task is marked **Inactive** by checking the option in the **Task Information** form **General** tab then the task is not considered in the scheduling process. Relationships to and from the task are ignored and Resource Hours and Costs are not included in the summary tasks rolled up values. The Baseline Values are maintained:

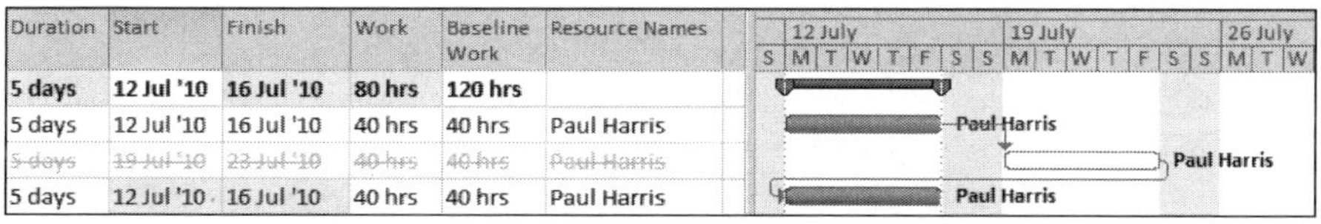

Duration	Start	Finish	Work	Baseline Work	Resource Names
5 days	**12 Jul '10**	**16 Jul '10**	**80 hrs**	**120 hrs**	
5 days	12 Jul '10	16 Jul '10	40 hrs	40 hrs	Paul Harris
~~5 days~~	~~19 Jul '10~~	~~23 Jul '10~~	~~40 hrs~~	~~40 hrs~~	~~Paul Harris~~
5 days	12 Jul '10	16 Jul '10	40 hrs	40 hrs	Paul Harris

  - ➢ **Manually Scheduled** and **Auto Scheduled** is covered in paragraph 22.3.1.
  - ➢ The **Bar** options are covered in the **Formatting Bars** section.
- **Predecessors** – This is where the task's predecessors are displayed. This is covered in the **ADDING THE DEPENDENCIES** chapter.
- **Resources** – This is where resources may be created, assigned to tasks and assignment information displayed. This topic is covered in the **RESOURCES** chapters.
- **Advanced** – Options are covered in the **CONSTRAINTS** chapter, paragraph 11.1.1.

- **Notes** – This is where notes about a task may be recorded. This field is handy to record assumptions.
- **Custom Fields** – Any **Custom Fields** that have been customized (by renaming the field) will be displayed in this tab. These are existing fields that may be renamed and customized by selecting **Project**, **Properties** group, **Custom Field**. These fields may hold different types of task information such as text, times, values, etc. There are options to define how these fields are summarized at the summary task level and may be assigned formulae to calculate their values.
- When multiple tasks are selected then the task form may be opened by right-clicking. Some of the attributes of all the tasks may be edited at the same time.

6.8 Elapsed Durations

A task may be assigned an **Elapsed** duration. The task will ignore all calendars and the task will take place 24 hours a day and 7 days per week. A 24-hour, 7-day per week calendar does not need to be created for these tasks. This is useful for tasks such as curing concrete but the Total Float will calculate three times longer than a task on an 8-hour a day calendar and this may be misleading.

To assign an elapsed duration type an "**e**" between the duration and units to enter an elapsed duration. The example below shows the difference between a 7-**Elapsed Day** task and a 7-day task on a **Standard** (5-day per week) calendar.

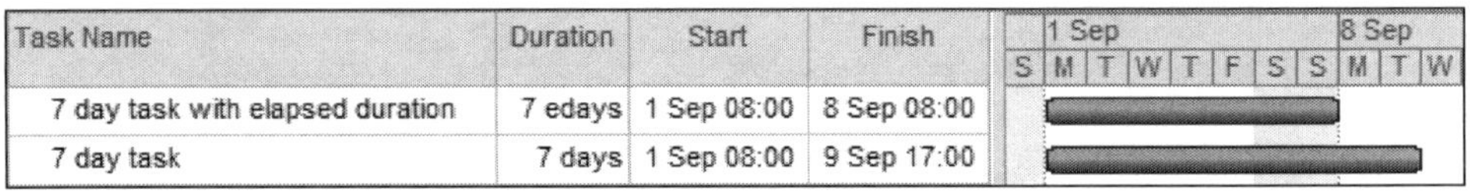

Task Name	Duration	Start	Finish
7 day task with elapsed duration	7 edays	1 Sep 08:00	8 Sep 08:00
7 day task	7 days	1 Sep 08:00	9 Sep 17:00

6.9 Indicators Column

The **Indicators** column, which has an icon in the column header, will display icons in the column when a task contains a non-default setting such as a **Note**, **Constraint,** or a **Task** calendar. Placing the mouse over the icon will display information about the task:

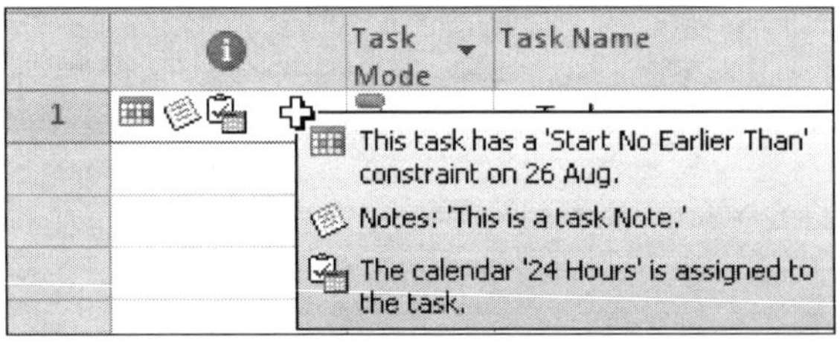

6.10 Assigning Calendars to Tasks

Tasks often require a different calendar from the **Project Calendar** and Microsoft Project allows each task to be assigned a unique calendar. A Task Calendar may be assigned by using the **Task Information** form or displaying the **Task Calendar** column.

6.10.1 Assigning a Calendar Using the Task Information Form

- Select one or more tasks that you want to assign to a different calendar by using Shift-click or Ctrl-click.
- Open the **Task Information** form when selecting a single task by double-clicking on a task.
- Open the **Task Information** form when selecting multiple tasks by:
  - ➢ Select **Task**, **Properties** group, **Information**, or
  - ➢ **Shift+F2**, or
  - ➢ Right-click and select **Task Information**.
- Then select the **Advanced** tab:

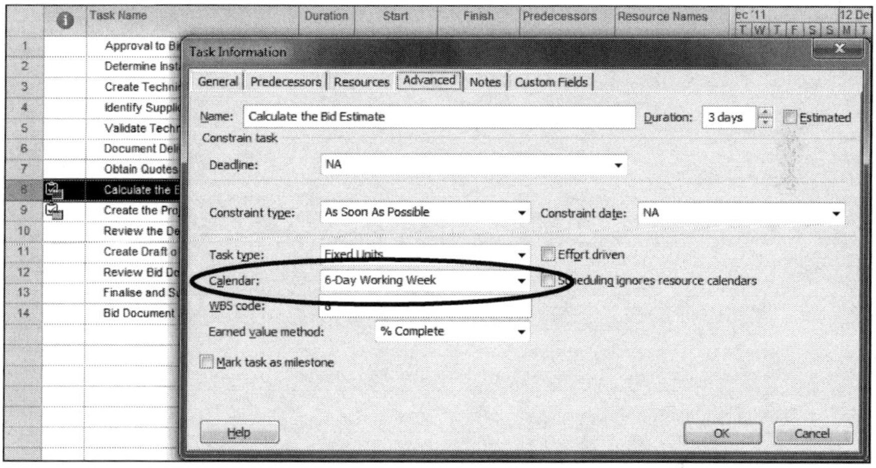

- From the **Calendar:** drop-down box select the calendar you want to assign to the task or tasks.

6.10.2 Assigning a Calendar Using a Column

You may also display the **Task Calendar** column and edit the task calendar from this column. The process of displaying a column is covered in the **FORMATTING THE DISPLAY** chapter. After a calendar has been assigned, an icon will appear in the **Indicators** column as displayed beside task 8 and 9 below:

	ℹ	Task Name	Task Calendar
7		Obtain Quotes from Suppliers	None
8		Calculate the Bid Estimate	6-Day Working Week
9		Create the Project Schedule	6-Day Working Week
10		Review the Delivery Plan	None

6.11 *Workshop 4 - Adding Tasks*

Background

If you do not have the default Microsoft Project settings installed on your computer or your Global.mpt has been edited then you may not have the same results as displayed in these workshops.

It is simpler to teach Microsoft Project by showing how to enter the tasks first and then creating the summary tasks to represent the WBS Nodes or Products or Deliverables. Once a user understands the process then the tasks and summary tasks may be entered in any order.

Assignment

1. We will assume that the Planning Process is complete and we are to produce a schedule with several tasks for each Product (Deliverable) in the Work Breakdown Structure - WBS.
2. The Work Breakdown Structure (WBS) and list of tasks below was created in ChangeAide. It displays all the Phases and Products, and the tasks in the Initiation Phase only:

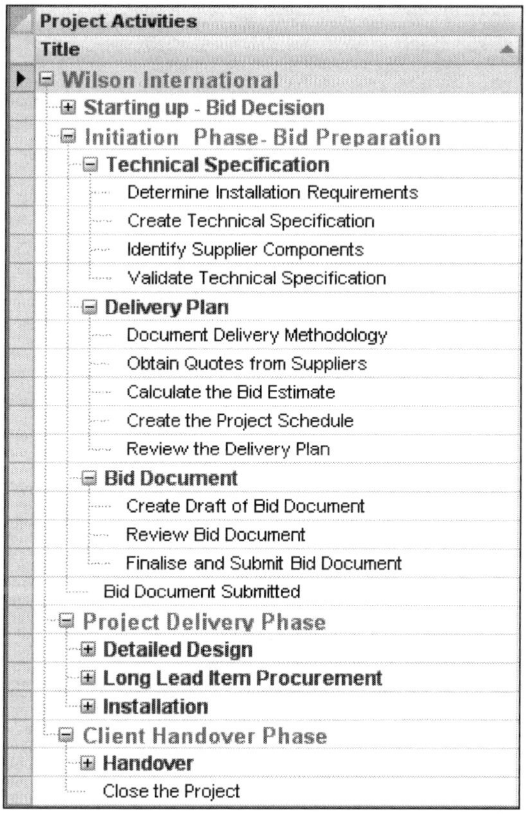

Continued...

3. Use the columns to enter the Name and Duration of the tasks as below.
   - The Estimate and Schedule will be completed by site personnel who work a 6 day week.
   - Assign the 6-Day Working Week calendar using the **Task Information** form to Tasks 8 and Task 9.
   - Double-click on the task to open this form and select the **Advanced** tab, **Calendar** drop-down box to assign the Task Calendar.
4. A task will become a milestone when assigned a zero duration.

ID	Task Name	Duration	Task Calendar
1	Approval to Bid	0 days	
2	Determine Installation Requirements	4 days	
3	Create Technical Specification	5 days	
4	Identify Supplier Components	2 days	
5	Validate Technical Specification	2 days	
6	Document Delivery Methodology	4 days	
7	Obtain Quotes from Suppliers	8 days	
8	Calculate the Bid Estimate	3 days	Assign the 6 Days Working Week calendar
9	Create the Project Schedule	3 days	Assign the 6 Days Working Week calendar
10	Review the Delivery Plan	1 day	
11	Create Draft of Bid Document	6 days	
12	Review Bid Document	4 days	
13	Finalize and Submit Bid Document	2 days	
14	Bid Document Submitted	0 days	

5. Your schedule should look like this:

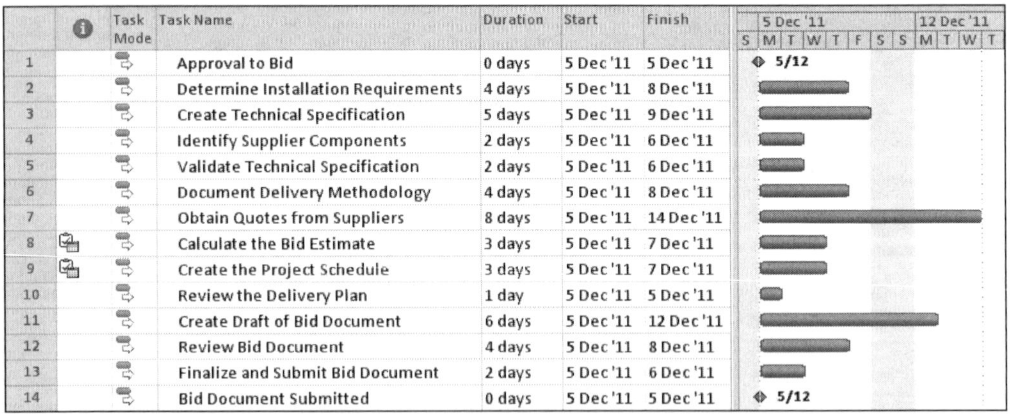

	Task Mode	Task Name	Duration	Start	Finish
1		Approval to Bid	0 days	5 Dec '11	5 Dec '11
2		Determine Installation Requirements	4 days	5 Dec '11	8 Dec '11
3		Create Technical Specification	5 days	5 Dec '11	9 Dec '11
4		Identify Supplier Components	2 days	5 Dec '11	6 Dec '11
5		Validate Technical Specification	2 days	5 Dec '11	6 Dec '11
6		Document Delivery Methodology	4 days	5 Dec '11	8 Dec '11
7		Obtain Quotes from Suppliers	8 days	5 Dec '11	14 Dec '11
8		Calculate the Bid Estimate	3 days	5 Dec '11	7 Dec '11
9		Create the Project Schedule	3 days	5 Dec '11	7 Dec '11
10		Review the Delivery Plan	1 day	5 Dec '11	5 Dec '11
11		Create Draft of Bid Document	6 days	5 Dec '11	12 Dec '11
12		Review Bid Document	4 days	5 Dec '11	8 Dec '11
13		Finalize and Submit Bid Document	2 days	5 Dec '11	6 Dec '11
14		Bid Document Submitted	0 days	5 Dec '11	5 Dec '11

NOTE: The icon in the Information column on the left-hand side indicates that Tasks 8 and 9 have a non-standard calendar, which is the **6-Day Working Week** calendar set in this workshop.

6. Ensure all tasks are assigned the **Task Mode** of **Auto Scheduled**.
7. Save your **OzBuild Bid** project.

7 ORGANIZING TASKS USING OUTLINING

Outlining is used to summarize and group tasks under a hierarchy of **Parent** or **Summary Tasks**. They are used to add structure to your project during planning, scheduling and updating. These headings are normally based on your project WBS.

Defining the project's breakdown structure can be a major task for project managers. The establishment of templates makes this operation simpler because a standard breakdown is predefined and does not have to be typed in for each new project.

Projects should be broken into manageable areas by using a structure based on a breakdown of the project phases, stages, deliverables, systematic functions, disciplines or areas of work. The Outline structure created in your project should reflect the primary breakdown of your project and often reflects the WBS.

Microsoft Project 2000 introduced a new feature titled **Grouping**, which is similar to the **Group and Sort** function found in Oracle Primavera software. This feature allows the grouping of tasks under headings other than the "Outline Structure." Unlike Oracle Primavera software, **Grouping** is not the primary method of organizing tasks and is covered in the **TABLES AND GROUPING TASKS** chapter.

7.1 Creating an Outline

To create an **Outline**, a summary task needs to be created above the detail tasks. This may be achieved two ways:

- Using the new 2010 **Insert Summary Task** function by:
  - Selecting all the tasks, **NOT JUST ONE TASK**, you wish to create a summary task above,

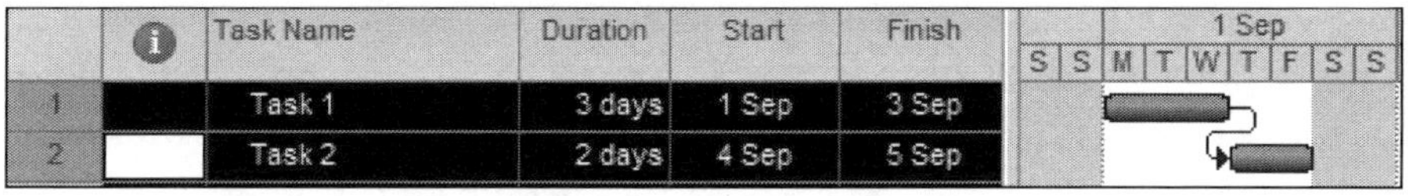

  - Click on **Task**, **Insert** group, **Summary** button,
  - Rename the newly created summary task:

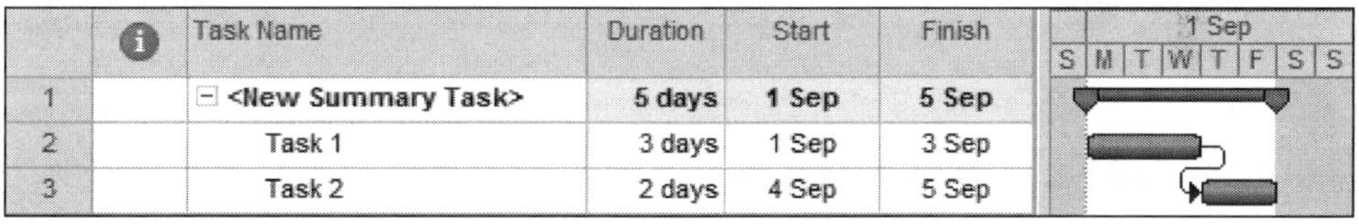

- The more traditional way is by:
  - Inserting a new **Summary task** above the **detail tasks** and
  - Then **Demoting** the **Detail tasks** below **Summary task**. (Demoting is explained in the next section.):

The Start and Finish dates of the **Summary task** are adopted from the earliest start date and latest finish date of the **Detail tasks**.

The duration of the **Summary** is calculated from the adopted start and finish dates over the **Summary** task calendar, which is by default the **Project Calendar**.

7.2 *Promoting and Demoting Tasks*

Demoting or **Indenting** tasks may be achieved in a number of ways. Select the task or tasks you want to **Demote**. You may use any of the following methods to **Demote a selected task**:

- Click on the Indent button on the **Task**, **Schedule** group, or
- Right-click on the tasks to open the task shortcut menu, click on , or
- Hold down the **Alt** and **Shift keys** and press the **Right Arrow Key** on your keyboard, or
- Move the mouse until you see a double-headed horizontal arrow in the task name field, left-click and drag the task right. A vertical line (see lower of the two pictures below) will appear indicating the outline level you have dragged the task(s) to:

Before dragging tasks to indent:

	Task Mode	Task Name	Duration	Start	Finish
1		Summary	1 day?	1 Nov	1 Nov
2		Task 1	3 days	1 Nov	3 Nov
3		Task 2	2 days	4 Nov	5 Nov
4		Task 3	3 days	8 Nov	10 Nov

After dragging tasks to indent:

	Task Mode	Task Name	Duration	Start	Finish
1		Summary	8 days	1 Nov	10 Nov
2		Task 1	3 days	1 Nov	3 Nov
3		Task 2	2 days	4 Nov	5 Nov
4		Task 3	3 days	8 Nov	10 Nov

Promoting or **Outdenting tasks** uses the same principle as demoting tasks. Select the task or tasks you want to promote, ensure you have selected the whole task and not just some cells, then you may:

- Click on the Outdent button, or
- Right-click on a selected task to open the task shortcut menu, click on the button, or
- Hold down the **Alt** and **Shift keys** together and press the **Left Arrow Key** on your keyboard, or
- Move the mouse until you see a double-headed horizontal arrow in the task name column, left-click and drag the tasks left.

Tasks may be added under a **Detail task** and demoted to a third level and so on.

	Task Mode	Task Name	Duration	Start	Finish
1		Summary	8 days	1 Nov	10 Nov
2		Task 1	3 days	1 Nov	3 Nov
3		Task 2	2 days	4 Nov	5 Nov
4		Task 3	3 days	8 Nov	10 Nov
5		Task 3.1	1 day	8 Nov	8 Nov
6		Task 3.2	1 day	9 Nov	9 Nov
7		Task 3.3	1 day	10 Nov	10 Nov

It is considered good practice to remove the link from "Task 2" to "Task 3" and replace it with a link from "Task 2" to "Task 3.1" thus not having any relationships between summary tasks.

7.3 Summary Task Duration Calculation

The summary task duration is calculated from the Start to the Finish over the calendar assigned to the task, thus changing the summary task calendar will change the displayed duration:

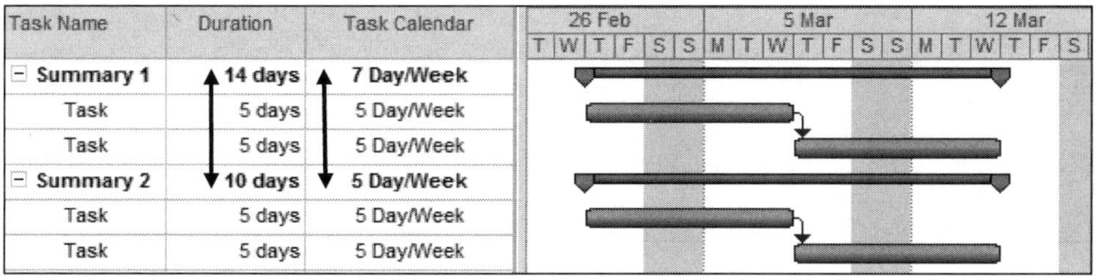

Task Name	Duration	Task Calendar
Summary 1	14 days	7 Day/Week
Task	5 days	5 Day/Week
Task	5 days	5 Day/Week
Summary 2	10 days	5 Day/Week
Task	5 days	5 Day/Week
Task	5 days	5 Day/Week

7.4 Summarizing Tasks

Once you have created summary tasks, the detail tasks may be rolled up or summarized under the summary tasks. Rolled up tasks are symbolized by the + sign to the left of the summarized task description:

- This picture shows **Detail Task 3** rolled up.

	Task Name	Duration	Start	Finish
1	Summary	8 days	1 Sep	10 Sep
2	Task 1	3 days	1 Sep	3 Sep
3	Task 2	2 days	4 Sep	5 Sep
4	+ Task 3	3 days	8 Sep	10 Sep

- This picture shows a **Summary Task** rolled up.

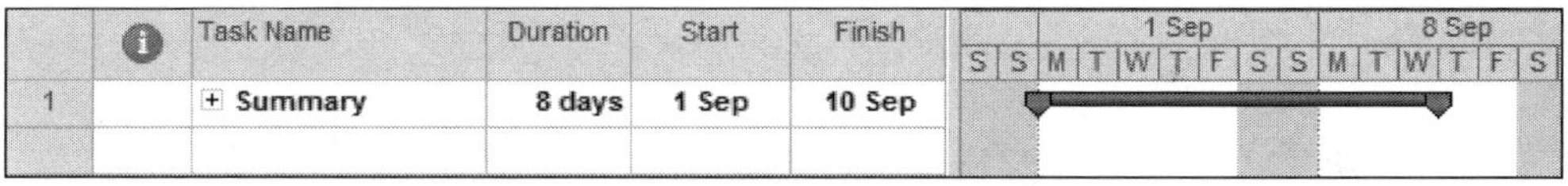

	Task Name	Duration	Start	Finish
1	+ Summary	8 days	1 Sep	10 Sep

7.4.1 Summarize and Expand Summary Tasks to Show and Hide Subtasks

Select the task you want to expand:

- Click on the ⊟ to the left of the Task Name, or
- Click on the **Hide Subtasks** button that may be added to the Quick Access Toolbar, or
- Double-click on the **Task ID** (not the **Task Name** as this will open the **Task** form).

Displaying rolled-up tasks is similar to rolling them up. To do this, select the task you want to expand. Then:

- Click on the ⊞ to the left of the Task Name, or
- Click on the **Show Subtasks** button, or
- Double-click on the **Task ID**.

7.4.2 Roll Up All Tasks to an Outline Level

A schedule may be rolled up to any Outline Level by selecting the desired Outline Level from the **View**, **Data** group, **Outline** button:

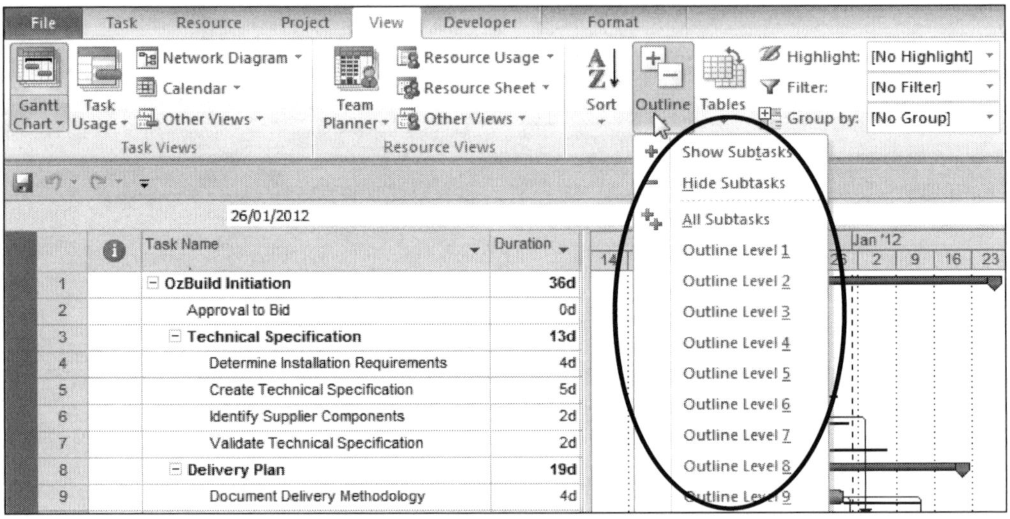

7.5 Project Summary Task

A **Project Summary Task** may be displayed by checking the **Format**, **Show/Hide** group, **Project Summary Task**. This task spans from the first to the last task in the project and is in effect a built-in Level 1 outline task. The description of the summary task is the Project Title entered in the **File**, **Info**, **Project Information**, **Advanced Properties** form. A Project summary task is a virtual task and may not have resources, relationships or constraints assigned and is assigned a Task ID of 0.

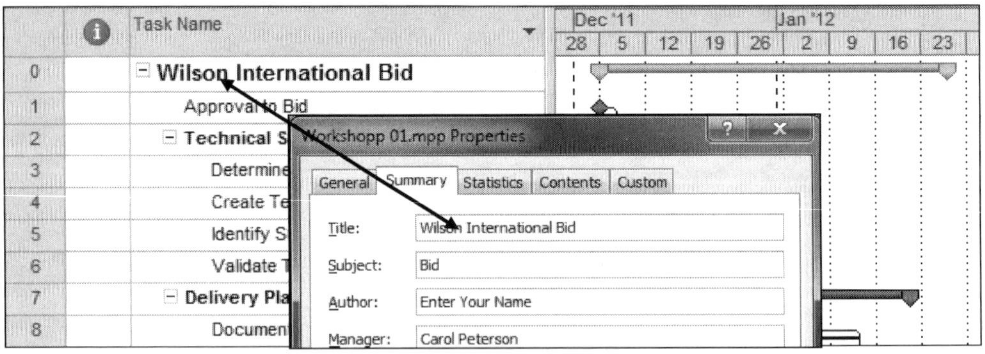

7.6 Workshop 5 - Entering Summary Tasks

Background

The summary tasks may be used to represent a Project, Deliverables/Products, WBS Nodes, Phase, Stages or Work Packages.

We will add summary tasks to represent the Initiation Phase and Deliverables/Products of the Initiation Phase.

Assignment

1. Display the Project Summary Task by checking the **Format**, **Show/Hide** group, **Project Summary Task** and close the form and observe how the Project summary task is formatted.
2. Hide the Project summary task as we will create an Outline Level for the Project summary task.
3. Create an Outline Level 1 for Phase entitled "OzBuild Initiation" and
4. Create an Outline Level 2 for each of the three Products:
   - Technical Specification
   - Delivery Plan
   - Bid Document.
5. Try using the various methods for indenting and outdenting tasks.
6. Your schedule should look like this:

		Task Mode	Task Name	Duration	Start	Finish
1			**OzBuild Initiation**	**8 days**	**5 Dec '11**	**14 Dec '11**
2			**Technical Specification**	**5 days**	**5 Dec '11**	**9 Dec '11**
3			Approval to Bid	0 days	5 Dec '11	5 Dec '11
4			Determine Installation Requirements	4 days	5 Dec '11	8 Dec '11
5			Create Technical Specification	5 days	5 Dec '11	9 Dec '11
6			Identify Supplier Components	2 days	5 Dec '11	6 Dec '11
7			Validate Technical Specification	2 days	5 Dec '11	6 Dec '11
8			**Delivery Plan**	**8 days**	**5 Dec '11**	**14 Dec '11**
9			Document Delivery Methodology	4 days	5 Dec '11	8 Dec '11
10			Obtain Quotes from Suppliers	8 days	5 Dec '11	14 Dec '11
11			Calculate the Bid Estimate	3 days	5 Dec '11	7 Dec '11
12			Create the Project Schedule	3 days	5 Dec '11	7 Dec '11
13			Review the Delivery Plan	1 day	5 Dec '11	5 Dec '11
14			**Bid Document Submitted**	**6 days**	**5 Dec '11**	**12 Dec '11**
15			Create Draft of Bid Document	6 days	5 Dec '11	12 Dec '11
16			Review Bid Document	4 days	5 Dec '11	8 Dec '11
17			Finalize and Submit Bid Document	2 days	5 Dec '11	6 Dec '11
18			Bid Document Submitted	0 days	5 Dec '11	5 Dec '11

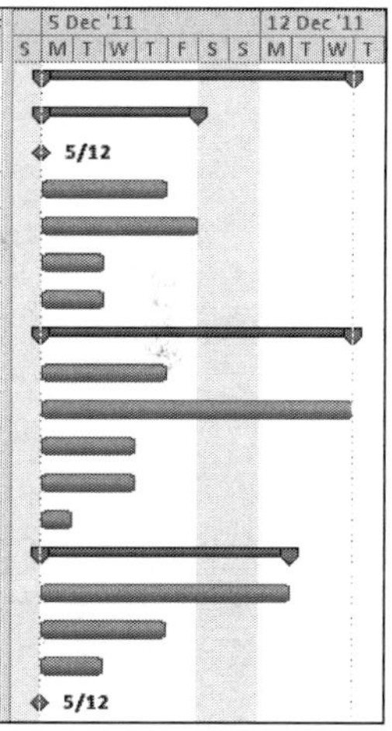

7. Save your **OzBuild Bid** project.

8 FORMATTING THE DISPLAY

This chapter covers the following topics, which are used to format the on-screen display which are also reflected in print preview and printouts:

Topic	Menu Command
Inserting Columns	• Highlight a column and strike the **Ins Key**, or • Select **Format**, **Columns** group, **Insert Column**, or • Right-click and select **Insert Column**.
Deleting Columns	• Highlight a column and strike the **Delete** key, or • Select **Format**, **Columns** group, **Column Settings**, **Hide Column**, or • Right-click and select **Hide Column**.
Adjusting the Width and Moving Columns	• Grab the right header border line with the mouse and drag or resize.
Table – formatting the columns of data	• **View**, **Data** group, **Tables**, **More tables...** or • Select a column and right-click to insert, or • Right-click on a column header and select **Field Settings**.
Formatting One Column	• Right-click on the column title and select **Field Settings**.
Format Bars	• Open the Bar Styles form by clicking anywhere in the Gantt Chart area, or • **Format**, **Bar Styles** group, or • **Format**, **Gantt Chart Styles** group, or • The **Gantt Chart Wizard**.
Formatting Time Units	• Select **File**, **Options**, **Advanced**, **Default options for this project:**
Row Height	• Drag one or more selected rows with the mouse, or • Edit the Table, or • **Wrap Text** command found on the **Format**, **Columns** group, **Column Settings**, **Wrap Text** which automatically adjusts the row height to fit the text into the available column width.
Timescale	• **Zoom Slider** at the bottom right-hand side of the screen, or • Double-click on the timescale opening the **Timescale** form, or • Use the **Zoom** buttons.
Gridlines	• **Format**, **Format** group, **Gridlines**, **Gridlines...**
Relationship Lines	• **Format**, **Format** group, **Layout**
Format Text Font	• Select the text to be formatted and right-click.

The formatting is applied to the current **View** only and is automatically saved as part of the View when another View is selected. Views are covered in more detail in the **VIEWS AND DETAILS** chapter.

8.1 Formatting the Columns

Microsoft Project has some column formatting functions which are intended to make it simple to add and format a new column.

There are two methods of formatting the columns:

- Inserting, editing and deleting columns of data using the **Column Definition** form.
- **Tables** – A table may be created or an existing table edited with required columns using the **Table Definition** form. You may set up the data columns in the way you want to see the information on the screen and in printouts. Therefore **Tables** may be created, edited and deleted and you may select which one is used to display the data with each View. One Table may be used with more than one View.

As time progresses with the option **File**, **Options**, **Advanced**, **Automatically add new views, tables, filters, and groups to the global** activated, a project that is created from the **Blank Project** will have many Views, Tables and Filters from old projects that may be irrelevant to the current project and it is suggested this be turned off.

8.1.1 Understanding Custom Fields

A Custom Field is a task or resource field that may be renamed and user defined data entered in columns. These fields may be formatted only to accept specific data such as dates, costs, durations or text. These are covered in more detail in the **TABLE AND GROUPING TASKS** chapter.

8.1.2 Inserting Columns

Insert a column by clicking on the column title where you require the new column. This will highlight the column. To insert a new column:

- Select **Format**, **Columns** group, **Insert**, **Column...**, or
- Hit the **Ins** Key, or
- Right-click and select **Insert Column...**.

Then select the column from the drop-down list. –

- You may immediately start typing, which will take you to the appropriate position in the list.
- In Microsoft Project 2010, when a column name that does not exist is typed into the header, then an existing Text column will be renamed with the new title. Therefore the inserted column is a renamed text **Custom Field**.

8.1.3 Format Columns Group

The **Format**, **Columns** group has the following functions:

- – Aligns the text to the left, center or right,
- – **Wraps Text** and increases the row height so all text is visible,
- – **Column Settings** has:
  - – **Hide Column** which hides a column but does not delete the data.

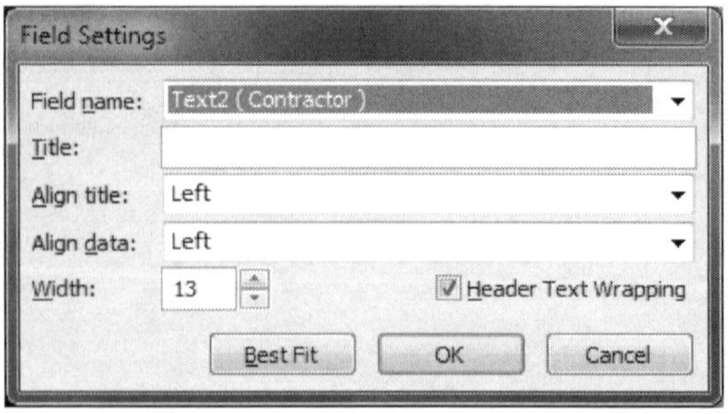

- – **Field Settings** that opens the **Field Settings** form:
  NOTE: The picture displays **Text2 Custom Field** that has been renamed Contractor.
- – **Data Type** which allows the data type of a Custom Field to be changed.

  This will result in the loss of data if a field is changed, say for example from Text to Cost.

- – **Display Add New Column** is a function new to Microsoft Project 2010. A column may be permanently displayed on the right-hand side of the screen titled ***Add New Column*** and clicking on this column will open up a drop-down box for the selection of the data type. This option will display or hide this column.
- – **Insert Column** inserts a new column.

- **Custom Fields** opens the **Custom Fields** form covered in the **TABLE AND GROUPING TASKS** chapter.

8.1.4 Deleting Columns

Delete a column by highlighting the column or by clicking on the title. Then:

- Select **Column Settings**, **Hide Column**,
- Hit the **Delete** key, or
- Right-click and select **Hide Column**.

1. There will be no confirmation of deleting a column, but you are allowed to undo the deletion.
2. The term "hide" means the column is removed from the Table in this project but the data is not deleted.

8.1.5 Adjusting the Width of Columns

You may adjust the width of the column either manually or automatically.

- For manual adjustment, move the mouse pointer to the right vertical line of the column in the header. A ↔ mouse arrow will then appear and enable the column to be adjusted.

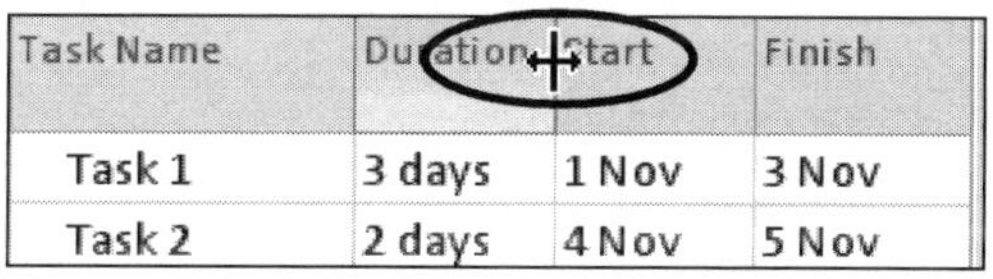

Task Name	Duration	Start	Finish
Task 1	3 days	1 Nov	3 Nov
Task 2	2 days	4 Nov	5 Nov

- For automatic adjustment, once again position the mouse pointer to the right vertical line of the column in the header and double left-click the mouse. The column width will automatically adjust to the best fit.

8.1.6 Moving Columns

Columns in a Table may be moved by clicking on the column header. The mouse pointer will change to a ✥ and the column may be dragged to a new location.

8.1.7 Formatting Columns Using the Table Function

- Select **View**, **Data** group, **Tables**, and select from the list of predefined **Tables** listed on the menu. Select the table you want to display:

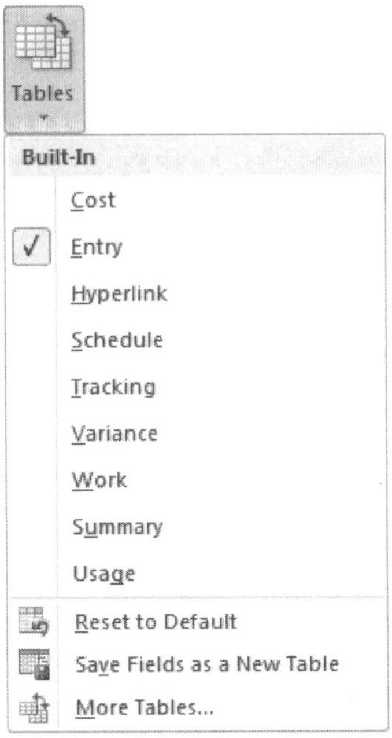

- Select **View**, **Data** group, **Tables**, **More Tables...** to open the **More Tables** form:

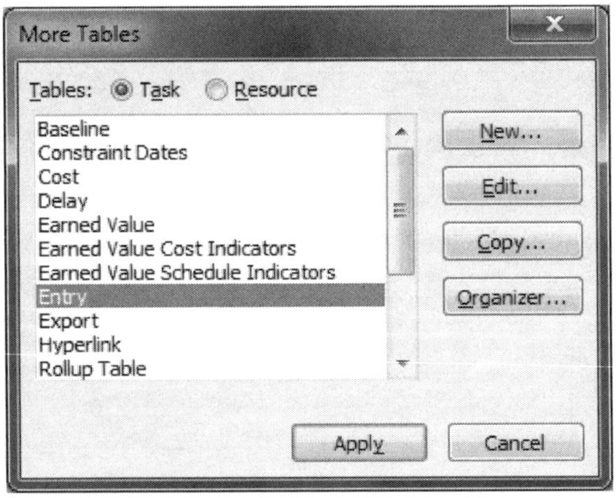

  - 

 – To create a new Table.
  - 

 – To edit the highlighted Table.
  - 

 – To copy the highlighted Table.
  - 

 – Opens the **Organizer** form which enables you to copy a Table from one opened project to another or to the Global Project.
  - 

 – Applies the selected Table making it visible on the screen.

- When you select New..., Edit... or Copy... you will be presented with the **Table Definition** form:

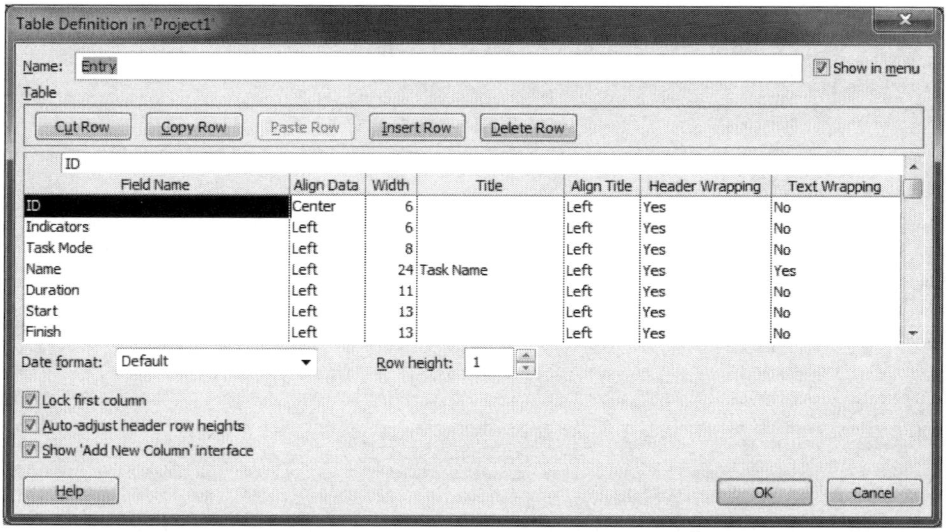

  - Click on the **Show in menu** box to display the Table in the **View**, **Data** group, **Tables** menu.
  - The columns of data will be displayed on screen from left to right in the same order as the rows in the form.
  - Highlight a row and then you may use the Cut Row, Copy Row, Paste Row, Insert Row or Delete Row buttons.
  - The data to be displayed may be selected from the drop-down box in the **Field Name** column.
  - **Align Data** and **Width** are used for formatting the data in the columns.
  - The Microsoft Project **Field Name** may be replaced by typing your own title in the **Title** box.
  - The **Date format:** drop-down box is used to change the format for this table only.

This is a very useful function to ensure that other users of the project file see the intended date format and not their system default date format.

- **Row Height:** sets the default height of all the rows in this table. A row height may be changed by dragging the cell boundary line once a task has been created.
  - **Lock first column** prevents the first column from scrolling and is useful when the first column contains the Task Name.
  - **Auto-adjust header row heights** will automatically adjust header row heights to the width of the column.
  - **Show 'Add New Column' interface** hides or displays the ***Add New Column*** column (new function to Microsoft Project 2010) on the right-hand side of the columns in all Views, used for adding new columns.

To save a table for use in all your new projects, copy the table to the **Global.mpt** template using **File**, **Info**, **Organizer** and select the **Tables** tab.

You may also copy a **Table** to another project or rename a **Table** using **File**, **Info**, **Organizer** and selecting the **Tables** tab.

Applying a Table to a View will permanently change the View unless the file is not saved. The Gantt Chart View has the Entry Table assigned by default.

8.2 Formatting Time Units

Select **File**, **Options**, **Advanced**, **Default options for this project:**

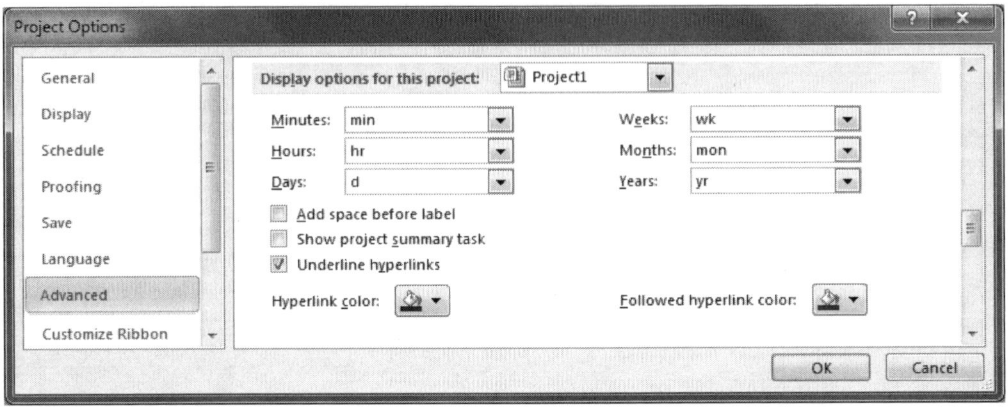

- The **Display options for this project:** always specifies the time units, for example **day**, **dy** or **d**.
- Uncheck the **Add space before label** check box to remove a space between the value and label in date columns which allows a narrower Duration column to be displayed.

To make the Duration column width narrow, **Days:** should be set to **d** and the **Add space before label** unchecked. The column header could also be edited to **Dur** to ensure the header is also narrow. This will provide more space for other data.

8.3 Formatting the Bars

Microsoft Project has several options for bar formatting:

- All the bars may be formatted to suit user definable parameters, or
- Individual bars may be formatted.

This section will cover the formatting of all the bars and the next section will cover formatting individual bars.

Most formatting only affects the current View.

All bars in the Gantt Chart may be formatted to suit your requirements for display by:

- Opening the **Bar Styles** form by double-clicking anywhere in the Gantt Chart area, or
- **Format**, **Bar Styles** group, or
- **Format**, **Gantt Chart Styles** group, or
- The **Gantt Chart Wizard**, which is a simple way to format bars.

Many of the formatting menu options are designed for a schedule created from a Microsoft Project 2010 template. Some menu options will not operate as expected if you have opened a project created in an earlier version of Microsoft Project. For example, the author found the baseline bar was placed on top of the current schedule bar using the Ribbon commands. Users may have to use the manual method of formatting bars by opening the bars form.

8.3.1 Formatting All Task Bars Using the Bar Styles Form

To format all the bars you must open the **Bar Style** form by:

- Double-click anywhere in the Gantt Chart area, but not on an existing bar, as this will open the **Format Bar** form for formatting an individual bar, or
- Select **Format**, **Bar Styles** group, **Format, Bar**:

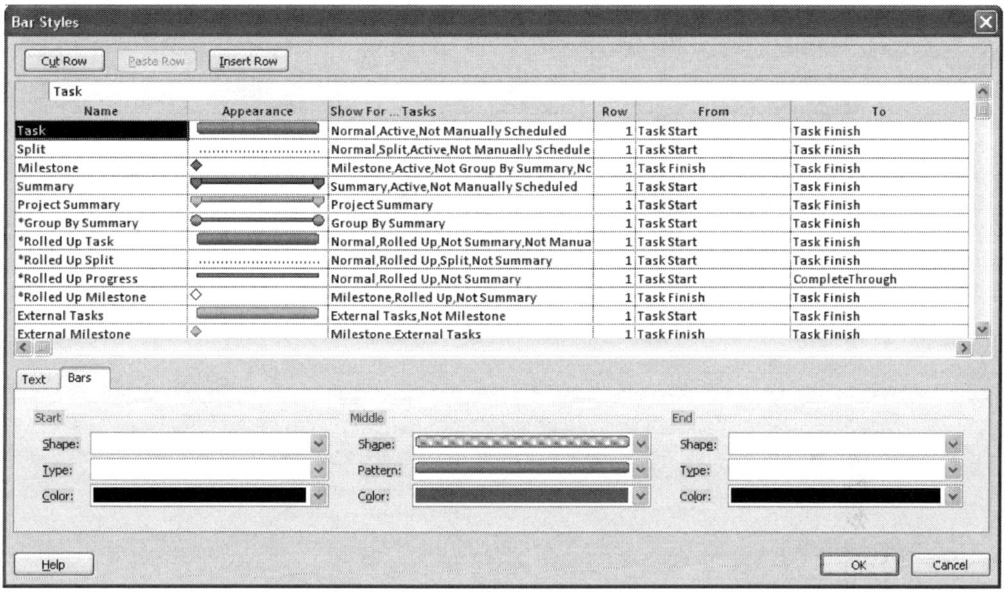

The following notes are the main points for using this function. Detailed information is available in the Help facility by searching for "Bar styles dialog box."

- Each bar listed in the table will be displayed on the bar chart.
- Bars may be deleted with the Cut Row button, pasted using the Paste Row button and new bars inserted using the Insert Row button.
- The **Name** is the title you may assign to the bar and is displayed in the printout legend. To hide the bar on the legend precede the **Name** with an *. There are many bars with an * by them as default, as displayed in the picture above.
- The appearance of each bar is edited in the lower half of the form. The bar's start point, middle and end points may have their color, shape, pattern, etc. formatted.
- When a new Milestone is created, the **From** and **To** must both be set to **Task Finish**.
- **Show For ... Tasks** allows you to select which tasks are displayed, similar to a filter. More than one task type may be displayed by separating each type with a ",". Bar types not required are prefixed with "**Not**." For example, the Normal,Rolled Up,Split,Not Summary bar would not display a bar for a summary task. Should you leave this cell blank then all task types will be displayed in this format.

The bars may be placed on one of four rows numbered from 1 to 4, top to bottom. If multiple bars are placed on the same row then the bar at the top of the list will be drawn first and the ones lower down the list will be drawn over the top, thus potentially hiding the ones below in the list.

- **From** and **To** allow you to establish where the bars start and finish. The picture below shows how to format **Total Float**, **Free Float** and **Negative Float**. Unlike some other planning and scheduling software, the Negative Float is drawn from the Start Date of a task and not the Finish Date and therefore a separate bar is required for Negative and Positive Float.

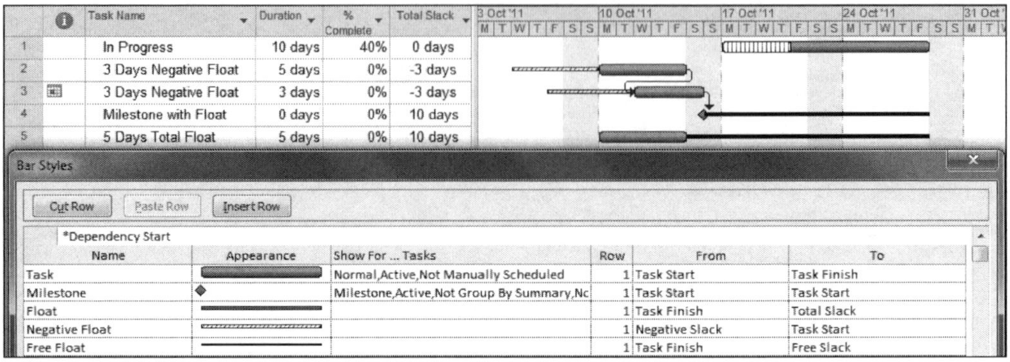

The Negative Float bar is not automatically displayed by any Microsoft Project function, nor is it included in any View. This is one of the most important bars to show when a project finish date has been set using a constraint and this must always be manually created. You may wish to consider recording a macro to create the bar and this can be run when a negative float bar is required. Recording a macro is covered in para 23.15.

- The **Text** tab allows you to place text inside or around the bar:

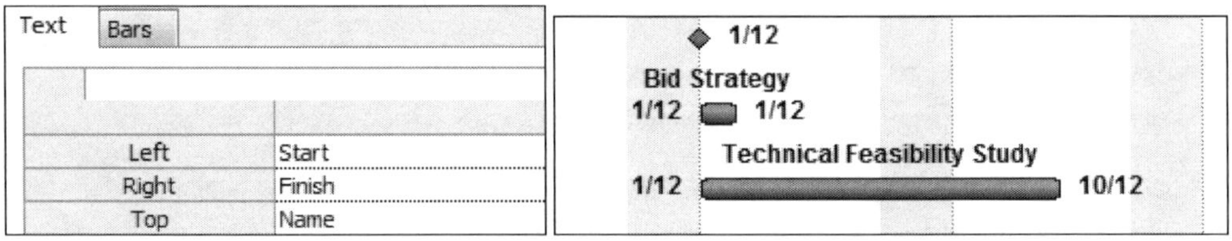

- It is not possible to format the font in the **Bar Styles** form. Select **Format**, **Format** group **Text Styles** to open the **Text Styles** form and select the bar text font.

To show Critical and Non-critical tasks, the bars should be formatted as shown below, with particular attention paid to the **Show For ... Tasks** column. Non-critical Tasks are formatted as **Normal**, **Non-critical** and Critical Tasks as **Normal**, **Critical**.

Name	Appearance	Show For ... Tasks	Row	From	To
Task		Normal,Active,Not Critical,Not Manually Sc	1	Task Start	Task Finish
Critical		Normal,Critical,Active,Not Placeholder	1	Task Start	Task Finish

8.3.2 Format Bar Styles Group Menu

Select the **Format**, **Bar Styles** group to view this group of commands:

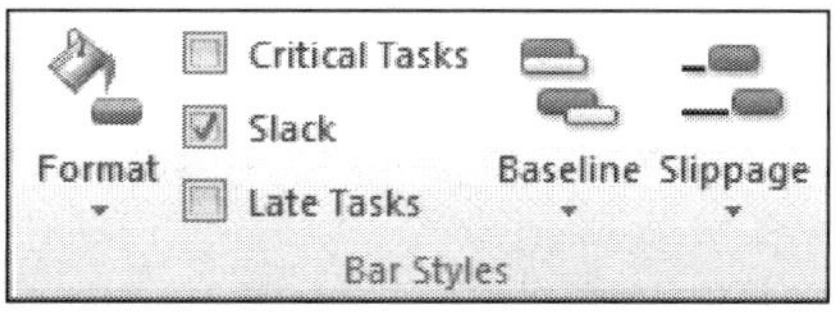

-  **Format** has two options:
  - **Bar** formats of one or more selected bars and is covered in the next section.
  - **Bar Styles** opens the **Bar Styles** form as discussed above to format all bars.
- The other buttons in the **Format**, **Bar Styles** groups will hide or display the bars as indicated, but these may not give the expected results with a project created in an earlier version of Microsoft Project.
  - **Critical Tasks** shades the Critical Tasks red.
  - **Slack** displays the Free Float and **NOT** Total Float bar.
  - **Late Tasks** displays tasks that are late compared to the **Status Date**.
  - **Baseline** displays the Baseline bar.
  - **Slippage** displays how much time the task is behind the Baseline.

Many of the formatting menu options are designed for a schedule created from a Microsoft Project 2010 template. Some menu options will not operate as expected if you have opened a project created in an earlier version of Microsoft Project. For example the author found the baseline bar was placed on top of the current schedule bar using the Ribbon commands. Users may have to use the manual method of formatting bars by opening the bars form or using the **Gantt Chart Wizard**.

8.3.3 Gantt Chart Styles Group Menu

Select **Format**, **Gantt Chart Styles** group to see the option for coloring bars. This function is new to Microsoft Project 2010.

The button at the bottom right-hand side opens the **Bar Styles** form.

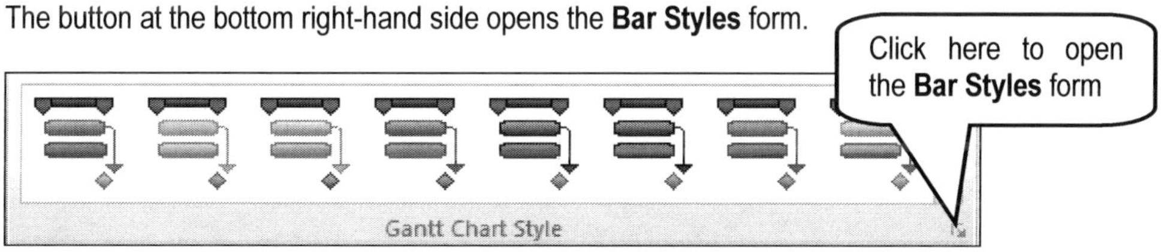

See warning above.

8.3.4 Formatting Bars Using the Gantt Chart Wizard

The Gantt Chart Wizard is a popular function for people who used earlier versions of Microsoft Project. The wizard will overwrite any formatting you may have created. This is a straightforward method of formatting your bars and often this is the best method of formatting bars. It is very simple to use but will not display the **Negative Float** and **Free Float** bars. These will have to be added manually using the **Bar Style** form as described in the **Bar Styles** form section.

If the **Gantt Chart Wizard** button is not on your Microsoft Project default toolbars then this may be added to either the **Quick Access Toolbar** or the **Ribbon**.

The author found that projects formatted with the **Gantt Chart Wizard** and projects created in earlier versions of Microsoft Project will have formatting that is incompatible with the Microsoft Project 2010 **Format**, **Bar Styles** group buttons. The use of the **Baseline** button resulted in the Baseline bar covering the current schedule bar so only the Baseline bar was visible. To resolve this issue users should either use only **Gantt Chart Wizard** or only the new Microsoft Project 2010 **Format**, **Bar Styles** group buttons, but not both. This issue may be rectified with software updates.

8.4 Row Height

8.4.1 Setting Row Heights

Row heights may be adjusted to display text that would otherwise be truncated by a narrow column.

The row height may be set in the **Table Definition** form by selecting **View**, **Data** group **Tables**, **More Tables....** From this view select the table in which you wish to edit the row height in and click on the [Edit...] button. Once the **Table Definition** form is open select the row height from the drop-down box next to **Row height:**.

The row height of one or more columns may also be adjusted in a similar way to adjusting row heights in Excel, by clicking on the row and dragging with the mouse:

- Highlight one or more rows that need adjusting by dragging or Ctrl-clicking. If all the rows are to be adjusted, then click on the **Select All** button above row number 1, to highlight all the tasks.

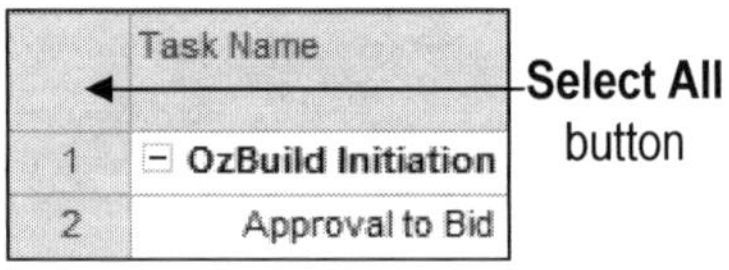

- Then move the mouse pointer to the left-hand side of a horizontal row divider line. The pointer will change to a double-headed arrow ⇕. Click and hold with the left mouse button and drag the row or rows to the required height.

8.4.2 Wrap Text Command

Microsoft Project 2010 has introduced a **Wrap Text** command found on the **Format**, **Columns** group, **Column Settings**, **Wrap Text** which automatically adjusts the row height to fit the text into the available column width.

8.5 Format Fonts

There are two basic options for formatting fonts:

- Either individual cells may be selected by Ctl-clicking or dragging with the mouse and formatted, or
- The fonts of tasks that meet preset criteria, such critical tasks may be formatted using the text **Styles** command.

8.5.1 Format Individual Cells Font Command

The **Format**, **Font...** function from Microsoft 2007 and earlier has been replaced with a right-click option and allows you to format any selected text in selected cells, rows or columns:

- Select the text to be formatted,
- Right-click and two toolbars are opened. The upper toolbar in the picture below has four buttons that may be used for formatting individual cells:

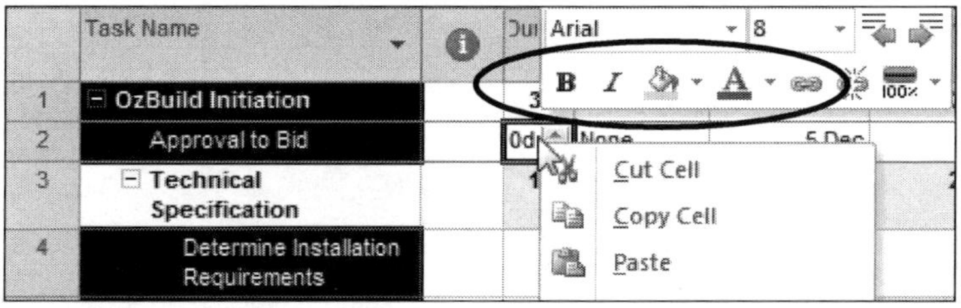

8.5.2 Format Text Styles

The **Format**, **Format** group, **Text Styles** command opens the **Text Styles** form and allows you to select a text type from the **Item to Change:** drop-down box and apply formatting to the selected item:

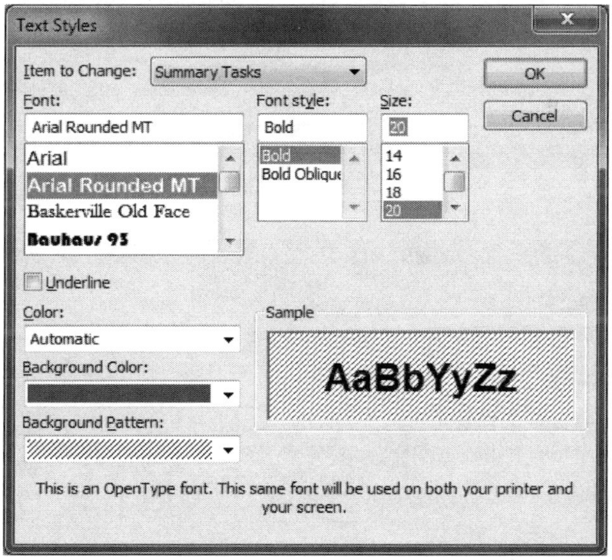

Text may be formatted by using any of the styles listed below:

- **All**: This is all text including columns and rows,

- **Non-critical**, **Critical**, **Milestone**, **Summary**, **Project Summary**, **Marked**, **Highlighted** and **External tasks**,
- **Row** and **Column** titles,
- **Top**, **Middle** and **Bottom Timescale Tiers**, and
- **Bar Text** left, right, below, above and inside.

8.6 Format Timescale

8.6.1 Zoom Slider

The **Zoom Slider** was introduced with Microsoft Project 2010 and replaced the **View**, **Zoom...** function. This may be found at the bottom right-hand side of the screen and provides a simple way of scaling the time scale in the Gantt Chart and all other time scaled views such as the Calendar, Usage and Network Diagram View.

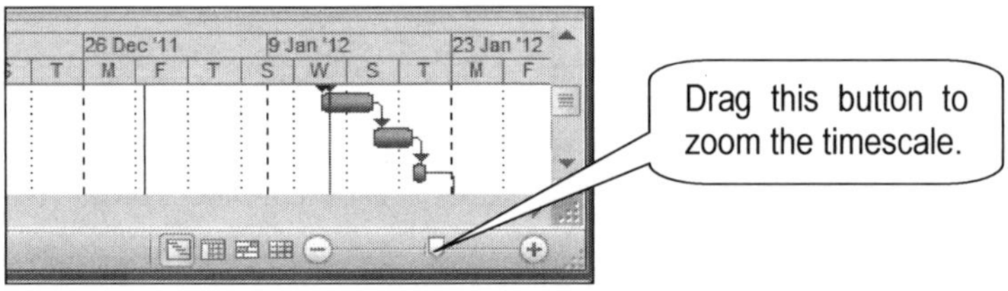

This function works differently than other scheduling software in that it changes the scale and the displayed time units at the same time and may result in some undesirable time units being displayed.

Once this function is used, your original timescale date formatting will be lost and may only be recovered with undo as this function applies its own formatting such as date formats.

The author has found that more predictable results are achieved by using the traditional **Zoom In** and **Zoom Out** functions which may be added to the **Quick Access Toolbar**.

8.6.2 Ribbon Menu

There are some new commands available with Microsoft Project 2010 on the **Ribbon**:

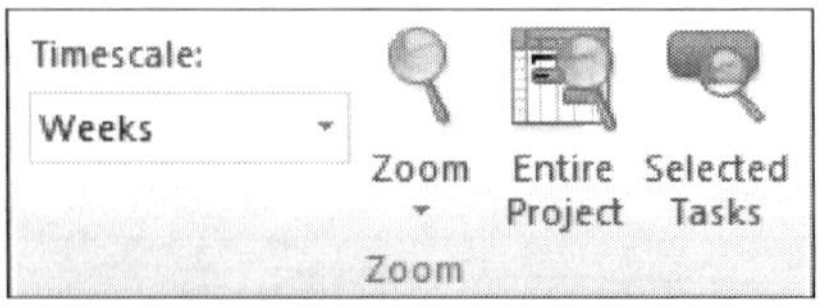

- The **Timescale:** option is a quick method of selecting the **Minor Timescale**, the lower line in the Timescale,
- Zoom opens a self-explanatory menu,
- **Entire Project** zooms the timescale to fit the whole project Gantt Chart to fit in the available space,
- **Selected Tasks** zooms the timescale to fit the bars of selected tasks to fit in the available space,

8.6.3 Format Timescale Command

The **Timescale** form provides a number of options for timescale display, which is located above the Bar Chart, and the shading of **Nonworking** time.

To open the **Timescale** form:

- Double-click on the timescale, or
- Add the **Timescale** button to the Ribbon or Quick Access Toolbar.

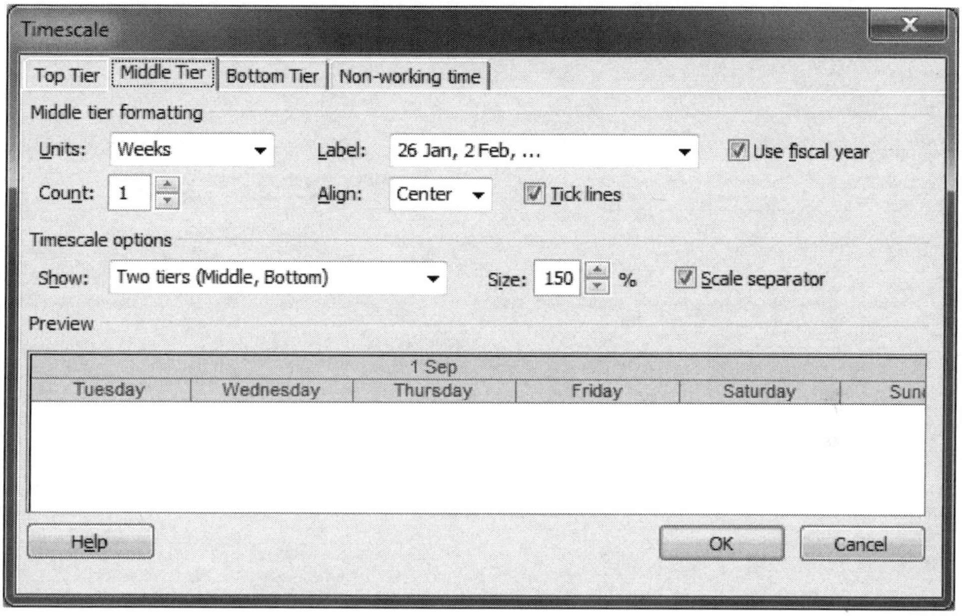

There are many options here which are intuitive and will not be described in detail.

Top Tier, **Middle Tier and Bottom Tier Tab**

- These three timescales may have different scales. These are often set at "weeks and days" or "months and weeks." By default, the Top Tier timescale has been disabled. You may enable the three tiers together by selecting Three Tiers (Top, Middle, Bottom) from the **Timescale options**, **Show:**.
- The **Label** will affect how much space the timescale will occupy, so the selection of a long label will result in longer Task bars.
- **Tick lines** and **Scale separator** hide and display the lines between the text.
- **Size:** controls the horizontal scale of the timescale and in association with the **Label:** are the two main tools for scaling the horizontal axis in the Gantt Chart.
- Choose the **Use fiscal year** function to display the financial year and then select the **File**, **Options**, **Calendar** tab to choose the month in which the fiscal year starts.
- Should you wish to number the time periods, for example; **Week 1**, **Week 2**, etc., there are a number of sequential numbering options available at the bottom of the label list.

Nonworking Time Tab

The **Nonworking time** tab allows you to format how the nonworking time is displayed. You may select only one calendar. The nonworking time may be presented as shading behind the bars, in front of the bars or hidden.

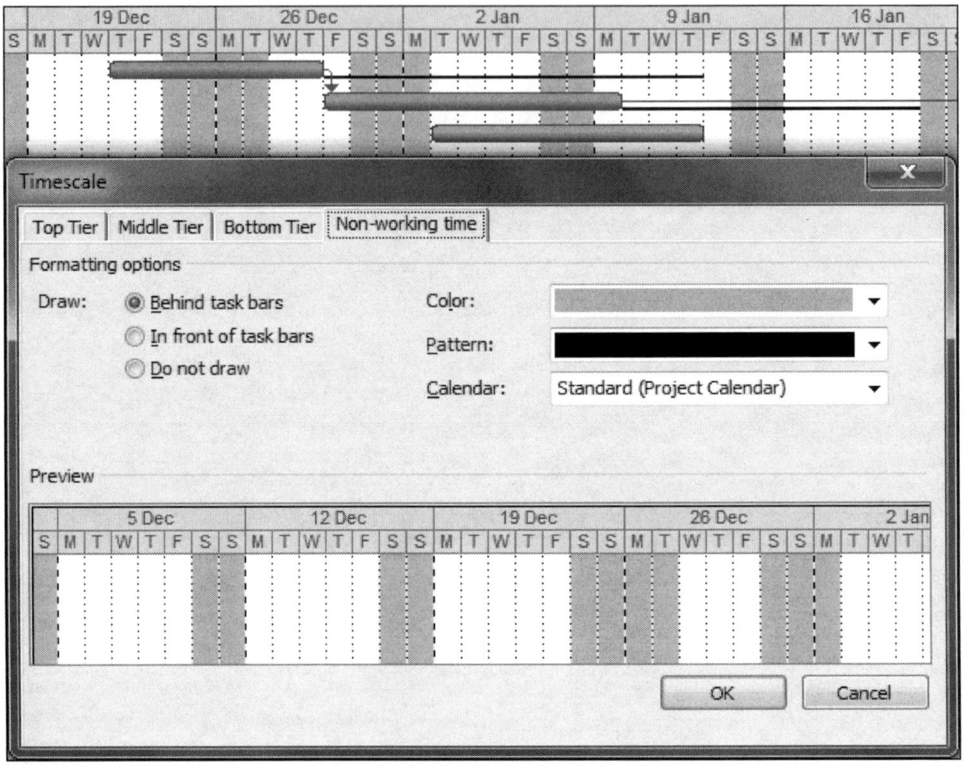

By default this is set to the Standard Calendar for each view and does not change when the Project Default Calendar is changed.

Therefore if you change the Project Base calendar in the **Project Information** and you wish to see this new calendar in all views you will have to edit all the views.

8.6.4 Format Timescale Font

To format the Timescale font, the **Format**, **Format** group, **Text Styles** command opens the **Text Styles** form:

The timescale fonts may be formatted separately by selecting the appropriate line item under **Item to Change:**.

A very tight timescale may be achieved by making the Bottom Timescale Tier a small font as displayed in the picture.

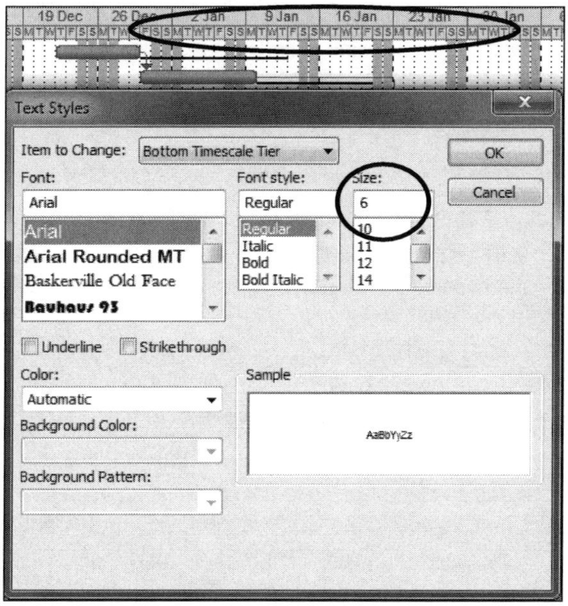

8.7 Format Gridlines

Gridlines are important to help divide the visual presentation of the Bar Chart. This example shows **Middle Tier Gridlines** every week and **Bottom Tier Gridlines** every day.

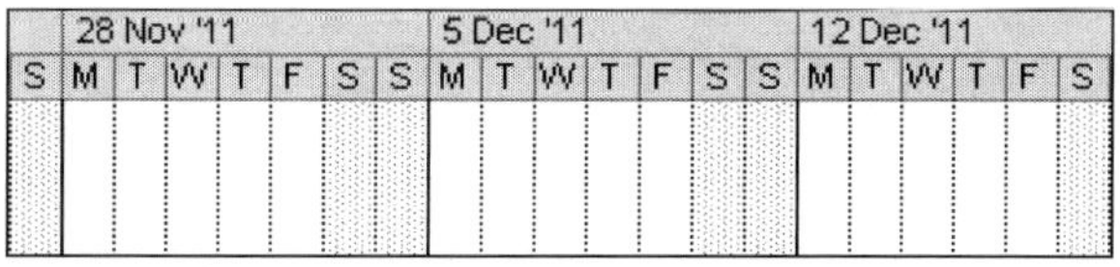

To format the Grid Line select **Format**, **Format** group, **Gridlines**, **Gridlines...** to open the **Gridlines** form:

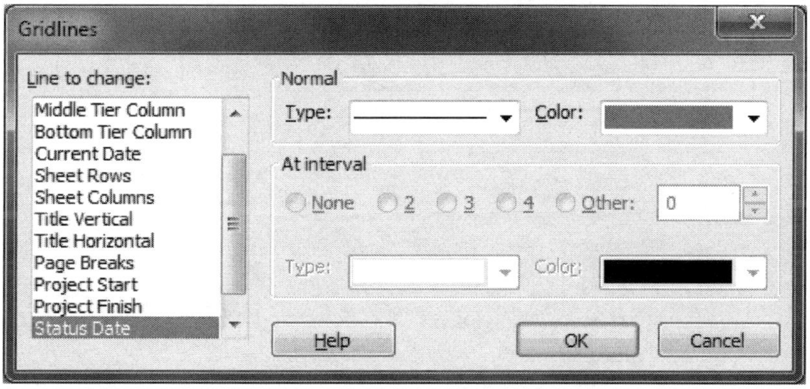

- Select the gridline from the drop-down box under **Line to change:**.
- Select color and type from under **Normal**.
- Date gridlines may be set to occur at intervals using the **At interval** option.

Some of the titles for the gridlines are not intuitive, so some interpretation is given below:

- For Data Column and Row dividing lines, use **Sheet Rows** and **Sheet Columns**.
- For Timescale and Column Titles, use **Horizontal** and **Title Vertical**.
- Gantt Chart area, including lines for **Project Start** and **Finish Date**, **Current** and **Status Date**, are clearly described.
- **Page Breaks** will only display manually-inserted breaks. You may need to add the **Insert Page Break** **Button** on the **Quick Access** Toolbar.

The earlier Microsoft Project option **Manual page breaks** check box in the **Print** form seemed to have disappeared from Microsoft Project 2010.

Microsoft Project has two dates that may be used to identify the **Data Date**, the date that the data has been collected for updating a project schedule. These two dates are the **Status Date** and **Current Date** which are set in the **Project Information** form:

- By default Microsoft Project displays the **Current Date** as a dark dotted vertical line but this is reset to the computer's system date each time the project file is opened. It is suggested that this line be removed using the **Gridline** form and the **Current Date** is not used to identify the **Data Date** because the software changes it every time the schedule is opened.
- The **Status Date** never changes once set and therefore it is suggested that this line should be displayed as per the picture above.

Many laser printers will not print light gray lines clearly, so it is often better to use dark gray or black Sight Lines for better output.

8.8 Format Links, Dependencies, Relationships, or Logic Lines

The Links, also known as Dependencies, Relationships, or Logic Lines, may be displayed or hidden by using the **Layout** form.

- Select **Format**, **Format** group, **Layout** to open the **Layout** form and click on one of the three radio buttons under **Links** to select the style you require:

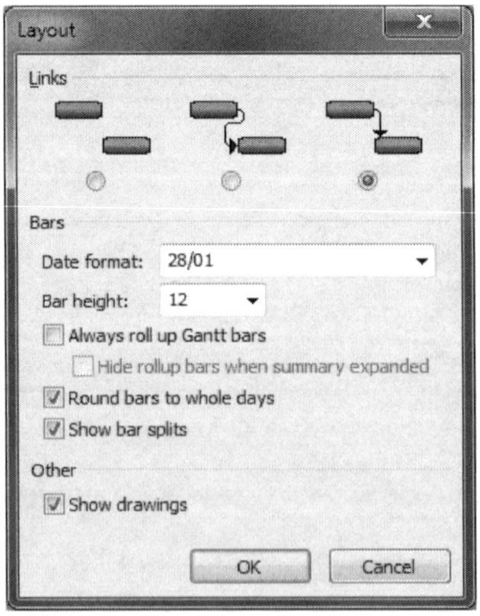

> ➢ The color of the **Link** is inherited from the color of the predecessor task.

- To display Critical Path on the relationship lines you will need to format the bars with a different color. This is often set to red.

The color of the successors' relationship lines is adopted from the task bar color. Therefore, re-formatting critical bars with the **Format Bar** form will also re-format the color of the successors' relationship lines and they may no longer display the Critical Path color on the Logic Lines. This will effectively mask the Critical Path and could provide misleading results.

The highest bar in the Bars form dictates the color of the relationship line and may not be the same as the color displayed in the Gantt Chart View.

Oracle Primavera products format the relationship separately from the bars and are able to identify the Critical, Driving and Non-Driving relationships, which is not possible with Microsoft Project.

8.9 Format Colors

Colors are formatted in a number of forms and there is no single form for formatting all colors:

- **Nonworking time** colors in the Gantt Chart are formatted in the **Timescale** form,; double-click on the timescale.
- **Text** colors are formatted in the **Text Styles** and **Font** forms, found in the **Format**, **Format** groups, **Text Style**.
- **Gridline** colors are formatted in the **Gridlines** form, also found under the **Format**, **Format** group, **Gridlines**.
- **Hyperlink** colors are formatted under **File**, **Options**, **Advanced**, **Display options for this project:**.
- **Timescale** colors are with the **File**, **Options**, **General** tab, **User Interface Options**, **Color scheme:** option.
- The **Logic Lines**, also known as **Dependencies**, **Relationships**, or **Links**, inherit their color from the predecessor's bar color in the Gantt Chart view and may be formatted in the Network Diagram view by selecting **Format**, **Format** group, **Layout**.

8.10 *Workshop 6 - Formatting the Bar Chart*

Background

Management has received your draft report and requests some changes to the presentation.

Assignment

Format your schedule as follows:

1. Select **View**, **Data** group, **Tables**, **More tables...** and create a new Table titled **Review** by copying the **Entry** table.
2. Add the **Task Calendar** column between **Start** and **Duration** columns in the **Table Definition** form.
3. Align Data for the **Task Calendar** to the left,
4. Remove the **Task Mode** column,

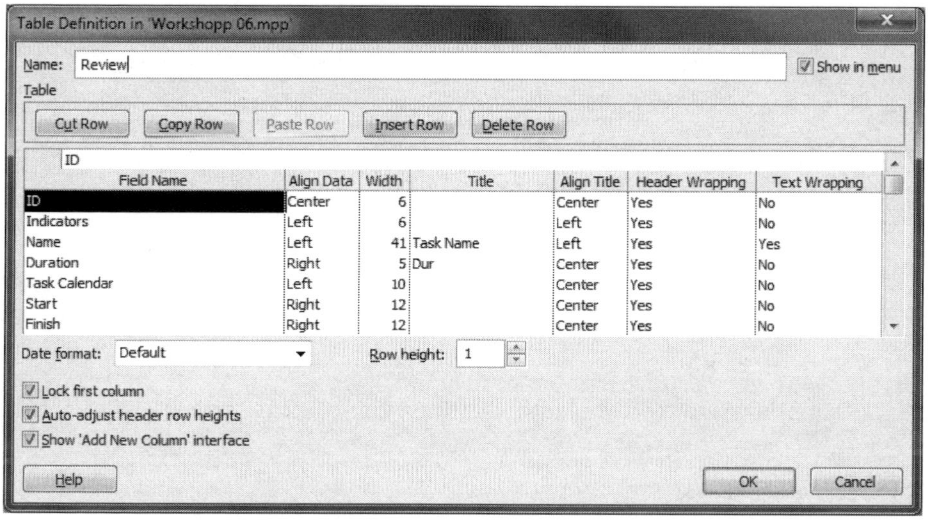

Table Definition in 'Workshopp 06.mpp'

Name: Review ☑ Show in menu

Table

Cut Row | Copy Row | Paste Row | Insert Row | Delete Row

ID

Field Name	Align Data	Width	Title	Align Title	Header Wrapping	Text Wrapping
ID	Center	6		Center	Yes	No
Indicators	Left	6		Left	Yes	No
Name	Left	41	Task Name	Left	Yes	Yes
Duration	Right	5	Dur	Center	Yes	No
Task Calendar	Left	10		Center	Yes	No
Start	Right	12		Center	Yes	No
Finish	Right	12		Center	Yes	No

Date format: Default Row height: 1

☑ Lock first column

☑ Auto-adjust header row heights

☑ Show 'Add New Column' interface

Help OK Cancel

5. Check the **Show in menu** option.
6. Click OK to close the form and apply the Table.
7. To make the Duration Column narrower, select from the **File**, **Options**, **Advanced** tab, **Display options for this project:** heading, select to display Days as "d" and uncheck **Add space before label**.
8. Right-click on the **Duration** column, select **Field Settings** to open the **Field Settings** form and enter a **Title:** of **Dur** and click Best Fit to produce a narrow column.
9. Add the **Zoom In** and **Zoom Out** buttons to the **Quick Access Toolbar** and test their function.

Continued Over...

10. Double-click on the timescale; format the **Middle Tier Timescale** with **Units:** of **Months** with **Label:** of **Jan '09** and **Count:** of 1 month, then format the **Bottom Tier Timescale** with **Units:** of **Weeks** with **Label:** of **26,2,...,** Size: of 150% and **Count:** of 1 Week.

11. Select **Format**, **Format** group, **Gridlines**, **Gridlines...** and format the Gridlines with **Middle Tier Columns** to dotted black lines and **Bottom Tier Columns** to dashed black lines.

12. Click on the **Format**, **Bar Styles**, **Critical Tasks** to display the Critical bar.

13. Double-click in the bar chart area to open the **Bar Styles** form, click on the Text tab and scroll through one bar at a time and remove all text from the all the bars. Ensure you highlight the text before deleting, if you make an error use the Undo key.

14. Add a new bar titled **Task Name** which does not display a bar and displays the Task **Name** to the right of the bar, as per the picture below. If you wish to remove the Task **Name** from the bars then you now only need to delete the one bar.

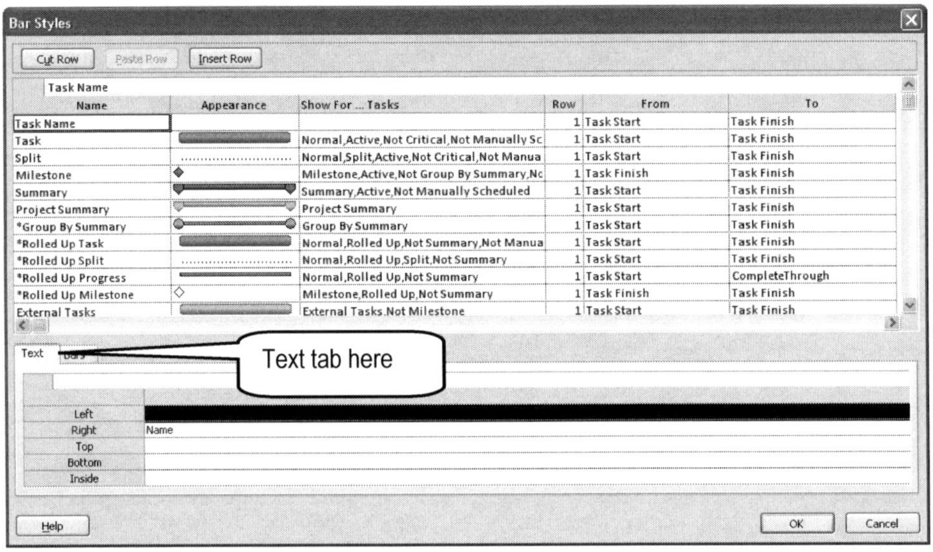

15. Check your result with the example shown below.

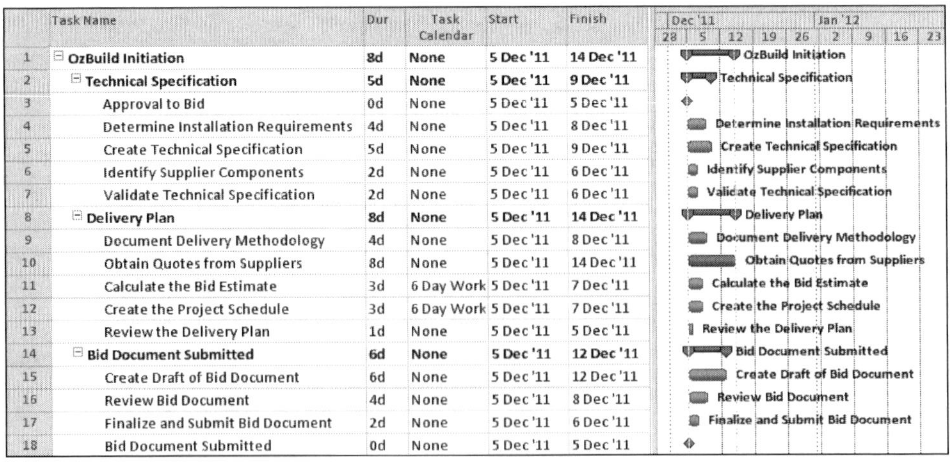

16. Save your **OzBuild Bid** project.

9 ADDING TASK DEPENDENCIES

This chapter will concentrate on the basis that all tasks are **Auto Scheduled**. There is a section that covers the relationships between **Manually Scheduled** tasks covered in para 22.3.1.

The next phase of a schedule is to add logic to the tasks. There are two types of logic that you may use:

- **Dependencies** (**Relationships** or **Logic** or **Links**) between tasks, and
- Imposed **Constraints** to task start or finish dates. These are covered in the **CONSTRAINTS** chapter.

Microsoft Project's Help file and other text uses the terms "**Dependencies**, **Relationships** and **Links**" for Dependencies but does not use the term "**Logic**."

There are a number of methods of adding, editing and deleting task **Dependencies**. We will look at the following techniques in this chapter:

Topic	Notes for creating a Finish-to-Start Dependency
• Graphically in the Gantt, Calendar or Network Diagram Views	Drag the 4-headed mouse pointer from one task to another to create an FS dependency.
• With the **Task**, **Schedule** group **Link** and **Unlink** buttons	Select the tasks in the order they are to be linked and click on the Link or buttons.
• By using the Menu command	Select the tasks in the order they are to be linked and select **Ctrl+F2**.
• By opening the **Task Information** form	Predecessor only may be added and deleted.
• Through the **Predecessor** and **Successor Details** forms	Open the bottom pane, **Windows**, **Split** and then right-click and select **Predecessors and Successors**.
• By editing or deleting a dependency using the **Task Dependency** form	Double-click on a task link (relationship line) in the **Bar Chart** or **Network Diagram** view.
• **Autolink inserted or moved tasks**	Select **File**, **Options**, **Schedule** tab, **Scheduling options for this project:** section, and check the **Autolink inserted or moved tasks** box. This option is NOT recommended.
• By displaying the **Predecessor** or **Successor** column	Edit the relationships in the columns.

Microsoft Project allows only one relationship between two tasks whereas Oracle Primavera software and Asta Powerproject allow two.

Dependencies

Generally, there are two types of dependencies that may be entered into the software:

- **Hard Logic**, also referred to as **Mandatory Logic**, are dependencies that may not be avoided. For example a footing would have to be excavated before it may be filled with concrete or a computer and software delivered before the software may be installed onto the computer.
- **Soft Logic**, also referred to as **Sequencing Logic** or **Preferred Logic**, which often may be changed at a later date to reflect planning changes. An example would be determining the order in which a number of footings are dug or which computer is installed with software first.

To create a **Closed Network** each task will require a Start predecessor and a Finish successor. Most schedules may be created using only Finish-to-Start relationships with positive or negative lags. This method ensures a Closed Network is created and the **Critical Path** flows through the tasks and not just through the relationships. When Start-to-Start relationships are used the Critical Path is calculated through the relationships only and is not a true Critical Path; the Critical Path must run through the task to be a true Critical Path.

A delay to the completion of the first task in the example on the left below will not delay subsequent tasks as the calculated Critical Path flows through the relationships and not the tasks, therefore a true Critical Path has not been created. The example on the right has created a true Critical Path because the driving path flows through the tasks and the relationships:

Open Network

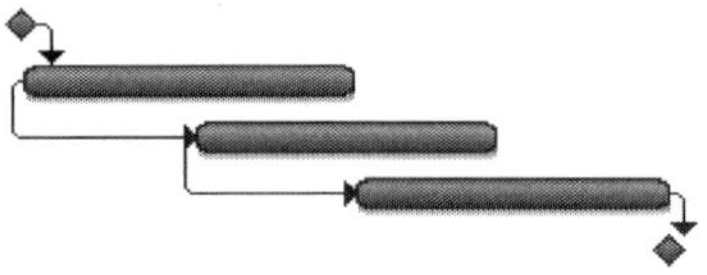

Closed Network

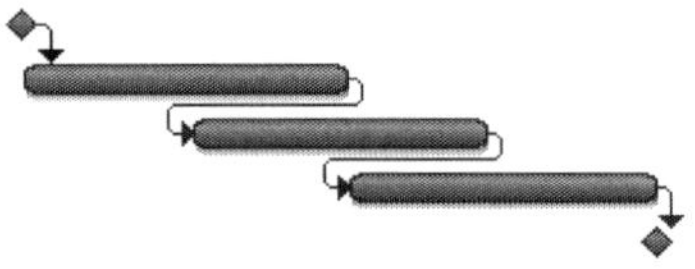

No delay to Finish Milestone

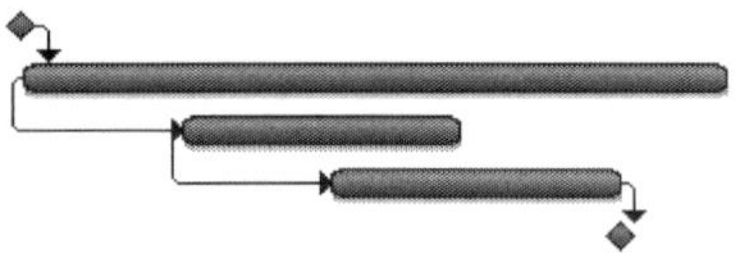

Delay to Finish Milestone

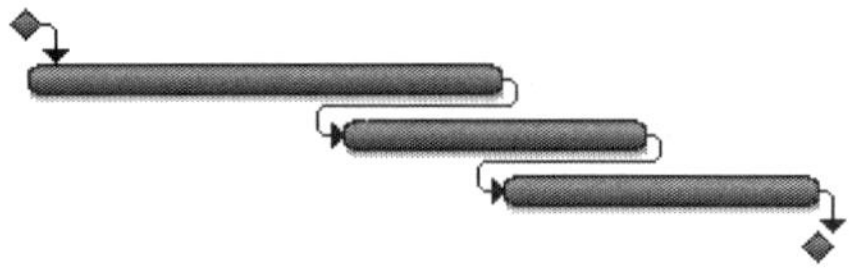

There is no simple method of documenting which is hard and which is soft logic. A schedule with a large amount of soft logic has the potential of becoming very difficult to maintain when the plan is changed. You will also find that soft logic converts to hard logic as a project progresses when commitments are made and tasks have started.

Constraints

Constraints are applied to tasks when relationships do not provide the required result. Typical applications of a constraint are:

- The availability of a site to commence work.
- The supply of information by a client.
- The required finish date of a project.

Constraints are often entered to represent contract dates or **External Logic** and may be directly related to contract items. It is often useful to make notes about contract dates reflected in the schedule in either the Task Note area or one of the Text columns. Constraints are covered in detail in the **CONSTRAINTS** chapter.

9.1 *Understanding Dependencies*

Two other terms you must understand are:

- **Predecessor**, a task that controls the start or finish of another immediate subsequent task.
- **Successor**, a task whose start or finish depends on the start or finish of another immediately preceding task.

	Task Name	Predecessors	Successors
1	A		2
2	B	1	3
3	C	2	

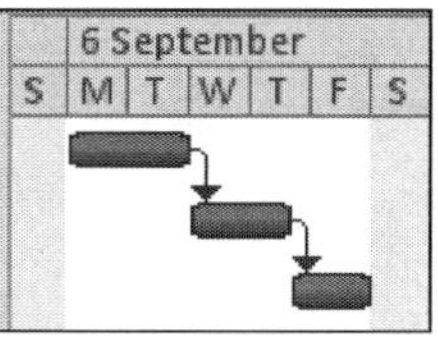

In the picture above A is the predecessor of B and C is the successor of B.

There are four types of dependencies available in Microsoft Project:

- Finish-to-Start (**FS**) – this is the default and also known as conventional
- Start-to-Start (**SS**)
- Finish-to-Finish (**FF**)
- Start-to-Finish (**SF**) – this relationship type is rarely used and should be avoided because it places the successor before the predecessor.

The following pictures show how the dependencies appear graphically in the **Gantt Chart** and **Network Diagram** (PERT) views:

The **FS** (or conventional) dependency looks like this:

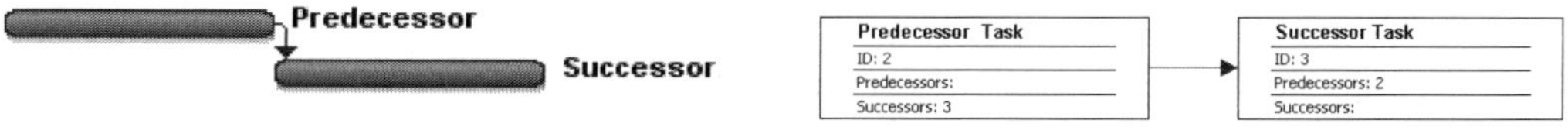

While the **SS** dependency is like this:

The **FF** dependency would be:

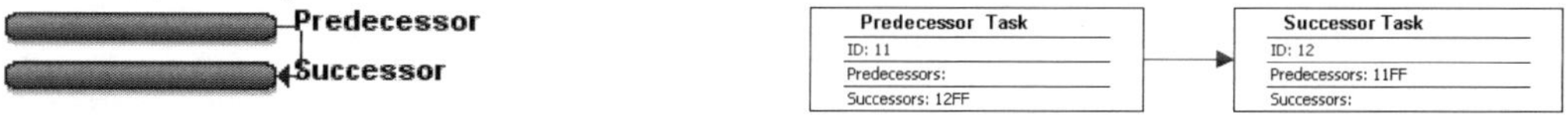

The **SF** dependency looks like:

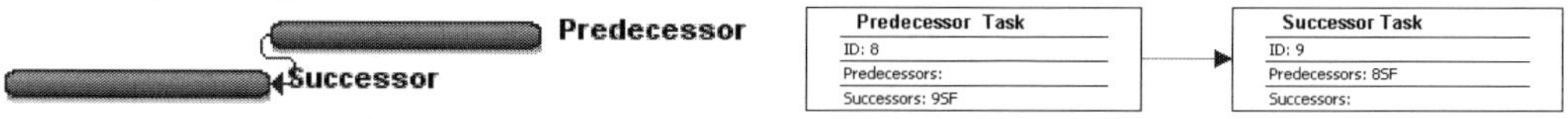

9.2 Understanding Lags and Leads

A **Lag** is a duration that is applied to a dependency to make the successor start or finish earlier or later and may be applied to any relationship type.

- A successor task will start or finish later when a positive **Lag** is assigned. Therefore, a task requiring a 3-day delay between the finish of one task and start of another will require a positive lag of 3 days.
- Conversely, a lag may be negative (also called a **Lead)** when a new task can be started before the predecessor task is finished.
- **Leads** and **Lags** may be applied to any relationship type including summary task relationships. Dependencies between summary tasks should be avoided and all relationships should be placed on detail tasks which makes following the logic simpler.

An example of an **FS** with positive lag

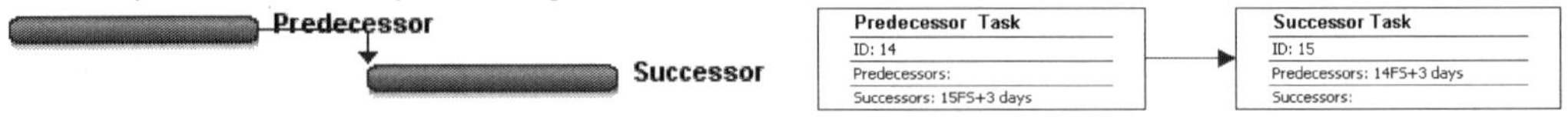

An example of an **FS** with negative lag:

Here are some important points to understand about lags.

- Lags are calculated on the **Successor Calendar** except with Microsoft Project 2002 and earlier which uses the **Project Calendar**, set in the **Project Information** form. Therefore files with lags and multiple calendars may calculate differently in earlier versions. (Oracle Primavera SureTrak and P3 use the predecessor's calendar, Primavera P6 has four user options and Asta Powerproject puts the lag on either or both the predecessors or successors and not the relationship.)
- Lags may be assigned **Elapsed** durations, therefore they will be based on a 24-hour, 7-day per week. To enter an elapsed lag type an "**e**" before the unit, e.g. **5 ed**.

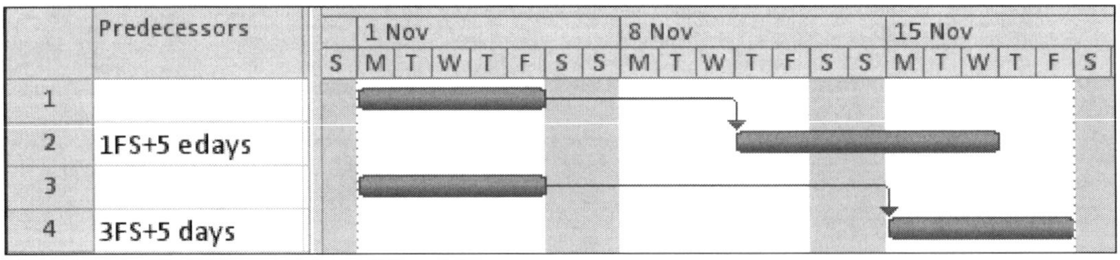

- Lags may be expressed in terms of percentage and in this situation the lag is a percentage of the predecessor's duration. The example below shows an FS dependency +250%; the predecessor is 1 day so the lag is 2.5 days. This results in the successor of 1 day duration spanning 2 days.

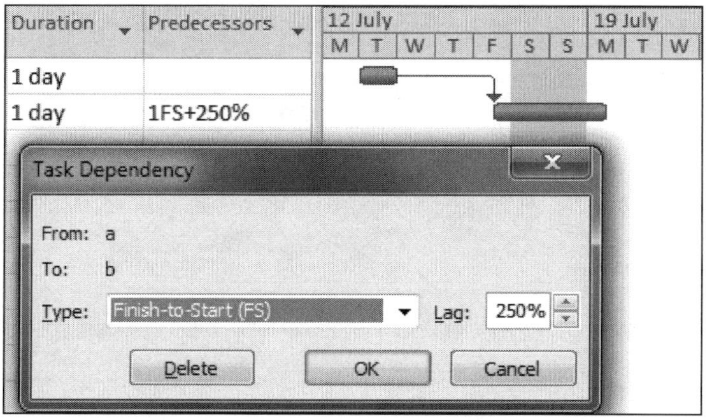

You must be careful when using a lag to allow for delays such as curing concrete when the Successor Calendar is not a 7-day calendar. Since this type of task lapses nonwork days, the task could finish before Microsoft Project's calculated finish date. You may want to use elapsed durations in a lag in this situation.

9.3 Restrictions on Summary Task Dependencies

Dependencies may be made between summary tasks and detail tasks of a different summary task. Consider the following points when using dependencies at summary task level:

- There is a built-in dependency between summary and detail tasks. Detail tasks may be considered as Start-to-Start successors and Finish-to-Finish predecessors of their summary task.
- Summary tasks may only have **FS** and **SS** dependencies; you will receive a warning message when you attempt to enter an illegal dependency.

It is recommended that dependencies be maintained at the detail level. This is particularly important when moving tasks from one summary task to another since the dependencies will still be valid. Again, be aware that there is a function found under the **File**, **Options**, **Schedule** tab, **Scheduling options for this project:** section, **Autolink inserted or moved tasks** which will change relationships when tasks are moved. This function should be turned off if you wish to move a task and keep the existing logic.

9.4 Assigning Dependencies

The dependencies may be displayed or hidden with the **Layout** form.

- Select **Format**, **Format** group, **Layout** to open the **Layout** form and click on the radio button under the style you require:

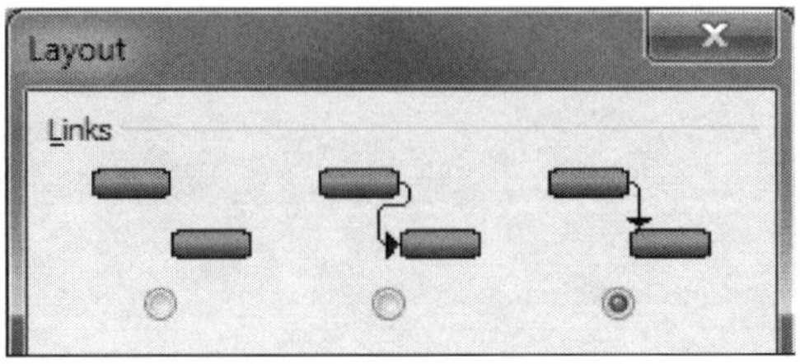

- The color of the dependency line is inherited from the color of the predecessor task.
- To display a Critical Path on the relationship lines you will need to format the bars as critical.

9.4.1 Graphically Adding a Dependency

You may graphically add a **Finish-to-Start** dependency only by:

- Selecting the **Gantt Chart**, **Calendar** or **Network Diagram**, then:
- Move the mouse pointer over a task until the mouse pointer changes to a ✥, left-click and drag to the successor task. The cursor will change to a 🔗 shape during this operation.

9.4.2 Using the Link and Unlink Buttons

The 🔗 **Link Tasks** button found the **Task**, **Schedule** group, which you should add to the **Quick Access Menu** may be used for linking tasks with a Finish-to-Start dependency:

- Highlight one or more tasks using Ctrl and left-click (to select one task at a time) or Shift and left-click (to select a contiguous group of tasks).
- Then click the 🔗 **Link Tasks** button on the toolbar and the tasks will be linked with Finish-to-Start dependencies in the order that they were selected.

To remove a dependency, select the tasks and click on the **Unlink Tasks** button.

The limit of a maximum of 10 groups of tasks that could be linked in this way has been removed from Microsoft Project 2010.

This function is not end sensitive as in Primavera products and Asta Power Powerproject and may only be used for assigning a Finish-to-Start relationship.

9.4.3 Task Linking Using the Keyboard

Multiple tasks may be linked with a Finish-to-Start dependency:

- Highlight one or more tasks using Ctrl-left-click (to select one task at a time) or Shift and left-click (to select a group of tasks).
- Then select **Ctrl+F2** and the tasks will be linked with Finish-to-Start dependencies in the order that they were selected.
- A group of tasks is created by dragging over two or more tasks. These are linked with FS relationships.

Primavera P3 and SureTrak software links tasks that have been highlighted from top to bottom and not in the order they are selected. Oracle Primavera P6 links in the order they are highlighted. Microsoft Project also links the tasks in the order they are highlighted.

9.4.4 Adding and Deleting Predecessors with the Task Information Form

The **Task Information** form may be used for adding and deleting predecessors only.

- Double-click on a task to open the **Task Information** form,
- Select the **Predecessors** tab,
- To select the predecessor, you may either:
  - ➢ Type in the Predecessor Task ID in the first line under ID, or
  - ➢ Use the drop-down box under task name:

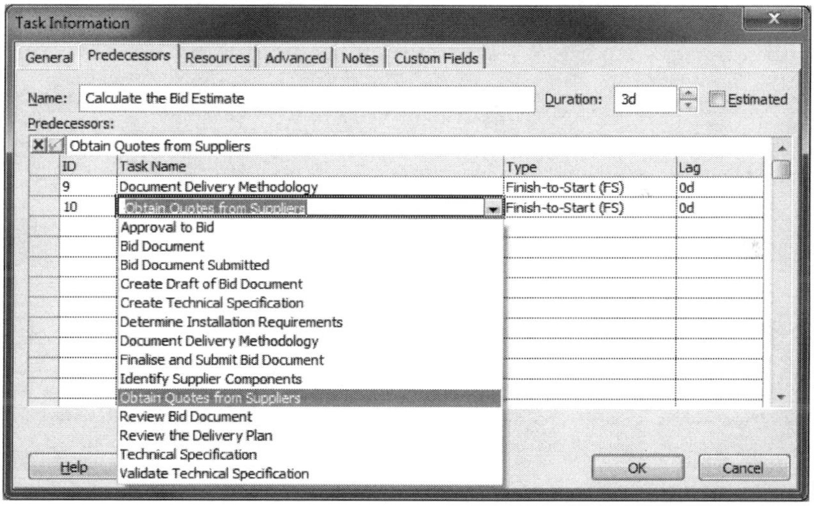

- Now enter the Relationship Type from the **Type** drop-down list and the lag, if required, from the **Lag** drop-down list.

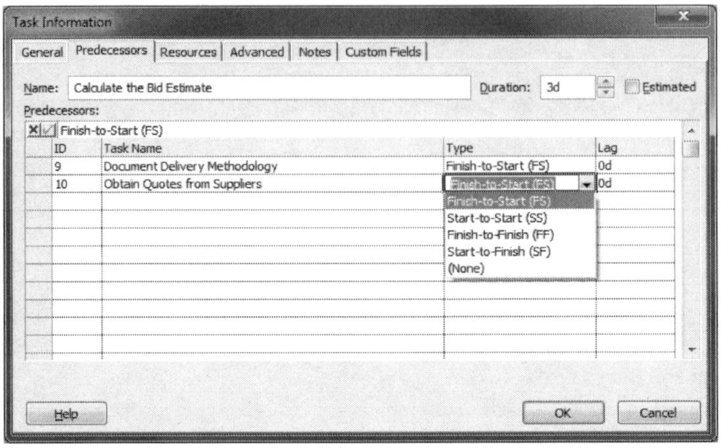

- To enter another relationship click on the next line.
- You are not able to scroll up or down to another task while the **Task Information** form is open.

To complete your operation, either:

- Press the **Enter Key** or click on the OK button to commit the changes, or
- Click on the **Esc Key** or click on the Cancel button to abort any changes.

9.4.5 Predecessor and Successor Details Forms

The Predecessor and Successor Details form may be displayed by:

- Opening the bottom pane by right-clicking in the Gantt Chart and selecting **Show Split**,
- Then making the bottom pane active by clicking anywhere in the bottom pane. The bar on the left-hand side of the bottom pane will turn blue when it is active,
- Displaying the **Task Details Form**, **Task Entry** or **Task Form** (shown below which is displayed by default),
- Then right-clicking in the bottom pane and select **Predecessors and Successors** to display the **Predecessors and Successors Detail** form:

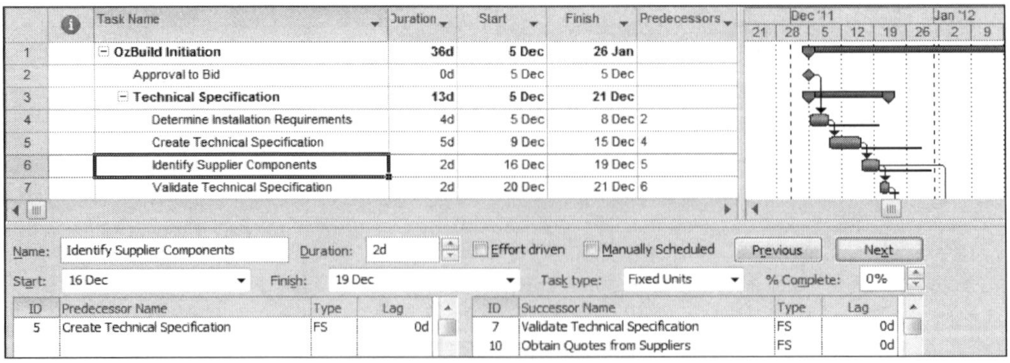

Predecessors and successors may be added using the same method as in the **Task Information** form.

Double-clicking on a Predecessor or Successor in any of these forms will display the Predecessor or Successor **Task Information** form, allowing the dates, constraints, etc. of related tasks to be examined.

9.4.6 Editing or Deleting Dependencies Using the Task Dependency Form

To use the **Task Dependency** form, a logic link between tasks must already exist. To open the **Task Dependency** form, double-click on a task link (relationship line) in the Bar Chart or Network Diagram.

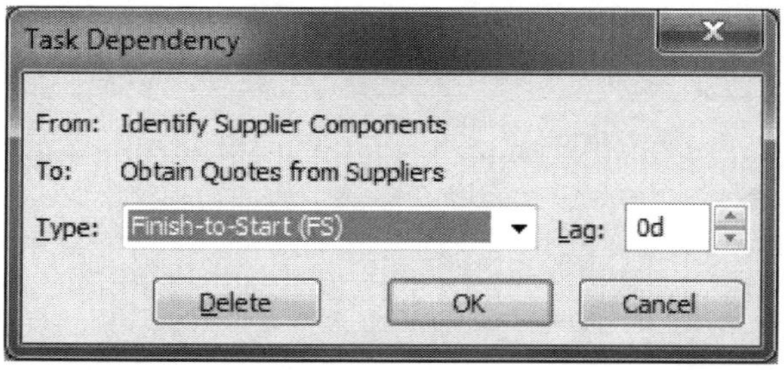

A link may only be edited or deleted from this form.

9.4.7 Autolink New Inserted Tasks or Moved Tasks

This function automatically creates predecessors to tasks above it and successors below it when a task is moved or inserted. This option may be activated by selecting the **File**, **Options**, **Schedule** tab, **Scheduling options for this project:** section and checking the **Autolink inserted or moved tasks** box.

When **Autolink inserted or moved tasks** is activated you must ensure that: you have selected the whole task by clicking on the Task ID and therefore highlighting all the columns before you drag the task to a new location. Otherwise, you will only move the cell contents.

When the task is moved, **Autolink inserted or moved tasks** will change the existing predecessor and successor logic without warning. This function potentially makes substantial changes to your project logic and may affect the overall project duration. It is suggested that the option is **NEVER** switched on as dragging a task to a new location may completely change the logic of a schedule.

9.4.8 Editing Relationships Using the Predecessor or Successor Columns

The **Predecessor** or **Successor** column may be displayed and edited following the example below.

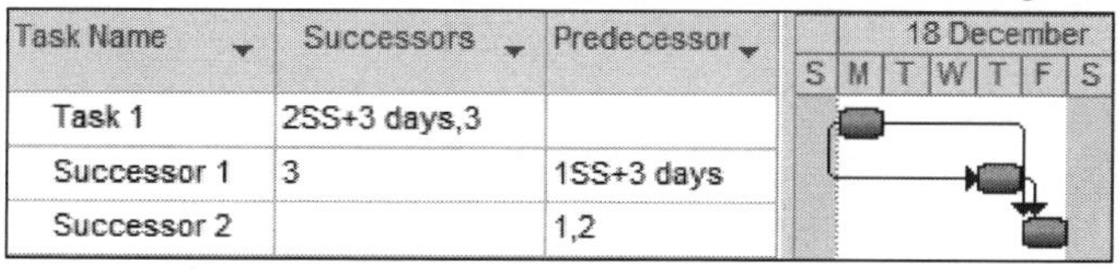

9.5 Scheduling the Project

Once you have your tasks and logic in place, Microsoft Project calculates the tasks' dates/times. More specifically, Microsoft Project has **Scheduled** the project to calculate the **Early Dates**, **Late Dates** and **Float**. This will allow you to review the **Critical Path** of the project. Microsoft Project uses the term **Slack** instead of the standard term **Float**. Both terms are used interchangeably throughout this book.

Sometimes it is preferable to prevent the **Automatic Calculation** of your project's start/end dates. To do this, select **File**, **Options**, **Schedule** tab, **Calculation**, click on **Off**. This is the same as **Manual Calculation** in earlier versions of the software.

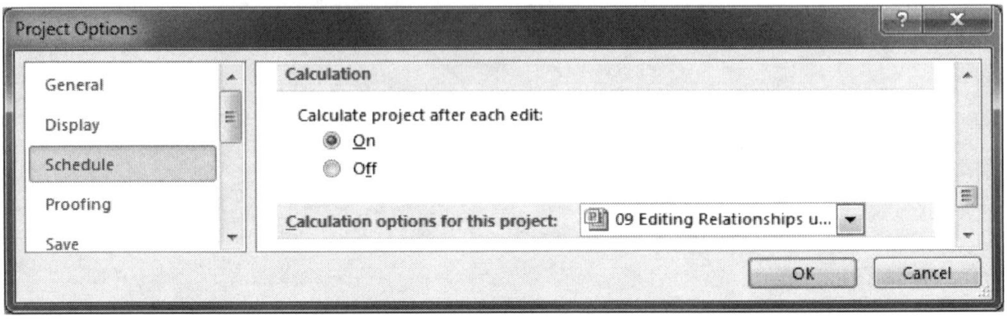

To calculate the schedule with the calculation mode set to manual:

- Press the **F9 Key**, or
- Click on the **Select All** button, top left-hand corner of the Gantt Chart view, right-click to open a menu and select **Calculate Project**, or
- Add a **Schedule Project** button to the **Ribbon** or **Quick Access Toolbar**.

9.6 Workshop 7- Adding the Relationships

Background

You have determined the logical sequence of tasks, so you may now enter the relationships.

Assignment

1. Remove the text from the bars by deleting .
2. Add the **Table** button from the **View**, **Data** group to the **Quick Access Toolbar**.
3. Apply the **Entry** table.
4. Remove the **Task Mode** column, right click on the header.
5. Input the logic below using several of the methods detailed in this chapter.

	ℹ	Task Name	Predecessors
1		⊟ **OzBuild Initiation**	
2		⊟ **Technical Specification**	
3		Approval to Bid	
4		Determine Installation Requirements	3
5		Create Technical Specification	4
6		Identify Supplier Components	5
7		Validate Technical Specification	6
8		⊟ **Delivery Plan**	
9		Document Delivery Methodology	7
10		Obtain Quotes from Suppliers	6
11		Calculate the Bid Estimate	9,10
12		Create the Project Schedule	11
13		Review the Delivery Plan	12
14		⊟ **Bid Document Submitted**	
15		Create Draft of Bid Document	9
16		Review Bid Document	13,15
17		Finalize and Submit Bid Document	16
18		Bid Document Submitted	17

6. Add the **Format**, **Format** group, **Layout** to the **Quick Access Toolbar**.
7. Hide and display the Logic Links using **Format**, **Format** group, **Layout** to open the **Layout** form (If your links are displayed by default, then hide and then display them again.)
8. Check your results against the diagram on the next page.
9. Save your **OzBuild Bid** project.

Answers to Workshop 7

		Task Name	Duration	Start	Finish	Predecessors
1		**OzBuild Initiation**	**31d**	**5 Dec '11**	**19 Jan '12**	
2		**Technical Specification**	**13d**	**5 Dec '11**	**21 Dec '11**	
3		Approval to Bid	0d	5 Dec '11	5 Dec '11	
4		Determine Installation Requirements	4d	5 Dec '11	8 Dec '11	3
5		Create Technical Specification	5d	9 Dec '11	15 Dec '11	4
6		Identify Supplier Components	2d	16 Dec '11	19 Dec '11	5
7		Validate Technical Specification	2d	20 Dec '11	21 Dec '11	6
8		**Delivery Plan**	**14d**	**20 Dec '11**	**11 Jan '12**	
9		Document Delivery Methodology	4d	22 Dec '11	29 Dec '11	7
10		Obtain Quotes from Suppliers	8d	20 Dec '11	3 Jan '12	6
11		Calculate the Bid Estimate	3d	4 Jan '12	6 Jan '12	9,10
12		Create the Project Schedule	3d	7 Jan '12	10 Jan '12	11
13		Review the Delivery Plan	1d	11 Jan '12	11 Jan '12	12
14		**Bid Document Submitted**	**14d**	**30 Dec '11**	**19 Jan '12**	
15		Create Draft of Bid Document	6d	30 Dec '11	9 Jan '12	9
16		Review Bid Document	4d	12 Jan '12	17 Jan '12	13,15
17		Finalize and Submit Bid Document	2d	18 Jan '12	19 Jan '12	16
18		Bid Document Submitted	0d	19 Jan '12	19 Jan '12	17

		Task Name
1		**OzBuild Initiation**
2		**Technical Specification**
3		Approval to Bid
4		Determine Installation Requirements
5		Create Technical Specification
6		Identify Supplier Components
7		Validate Technical Specification
8		**Delivery Plan**
9		Document Delivery Methodology
10		Obtain Quotes from Suppliers
11		Calculate the Bid Estimate
12		Create the Project Schedule
13		Review the Delivery Plan
14		**Bid Document Submitted**
15		Create Draft of Bid Document
16		Review Bid Document
17		Finalize and Submit Bid Document
18		Bid Document Submitted

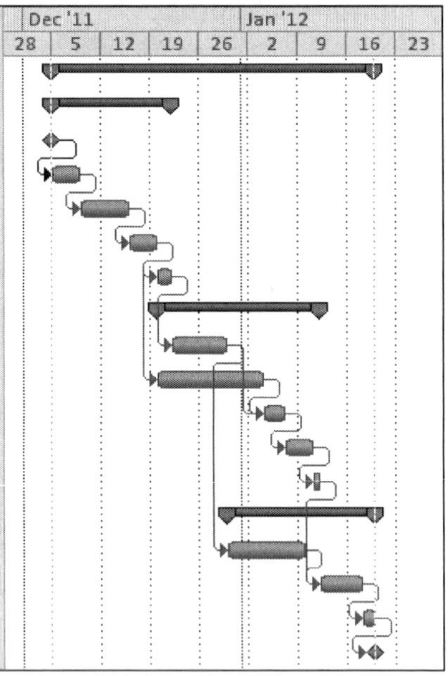

10 NETWORK DIAGRAM VIEW

The **Network Diagram View** is an enhancement of the earlier versions of Microsoft Project **Pert View** and displays tasks as boxes connected by the relationship lines. This chapter will not cover this subject in detail but will introduce the main features.

To view your project in the Networking View:

- Select **View**, **Task Views** group **Networking Diagram**, or
- Select **Task**, **View** group and select **Networking Diagram** from the drop-down list.

Topic	Menu Command
• Add new tasks	Click and drag into a blank area. This will add a new task with a Finish-to-Start relationship, or Use the **Insert Key** and a new task is added after the highlighted task without a relationship.
• Delete tasks	Select the task and press the **Delete** key.
• Display the **Task Information** form	Double-click on a Task Box, or Highlight a task and right-click on it then select **Task Information...** for the menu.
• Format Dependencies	Select **Format**, **Format** group, **Layout**
• Display the **Task Dependency** form	Double-click on a relationship line.
• Display information in the bottom pane	Right-click and select **Show Split**, or Drag the dividing bar.
• Format Task Boxes	Select **Format**, **Format** group, **Box Styles**, or Double-click on the outside edge of a box.
• Format an individual Task Box	Select **Format**, **Format** group, **Box**
• Change the scale of the display	Select **View**, **Zoom** group, **Zoom** ,or Use the **Zoom Slider** at the bottom right-hand side of the screen.

10.1 Understanding the Network Diagram View

The following list describes the main display features of the Network Diagram View:

- Summary tasks, detail tasks and Milestones are normally formatted with a different shape. Typical shape examples are provided as follows:
  - Summary tasks are trapezoidal –
  - Detail tasks are rectangular –
  - The Milestone Task is an elongated diamond –

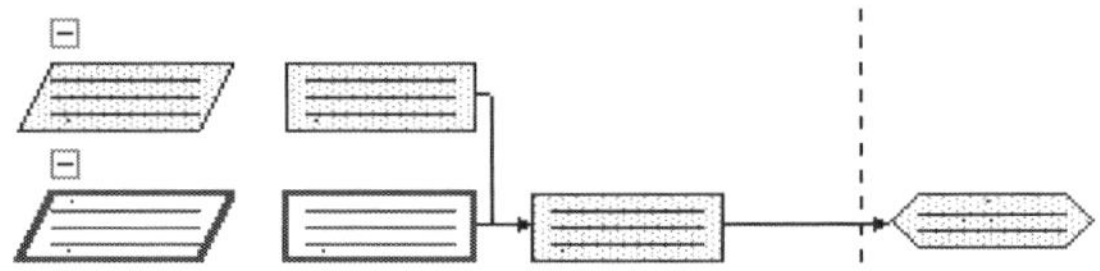

- Summary tasks are positioned to the left at the same level or above detail tasks.
- Summary tasks may be rolled up by clicking on the ⊟ above the task and expanded by clicking on the ⊞ above a rolled up summary task.
- All relationship lines are drawn as **Finish-to-Start** even when they are not linked as a **Finish-to-Start** relationship. The link type may be displayed on the arrow. See **Link style** later in this chapter.
- Critical tasks may be formatted to have different borders and backgrounds.
- The contents of the Task Boxes and relationship lines may also be formatted.

10.2 Adding and Deleting Tasks in the Network Diagram View

- A **New Task** may be created with a **Finish-to-Start** relationship by dragging from the center of a Task Box into a blank part of the screen.
- A **New Task** may be created without a relationship below the tasks position in the Gantt Chart by:
  - Using the **Insert Key**, or
  - Selecting **Task**, **Insert** group, **Task** **Task** (New Task).

10.3 Adding, Editing and Deleting Dependencies

Dependencies may be added, edited or deleted using the following methods:

- Graphically add a relationship by clicking on the center of one task and dragging to the successor.
- Hold the **Ctrl Key** to select two or more tasks and then use the **Task**, **Schedule** group, **Link Task** function.
- The **Task**, **Schedule** group, **Unlink Task** function removes dependencies between selected tasks.
- Open the **Task Information** form by double-clicking on a task and selecting the **Predecessors** tab.
- Double-click on a **Relationship line** to open the **Task Dependency** form and edit or delete a dependency.
- Create a split window by right-clicking and selecting **Show Split** and then display the predecessors and successors in the bottom pane by right-clicking and selecting **Predecessors and Successors**.

10.4 Formatting the Task Boxes

Task Boxes may be formatted from the **Box Styles** form, which is displayed by:

- Selecting **Format**, **Format** group, **Box Styles**:

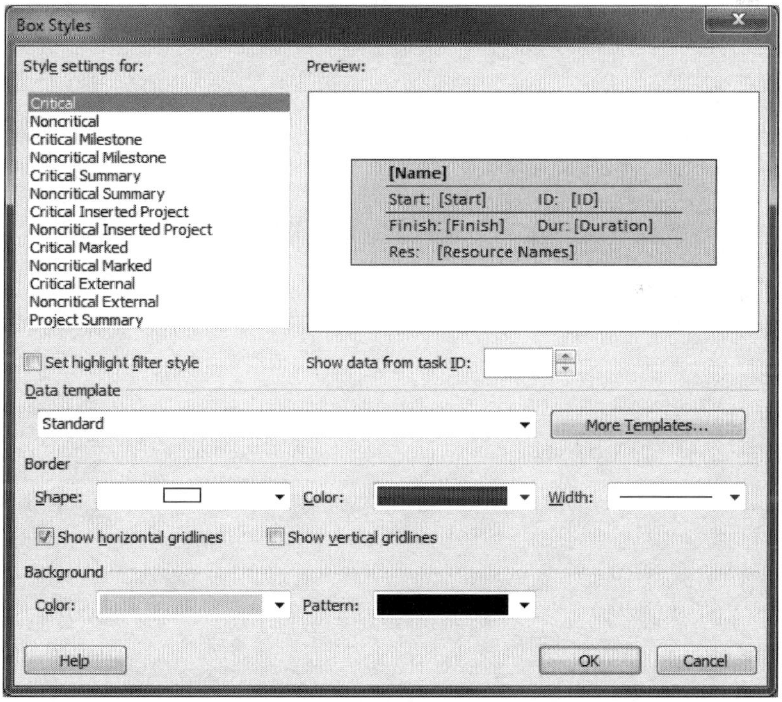

- A new template may be created to display other data by clicking on the More Templates... button which will open the **Data Templates** form.

10.5 Formatting Individual Boxes

Once highlighted, a **Task Box** may be formatted differently from all the others by:

- Selecting **Format**, **Format** group, **Box** to open the **Format Box** form, or
- Double-clicking on the outside edge of a box.

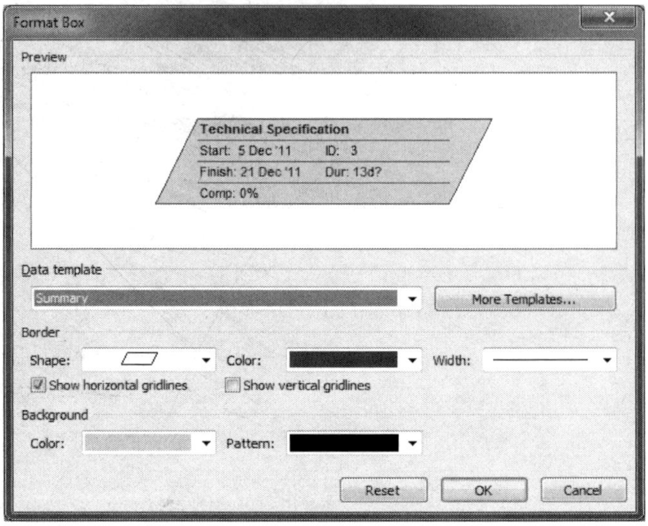

The [Reset] button is used to set the formatting back to default.

10.6 Formatting the Display and Relationship Lines

Most formatting, except formatting the boxes, is set within the **Layout** form. Select **Format**, **Format** group, **Layout** to open the **Layout** form:

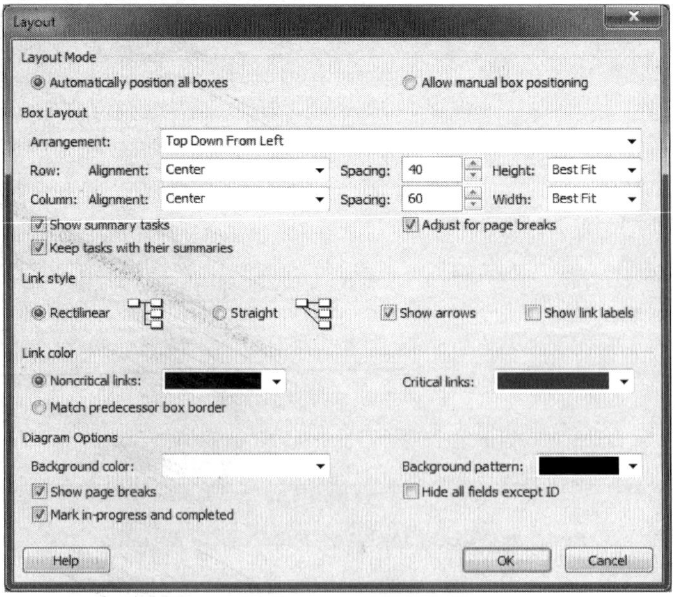

- The **Layout Mode** allows you to drag a Task Box to a new position. When **Allow manual box positioning** is selected, place the mouse over the Task Box and then when it changes to a ✥, drag the box to the required location.
- **Box Layout** allows you to specify how the Task Boxes are arranged. This option will only work when **Layout Mode** is set to **Automatically position all boxes**. For example, when "Top Down by Week" is selected, all the Tasks that start in the first week will be placed in the first column. The other options under **Box Layout** should be self-explanatory.

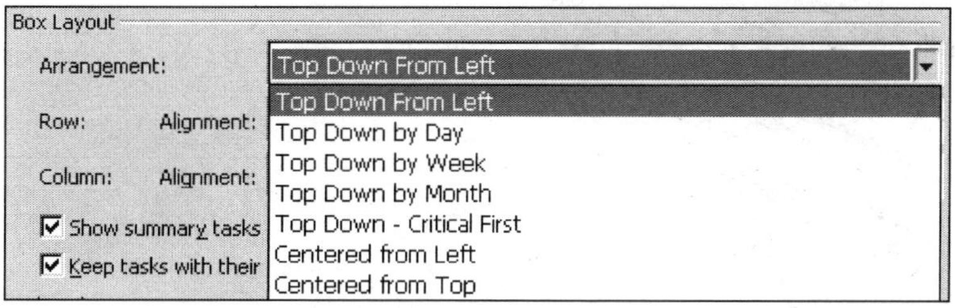

- **Link style** is an option to display relationships. Checking **Show link labels** will place the relationship type and lag on the relationship line and is useful when all your relationships are not Finish-to-Start. See below.

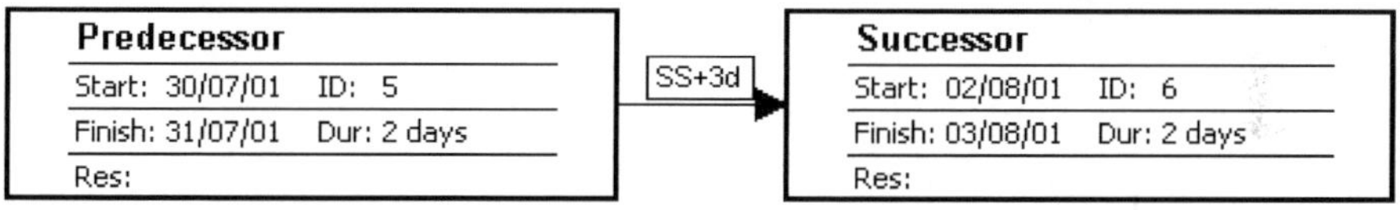

- **Link color** allows you to specify the color of the critical links and other link types. Selecting the option **Match predecessor box border** sets the format of the relationship lines to the predecessor's box border format. The formatting of links is not available in the Gantt Chart view.
- **Diagram Options** are self-explanatory. The **Hide all fields except ID** will display the Task Boxes, as below. In the example, note that **Show link labels** has also been checked:

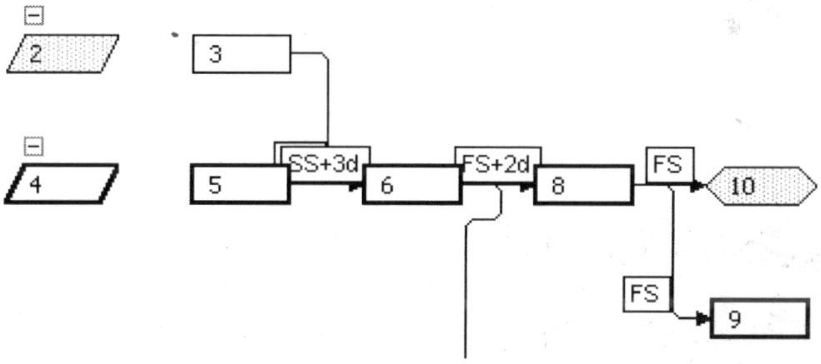

10.7 Early Date, Late Date and Float/Slack Calculations

To help understand the calculation of late and early dates, float and Critical Path, we will now manually work through an example. The boxes below represent tasks on a 7 day per week calendar..

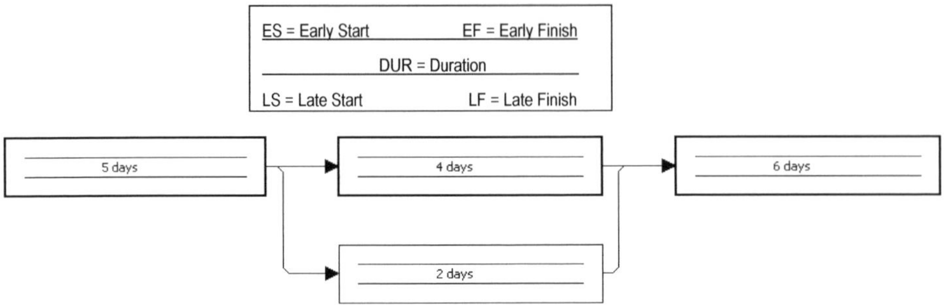

The forward pass calculates the early dates: EF = ES + DUR – 1

Start the calculation from the first task and work forward in time.

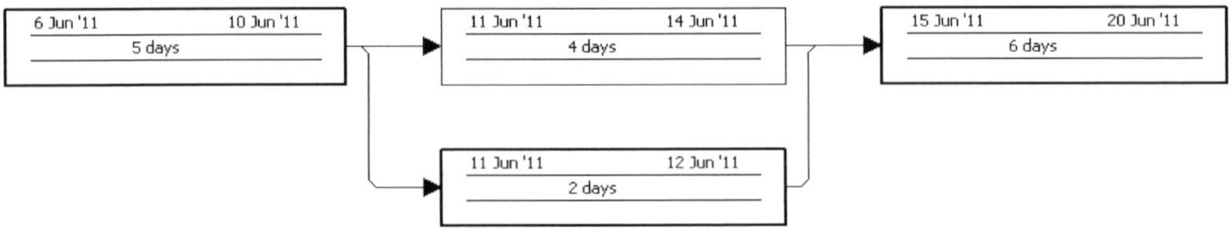

The backward pass calculates the late dates: LS = LF – DUR + 1

Start the calculation at the last task and work backward in time.

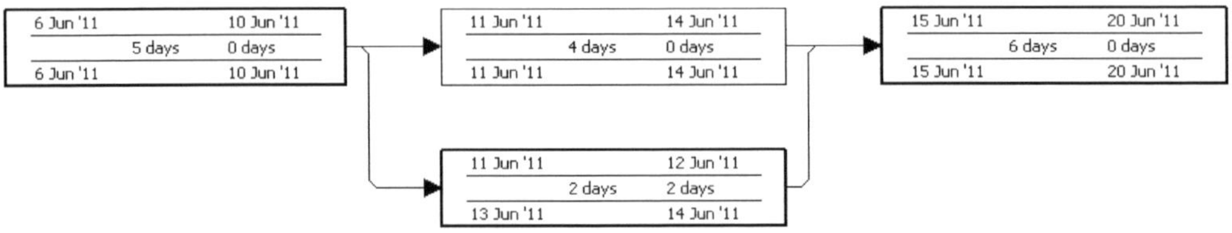

The **Critical Path** is the path where any delay causes a delay in the project end date and runs through the top row of tasks.

Total Float is the difference between either the **Late Finish** and the **Early Finish** or the difference between the **Late Start** and the **Early Start**.

- The 2 days' task has float of 14 – 12 = 2 or 13 – 11 = 2 days. None of the other tasks has float.

The example above would look like the picture below in the Gantt Chart view:

Duration	Start	Finish	Total Float
5 days	6 Jun '11	10 Jun '11	0 days
4 days	11 Jun '11	14 Jun '11	0 days
6 days	15 Jun '11	20 Jun '11	0 days
2 days	11 Jun '11	12 Jun '11	2 days

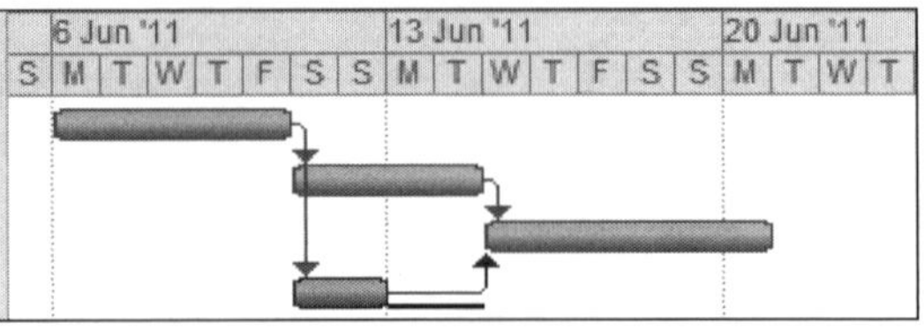

10.8 *Workshop 8 - Scheduling Calculations*

Background

We want to look at the Network Diagram and practice calculating Early and Late dates with a simple manual exercise.

Assignment

1. Apply the **Network Diagram** View, right click in the dark band on the left hand side of the screen.
2. Hide the Summary tasks by selecting **Format**, **Show/Hide** group, **Summary Tasks**.
3. Use the buttons to zoom in and out.
4. Right-click in the **Network Diagram,** select **Layout** to open the **Layout** form and select **Allow manual box positioning**.
5. You should now be able to reposition the boxes manually by left-clicking and dragging.
6. Reapply the **Gantt Chart** View.
7. Calculate the early and late start and finish dates for the following tasks, assuming a Monday to Friday working week and the first task starts on 06 Jun 11.

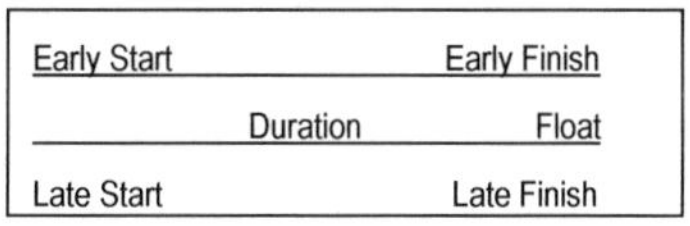

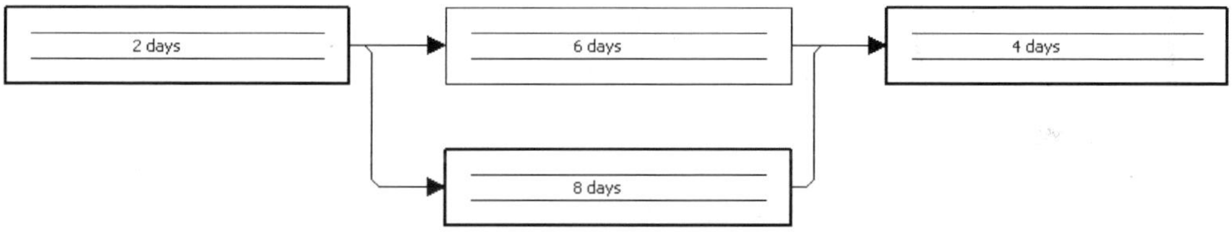

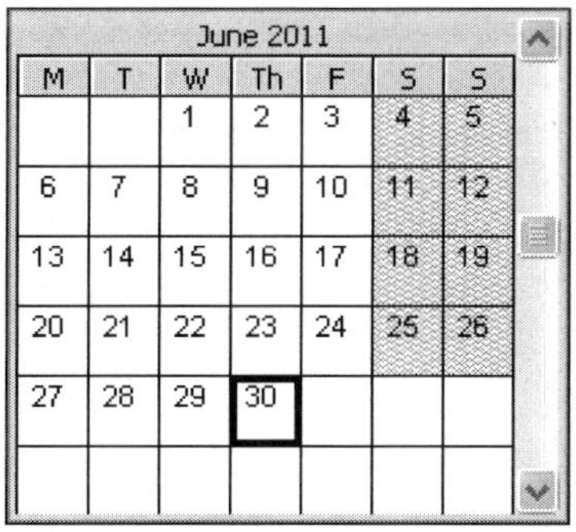

Answers to Workshop 8

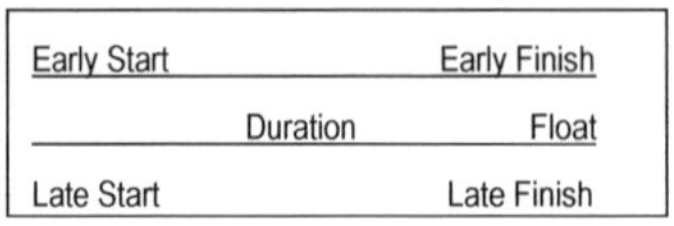

Forward Pass EF = ES + DUR –1

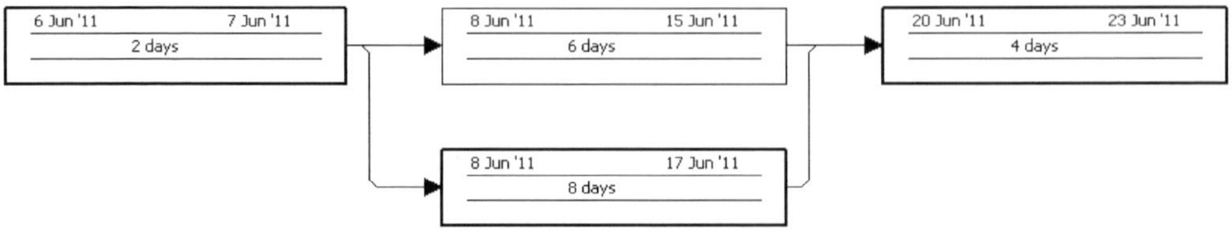

Backward Pass LS = LF – DUR +1

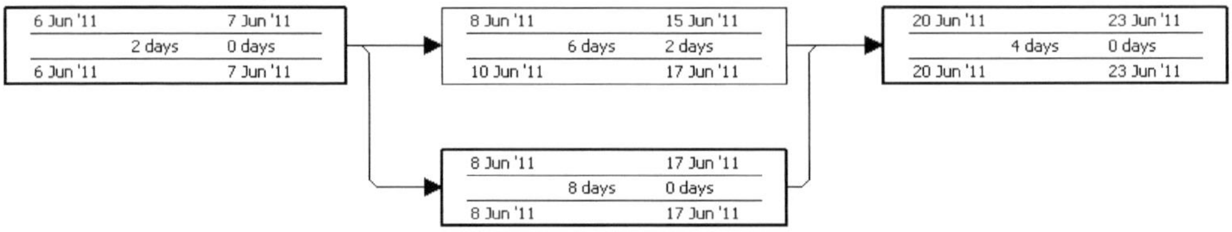

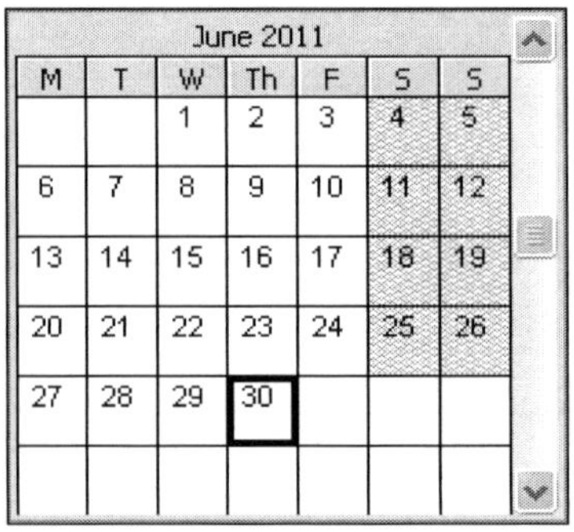

Duration	Start	Finish	Total Float
2 days	6 Jun '11	7 Jun '11	0 days
6 days	8 Jun '11	15 Jun '11	2 days
4 days	20 Jun '11	23 Jun '11	0 days
8 days	8 Jun '11	17 Jun '11	0 days

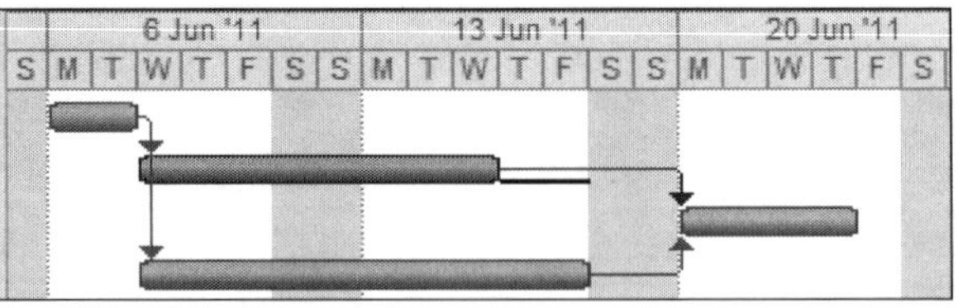

11 CONSTRAINTS

Constraints are used to impose logic on tasks that may not be realistically scheduled with logic links. Microsoft Project will only allow one constraint against a given task with the exception of a **Deadline Date**. This chapter will deal with the following constraints in detail, which are the minimum number of constraints that are required to effectively schedule a project:

- **Start No Earlier Than**
- **Finish No Later Than**

These two constraints may be applied to summary and detail tasks; all others may only be applied to detail tasks.

- **Start No Earlier Than** (also known as an "Early Start" constraint) is used when the start date of a task has been set by a client or an external event. Microsoft Project will not schedule the task early start date prior to this date.
- **Finish No Later Than** (also known as a "Late Finish" constraint) is used when the latest finish date is stipulated. Microsoft Project will not show the task's Late Finish date after this date, but the Early Finish date will be able to exceed this date and Negative Float will be generated when the Late Date is earlier than the Early Date. This represents the amount of time to be "caught up" to finish the project on time.

The following chart summarizes the methods used to assign Constraints to Tasks:

Topic	Notes for Creating a Constraint
• Open the **Task Information** form.	Double-click on the task and select the **Advanced** tab.
• Display the **Constraint Type** and **Constraint Date** columns.	Apply the **Constraint Table** or insert the columns in an existing table.
• Type a date into a task Start or Finish date field of the **Task Information** form or the **Details** form or a column.	A date typed in an task Start field will apply a **Start No Earlier Than** constraint of that date, without warning. A date typed in an task Finish field will apply a **Finish No Later Than** constraint, without warning.
• Display a **Combination** view displaying the **Task Details** form in the bottom pane.	Open the bottom pane by right-clicking n the Gantt Chart and selecting **Show Split**, Right-click on the vertical band on the bottom left-hand side of the screen labeled **Task Form** and select from the menu **Task Details** form.

There is an option found under the **File**, **Options**, **Schedule** tab, **Scheduling options for this project:** section, titled **Tasks will always honor their constraint dates**. This function is described in detail in the **OPTIONS** chapter, **Schedule** section. When this option is checked, which is the default, constraints override a logic link. When unchecked, a logic link will override a constraint and a task may be delayed.

Tasks will always honor their constraint dates should never be checked.

Only one constraint may be applied to a task or milestone except when a **Deadline Date** is assigned. Oracle Primavera products and Asta Powerproject allow two constraints per task.

A full list of **constraints** available in Microsoft Project is:

- **As Soon As Possible** — This is the default for a new task. A task is scheduled to occur as soon as possible and does not have a Constraint Date.
- **As Late As Possible** — A task will be scheduled to occur as late as possible and does not have any particular Constraint Date. The Early and Late dates have the same date. A task with this constraint has no Total Float and will delay the start of all the successor tasks.
- **Start No Earlier Than** — This constraint sets a date before which the task will not start.
- **Start No Later Than** — This constraint sets a date after which the task will not start.
- **Must Start On** — This constraint sets a date on which the task will start. Therefore the task has no float. The early start and the late start dates are set to be the same as the Constraint Date.
- **Must Finish On** — This constraint sets a date on which the task will finish. Therefore has no float. The early finish and the late finish dates are set to be the same as the Constraint Date.
- **Finish No Earlier Than** — This sets a date before which the task will not finish.
- **Finish No Later Than** — This sets a date after which the task will not finish.
- **Deadline Date** — This is similar to applying a **Finish No Later Than** constraint. This offers the opportunity of putting a second constraint on a task.

Earlier Than constraints operate on the **Early Dates** and **Later Than** constraints operate on **Late Dates**. The picture below demonstrates how constraints calculate Total Float (Total Slack) of tasks (without predecessors or successors) against the first task of 10 days' duration:

Constraint Type	Constraint Date	Early Start	Early Finish	Late Start	Late Finish	Total Slack
As Soon As Possible	NA	15 Nov	28 Nov	15 Nov	28 Nov	0d
As Late As Possible	NA	15 Nov	17 Nov	24 Nov	28 Nov	0d
Start No Earlier Than	21 Nov	21 Nov	23 Nov	24 Nov	28 Nov	3d
Start No Later Than	22 Nov	15 Nov	17 Nov	22 Nov	24 Nov	5d
Must Start On	22 Nov	22 Nov	24 Nov	22 Nov	24 Nov	0d
Must Finish On	18 Nov	16 Nov	18 Nov	16 Nov	18 Nov	0d
Start No Earlier Than	22 Nov	22 Nov	24 Nov	24 Nov	28 Nov	2d
Finish No Later Than	22 Nov	15 Nov	17 Nov	18 Nov	22 Nov	3d

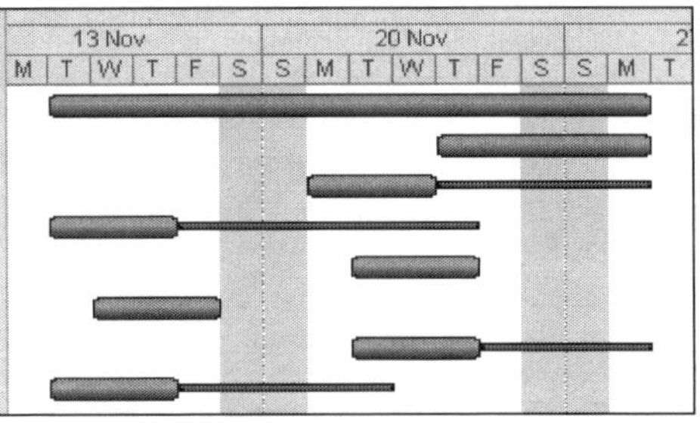

1. An **Expected Finish** is used in Oracle Primavera software to calculate the remaining duration of a task. There is no equivalent of this constraint in Microsoft Project 2010.
2. A task assigned with an **As Late as Possible** constraint in Oracle Primavera software will schedule the task so it absorbs only **Free Float** and will not delay the start of successor tasks. In Microsoft Project, a task assigned with an **As Late as Possible** constraint will be delayed to absorb the Total Float and delay all its successor tasks, not just the task with the constraint. Therefore an **As Late as Possible** constraint should be used with care in Microsoft Project.

11.1 Assigning Constraints

11.1.1 Using the Task Information Form

To assign a constraint using the **Task Information** form:

- Double-click on a task to open the form,
- Select the **Advanced** tab,
- Select the **Constraint type:** from the drop-down box,
- Select the **Constraint date:** from the calendar, or type the date in the box, and
- Click on the OK button to accept the constraint.

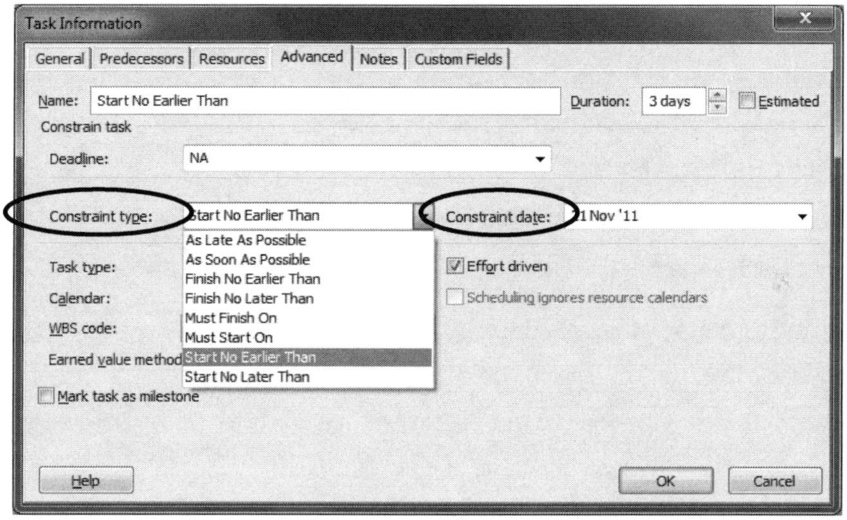

11.1.2 Using the Constraint Type and Constraint Date Column

To assign a constraint using the **Constraint Type** and **Constraint Date** columns:

- Either
  - ➢ Insert the **Constraint Type** and **Constraint Date** columns in your existing table by right-clicking on a column header and selecting **Insert Column**, or
  - ➢ Apply the **Constraint Dates** table by selecting **View**, **Data** group, **Tables**, **More Tables....**
- Assign your **Constraint Type** and **Constraint Date** from the drop-down boxes in the columns.

	Task Name	Duration	Constraint Type	Constraint Date
10	Obtain Quotes from	8d	Start No Earlier Than	3 Jan
11	Calculate the Bid Est	3d	As Soon As Possible	NA
12	**⊟ Bid Document**	**19d**	**As Soon As Possible**	**NA**
13	Create Draft of Bid D	6d	As Soon As Possible	NA
14	Finalise and Submit I	2d	As Soon As Possible	NA
15	Bid Document Submitte	0d	Finish No Later Than	26 Jan

11.1.3 Typing a Date into the Task Information or Details Form

You may assign some constraints from the **Task Information** or **Task Details** form:

- A **Start No Earlier** constraint is assigned by overtyping the Start date, and
- A **Finish No Earlier** constraint is assigned by overtyping the Finish date.

You may overtype or select a date from the drop-down box.

> *i* This function provides no warning that a constraint has been set and new users need to be careful when they enter a date into a Start or Finish field.

11.1.4 Using the Task Details Form

Constraints may be set in the **Task Details** form, which is covered in detail in the **VIEWS AND DETAILS** chapter.

The **Task Details** form should first be made visible in the **View** menu by:

- Opening the **More Views** form available from many menus,
- Select the **Task Details Form**,
- Open the **Task Details Form - View Definition** by clicking on the [Edit...] button,
- Checking the **Show in menu** in the form.

Then **Task Details** form may be displayed by:

- Opening the bottom pane by right-clicking and selecting **Show Split**,
- Right-clicking on the vertical band on the bottom left-hand side of the screen labeled **Task Form,**
- Select from the menu the **Task Details** form:

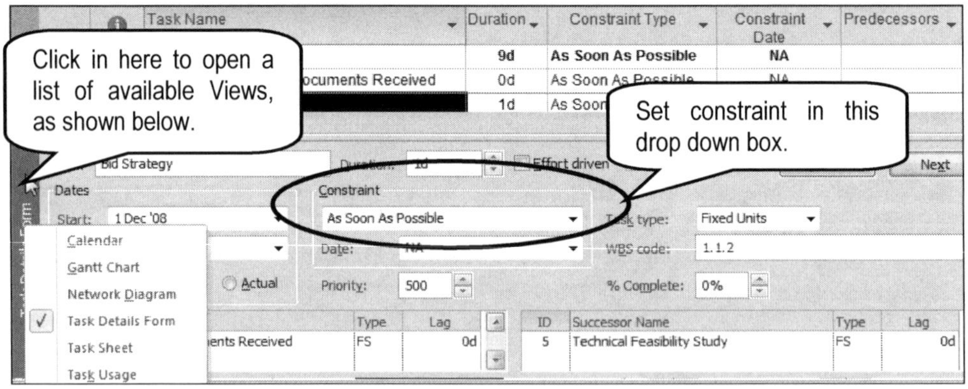

11.2 Deadline Date

Deadline Date was a new to Microsoft Project 2000 feature, which allows the setting of a date that a task should be complete. A **Deadline Date** is similar to placing a **Finish No Later Than** constraint on a task and affects the calculation of the **Late Finish** date and float of the task. A second constraint such as an Early Start constraint may also be assigned to a task with a Deadline Date.

The Deadline Date may be displayed as a column and the Indicator displayed on the bar chart may be formatted in the **Bars** form. This is covered in the **FORMATTING THE DISPLAY** chapter.

An Indicator icon ◆ is placed in the Indicator column when the Deadline Date creates Negative Float.

The Move Project function moves a Deadline Date, see para 16.4.1.

11.3 Changing Manually Scheduled Tasks to Auto Scheduled

When a task is changed from **Manually Scheduled** to **Auto Scheduled in** the **File**, **Options**, **Schedule** tab, **Scheduling options for this project:** section, **Keep Tasks on nearest working day when changing to Automatically Scheduled mode** will:

- When checked set a **Start No Earlier** constraint on the task so it does not move back in time if it has no predecessors, or
- When unchecked the task will not have a constraint set and will move back when it has no predecessors.

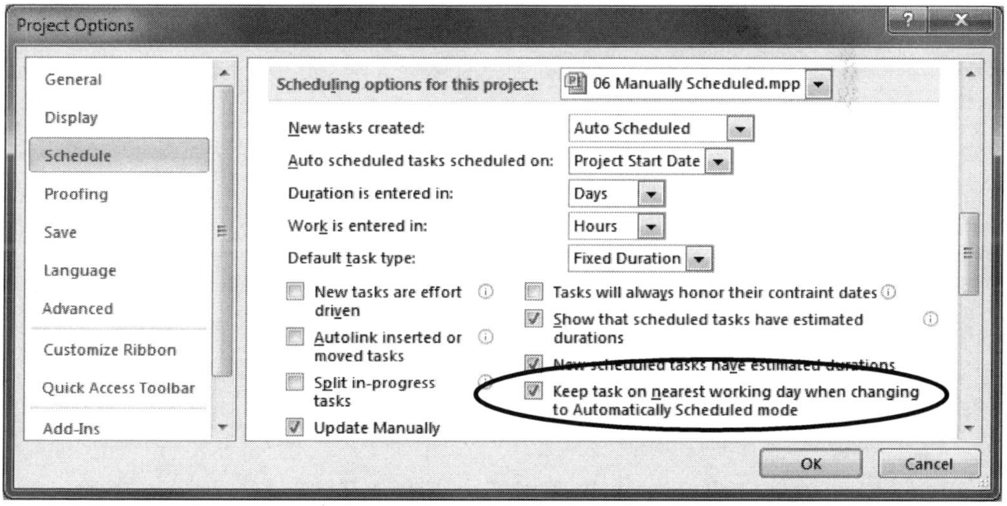

11.4 Task Notes

It is often important to note why constraints have been set. Microsoft Project has functions that enable you to note information associated with a task, including the reasons associated for establishing a constraint.

The **Task Information** form has a **Note** tab, which has some word processing-type formatting functions.

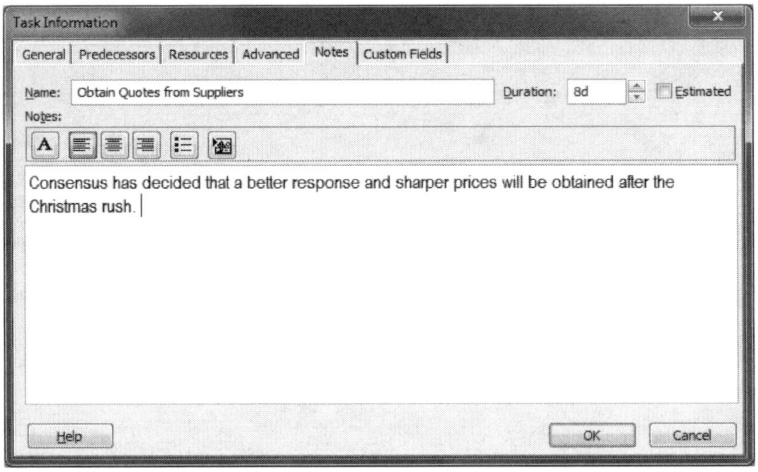

The notes may be displayed by:

- Inserting the **Notes** column. The Indicators column has a icon to indicate a note and a icon to indicate a constraint:

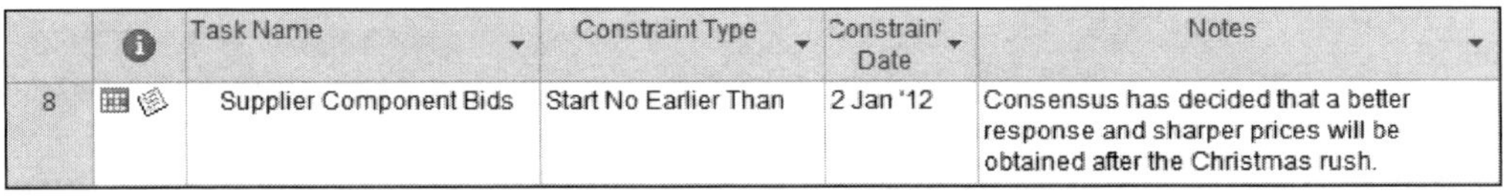

- Displaying the note next to the task bar chart:

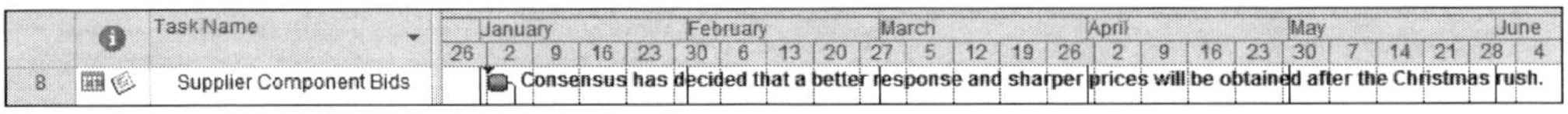

- There is an option for printing task notes in the **Page Setup...**, **View** form and this option prints the Task ID, Task Name and Note on a separate sheet:

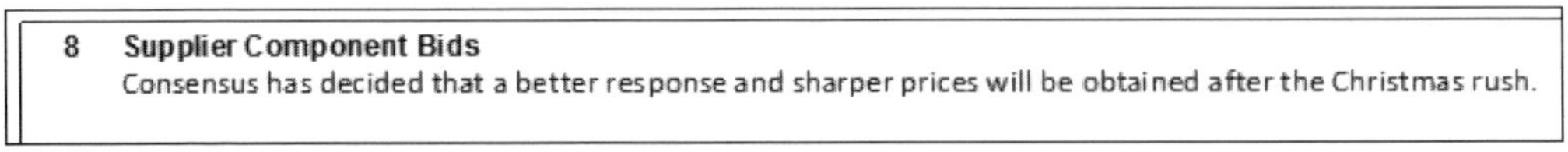

Other options for recording task notes are:

- Display and use one of the Text columns where the title may be renamed or customized.
- Insert a Text Box on the Gantt Chart using **Format**, **Drawing** group, **Drawings** and clicking on the Text Box , , and placing a note in the Text Box.

11.5 Workshop 9 - Constraints

Background

Management has provided further input to your schedule. The client requires the submission on 26 Jan 12. Because the **Format**, **Bars Styles** group **Slack** button only displays the Free Float and does not display the Total Float or Negative Float we will use the Gantt Chart Wizard to format the bars to show these important pieces of information.

Assignment

1. Insert the **Total Slack** (Float) column into the **Entry** table between the **Finish** and **Predecessor** column using the **Add New Column** column.
2. Run the **Gantt Chart Wizard** using the **Gantt Chart Wizard** button . Select **Custom Gantt** Chart. Display the Critical Path and Total Slack (Float) in the Gantt Chart, do not display resources and dates, and show the link lines between dependent tasks. **NOTE:** The Total Slack (Float) bar should now be displayed.
3. Create a **Negative Slack** (Float) bar manually in the **Bar Styles** form by selecting **Format**, **Bar Styles** group, **Format**, **Bar Styles** and adding a bar in red as displayed below:

Name	Appearance	Show For ... Tasks	Row	From	To
Negative Slack			1	Negative Slack	Task Start

   NOTE: No Negative Float bar will be displayed at this point in time.

4. Observe the calculated finish and the Critical Path before applying any constraints.
5. Apply a **Finish No Later Than** constraint with a constraint date of 26 Jan 12 to task **18 Bid Document Submitted** task. If you are presented with an error message, read the message carefully and then set the constraint. Now review float, there should be no change in the Total Float. This demonstrates that a **Finish No Later Than** constraint after the calculated early finish date does not create positive float.
6. Due to proximity to Christmas, management has requested we delay task **10 Obtain Quotes from Suppliers** until first thing in the New Year, 03 Jan 12. It is hoped that sharper prices will be obtained after the Christmas rush. You may record this decision in the task notes.
   - To achieve this, set a **Start No Earlier Than** constraint and a constraint date of 03 Jan 12 on task **10 Obtain Quotes from Suppliers**. Should you be presented with an error message, allow scheduling conflict and set the constraint.
   - Now observe the impact on the Critical Path and end dates.
7. After review, it is agreed that 2 days can be deducted from task **16 Review Bid Document**. Change the duration of this task to 2 days.
8. Press **F9** to ensure the schedule is recalculated as Microsoft Project sometimes does not calculate the Float automatically.
9. You will notice that the Total Float of all critical tasks is now zero and the Critical Path runs between the two tasks with constraints.
10. Save your **OzBuild Bid** project.

Answers to Workshop 9

Before delaying the **10 Obtain Quotes from Suppliers** until 03 Jan 12:

	Task Name	Duration	Start	Finish	Total Slack
1	**OzBuild Initiation**	**31d**	**5 Dec '11**	**19 Jan '12**	**0d**
2	**Technical Specification**	**13d**	**5 Dec '11**	**21 Dec '11**	**0d**
3	Approval to Bid	0d	5 Dec '11	5 Dec '11	0d
4	Determine Installation Requirements	4d	5 Dec '11	8 Dec '11	0d
5	Create Technical Specification	5d	9 Dec '11	15 Dec '11	0d
6	Identify Supplier Components	2d	16 Dec '11	19 Dec '11	0d
7	Validate Technical Specification	2d	20 Dec '11	21 Dec '11	2d
8	**Delivery Plan**	**14d**	**20 Dec '11**	**11 Jan '12**	**0d**
9	Document Delivery Methodology	4d	22 Dec '11	29 Dec '11	2d
10	Obtain Quotes from Suppliers	8d	20 Dec '11	3 Jan '12	0d
11	Calculate the Bid Estimate	3d	4 Jan '12	6 Jan '12	0d
12	Create the Project Schedule	3d	7 Jan '12	10 Jan '12	0d
13	Review the Delivery Plan	1d	11 Jan '12	11 Jan '12	0d
14	**Bid Document Submitted**	**14d**	**30 Dec '11**	**19 Jan '12**	**0d**
15	Create Draft of Bid Document	6d	30 Dec '11	9 Jan '12	2d
16	Review Bid Document	4d	12 Jan '12	17 Jan '12	0d
17	Finalize and Submit Bid Document	2d	18 Jan '12	19 Jan '12	0d
18	Bid Document Submitted	0d	19 Jan '12	19 Jan '12	0d

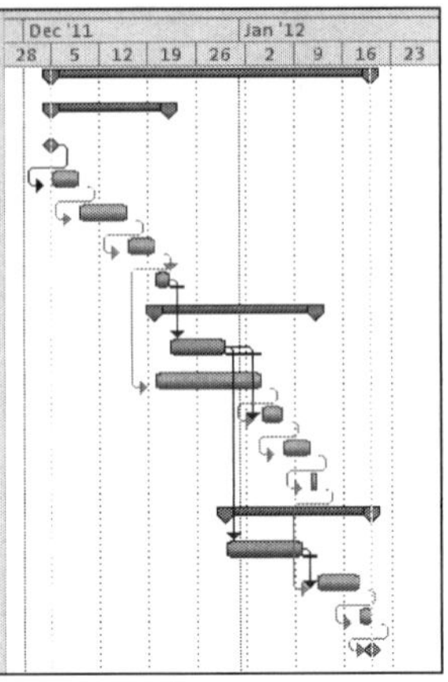

After delaying the **10 Obtain Quotes from Suppliers** until 03 Jan 12

	Task Name	Duration	Start	Finish	Total Slack
1	**OzBuild Initiation**	**38d**	**5 Dec '11**	**30 Jan '12**	**-2d**
2	**Technical Specification**	**13d**	**5 Dec '11**	**21 Dec '11**	**5d**
3	Approval to Bid	0d	5 Dec '11	5 Dec '11	5d
4	Determine Installation Requirements	4d	5 Dec '11	8 Dec '11	5d
5	Create Technical Specification	5d	9 Dec '11	15 Dec '11	5d
6	Identify Supplier Components	2d	16 Dec '11	19 Dec '11	5d
7	Validate Technical Specification	2d	20 Dec '11	21 Dec '11	7d
8	**Delivery Plan**	**19d**	**22 Dec '11**	**20 Jan '12**	**-2d**
9	Document Delivery Methodology	4d	22 Dec '11	29 Dec '11	7d
10	Obtain Quotes from Suppliers	8d	3 Jan '12	12 Jan '12	-2d
11	This task has a 'Start No Earlier Than' constraint on 3 Jan '12. ate	3d	13 Jan '12	16 Jan '12	-2d
12	Create the Project Schedule	3d	17 Jan '12	19 Jan '12	-2d
13	Review the Delivery Plan	1d	20 Jan '12	20 Jan '12	-2d
14	**Bid Document Submitted**	**21d**	**30 Dec '11**	**30 Jan '12**	**-2d**
15	Create Draft of Bid Document	6d	30 Dec '11	9 Jan '12	7d
16	Review Bid Document	4d	23 Jan '12	26 Jan '12	-2d
17	Finalize and Submit Bid Document	2d	27 Jan '12	30 Jan '12	-2d
18	Bid Document Submitted	0d	30 Jan '12	30 Jan '12	-2d

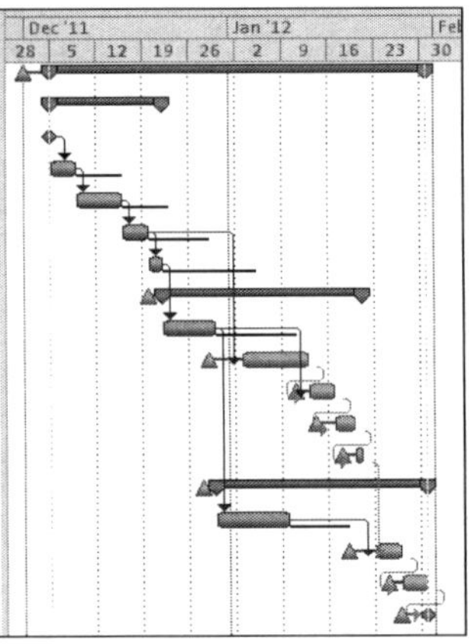

After trimming 2 days from **16 Review Bid Document**:

	Task Name	Duration	Start	Finish	Total Slack
1	**OzBuild Initiation**	**36d**	**5 Dec '11**	**26 Jan '12**	**0d**
2	**Technical Specification**	**13d**	**5 Dec '11**	**21 Dec '11**	**7d**
3	Approval to Bid	0d	5 Dec '11	5 Dec '11	7d
4	Determine Installation Requirements	4d	5 Dec '11	8 Dec '11	7d
5	Create Technical Specification	5d	9 Dec '11	15 Dec '11	7d
6	Identify Supplier Components	2d	16 Dec '11	19 Dec '11	7d
7	Validate Technical Specification	2d	20 Dec '11	21 Dec '11	9d
8	**Delivery Plan**	**19d**	**22 Dec '11**	**20 Jan '12**	**0d**
9	Document Delivery Methodology	4d	22 Dec '11	29 Dec '11	9d
10	Obtain Quotes from Suppliers	8d	3 Jan '12	12 Jan '12	0d
11	Calculate the Bid Estimate	3d	13 Jan '12	16 Jan '12	0d
12	Create the Project Schedule	3d	17 Jan '12	19 Jan '12	0d
13	Review the Delivery Plan	1d	20 Jan '12	20 Jan '12	0d
14	**Bid Document Submitted**	**19d**	**30 Dec '11**	**26 Jan '12**	**0d**
15	Create Draft of Bid Document	6d	30 Dec '11	9 Jan '12	9d
16	Review Bid Document	2d	23 Jan '12	24 Jan '12	0d
17	Finalize and Submit Bid Document	2d	25 Jan '12	26 Jan '12	0d
18	Bid Document Submitted	0d	26 Jan '12	26 Jan '12	0d

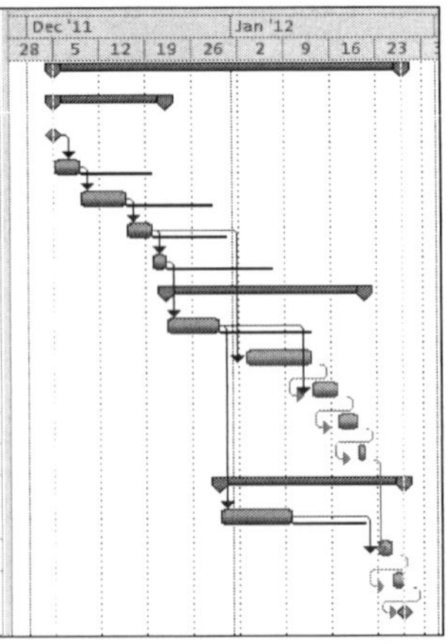

NOTE: If your Total Float is not calculating as above, press F9 to recalculate.

12 FILTERS

This chapter covers the use of **Filters** to select which tasks are displayed on the screen and in printouts.

12.1 Understanding Filters

Microsoft Project has the ability to display tasks that meet specific criteria. You may want to see only the incomplete tasks, or the work scheduled for the next couple of months, or the tasks that are in-progress, assigned a specific resource, responsibility, phase, discipline, system or belong to a physical area of a project.

Microsoft Project defaults to displaying all tasks. It has a number of predefined filters available that you may use or edit and you may also create one or more of your own.

There are **Task** filters that apply to **Task** views and **Resource** filters that apply to **Resource** views. Both types are created and applied in the same way. In this chapter we will focus on Task Filters but resource Filters are created in a similar way.

There are two types of filters:

- The first is where you select a **Filter** which exists or has been created using the **Filters** form.
- The second is to create an **AutoFilter** which is very similar to the Excel **AutoFilter** (Drop-down filter) function which is based on the selected column.

Topic	Menu Command
• Apply a **Filter**	Select **View**, **Data** group, **Filter:** drop-down box, and then either: • Select a filter from the list, or • Select **More Filters...** for a complete list of filters.
• Create or modify a **Filter**	Select **View**, **Data** group, **Filter:** drop-down box, **More Filters...** to open the **More Filter** form.
• Turn on **AutoFilter**	Select **View**, **Data** group, **Filter:** drop-down box, **Display AutoFilter**.
• Apply an **AutoFilter**	Click on the button in the column headers.

12.2 *Understanding the Filter Menu*

The **Filter** menu is opened from the **View**, **Data** group, **Filter:** drop-down box, or you may put a **Filter** menu item on your **Quick Access Toolbar**. This may not display a complete list of available filters, as this list displays only filters selected to be displayed in the **Filter Definition** form and more may be available when selecting the **More Filters...** option.

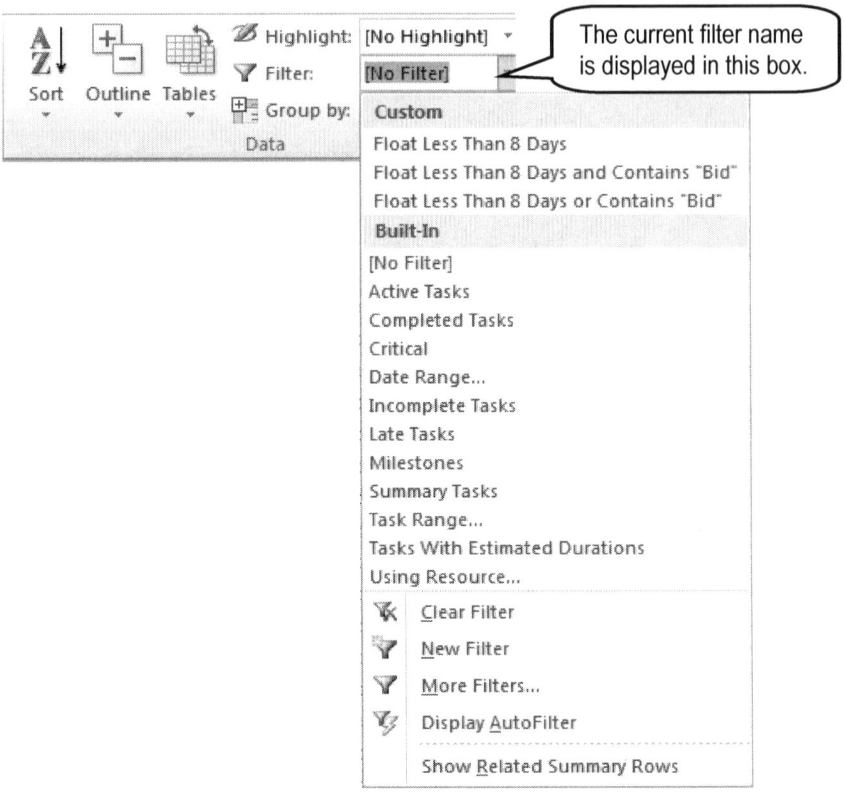

- **Custom** filters are those that the user has created or were created as part of a template.
- **Built-In** filters are those that exist as part of the Microsoft Project Global.mpt which is used to create a project when no template has been used.
- **Clear Filter** will remove all filters, both **Filters** and **AutoFilters**, and display all tasks.
- **New Filter** will open the **Filter Definition** form, allowing the creation of a new filter.
- **More Filters...** opens the **More Filters** form which will list all the filters available to the current project. Only filters with the **Show in menu** check box checked in the **Filter Definition** form are displayed in the menu above.
- **Display AutoFilter** turns on and off the ability to use AutoFilters and hides or displays the arrow in the column headers which in turn enables or disables the **AutoFilter** function:

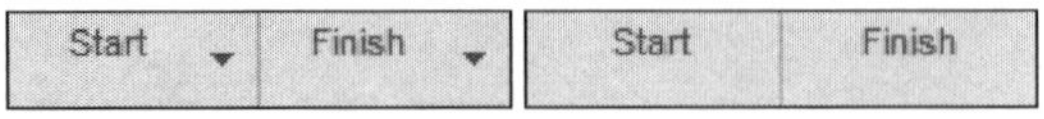

- **Show Related Summary Rows** will display any related and hidden Summary Rows as a result of applying a filter.

12.3 Applying an Existing Filter

To apply a filter:

- Select **View**, **Data** group, **Filter:** and select a filter from the drop-down list.
- Select **View**, **Data** group, **Filter**, **More Filters...** to open the **More Filters** form.

The **More Filters** form displays all filters available in a project, some of these may not be displayed in the Filter menu

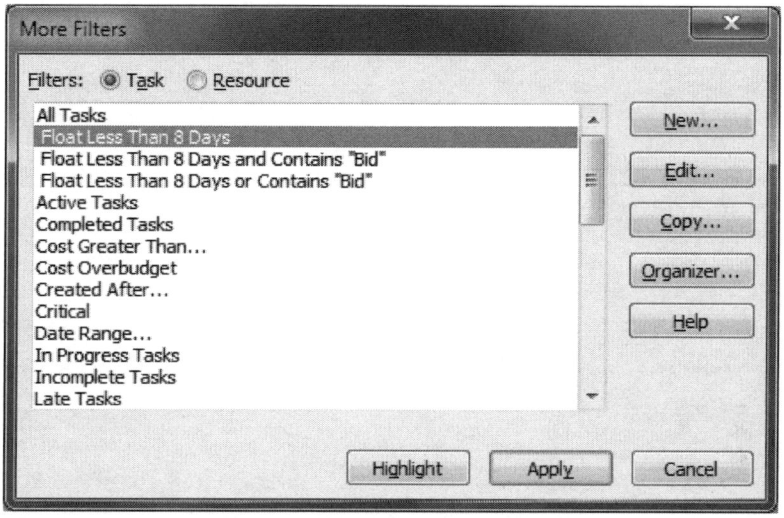

- The two radio buttons at the top of the form allow you to select filters that operate either on a **Task** view or on a **Resource** view.
  - ➢ **Task** filters will operate using most task data such as dates, durations, text columns, number columns, outline and WBS.
  - ➢ **Resource** filters will operate on resource criteria only and not the task criteria.
- Select the required filter from the list, and
- Select either:
  - ➢ 

 to shows all tasks but highlights the tasks that meet the criteria, or
  - ➢ 

 to display only the tasks that meet the criteria.

12.4 *Creating and Modifying Filters*

New filters are created from the **More Filters** form. This may be opened by selecting **View**, **Data** group, **Filters:**, **More Filters ...**:

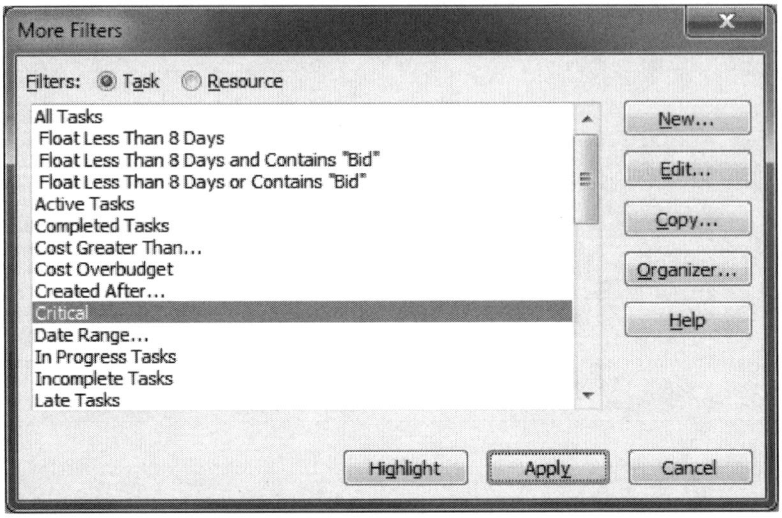

- Click on Organizer... to open the **Organizer** form where you may copy a filter to and from another open project, rename or delete a filter:

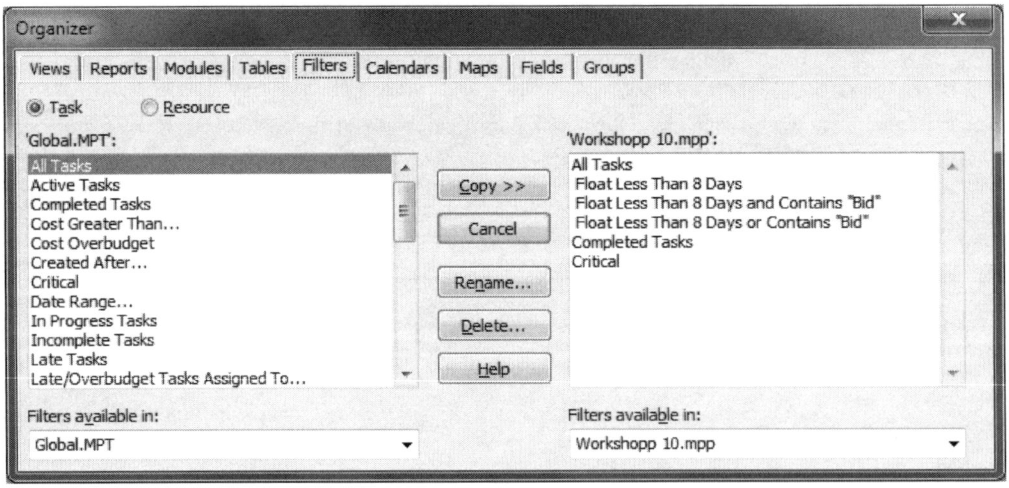

- Click on:
  - New... to create a new filter, or
  - Edit... to edit an existing filter, or
  - Copy... to copy an existing filter.

- The **Filter Definition** form will be displayed. The one-line example below will only display critical tasks.

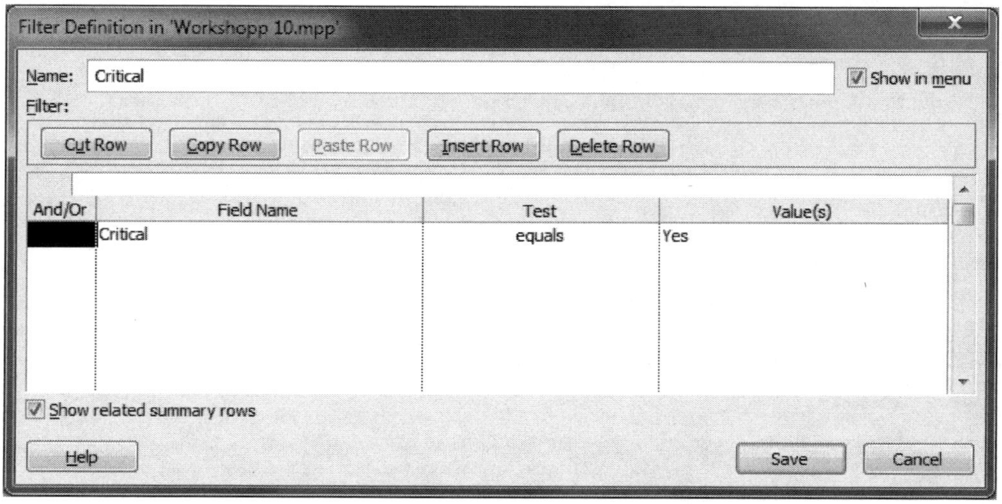

- The filter may be edited in the **Filter Definition** form to display or highlight the required tasks.
- Checking the **Show in menu** box will place the **Filter** in the menu.
- Checking **Show related summary rows** will display any associated Summary tasks.
- Select OK to return to the **More Filters** form.

i It is useful to place a space at the start of the filter name when creating a new filter as this will place the filter you have just created at the top of the **More Filters** form list.

12.5 Defining Filter Criteria

The filter criteria are determined by four columns of information in the **Filter Definition** form:

- **And/Or** functions when you have two or more lines of data in the **Filter Definition** form to operate on.
- **Field Name** defines the data field you want to operate on.
- **Test** sets the criteria such as "Greater Than" or "Less Than" or "Equals."
- **Value(s)** is/are a date, number, Yes/No or text for the **Test** field to operate on. If more than one value is to be considered, for example when a **Test** is "Between," the two values are separated by a comma ",". The example below is a filter that will only display detail tasks that will start between 1 Jan '12 and 20 Jan '12.

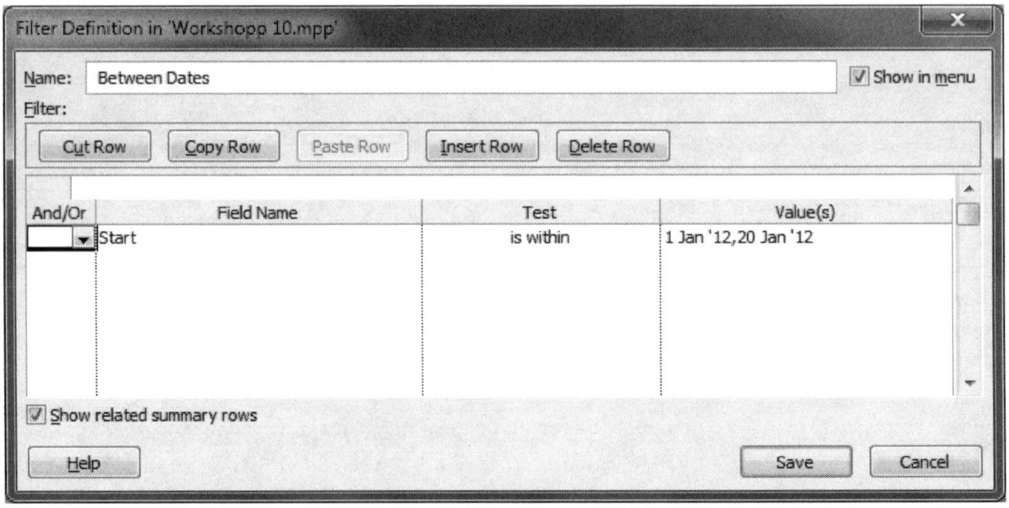

This chapter will not cover all the aspects of filter definitions but will cover the major principles, so you may experiment when you require a filter.

There are a number of predefined filters with a standard Microsoft Project installation. You should inspect these to gain an understanding of how filters are constructed and applied.

12.5.1 Simple Filters, Operator and Wild Cards

A simple **Filter** contains one line of data, therefore the **And/Or** function is not used. These are the most common filters and meet most common filtering requirements.

These filters are used for purposes such as displaying tasks which:

- Are not started, complete, or in-progress tasks.
- Have a Start or Finish before or after a particular date.
- Contain specific text.
- Are within a range of dates.

There are some operands you should be aware of:

- Some fields may have "**Yes**" or "**No**" entered in the **Value(s).** The task fields that may be filtered using a "**Yes**" or "**No**" include:
  - Summary – Indicates if the task is a summary or detail task,
  - Critical – Indicates if the task is critical when the Total Slack is less than or equal to the value entered in the **Calculation** tab or the **Options** form,
  - Milestones and
  - Effort-Driven.

  The filter below will select all tasks that are Milestones:

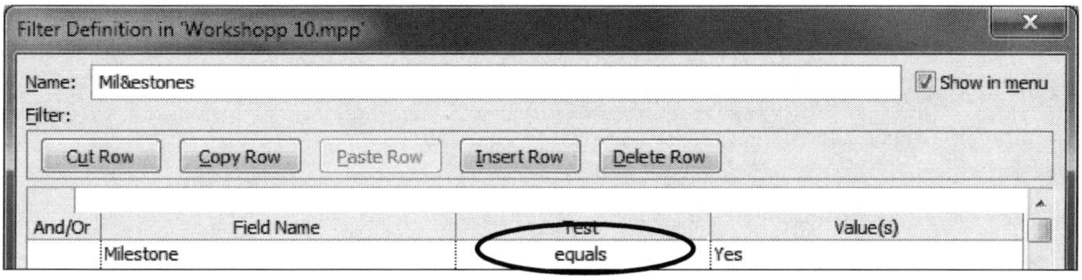

- The **Wildcard** functions are similar to the DOS Wildcard functions and are mainly used for filtering text:
  - You may replace a single character with a "**?**". Thus, a filter searching for a Task Name only containing "b**?**t" will display words like "bat", "bit" and "but".
  - You may replace a group of characters with an *****. Thus, a filter searching for a word in a Task Name containing "b*t" will display words like "blot", "blight" and "but".

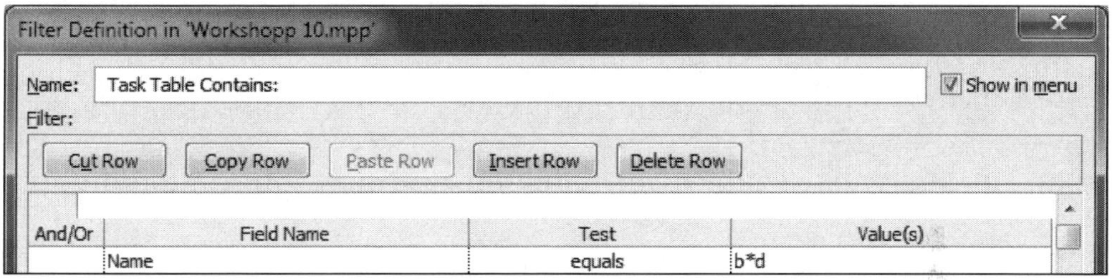

NOTE: For the Wildcard function to operate the **equals Test** must be used. This function does not work with other operands and in this mode works as a **contains** operand.

- **NA** allows the selection of a blank value. The filter below displays tasks without either a Baseline Start or Baseline Finish date:

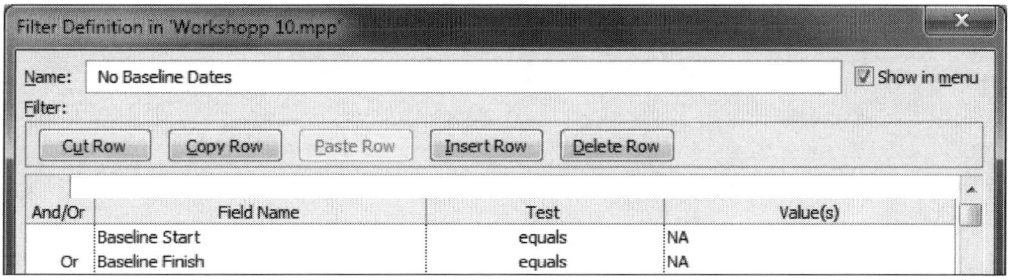

- A **Calculated Filter** compares one value with another. The **Value(s)** field is selected from the drop-down box. The example below will display those tasks that are scheduled to start later than the Baseline start:

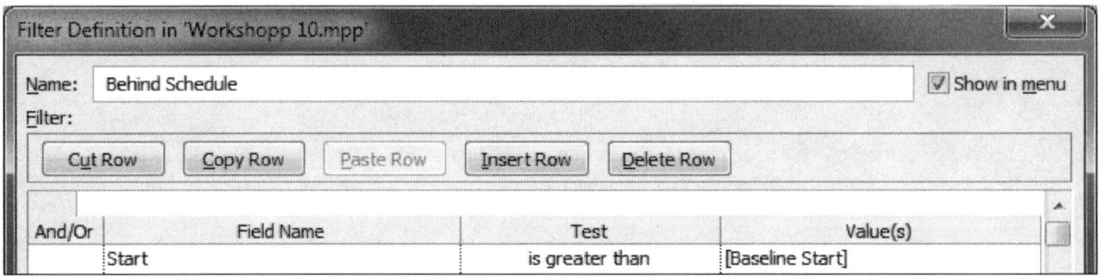

12.5.2 And/Or Filters

The **And/Or** function allows a search for tasks which meet more than one criteria by using the **And/Or** option:

- The filter below displays tasks with Slack less than 8 days **And** contain the word "Bid":

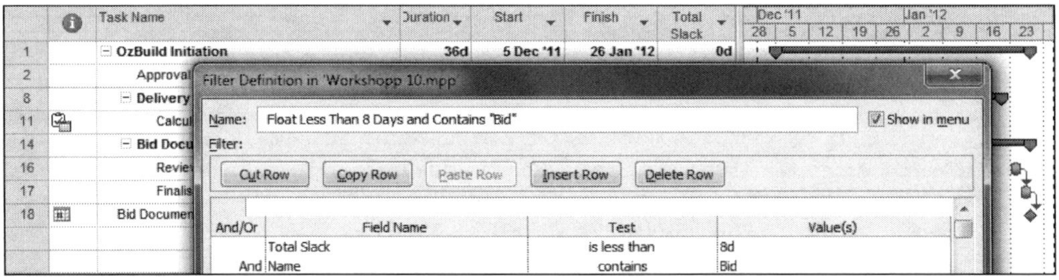

- The filter below is similar to the one above but displays tasks with Slack less than 5 days **Or** contain the word "Bid". It displays many more tasks:

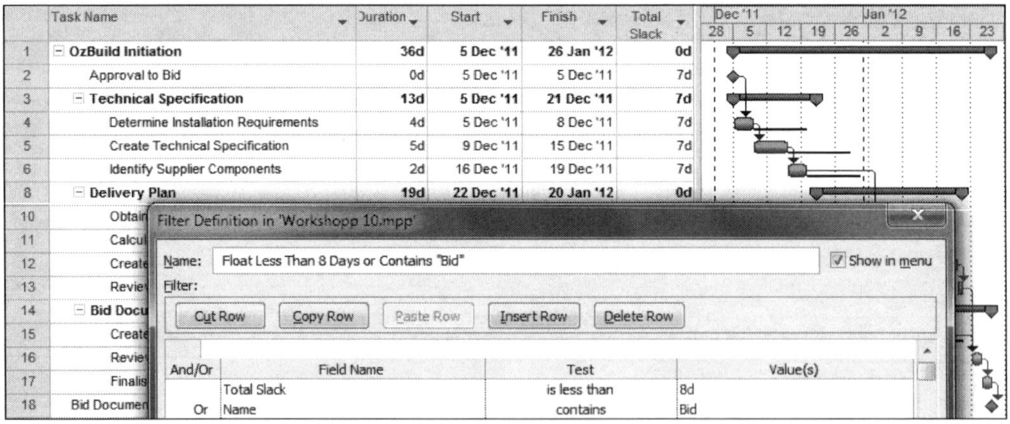

12.5.3 Multiple And/Or

Multiple **And/Or** statements are possible by placing a line with only an **And/Or** statement. The filter below selects tasks that have a Baseline Finish and are scheduled to finish late or are not completing their work quickly enough, shown as the Budgeted Cost of Work Performed (Earned Value) is less than the Budgeted Cost of Work Scheduled (Planned Value):

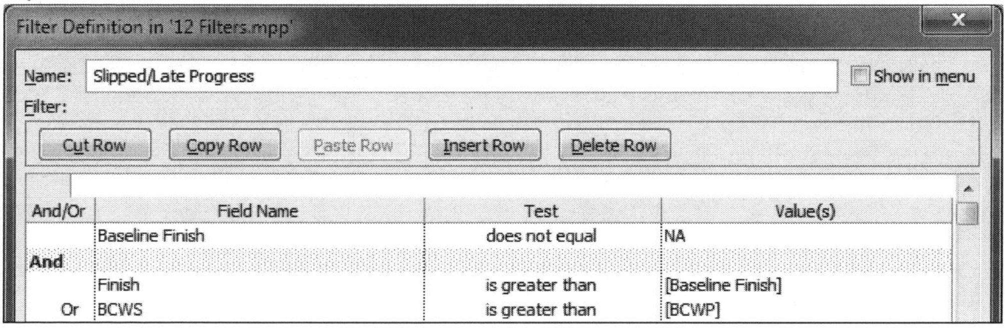

12.5.4 Interactive Filter

These filters allow you to enter the **Value(s)** of the filtered field after applying the filter. The filter is tailored each time it is applied via a user-prompt. The filter below will ask you to enter a word in the task name.

For this function to operate properly, the text in the **Value(s)** field must commence with a double quotation mark **"**and end with a double quotation and question mark**"?** :

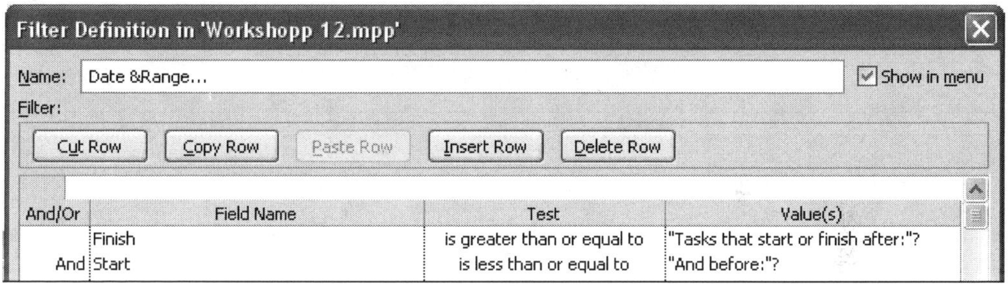

After the filter is applied, you will be presented with the **Interactive Filter** form to enter the required text:

12.6 AutoFilters

This function has been greatly enhanced in Microsoft project 2010. Microsoft Project **AutoFilters** are similar to the Excel **AutoFilter** function and allow you to select the filter criteria from drop-down menus in the column headers. This function allows both **Grouping** and **Sorting** of tasks, which will be covered in the **TABLES AND GROUPING TASKS** chapter.

To create an **AutoFilter** based on one parameter:

- Turn on the **AutoFilter** function by selecting **View**, **Data** group, **Filter:** drop-down box, **Display AutoFilter**.
- The column headers will display the button in the column header. Click on this button in one of the columns to display a drop-down box:

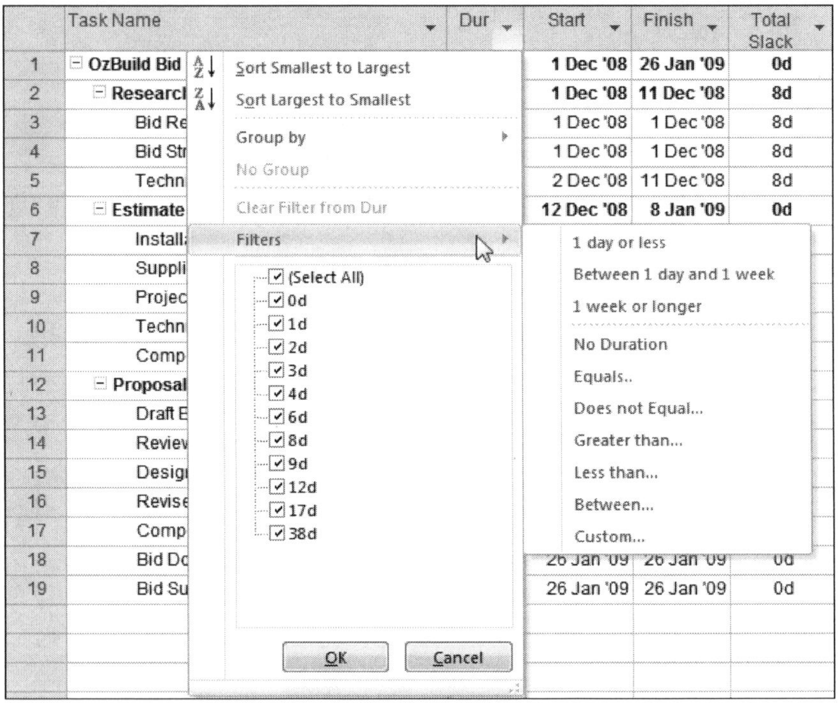

- Select the required criteria from the check box list, or
- Click on the **Filters** heading, as displayed above, to open up a second set of selections, which in turn will provide many more options which will open the **Custom AutoFilter** form:

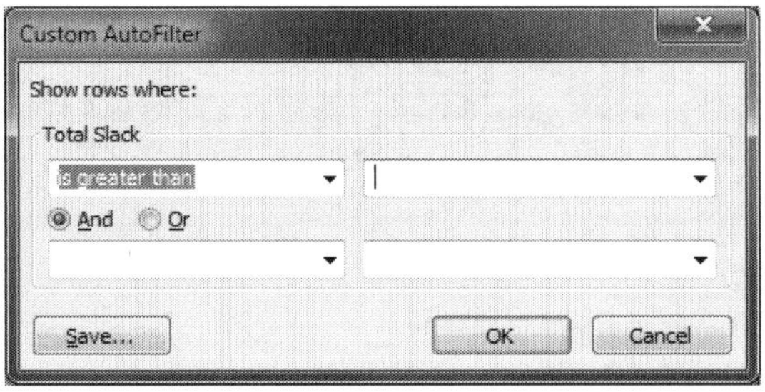

- Select the parameters you want to operate on from the four drop-down boxes and check the **And** or **Or** radio button.
- To save a drop-down filter as a normal filter, click on the Save... button, which opens the **Filter Definition** form.
- You may now select another column and create a filter based on two parameters to reduce the number of tasks displayed.
- After an AutoFilter has been applied the indicator in the column heading changes to a 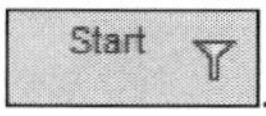

.

AutoFilters always select the associated summary tasks of any selected detail tasks.

12.7 Workshop 10 - Filters

Background

Management has asked for some reports to suit their unique requirements.

Assignment

1. They would like to see all the critical tasks.
   - Add the **Filter** button, found under **View**, **Data** group, to the **Quick Access Toolbar**.
   - Apply the **Critical** tasks filter, found under **View**, **Data** group **Filter** button.
   - You will see only tasks that are on the Critical Path and their associated Summary tasks.

2. They would like to see all the tasks with float less than 8 days:
   - Create a new filter titled **Float Less Than 8 Days**,
   - Use the **Filter** button, or the **View**, **Filter**, **More Filters...** to open the **Filters** form.
   - If you place a space at the start of the Filter name the filter will be placed at the top of the list and make it easier to find filters you have created.
   - Create a criteria to display a **Total Slack** of less than 8 days,
   - Show the Summary tasks by checking **Show related summary rows** box,
   - Show the filter in the menu, and
   - Apply the filter.

   You should see that extra tasks with float less than 8 days are now displayed.

3. They would like to see all the tasks with float less than, or equal to 8 days, **OR** contains the word "Bid."
   - Copy the **Float Less Than 8 Days** filter,
   - Assign a title to the filter: **Float Less Than 8 Days or Contains "Bid"**,
   - Add the condition: **Or** Name (Task Name) contains **Bid**,
   - Show in the menu, and
   - Apply the filter.
   - You should find that one extra task is now shown.

4. Copy the filter, title it **Float Less Than 8 Days and Contains "Bid"** and change the condition to **And** to see the difference between **Or** and **And** options.

5. We now wish to create an **AutoFilter** that displays all the tasks containing the word "document".
   - Apply the **(No Filter)** option, which is the same as the **All Tasks** option used in other forms.
   - Add the **Display Auto Filter** button to the **Quick Access Toolbar** and use this to ensure the Auto Filters are activated and each column header has a down arrow as per this picture:

   - Click on the down arrow in the Task Name header,
   - Select **Filters, Custom...** to open the **Custom Auto Filter** form,
   - Create a Custom Auto filter to contain tasks containing the word "document".

6. Now apply the **(No Filter)** or the **All Tasks** Filter to remove the **AutoFilter**.
7. Save your **OzBuild Bid** project.

Answers to Workshop 10

After applying the Critical Filter:

	Task Name	Duration	Start	Finish	Total Slack
1	OzBuild Initiation	36d	5 Dec '11	26 Jan '12	0d
8	Delivery Plan	19d	22 Dec '11	20 Jan '12	0d
10	Obtain Quotes from Suppliers	8d	3 Jan '12	12 Jan '12	0d
11	Calculate the Bid Estimate	3d	13 Jan '12	16 Jan '12	0d
12	Create the Project Schedule	3d	17 Jan '12	19 Jan '12	0d
13	Review the Delivery Plan	1d	20 Jan '12	20 Jan '12	0d
14	Bid Document Submitted	19d	30 Dec '11	26 Jan '12	0d
16	Review Bid Document	2d	23 Jan '12	24 Jan '12	0d
17	Finalize and Submit Bid Document	2d	25 Jan '12	26 Jan '12	0d
18	Bid Document Submitted	0d	26 Jan '12	26 Jan '12	0d

Creating the **Float Less Than 8 Days** Filter:

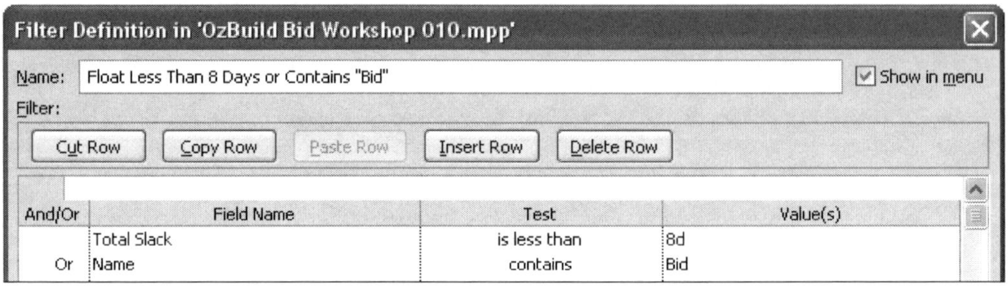

And/Or	Field Name	Test	Value(s)
	Total Slack	is less than	8d
Or	Name	contains	Bid

After applying the **Float Less Than 8 Days or Contains** Filter:

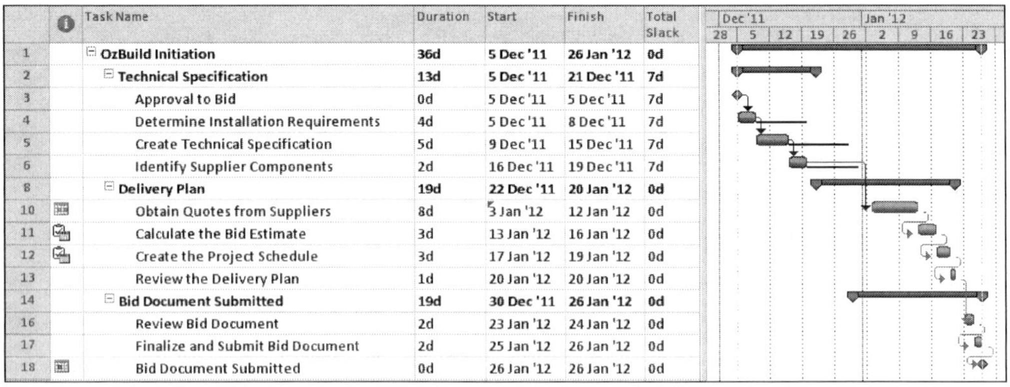

	Task Name	Duration	Start	Finish	Total Slack
1	OzBuild Initiation	36d	5 Dec '11	26 Jan '12	0d
2	Technical Specification	13d	5 Dec '11	21 Dec '11	7d
3	Approval to Bid	0d	5 Dec '11	5 Dec '11	7d
4	Determine Installation Requirements	4d	5 Dec '11	8 Dec '11	7d
5	Create Technical Specification	5d	9 Dec '11	15 Dec '11	7d
6	Identify Supplier Components	2d	16 Dec '11	19 Dec '11	7d
8	Delivery Plan	19d	22 Dec '11	20 Jan '12	0d
10	Obtain Quotes from Suppliers	8d	3 Jan '12	12 Jan '12	0d
11	Calculate the Bid Estimate	3d	13 Jan '12	16 Jan '12	0d
12	Create the Project Schedule	3d	17 Jan '12	19 Jan '12	0d
13	Review the Delivery Plan	1d	20 Jan '12	20 Jan '12	0d
14	Bid Document Submitted	19d	30 Dec '11	26 Jan '12	0d
16	Review Bid Document	2d	23 Jan '12	24 Jan '12	0d
17	Finalize and Submit Bid Document	2d	25 Jan '12	26 Jan '12	0d
18	Bid Document Submitted	0d	26 Jan '12	26 Jan '12	0d

Creating an AutoFilter that displays Task Names containing **document**:

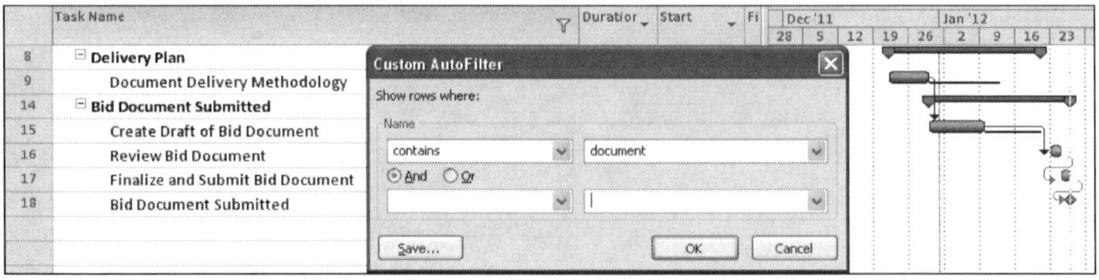

	Task Name
8	Delivery Plan
9	Document Delivery Methodology
14	Bid Document Submitted
15	Create Draft of Bid Document
16	Review Bid Document
17	Finalize and Submit Bid Document
18	Bid Document Submitted

13 TABLES AND GROUPING TASKS

Outlining was discussed earlier as a method of organizing detail tasks under summary tasks. There are alternative data fields and functions available in Microsoft Project for recording task information, then organizing, grouping and displaying task information:

- Text Columns, Custom Fields and Grouping
- Custom Outline Codes – covered in the **MORE ADVANCED SCHEDULING** chapter.
- User Defined WBS (Work Breakdown Structure) – covered in the **MORE ADVANCED SCHEDULING** chapter.

These functions are addressed in this book but are not examined in detail. These functions enable the presentation of the tasks under other project breakdown structures.

Topic	Menu Command
• Applying a Table to a View	• Click the **Select All** button and right-click, or • Select **View**, **Data** group, **Tables** and select a Table from the list in the menu.
• Creating or Editing a Table	Select **View**, **Data** group, **Tables** to open the **Customize Fields** form.
• Create a Custom Field	Adding the **Custom Fields** button to your **Ribbon** or **Quick Access Toolbar**.
• Grouping	Select **View**, **Data** group, **Group by:**
• Custom Outline Codes	Add the **Custom Fields** button to your **Quick Access Toolbar** or **Ribbon**.
• Assign Custom Outline Codes	• Display the Custom Field column, or • Open the **Task Information** form **Custom Field** tab.
• Display Outline Codes	• Display the **Outline Code** column, or • Display the **Outline Code** with the **Task Name** by selecting the **File**, **Options**, **View** tab and checking the **Show outline number**.
• User-defined WBS	• Add the **WBS** button on your **Ribbon** or **Quick Access Toolbar** and click on the **WBS** button.

13.1 Understanding Project Breakdown Structures

A Project Breakdown Structure often represents a hierarchical breakdown of a project into logical functional elements. Some organizations have highly organized and disciplined structures with "rules" for creating and coding the elements of the structure. Some clients also impose a WBS code on a contractor for reporting and/or claiming payments. The following are examples of such structures:

- WBS **Work Breakdown Structure**, breaking down the project into the elements of work required to complete a project.
- PBS **Product Breakdown Structure**, used in the PRINCE2™ Project Management Methodology.
- OBS **Organization Breakdown Structure**, showing the hierarchical management structure of a project.
- CBS **Contract Breakdown Structure**, showing the breakdown of contracts.
- SBS **System Breakdown Structure**, showing the elements of a complex system.

We will discuss the following functions available in Microsoft Project to represent these structures in your schedule.

13.2 Tables

A table selects and formats the columns of data to be displayed in a View. The formatting of tables is covered in the **FORMATTING THE DISPLAY** chapter.

- A table may be applied to one or more Views which display data in tables. This includes Views such as the Gantt Chart, Resource Sheet, Resource Usage, Task Sheet and Task Usage.
- There are two types of tables:
  - **Task** tables that are applied to **Task Views** and
  - **Resource** tables that are applied to **Resource Views**.
- When the View is active and you assign it a different Table, the View is permanently changed and the Table permanently associated with the View. Unlike Oracle Primavera software, the user does not have the option to save or not save changes to a view when another is selected.

Formatting a table by adding or removing columns, etc., is editing the current table on a permanent basis. These changes will appear when the table is next applied and this will affect any View the table is associated with. It is therefore strongly recommended that each View be paired with a unique table of the same name. Consider carefully when adding or deleting columns from a table as the changes are permanent, unless you do not save your file.

13.2.1 Applying a Table to a View

A table may be applied to the active View by:

- Clicking the **Select All** button, the box above the row 1 number, then right-clicking the mouse to display a sub-menu with the table options, or
- Selecting **View**, **Data** group **Tables** and selecting a Table from the list in the menu.

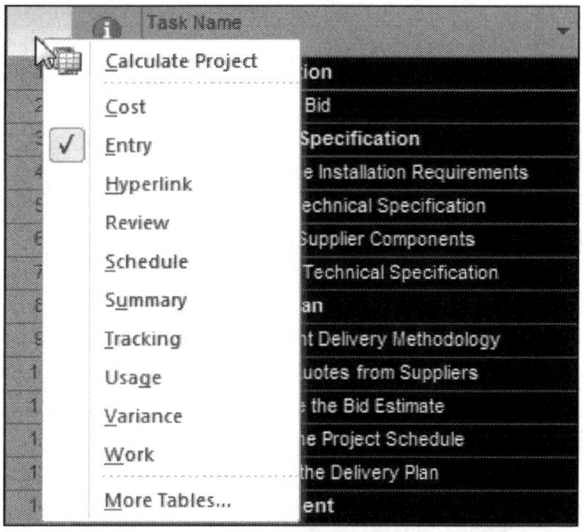

Both of these Table menus have a **More Tables...** option which will open the **More Tables...** form:

- Tables that have not been selected to appear on the menu list will be displayed here.
- Select a table from the list and click on [Apply].

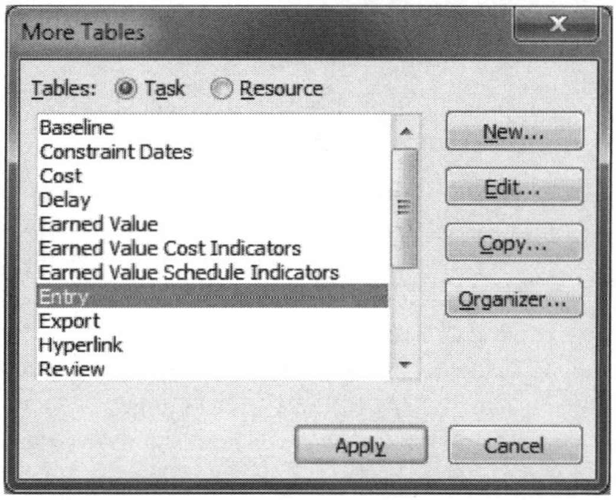

13.2.2 Creating and Editing a Table

A **Table** may be created or edited by opening the **View**, **Data** group **Tables**, **More Tables...**form:

- [New...] creates a new table,
- [Edit...] edits an existing table, or
- [Copy...] creates a copy of an existing selected table.
- [Apply] – Applies the table to a view.

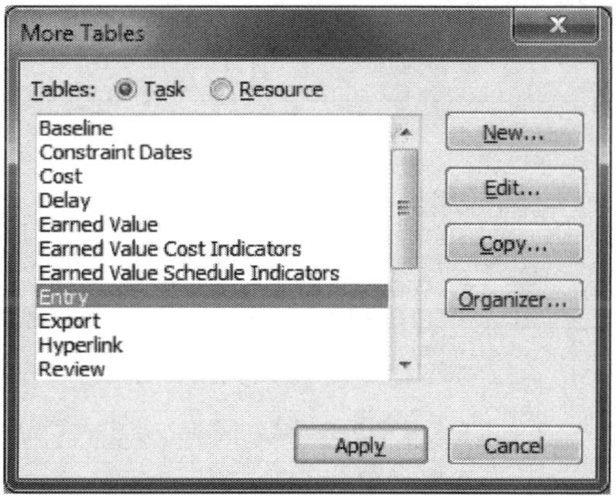

All these buttons open the Table Definition form shown below:

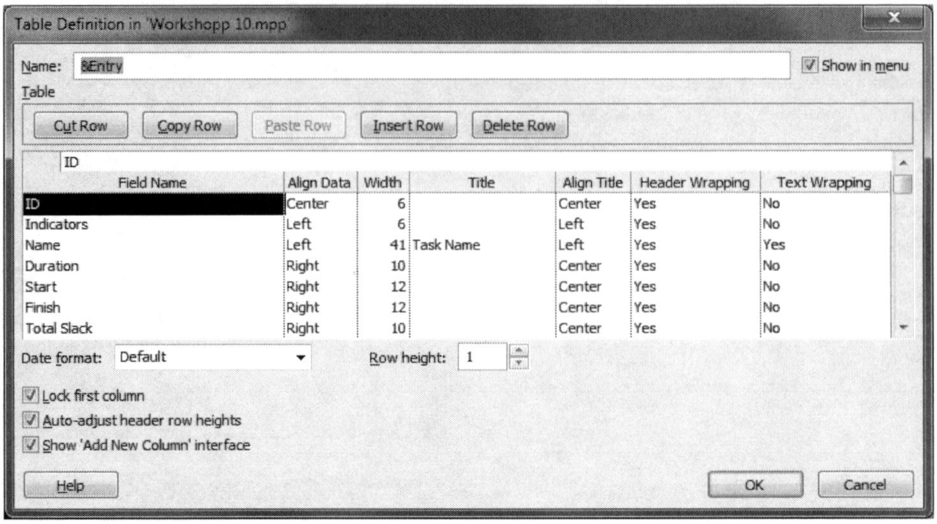

- The functions in this form are similar to those in many other forms. The functions that are unique to this form are listed below:
  - **Show in menu** – Decides if the Table is displayed in menus.
  - **Date format:** – Changes the format of the dates in this project and table only.
  - **Row height:** – Allows you to specify the row height for this table.
  - **Lock first column** – Ensures the first column is always displayed when scrolling to the right.
  - **Auto-adjust header row heights** – Automatically adjusts the header height when the width of the column is adjusted so the column text wraps.
  - **Show 'Add New Column' interface** shows the **New Column** column at the right of all columns. Clicking on this column creates a new column.

The **Date Format** selected in the **File**, **Options**, **General** tab is overridden by a date format selected in a Table. Therefore, if you have a project that requires a unique date format then the option of selecting a date format in a Table overrides the default on any computer for anyone who opens the project file.

13.3 Custom Fields

A **Custom Field** is an existing Microsoft project field that may be:

- Renamed to suit your projects requirements,
- Tailored to display specific data in a specific format,
- Assigned a list, such as a list of values or people, that may be assigned from a drop-down list, or
- Assigned a formula for calculating data from other fields.

To create or edit a **Custom Field** the **Custom Fields** form must be opened by:

- Displaying the **Custom Fields** button Ribbon or Quick Access Toolbar, or
- Selecting **Custom Fields** when inserting a new column, or
- Selecting **Custom Fields** when right-clicking on an existing column.

Task fields may be used for:

- Recording additional information about Tasks (such as responsibility, location, floor, system)
- Recording additional information about Resources such as telephone number, address and skills.
- Formulas may be created to populate the fields with calculated data.
- Tasks or resources may be grouped using these fields.

These predefined fields fall into the following categories:

- Cost
- Date
- Duration
- Finish (date)
- Flag
- Number
- Start (date)
- Text
- Outline Code

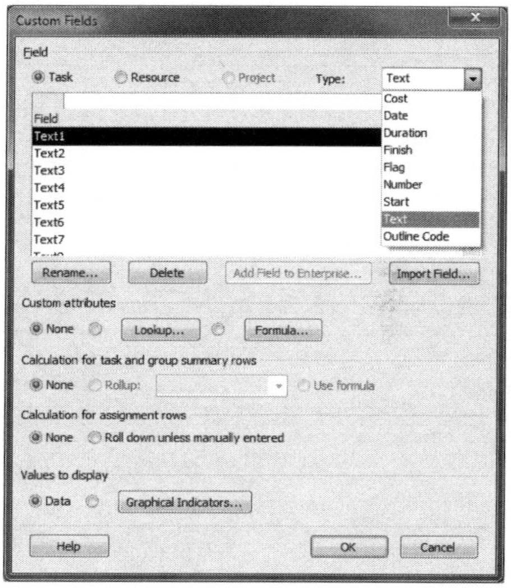

Both the title and content of these fields may be edited with options including:

- Rename... allows the renaming of the field name.
  - This new name is then available when inserting columns and is displayed in the column header.
  - After Custom Field is renamed, the new name will be displayed in the **Custom Fields** tab of the **Task** or **Resource Information** form and the appropriate information may then be entered in this form.
- Import Field... allows importing from other fields or project files.
- **Custom Attributes**:
  - **None** allows data to be entered into the field without any restrictions.
  - Lookup... opens the **Edit Lookup Table** where a table of values and descriptions may be entered. The Value is displayed in columns and Description in bands when the tasks are grouped by this field. These value may be copied and pasted from other applications such as Excel.
  - Formula... allows the assigning of formulae for the calculation of field value from other task and project fields.

- **Calculation for task and group summary rows** specifies how Summary tasks calculate their value, such as Maximum, Minimum, Sum, None and Average. For example, the following options may be used:
  - A Start Date would select Minimum,
  - A Finish Date would select Maximum,
  - Cost would use Sum.
- **Calculation for assignment** rows determines if the field value is displayed only against the resource in Task Usage and Resource Usage fields or against the resource and assignment.

Resource Only

	Resource Name	Wor	Location
1	Paul Harris	16 hrs	Melbourne
	Electrical Design	*8 hrs*	
	Mechanical Design	*8 hrs*	
2	Samantha Harris	16 hrs	Brisbane
	Electrical Design	*8 hrs*	
	Mechanical Design	*8 hrs*	

Resource and Assignment

	Resource Name	Wor	Location
1	Paul Harris	16 hrs	Melbourne
	Electrical Design	*8 hrs*	*Melbourne*
	Mechanical Design	*8 hrs*	*Melbourne*
2	Samantha Harris	16 hrs	Brisbane
	Electrical Design	*8 hrs*	*Brisbane*
	Mechanical Design	*8 hrs*	*Brisbane*

- **Value to display** allows the options of displaying the value in the cell or generating graphical indicators such as traffic lights. A very simple example is displayed below when the Number 1 Custom Field has been renamed Risk and three values entered and three different images displayed:

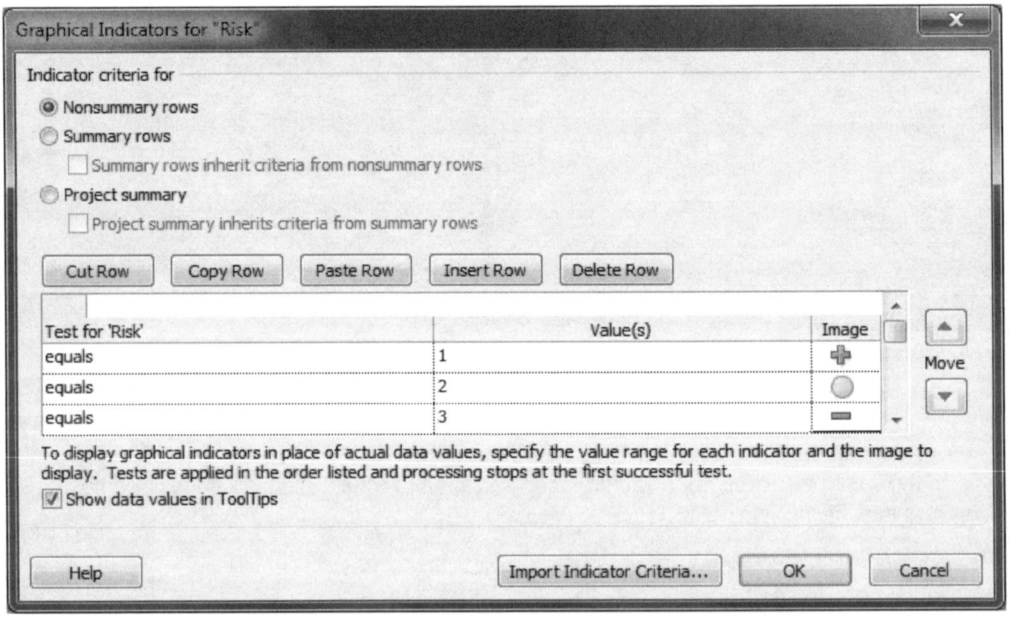

Outline Codes will be covered in more detail later in this chapter.

Oracle Primavera P3 and SureTrak software users will find the formatting options available when using Value and Description restrictive, because the description may not be displayed in columns and the value not displayed when Grouping. This is similar to the way Oracle Primavera P6 works.

13.4 Grouping

Grouping allows grouping of tasks under data items such as Customized fields, Durations, Constraints, etc. This function is particularly useful with schedules with a number of tasks and there is a requirement to work with a related group of tasks throughout a project. The picture below displays a simple project where the relationship between each Task is difficult to check by inspection of the Gantt Chart organized with Outlining by Phase:

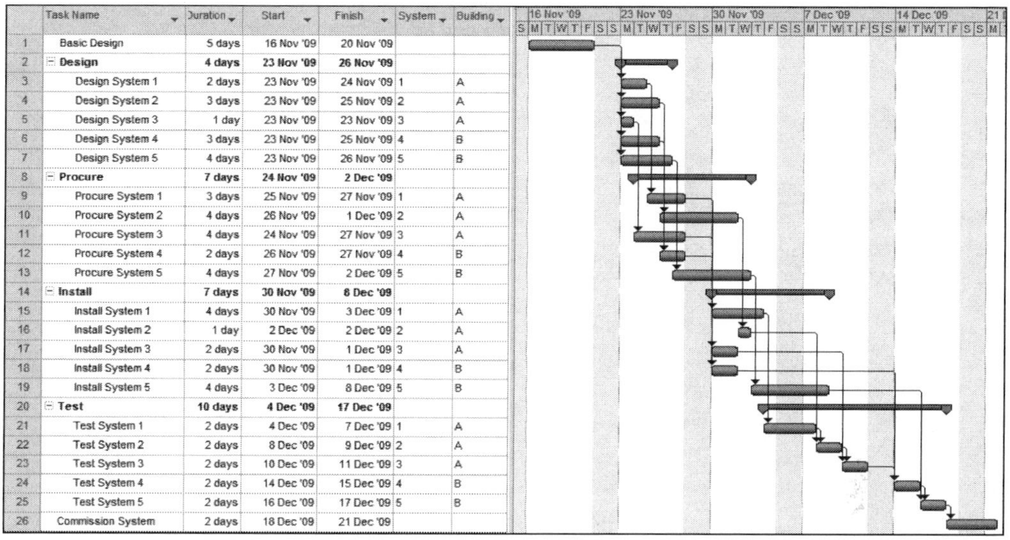

	Task Name	Duration	Start	Finish	System	Building
1	Basic Design	5 days	16 Nov '09	20 Nov '09		
2	**Design**	**4 days**	**23 Nov '09**	**26 Nov '09**		
3	Design System 1	2 days	23 Nov '09	24 Nov '09	1	A
4	Design System 2	3 days	23 Nov '09	25 Nov '09	2	A
5	Design System 3	1 day	23 Nov '09	23 Nov '09	3	A
6	Design System 4	3 days	23 Nov '09	25 Nov '09	4	B
7	Design System 5	4 days	23 Nov '09	26 Nov '09	5	B
8	**Procure**	**7 days**	**24 Nov '09**	**2 Dec '09**		
9	Procure System 1	3 days	25 Nov '09	27 Nov '09	1	A
10	Procure System 2	4 days	26 Nov '09	1 Dec '09	2	A
11	Procure System 3	4 days	24 Nov '09	27 Nov '09	3	A
12	Procure System 4	2 days	26 Nov '09	27 Nov '09	4	B
13	Procure System 5	4 days	27 Nov '09	2 Dec '09	5	B
14	**Install**	**7 days**	**30 Nov '09**	**8 Dec '09**		
15	Install System 1	4 days	30 Nov '09	3 Dec '09	1	A
16	Install System 2	1 day	2 Dec '09	2 Dec '09	2	A
17	Install System 3	2 days	30 Nov '09	1 Dec '09	3	A
18	Install System 4	2 days	30 Nov '09	1 Dec '09	4	B
19	Install System 5	4 days	3 Dec '09	8 Dec '09	5	B
20	**Test**	**10 days**	**4 Dec '09**	**17 Dec '09**		
21	Test System 1	2 days	4 Dec '09	7 Dec '09	1	A
22	Test System 2	2 days	8 Dec '09	9 Dec '09	2	A
23	Test System 3	2 days	10 Dec '09	11 Dec '09	3	A
24	Test System 4	2 days	14 Dec '09	15 Dec '09	4	B
25	Test System 5	2 days	16 Dec '09	17 Dec '09	5	B
26	Commission System	2 days	18 Dec '09	21 Dec '09		

With the Grouping function it is possible to Group on a text field to reorganize the data. In this example, the schedule has been reorganized by the Text 1 - System and Text 2 - Building fields, which have been renamed using the **Custom Fields** form to System and Building. You may now clearly see the logic between the Items:

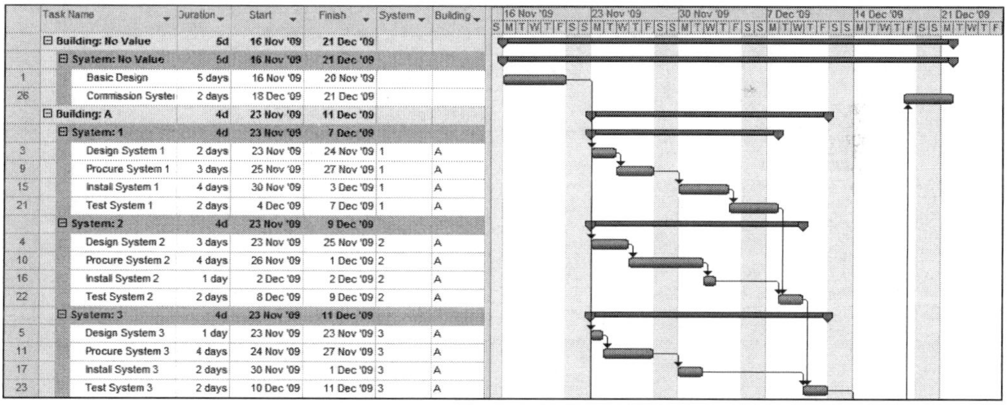

	Task Name	Duration	Start	Finish	System	Building
	Building: No Value	**5d**	**16 Nov '09**	**21 Dec '09**		
	System: No Value	**5d**	**16 Nov '09**	**21 Dec '09**		
1	Basic Design	5 days	16 Nov '09	20 Nov '09		
26	Commission Syste	2 days	18 Dec '09	21 Dec '09		
	Building: A	**4d**	**23 Nov '09**	**11 Dec '09**		
	System: 1	**4d**	**23 Nov '09**	**7 Dec '09**		
3	Design System 1	2 days	23 Nov '09	24 Nov '09	1	A
9	Procure System 1	3 days	25 Nov '09	27 Nov '09	1	A
15	Install System 1	4 days	30 Nov '09	3 Dec '09	1	A
21	Test System 1	2 days	4 Dec '09	7 Dec '09	1	A
	System: 2	**4d**	**23 Nov '09**	**9 Dec '09**		
4	Design System 2	3 days	23 Nov '09	25 Nov '09	2	A
10	Procure System 2	4 days	26 Nov '09	1 Dec '09	2	A
16	Install System 2	1 day	2 Dec '09	2 Dec '09	2	A
22	Test System 2	2 days	8 Dec '09	9 Dec '09	2	A
	System: 3	**4d**	**23 Nov '09**	**11 Dec '09**		
5	Design System 3	1 day	23 Nov '09	23 Nov '09	3	A
11	Procure System 3	4 days	24 Nov '09	27 Nov '09	3	A
17	Install System 3	2 days	30 Nov '09	1 Dec '09	3	A
23	Test System 3	2 days	10 Dec '09	11 Dec '09	3	A

i The first few characters of the field determine the sort order when tasks are grouped by a Text Field. To order items differently from the fields' text values, place a number or letter at the start of the description, or create a **Custom Outline Codes** which will take a little more effort but provide a more satisfactory result.

13.4.1 Group by: Function

The **View**, **Data** group, **Group by:** option allows you to Group scenarios in the same way as filters are created and saved:

- **Custom** are user defined groups,
- **Built-In** are system defined groups,
- **Clear Group** removes any grouping applied to a View,
- **New Group By...** opens the **Group Definition** form allowing the defining and saving of a new group scenario,
- **More Groups...** opens the **More Groups** form allowing access to Groups that may not be listed in the **View**, **Data** group, **Group by:** list.

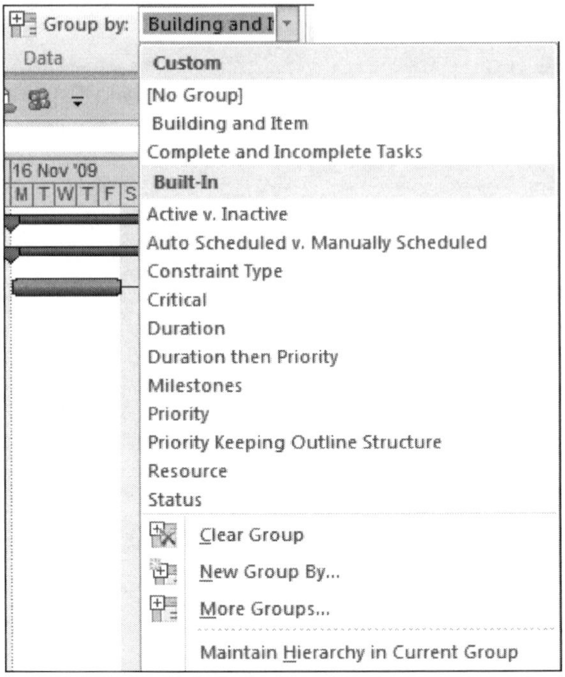

- **Maintain Hierarchy in Current Group** is a new feature to Microsoft Project 2010 and allows the user to see the Outline hierarchy when Grouping. The picture below displays the effect of grouping by two Custom Text columns, with the lower picture having this option turned on:

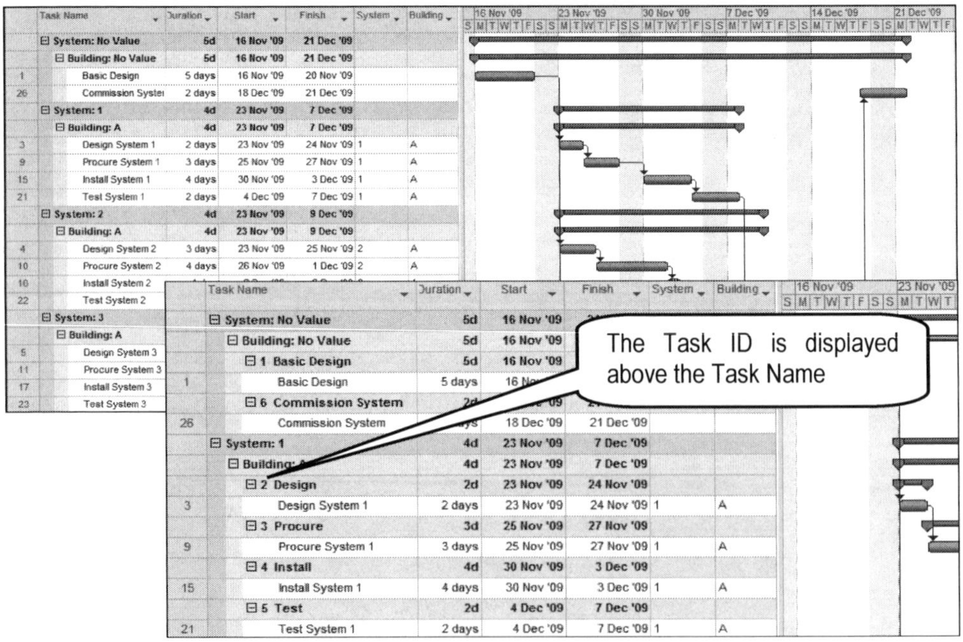

13.4.2 Using a Predefined Group

The Grouping function works in a similar way to Filters and Tables. A predefined Group may be assigned by:

- Selecting **View**, **Data** group, **Group by:**
- Then either:
  - Selecting a grouping from the list, or
  - Selecting **More Groups…** to open the **More Groups** form and then selecting one from the list after clicking on the **Task** or **Resource** radio button.

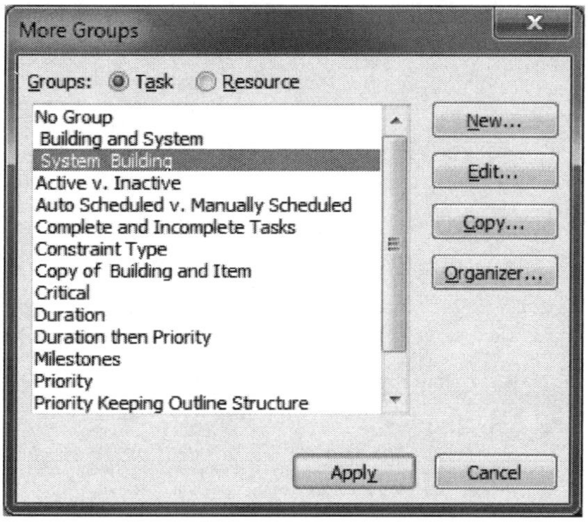

13.4.3 Creating a New Group

Create a new Group by:

- Selecting **View**, **Data** group, **Group by:**,
- Selecting **More Groups…** to open the **More Groups** form,
- Clicking on the  button to open the **Group Definition** form,
- Now create a "Grouping" which may be reapplied at a later date or copy to another project using **Organizer**.

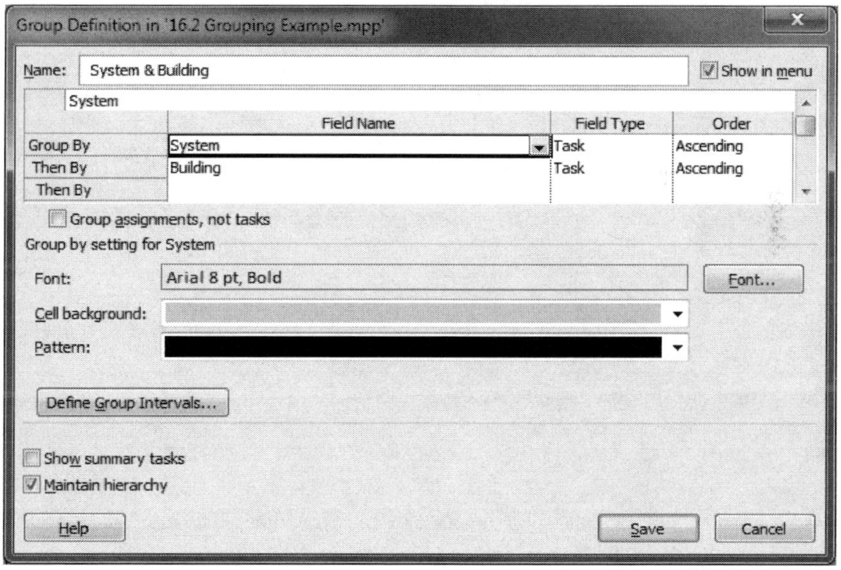

- The **Define Group Interval** form is available with many **Group By** options, such as Start or Finish, and allows further formatting options by defining the intervals of the banding.

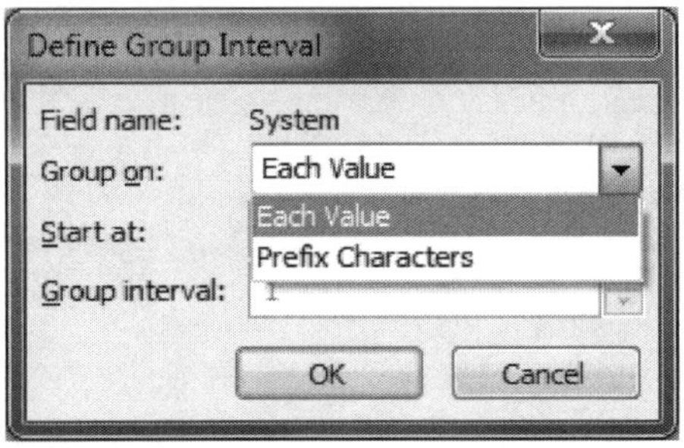

Grouping is similar to the Oracle Primavera organize function. It is possible to mimic this Oracle Primavera function using the text columns as Task Code dictionaries. Projects converted from Oracle Primavera software format often translate Primavera's Task Codes to Microsoft Project's Text fields. After conversion, the project may be **Grouped** by Text fields. **Custom Outline Codes** may produce a better result as bands may be ordered with this function.

13.4.4 Grouping Resources in the Resource Sheet

Resources may be created in the **Resource Sheet**. Then the resources may be grouped by a number of attributes. The standard options are shown below:

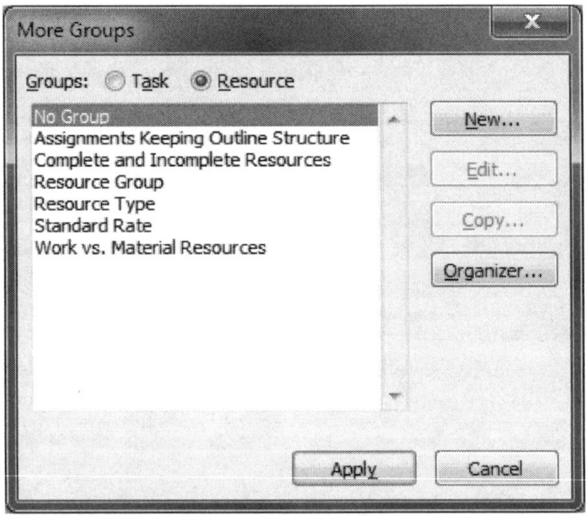

Resources are covered in more detail in the **RESOURCES** chapters.

There are many uses for Grouping Resources which may be used in conjunction with Customized Fields:

- A project hierarchical organizational structure may be created using these Customized Outline Codes and resources summarized under this hierarchical structure in the Resource Sheet.
- Resources details such as skill, trade, address, office, department and telephone number may be recorded in Customized Fields and the resources grouped by this data.

13.5 Workshop 11 - Reorganizing the Schedule

Background

We want to issue reports for comment by management. We will group the tasks by their float value and show the WBS columns. We will also look at the Outline Codes and then Group the Tasks by the people responsible for the work, which we will enter into a text column.

Assignment

1. Grouping – to group tasks without float:
   - Ensure there is no filter applied.
   - Apply the **Entry** table and ensure the **Total Slack** column is displayed.
   - Add the **Group by:** button to the **Quick Access toolbar** by selecting **View**, **Data** group,
   - Create a new Group titled **Total Float** and group the tasks by **Total Slack**.
   - Check the **Show in menu** option, **DO NOT** show Summary tasks and apply.
   - All the tasks with zero days' float are grouped at the top under the heading **Total Slack: 0 days**.

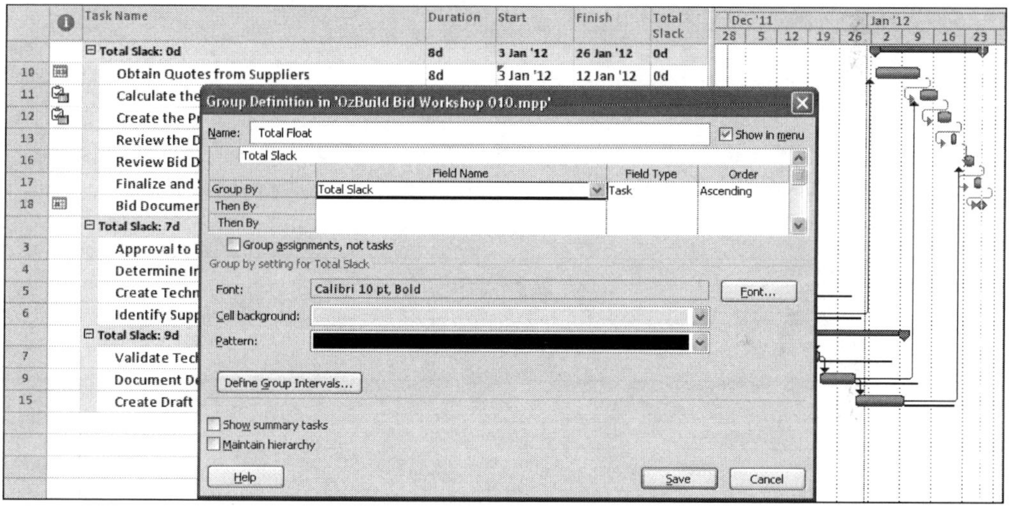

2. Grouping by Responsibility
   - Use the **Add New Column** to add a new column by typing **Responsibility** in the header. This will rename Text 1.
   - Drag this new column so it is beside the Task name.
   - Assign the Responsibilities in the table below, use Copy & Paste cells:

ID	Task Name	Responsibility
2	**Technical Specification**	
3	Approval to Bid	
4	Determine Installation Requirements	Scott Morrison - Engineering
5	Create Technical Specification	Scott Morrison - Engineering
6	Identify Supplier Components	Angela Lowe - Purchasing
7	Validate Technical Specification	Scott Morrison - Engineering
8	**Delivery Plan**	
9	Document Delivery Methodology	Scott Morrison - Engineering
10	Obtain Quotes from Suppliers	Angela Lowe - Purchasing
11	Calculate the Bid Estimate	Carol Peterson - Bid Manager
12	Create the Project Schedule	Carol Peterson - Bid Manager
13	Review the Delivery Plan	Carol Peterson - Bid Manager
14	**Bid Document**	
15	Create Draft of Bid Document	Carol Peterson - Bid Manager
16	Review Bid Document	Carol Peterson - Bid Manager
17	Finalize and Submit Bid Document	Carol Peterson - Bid Manager
18	Bid Document Submitted	

   - Create a Group titled **Responsibility** by clicking the **Group by: button**  and grouping the tasks by Responsibility showing in the menu but do not show Summary tasks.

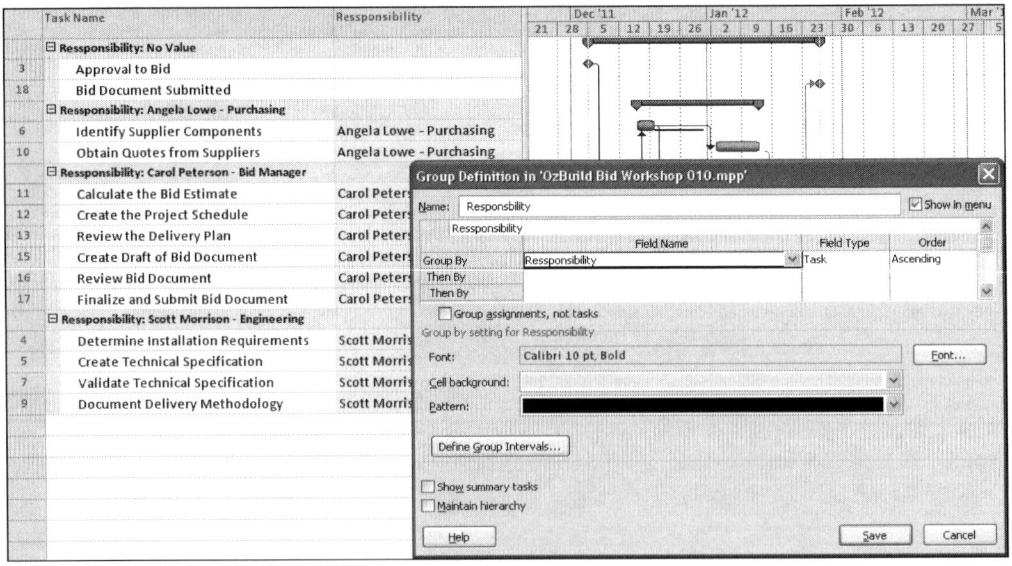

3. Remove all Grouping and the **Responsibility** column.

4. Save your **OzBuild Bid** project.

14 VIEWS AND DETAILS

A **View** is a function where the formatting such as **Grouping**, **Table**, **Filter, Print Settings** and **Bar** formatting are saved as a **View** and reapplied later.

All Views, except the **Timescale** view which is normally displayed above the Gantt Chart, may be applied by:

- Clicking the appropriate button from the **Ribbon View**, **Task Views** and **Resource Views** groups.

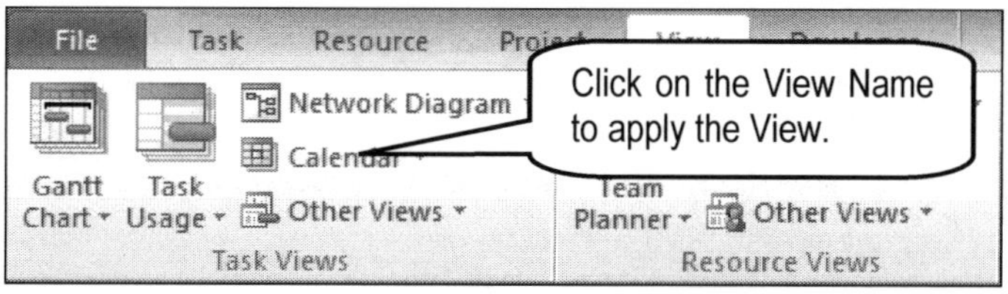

- Clicking on the down arrow ▼ by a View Name on **View**, **Task Views** and **Resource Views** groups to open a submenu and then click on the View name to apply the View:

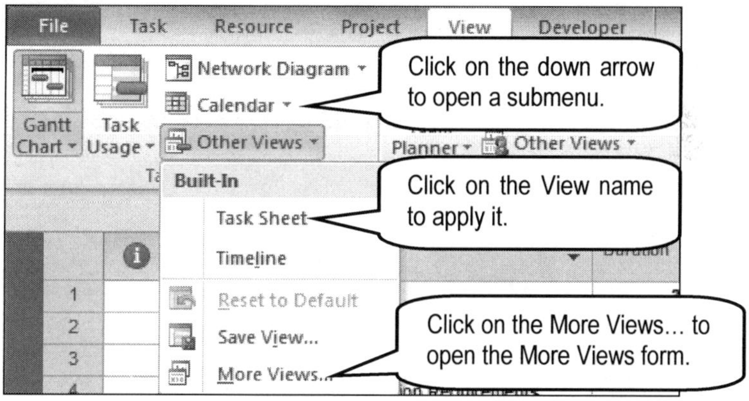

- There are more views available than the Views listed on the **Ribbon** menu. These may be applied from the **More Views...** form. This may be accessed from all the **View**, **Task Views** and **Resource Views** groups, by placing a button on the **Quick Access Toolbar** and, possible the simplest way, to right click in the dark band on the left-hand side of the active pane:

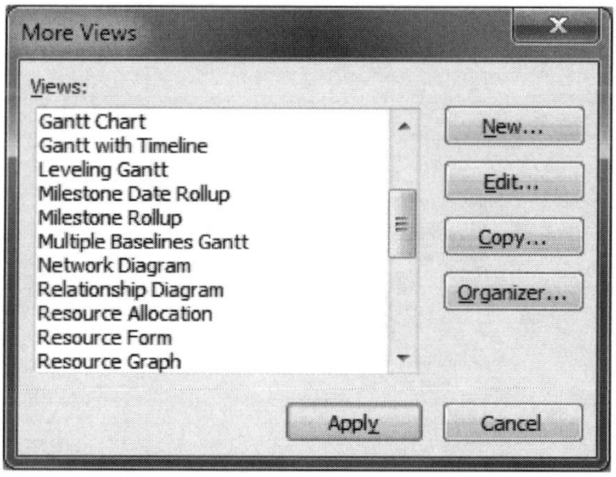

- A View may be displayed by right-clicking in the bar on the left had side of the screen which will open a menu with a list of Views:

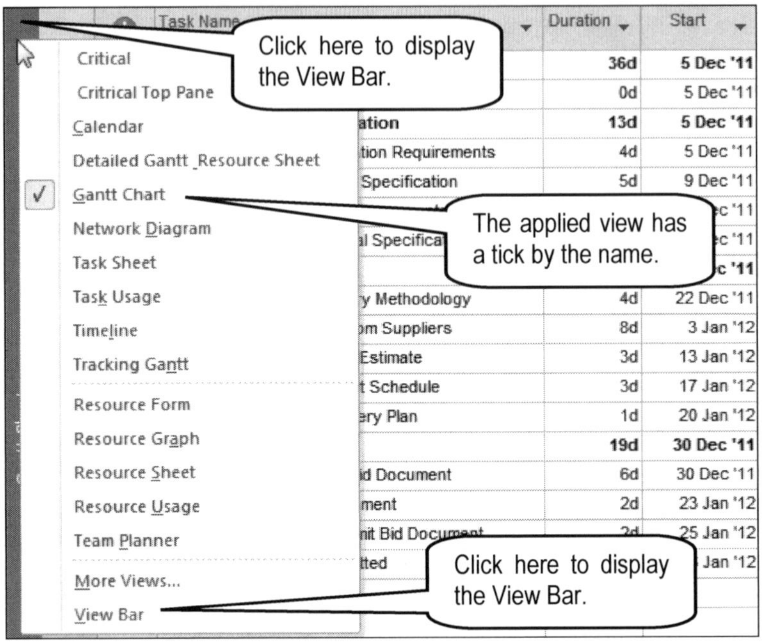

- A View may also be applied by displaying the **View Bar** and clicking on a **View** button. The **View Bar** is displayed as shown in the picture below.

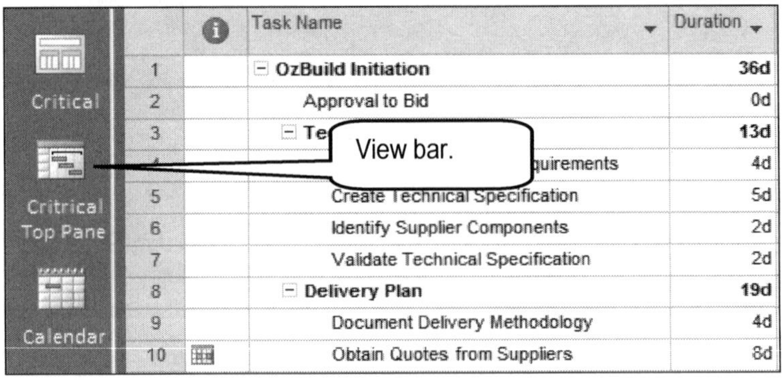

- There is also a button on the **Task**, **View** group that displays a list of available task related Views:

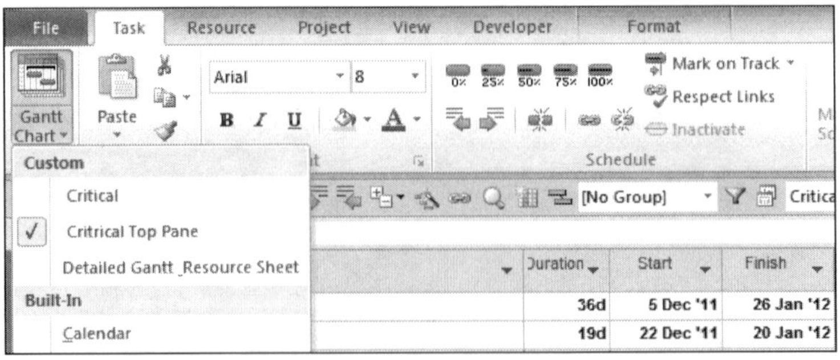

The **Timeline** view is shown above the Gantt Chart by selecting **View**, **Split View** group and checking the **Timeline** check box. This View is covered in more detail at the end of this chapter.

The views displayed in the **Ribbon** menu and displayed on the **View Bar** with a standard install of Microsoft Project are listed below:

View Name	Ribbon Command	Comments
Calendar	**Task**, **View** group, **Calendar**	This may be applied to the top window only and displays the tasks overlaid on a calendar.
Gantt Chart	**Task**, **View** group, **Gantt Chart**	Displays a Table on the left of the screen and Bar Chart on the right.
Network Diagram	**Task**, **View** group, **Network Diagram**	This view is a graphical PERT-style display and is covered in the **NETWORK DIAGRAM VIEW** chapter.
Relationship Diagram	Not on the **Ribbon** as a default.	This is a graphical view showing the relationship among tasks. Usually placed in the bottom pane.
Resource Form*	**Resource**, **View** group, **Other View**	This displays one Resource at a time and list the tasks assigned to the resource. Usually placed in the bottom pane.
Resource Graph*	**Resource**, **View** group, **Other View**	A split table displaying the Resource name on the left-hand side and resource usage in bar chart format on the right-hand side.
Resource Sheet*	**Resource**, **View** group, **Resource Sheet**	A single table used to create resources and displaying Resource information such as costs and calendars.
Resource Usage*	**Resource**, **View** group, **Resource Usage**	Similar to the Task usage, displays a Table with Resources with associated Tasks on the left and the Resources usage data apportioned over time on the right.
Task Form	**Task**, **View** group, **Other Views**	This is the form that is normally displayed in the bottom pane when the Gantt Chart view is split.
Task Sheet	**Task**, **View** group, **Other Views**	This is the same as a Gantt Chart view button bars are displayed.
Timeline	**Task**, **View** group, **Other Views**	This is a new Microsoft Project 2010 view displaying the whole project graphically above the Gantt Chart.
Tracking Gantt	**Task**, **View** group, **Gantt Chart**	This is a Gantt Chart view for entering progress which uses the tracking table and displays the Baseline.

* The Views containing resource information are covered in more detail in the **UPDATING PROJECTS WITH RESOURCES** chapter.

The **Calendar** view is not covered in detail in this book. The **Network** view is covered in the **NETWORK DIAGRAM VIEW** chapter.

14.1 Understanding Views

There are two types of Views:

- A **Single View** is normally applied to the active pane only; when the pane is split, or the whole screen when not split.
- A **Combination View** is comprised of two **Single Views**, one displayed in the top pane and one in the bottom pane.

The top pane is usually used to display all data and the bottom pane display specific data relating to the selected task or tasks in the top pane.

All **Single Views** may be applied to the top pane and when the window is split, most may be applied to the bottom pane. When a **Single View** is applied to the bottom pane, it will only display the information attributed to the task that is highlighted in the top pane.

When a **Single View** is applied to the top or bottom pane, the other pane is left with the contents of the previous **Combination View**.

A **View** is based on a **Screen** when it is created. The **Screen** may not be changed after the **View** is created. There are 16 **Screens**:

- Calendar
- Network Diagram
- Resource Form
- Resource Name Form
- Resource Usage
- Task Form
- Task Sheet
- Team Planner – New to 2010
- Gantt Chart
- Relationship Diagram
- Resource Graph
- Resource Sheet
- Task Details Form
- Task Name Form
- Task Usage
- Timeline – New to 2010

The Table in **APPENDIX 1 – SCREENS USED TO CREATE VIEWS** lists the Screens and provides further detail about formatting the screens. A few important points to consider are:

- The **Calendar** screen may only be displayed in the top pane.
- The **Gantt Chart** and **Network Diagram** are often best displayed in the top pane and have limited use when displayed in the bottom pane.
- **Relationship Diagram** is best displayed in the bottom pane.
- The **Forms** are best displayed in the bottom pane and convey **Task** or **Resource** information about a task that is highlighted in the top pane. **Forms** may be further formatted by right-clicking in the form to open a menu.
- The **Task Sheet** is similar to the **Gantt Chart** but does not display bars and is best displayed in the top pane.
- The **Resource**, **Task Usage** and **Team Planner** screens display resource information and are further discussed in the **RESOURCE OPTIMIZATION** chapter.
- **Resource Graph** and **Resource Tables** are best displayed in the bottom pane.

14.2 *Creating a New View*

A new View may be created by copying and editing an existing View, or creating a new View.

14.2.1 Creating a New Single View

To create a new Single View:

- Open the **More Views** form, which is available from many view buttons,
- Click on the 

button to open the **Define New View** form:

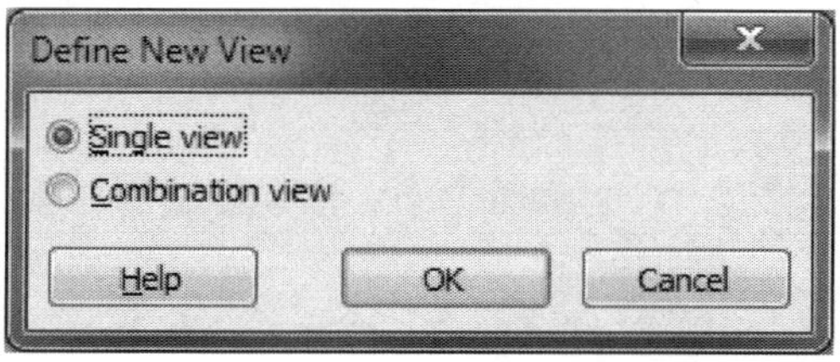

- Click on the **Single view** radio button to open the **View Definition** form:
- You may now enter:
  - ➢ The new View name in the **Name:** box by overtyping the "**View 1**" name assigned by default by Microsoft Project,
  - ➢ Select the **Screen:** View. (see **APPENDIX 1** for more information on the screens). A list of available screens is displayed below:

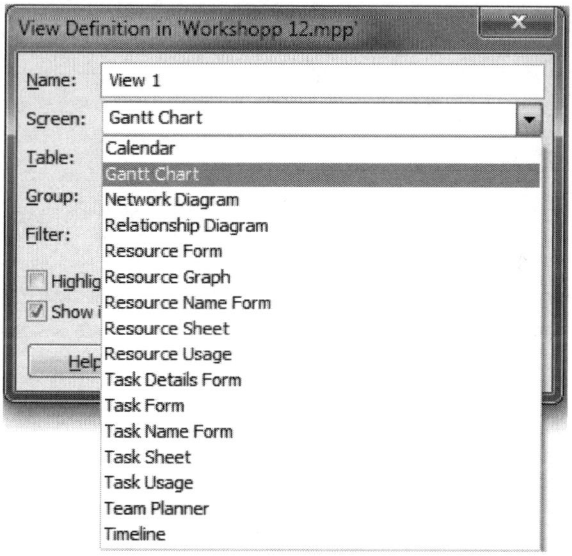

  - ➢ Select the **Table:** you want to apply with the view.
  - ➢ You may not want to display your tasks using the Outline display mode. The **Group:** function allows you to group your tasks by other data items such as a **Text Column** or **Constraint Type** and is covered in the **TABLES AND GROUPING TASKS** chapter.
  - ➢ You may also select a filter to apply with the View from the **Filter:** drop-down box.
  - ➢ Click the **Highlight filter** box to highlight the tasks that meet the filter specification as opposed to applying the filter.
  - ➢ Click on the **Show in menu** box to display the View in a menu.

- Click on the OK button to create the new **View**.
- From the **More Views** form click on the Apply button to apply the new **View**.

Inserting a space before the View name will put the View to the top of the list making it simpler to identify those Views that you have created or edited.

14.2.2 Creating a Combination View

Before creating a new Combination View the two Views that are to be displayed in the top and bottom pane must have been created:

- Open the **More Views** form,
- Click on the New... button to open the **Define New View** form:

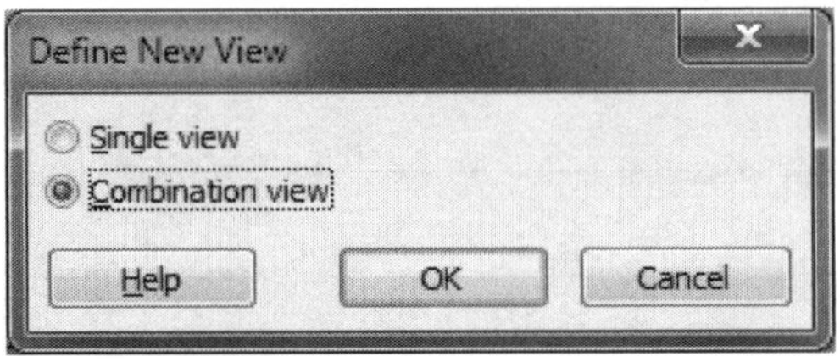

- Select C**ombination view** and click OK; this will open the **View Definition** form:

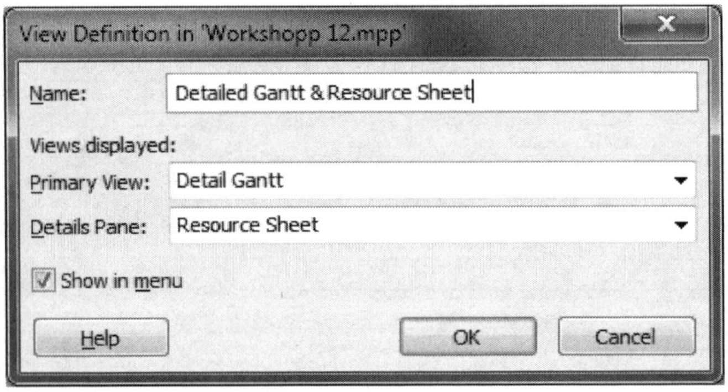

- Enter your View name and select the Views you want to display in the top and bottom pane,
- Click on **Show in menu** to display the View in the menu and on the **View Bar**, and
- Click on the OK button to create the new **View**.

A useful technique is to create a View, and associated Table and Filter, with the same name and keep them together as a set. For example, a View created to show critical tasks could have a View, Table and Filter all titled "Critical."

14.2.3 Copying and Editing a View

To copy an existing View:

- Open the **More Views** form:

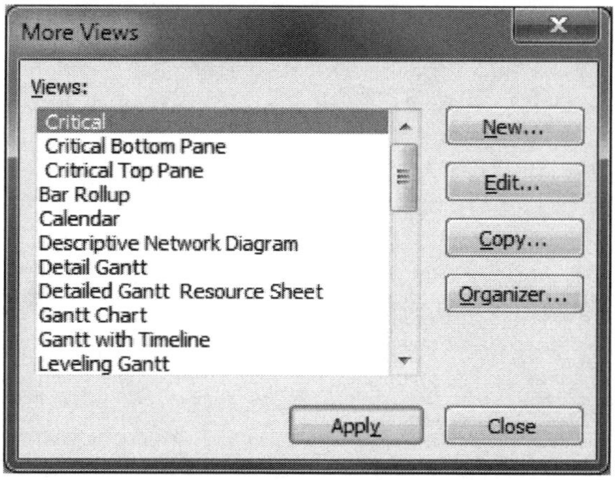

- Select the View you want to copy from the drop-down list and click on the Copy... button to open the **View Definition** form. This form is different for Single and Combination Views. The example below is a **Single View** created from the **Gantt Chart** Screen:

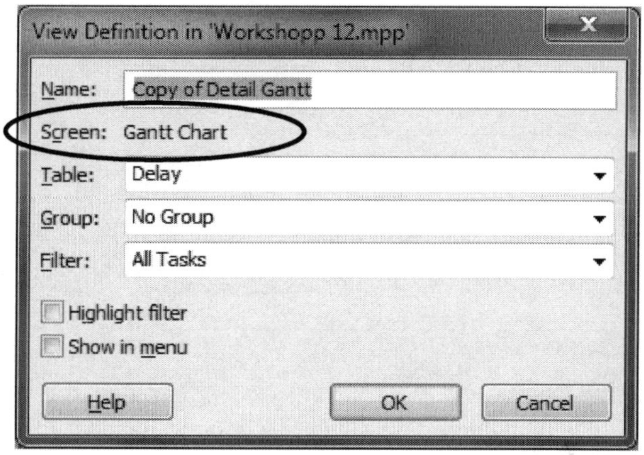

- The **Screen:** may not be changed in an existing or copied view and the screen option is shown as gray. See picture above.
- Change the name and any other parameters and then click on OK to create the **View**.

14.2.4 Copying a View to and from Another Project

Views may be copied from one project to another with the **Organizer** function. The **Organizer** function may be accessed by selecting:

- Organizer... from the **More Views** form, or
- Placing the **Organizer** button on the **Ribbon** or the **Quick Access Toolbar**.

If a View is copied to another project then the associated Tables, Filters and Grouping may also need to be copied.

14.3 Details Form

Details forms are the third level of formatting that may be assigned in some views. An extensive list of the Details forms is outlined in **APPENDIX 1 – SCREENS USED TO CREATE VIEWS**.

Each view has a number of Details options, which tends to make this aspect of Microsoft Project difficult for all levels of users.

The **Details** forms may be selected in the bottom pane by right-clicking in the active pane to open a menu. Examples of Details forms are displayed below:

- **Task Form** with Resource Costs Details form:

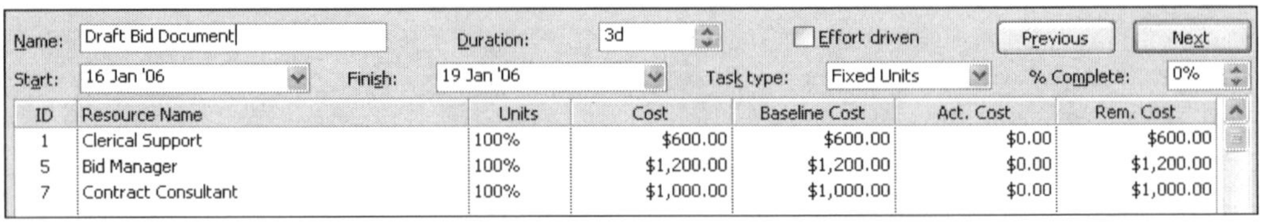

- **Task Details Form** with Predecessors and Successors Details form which displays more information than the **Task Form**:

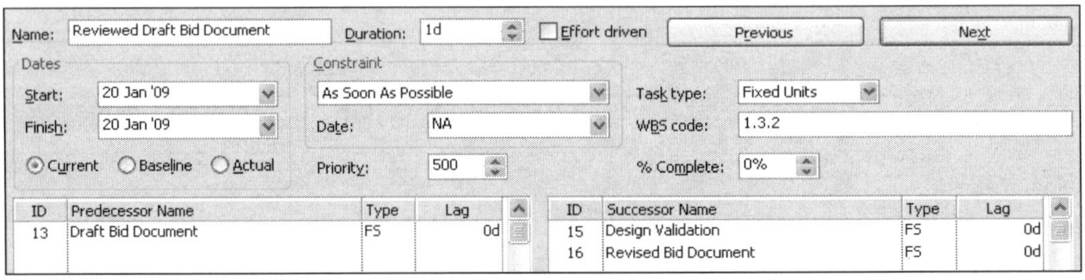

14.4 Timeline View

This view, new to Microsoft Project 2010, allows you to clearly understand how much of the Gantt Chart is displayed on the screen. The picture below demonstrates that about one-third of the project is displayed in the Gantt Chart.

The **Timescale** view is shown above the Gantt Chart by selecting **View**, **Split View** group and checking the **Timeline** check box. Right-clicking in the **Timeline** will show a menu, as displayed in the picture below:

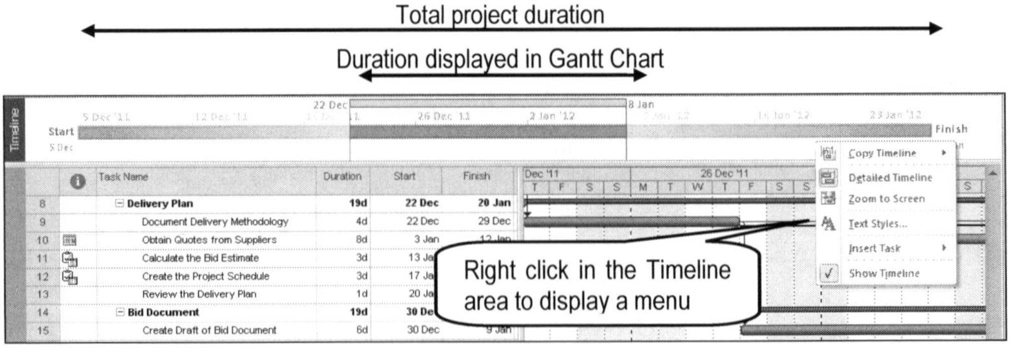

A task may be added to the **Timeline** view by selecting the **Add to Timeline** found in many menus. Important tasks that need to be highlighted should be considered for this type of display. In the picture below the Start and Finish Milestones and Obtain Quotes have been added to the Timeline view:

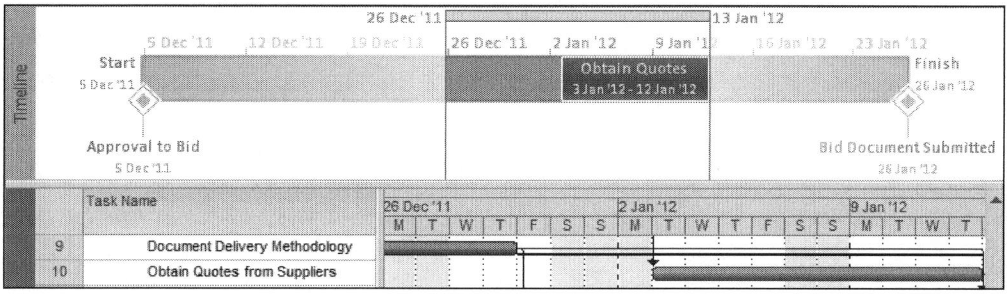

14.5 A Logical Process for Developing a View

A View may be used to create a management report or to manipulate a schedule. The following tips should be considered when creating a view that will be used for reporting:

- It is important that you plan the process you wish to use to create Views. A small amount of planning at the start of a project will save a large amount of time later in a project lifecycle and avoid changing a number of views.
- When there is a requirement to create a number of Views that will all have the same headers and footers when printed out, then it is best to create one View and spend time ensuring that the print settings are correct. Then copy the View, which copies the print settings, to create the remainder of the Views.
- It is also advisable to name the Filters, Table and Groupings with the same name so that it can easily be understood where Filters, Table and Groupings belong.
- When there are a large number of views to be created a numbering or coding system should be considered and used as a prefix to their names which will group and order the Filters, Table and Groupings.
- Filters, Table and Groupings that are part of Views should not be shown in the menu so their names not inadvertently changed.

The following process is suggested for creating a new View;

- Collect the View requirements,
- Plan the naming/coding system to be used if there are a number of views to be created,
- Create any Custom fields required,
- Create the Table, Filter and Grouping to be used with the View,
- Create the View and assign the Table, Filter and Grouping,
- Create the print headers and page setup,
- Format the Timescale, Gridlines, Bars,
- Apply any special sorting or font formatting,
- Save the file.

14.6 *Workshop 12- Organizing Your Data Using Views and Tables*

Background

Having completed the schedule you want to report the project schedule with different views.

Assignment

Display your project in the following formats, noting the different ways you may represent the same data. Open your **OzBuild Bid** project from the previous workshop to complete the following exercise.

1. Right click in the dark bar on the right hand side and display the **Calendar** view and scroll through a few months. Right-click in different parts of the screen and view the menu options. When there are many tasks on one day they may not all be displayed.
2. Display the **Network Diagram** view and zoom to 50%, using **View**, **Zoom** group, **Zoom** or the buttons.
3. Scroll around the schedule and then summarize the task by clicking on the [+] and the [-].
4. Display the **Gantt Chart** view and split the screen.
5. Display the **Relationship Diagram** view in the bottom pane by first making the bottom pane active and then right clicking in the dark band on the left of the screen to open **More Views** form. Scroll around the schedule by clicking on tasks in the top pane and review the changes in the bottom pane.
6. Edit the **Task Details** form to show in the menu and apply it in the bottom pane. Notice the additional fields that are available in this form compared to the **Task Information** form.
7. Apply each one of the following **Details** forms to the **Task Details** view in the bottom screen by right-clicking in the bottom pane.

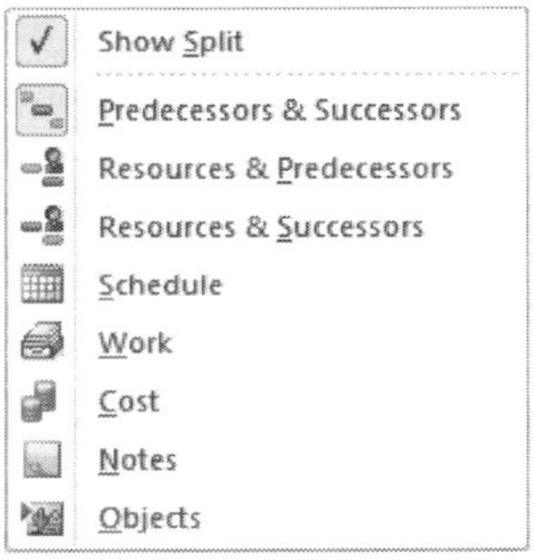

8. Display the Timeline View by selecting **View**, **Split View** group and check the **Timeline** box.
9. Add the Milestones and the **Obtain Quotes from suppliers** task to the **Timeline** by right clicking and selecting **Add to Timeline**.
10. Remove the **Timeline** by right clicking in the Gantt Chart and click on **Show Timeline**.
11. Apply the following Tables to the **Gantt Chart** view in the top pane:
    - Schedule, then
    - Tracking, then
    - Entry.
12. Close the split.

Continued Over...

13. We now will create a Combination View titled **Critical Top Pane** to show only Critical Tasks in the top pane with the Task Details form in the bottom pane.
    - Copy the **Entry** table and create a **Critical** table with the following columns: ID, Indicators, Name, Duration, Start, Finish, Total Slack and Free Slack.
    - Do not check **Show in the menu**,
    - Close the **More Tables...**form without applying the **Critical** table by clicking on Close,
    - Create a Single Pane Gantt Chart View titled **Critical Top Pane** by opening the **More Views....** And selecting New..., as per the picture on the right:

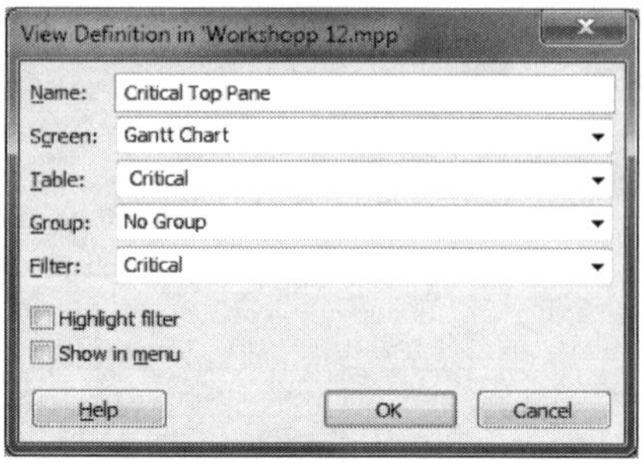

    - Create a Single Pane View titled **Critical Bottom Pane** using the Task Details form and All Tasks filter, as per the picture on the right:

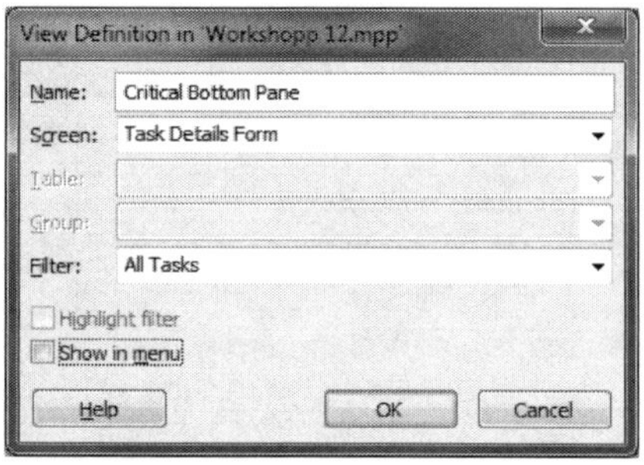

    - Create a Combination View titled **Critical** and apply it, as per the picture on the right:

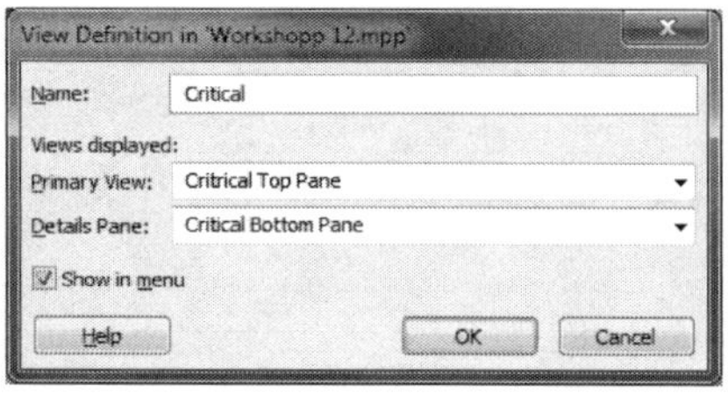

    - Apply the Critical View and you should see that the Critical Filter and Critical Table are applied in the Top Pane and Task Details Form in the bottom pane:

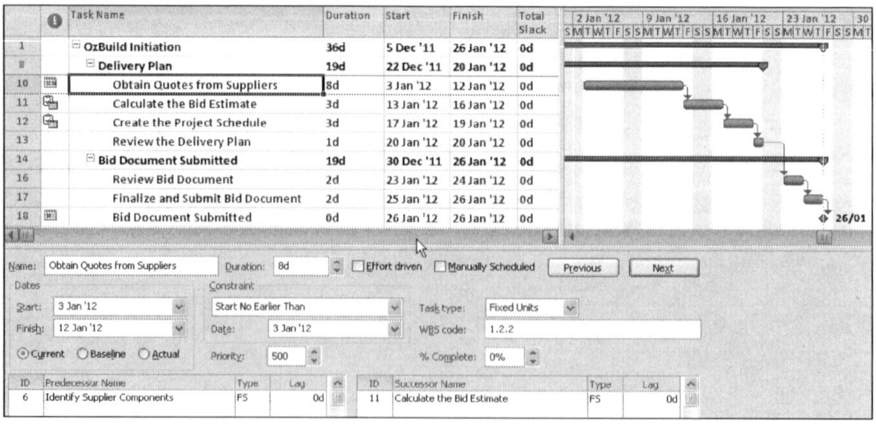

14. Save your **OzBuild Bid** project.

15 PRINTING AND REPORTS

You are now at the stage to print the schedule so the project team may review and comment on it. This chapter will examines some of the many options for printing your project schedule.

There are two tools available to output your schedule to a printer:

- The **Printing** function prints the data displayed in the current Active View.
- The **Reporting** function prints reports, which are independent of the current View. Microsoft Project supplies a number of predefined reports that may be tailored to suit your own requirements.

It is recommended that you consider using a product such as Adobe Acrobat to output your schedule in pdf format. There are many lower costs pdf creating software packages available on the internet. You will then be able to email high quality outputs that recipients may print or review on screen without needing a copy of Microsoft Project.

It is also easier to fit a Gantt Chart View which has many columns on an A3 or 11"x17" than an A4 or Letter sized output. Therefore it is often best to print to an A3 or 11"x17" pdf and then print to an A4 or Letter sized piece of paper using the pdf printing software.

15.1 Printing

Only the active View may be printed when a screen is split. The active view normally has a dark highlighted bar down the left-hand side of the screen. Views created from **Forms** (for example, the Task Form) may not be printed, so the printing options will be shown in gray when the forms are active.

Print settings are applied to the individual Views and the settings are saved with the currently displayed View.

In Microsoft Project 2010 the printing commands have been consolidated under the **File**, **Print** command.

Microsoft Project sometimes makes it difficult to print a Gantt Chart on one page. The author recommends adjusting the timescale so the whole project fits into half the screen before selecting **Print Preview** makes this process simpler.

Each time you report to the client or management, it is recommended that you save a complete copy of your project and change the name slightly (perhaps by appending a date to the file name or using a revision or version number) or create a subdirectory for this version of the project. This allows you to reproduce these reports at any time in the future and an electronic copy is available for dispute resolution purposes.

15.2 File, Print Form

The Microsoft Project 2010 **File**, **Print** form has replaced the earlier versions **Print Preview** and **Print** form. To preview the printout:

- Select **File**, **Print**, or
- Click on the **Quick Access Toolbar**  **Print Preview** button or the **Ribbon**.

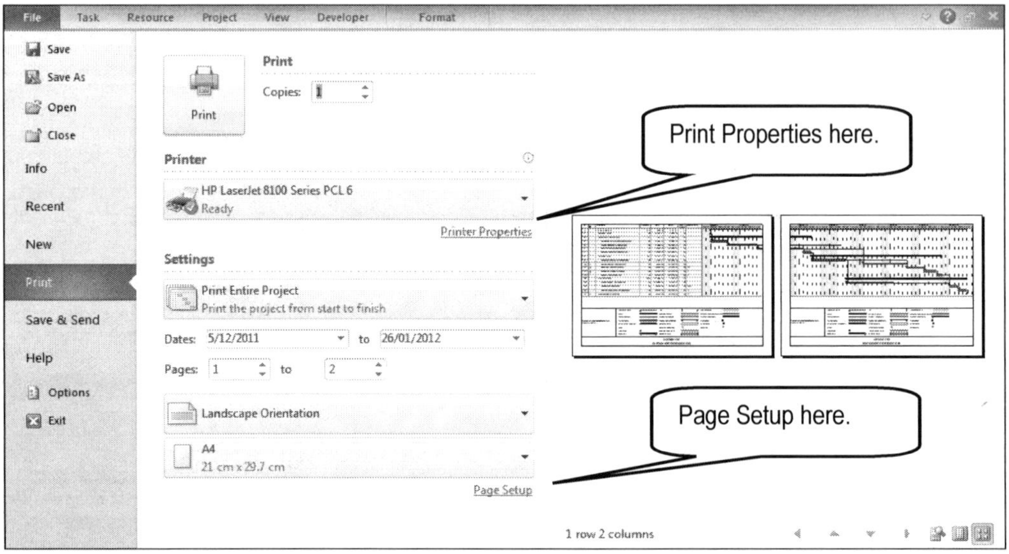

15.2.1 Print and Printer Heading

This heading allows the selection of:

- The printer and number of copies
- Printer properties.

15.2.2 Setting Heading

This heading has several options that allow the selection of the dates, pages to be printed and which columns to be printed:

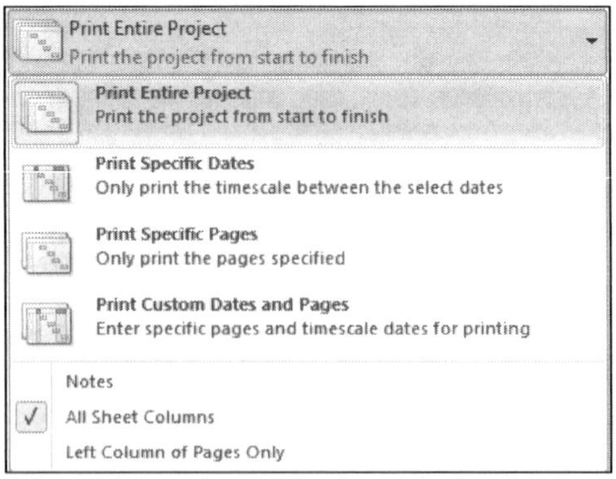

- **Print Entire Project** – prints the whole Gantt Chart
- **Print Specific Dates** – prints the selected dates. Changing the dates will change the option.
- **Print Specific Pages** – allows the selection of specific pages to be printed when multiple pages are displayed.
- **All Sheet Columns** – when unchecked will only print the visible columns displayed in the Gantt Chart.
- **Left Column of Pages only** – will print only the left pages of a printout when they are more than one page wide.

15.2.3 Buttons at the Bottom Right Hand Side of Print Form

The following paragraphs describe the functions of the buttons at the bottom right-hand side of the Print Preview screen from left to right:

- The first four buttons on the left, ◄ ► ▲ ▼, allow scrolling when a printout has more than one page.
- The magnifying glass zooms in only. You will need to click on the bottom of the preview screen to zoom out again. You may also click on the preview screen to zoom in.
- The next two buttons, and , display one or all pages, respectively.

15.3 Page Setup

Page Setup is unique to each View. To open the **Page Setup** form:

- Click the **Page Setup** link at the bottom of the **Settings** section, or
- Place a **Page Setup** button on the **Quick Access Toolbar** or **Ribbon**:

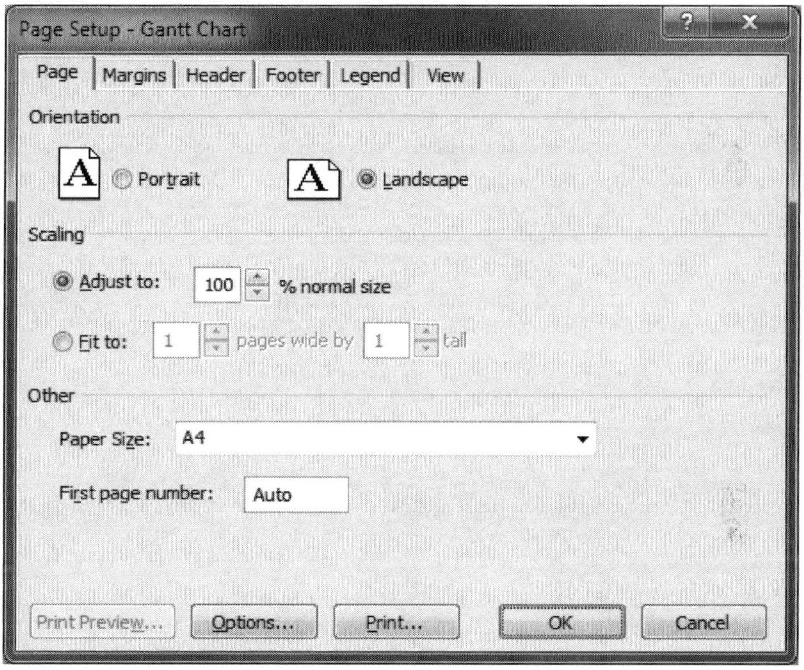

The **Page Setup** form contains the following tabs:

- Page
- Margins
- Header
- Footer
- Legend
- View.

Depending on the View being printed, some options in the **Print Setup** form will be unavailable and shown in gray.

The Options... button opens the printer setup/options form.

When the **Page Setup** form is opened from the **Quick Access Toolbar** or **Ribbon** then the Print Preview... button becomes available and takes you to the **Print** form.

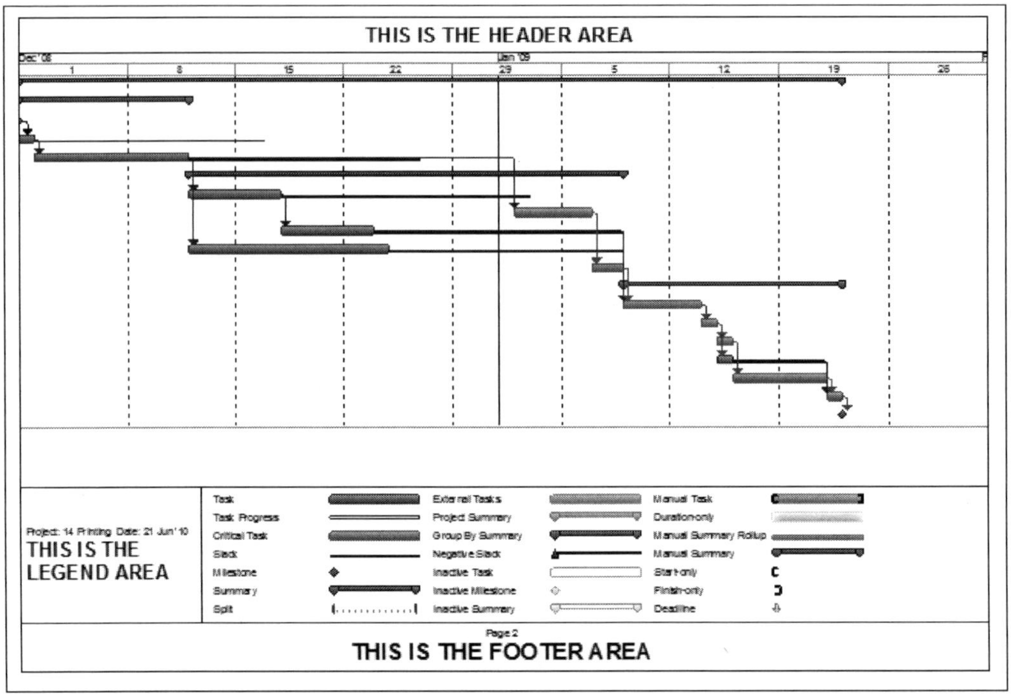

15.3.1 Page Tab

The Microsoft Project options in the **Page** tab are:

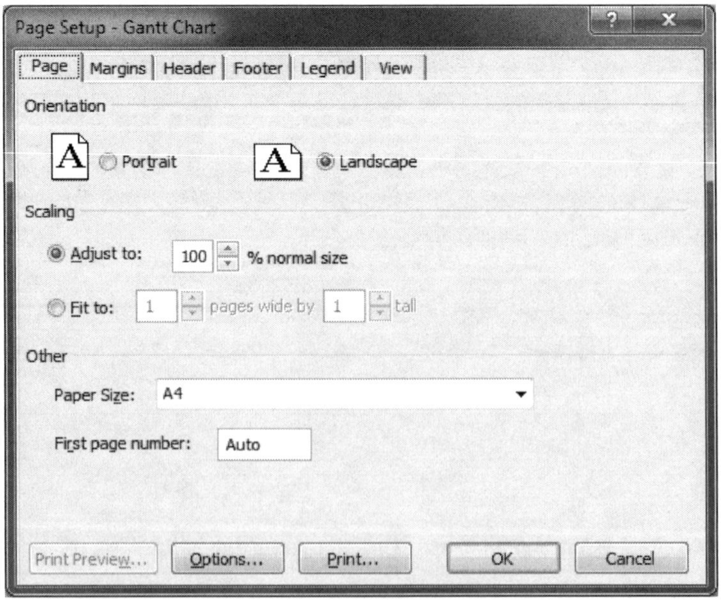

- **Scaling** allows you to adjust the number of pages the printout will fit onto:
  - **Adjust to:** – Allows you to choose the scale of the printout that both the bars and column text are scaled to. Microsoft Project will calculate the number of pages across and down for the printout.
  - **Fit to:** – Allows you to choose the number of pages across and down and Microsoft Project will scale the printout to fit.
- The **First page number:** – Allows you to choose the first page number of the printout. This is useful when enclosing the printout as an attachment or an appendage to another document.
- Pages are numbered down first and then across:

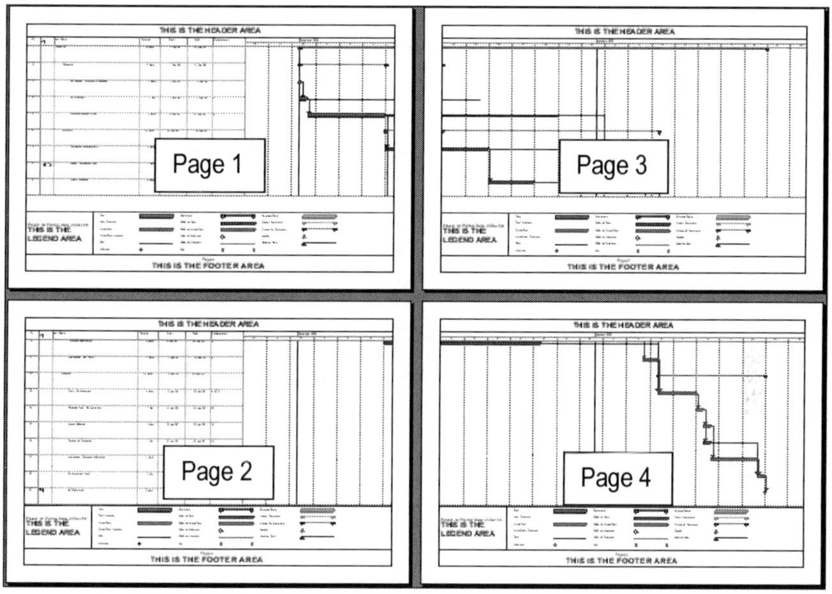

15.3.2 Margins Tab

With this option you may choose the margins around the edge of the printout.

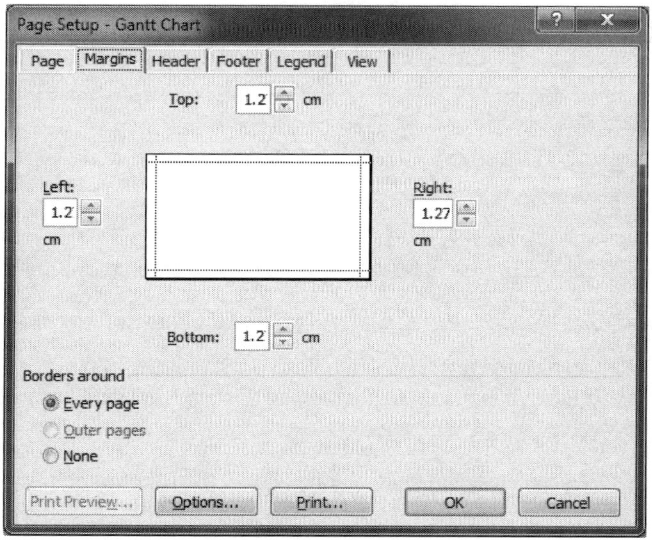

- Type in the margin size around the page. It is best to allow a wider margin for an edge that is to be bound or hole-punched; 1 inch or 2.5 cm is usually sufficient. The units of measurement, in. or cm, are adopted from the operating system **Control Panel**, **Regional and Language Option** settings.
- Microsoft Project will print a border around the Gantt Chart bars and Columns. **Borders around** places a border line around the outside of all text in the Headers and Footers. There are three options:
  - **Every page** – This places a border around every page.
  - **Outer pages** – This capability is only available with a **Network Diagram v**iew. It allows you to join all the pages into one large printout with a border only on the outside edge of all the pages once they are joined up.
  - **None** – Does not place a border on any sheets of the printout.

15.3.3 Header, Legend and Footer Tabs

Headers appear at the top of the screen above all schedule information and footers are located at the bottom, below the **Legend** if it has been selected to be displayed. Both the headers and footers are formatted in the same way. We will discuss the setting up of footers in this chapter.

Click on the **Footer** tab from the **Page Setup** form. This will display the settings of the default footers and headers.

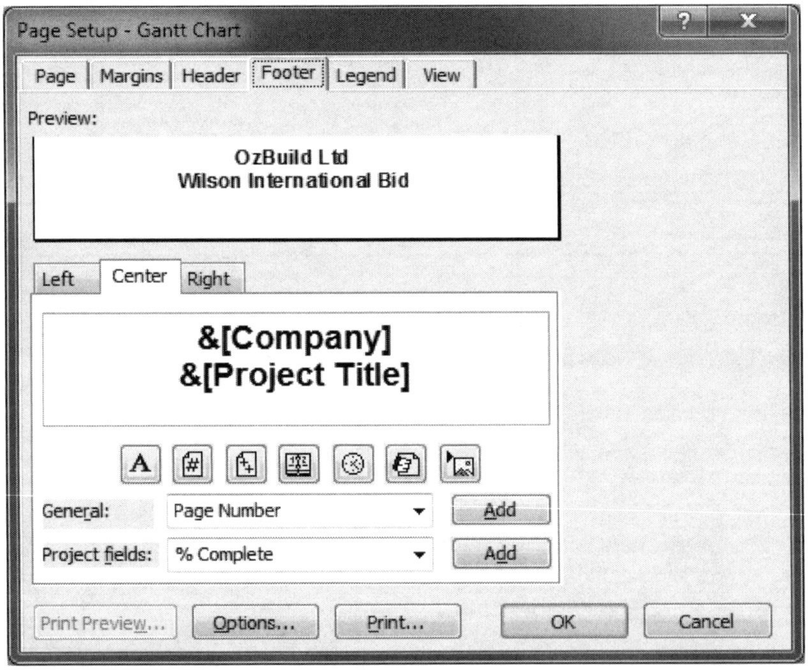

- **Preview:** – The box at the top of the form shows how your Footer will be displayed.
- Text may be placed in all three positions in the Footer and Header – on the Left, Center. Right-click on the required tab to insert new text or remove existing text in the box below.
- Text may be added by using a number of methods:
  - Freeform text may be typed into the footer box below the **Alignment:** box,

- Add data in the footer by clicking one of these buttons, **Page Number**, **Total Page Count**, **Current Date**, **Current Time**, **File Name** or **Insert Picture** (for example a corporate logo),
- To insert Microsoft Project field-type information to your footer, click on Add to insert the field into the footer. You may select from the drop-down box to the right of **General:** or **Project fields:**,
- To format the text you must first highlight the text and then click on the **Format Text Font** button A to open the **Font** form.
- Print Preview... – Returns you to the **Print Preview** form.
- Options... – Opens the **Printer Properties** form.
- Print... – Opens the **Print** form.
- OK – Accepts the changes.
- Cancel – Cancels any recent changes that have not yet been saved.

15.3.4 Legend Tab

The **Legend Text** is printed to the left of the **Legend**:

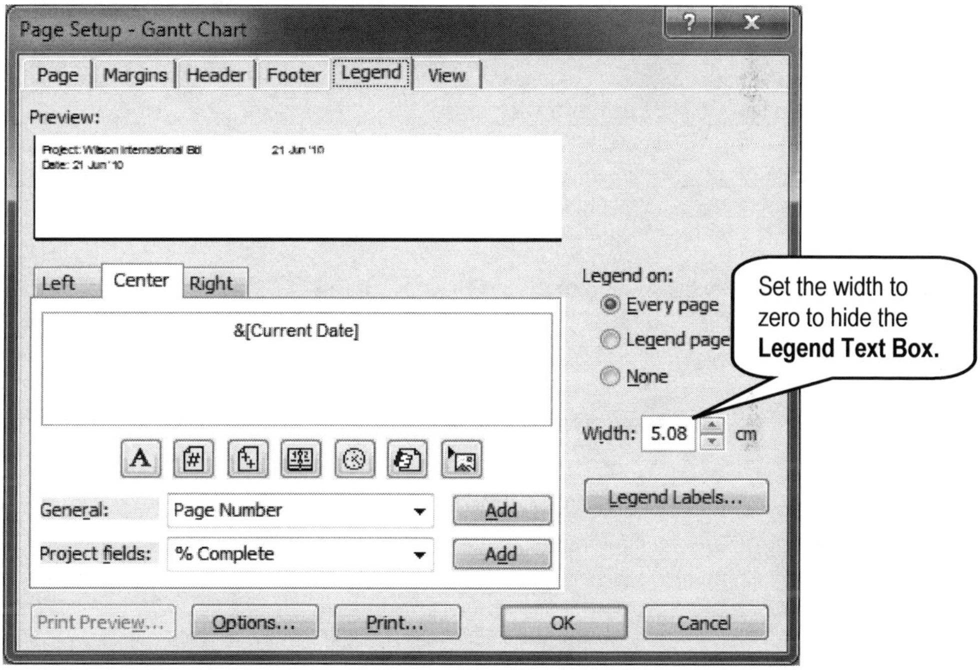

The **Legend Text** is formatted in the same way as the **Header** and **Footer**.

The **Legend** has three additional options not available in the **Header** and **Footer**.

- Click on the radio button below **Legend on:**
  - **Every page** will print the legend at the bottom of every page.
  - **Legend page** will print the legend on a separate page with no detailed schedule data, bars, or columns.
  - **None** will not print a legend.

- **Width:** sets the width of the **Legend Text**. Set the width to zero to hide the legend.
- Legend Labels... Opens the **Font** form for formatting the font of the text in the legend next to each of the bars and milestones.
- To hide a bar type in the Legend, type an "*" in front of the description in the **Bar Styles** form. This bar will still be displayed but will not be displayed in the Legend:

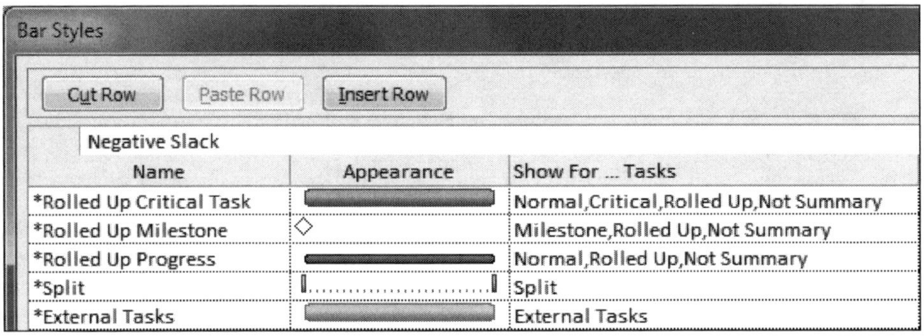

15.3.5 View Tab

The View tab has five options:

- **Print all sheet columns:** – This option applies to the left-most horizontal pages only when there is more than one page across a printout.
  - When checked, this option will print all the sheet columns displayed by the current table in the Gantt Chart, even if the columns are hidden by the vertical divider in the normal view.
  - When unchecked, this option will only print the completely visible columns.

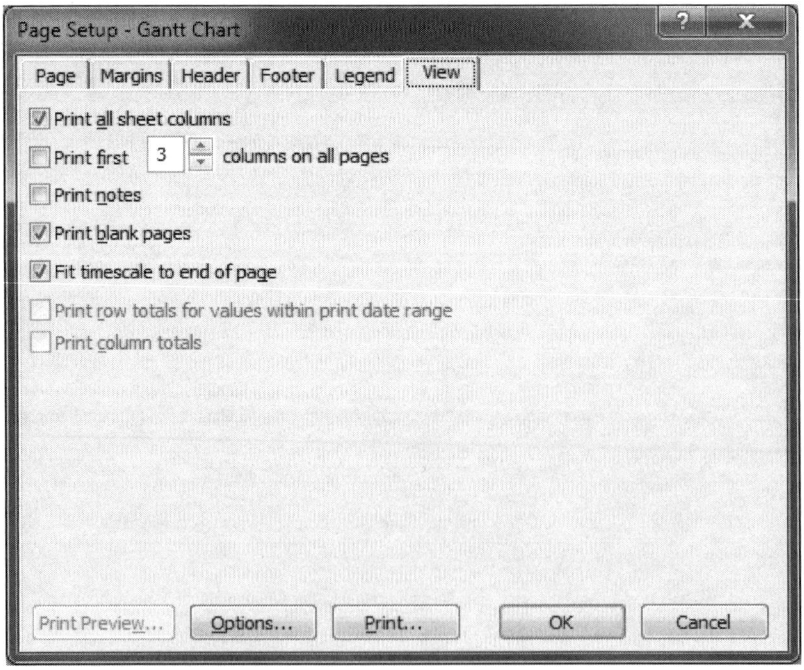

- **Print first ... columns on all pages** – Applies to all pages. The greater of the number of columns between this option and the options above will be printed on the first page.
  - **When checked**, this will allow repetitiously printing the selected number of columns on all pages.
  - **When unchecked**, this will not print any columns on the second and subsequent pages.
- **Print notes** will allow the printing of any **Notes** such as **Task Notes** on a separate page.
- **Print blank pages** will prevent the printing of all pages in the Gantt Chart, when there are no bars.
- **Fit timescale to end of page** will extend the timescale and associated bars so they fit to the end of a page, but sometimes you may find better results by turning this option off:
  - Option is checked, bars and timescale extend to the end of a page:

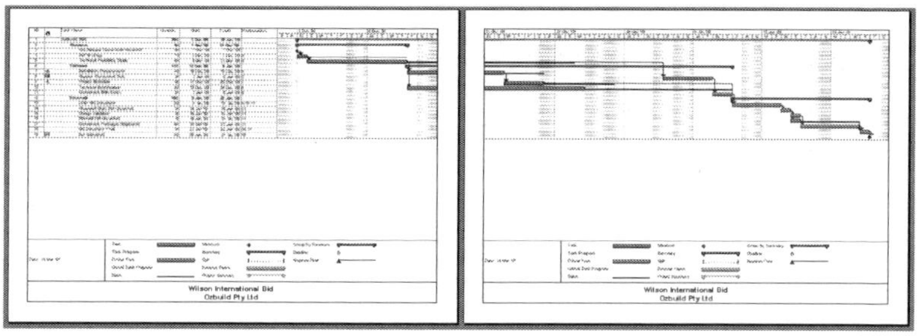

  - Option is unchecked, the bars stop in the middle of a page:

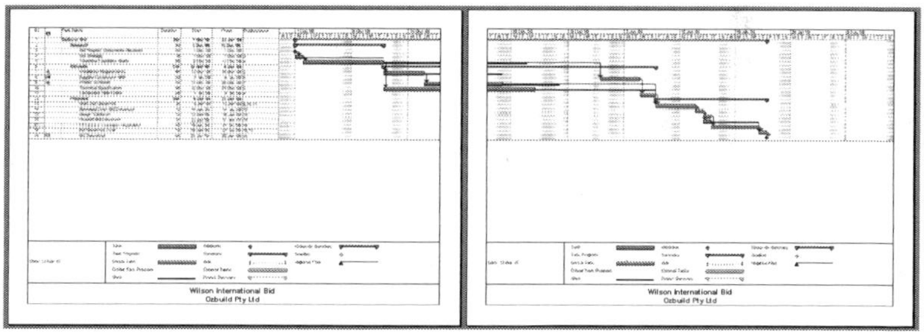

- **Print row totals for values within date range** and **Print column totals** options become available when tabular data is selected for printing such as a Resource Sheet view.

15.4 Manual Page Breaks

Manual page breaks may be inserted but these did not print on the author's install of Microsoft Project 2010 as the **Print** form **Manual page breaks** check box from the earlier version of Microsoft Project was missing and could not be found on any list of commands. This issue may be resolved at a later time with a software upgrade.

- Manual page breaks are inserted by:
- Placing the **Manual Page Break** button on the **Ribbon** or **Quick Access Toolbar**,
- Highlighting the row above where a page break is required. Then click on the **Manual Page Break** button. A dotted line will indicate the location of the manual page break.
- To remove a manual page break, highlight the row above where there is a page break and the **Manual Page Break** button.

15.5 Reports

The **Reports** are found at the **Project**, **Reports** group. There are two types of reports:

- **Visual** which were introduced with Microsoft Project 2007 and
- **Reports** which have been available for a long time.

15.5.1 Visual Reports

Select **Project**, **Reports** group **Visual Reports** to open the **Visual Reports - Create Report** form.

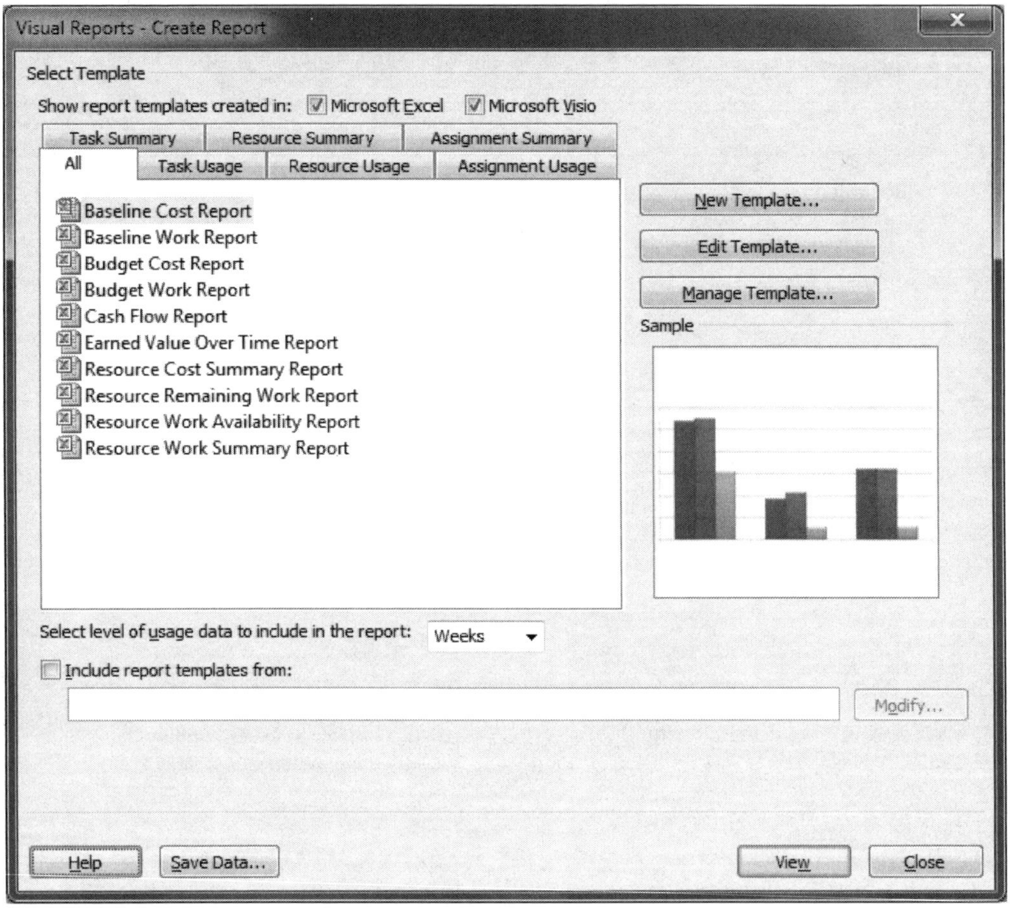

Visual Reports allow:

- The creation of reports, such as Histograms and Cash Flows, These are generated from templates to be exported and displayed in Excel or Visio.
- The templates may be modified and new ones created.

15.5.2 Reports

Select **Project**, **Reports** group, **Reports** to open the **Reports** form which displays six buttons.

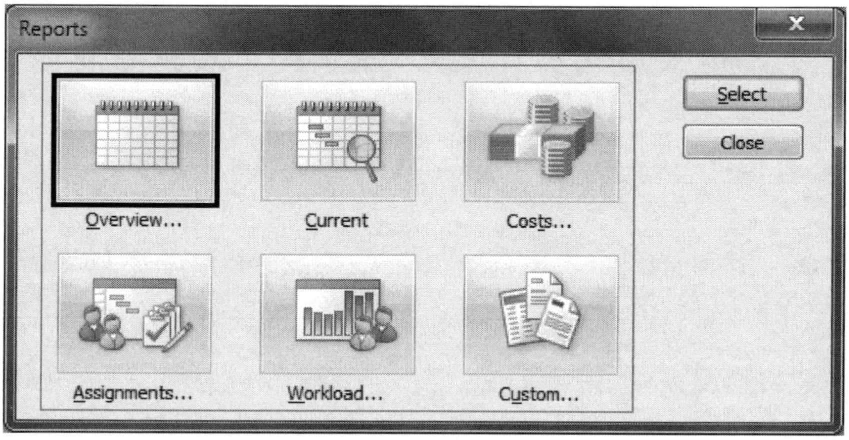

- Select a Report option by:
  - Double-clicking on any one of the buttons, or
  - Clicking on a button and clicking on the Select button.
- This will open up a menu of reports under the chosen heading. The picture below displays the **Current Tasks Reports** menu. The remaining five headings are done similarly and therefore are not explained in detail:

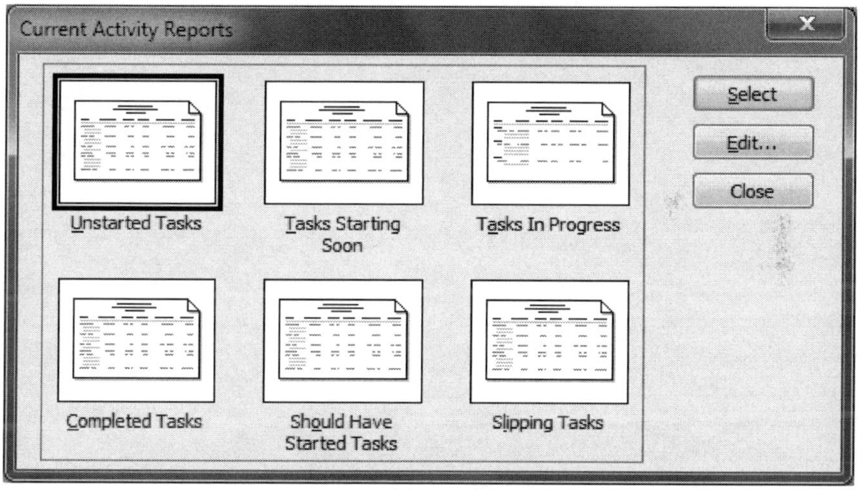

Double-click on any report and it will be sent to **Print Preview.** Here the print settings may be edited prior to printing.

Some of the report parameters may be further edited; for example, select the **Unstarted Tasks** report and click on the Edit... button to open the **Task Report** form.

15.6 Completed Schedule Check List

The following list could be used to check a completed schedule before submission:

- Check all calendars.
- Ensure there is a closed network with all tasks having a start predecessor and finish successor. This may be achieved by displaying the predecessor and successor columns.
- Check all relationships are valid.
- Review float. Tasks with excessive float should be assigned dummy successors or delayed if they are not scheduled in a realistic timeframe with sequencing logic or Early Start constraints.
- Check all constraints are valid and cross referenced to contract documentation or project management plan
- Check the full scope of the project has been captured.
- Ensure all stakeholders are represented and agree to their scope or work.
- Ensure all risk mitigation tasks have been added.
- Check the Critical Path is realistic and aligned with what project personnel consider critical.
- A resourced schedule should be optimized by checking the histograms and tables.
- Evaluate the contingent time.
- Ensure all project personnel are in agreement with the schedule.

15.7 Workshop 13 - Reports

Background

We want to issue a report for comment by management.

Assignment

Open your **OzBuild Bid** project from the previous workshop to complete the following steps:

1. Apply the **Gantt Chart** view.
2. Select the top pane and apply the **Entry** Table.
3. Ensure there is no filter applied.
4. Display only the Task ID, Indicators, Name, Duration, Start Date, Finish Date, Total Slack and Predecessors columns.
5. Adjust the columns to the best fit.
6. To fit all the tasks on one A4 or letter-size landscape page adjust the middle tier unit of timescale to **Months** with **Label** of **Jan '09** and bottom tier to **Weeks** with **Label** of **26**,2**...** and **Size** of **150%**.
7. Hide all the Rolled Up, Manual and External task bars by placing a * in front of the Bar Name of all Rolled Up, Manual, Inactive and External task bars in the **Bar Styles** form. These will then not be displayed in the legend.
8. Selecting **File**, **Print**, **Page Setup**
   - Set the page size to fit to 1 page wide by 1 page tall from the **Page** tab.
   - Remove any text from the **Header**.
   - Place only the **Company Name** and **Project Title** in the center of the **Footer** with a font of Calibri Bold 14.
   - Place only the System Date (Date) in the **Legend** at Calibri 8.
   - Select **Print all sheet columns** in the **View** tab.
9. Save your **OzBuild** project.
10. Compare your result with the picture on the next page.
11. We will baseline and progress the project in the next workshop, but we will require an unprogressed schedule for the resources workshops.
    - Save your OzBuild project as **OzBuild With Resources**.
    - Close this project and open your **OzBuild** project.

Answers to Workshop 13

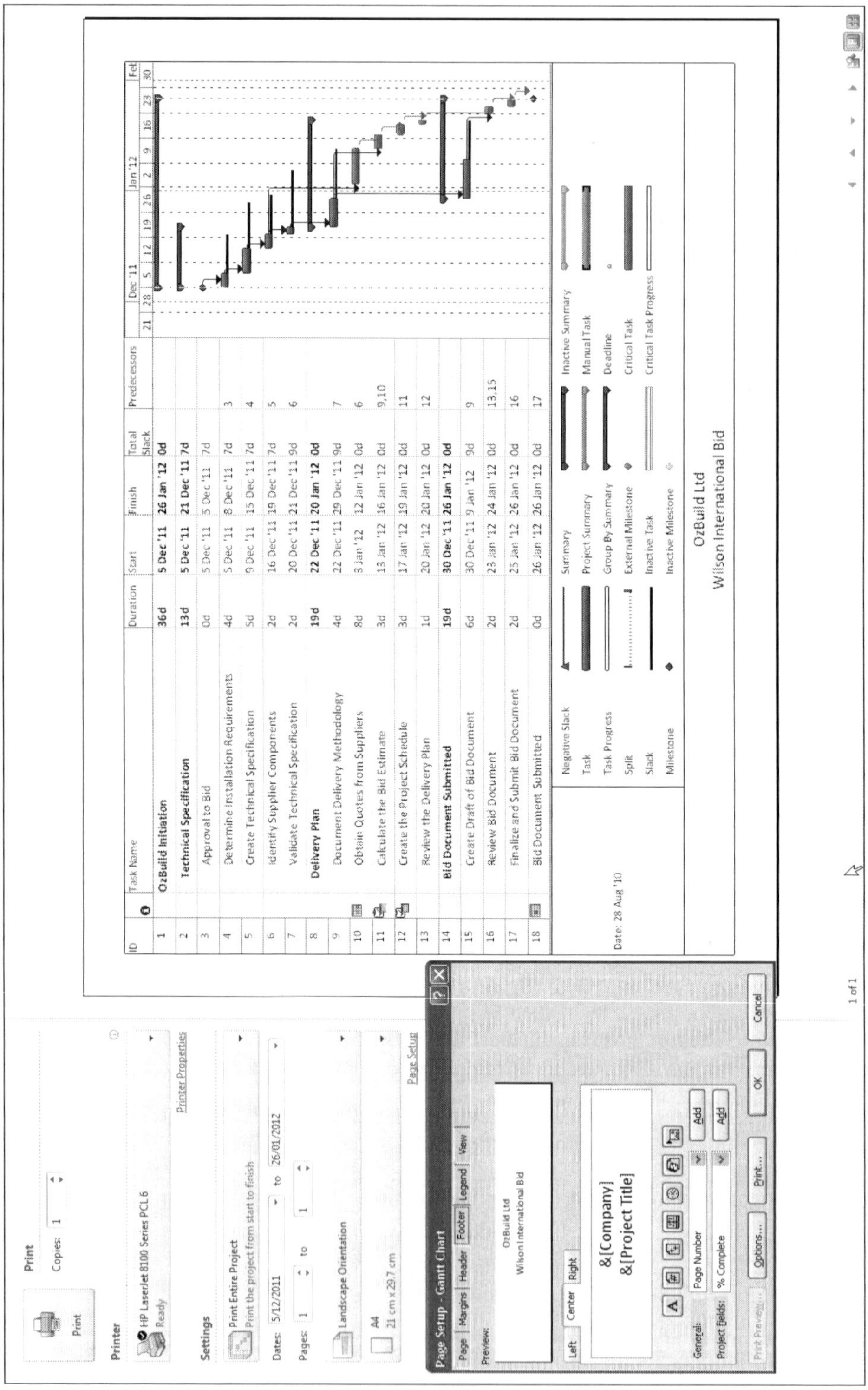

16 TRACKING PROGRESS

The process of tracking progress is used after the plan has been completed, the Baseline set and the project is underway. Now the important phase of regular monitoring begins. Monitoring is important to help predict problems as early as possible, and thus minimize the impact of problems on the successful completion of the project.

Many schedules are updated in Microsoft by just entering the task % Complete and not adjusting the Actual dates and durations. The result of this process is an un-impacted progressed schedule which will visually indicate which tasks are ahead of time or behind time, but the current dates are always equal to the Baseline dates. This process results in a schedule that:

- Does not reforecast a revised project finish date,
- May not be used to calculate delays, extensions of time or acceleration,
- May result with completed work in the future and incomplete work in the past which is not logical.

This book will focus on the process of updating a schedule to create an impacted schedule which will reforecast a revised project finish date. The main steps for monitoring progress are:

- Set the **Baseline Dates**, also known as **Target Dates** in some software. These are the dates against which progress is compared.
- Approve the work to commence in accordance with the plan.
- Record or mark-up progress as of a specific date, the **Status Date**. This date is also known as the **Data Date**, **Current Date**, **Report Date, Update Date**, **Time Now** and **As-of-Date**.
- **Update** or **Status** the schedule with **Actual Start** and **Actual Finish** dates where applicable, and adjust the task Actual and Remaining durations and/or % Complete.
- Compare and **Report** actual progress against planned progress and revise the schedule, if required, to forecast future tasks and milestones.
- Implement any corrective action to bring the project back on schedule.

By the time you get to this phase you should have a schedule that compares your original plan with the current plan, showing where the project is ahead or behind. If you are behind, you should be able to use this schedule to plan appropriate remedial measures to bring the project back on target.

This chapter will cover the following topics:

Topic	Menu Command
• Setting, resetting and clearing the **Baseline**	Select **Project**, **Schedule** group, **Set Baseline**, **Set Baseline...**
• **Current Date** and **Status Date**	May be edited from the **Project**, **Properties** group, **Project Information** form.
• Automatically update the schedule	Select **Project**, **Status**, **Update Project**
• Move the **Incomplete Work** of an **In-progress** task into the future	Select **Project**, **Status**, **Update Project**
• Updating the Tasks	Select **Task**, **Schedule** group

16.1 Setting the Baseline

Setting the Baseline copies the following information into Baseline fields in the existing file:

- **Start** and **Finish** dates into fields titled **Baseline Start** and **Baseline Finish**.
- **Duration** into the **Baseline Duration**.
- Each resource's **Costs** and **Work** into **Baseline Costs** and **Baseline Work** (work is typically the number of hours) when resources are assigned to tasks.

Once the Baseline is set and changes are made to the schedule, you will be able to compare your progress with your original plan and you will be able to see if you are ahead or behind schedule and by how much.

Some important points you should understand before setting the Baseline:

- The Baseline Dates should be established before you update the schedule for the first time and are usually subject to an official approval process.
- The Baseline Dates and Duration fields are not calculated fields, so they may be edited in columns and forms. Caution should be used before changing a Baseline Date or Duration, since it is the basis for all project deviation measurements.
- Summary tasks scheduled Start, Finish, Duration, Costs and Work are recalculated as detail tasks are added or deleted. Setting the Baseline copies these values but the Baseline values are **NOT** recalculated when new tasks are created or existing tasks are moved to a different Summary task.
- Setting the Baseline Date does not store the logic, float/slack times, or constraints.
- A Baseline is normally applied to all tasks irrespective of their Outline levels.
- New tasks do not have a baseline when created.

16.1.1 Setting Baseline Dates

To set the Baseline, select **Project**, **Schedule** group, **Baseline**, **Set Baseline...** to display the **Set Baseline** form.

- The **Set Baseline** option copies the **Start** and **Finish** dates and **Duration** into the **Baseline** fields.
- When resources and costs have been assigned then these are baselined at the same time.
- You may highlight some tasks before opening the **Set Baseline** form and click on the **Selected tasks** radio button to set the Baseline for the specified tasks only.

This operation will overwrite any previous Baseline settings.

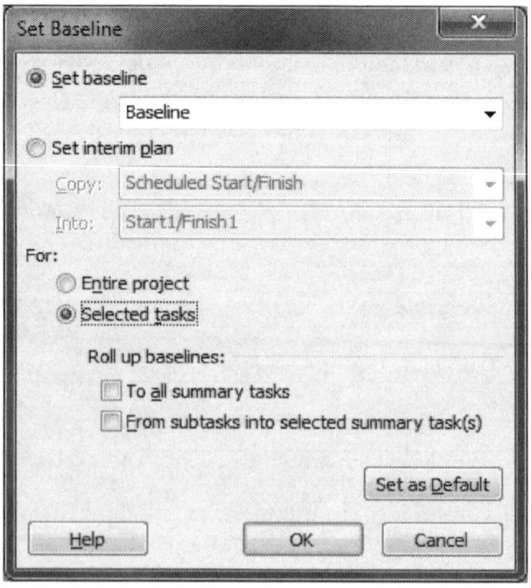

The **Set Baseline** form default settings selects and baselines **All Tasks** and the task Start and Finish dates which are titled **Start/Finish**. This is the normal method of setting the Baseline.

After establishing the Baseline, you can input the progress data without fear of losing the original dates. This will also enable you to compare the progress with the original plan.

16.1.2 Clearing and Resetting the Baseline

You may clear some or all of the Baseline fields using the **Clear Baseline** form. This is opened by selecting **Project**, **Schedule** group, **Baseline**, **Clear Baseline plan**:

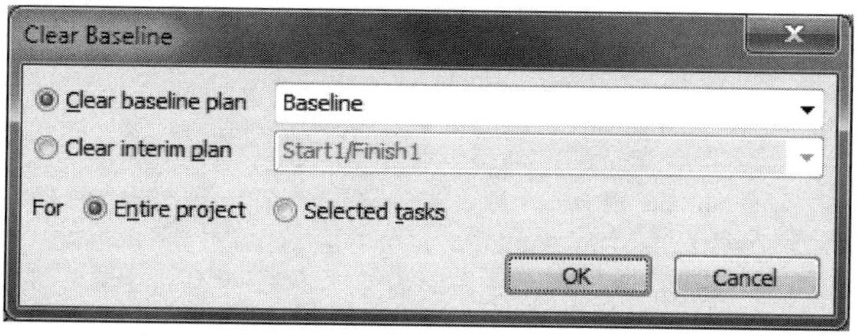

16.1.3 Displaying the Baseline Data

The Baseline dates data may be displayed by:

- Displaying the Baseline columns where the data may be edited, or
- Displaying the dates in a form such as the Resources Details Form. This will only display the **Baseline** data and not **Baseline 1** to **10**, or
- Show a baseline bar on the Bar Chart.

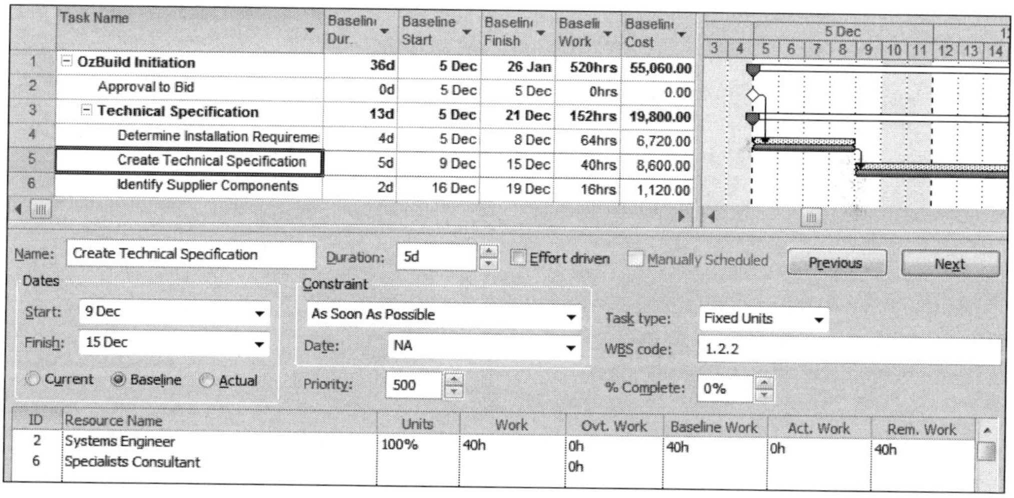

The Baseline Start Dates, Finish Dates and Durations may be edited and are not linked by logic. Therefore, a change to a Baseline Duration will not affect either the Baseline Start Date or the Baseline Finish date.

16.2 Practical Methods of Recording Progress

Normally a project is updated once a week, fortnightly, or monthly. Very short projects could be updated daily or even by the shift or hour. As a guide, a project would typically be updated between 12 and 20 times in a project life cycle. Progress is recorded on or near the **Status Date** and the scheduler updates the schedule upon the receipt of the progress information.

The following information is typically recorded for each task when updating a project:

- The task Actual Start date and time if required,
- The number of days/hours remaining on the **Task** or when the task is expected to finish,
- The percentage complete, and
- If complete, the task Actual Finish date and time, if required.

A marked-up copy recording the progress of the current schedule is often produced prior to updating the data in Microsoft Project. Ideally, the mark-up should be prepared by a physical inspection of the work or by a person who intimately knows the work. It is good practice to keep this marked-up record for your own reference at a later date. Ensure that you note the date of the mark-up (i.e., the data date) and, if relevant, the time. It is important to ensure that each Actual Start and Actual Finish date be tied to independent evidence such as daily reports or photographs when a project is likely to be subject to dispute resolution.

Often an Updating Report or mark-up sheet, such as the one below, is distributed to the people responsible for marking up the project progress. The marked-up sheets are returned to the scheduler for data entry into the software system.

A View, such as the one below, could be created for recording progress:

- It may have a filter applied to display only tasks that are in-progress or due to start in the next few weeks.
- A manual page break could be placed at each responsible person's band, so when the schedule is printed each team member would have a personal listing of their tasks that are either in-progress or due to commence. This is particularly useful for large projects.

	Task Name	Duration	% Comp	Start	Actual or Expected Start	Finish	Actual or Expected Finish
	⊟ **Reponsibility: Angela Lowe - Purchasing**	**4d**	**0%**		**NA**		**NA**
8	Supplier Component Bids	3 days	0%	2 Jan	NA	6 Jan	NA
11	Component Bids Costs	2 days	0%	7 Jan	NA	8 Jan	NA
17	Component Packages Negotiated	4 days	0%	16 Jan	NA	21 Jan	NA
	⊟ **Reponsibility: Carol Peterson - Bid Manager**	**4d**	**0%**		**NA**		**NA**
4	Bid Strategy	1 day	0%	1 Dec	NA	1 Dec	NA
9	Project Schedule	4 days	0%	18 Dec	NA	23 Dec	NA
14	Reviewed Draft Bid Document	1 day	0%	14 Jan	NA	14 Jan	NA
16	Revised Bid Document	1 day	0%	15 Jan	NA	15 Jan	NA
18	Bid Document Final	1 day	0%	22 Jan	NA	22 Jan	NA
	⊟ **Reponsibility: David Williams - Account Manager**	**3d**	**0%**		**NA**		**NA**
3	Bid Request Documents Received	0 days	0%	1 Dec	NA	1 Dec	NA
13	Draft Bid Document	3 days	0%	9 Jan	NA	13 Jan	NA

Other electronic methods, discussed next, may be employed to collect the data. Irrespective of the method used, the same data needs to be collected.

The above View has been created by:

- Renaming Text 1 as Responsibility using **Project**, **Properties** group, **Custom Fields** form
- Entering the responsible person in Text ,and
- Grouping by Text 1, which has been renamed **Responsibility**.

There are several methods of collecting the project status:

- By talking to the responsible people,
- By sending a hard copy to each responsible person to mark up and return to the scheduler.
- By cutting and pasting the data from Microsoft Project into another tool, such as Excel, and emailing the data to each responsible person as an attachment.
- By giving the responsible party direct access to the schedule software to update it. This approach is not recommended, unless the project is broken into sub-projects. By using the sub-project method, only one person updates each part of the schedule.
- Microsoft Project Server, a companion Microsoft Project product that allows collaborative scheduling, and time sheeting could be implemented. This topic is beyond the scope of this book.
- By using a task-based timesheet system which would also collect the hours expended on each task, and potentially the estimated remaining work and duration required to complete the task.

Some projects involve a number of people. In such cases, it is important that procedures be written to ensure that the status information is collected:

- In a timely manner,
- Consistently,
- In a complete manner, and
- In a usable format.

It is important for a scheduler to be aware that some people have great difficulty in comprehending a schedule. When there are a number of people with different skill levels in an organization, it will be necessary to provide more than one method of updating the data. You even may find that you have to sit down with some people to obtain the correct data, yet others are willing and comfortable to email you the information.

16.3 Understanding Tracking Progress Concepts

There are some terms and concepts used in Microsoft Project that must be understood before we update a project schedule:

16.3.1 Task Lifecycle

There are three stages of a task's lifecycle:

- **Not Started** – The **Early Start** and **Early Finish** dates are calculated from the logic, **Calendars**, **Constraints** and the **Task Duration**.
- **In-Progress** – The task has an **Actual Start** but is not complete. Milestones may be in-progress in Microsoft Project but in reality they should either be Not Started or Complete.
- **Complete** – The task is in the past, the **Actual Start** and **Actual Finish** dates have been entered into Microsoft Project, and they override the logic and constraints.

16.3.2 Actual Start Date Assignment

This section will explain how Microsoft Project assigns the **Early Start** of an **In-Progress** task.

- When an **Actual Start** is entered into the **Actual Start** field, this date overrides the **Early Start date**. The predecessor logic and start date constraints are ignored. **NOTE:** If **Split in-progress tasks** is checked in the **File**, **Options**, **Schedule** tab, **Scheduling options for this project:** section, then a successor may split a task when the successor is commenced before the predecessor finish date.
- For an un-started task, **Actual Start** date is set to equal the **Early Start** date when:
  - A **% Complete** between 1% and 100% is entered, or
  - An **Actual Duration** is entered, or
  - An **Actual Finish** is entered, or
  - An update schedule or task function is used.
- When a % Complete of 100% is entered, then an **Actual Start** date is set equal to the **Early Start** and an **Actual Finish** date equal to the **Early Finish** date are both set.

16.3.3 Calculation of Actual & Remaining Durations of an In-Progress Task

- The **Actual Duration** is normally the worked duration of a task.
- The **Remaining Duration** is the un-worked duration of a task.
- **Duration** = **Actual Duration** + **Remaining Duration**. Before a task is commenced the **Actual Duration** is zero and the **Remaining Duration** equals the **Duration** assigned to the task.
- There is an in-built proportional link between **Duration**, **Actual Duration**, **Remaining Duration** and **% Complete**. It is not possible to unlink these fields (as in other scheduling software) and therefore not possible to enter the **Remaining Duration** independently of the **% Complete**. The following explains the relationship between these fields:
  - Change the **Duration**: the **Actual Duration** remains constant and the **% Complete** and the **Remaining Duration** changes proportionally.
  - Change the **% Complete**: the **Duration** remains constant and the **Actual Duration** and the **Remaining Duration** changes proportionally.
  - Change the **Actual Duration**: the **Duration** remains constant and the **% Complete** and the **Remaining Duration** changes proportionally.
  - Change the **Remaining Duration**: the **Actual Duration** remains constant and the **% Complete** and the **Duration** changes proportionally.

- When the **% Complete** is set to 100 or the **Remaining Duration** is set to zero, the **Actual Finish** date is set to the **Early Finish date** and the **Actual Duration is** set to the **Duration**.

The **Physical % Complete** column maybe displayed and updated when a task % Complete is required that is not related to the Durations. This leaves % complete as % time complete. **The Physical % Complete** field does not summarize to summary tasks.

The example below shows three tasks, the first un-started, the second in-progress and the third complete. You should observe:

- The relationship between the **Duration**, **Actual Duration**, **Remaining Duration** and **% Complete** in each of the tasks, and
- How the **Actual Start** and **Actual Finish** are set.

	Start	Act. Start	Finish	Act. Finish	% Comp.	Dur	Act. Dur.	Rem. Dur.
1	2 Nov	NA	13 Nov	NA	0%	10d	0d	10d
2	2 Nov	2 Nov	13 Nov	NA	25%	10d	2.5d	7.5d
3	2 Nov	2 Nov	13 Nov	13 Nov	100%	10d	10d	0d

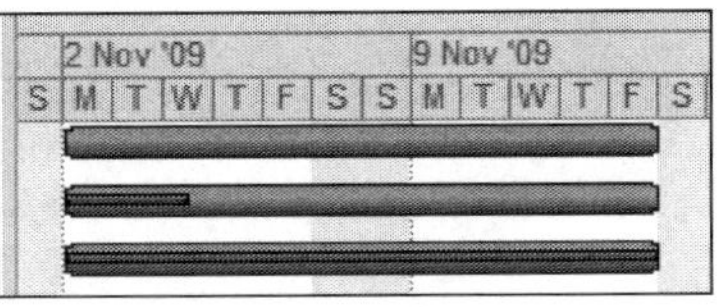

Unlike in Oracle Primavera software, it is not possible in Microsoft Project to unlink the **Remaining Duration** and **% Complete**. This may prove frustrating to some schedulers, as you will not be able use the **% Complete** column to represent the amount of deliverables complete when the task is not progressing at a linear rate. The Physical % Complete could be used to represent the amount of deliverables complete when the task is not progressing at a linear rate.

Furthermore, Microsoft Project calculates the Finish Date of a task from the Actual Start plus the Duration. It ignores the Remaining Duration, the Current Date and Status Date when calculating the Finish Date of a task. Oracle Primavera users will find this a difficult concept to understand but these concepts must be understood to use Microsoft Project effectively.

16.3.4 Calculating the Early Finish Date of an In-Progress Task

Retained Logic and Progress Override are not terms used by Microsoft Project documentation. These terms are used by other Oracle Primavera software and are used here to help clarify how Microsoft Project performs its calculations. In the example below, there are two tasks with a Finish-to-Start relationship:

	Act. Start	Act. Finish	% Comp.
1	NA	NA	0%
2	NA	NA	0%

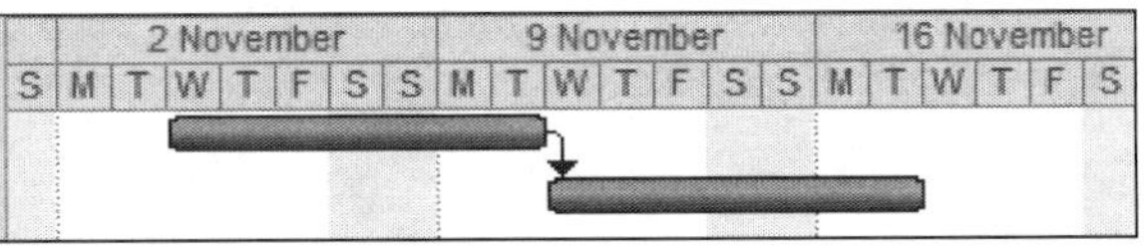

There are two options for calculating the finish date of the successor when the successor task starts before the predecessor task is finished:

- **Retained Logic**. In the example below, the logic relationship is maintained between the predecessor and successor for the un-worked portion of the Task, the Remaining Duration, and continues after the predecessor has finished.

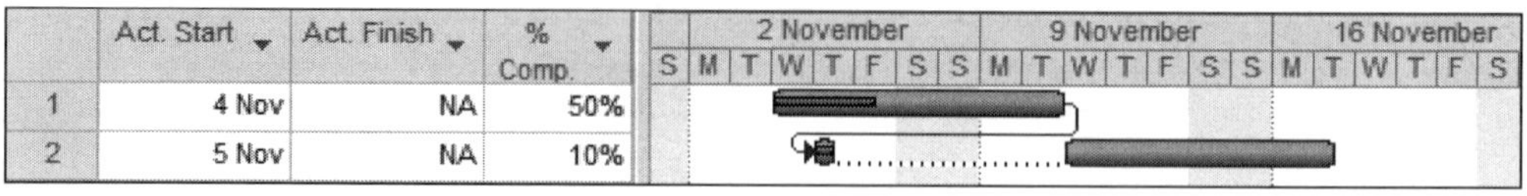

This option will operate when:

- ➢ The Project Option **Split in-progress tasks** is checked, and
- ➢ There is an **Actual Start**, and
- ➢ A **% Complete** between 1% and 99% is assigned to the successor task.

- **Progress Override**. In the example below, the Finish-to-Start relationship between the predecessor and successor is disregarded, and the un-worked portion of the Task, the Remaining Duration, continues before the predecessor has finished:

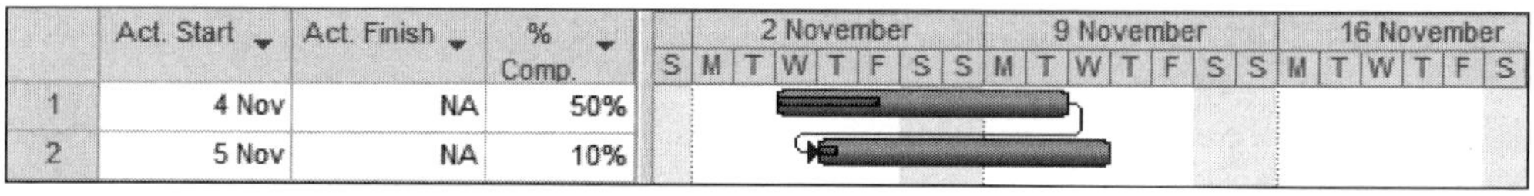

Progress Override option will operate when:

- ➢ The Project Option **Split in-progress tasks IS NOT** checked, and
- ➢ The task has an **Actual Start** and 0% Complete and Project Option **Split in-progress tasks IS** checked.

Be aware that this function calculates differently to earlier versions of Microsoft Project and will split a successor task when an actual start is assigned to a successor that is earlier than the Start date and the % Complete is zero.

This function may result in some problems in reporting a schedule when the **Split in-progress tasks** option is used. The two examples below are from the same schedule, both with the **Split in-progress tasks** option checked but the Actual date and % Complete were entered in a different order so different results are obtained:

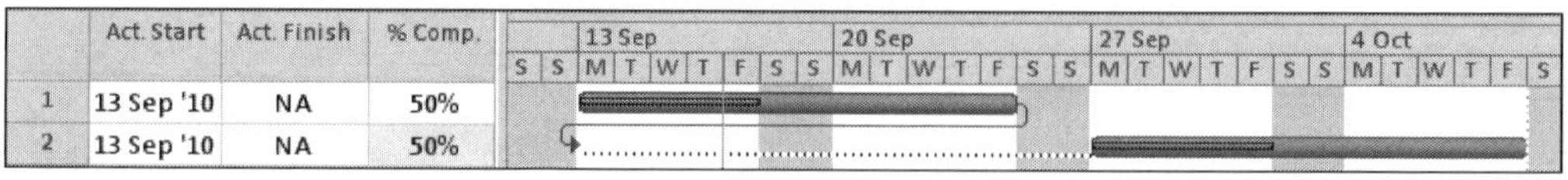

NOTE: You may wish to experiment with a Finish-to-Finish lag if these options do not give a satisfactory result.

16.3.5 Updating Completed tasks

Normally completed tasks are updated with actual dates that match when the task started and finished. To update a completed task:

- Enter the Actual Start date, the date the task actually started and then either:
  - Enter the Actual Finish Date and then the % Complete will be set to 100% or
  - Adjust the Remaining Duration until the task Finish Date is the same as when the task actually finished, then enter 100%.
- Alternatively enter 100% and adjust the Actual Start and then the Actual Finish.

16.3.6 Summary Bars Progress Calculation

Summary bars are not normally updated by entering the **Actual Start** date, **Actual Finish** date, or **% Complete** against them. This is possible in Microsoft Project and is covered later in the section titled **Marking Up Summary Tasks**, see para 22.9.6.

This status information is usually entered against the detail tasks, so the summary tasks inherit the status data from the detail tasks.

- An **Actual Start** is assigned against a summary task when any detail task has an **Actual Start**.
- A summary task's **% Complete** is calculated from the total of all the detail tasks' **Actual Durations** divided by the total of all the detail tasks' **Durations**. This may be misleading when Milestones have been marked complete and no progress is calculated on the summary bar.
- A summary task's **Actual** and **Remaining Durations** are calculated from the **Duration** and **% Complete**.
- An **Actual Finish** is assigned against a summary task when all detail tasks have an **Actual Finish**.

16.3.7 Understanding the Current Date, Status Date & Update Project Date

Microsoft Project has two project Data Date fields that may be displayed as vertical lines on the schedule. These dates may be edited from the **Project**, **Properties** group, **Project Information** form:

- **Current Date** – This date is set to the computer's date each time a project file is opened. It is used for calculating **Earned Value** data when a **Status Date** has not been set. By default this is set to **Default start time:** in the **File**, **Options**, **Schedule** tab, **Calendar options for this project:** section. This is not generally used.
- **Status Date** – This field is blank by default with a value of **NA**. When this date is set, it will not change when the project is saved and reopened at a later date. When set, this date overrides the **Current Date** for calculating **Earned Value** data. After this date has been set then it may be displayed as a gridline and you remove the date by typing **NA** into the field. By default this is set to **Default end time** in the **Options** form.

NOTE: The **Current Date** is set to the **Default start time** and the **Status Date** is set to **Default end time**, so when both are set to the same date and displayed as grid lines, they will both be displayed, one at the start and one at the end of the day. See the picture below:

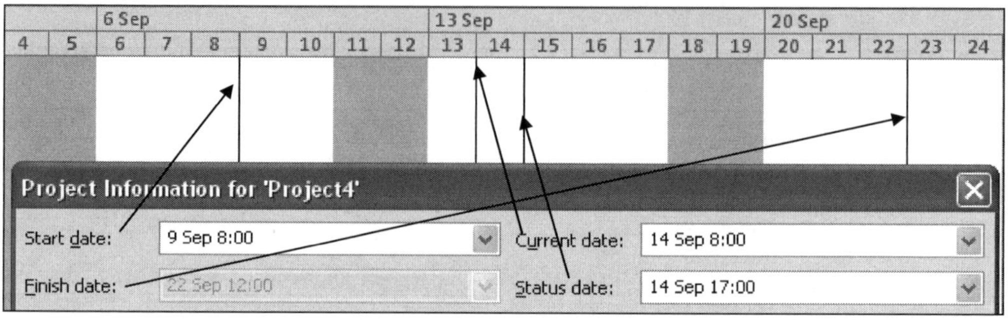

It is recommended that the **Status Date** be set and displayed as a vertical line on a progressed schedule and that the **Current Date** not be displayed, as the **Current Date** represents the date today and does not normally represent any scheduling significance.

The **Update Project Date** may also influence how Microsoft Project calculates the end date of some tasks. This date may not be displayed as a vertical line on the screen but may be used in conjunction with the **Reschedule uncompleted work to start after:** function covered later in this chapter.

NEITHER the **Current Date** nor the **Status Date** is used to calculate the **Early Finish** of an **In-Progress** task of a schedule using **F9** or **Automatic Scheduling**, unless one of the following two functions is used:

- The **Project**, **Status** group, **Update Project...**, **Reschedule incomplete to start after:** date, or
- The **Status Date** may be used to move the start of incomplete and the finish of completed parts of a task back or forward to the **Status Date** with the function **Status Date Calculation Options** (new to Microsoft Project 2002). This option will be discussed later in this chapter in para 16.4.7. It has restrictions that could make the function difficult to use on a project.

Project, **Status** group has the **Status Date** function that displays the **Current Status Date**, it will open the **Status Date** form where the status date may also be edited.

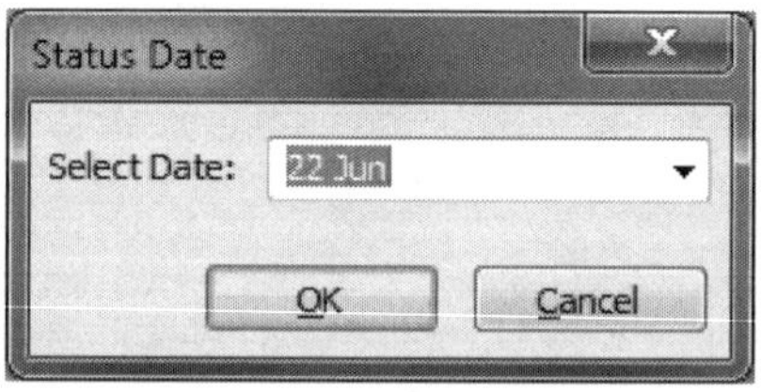

Ideally, scheduling software has one current **Data Date** and the function of it is to:

- Separate the completed parts of tasks from incomplete parts of tasks,
- Calculate or record all costs and hours to date before the data date, and to forecast costs and hours to go after the data date.
- Calculate the **Finish Date** of an in-progress task from the **Data Date** plus the **Remaining Duration** over the **Task Calendar**.

It is relatively easy to be in a situation where you have complete or in-progress tasks with start dates later than the data date, and/or incomplete or un-started tasks with a finish date earlier than the data date. This is an unrealistic situation, which is more difficult to achieve in other scheduling software packages. Care should be taken to avoid this situation and checks made after the schedule has been updated.

16.4 Updating the Schedule

The next stage is to update the schedule by entering the mark-up information against each task.

When dealing with large schedules, it is normal to create a look-ahead schedule with a filter to display incomplete and un-started tasks commencing in the near future only.

Microsoft Project provides several methods of updating the schedule:

- **Update Project** – This is an automated process that assumes all tasks have progressed as planned. After updating a project, you may adjust the dates and percent complete to the recorded progress.
- **Update Tasks** – This function is used to update tasks one at a time.
- Update tasks using the **Task** or **Task Details** form.
- Update tasks by displaying the appropriate tracking columns by:
  - Selecting the **Tracking** table, or
  - Creating your own table, or
  - Inserting the required columns in an existing table.

Each of these methods is discussed in the following sections. Then we will discuss the following two functions which are designed to assist you in moving tasks to their logical places in relation to the **Status Date**:

- Move incomplete work into the future, using the **Reschedule uncompleted work to start after: function**, see para 16.4.7 and
- Positioning tasks in a logical place in relation to the Status Date using the **Status Date Calculation Options** function, see para 22.9.4.

16.4.1 Move Project

This function is new to Microsoft Project 2010.

Project, **Schedule** group has the **Move Project** button which opens the **Move Project** form and allows the user to change the **Project Start Date**. When the **Move deadlines** check box is checked any Deadline Dates and constraints are also moved based on a 7-day per week calendar so moving a project one day will move a **Deadline Date** on a Friday to a Saturday:

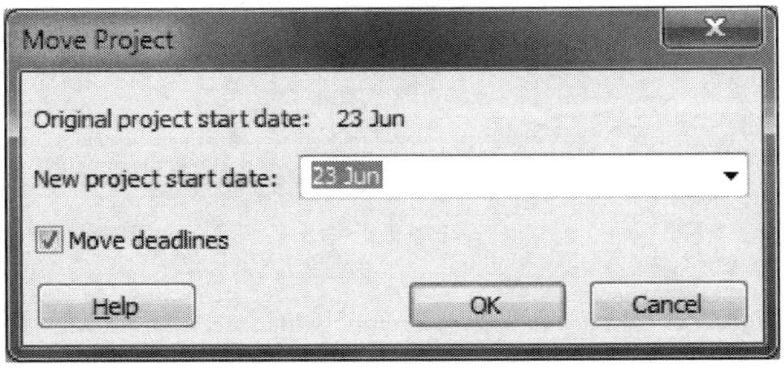

Baselines are not moved with this function.

16.4.2 Using Update Project

Microsoft Project has a function titled **Update Project** for updating a project as if it had progressed according to plan. This function sets **Actual Start** and **Actual Finish** dates, **% Complete** and **Renaming Durations** in proportion to a user-assigned date.

Add a button to the **Quick Access Toolbar** or select **Project**, **Status** group, **Update Project...** to open the **Update Project** form::

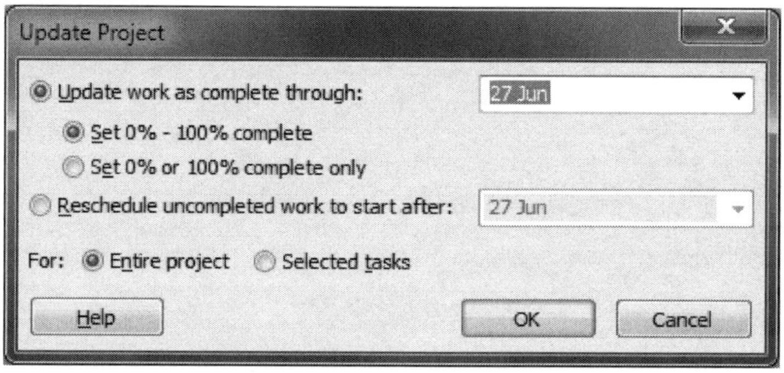

The two options under **Update work as complete through:** which apply to in-progress tasks only:

- **Set 0% – 100 % Complete**:
  - ➢ This option sets the **Status Date** to the date you have nominated as the update date. This is displayed as the vertical line in the Gantt Chart below create using the **Format Gridlines** function,
  - ➢ Sets the **Actual Start** to the **Start**, and
  - ➢ Sets the **% Complete** and **Actual Duration** in proportion to the amount of time worked for any in-progress tasks.

	Act. Start	Act. Finish	% Comp.	Duration	Act. Dur.	Rem. Dur.
1	4 Nov	10 Nov	100%	5 days	5 days	0 days
2	11 Nov	NA	40%	5 days	2 days	3 days
3	NA	NA	0%	5 days	0 days	5 days

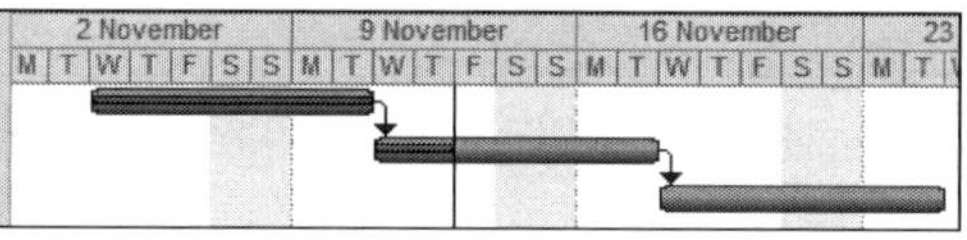

- **Set 0% or 100 % Complete only**. This option sets:
  - ➢ The **Actual Start** to the **Early Start** but leaves the **% Complete** and **Actual Duration** at zero.
  - ➢ The **% Complete** is set to 100% only when the task is complete.
  - ➢ Does not set the **Status Date** (or reset if it has been set in a previous update) to the date you have chosen as the update date. There is no vertical line representing the **Status Date** in the picture below:

	Act. Start	Act. Finish	% Comp.	uration	Act. Dur.	Rem. Dur.
1	4 Nov	10 Nov	100%	5 days	5 days	0 days
2	11 Nov	NA	0%	5 days	0 days	5 days
3	NA	NA	0%	5 days	0 days	5 days

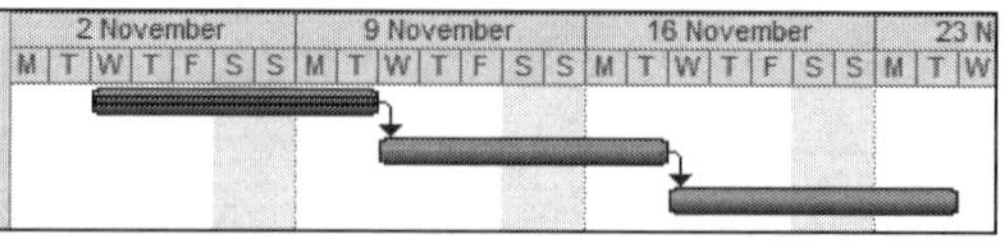

You may use the **Selected tasks** option when you highlight the tasks to be progressed before opening the **Update Project** form. Unselected tasks will not be progressed, but these tasks may be scheduled to occur after the **Status Date** by using the **Reschedule uncompleted work to start after:** function. This is covered later in this section.

You may not reverse progress with this option as one is able to do with SureTrak and Asta Powerproject.

16.4.3 Update Tasks Form

Microsoft Project has a function that may be used for updating tasks one at a time or may be used for updating selected tasks with the same information. For example, there may be several tasks with the same Actual Start or % Complete:

- Select one or more tasks that you want to update with the same information such as the same Actual Start date.
- Select **Task**, **Schedule** group, **Mark on Track**, **Update Tasks...** to open the **Update Tasks** form:

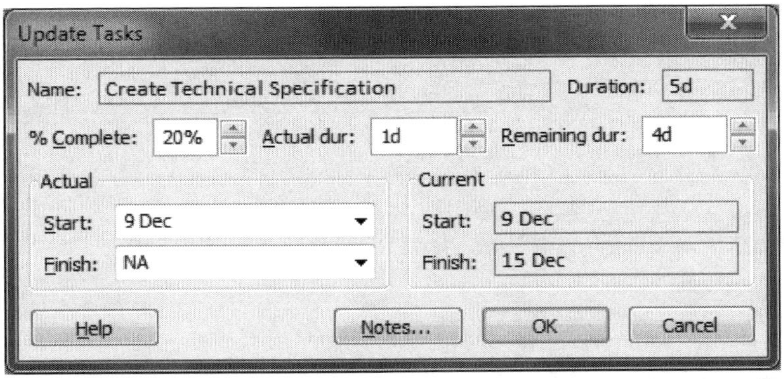

- Enter the required data and click on the OK button to close the form.

16.4.4 Updating Tasks Using the Task Information Form

You may use the **Task Information** form to update progress:

- Open the **Task** form by double-clicking on a task,
- Then the Percent complete and the dates may be edited.

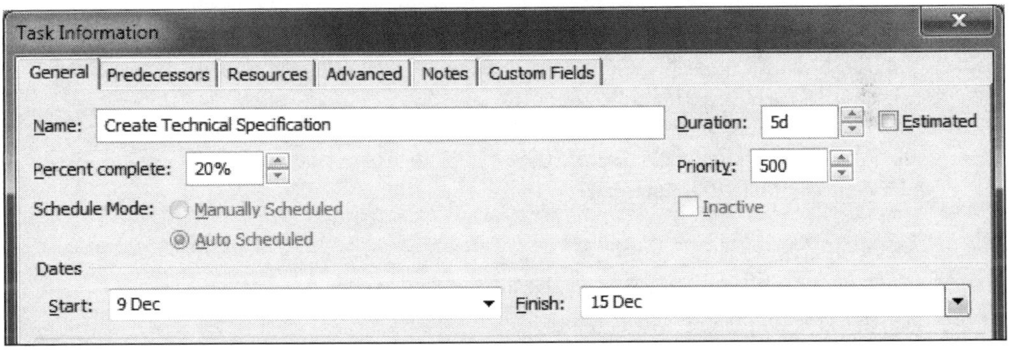

The **Task Information** form should not be used when the Actual and remaining durations are being adjusted to update a project.

Using the **Update Tasks** form or the **Task Information** form are cumbersome methods for updating a large number of individual tasks since the form has to be closed after each task has been updated, the cursor moved to the next task and the form reopened.

If you have a large number of tasks to be updated then it is quicker to use:

- Columns, or
- A Detailed form in the bottom pane, or
- The Task, Schedule group buttons.

16.4.5 Updating Tasks Using the Task Details Form

- To open the **Task Details** form, open the dual-pane view using the right-click **Show Split** command,
- Now open the **Task Details Form** by right-clicking in the dark band on the right-hand side of the screen,
- Select **More Views…** to open the **More Views** form,
- Select **Task Details Form**.

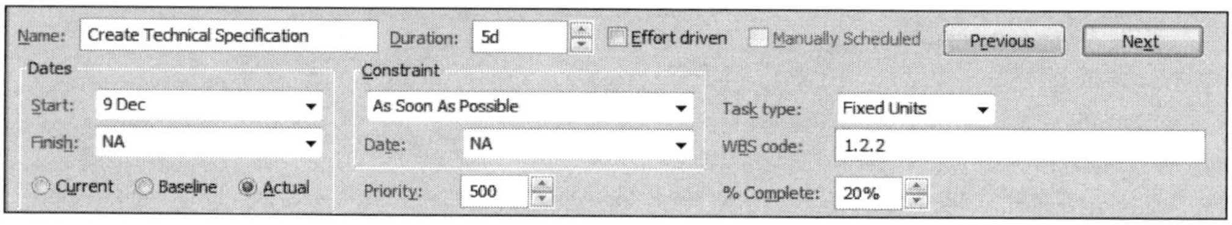

- Updating a task:
  - ➢ Click on the **Actual** radio button,
  - ➢ Enter the Actual Start date,
  - ➢ Enter a **% Complete**. An **Actual Start** date will be set by Microsoft Project when a % Complete is entered and may be edited from the **Start:** drop-down box,
  - ➢ The **Duration** may be edited in order to calculate a new finish date. You will note that the % Complete will change when durations are edited.
  - ➢ When a date is typed into the **Finish:** drop-down box, a **Finish Constraint** may be set without warning when the task is not 100% complete. These may be edited from the **Task Information** form's **Advanced** tab.

16.4.6 Updating Tasks Using Columns

An efficient method of updating tasks is by displaying the data in columns. This may be achieved by:

- Applying the **Tracking Gantt** view and the **Tracking Table**, or
- Creating your own table, or
- Inserting the required columns.

The tracking Table may not exist if you are working on a schedule that has had this table deleted or if you have a non-standard install of Microsoft Project in which this table has been deleted from the Global.mpt. If you do not use the tracking table, be sure to add the following columns: **Actual Start**, **Actual Finish**, **% Complete**, **Actual Duration**, and **Remaining Duration**.

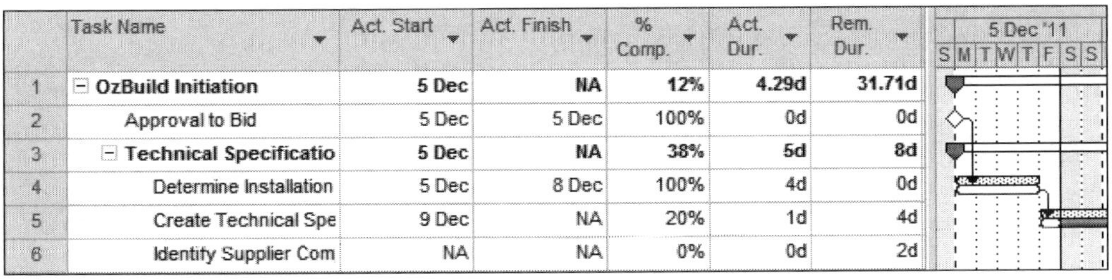

	Task Name	Act. Start	Act. Finish	% Comp.	Act. Dur.	Rem. Dur.
1	**OzBuild Initiation**	**5 Dec**	**NA**	**12%**	**4.29d**	**31.71d**
2	Approval to Bid	5 Dec	5 Dec	100%	0d	0d
3	**Technical Specificatio**	**5 Dec**	**NA**	**38%**	**5d**	**8d**
4	Determine Installation	5 Dec	8 Dec	100%	4d	0d
5	Create Technical Spe	9 Dec	NA	20%	1d	4d
6	Identify Supplier Com	NA	NA	0%	0d	2d

The status data may now be entered directly into the columns.

16.4.7 Reschedule Uncompleted Work To Start After

There is a feature available in the **Update Project** form titled **Reschedule uncompleted work to start after:** which will schedule the **Incomplete Work** of an **In-Progress** task to start on a specific date in the future.

If you want to apply this operation to some tasks, then these options should be selected first.

- Add a button to the **Quick Access Toolbar** or select **File**, **Options**, **Schedule** tab and ensure the **Split in-progress tasks** option is checked. If this option is not checked, then this function will not operate.

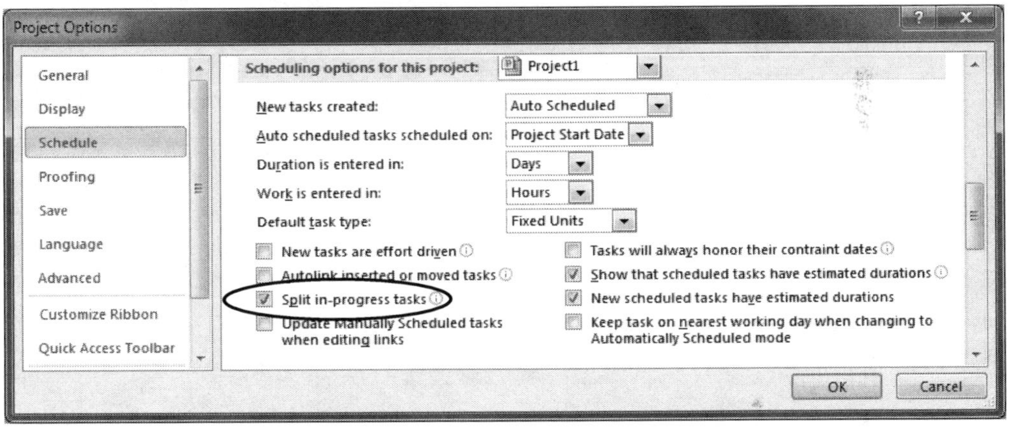

- Add a button to the Quick Access Toolbar or select Project, Status group, Update Project... to open the **Update Project** form:

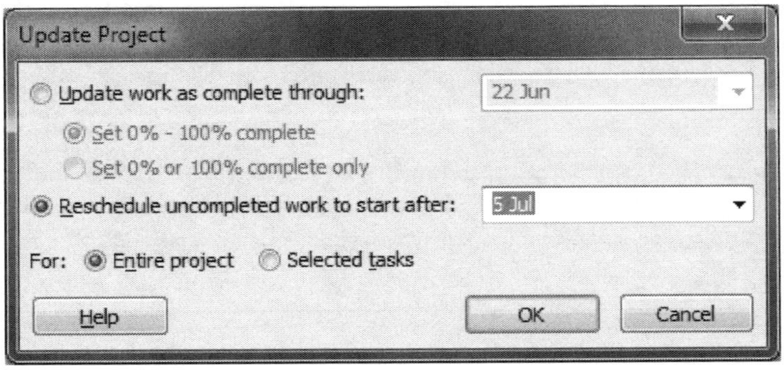

- Click on the **Reschedule uncompleted work to start after:** radio button.
- In the drop-down box to the right, specify the date after which incomplete work should commence. Then click on the OK button.

A task may be split without the split being displayed in the Gantt Chart by un-checking the **Show bar splits** in the **Format**, **Format** group **Layout** form. In the examples below, the **Incomplete Work** has been moved after 11 November:

- The task has been split in the picture below, the splits are displayed and the **Remaining Duration** is dependent on the Task Type, **Fixed Duration** tasks have a longer duration than **Fixed Units** and **Fixed Work**:

% Comp.	Duration	Act. Dur.	Rem. Dur.	Type
20%	15 days	3 days	12 days	Fixed Duration
20%	10 days	2 days	8 days	Fixed Units
20%	10 days	2 days	8 days	Fixed Work

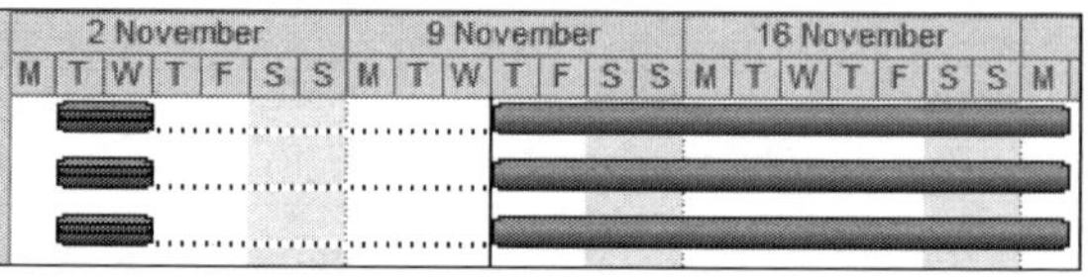

- The task has been split in the picture below and the splits **NOT** displayed; **Format**, **Format** group **Layout** form to hide splits and the **Remaining Duration** depends of the Task Type:

% Comp.	Duration	Act. Dur.	Rem. Dur.	Type
20%	15 days	3 days	12 days	Fixed Duration
20%	10 days	2 days	8 days	Fixed Units
20%	10 days	2 days	8 days	Fixed Work

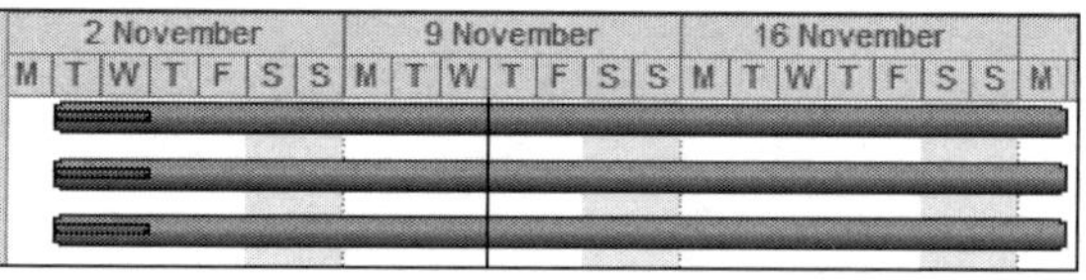

When a project is updated using the **Update Project** function, the **Status Date DOES NOT** change to equal the **Project Update Date**. You may end up with two dates that represent the **Data Date**—the **Update Project** date and the **Status Date**, which may both reflect different dates. The picture below shows the Status Date in the black vertical line at 11 November and the **Update Project** date set at 17 November, which has split the last task. In this situation the Status Date should be set manually.

	Act. Start	Act. Finish	% Comp	Dur	Act. Dur.	Rem. Dur.
1	2 Nov	6 Nov	100%	5 days	5 days	0 days
2	9 Nov	NA	60%	5 days	3 days	2 days
3	NA	NA	0%	5 days	0 days	5 days

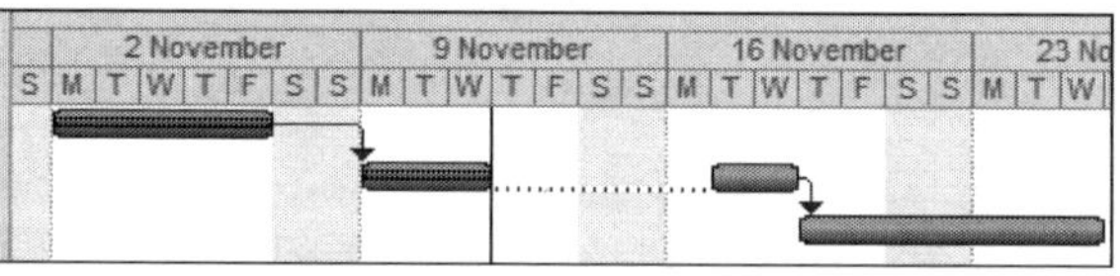

For tasks that are behind schedule, you may use the **Update Project** function to reschedule them after the **Update Project** date. This date will effectively become the **Data Date**. However, it is not possible to show the **Update Project** date as a vertical line on the bar chart. You may set and display the **Status Date** at the same date so incomplete work is all scheduled after a line displayed on the Gantt Chart.

i It is recommended when you use the **Update Project** function that you should open the **Project Information** form and set the **Status Date** to the same date as the **Update Project** date. This enables you to display a **Data Date** on the bar chart in the correct place.

16.4.8 Updating Tasks Using Task, Schedule Functions

The **Task**, **Schedule** group has the following functions. It has replaced the original **Tracking Toolbar** from earlier versions of Microsoft Project

- The 0% 25% 50% 75% 100% buttons will set the Percentage Complete as indicated. These will set an Actual Start Date and may be used to remove progress from a task.
- The **Mark on Track** button will progress the task to the Status Date as if it has progressed according to plan.

16.5 Simple Procedure for Updating a Schedule

For those people who require just one simple method of updating a schedule utilizing the **Update Project** function then the following process should be considered. It may not suit all situations especially when a project is way off plan. It is ideally suited to a situation when the plan is being closely followed and only minor adjustments are required to the actual dates and durations:

- Ensure that everyone on the project team is aware of the reporting cycle, the updating procedure and review process.
- Collect accurate and complete status information relative to the Status Date.
- Apply a suitable layout and table such as the Tracking layout and Tracking table.
- Set the Baseline by selecting **Project**, **Schedule** group, **Set Baseline**, **Set Baseline....**
- Display the Baseline bars by selecting **Format**, **Bar Styles** group and selecting **Baseline** or running the **Gantt Chart Wizard...** or use the **Format**, **Bar Styles** group, **Baseline** button.
- Display the Status Date Gridline, select **Format**, **Format** group, **Gridlines**, **Gridlines...**, select **Status Date**.
- Select **Project**, **Status** group, **Update Project** to open the **Update Project** form and select **Set 0% – 100 % Complete**, set the date in the form to the new **Status Date**.
- The project should be updated as if it has progressed exactly as planned and the Status Date should now be displayed in the bar chart.
- Now adjust the task dates by dragging the bars or entering the dates in the appropriate column; the order that the actions take place is important:
  - **Complete** tasks should have the Actual Start and then the Actual Finish dates adjusted to when the task actually started and actually finished.
  - **In-Progress tasks** should have the Actual Start adjusted first, then the task bar dragged so the finish date is where it is expected to finish and finally the % Complete adjusted.
  - **Unstarted** tasks should have their logic and durations revised.
  - Consider using the **Task**, **Schedule** group buttons at this point.
- Add any scope changes to the schedule.
- Unstarted tasks should have their logic and durations revised.
- Save the project with a new filename and save for future reference.

16.6 Procedure for Detailed Updating

This procedure is suited to people who wish to update a schedule properly and make sure the Actual dates and durations are correct. It has small but important differences to the previous process:

- Ensure that everyone on the project team is aware of the reporting cycle, the updating procedure and review process.
- Collect accurate and complete status information relative to the Status Date.
- Apply a suitable layout and table such as the Tracking layout and Tracking table.
- Set the Baseline by selecting **Project**, **Schedule** group, **Set Baseline**, **Set Baseline...**.
- Display the Baseline bars by selecting **Format**, **Bar Styles** group and selecting **Baseline** or running the **Gantt Chart Wizard...** or use the **Format**, **Bar Styles** group, **Baseline** button.
- Select the **Tracking Gant** view and you may find the **Tracking Table** useful to apply.
- Display the Variance columns; the **Finish Variance** is always a popular column to display.
- Display the **Status Date Gridline** and hide the **Current Date** gridlines by selecting **Format**, **Format** group, **Gridlines**, **Gridlines...**.
- Now enter the task status for each task one at a time by entering the information in the appropriate column.
- The order in which the data entry take place is important as different results will be obtained when data is entered in a different order:
  - **Complete tasks** should have the **Actual Start** and then the **Actual Finish** dates adjusted, in this order, to the date that the task actually started and actually finished. If you adjust the Finish date first, then the Start date, you will have to readjust the Finish date again.
  - **Completed Milestones** will be changed to a Task if an Actual Finish date is entered, so only enter an Actual Start and 100% when a Milestone is complete,
  - **In-Progress tasks** should have the **Actual Start** entered first, then there are two option for updating the task:
    1. The task bar may be dragged or Duration adjusted so the finish date is where it is estimated to finish and the **% Complete** may be adjusted manually by typing in the value or dragging the % Complete in the Gantt Chart, or
    2. When you have been provided with tasks' Remaining Durations or expected finish dates. The Actual Duration should be entered so that progress is up to the **Status Date** and then the Remaining Duration may then be entered and the Actual Duration will not change.

Tasks that are behind schedule may be split with the **Reschedule Work** button. This may be added to the **Quick Access Toolbar** or **Ribbon** or selecting **Project**, **Status** group, **Update Project...** to open the **Update Project** form and clicking on the **Reschedule uncompleted work to start after:** radio button. Make sure that the **File**, **Options**, **Schedule** tab, **Split in-progress tasks** box is checked:

- Unstarted tasks should be in the future and have their logic and durations revised.
- Add new activities to reflect scope changes or adding further detail to the schedule.
- Save the project with a new filename and save for future reference.

16.7 Comparing Progress with Baseline

There will normally be changes to the schedule dates and more often than not these are delays. The full extent of the change is not apparent without having a Baseline bar to compare with the updated schedule.

To display the **Baseline Bar** in the **Gantt Chart** you may use any of the functions covered in the **FORMATTING THE DISPLAY** chapter,

- The **Format**, **Bar Styles** group, **Baseline** button, or
- The **Format**, **Bar Styles** group, **Format**, **Bar Styles** function, or
- You may use the **Gantt Chart Wizard** as follows:
  - Add the **Gantt Chart Wizard button** to your Quick Access Toolbar or Ribbon,
  - Click on the **Gantt Chart Wizard button** to open the Gantt Chart Wizard.
  - Select the **Baseline** or **Custom Gantt Chart** option. This will display both the current schedule and the baseline.

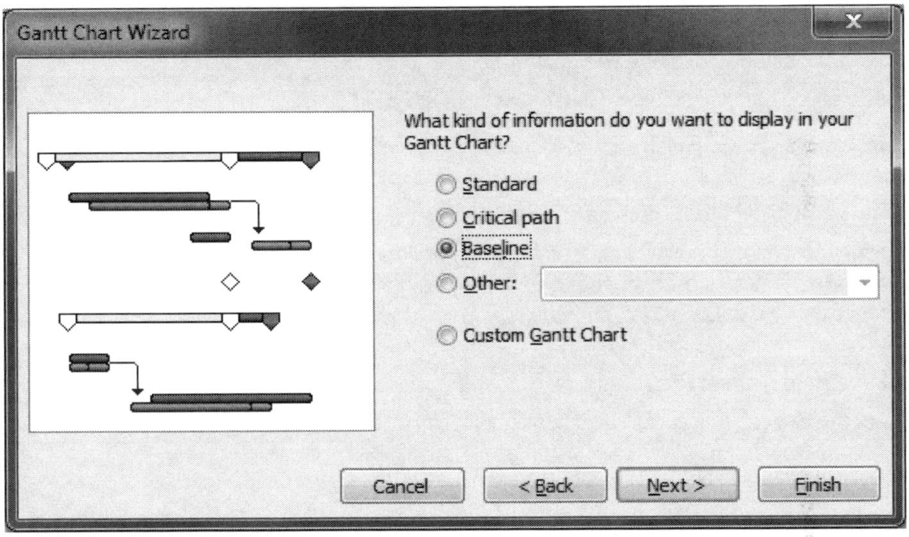

  - Hit the Next > button and follow the remainder of the instructions to complete the formatting. You will be given options for applying text and relationships in the Gantt Chart.

This wizard will overwrite any customized formatting you have made using the **Format**, **Bar Styles** group options.

The author found the bar formatting with the **Gantt Chart Wizard** is not compatible with the other formatting options provided with the new Microsoft Project 2010 **Format**, **Bar Styles** options as the **Gantt Chart Wizard** puts the Baseline bar in the lower half of the bar and the **Format**, **Bar Styles** group options puts the Baseline Bar in the upper half of the bar.

The Start and Finish Date variances are available by displaying the **Start Variance** and **Finish Variance** columns. These variance columns compare the **Baseline** dates with the current schedule dates. Variance columns and are not available for **Baseline 1** to **10 dates**, only the **Baseline** dates.

16.8 In-Progress Schedule Check List

The following check list may be used to check an in-progress schedule.

Complete Tasks

- All tasks have an Actual Start and an Actual Finish before the Status Date.

In-Progress Tasks

- Actual Start dates should all be in the past and Early Finish dates in the future.
- Check tasks with Constraints, are the constraints still valid?
- Do all tasks have Finish successors?
- Are there any tasks with progress greater than planned and require the duration shortened?
- Are there any tasks that have progressed slower than planned and require the duration lengthened or split.

Not Started Tasks

- All Start date should be in the future.
- Check that all the constraints on these tasks are still valid.
- All tasks should have Finish successors except the Project Finish Milestone(s).

Open Ends and Total Float

- Confirm that all tasks have successors and review float. Tasks with excessive float should be assigned dummy successors or delayed if they are not scheduled in a realistic timeframe with sequencing logic or Early Start constraints.

Critical and Near Critical Path

- Check the Critical Path is realistic and aligned with what project personnel consider critical.

Scope Changes

- Ensure that all project changes have been reflected in the schedule.
- It is good practice to add new activities for new work and cross reference the task to the change documentation using the Notes or a Text column.

Performance

- Has the performance of complete and in-progress tasks been reflected in un-started tasks, thus revising the un-started work durations based on achievements to date.

Baseline Comparison

- Review the Baseline dates with the current schedule and confirm that any delays are legitimate.
- Have there been many changes and delays and therefore should the schedule be re-baselined?

16.9 Corrective Action

There are two courses of action available with date slippage:

- The first is to accept the slippage. This is rarely acceptable, but it is the easiest answer.
- The second is to examine the schedule and evaluate how you could improve the end date.

Solutions to return the project to its original completion date must be cleared with the person/people responsible for the project, since they can have the most impact on the work.

Suggested techniques to bring the project back on track include:

- Reducing the durations of tasks on, or almost on, the Critical Path. When tasks have resources, increasing the number of resources working on the tasks may reduce duration. Changing longer tasks is often more achievable than changing the length of short duration tasks.
- Providing more time by changing calendars, say from a five-day to a six-day calendar, so that tasks are being worked on for more days per week or providing more hours per week.
- Changing task relationships so tasks take place concurrently. This may increase the peak resource requirements and this issue needs to be taken into account. This may be achieved by:
  - Introducing negative lags to Finish-to-Start relationships which maintains a Closed Network, or
  - Changing Finish-to-Start relationships to Start-to-Start which may result in open ends which will have to be closed by adding a Finish successor.
- Change the method of execution, for example moving work off-site.
- Reducing the project scope and hence deleting tasks.

16.10 Workshop 14 - Updating the Schedule and Baseline Comparison

Background

At the end of the first week you have to update the schedule and report progress and slippage.

Assignment

Open your **OzBuild Bid** project file and complete the following steps:

1. Ensure you have saved a copy of your project as **OzBuild With Resources** for use in the resources workshop and open your **OzBuild Bid** project.
2. Apply the **Gantt Chart** view.
3. Apply the **Tracking** table.
4. Set the Baseline for all the tasks on your project using the **Project, Schedule** group, **Set Baseline, Set Baseline...** command.
5. Display the baseline bar by selecting **Format**, **Bar Styles** group **Baseline**. If the Baseline bar does not display you may have to run the Gantt Chart Wizard.
6. Set the timescale as per the pictures below.
7. Hide the **Physical % Complete**, **Actual Costs** and **Actual Work** columns.
8. Add the **Finish Variance** column on the right.
9. Use the **Format**, **Format** group, **Gridlines** to display the **Status Date** as a solid black line, it will not be displayed yet.

	Task Name	Act. Start	Act. Finish	% Comp.	Act. Dur.	Rem. Dur.	Finish Variance
1	⊟ **OzBuild Initiation**	**NA**	**NA**	**0%**	**0d**	**36d**	**0d**
2	⊟ **Technical Specification**	**NA**	**NA**	**0%**	**0d**	**13d**	**0d**
3	Approval to Bid	NA	NA	0%	0d	0d	0d
4	Determine Installation Require	NA	NA	0%	0d	4d	0d
5	Create Technical Specification	NA	NA	0%	0d	5d	0d
6	Identify Supplier Components	NA	NA	0%	0d	2d	0d
7	Validate Technical Specificatio	NA	NA	0%	0d	2d	0d
8	⊟ **Delivery Plan**	**NA**	**NA**	**0%**	**0d**	**19d**	**0d**
9	Document Delivery Methodolo	NA	NA	0%	0d	4d	0d
10	Obtain Quotes from Suppliers	NA	NA	0%	0d	8d	0d
11	Calculate the Bid Estimate	NA	NA	0%	0d	3d	0d
12	Create the Project Schedule	NA	NA	0%	0d	3d	0d
13	Review the Delivery Plan	NA	NA	0%	0d	1d	0d
14	⊟ **Bid Document Submitted**	**NA**	**NA**	**0%**	**0d**	**19d**	**0d**
15	Create Draft of Bid Document	NA	NA	0%	0d	6d	0d
16	Review Bid Document	NA	NA	0%	0d	2d	0d
17	Finalize and Submit Bid Docum	NA	NA	0%	0d	2d	0d
18	Bid Document Submitted	NA	NA	0%	0d	0d	0d

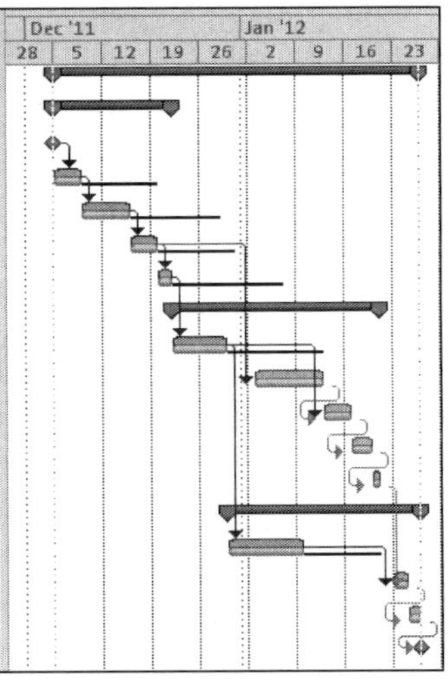

NOTE: The **Status Date** gridline will not display until the **Status Date** has been set.

10. Use **Project**, **Status** group, **Update Project...** to update progress to 9 Dec 11. The time will be at 5:00pm or 17:00 hrs on the Friday.
11. Check the **Status date** in the **Project**, **Properties** group, **Project Information** form; it should be 9 Dec 11 and the black **Status Date** line should now be displayed.
12. Expand the time scale to days using the **Zoom** button, you also may need to adjust the **Size** in the **Timescale** form.
13. Display the Non-working time behind the bars form the **Timescale** form:

	Task Name	Act. Start	Act. Finish	% Comp.	Act. Dur.	Rem. Dur.	Finish Variance
1	**⊟ OzBuild Initiation**	**5 Dec '11**	**NA**	**12%**	**4.29d**	**31.71d**	**0d**
2	**⊟ Technical Specific**	**5 Dec '11**	**NA**	**38%**	**5d**	**8d**	**0d**
3	Approval to Bic	5 Dec '11	5 Dec '11	100%	0d	0d	0d
4	Determine Inst	5 Dec '11	8 Dec '11	100%	4d	0d	0d
5	Create Technic	9 Dec '11	NA	20%	1d	4d	0d
6	Identify Suppli	NA	NA	0%	0d	2d	0d

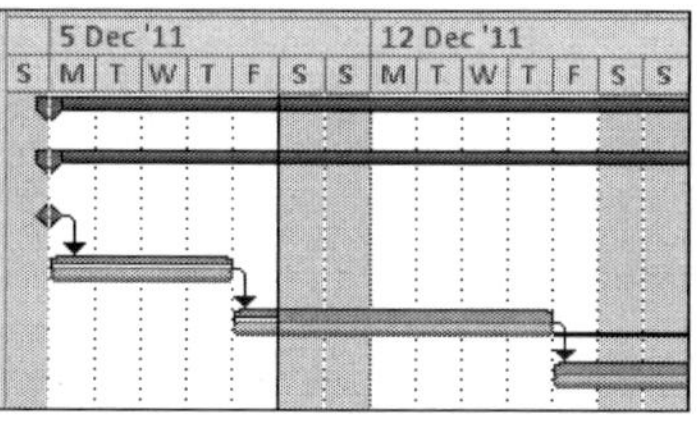

14. Update the following tasks using the table below. Enter the data in the order below against the detail tasks only.
    - Actual Start and 100 % against complete Milestones, Task 3. Do not enter an Actual Finish against Milestone as they will change to tasks.
    - Actual Start and Actual Finish against complete tasks, Task 4.
    - Actual Start, Actual Duration so the actual duration meets the **Status Date**, Remaining Duration for in progress tasks, Task 5.

	Task Name	Act. Start	Act. Finish	% Comp.	Act. Dur.	Rem. Dur.
3	Approval to Bid	6 Dec '11	6 Dec '11	100%	0d	0d
4	Determine Installation Requirements	6 Dec '11	8 Dec '11	100%	3d	0d
5	Create Technical Specification	8 Dec '11	NA	25%	2d	6d

15. Your schedule should look like the picture below:

	Task Name	Act. Start	Act. Finish	% Comp.	Act. Dur.	Rem. Dur.	Finish Variance
1	**⊟ OzBuild Initiation**	**6 Dec '11**	**NA**	**11%**	**3.98d**	**31.02d**	**0d**
2	**⊟ Technical Specificat**	**6 Dec '11**	**NA**	**33%**	**4.67d**	**9.33d**	**2d**
3	Approval to Bid	6 Dec '11	6 Dec '11	100%	0d	0d	1d
4	Determine Install	6 Dec '11	8 Dec '11	100%	3d	0d	0d
5	Create Technical	8 Dec '11	NA	25%	2d	6d	2d
6	Identify Supplier	NA	NA	0%	0d	2d	2d
7	Validate Technica	NA	NA	0%	0d	2d	2d
8	**⊟ Delivery Plan**	**NA**	**NA**	**0%**	**0d**	**17d**	**0d**
9	Document Delive	NA	NA	0%	0d	4d	2d
10	Obtain Quotes fr	NA	NA	0%	0d	8d	0d
11	Calculate the Bid	NA	NA	0%	0d	3d	0d
12	Create the Projec	NA	NA	0%	0d	3d	0d
13	Review the Deliv	NA	NA	0%	0d	1d	0d
14	**⊟ Bid Document Subn**	**NA**	**NA**	**0%**	**0d**	**17d**	**0d**
15	Create Draft of Bi	NA	NA	0%	0d	6d	2d
16	Review Bid Docur	NA	NA	0%	0d	2d	0d
17	Finalize and Subn	NA	NA	0%	0d	2d	0d
18	Bid Document Su	NA	NA	0%	0d	0d	0d

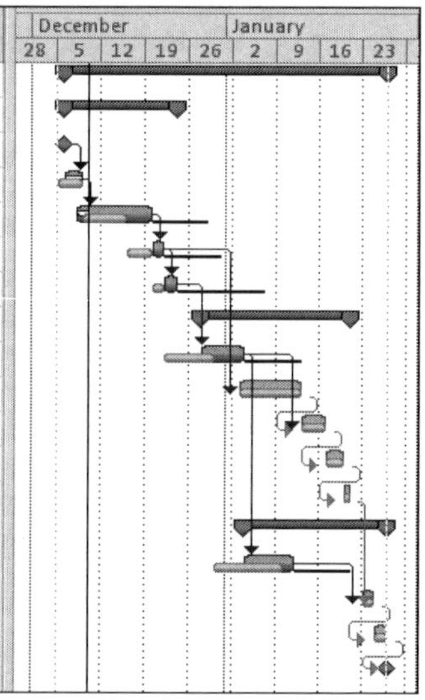

16. **NOTE:** there is no change in the end date of the project as there is sufficient Float to absorb the delay.

17. We will now update the schedule without using the **Update Progress** function.
18. Move the **Status Date** to 16 Dec 11 by selecting **Project**, **Properties** group, **Project Information**.

Project Information for 'OzBuild Workshop 14.mpp'

Start date:	5 Dec '11	Current date:	18 Sep '10
Finish date:	26 Jan '12	Status date:	16 Dec '11
Schedule from:	Project Start Date	Calendar:	Standard

19. Update the project detail tasks only with the following information. Enter the data in the order below against the detail tasks only. **NOTE** Do not edit the % Comp, the software will calculate this:
    - Actual Start
    - Actual Duration, so the actual duration meets the **Status Date**.
    - Remaining Duration
    - The % Complete will calculate automatically.

	Task Name	Act. Start	Act. Finish	% Comp.	Act. Dur.	Rem. Dur.
5	Create Technical Specification	8 Dec '11	16 Dec '11	100%	7d	0d
6	Identify Supplier Components	15 Dec '11	NA	33%	2d	4d
7	Validate Technical Specification	16 Dec '11	NA	10%	1d	9d

20. Add the **Total Float** (Total Slack) column.
21. Your project should look like the following pictures, without a delay to the end of the project as there is sufficient Float to absorb the delay:

	Task Name	Act. Start	Act. Finish	% Comp.	Act. Dur.	Rem. Dur.	Finish Variance	Total Slack
1	⊟ **OzBuild Initiation**	**6 Dec '11**	**NA**	**24%**	**8.27d**	**26.73d**	**0d**	**0d**
2	⊟ **Technical Specification**	**6 Dec '11**	**NA**	**50%**	**9d**	**9d**	**6d**	**3d**
3	Approval to Bid	6 Dec '11	6 Dec '11	100%	0d	0d	1d	0d
4	Determine Installation Requ	6 Dec '11	8 Dec '11	100%	3d	0d	0d	0d
5	Create Technical Specificatio	8 Dec '11	16 Dec '11	100%	7d	0d	1d	0d
6	Identify Supplier Componen	15 Dec '11	NA	33%	2d	4d	3d	-1d
7	Validate Technical Specificat	16 Dec '11	NA	10%	1d	9d	6d	3d
8	⊟ **Delivery Plan**	**NA**	**NA**	**0%**	**0d**	**14d**	**0d**	**0d**
9	Document Delivery Methodc	NA	NA	0%	0d	4d	6d	3d
10	Obtain Quotes from Supplie	NA	NA	0%	0d	8d	0d	0d
11	Calculate the Bid Estimate	NA	NA	0%	0d	3d	0d	0d
12	Create the Project Schedule	NA	NA	0%	0d	3d	0d	0d
13	Review the Delivery Plan	NA	NA	0%	0d	1d	0d	0d
14	⊟ **Bid Document Submitted**	**NA**	**NA**	**0%**	**0d**	**13d**	**0d**	**0d**
15	Create Draft of Bid Documen	NA	NA	0%	0d	6d	6d	3d
16	Review Bid Document	NA	NA	0%	0d	2d	0d	0d
17	Finalize and Submit Bid Docu	NA	NA	0%	0d	2d	0d	0d
18	Bid Document Submitted	NA	NA	0%	0d	0d	0d	0d

22. Task 6 has negative Total Float because Task 7 (its predecessor) has started before Task 6 has finished.

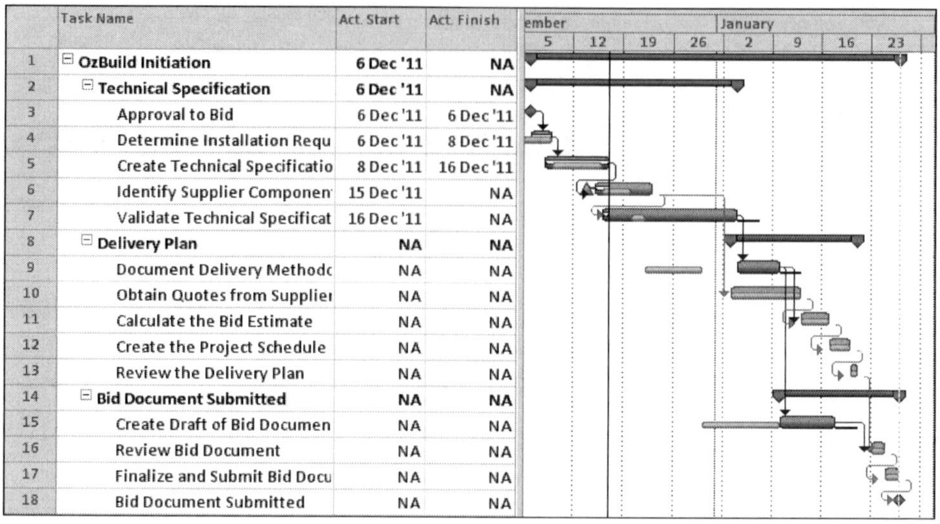

	Task Name	Act. Start	Act. Finish
1	OzBuild Initiation	6 Dec '11	NA
2	Technical Specification	6 Dec '11	NA
3	Approval to Bid	6 Dec '11	6 Dec '11
4	Determine Installation Requ	6 Dec '11	8 Dec '11
5	Create Technical Specificatio	8 Dec '11	16 Dec '11
6	Identify Supplier Componen	15 Dec '11	NA
7	Validate Technical Specificat	16 Dec '11	NA
8	Delivery Plan	NA	NA
9	Document Delivery Methodc	NA	NA
10	Obtain Quotes from Supplie	NA	NA
11	Calculate the Bid Estimate	NA	NA
12	Create the Project Schedule	NA	NA
13	Review the Delivery Plan	NA	NA
14	Bid Document Submitted	NA	NA
15	Create Draft of Bid Documen	NA	NA
16	Review Bid Document	NA	NA
17	Finalize and Submit Bid Docu	NA	NA
18	Bid Document Submitted	NA	NA

23. Select **File**, **Options**, **Schedule**, **Scheduling options for this project :** and check the **Split in-progress tasks** box:
24. Task 7 has **Split** as the Remaining Duration is acknowledging the predecessor.

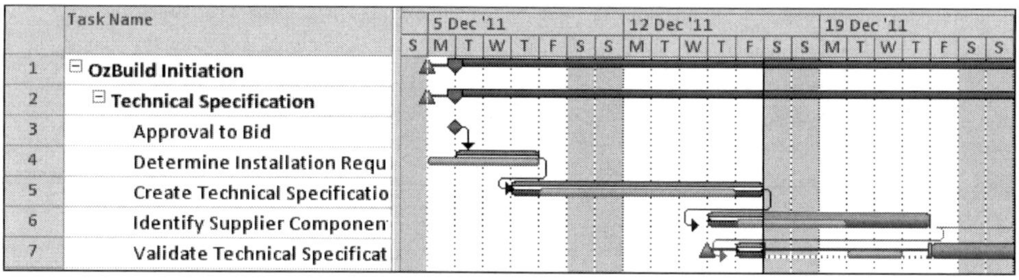

	Task Name
1	OzBuild Initiation
2	Technical Specification
3	Approval to Bid
4	Determine Installation Requ
5	Create Technical Specificatio
6	Identify Supplier Componen
7	Validate Technical Specificat

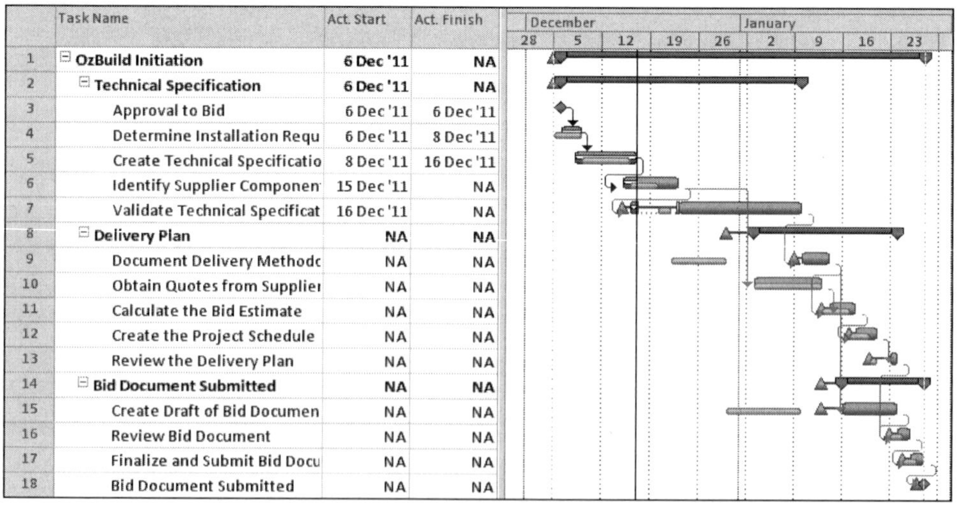

	Task Name	Act. Start	Act. Finish
1	OzBuild Initiation	6 Dec '11	NA
2	Technical Specification	6 Dec '11	NA
3	Approval to Bid	6 Dec '11	6 Dec '11
4	Determine Installation Requ	6 Dec '11	8 Dec '11
5	Create Technical Specificatio	8 Dec '11	16 Dec '11
6	Identify Supplier Componen	15 Dec '11	NA
7	Validate Technical Specificat	16 Dec '11	NA
8	Delivery Plan	NA	NA
9	Document Delivery Methodc	NA	NA
10	Obtain Quotes from Supplie	NA	NA
11	Calculate the Bid Estimate	NA	NA
12	Create the Project Schedule	NA	NA
13	Review the Delivery Plan	NA	NA
14	Bid Document Submitted	NA	NA
15	Create Draft of Bid Documen	NA	NA
16	Review Bid Document	NA	NA
17	Finalize and Submit Bid Docu	NA	NA
18	Bid Document Submitted	NA	NA

25. The project is now one day late and represented by the Negative Float of one day and the Finish Variance of one day.
26. What options do you have to bring the project back on schedule? Use your option to remove the negative float.
27. Save your **OzBuild Bid** project.

17 CREATING RESOURCES AND COSTS

A resource may be defined as something or someone that is assigned to a task and is required to complete the task. This includes people or groups of people, materials, equipment and money. The following reasons may be driving the use of resources in a schedule and each will command a different approach to the creation and updating of a resourced schedule:

- Estimating the cost or manning requirements of a project,
- Creating a platform for recording effort through time sheeting,
- Forecasting future resource requirements, with and without effort recording and
- For cash flow forecasting and/or Earned Value Performance Management.

When it is planned to update a resourced schedule it is recommended that the minimum number of resources be assigned to tasks. Avoid cluttering the schedule with resources that are in plentiful supply or are of little importance. Every resource added to the schedule will need to be updated. Therefore the scheduler's workload increases as resources are added to tasks.

When you create your resources, you should consider them under the following headings:

- Resources used as **Input Resources** – Those that are required to complete the work:
  - Individual people by name.
  - Groups of people by trade or skill.
  - Individual equipment or machinery by name.
  - Groups of resources such as Crews or Teams made up of equipment and machinery.
  - Materials or Money.
- Resources used as **Output Resources** – Things that are being delivered or produced:
  - Specifications completed.
  - Bricks laid.
  - Lines of code written.
  - Tests completed.

After planning your resource requirements, the following steps should be followed to create and use resources in a Microsoft Project schedule:

- Create your resources in the **Resource Sheet**.
- Manipulate the resource calendar if resources have special timing requirements.
- Assign the resources to tasks.
- Review the resource requirements through **Resource Graph** and **Resource Usage** views.

This chapter will concentrate on:

- The creation of resources in the **Resource Sheet**,
- Understanding **Task Type** and **Effort-Driven Tasks**,
- Assigning the resources to tasks, and
- Editing **Resource Calendars**.

Resources may be shared between projects using the **Resource**, **Assignments** group, **Resource Pool**, **Share Resources...** function. This is out of the scope of this book.

17.1 Creating Resources in the Resource Sheet

To add resources to the Resource Sheet, select **View**, **Resource Views** group, **Resource Sheet**.

	i	Resource Name	Type	Materia Label	Initials	Group	Max. Units	Std. Rate	Base Calendar	Cost/Use	Ovt. Rate	Accrue At
1		Project Manager	Work		PM	Office	00%	120.00/hr	Standard	0.00	0.00/hr	Prorated
2		Systems Engineer	Work		SE	Office	00%	90.00/hr	Standard	0.00	0.00/hr	Prorated
3		Project Support	Work		PS	Site	00%	80.00/hr	6-Day Working Week	0.00	0.00/hr	Prorated
4		Purchasing Officer	Work		PO	Office	00%	70.00/hr	Standard	0.00	0.00/hr	Prorated
5		Clerical Support	Work		CS	Office	00%	50.00/hr	Standard	0.00	0.00/hr	Prorated
6		Specialists Consultant	Cost		SC	Contractor						Prorated
7		Report Binding	Material	each	RB			100.00		0.00		Prorated

- To add a new resource:
  - ➢ Click on the first blank line and enter the resource data, or
  - ➢ Highlight the line where you would like to insert your resource, right-click and select **Insert Resource**, or
  - ➢ Use the **Ins Key**.
- The first column, with a [i] in the header, is the indicator column; [notes icon] is the Notes indicator; and [over-allocation icon] is the resource over-allocation indicator.
- Enter the **Resource Name**. Microsoft Project allows duplicate Resource Names to be entered into the Resource Table, but this situation should be avoided by visually checking all your Resource Names. When resources are to be shared amongst projects the spelling and coding of the resources must be carefully planned.
- Enter one of the three Resource **Types**: **Work** or **Materials** or **Cost**. They function differently:
  - ➢ **Work** resources, such as people, often have a limit to the number that are available. This type of resource may have a maximum number assigned, a standard and an overtime rate and may also have a calendar assigned.
  - ➢ **Materials** resources have a **Material Label** which is not available with a **Work** resource, have a quantity but do not have a maximum availability. They are considered unlimited and do not have a calendar.
  - ➢ **Cost** resources have no quantity or calendar but may be graphed.
- A **Material** resource may be assigned a **Material Label**, which may be the unit of measurement, such as m^3 or feet.
- The **Initials** are filled out by Microsoft Project with the first character of the **Resource Name**. This Initial field should be unique. Because it is displayed in some Views. It should be edited so it makes sense to you. For example, you could use a person's initials, log-in name or payroll number.
- You may enter any text in the **Group** field if you want to group, filter or sort your resources by this field. This could be used for Department, Branch or Skill.
- The method of entering the **Resource Units** may be formatted as a percentage or as a decimal via options. Enter the **Max Units** for **Work** resources only. 100% (or 1.00) would represent one person and 400% (or 4.00) would represent four people. This value is used in Usage views to display overloading.

- Select the **File**, **Options**, **Schedule** tab to set your option of Percentage or Decimal, 2 or 200% is two resources:

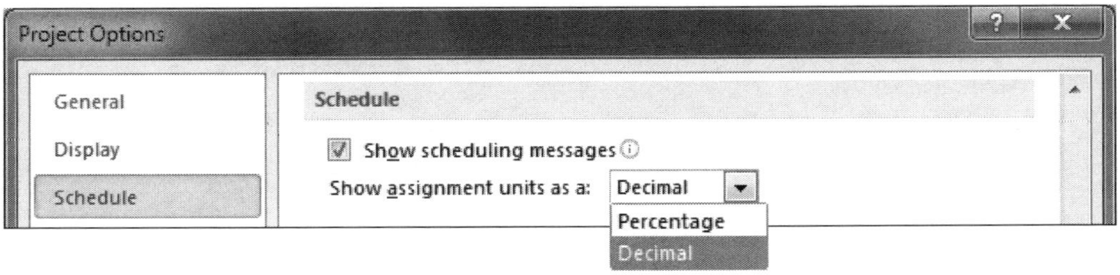

- Edit the **Standard Rate** for **Work** and **Material** resources only, if required. The resource default units are "hours" (hr), but this may be edited to be the cost per:
  - minute – min
  - hour – hr
  - day – day
  - week – wk
  - month – mon
- Enter the **Overtime Rate** for the **Work** resources only. A salaried person may not be paid overtime and would have a zero rate for overtime.
- Enter the **Cost per Use** for **Work** and **Material** resources only. This could represent a mobilization cost and is applied each time a resource is assigned to a task. The **Cost per Use** is accrued when an actual start date is entered.
- **Accrue At**:
  - **Start** – The costs for this resource are incurred when the task commences.
  - **Prorated** – The costs for this resource are spread over the duration of the task.
  - **End** – The costs for this resource are incurred when the task is complete.
- **Base Calendar** – When a new resource is created it is assigned the **Project Base** Calendar and may be changed. This is the calendar assigned to **Work** resources and may be edited to suit each individual resource availability including editing for individual holidays. See paragraph 17.4.2

17.2 Grouping Resources in the Resource Sheet

Resources may be grouped on any data fields, such as Custom Fields and Custom Outline Codes, using the **View**, **Data**, **Group by:** function. The example below shows resources grouped by **Resource Group**:

	i	Resource Name	Type	Material Label	Initials	Group	Max. Units	Std. Rate	Base Calendar	Cost/Use	Ovt. Rate	Accrue At
		⊟ Type: Work	**Work**				**00%**			**0.00**		
1		Project Manager	Work		PM	Office	00%	120.00/hr	Standard	0.00	0.00/hr	Prorated
2		Systems Engineer	Work		SE	Office	00%	90.00/hr	Standard	0.00	0.00/hr	Prorated
3		Project Support	Work		PS	Site	00%	80.00/hr	Standard	0.00	0.00/hr	Prorated
4		Purchasing Officer	Work		PO	Office	00%	70.00/hr	Standard	0.00	0.00/hr	Prorated
5		Clerical Support	Work		CS	Office	00%	50.00/hr	Standard	0.00	0.00/hr	Prorated
		⊟ Type: Material	**Materi:**							**0.00**		**Prorated**
7		Report Binding	Material	each	RB			100.00		0.00		Prorated
		⊟ Type: Cost	**Cost**									**Prorated**
6		Specialists Consultant	Cost		SC	Contractor						Prorated

17.3 Resource Information Form

The **Resource Information** form is opened by double-clicking on a specific row within the **Resource Sheet** view.

17.3.1 General Tab

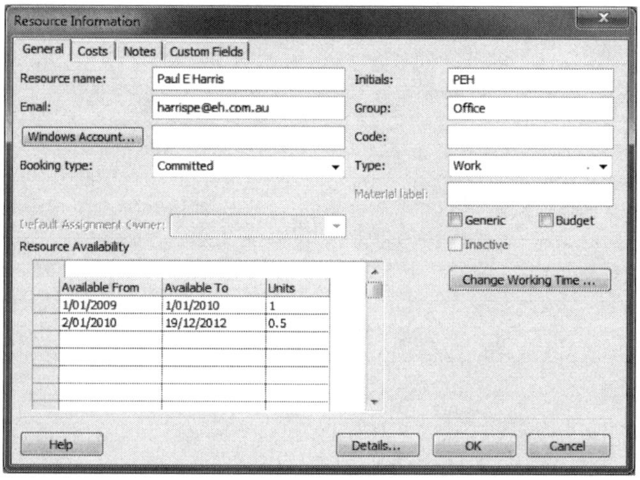

- The **Resource name:** is the name of the resource and may be displayed in columns with assignment **Units** (per time period). It is best to keep this name as short as possible.
- The **Email** field is used in email communication and is not covered in this book.
- [Windows Account...] allows the assignment of a resource to a Windows account and is not covered in this book.
- **Booking Type:** is an option to tag the assignment as **Committed** or **Proposed**. A **Proposed** resource does not affect the availability of a resource.
- **Resource Availability** is used to identify the resource availability over time.
- **Initials:** should be kept unique and may be displayed in columns.
- **Group** and **Codes** are fields that may be used to group resources by any user defined description such as Office, Site, City etc.
- **Work** has three options discussed earlier, **Work**, **Material** or **Cost**.
- **Generic** resources are used to indicate long term resource requirements and may be substituted with people as the work appears on the immediate horizon.
- **Budget** indicates that the resource is being used for budget purposes and the **Resource Availability** features are disabled when a resource is marked as Budget. New to Microsoft Project 2007.
- **Inactive** in an enterprise environment indicates the resource is no longer available but may be assigned to tasks in the past so it is preferable not to delete the resource. They are excluded from assignment lists.
- The [Change Working Time ...] button opens the **Change Working Time (Resource)** form editing the resource calendar. Select each resource's **Base calendar** and edit the calendar to suit the resource's individual availability dates and times.

17.3.2 Costs Tab

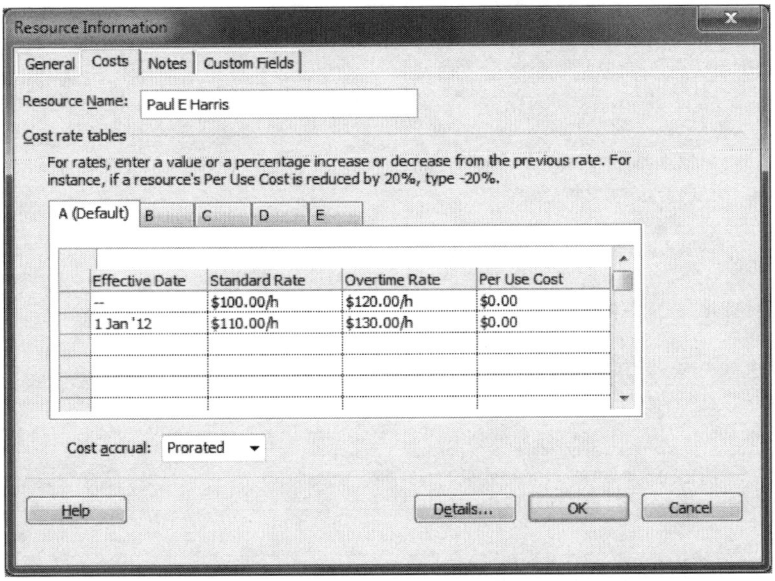

The **Cost rate tables** allow the adjustment of resource rates over time and allows the assignment of up to five different rates to a resource. The rate is assigned in the **Resource Information** form. This form is opened by double-clicking on the **Resource Name** for any assigned resource in either the **Resource Sheet**, **Task Usage** view or the **Resource Usage** view.

17.3.3 Notes

This is where notes are made about the resource such as assumptions.

17.3.4 Custom Fields

Custom Fields are for assigning user defined information to resources and are not covered in detail in this book. These are different to the task Custom Fields.

- Custom Resources fields may be created in the **Custom Fields** form by selecting **Project**, **Properties** group, **Custom Fields**.
- After the fields have been defined in the **Custom Fields** form, these fields appear in the **Resource Information** form and may be used to assign custom-defined costs and other information to resources from the **Custom Fields** tab of the **Resource Information** form or by adding columns to views such as the **Resource Sheet**.

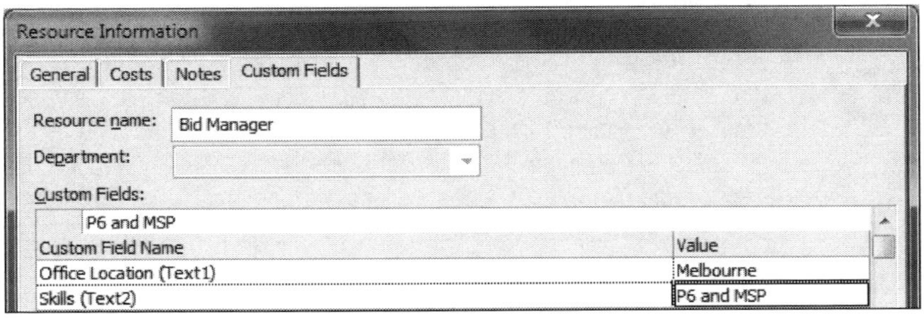

17.4 Resource Calendars

Tasks calendars may not accommodate specific resource availability. For example, a Project Calendar would not usually reflect when a person takes a holiday. Resource Calendars, on the other hand, can be used to schedule this resource-specific nonworking time. Therefore Resource Calendars could be used to schedule work when specific resources have a unique availability.

A unique resource calendar is created automatically when a resource is created and is a copy of the project **Base Calendar** when the resource is created.

When a resource is assigned to a task in the situation where the Project Calendar, Task Calendar and Resource Calendar and are all different; then the work is calculated based on some very complex parameters. This topic is extremely complex and is covered in more detail in below.

17.4.1 Editing a Resource calendar

The Resource Calendar may be edited in the same manner as Base Calendars from the **Change Working Time** form. This form may be opened by opening the **Resource Information** form (double-clicking on a **Resource Name** in most forms) and selecting the [Change Working Time ...] in the **Resource Information** form, **General** tab.

17.4.2 Resource Calendars Calculations

The hierarchy of Calendars is interesting and is documented below. The table over the page summarizes this hierarchy.

NO RESOURCES ASSIGNED TO TASKS

- The **Project Calendar** is used to calculate the Task Dates and Task Duration when no Task Calendar or resources are assigned.
- **Task Calendar** is used to calculate the Task Dates and Task Duration when a Task Calendar is assigned and no resources are assigned.

RESOURCES ASSIGNED AND NO TASK CALENDAR ASSIGNED

- The **Resource Calendar** is used to schedule resource work when resources are assigned to an activity without a **Task Calendar**.
  - **Fixed Units** and **Fixed Work** tasks calculate the Task Dates, Task Duration using the **Resource Calendar** only. The **Project Calendar** is not considered.
  - **Fixed Duration** tasks calculate the Task Dates and Task Duration using the **Project Calendar** and the resources work when their **Resource Calendar** allows, within the Task Duration.

A **Fixed Duration** task will schedule work when the task duration spans over a period that the resource may work. Work will be scheduled when the **Task Calendar** and **Project Calendar** have no common working time as long as the Task spans a Resource Work availability period. This may happen if a **Project Calendar** has Monday to Friday working and the **Resource Calendar** assigned a Saturday and Sunday working.

A task may not schedule work when a task is **Fixed Duration** and does not span the **Resource Calendar** availability.

RESOURCES ASSIGNED AND TASK CALENDAR ASSIGNED

- Resource Work is scheduled using a combination of the remaining available work time from the **Resource Calendar** and **Task Calendar**. For example a resource that is only available Friday and Saturday and assigned to a Task with a Monday to Friday calendar will only have Work scheduled on Fridays.
  - **Fixed Units** and **Fixed Work** tasks calculate Task Dates and Task Duration based on the **Resource Calendars** only. The **Task Calendar** is ignored for date calculation and is only used to allow the scheduling of work in combination with the Resource Calendar.
  - **Fixed Duration** calculates the Task Dates and Task Duration using the **Task Calendar**.

A task may not be scheduled and an error message will be displayed when a task is **Fixed Duration** and there is no common available working time from the **Resource Calendar** and **Task Calendar**. This would happen when a task is assigned a **Task Calendar** with Monday to Friday working and the **Resource Calendar** working on Saturday and Sunday.

- **Scheduling ignores resource calendars** – when checked the **Resource Calendar** is ignored and **Task Calendar** is used to calculate the Task Dates, Task Duration and schedule Work. **NOTE:** This option is not available when a Task Calendar has not been assigned.

Task Calendar	Resource assigned	Scheduling ignores resource calendars	Task Type	Calendar Used to Calculate Work	Calendar Used to Calculate Dates
None	No	N/A	Any	N/A	Project
Yes	No	N/A	Any	N/A	Task
None	Yes	N/A	Fixed Units or Fixed Work	Resource	Resource
None	Yes	N/A	Fixed Duration	Resource	Project
Yes	Yes	No	Fixed Units or Fixed Work	Remaining Availability of the combination of the Task and Resource.	Resource
Yes	Yes	No	Fixed Duration	Remaining Availability of the combination of the Task and Resource.	Task
Yes	Yes	Yes	Any	Task	Task

17.4.3 Issues Using Resource Calendars

The user must be aware that:

- The assignment of a Resource with a calendar that is different to the Task Calendar will change the task dates, durations and float values.
- The option to ignore Resource Calendars when no Task Calendar has been assigned is not available. So when a Task Calendar is NOT assigned, the Resource Calendar will always be acknowledged and the schedule dates will often change when a assigning a resource with a different calendar to the Project Calendar. To simplify the schedule calculation you may consider ensuring all Resource Calendars are the same as the Task Calendars.
- The Start and Finish dates of a Fixed Duration task may be different to the Start and Finish of the scheduled work. This is often longer when the Resource Calendars are different to the Task Calendars. The Start and Finish Dates therefore represent when the work may be completed and resources are scheduled within the task duration according to their calendar availability. Durations may be longer and Float shorter than Fixed Units or Fixed Work tasks.
- The Start and Finish dates of a Fixed Units or Fixed Work task are the same as the Start and Finish of the work. If you wish to display bars that depict when the work is to start and finish, then this option may be appropriate.
- The difference between the calculation of Fixed Duration, Fixed Units and Fixed Work tasks is significant and very complex; changing these options may have a significant effect of schedule calculations. Especially when changing Resource assignments.
- Increasing or decreasing the duration of tasks or changing the assignment of resources will calculate different values depending of the Task Type and the task Effort Driven setting.
- A split may be created at the end of a task when changing assignments or Task Calendars. This is represented by dots at the end of the task and may be removed by dragging the end of the task.
- The order that data is entered may result in different work or duration values; which in turn leads to confusion of inexperienced users. Try to be consistent in the order that data is entered.
- Users must spend considerable time playing with the software in order to master these complex options. You may wish to consider creating a schedule with a resource that is available Saturday and Sunday and a Task calendar that is available Friday and Saturday. Then create a number of tasks which have been assigned the resource and assign each task with a different permutation of Task Types and Task Calendars of None, Standard (5days/week) and the Friday and Saturday calendar. Display the Task Usage form to see how the resource Work is scheduled.
- Users must be careful when creating and assigning resources. To simplify the scheduling process you may wish to only use one or two set of parameters on all your tasks that you understand and not try to master them all.
- The author recommends the following set of options should be considered for basic schedules when assigning Resources:
  - Fixed Duration or Fixed Work, Non Effort Driven Tasks,
  - Not to use Task Calendars, except by exception,
  - Ensuring all Resource Calendars are the same as the Project Calendar.

17.5 *Workshop 15 - Defining Resources*

Background

The resources must now be added to this schedule. Since we have updated our project, we need to revert to the original schedule that we saved prior to updating the current schedule.

Assignment

1. Save and close your current project.
2. Open the **OzBuild With Resources**.
3. Select **File**, **Options** from the menu. From the **Schedule** tab, set **Show assignment unit as a: Decimal**.
4. Open the **Resource Sheet** view, by right-clicking in the dark band on the left-hand side, and add the resources displayed in the picture below to the project, leaving **Cost/Use** and **Ovt.Rate** (Overtime Rate) as zero and Accrue At as Prorated.
5. The Project Support resource will be assigned to activities that are on a 6-Day Working Week calendar, so these resources should be assigned a 6-Day Working Week calendar so the schedule calculates the same dates.
6. **NOTE:** No currency has been displayed in these workshops so you should use your default currency.

	ℹ	Resource Name	Type	Material Label	Initials	Group	Max. Units	Std. Rate	Ovt. Rate	Cost/Use	Accrue At	Base Calendar
1		Project Manager	Work		PM	Office	1	120.00/hr	0.00/hr	0.00	Prorated	Standard
2		Systems Engieer	Work		SE	Office	1	90.00/hr	0.00/hr	0.00	Prorated	Standard
3		Project Support	Work		PS	Site	1	80.00/hr	0.00/hr	0.00	Prorated	6-Day Working Week
4		Purchasing Officer	Work		PO	Office	1	70.00/hr	0.00/hr	0.00	Prorated	Standard
5		Cleical Support	Work		CS	Office	1	50.00/hr	0.00/hr	0.00	Prorated	Standard
6		Specialists Consultant	Cost		SC	Office					Prorated	
7		Report Binding	Material	Each	RB			100.00		0.00	Prorated	

5. Now select **View**, **Data** group, **Group by:**, **Resource Group** to see the resource grouping function:

	ℹ	Resource Name	Type	Material Label	Initials	Group	Max. Units	Std. Rate	Ovt. Rate	Cost/Use	Accrue At	Base Calendar
		⊟ **Group: No Value**								**0.00**	**Prorated**	
7		Report Binding	Material	Each	RB			100.00		0.00	Prorated	
		⊟ **Group: Office**				**Office**	**4**			**0.00**		
1		Project Manager	Work		PM	Office	1	120.00/hr	0.00/hr	0.00	Prorated	Standard
2		Systems Engieer	Work		SE	Office	1	90.00/hr	0.00/hr	0.00	Prorated	Standard
4		Purchasing Officer	Work		PO	Office	1	70.00/hr	0.00/hr	0.00	Prorated	Standard
5		Cleical Support	Work		CS	Office	1	50.00/hr	0.00/hr	0.00	Prorated	Standard
6		Specialists Consultant	Cost		SC	Office					Prorated	
		⊟ **Group: Site**				**Site**	**1**			**0.00**	**Prorated**	
3		Project Support	Work		PS	Site	1	80.00/hr	0.00/hr	0.00	Prorated	6-Day Working Week

6. Save your **OzBuild With Resources** project.

18 ASSIGNING RESOURCES AND COSTS TO TASKS

Microsoft Project has the following types of resources:

- **Fixed Costs** are costs allocated to tasks (without assigning a resource) in order to calculate the total cost of a project. A Cost Resource has more options and will give a better result.
- **Work** may be assigned to a task without a resource in order to calculate the total number of hours required for a project without adding a resource and display in the **Task Usage** form.
- **Work resources** that are used for people or equipment. The **Work** (quantity) is usually measured in hours and the **Work** resource components are linked to the Task Duration. These resources may be assigned a **Rate** to calculate their cost and a calendar.
- **Material resources**, which have a Quantity and a Unit Rate to calculate a costs. The quantity is not linked to the task duration and may not be assigned a calendar.
- **Cost resources** were introduced in Microsoft Project 2007. This is a resource that does not have a quantity, is not affected by the task duration and may not be assigned a calendar.

Resources may be assigned to tasks using a number of methods including:

Method	Menu Command
• **Fixed Costs** assignment	Display the **Fixed Costs** and **Fixed Costs Accrual** columns.
• **Work** assignment	To assign work to a task which does not have resources display the **Work** column and type in the hours. A resource assigned to a task with work will inherit the work value assigned to the task.
• **Resource Assignment** form	Click on the **Assign Resource** button. You may assign **Units** and **Costs**.
• **Task Information** form	Double-click on a **Task** name or click on the **Task Information** button. You may assign **Resource Units** and **Costs**.
• The **Resource Task Details** forms	In the bottom window, select the **Task Details Form**, **Task Form** or **Task Name Form**, and then select the appropriate form from the **Details** option. Each form has different options.
• The **Resources Names** and **Resource Initials** columns	Insert appropriate columns by right-clicking on the column heading where you want to insert a column and then assign a Resource.
• **Contoured** Resource assignment	Open the **Assignment Information** form by: • Double-clicking on a resource in the **Task Usage** or **Resource Usage** view, or • Right-clicking on a resource and selecting **Assignment Information** from the menu.
• **Shared Resources**	Select **Resource**, **Assignments** group, **Resource Pool**, **Share Resources...** to open the **Share Resources** form to share resources with other projects.

18.1 Fixed Costs

Fixed costs are a function whereby you may assign costs to a task without creating resources. It is a useful function if you require a cash flow only but not so useful with a progressed schedule.

- A fixed cost is assigned using the **Fixed Cost** column.
- The fixed cost may be accrued at the **Start**, **End** or **Prorated** over the duration of the task. This option is selected from the **Fixed Cost Accrual** column. The default for the **Fixed Cost Accrual** is set in the **File**, **Options, Schedule** tab:

Task Name	Duration	Fixed Cost	Fixed Cost Accrual	1 March M	T	W	T	F
⊟ **Summary**	**5 days**	**$0.00**	**Prorated**	$240.00	$40.00	$40.00	$40.00	$240.00
$200.00 Fixed cost accrued at Start	5 days	$200.00	Start	$200.00				
$200.00 Fixed cost Prorated	5 days	$200.00	Prorated	$40.00	$40.00	$40.00	$40.00	$40.00
$200.00 Fixed cost accrued at End	5 days	$200.00	End					$200.00

- Fixed Costs will not be displayed in the **Resource Sheet** or **Resource Usage** views but are available in the **Task Usage** view and in a **Report**. The **Cash Flow** report will only give you the cash flow in weeks but may be exported to Excel.
- Fixed Costs are added to resource costs and the total is shown in the **Cost** column.

Task Name	Fixed Cost	Fixed Cost Accrual	Resource Initials	Cost
⊟ **Summary**	**$0.00**	**Prorated**		**$8,800.00**
$200.00 Fixed cost accrued at Start	$200.00	Start		$200.00
$200.00 Fixed cost Prorated	$200.00	Prorated		$200.00
$200.00 Fixed cost accrued at End	$200.00	End		$200.00
Activity With Resources Only	$0.00	Prorated	PEH	$4,000.00
Activity With Costs & Resources	$200.00	Prorated	PEH	$4,200.00

When both **Fixed Costs** and **Resource Costs** are assigned to a task, there is no column to display only the total **Resource Costs**. It is therefore recommended to be able to clearly understand the contents of a Cost column that either Fixed Costs or Resource Costs be assigned to a task but not both.

When a Baseline is set, the Fixed costs and the Resource costs are added together.

The Cost resource has more functionality and should be used in place of Fixed Costs.

18.2 Assigning Work without a Resource

To assign work to a task which does not have resources; display the **Work** column and type in the hours. A resource assigned to a task with work will inherit the work value assigned to the task.

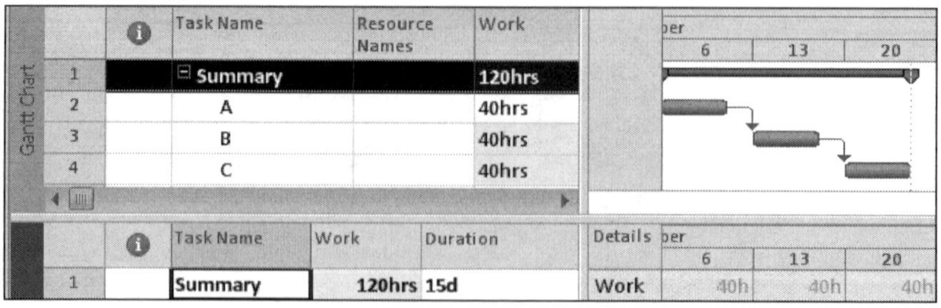

18.3 Resource Definitions

When a resource is assigned to a task, it has three principal components:

- **Quantity**, in terms of **Work** or **Material** required to complete the task,
- **Units**, which represents the number of people working on a task or material quantity and
- **Cost**, calculated from the **Standard Rate**, **Overtime Rate** and **Cost per Use**.

The **Units** (per Time Period) of a **Work** resource may be entered against a task, the **Work** (Quantity) will be calculated, or the **Work** entered and the **Units** calculated. The resource cost is calculated from the resource **Work** times the resource **Rate**.

In Oracle Primavera software **Units/Time** is the same as Microsoft Project **Units** and the Oracle Primavera software **Units** is the same as Microsoft Project **Work**.

18.4 Task Type and Effort-Driven

The **Task type** and **Effort-driven** options operate after the first **Work** resource has been assigned to a task. The relationship among the following four variables are controlled by these options:

- The number of different **Resources**, i.e., painters and testers are two different resources.
- The **Task duration**.
- The resource **Units** (per Time Period), i.e., two testers would be 2 Units per Time Period.
- The amount of **Work** to be performed, i.e., the total number of hours.

The **Task type** and **Effort-driven** functions control which variable changes when one of these four parameters is changed when **Work** resources are added or removed from a task. These options may be set in a number of forms including the **Task** and the **Task Details** form. **Material** resources, **Cost** resources and **Fixed Costs** do not change values after they have been assigned.

18.4.1 Task Type – Fixed Duration, Fixed Units, Fixed Work

There is a relationship between the **Duration** of a task, the **Work** (the number of hours required to complete a task) and the **Units** (per Time Period), (the rate of doing the work or number of people working on the task). The relationship is:

Duration x Units (per Time Period), **= Work**

There are three options for the **Default task type:** which decide how this relationship operates. They are:

- **Fixed Duration** — The **Duration** stays constant when either the **Units** (per Time Period) or **Work** is changed. If you change the **Duration**, then the **Work** changes.
- **Fixed Units** — The **Units** (per Time Period) stays constant when either the **Duration** or **Work** is changed. If you change the **Units** (per Time Period), then the **Duration** changes.
- **Fixed Work** — The **Work** stays constant if either **Duration** or **Units** (per Time Period) is changed. Therefore your estimate will not change when you change **Duration** or **Units** (per Time Period). If you change the **Work**, then the **Duration** changes.

18.4.2 Effort-Driven

Once a resource has been assigned to a task, the task **Effort** is the combined number of hours of all resources assigned to a task. The **Effort-driven** option decides how the effort is calculated when a resource is added or when a resource is removed to a **Fixed Units** or **Fixed Duration** task. There are two options:

- **Effort-driven** When a resource is added or removed from a task, the **Task Effort** assigned to a task remains constant. Adding or removing resources leaves the total effort assigned to a task as a constant unless all resources are removed. The work is shared amongst the resources and the resources are considered equal in value.
- **Non Effort-driven** When a resource is added to or removed from a task, the **Resource Effort** or **Work** of other resources remains constant. Adding or deleting resources increases or decreases the total task effort.

Some resource options to consider in the **File**, **Options**, **Schedule** tab are:

- When you do not want the **Duration** to change as the resource work is edited, set the **Default task type:** as **Fixed Duration** and **Non Effort Driven.** Each resource work is independent of all other resources and the total work remains constant when the duration is changed. The **Units per Time Period** i.e. the crew size will change if the duration is changed. The Estimate to Complete will not change.
- When you do not want the **Units (**per Time Period) to change as the duration is changed then set the **Default task type:** as **Fixed Units** and **Non Effort Driven**. Therefore the crew size will NOT change if the duration is changed but the work will change. For example a task with three resources assigned will always have three resources assigned and the work will increase or decrease as the duration is increased or decreased. The Estimate to Complete will change.

When tasks are Effort Driven and multiple resources are to be assigned a different result is obtained if one resource is assigned at a time to the option of assigning multiple resources at a time.

18.5 Resource Calendars

The simplest method of scheduling is when all tasks and resources share the same calendar. This is often not desirable and Microsoft Project allows three levels of calendars, project, task and resource.

The interaction among these calendars when resources are assigned is difficult to understand and the order that resources are assigned to tasks and assignment of task calendars may result in different calculated task durations and work. It is recommended that you practice with a small schedule with one or two tasks and resources until you are confident on how the software is calculating. The calendar rules are described in detail in paragraph 17.4.

A common mistake is assigning a task an edited task calendar, then at a later date assigning resources without editing the resource calendars to match the task calendars and not realizing that the task durations no longer calculate the same.

18.6 Assigning Resources using the Resource Assignment Form

Highlight one or more tasks that you want to assign resources. To open the **Assign Resources** form:

- Add the **Assign Resources** button to the **Quick Access Toolbar**, or
- Select a task and right-click and select the **Assign Resources...**, or
- Select **Resource**, **Assignments** group, **Assign Resources**

The **Units** represent the number of people working on a task and may be displayed as **Units** shown in the picture on the left, or as a **Percentage** shown on the right. The value of 1.00 is the same value as 100%. This option may be changed in the **Schedule** tab of the **Options** form:

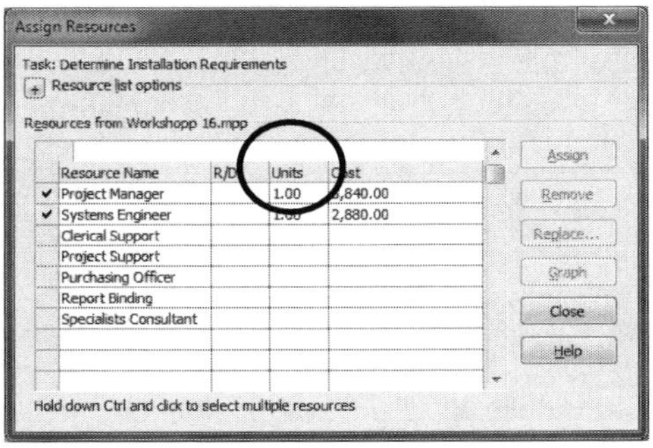

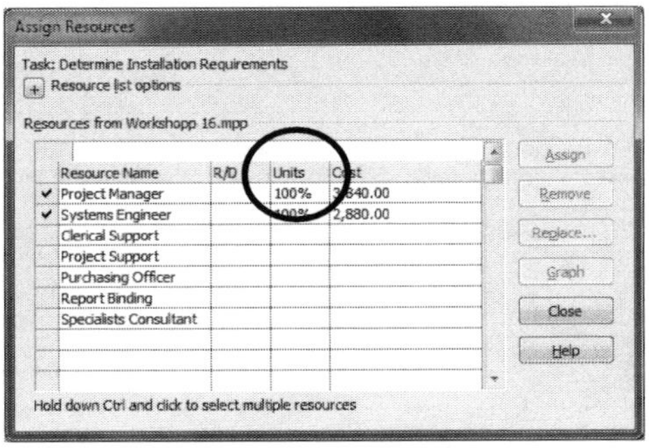

- Select the **Resource** from the form.
  - ➢ Type in the number of resources you want to assign under **Units**. This may be in % or whole numbers depending on how your options are set.
  - ➢ Click on the Assign button to assign a resource to a task.
- You may then assign another resource to a task.
- Select a resource and click on the Remove button to remove a resource.
- Select a resource and click on the Replace... button to open the Replace Resource form to replace a resource.

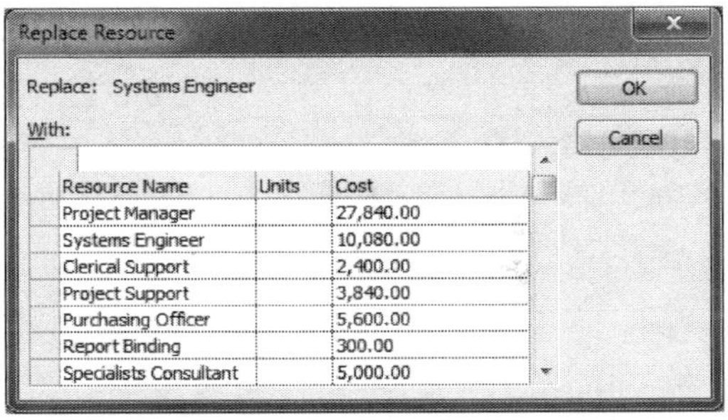

- The **Resource list options** at the top of the screen allows the resource list to be reduced by the use of filters and is very useful when there is a large number of resources or to create new resources be from your address book.

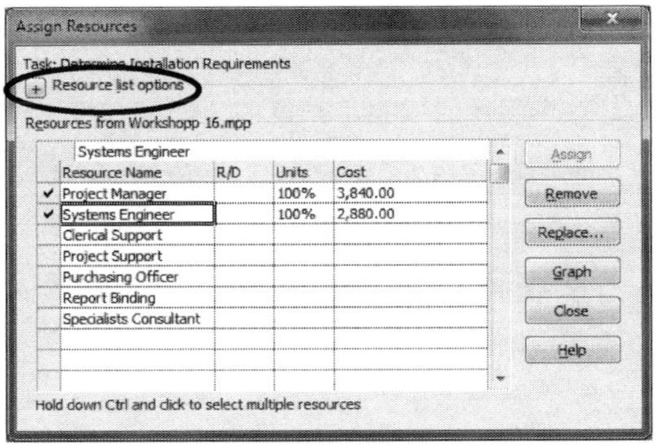

18.7 Assigning Resources Using the Task Details Form

Open the bottom window displaying the **Task Detail Form**, **Task Form** or **Task Name Form**. Then select the appropriate option by right-clicking in the form. See the picture on the right:

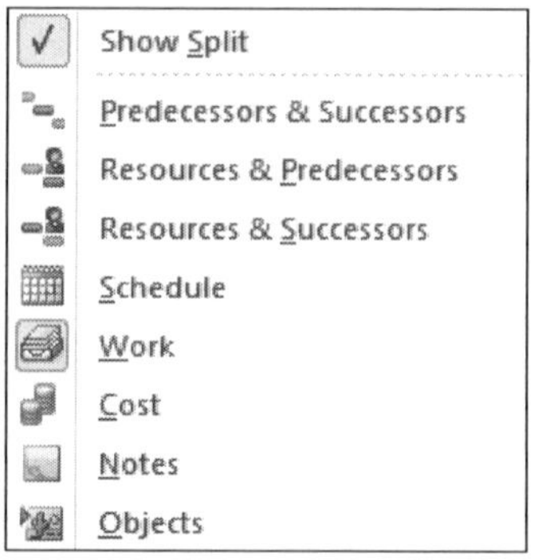

The table below lists the resource component options available in these forms:

Form	Assignment Option
• Resources & Predecessors	**Units** and **Work**
• Resources & Successors	**Units** and **Work**
• Schedule	**Work** only
• Work	**Units** and **Work**
• Cost	**Units** only with calculated **Costs**

The **Task Entry** form with the Resource **Work** details form is displayed below.

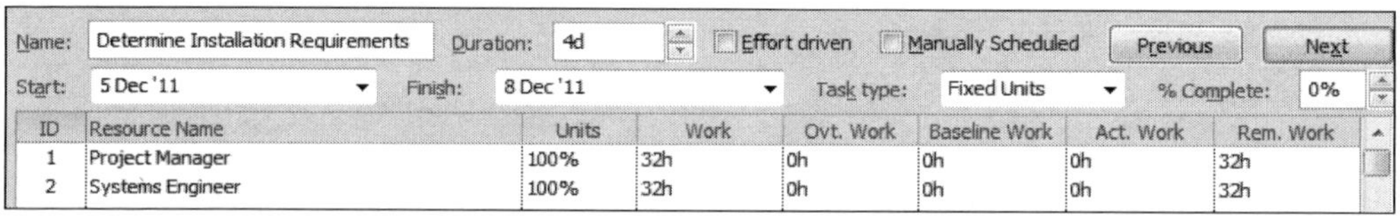

- Select the required resource in the drop-down box under the **Resource Name** heading.
- Enter the number of resources under **Units**, or
- Enter the amount of **Work** – the number of hours may be entered under this heading.
- **Ovt. Work** – Overtime Work may be assigned to reduce the duration of the task. The **Work** remains the same, but the **Overtime** value represents the amount of work being done on overtime. Overtime work is not displayed as an overload in the Usage Views.

When **Overtime** work is assigned and costs are being calculated. If an Overtime Rate is not entered the cost will decrease as more overtime is assigned.

- **Baseline Work** is copied from **Work** when a **Baseline** is set.
- **Act. Work** – Actual Work is entered when work is in-progress.
- **Rem. Work** – Remaining Work is calculated by subtracting **Actual Work** from **Work**.

18.8 Assigning Resources Using the Task Information Form

Open the **Task Information** form:

- Select the required resource from the drop-down box.
- Type in the number of required resources in the Units box.

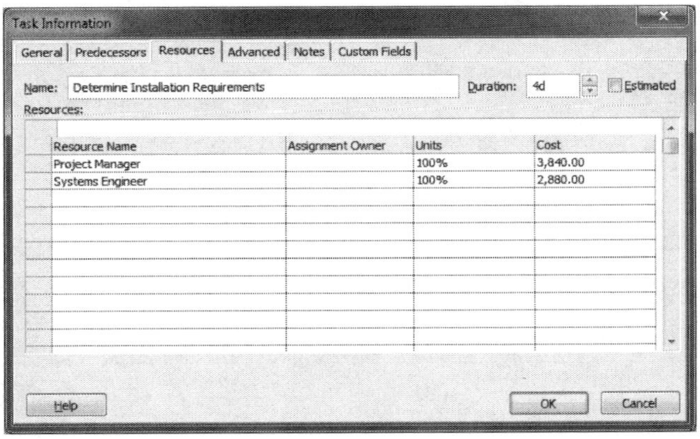

18.9 Assigning Resources from the Resource Column

Resources may be assigned by displaying the Resource Names column and clicking in the cell to display the available resources. This feature is new to Microsoft project 2010.

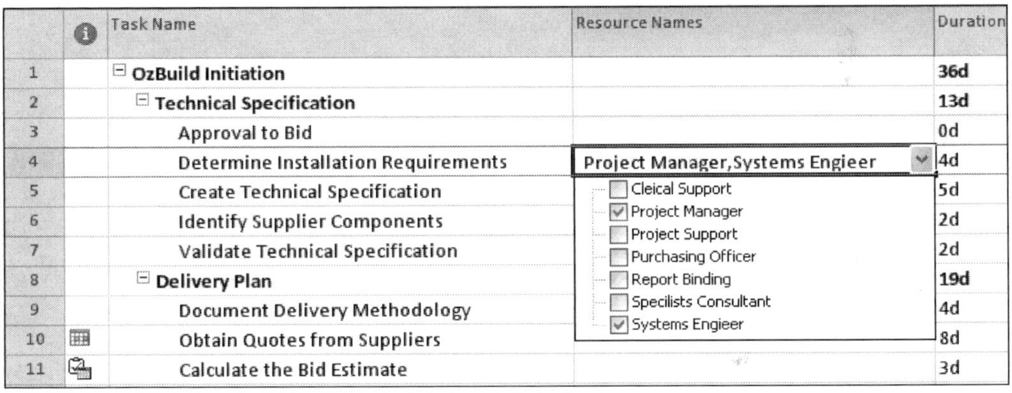

18.10 Assignment of Resources to Summary Tasks

Summary tasks may be assigned **Fixed Costs**, **Work Resources**, **Costs Resources** and **Material Resources**.

You must also be aware that when a Work resource is assigned to a summary task the task type is set to **Fixed Duration** and that setting may not be changed. Thus, any change in duration of a summary task due to rescheduling of associated detail tasks will result in a change to the work assignment and the calculated costs of a summary task.

It is recommended that unless a summary task Work resource assignment is required to vary in proportion to the summary task duration, then Work Resources should not be assigned to a summary task. You should consider using Fixed Costs, Cost resource or a Material resource if appropriate.

18.11 *Rollup of Costs and Hours to Summary Tasks*

The summary task **Cost** and **Work** fields are calculated from the sum of the costs and work assigned to the related detail tasks and those of the summary task.

> It becomes difficult for a scheduler to check the total cost of a summary task after costs and work have been assigned to both the summary task and associated detail tasks. It is therefore recommended that you consider only assigning costs and work to detail tasks.

Summary tasks have the costs and work rolled up to give you a cost at any Outline level.

	Task Name	Work	Cost
1	**⊟ OzBuild Initiation**	**520hrs**	**55,060.00**
2	Approval to Bid	0hrs	0.00
3	**⊟ Technical Specification**	**152hrs**	**19,800.00**
4	Determine Installation Requirements	64hrs	6,720.00
5	Create Technical Specification	40hrs	8,600.00
6	Identify Supplier Components	16hrs	1,120.00
7	Validate Technical Specification	32hrs	3,360.00
8	**⊟ Delivery Plan**	**224hrs**	**21,520.00**
9	Document Delivery Methodology	32hrs	3,840.00
10	Obtain Quotes from Suppliers	128hrs	12,160.00
11	Calculate the Bid Estimate	24hrs	1,920.00
12	Create the Project Schedule	24hrs	1,920.00
13	Review the Delivery Plan	16hrs	1,680.00
14	**⊟ Bid Document**	**144hrs**	**13,740.00**

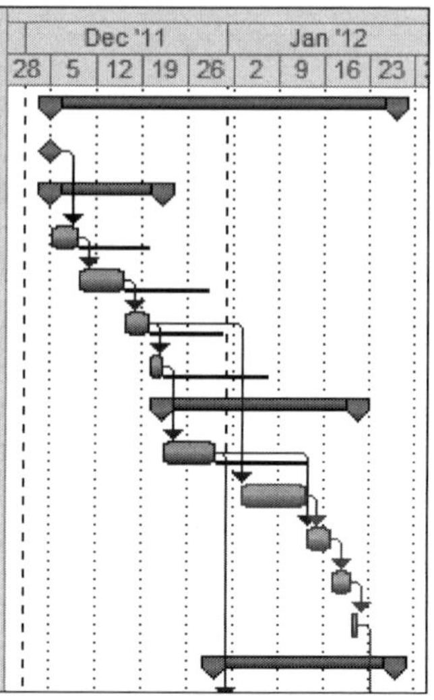

The Baseline Costs and Work are copied from the Cost and Work fields at the time that the Baseline is set and are not calculated from their detail tasks. Thus, when tasks are added, deleted or moved to different summary tasks then the Baseline Costs and Work are no longer the sum of their detail tasks.

There is a function titled **Summary Task Interim Baseline Calculation**, which is covered in the **UPDATING PROJECTS WITH RESOURCES** chapter. This will allow the summary tasks Baseline Dates and Costs to be recalculated.

18.12 Contour the Resource Assignment

A Resource Assignment may be assigned to a task with a non-linear profile. This function is titled **Work Contour** and is similar to the Resource Curve function in Oracle Primavera software. To assign a contour to a resource assignment:

- Open the **Assignment Information** form by:
  - ➢ Double-clicking on a resource in the **Task Usage** or **Resource Usage** view, or
  - ➢ Right-clicking on a resource and selecting **Information** (Assignment) from the menu.
- The picture below shows the Sales Engineer being assigned as **Back Loaded**.

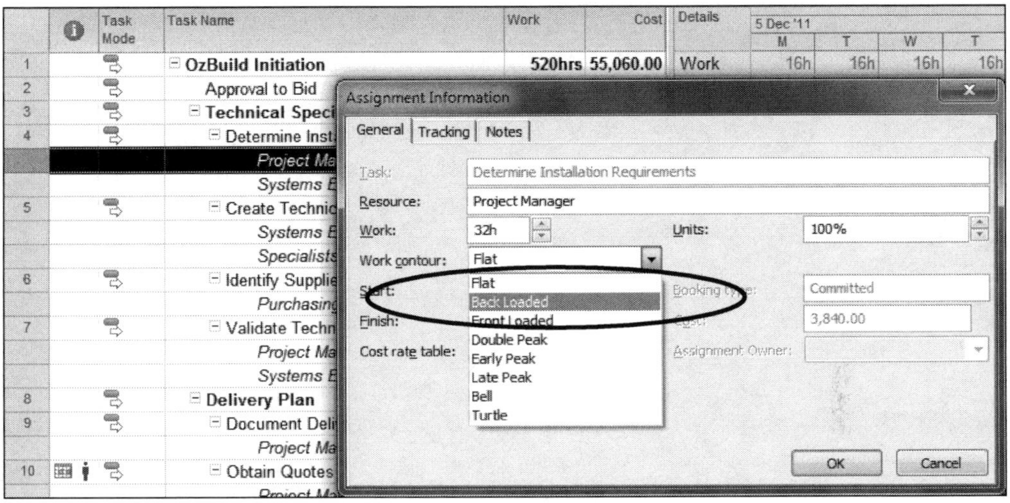

- From the **Work contour:** drop-down box, select the **Work Contour** type.
- The picture below is the **Resource Usage** form. It shows one task titled **Example Task** with nine resources. Each resource name has been made the same as the assigned **Work** contour. The picture shows:
  - ➢ The effect of the assignment for each of the **Work Contour** types, and
  - ➢ The icon in the **Task Information** column is a graphical representation of the contour.

		Task Name	Work	Details	10 June				
1		Example Task	360 hrs	Work	47.68h	103.27h	76.1h	86.27h	46.68h
		Flat	40 hrs	Work	8h	8h	8h	8h	8h
		Back Loaded	40 hrs	Work	1.67h	5h	8.33h	11.67h	13.33h
		Front Loaded	40 hrs	Work	13.33h	11.67h	8.33h	5h	1.67h
		Double Peak	40 hrs	Work	6h	12h	4h	12h	6h
		Early Peak	40 hrs	Work	6h	16h	10h	6h	2h
		Late Paek	40 hrs	Work	2h	6h	10h	16h	6h
		Bell	40 hrs	Work	2.4h	9.6h	16h	9.6h	2.4h
		Turtle	40 hrs	Work	4.28h	10h	11.43h	10h	4.28h
		Contoured	40 hrs	Work	4h	25h	0h	8h	3h

The **Flat** option allows you to type in any value into each of the cells. A resource assignment is automatically set to **Contoured** when one manual entry is made in the table.

18.13 Workshop 16 - Assigning Resources to Tasks

Background
The resources must now be assigned to their specific tasks.

Assignment
Open the **OzBuild With Resources** project and complete the following steps:

1. Select the **Gantt Chart** view.
2. Add the **Resource Names** column to the right of the **Task Name** and align the data to the left.
3. Split the pane by right-clicking in the Gantt Chart and selecting **Show Split**.
4. Display the **Task Details Form** in the bottom pane window.
5. Right-click in the **Task Details Form** and choose **Work**.
6. Ensure all Detail Tasks are **NOT Effort Driven** and are **Fixed Units.**
7. Add the **Assign Resources** button to the **Quick Access Toolbar.**
8. Using the **Resource Work** or the **Assign Resources** form assign the following resources:

NOTES: Once you have entered the **Resource Name** in the **Resources Work** form and assigned the **Units**, Microsoft Project will calculate the worked hours automatically after you click out of the form or press the enter key. Ensure the tasks are **NOT Effort-Driven** as you enter resources, otherwise the Total Work may stay constant and the duration change as you add additional resources. As resources are assigned to tasks 10 and 11 the task calendars will be ignored but as the resource has been assigned a 6-Day Working Week calendar these tasks will be scheduled with the same dates.

ID	Task Name	Resources
4	Determine Installation Requirements	Project Manager, Systems Engineer
5	Create Technical Specification	Systems Engineer, Specialists Consultant and assign a cost of $5,000.00
6	Identify Supplier Components	Purchasing Officer
7	Validate Technical Specification	Project Manager, Systems Engineer
9	Document Delivery Methodology	Project Manager
10	Obtain Quotes from Suppliers	Purchasing Officer, Project Manager
11	Calculate the Bid Estimate	Project Support
12	Create the Project Schedule	Project Support
13	Review the Delivery Plan	Project Manager, Systems Engineer
15	Create Draft of Bid Document	Clerical Support, Project Manager
16	Review Bid Document	Systems Engineer, Project Manager
17	Finalize and Submit Bid Document	Project Manager, Report Binding [3 each]

Workshop 16 CONTINUED

1. Format your columns as per below to check your answer:

	ⓘ	Task Name	Resource Names	Duration	Work	Cost
1		⊟ **OzBuild Initiatio**		**36d**	**520hrs**	**55,060.00**
2		⊟ **Technical Spe**		**13d**	**152hrs**	**19,800.00**
3		Approval to		0d	0hrs	0.00
4		Determine	Project Manager,Systems Engieer	4d	64hrs	6,720.00
5		Create Tech	Systems Engieer,Specialists Consultant[5,000.00]	5d	40hrs	8,600.00
6		Identify Su	Purchasing Officer	2d	16hrs	1,120.00
7		Validate Te	Project Manager,Systems Engieer	2d	32hrs	3,360.00
8		⊟ **Delivery Plan**		**19d**	**224hrs**	**21,520.00**
9		Document [	Project Manager	4d	32hrs	3,840.00
10		Obtain Quo	Project Manager,Purchasing Officer	8d	128hrs	12,160.00
11		Calculate th	Project Support	3d	24hrs	1,920.00
12		Create the I	Project Support	3d	24hrs	1,920.00
13		Review the	Project Manager,Systems Engieer	1d	16hrs	1,680.00
14		⊟ **Bid Document**		**19d**	**144hrs**	**13,740.00**
15		Create Draf	Cleical Support,Project Manager	6d	96hrs	8,160.00
16		Review Bid	Project Manager,Systems Engieer	2d	32hrs	3,360.00
17		Finalize anc	Project Manager,Report Binding[3 Each]	2d	16hrs	2,220.00
18		Bid Docume		0d	0hrs	0.00

2. Now display the **Task Usage** view in the Bottom Pane, display the columns shown below, select all the tasks in the top pane and check that your data matches the table.

	ⓘ	Task Name	Resource Names	Dur
1		⊟ OzBuild Initiatio		36d
2		⊟ Technical Spe		13d
3		Approval to		0d
4		Determine	Project Manager,Systems Engieer	4d
5		Create Tech	Systems Engieer,Specialists Consultant[5,000.00]	5d
6		Identify Su	Purchasing Officer	2d
7		Validate Te	Project Manager,Systems Engieer	2d

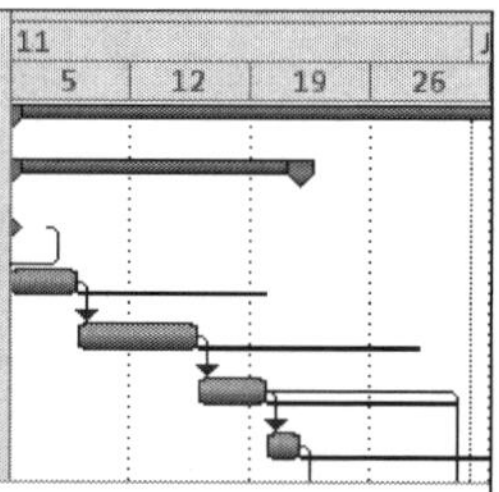

	Task Name	Assignment Units	Work	Total Cost	Duration	Details	11: 5	12	19	26
1	**OzBuild Initiation**		**520hrs**	**55,060.00**	**36d**	Work	72h	40h	56h	32h
2	**Technical Specification**		**152hrs**	**19,800.00**	**13d**	Work	72h	40h	40h	
3	Approval to Bid		0hrs	0.00	0d	Work				
4	Determine Installation Req		64hrs	6,720.00	4d	Work	64h			
	Project Manager	1	*32hrs*	*3,840.00*		Work	32h			
	Systems Engieer	1	*32hrs*	*2,880.00*		Work	32h			
5	Create Technical Specificat		40hrs	8,600.00	5d	Work	8h	32h		
	Systems Engieer	1	*40hrs*	*3,600.00*		Work	8h	32h		
	Specialists Consultant			*5,000.00*		Work				
6	Identify Supplier Compone		16hrs	1,120.00	2d	Work		8h	8h	
	Purchasing Officer	1	*16hrs*	*1,120.00*		Work		8h	8h	
7	Validate Technical Specific		32hrs	3,360.00	2d	Work			32h	
	Project Manager	1	*16hrs*	*1,920.00*		Work			16h	
	Systems Engieer	1	*16hrs*	*1,440.00*		Work			16h	
8	**Delivery Plan**		**224hrs**	**21,520.00**	**19d**	Work			16h	16h

3. Save your **OzBuild Bid** project.

19 RESOURCE OPTIMIZATION

At this point in the preparation of the schedule the resources should be reviewed and optimized to ensure that they are being efficiently used and sufficient resources are available.

This chapter will briefly cover the following topics which will enable you to review your resources:

- **Resource Histograms** – Allow the display of each resource on a time-phased vertical bar graph. These are termed **Resource Graphs** in Microsoft Project.
- **Resource Tables** – Allow the display of one or more resource requirements in a table on a time-phased basis. This information is displayed by the **Task Usage** and **Resource Usage** views.
- **S-Curves** – Allow the display of the planned, earned or actual consumption of resources or costs as a line graph. A single S-Curve may be produced for one or selected resource costs or hours using the Resource Graph view. The display of multiple S-Curves showing the Planned, Actual and Earned cost or hours of resources is not possible. It is also not possible to display Fixed Costs on the S-Curves, but the source data for resources may be exported to a spreadsheet where multiple S-Curves may be readily created. They are displayed via customized Resource Graphs
- **Leveling** – There are several techniques available for smoothing resource peaks or overloads in resource requirements.

19.1 Resource Graph Form

The **Resource Graph** form was a new feature to Microsoft Project 2002 and was removed in Microsoft Project 2010.

Selecting the Graphs... from the **Assign Resources** form will now display the **Resource Graph** form in the Bottom Pane:

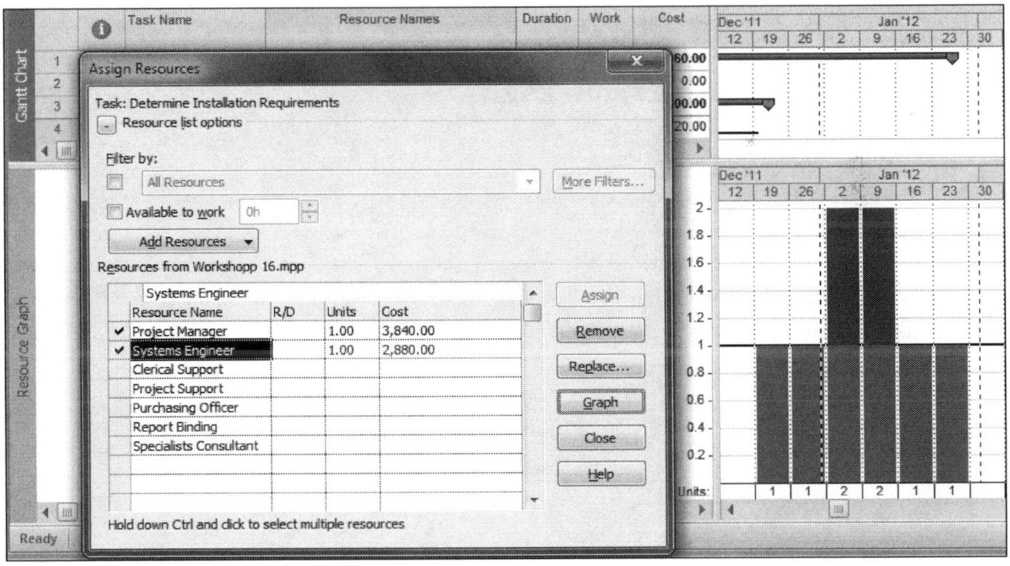

19.2 Resource Graph View

A **Resource Graph** may be displayed with the **Resource Graph** view.

The **Resource Graph** may be viewed in the top or bottom pane. The view below displays the Resource Usage in the top pane and Resource Graph in the bottom pane and shows the Project Manager is overloaded:

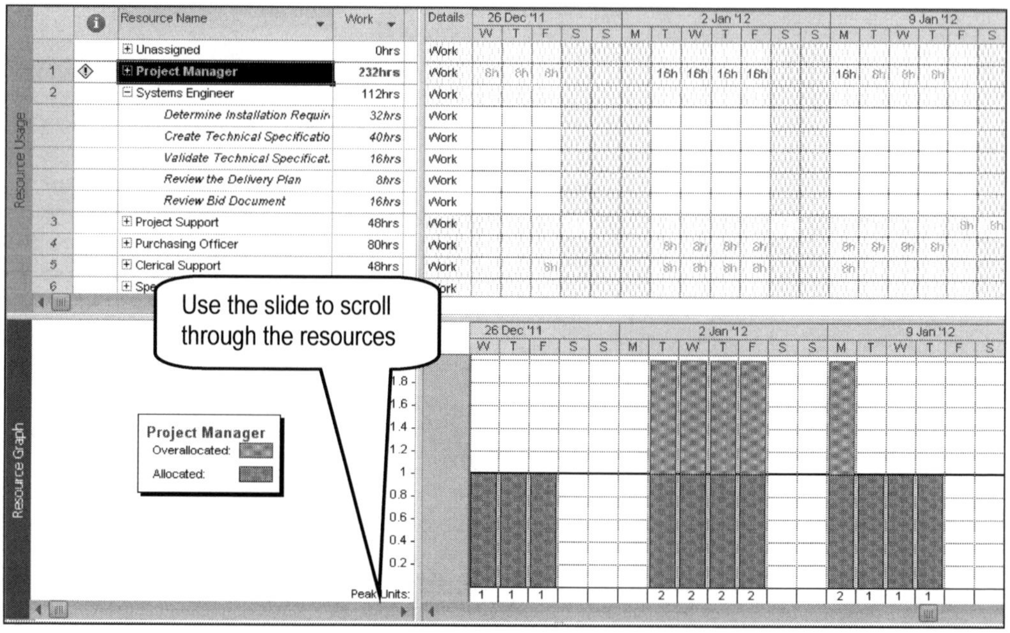

- Only one resource is displayed at a time unless specially formatted as discussed next. You may scroll through the resources by:
  - Pressing the **Page Up** and **Page Down Keys**, or
  - Clicking on the scroll bar in the lower left-hand side of the **Resource Graph** view.
- The **Resource Graph Units** options include Cumulative Costs and Work, Costs, Work and Percentage Allocation.
- Right-clicking in the graph area of the screen to display the options.
- The **Resource Graph** gridlines and colors may be formatted by right-clicking in the graph area of the screen and selecting the **Bar Styles** option.
- The **Timescale** of the graph is adopted from the timescale setting. You will find the **Zoom** buttons useful for changing the timescale.

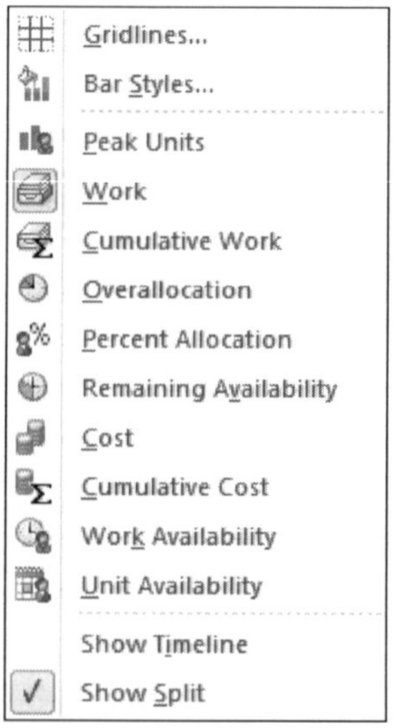

- To show a histogram for selected resources:
  - Display the **Resource Usage** in the top pane,
  - Display the **Resource Graph** in the bottom pane,
  - Right-click in the **Resource Graph** and open the **Bar Styles** form,
  - Ensure there is a **Bar** displayed for **Selected Resources**,
  - Close the form,
  - Select one or more resources in the Resource Usage view.
  - The result is as per the picture below:

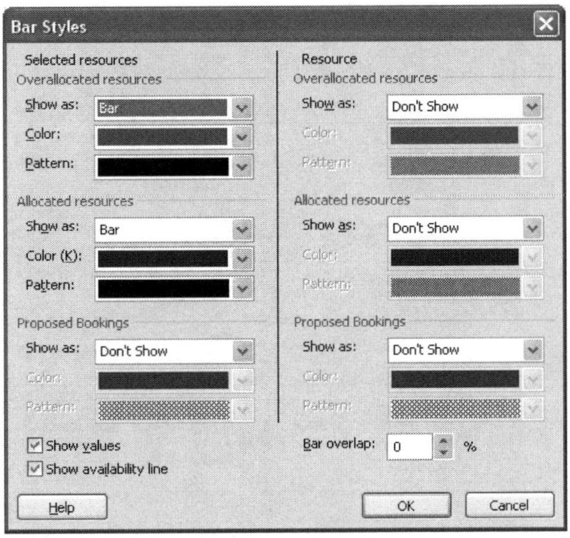

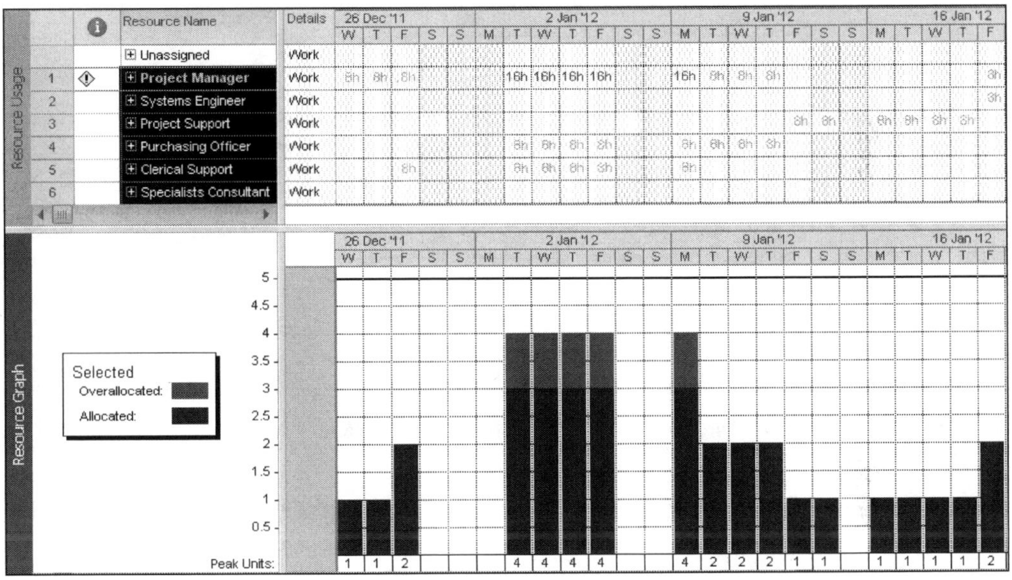

19.3 *Resource Tables View*

Resource tables are displayed using the **Task Usage** or **Resource Usage** views.

- The **Task Usage v**iew organizes the schedule by **Task** and then by **Resource,**
- Summarizing in the **Gantt Chart** view will summarize the **Task Usage v**iew when the :

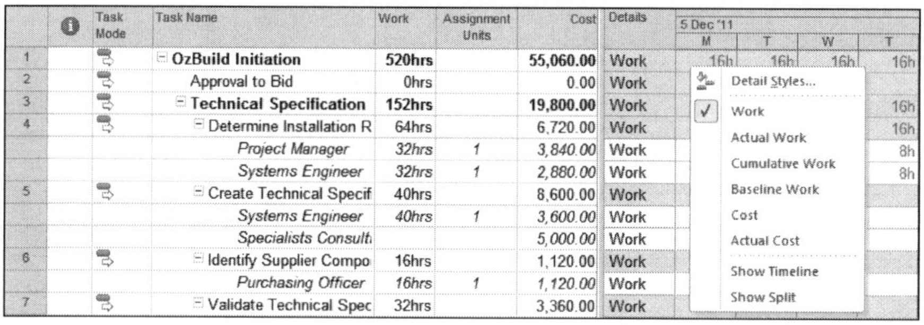

- The **Resource Usage** view organizes the schedule by **Resource** and then by **Task**. Note the Sales Engineer is overloaded as indicated by the icon in the indicators column:

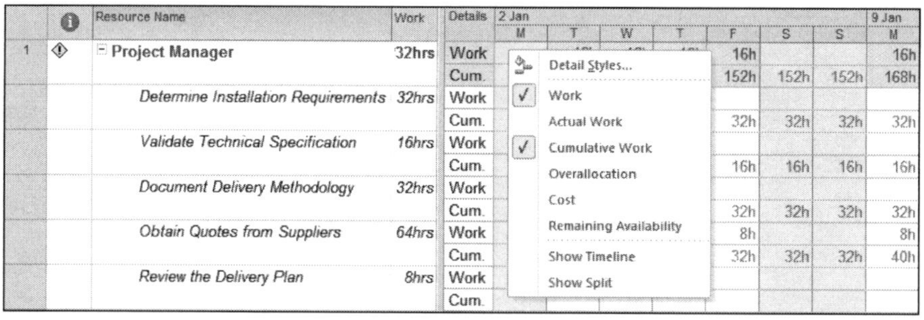

- When these views are displayed in the top **Pane** they display all resources and all tasks.
- When these views are displayed in the bottom **Pane** they display values for the resources or tasks that have been selected in the top **Pane**.
- More than one line of data may be displayed by right-clicking in the display and selecting from the menu as shown above.
- There are some interesting additional Resource Assignment fields available in this view that you may wish to experiment with.

19.4 Detailed Styles Form

This form may be opened from the **Resource Usage** and **Task Usage** forms by right-clicking and selecting **Detailed Styles...**. This allows further options for formatting these views including creating a single S-Curve:

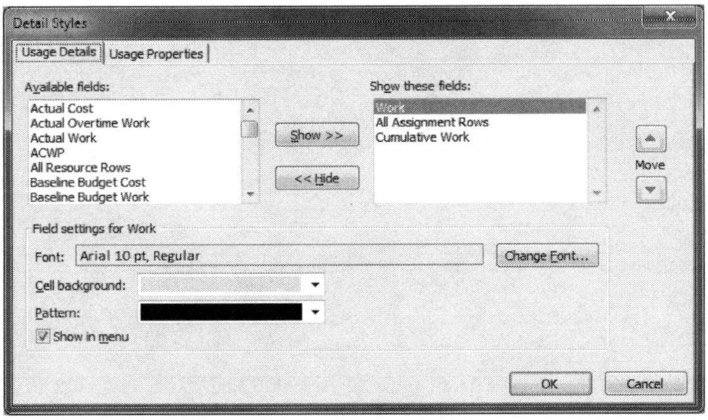

19.5 Creating an S-Curve from Microsoft Project

A single S-Curve may be created graphically and displayed by Microsoft Project. The example below is produced by:

- Displaying the **Resource Sheet** in the top pane and selecting all the resources,
- Displaying the **Resource Graph** in the bottom pane,
- Right-clicking and displaying the **Cumulative Costs** and
- Right-clicking, opening the **Bar Styles...** form and formatting as displayed below:

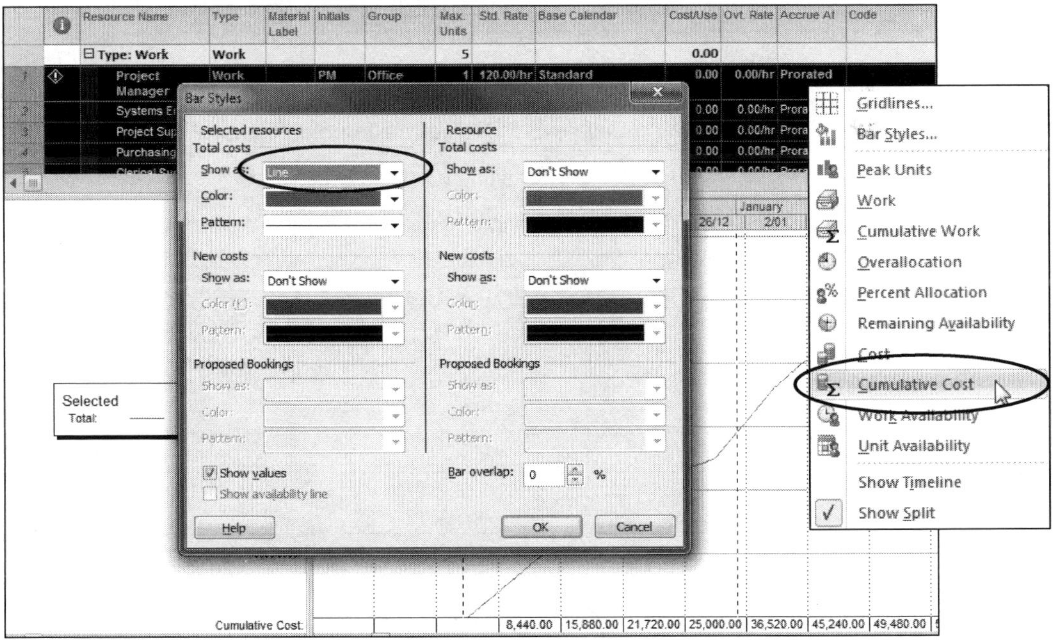

19.6 Team Planner View

The Team Planner View is new to Microsoft Project 2010 and is a very useful view for analyzing a schedule. This view allows a **Production Planning** type view where tasks may be assigned to resources as opposed to **Project Planning** where resources are assigned to tasks. The picture below clearly shows where the Project Manager is overloaded as he/she is assigned to two tasks at the same time:

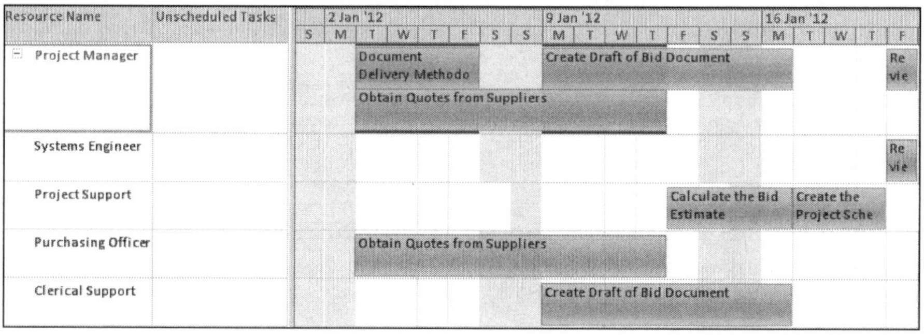

An overloaded resource may have an assignment reassigned by selecting the resource and then right-clicking and selecting **Reassign To** and select an alternative resource from the list:

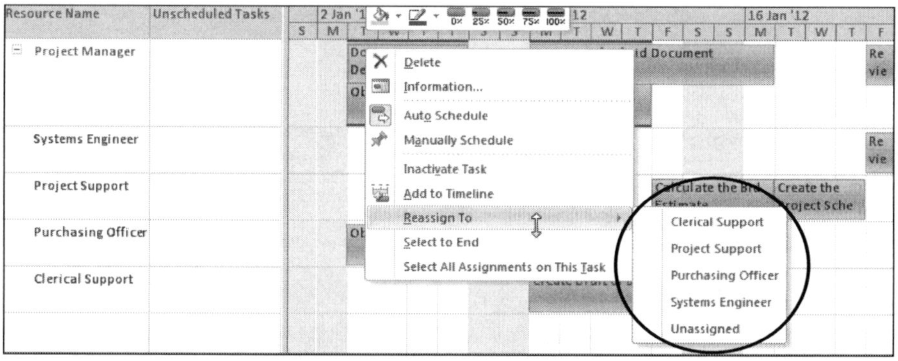

- Double-clicking on the Task will open up the **Task Information** form.
- Double-clicking on the Resource will open up the **Resource Information** form.
- Dragging a Task to another Resource will reassign the task to a resource.
- If Work is assigned to a task (without assigning a resource) using the Work column then a task will be shown as **Unassigned**:

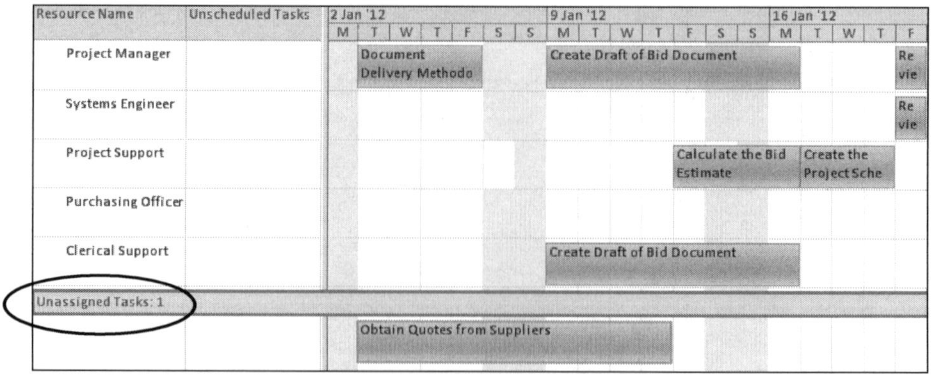

19.7 Printing Resource Profiles and Tables

To **Print** a **Task Usage**, **Resource Usage**, or **Resource Graph**, make the appropriate **Pane** active and use the print functions as described in the **PRINTING AND REPORTS** chapter.

19.8 Creating Resource Graphs, Crosstab Tables, S-Curves in a Spreadsheet

Resource Graphs, Crosstab Tables, S-Curves and may be created for displaying:

- Planning information, such as the number of people required or a project cash flow,
- Progress in terms of hours spent or cost to date, and
- Performance, for example comparing planned and actual hours or costs to date.

Earned Value also known as **Earned Value Performance Measurement** (**EVPM**) is a well-documented technique used for the management of projects. This technique requires the results output in a number of formats which Microsoft Project is not able to reproduce. Spreadsheets or specialists software will produce these outputs from data exported from Microsoft Project. There are many good Earned Value reference documents that may be used to assist in the establishment of an Earned Value Performance Measurement system including:

- The Australian Standard "AS 4817-2008 Project performance measurement using Earned Value", and
- The Project Management Institute Practice "Standard For Earned Value Management"

Excel is often used to create S-Curves and Graphs (Histograms) for the following reasons:

- The ability to easily record and display historical period information, this may be hours consumed or dollars spent per week or per month.
- The ability to simply record and enter actuals at a summary level in Excel. It is simpler to record cost and hours at project or at WBS component than at a detail task level.
- The superior graphical output of Excel and flexibility compared to Microsoft Project; such as the ability to display both tabular and graphical information on a single printout.

Many people are familiar with exporting or copying and pasting tabular data from one software program to another and are also comfortable with creating S-Curves and Histograms in spreadsheets which are titled charts in Excel. This section of this book will cover the basics of transferring the data from Microsoft Project to a spreadsheet for the creation of S-Curves and Histograms.

19.8.1 Export Time Phased Data Using Visual Reports

In Microsoft Project 2007 the **Analysis** toolbar export function was moved to the **Visual Reports - Create** form. Reports like the **Cash Flow Report** and the **Earned Value Over Time Report** are intended to be used to display time-phased data.

You may find this function difficult to use as the data is exported in pivot table format and dates are, by default, seen as week numbers.

19.8.2 Export Using Time Phased Data Copy and Paste

A **Resource Usage** view may be highlighted, copied, and then pasted into spreadsheets to create S-Curves. The Microsoft Project headings are not copied, and the data on the left-hand side of the **Pane** and the data on the right-hand side of the **Pane** have to be copied separately and aligned with manually created headings in Excel.

To transfer the data into Excel by copy and paste:

- Organize the **Task Usage** or **Resource Usage** view and **Details** so it displays the rows, columns, units and timescale you require in your graph.

	Task Name	Work	Details	5 Dec							12 Dec	
				M	T	W	T	F	S	S	M	T
1	⊟ **OzBuild Initiation**	**520hrs**	Work	16h	16h	16h	16h	8h			8h	8h
2	Approval to Bid	0hrs	Work									
3	⊟ **Technical Specification**	**152hrs**	Work	16h	16h	16h	16h	8h			8h	8h
4	⊟ Determine Installation Requirements	64hrs	Work	16h	16h	16h	16h					
	Project Manager	*32hrs*	Work	8h	8h	8h	8h					
	Systems Engineer	*32hrs*	Work	8h	8h	8h	8h					

- Highlight the rows on the left-hand side of your pane that you want to copy to the spreadsheet. This would be the Task name and Work in the picture above.
- Position the cursor under the spreadsheet heading and paste. The heading rows are copied and pasted with Microsoft Project 2010. These will paste as columns A and B in the picture below.
- Type the dates along the top row of your spreadsheet in the same format as the right-hand pane of Microsoft Project. As per cells C1 to K1 in the picture below.
- Select the data required to be pasted into Excel from the right-hand side of the pane in Microsoft Project by dragging. Ensure the top left-hand cell matches the first date typed in the spreadsheet.
- Paste into the spread sheet by placing the mouse in cell C2:

	A	B	C	D	E	F	G	H	I	J	K
1	Task Name	Work	5-Dec	6-Dec	7-Dec	8-Dec	9-Dec	10-Dec	11-Dec	12-Dec	13-Dec
2	**OzBuild Initiation**	**520hrs**	16h	16h	16h	16h	8h			8h	8h
3	Approval to Bid	0hrs									
4	**Technical Specification**	**152hrs**	16h	16h	16h	16h	8h			8h	8h
5	Requirements	64hrs	16h	16h	16h	16h					
6	*Project Manager*	*32hrs*	8h	8h	8h	8h					
7	*Systems Engineer*	*32hrs*	8h	8h	8h	8h					

You may now create your S-Curves in the spreadsheet using its built-in Excel graphing function.

19.8.3 Creating S-Curves in Excel

Earned Value Performance Measurement (EVPM) data may be calculated in Microsoft Project (an example is shown at the end of the **UPDATING PROJECTS WITH RESOURCES** chapter) or in Excel. The table below is a simple example of EVPM data and this data may be displayed at any level such as at Project, Phase, WBS Node or task.

- The **Planned Value** is usually exported from Microsoft Project when the schedule is Baselined.
- The **Earned Value** could be calculated either:
  - In Microsoft Project after the project has been updated and transferred to Excel, or
  - Calculated in Excel from the original Baseline Costs multiplied by the % Complete.
- The **Actual Costs** could be calculated either:
  - Outside Microsoft Project and entered into Excel, or
  - In Microsoft Project by entering the detail cost information against each task in Microsoft Project and exporting the rolled up cost into Excel each period.
- The **Estimate To Complete** is displayed in an EVPM graph and may be generated in Microsoft Project after the schedule, resources and costs have been revised and the Estimate To Complete exported to Excel at the required level. This is a very time consuming exercise if performed manually without a time sheet system.

	Jan	Feb	Mar	Apr	May	Jun	Jul	Aug
Planned or BCWS	$ -	$ 6,000	$ 15,000	$ 30,000	$ 43,000	$ 50,000	$ -	$ -
Earned or BCWP	$ -	$ 4,000	$ 10,000	$ 20,000	$ -	$ -	$ -	$ -
Actual or ACWP	$ -	$ 8,000	$ 20,000	$ 40,000	$ -	$ -	$ -	$ -
Estimate At Completion	$ -	$ -	$ -	$ 40,000	$ 55,000	$ 65,000	$ 70,000	$ 75,000

The Excel S-Curve Chart below may be created by highlighting the data in Excel, selecting a **Line** Chart Type and following the Wizard instructions. Histograms are created in a similar way by selecting a different Chart Type.

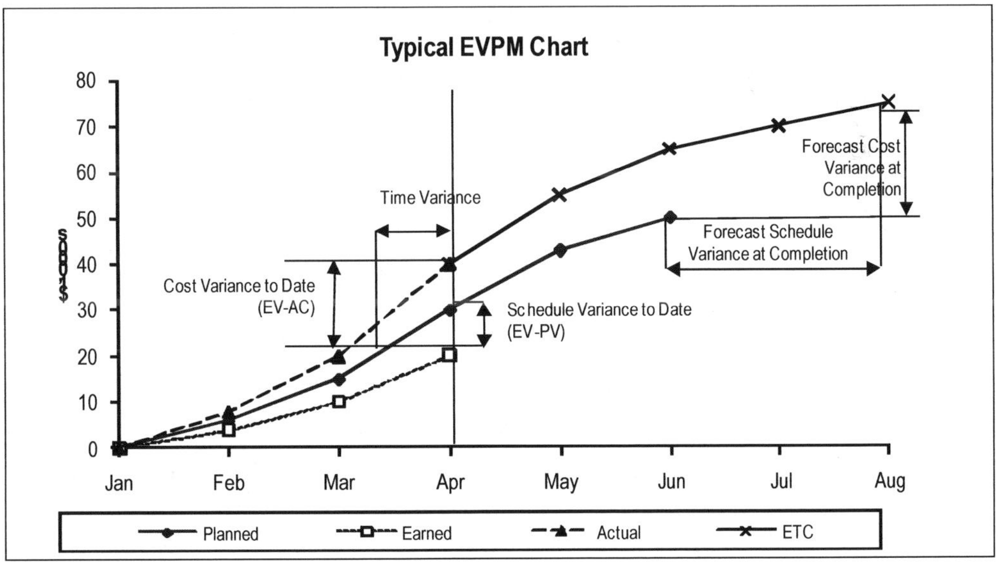

19.9 Resource Optimization

There are many techniques to optimize resource requirements caused by:

- Overloading or peaks in resource requirements, or
- To resolve uneconomical use of resources due intermittent resource use resulting in additional costs required to demobilize and remobilize crews.

19.9.1 Resource Optimization through Leveling

After resource overloads or inefficient use of resources have been identified with Resource Graphs and Usage views the schedule may have to be leveled to reduce peaks and troughs in resource demands. The process of leveling is defined as delaying tasks until resources become available. There are several methods of delaying tasks and thus leveling a schedule:

- **Turning off Automatic Calculation and Dragging Tasks**. This option does not maintain a Critical Path and reverts back to the original schedule when recalculated. This option should not be used when a contract requires a Critical Path schedule to be maintained as the schedule will no longer be calculating correctly.
- **Constraining Tasks**. A constraint may be applied to delay a task until the date that the resource becomes available from a higher priority task. This is not a recommended method because if the higher priority task is delayed the schedule may become unleveled. A delay Milestone should be added so the cause of the delay is easily seen when the plan is reviewed.
- **Sequencing Logic**. Relationships may be applied to tasks sharing the same resource(s) in the order of their priority. In this process a resource-driven Critical Path will be generated. If the first task in a chain is delayed then the chain of tasks will be delayed. But the schedule will not become unleveled and the Critical Path maintained. In this situation a successor task may be able to take place earlier and the logic will have to be manually edited.
- **Leveling Function**. The Leveling function will level resources by automatically delaying tasks without the need for Constraints or Logic and will find the optimum order for the tasks based on nominated parameters. Again, as this option does not maintain a Critical Path it should not be used when a contract requires a Critical Path schedule to be maintained. The Leveling function may be used to establish an optimum scheduling sequence and then Sequencing Logic applied to hold the leveled dates and to create a Critical Path.

19.9.2 Other Methods of Resolving Resource Peaks and Conflicts

Other methods of resolving resourcing problems that are not strictly under the definition of leveling are:

- **Revising the Project Plan**. Revise a project plan to mitigate resource conflicts such as changing the order of work, contracting work out, prefabricating instead of site fabrication, etc.
- **Duration Change**. Increase the task duration to decrease the resource requirements, so a 5-day task with 10 people could be extended to a 10-day task with 5 people.
- **Resource Substitution**. Substitute one resource with another available resource.
- **Increase Working Time**. This will reduce the overall duration of the task may release the resource for other tasks earlier.
- **Splitting** tasks around peaks.
- Manually adjusting hours in **Usage** views.

19.9.3 Resource Leveling Function

Microsoft Project has a basic resource leveling function that is set up through the **Resource Leveling** form by selecting **Resource**, **Level** group, **Leveling** Options.

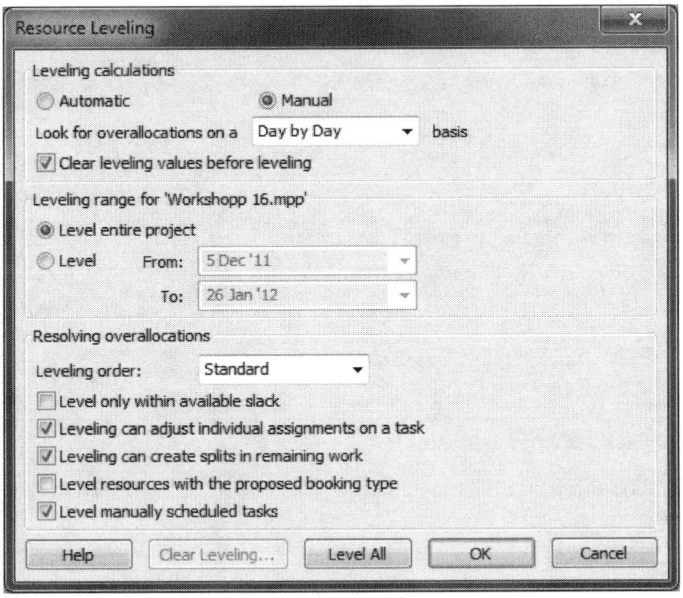

- **Leveling calculations**
  - **Automatic/Manual**. When **Manual** is selected, the buttons in the **Resource Leveling** form are operational. When Automatic is selected, the schedule is always leveled according to the parameters selected in the **Resource Leveling** form.
  - **Look for overallocations on a ... basis** considers the average allocation in the time period selected and only levels when average exceeds the available, thus allowing for short periods of overloading.
  - **Clear leveling values before leveling** un-levels the schedule and then re-levels.
- **Leveling range for...** allows for the whole project or a time portion of a schedule to be leveled, such as a Stage or Phase.
- **Resolving overallocations**
  - **Leveling order:** allows three options for the order that tasks are prioritized for leveling. One option is the task **Priority** field which may be set in a column or in the **General** tab of the **Task Information** form. A **Priority** of 0 is the lowest priority and 1000 is the highest and tasks that must not be delayed should be set at 1000.
  - **Level only within available slack** will not delay the end date of the project but will attempt to level the schedule in the available Total Slack (Total Float).
  - **Leveling can adjust individual assignments on a task** allows one resource assigned to a task to be delayed in relation to others assigned to the same task, thus allowing other resources to work as scheduled. This will in effect increase the duration of a task and may result in a split task. This function works in conjunction with the **Level Assignments** field that may be displayed in a column. Individual tasks may or may not be allowed to have their resource assignments adjusted. This function has a similar effect to the Oracle Primavera P3 and SureTrak Task Type Independent which has been omitted from Oracle Primavera P6.
  - **Leveling can create splits in remaining work** allows leveling to split or not to split tasks during leveling.

- ➢ **Level resources with proposed booking type** will include these resources when leveling.
- ➢ **Level manually scheduled tasks** will also include these tasks in the leveling calculations.

- Clear Leveling... allows the option of clearing leveling for selected task or all tasks and returns the schedule to the unleveled state.

19.9.4 Resource, Level group Ribbon Commands

This group of commands has the following options:

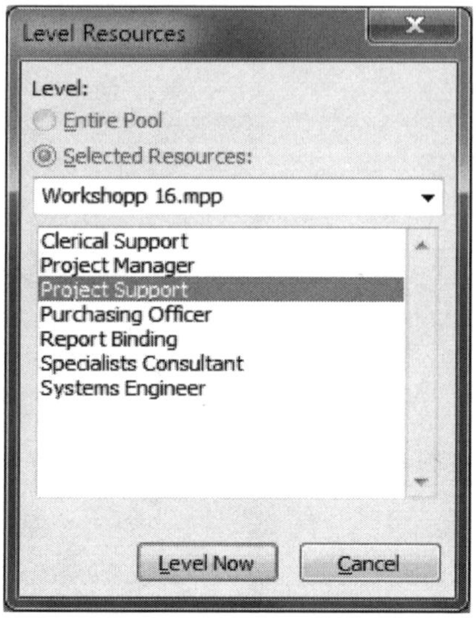

- **Level Selection** levels two or more tasks that have been selected.
- **Level Resources** opens the **Level Resources** form allowing the selection of one or more resources for leveling.
- **Level All** levels the project based on the parameters set in the **Resource Leveling** form.
- **Clear Leveling** un-levels the project.
- **Next Overallocation** scrolls through one overallocated task to another.

19.10 Workshop 17 – Resource Graphs and Tables

Background

We will create a copy of our current project file for this workshop, then use Usage Views and Graphs to isolate the resources that are overallocated and level the schedule.

Assignment

1. Save your OzBuild Bid project file and then resave as **OzBuild Leveling**.
2. Display the **Gantt Chart** view in the top pane, the **Resource Usage** view in the bottom pane and adjust the timescale to show days only as per the picture below.
3. Click on **Select All button** to display all resources. The overloaded resources are highlighted in red.
4. Set the Timescale to daily.
5. Right-click in the bottom pane and display both the Work and Overallocation resources. The overallocated resources are highlighted in red and the overallocated lines of data show by how much:

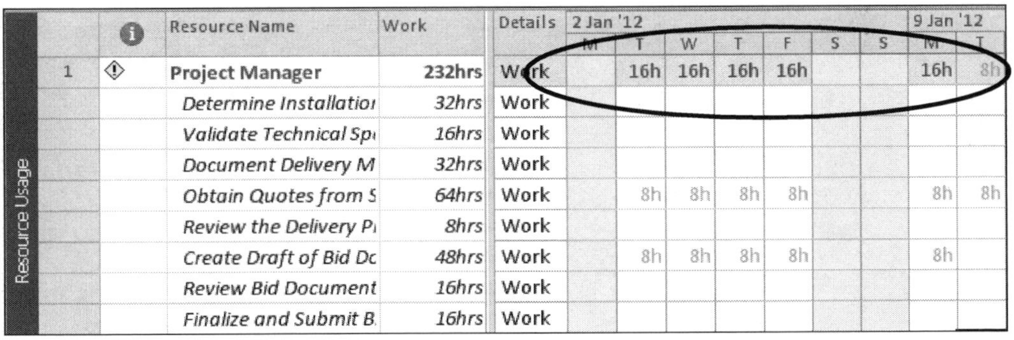

		Resource Name	Work	Details	2 Jan '12 M	T	W	T	F	S	S	9 Jan '12 M	T
1		Project Manager	232hrs	Work		16h	16h	16h	16h			16h	8h
		Determine Installatio	*32hrs*	Work									
		Validate Technical Sp	*16hrs*	Work									
		Document Delivery M	*32hrs*	Work									
		Obtain Quotes from S	*64hrs*	Work		8h	8h	8h	8h			8h	8h
		Review the Delivery P	*8hrs*	Work									
		Create Draft of Bid Dc	*48hrs*	Work		8h	8h	8h	8h			8h	
		Review Bid Document	*16hrs*	Work									
		Finalize and Submit B	*16hrs*	Work									

6. Display the **Resource Graph** form in the bottom pane and check the Histograms for the resources. Note again the overallocated resources:

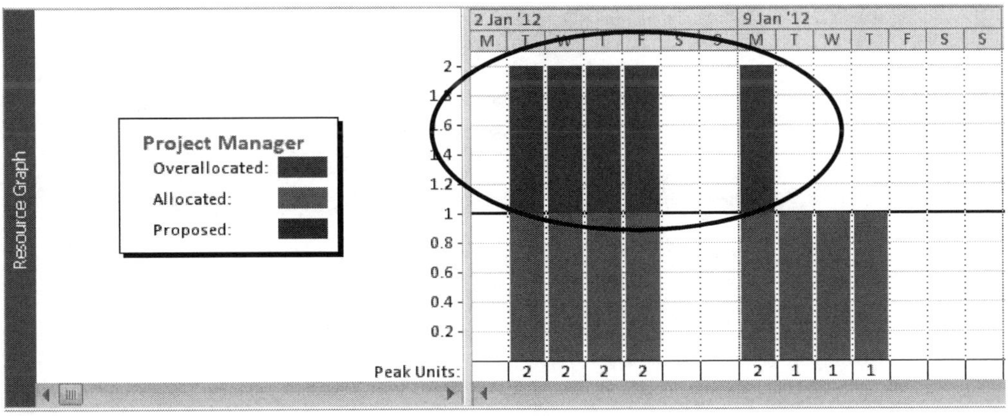

7. Set the Baseline and display the Baseline bars.
8. Now level the schedule, select **Resource**, **Leveling Options** to open the **Resource Leveling** form:
9. Set the options as per below and click on Level All:

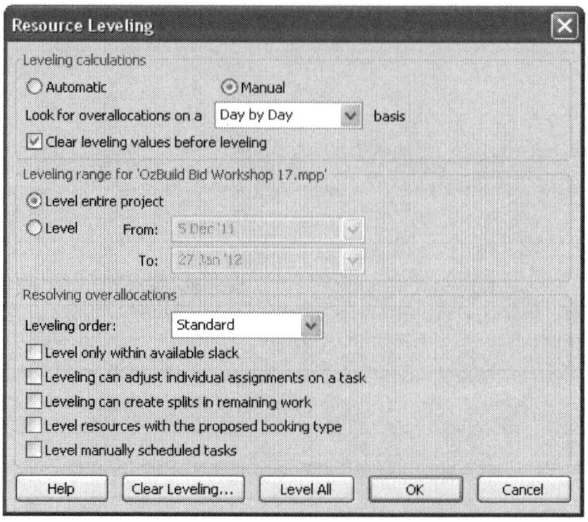

10. Your answer should look like this, with task 13 delayed and the end data delayed:

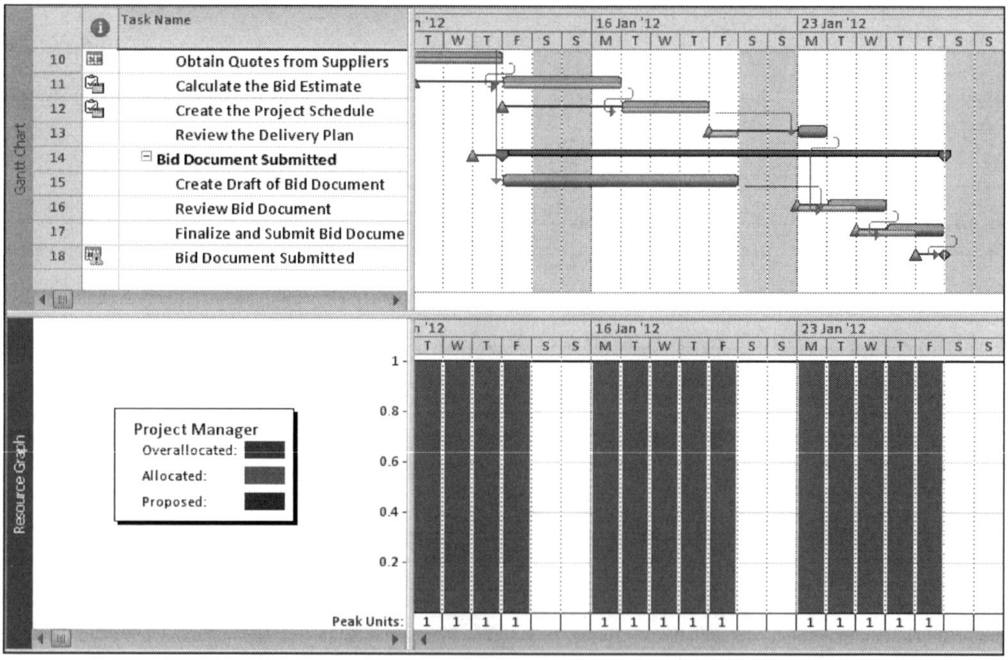

11. Now clear the leveling and try with different options.

20 UPDATING PROJECTS WITH RESOURCES

Updating a project with resources uses a number of features that are very complex and interactive. It is suggested that after you have read this chapter and before you work on a live project that you create a simple schedule with a couple of tasks and assign two or three resources against each task. Set the **Options** to reflect the way you want to enter the information and how you want Microsoft Project to calculate. Go through the updating process with dummy data and then check that the results are as you expected. The options to consider are:

- How is the measure of progress at the summary task level displayed? The summary **% Work** is based on hours of effort, which is more meaningful than the summary **% Complete**, which is based on durations. Or are you displaying the **Physical % Complete** which does not roll up to the summary tasks?
- Have you linked **% Complete** and **% Work** with the **File**, **Options**, **Schedule** tab, **Calculation options for this project:**, **Updating task status updates resource status** option? If unlinked, the **% Work** may be different from **% Complete**.
- Do you want Microsoft Project to calculate the resource **Actual Costs** with the option **File**, **Options**, **Schedule** tab, **Calculation options for this project:**, **Actual costs are always calculated by Project**?
- Are your tasks scheduled to start after a date using the **Project**, **Status** group, **Update Project**, **Reschedule uncompleted tasks to start after:** in conjunction with the **File**, **Options**, **Schedule** tab, **Scheduling options for this project:** section, **Split in-progress tasks** option?

Updating a project with resources takes place in two distinct steps:

- The dates are updated using the methods outlined in the **TRACKING PROGRESS** chapter, then
- The resources' hours and costs are updated.

This chapter covers the following topics:

- Understanding **Baseline Dates** (Target Dates), **Baseline Costs** (Budget) and **Baseline Work**.
- Understanding the **Status Date**, **Work After Date** and **Current Date** with respect to resources.
- Information Required to Update a Resourced Schedule.
- Updating Resources.
- Splitting Tasks.
- Summary Task Interim Baseline Calculation.

Microsoft Project does not provide the capability of producing multiple S-Curves. The data may be exported or copied and pasted to products such as Excel where S-Curves may be created.

20.1 Understanding Baseline Dates, Duration, Costs and Hours

Baseline Dates are also known as Target Dates and are normally the original Project Early Start and Early Finish dates. These are the dates against which project progress is measured.

Baseline Duration is the original planned duration of a task.

Baseline Costs are also known as Budgets and represent the original project cost estimate. These are the figures against which the expenditures and Cost at Completion (or Estimate at Completion) are measured.

Baseline Work is also known as Budgeted Quantity and represents the original estimate of the project quantities. These are the quantities against which the consumption of resources are measured.

The **Baseline Costs** and **Work** of resources are **NOT** automatically recorded in the Baseline fields of each resource as the resource is assigned to a task. All **Baseline** information **(Dates**, **Costs** and **Work)** is saved when the project or selected tasks have the Baseline set. Baseline data is saved at task and resource assignment level.

If resources have been assigned then the Baseline Costs and Work are recorded at the same time as the Baseline dates.

Setting the **Baseline Dates** is covered in the **TRACKING PROGRESS** chapter.

Baseline Dates may be displayed by using the following methods:

- Baseline Date Start and Finish columns, or
- Bar Chart Bars, or
- Dates on the Bars, or
- In forms such as the **Task Details** form.

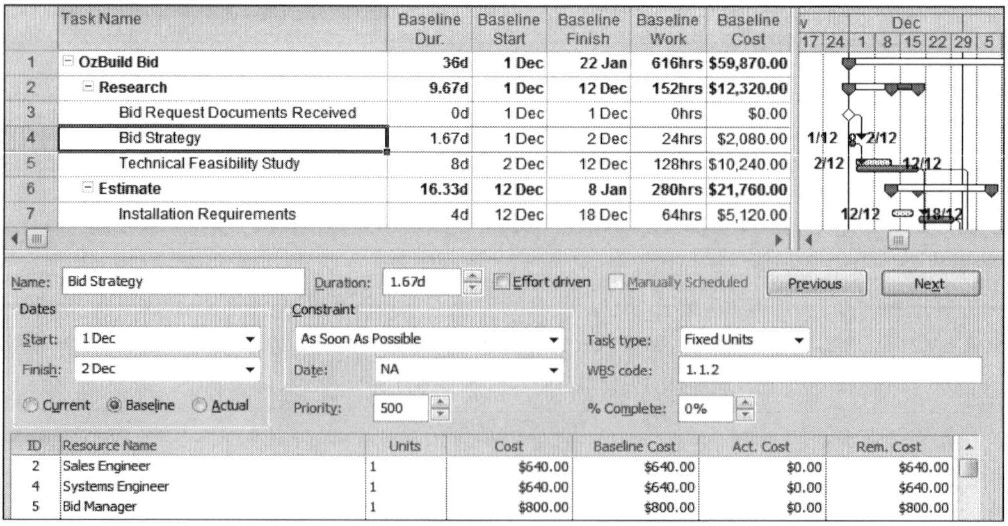

20.2 Understanding the Status Date

The **Status Date** is a standard scheduling term. It is also known as the **Data Date**, **Review Date**, **Status Date**, **As of Date**, **Report Date** and **Update Date**.

- The **Status Date** is the date that divides the past from the future in the schedule. The **Status Date** is not normally in the future but is often in the recent past due to the time it may take to collect the information to update the schedule.
- **Actual Costs** and **Quantities/Hours** or **Actual Work** occur before the **Status Date**.
- **Costs** and **Quantities/Hours To Complete** or **Work to Complete** occur after the **Status Date**.
- **Remaining duration** is the duration required to complete a task. It is calculated forward from the **Data Date**.

Microsoft Project has four dates associated with updating a schedule. These are covered in the **TRACKING PROGRESS** chapter. In summary, these date fields are:

- **Current Date** – This date is set to the computer's system date, by default at 08:00hrs, each time a project file is opened. It is used to calculate **Earned Value** data when a **Status Date** is not set.
- **Status Date** – By default this is blank. After assigning this date, by default at 17:00hrs, it will not change (the **Current Date** does) when the project is saved or reopened at a later date. When set, this date overrides the **Current Date** for calculating **Earned Value** data.
- **Update work as completed through:** (date) – When a project is updated using the **Update Project** form (the project is updated as if it were progressing exactly according to plan), the **Status Date** is set to the same date as **Project Update Date** at 17:00hrs.
- **Reschedule uncompleted work to start after:** date – This function is used to move the **Incomplete Work** of **In-Progress** tasks into the future.
  - **In-Progress** tasks must be able to **Split** for this function to operate. The option to split tasks is found on the **File**, **Options**, **Schedule** tab.
  - The **Status Date** is **NOT** set to the **Reschedule uncompleted work to start after:** date when this function is used.
  - This function will not move the incomplete portions of tasks back in time when a task is completed ahead of schedule. This causes the task's **Remaining Duration** to occur sometime in the future and not immediately after the selected date. The example below shows a schedule with the **Reschedule uncompleted work to start after:** date set to 10 June. The top task's Remaining Duration commences on 11 June, the task is split and the Remaining Duration occurs immediately after 10 June. The lower task's Remaining Duration does not commence until 18 June. This is not realistic and manual intervention is required to correct this.

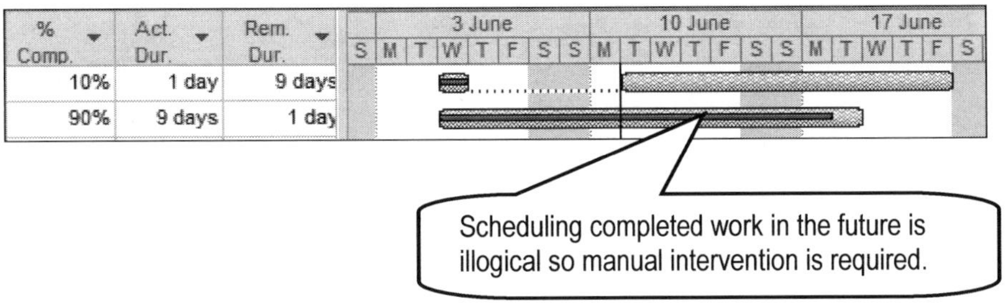

NEITHER the **Current Date** nor the **Status Date** is used to calculate the **Early Finish** of an **In-Progress** task when a schedule is calculated.

When **Automatic Scheduling** is disabled (e.g. the **File**, **Options**, **Schedule** tab, **Calculation** section **Calculate project after each edit is** not checked) then the schedule is recalculated using the **F9** key.

The end date of an in-progress task in Microsoft Project is normally calculated from the **Actual Start Date** plus the **Duration**. This is a different method of calculation than employed by other scheduling software, which normally calculates the end date of a task from a single **Data Date** plus the **Remaining Duration**. This ensures all incomplete work is in the future.

Users of Microsoft Project must spend more time checking the schedule to ensure that completed work is all in the past and incomplete work is in the future in relation to the **Status Date**.

There are a number of scheduling methods and functions available to achieve this situation but the software will not automatically make this happen.

20.3 Formatting the Current Date and Status Date Lines

To format the display of the **Current Date** and **Status Date** lines on the Bar Chart, select **Format**, **Format** group, **Gridlines...** to display the **Gridlines** form:

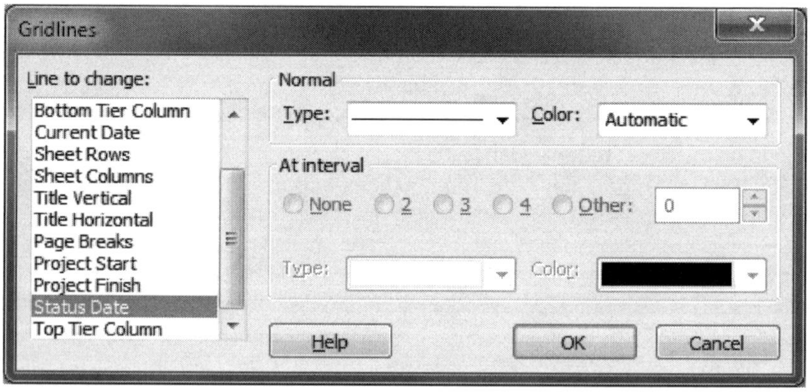

- These **Options** allow the selection of colors and line types for all sight lines as shown in the **Lines to Change** box on the left of the example above.
- All other sight lines may also be formatted in this form.

It is suggested that the **Current Date** be removed to avoid confusion with the **Status Date**.

The **Status Date** should be displayed in a color that is different to the relationship and grid lines so it stands out, for example solid black.

20.4 Information Required to Update a Resourced Schedule

A project schedule is usually updated at the end of a period, such as each day, week or month. One purpose of updating a schedule is to establish differences between the plan and the current schedule and if necessary, take action to bring the project back on track.

Microsoft Project may calculate task **Actual Costs** from the rates entered in the **Resource Table** or the costs may be entered manually. This option is set in the **File**, **Options**, **Schedule** tab. If the **Actual Costs** are to be calculated by Microsoft Project then the **Actual Costs** do not need to be collected. The following information is required to update a resourced schedule:

Tasks completed in the update period:

- **Actual Start** date of the task.
- **Actual Finish** date of the task.
- **Actual Costs** spent, **Actual Resource Hours** spent, and/or **Actual Material Quantities**.

Tasks commenced in the update period:

- **Actual Start** date of the task.
- **Remaining Duration** or **Expected Finish** date.
- **Actual Costs** and **Actual Resource Hours** and/or **Actual Material Quantities**.
- **Hours** or **Quantities** to complete. Costs to complete are always calculated using the resource rates in the Resource Table.
- **Stop** date and **Resume** date for tasks that have had their work suspended. These may be used for splitting tasks.

Tasks Not Commenced:

- Changes in logic or date constraints.
- Changes in estimated **Costs**, **Hours** or **Quantities**.
- Any additional tasks to represent new work.

The schedule may be updated once this information is collected.

You have the option of allowing Microsoft Project to calculate many of these fields from the **% Complete** by selecting the appropriate option found in the **File**, **Options, Schedule** tab.

20.5 Updating Dates and Percentage Complete

The schedule should be first updated as outlined in the **TRACKING PROGRESS** chapter. In summary, this is completed by entering:

- The **Actual Start** and **Actual Finish** dates of **Complete** tasks.
- The **Actual Start**, **% Complete**, **Remaining Duration** or **Expected Finish** of **In-Progress** tasks.
- Adjust Logic and **Durations** of **Un-started** tasks.

Before you do this, you should set the **File**, **Options, Schedule** tab to ensure that the actual costs and hours calculate the way you want.

20.6 Updating Resources

There are many permutations available in the **File**, **Options** form for calculating resource data. Due to the number of resource options and numerous forms available in Microsoft Project, it is not feasible to document all the combinations available for resource calculation.

This book, therefore, outlines some typical scenarios and examples of entering the update data that you may want to try on your projects.

Material and **Cost** resources are updated in a similar way as **Work** resources and are not covered separately.

20.6.1 Updating Tasks with Fixed Costs Only

A project with fixed costs only is the simplest option for managing costs. The example below displays:

- A 10-day **Duration** task which is 50% Complete.
- A **Baseline Cost** of $1,000.00 which was created by an original **Fixed Cost** of $1000.00 when the **Baseline** was set.
- A **Fixed Cost** of $800.00 representing a revised estimate that has reduced the original estimate by $200.00 to $800.00.
- An **Actual Cost** of $400.00 and **Remaining Cost** of $400.00, which are calculated from the 50 **% Complete**.
- The **Current Bar** (the upper bar in the picture below) shows that the task started 2 days late and is scheduled to end 2 days late as compared to the **Baseline Bar** (the black lower bar).

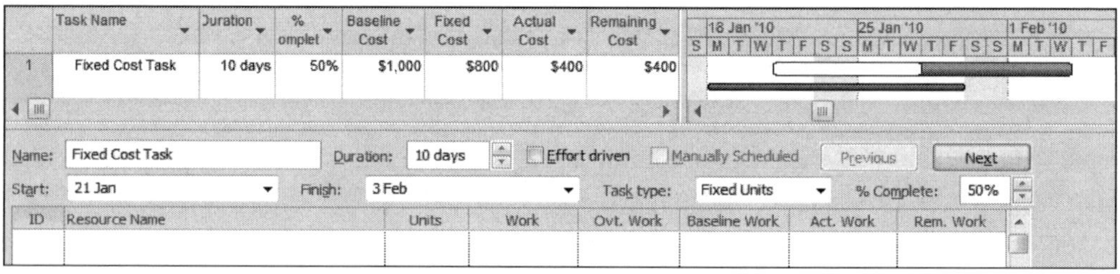

You will notice that the **Task Details** view with the **Resource Cost** details form does not show any resources or costs when **Fixed Costs** are used.

The disadvantage of fixed costs is that they are always linked to the % Complete and an independent Actual Fixed Cost may not be entered. Microsoft Project 2007 introduced Cost Resources which has resolved this problem.

20.6.2 Forecasting Resource Hours

The next level of complexity usually occurs when a schedule is used for the management of resource hours but not costs.

One or more resources may be applied to a task and you may want to enter both the **Actual Work** and the **Remaining Work** independently. In this situation you will need to unlink **% Complete** and **Actual Work** with the **Updating task status updates resource status** option in the **File**, **Options**, **Schedule** tab. Now the **% Work** field will be linked to the **Work**, **Actual Work** and **Remaining Work** fields and will now operate independently of the **% Complete** field.

The example below uses the **Task Details** form.

- A 10-day **Duration** task which is 40% Complete.
- The task's **Baseline Work** of 240 hours is from the addition of the two resource allocations when the **Baseline** was set.
    - The Bid Manager was originally assigned at 100%, or full-time, giving a Baseline Work of 80 hours.
    - The **Clerical Support** was originally assigned at 200%, or 2 full-time people, giving a **Baseline Work** of 160 hours.
- The task's **Actual Work** of 90 hours is the addition of the two resources' **Actual Work** of 20 hours and 70 hours.
- The task's **Remaining Work** of 220 hours is the addition of the **Remaining Work** of 70 hours and 150 hours.
- The **% Work** of 29% is calculated by dividing the **Actual Work** by the **Work.** This is different to from the **% Complete**, which represents the elapsed time.
- Again, the **Current Bar** shows the task started two days late and is scheduled to end two days late.

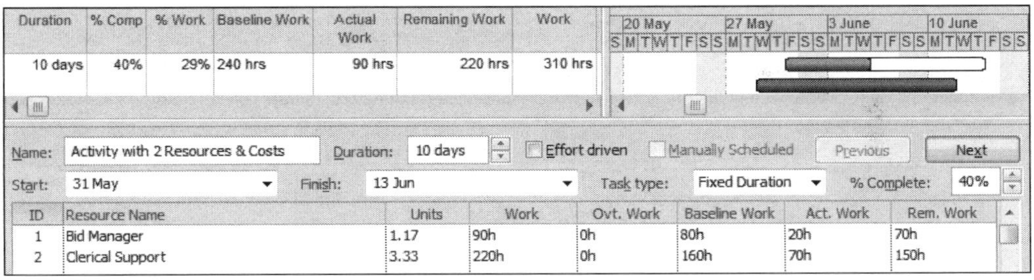

- The **Actual Work** and **Remaining Work** were entered manually and have not been calculated by Microsoft Project from the **% Complete**.
- The duration of the task is still 10 days long because it is a **Fixed Duration** task. The **Units** have increased from 1 to 1.17 and 2 to 3.33 for the Bid Manager and Clerical Support, respectively, as the **Work** is now greater than the **Baseline Work** due to the increase in the number of hours required to complete the task.

20.6.3 Forecasting Resource Hours and Costs Form

The example below is similar to the previous example, but it now displays the **Resource Costs** (not the **Work)** calculated by Microsoft Project with **% Complete** and **Actual Work** unlinked.

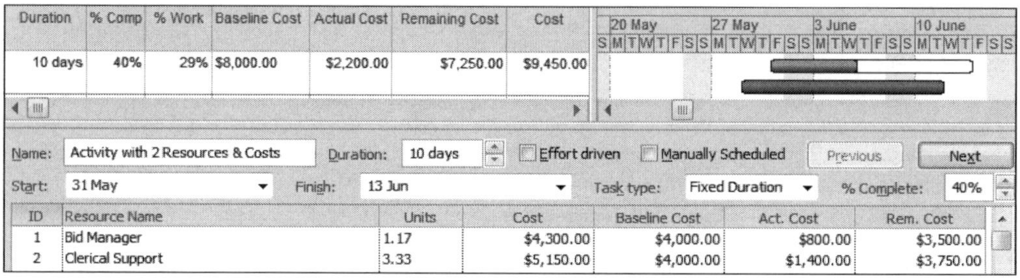

The next level of complexity occurs usually when a schedule is used for the management of resource hours and costs.

You may want to enter both the **Actual Work** and **Actual Costs** separately. For example, you may want to take the costs and hours from a timesheet and/or an accounting system that may have a different resource rate than your schedule. Input your data in the bottom pane of the window, which is known as the **Resource Details** form. This process is very time consuming and requires significant organizational commitment to succeed.

In this situation you will need to:

- Unlink **% Complete** and **Actual Work** with the **Updating task status updates resource status** option in the **File**, **Options, Schedule** tab, and
- Unlink the **Actual Work** and **Actual Costs** by disabling the **Actual costs are always calculated by Project** option in the **File**, **Options, Schedule** tab.

The example below shows how the costs are calculated with:

- **Work** and **Costs** unlinked, and
- Updated hours as per the previous example.

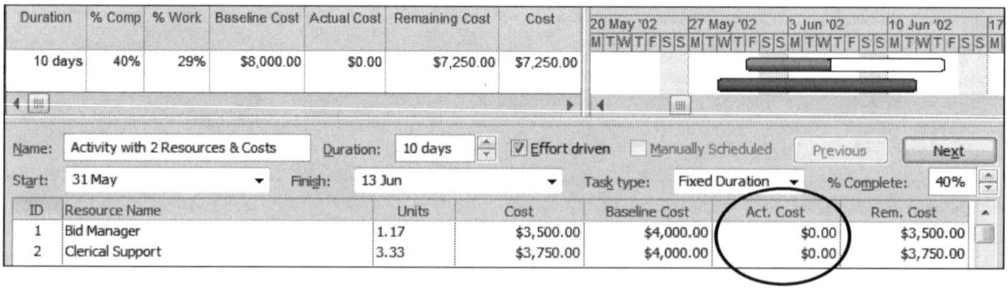

The **Actual Costs** have not been calculated by Microsoft Project and remain at zero. The **Remaining Costs** are based on the resources' **Standard Rate**. The **Actual Costs** should be entered by the user to update the schedule.

Now that the Actual Costs and Actual Work are unlinked, you may type in the **Actual Costs** per resource in the bottom pane of the window (i.e., the **Resource Details** form) without affecting the **Actual Work.**

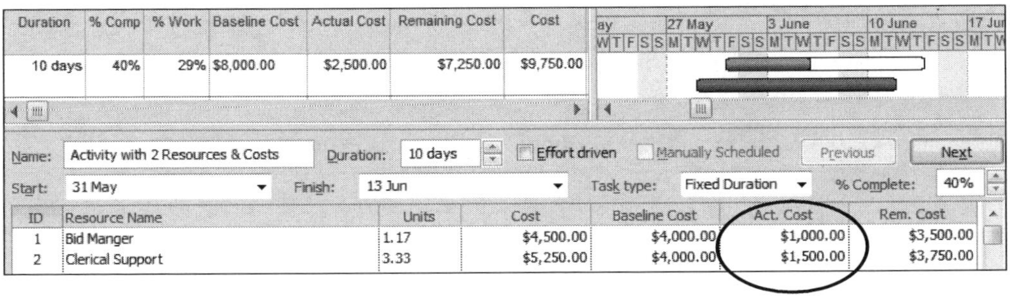

20.6.4 Using the Task Usage and Resource Usage Views

The **Task Usage** and **Resource Usage** forms allow the most flexibility when entering resource quantities and costs to used date, e.g. **Actual Work** and **Actual Cost**. The picture below is the **Task Usage** form from the OzBuild workshops showing the **Work**, **Actual Work** and **Baseline Work** rows. Additional rows of information may be obtained by right-clicking to display a menu.

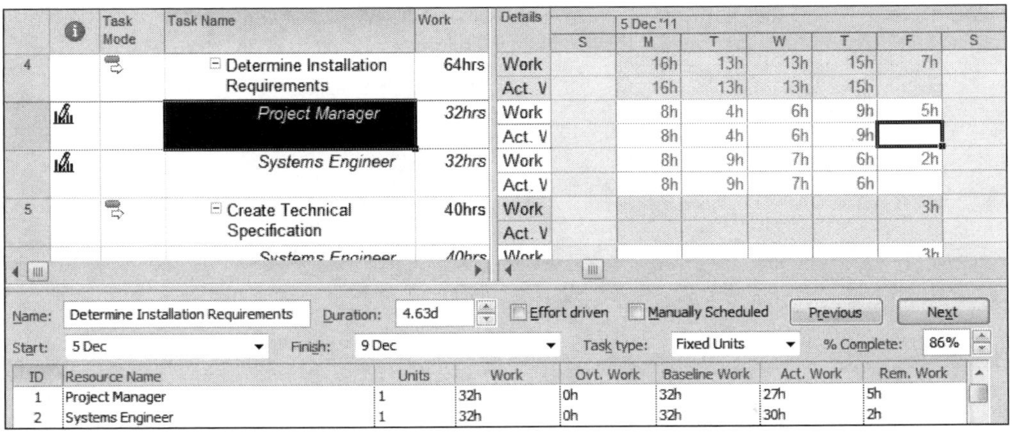

A timesheet-style view may be created with the **Resource Usage** view. This view may be printed or used by team members to directly update their hours to-date in the **Act. Work** (Actual Work) rows and their estimated hours in the **Work** rows. The advantage of this view is that all tasks are grouped together in one band under each name. The Project Manager's hours for Fri 9 Dec could be typed into the highlighted square above.

Calculated fields that may not have data entered into them are shaded, such as the task rows in the picture above.

20.7 Splitting Tasks

When the **Split in-progress tasks** option is enabled, a task may be **Split** by:

- Dragging the incomplete portion of a task in the bar chart, or
- Clicking on the button and then moving your cursor over the point on the task bar where you want a split and dragging the task, or
- Using the **Project**, **Status** group, **Update Project**, **Reschedule uncompleted work to start after:** function, or
- Commencing a task before its predecessor finishes.

In the picture below the upper task was split using the button and the lower task was split because it commenced before its predecessor.

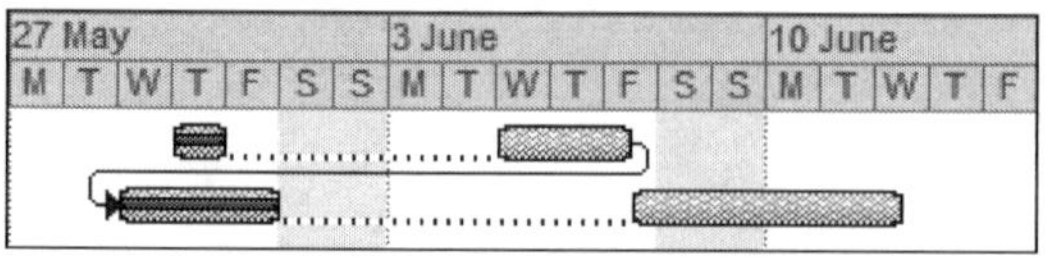

A **Split** may be reversed by dragging the split portion back in the bar chart if there is no predecessor pushing the split out. The first task in the example below has been dragged back. The second task may not be dragged back due to the FS relationship. The relationship could be removed.

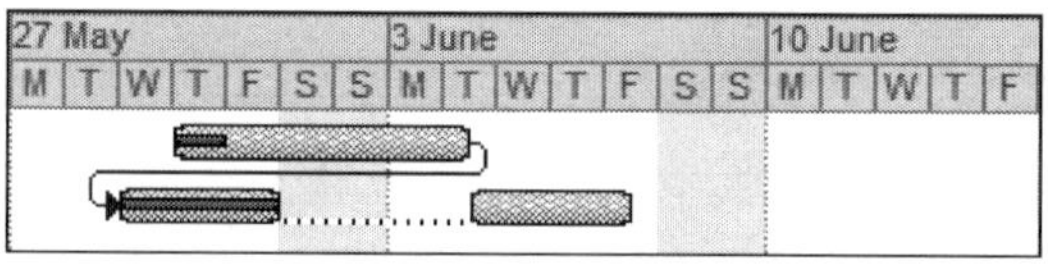

Once a task is **Split**, then the resources are not scheduled to work during the split period. This concept is demonstrated in the **RESOURCE OPTIMIZATION** chapter.

Sometimes a split occurs at the end of the task as per the picture below and the task has a series of dots at the end. This is as a result of the last part of a split task having a zero duration. This may often be removed by dragging the end of the split to create a duration in the last part, and then dragging the split task together:

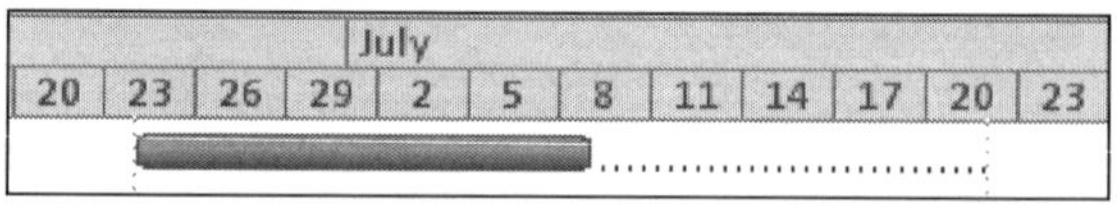

20.8 Summary Tasks and Earned Value

Actual Costs and **Work** may be summarized at any level in the same way as **Work** and **Costs**. The picture below is showing the **Earned Value** table. The costs have been summarized up to the Project Level:

	Task Name	Planned Value - PV (BCWS)	Earned Value - EV (BCWP)	AC (ACWP)	SV	CV	EAC	BAC	VAC
1	**OzBuild Initiation**	**7,440.00**	**7,908.00**	**8,040.00**	**468.00**	**-132.00**	**55,979.06**	**55,060.00**	**-919.06**
2	Approval to Bid	0.00	0.00	0.00	0.00	0.00	0.00	0.00	0.00
3	**Technical Specificati**	**7,440.00**	**7,908.00**	**8,040.00**	**468.00**	**-132.00**	**20,130.50**	**19,800.00**	**-330.50**
4	Determine Installation	6,720.00	6,720.00	5,040.00	0.00	1,680.00	5,040.00	6,720.00	1,680.00
5	Create Technical Sp	720.00	1,188.00	3,000.00	468.00	1,812.00	21,717.17	8,600.00	13,117.17
6	Identify Supplier Cor	0.00	0.00	0.00	0.00	0.00	1,120.00	1,120.00	0.00
7	Validate Technical S	0.00	0.00	0.00	0.00	0.00	3,360.00	3,360.00	0.00
8	**Delivery Plan**	**0.00**	**0.00**	**0.00**	**0.00**	**0.00**	**21,520.00**	**21,520.00**	**0.00**
14	**Bid Document**	**0.00**	**0.00**	**0.00**	**0.00**	**0.00**	**13,740.00**	**13,740.00**	**0.00**
18	Bid Document Submitte	0.00	0.00	0.00	0.00	0.00	0.00	0.00	0.00

The terminology below is used by a large number of companies and organizations. It provides standard terms to describe Earned Value calculations, which many people understand. Below are some of the terms that are in common use:

- AC or ACWP — Actual Cost or Actual Cost of Work Performed
- EV or BCWP — Earned Value or Budget Cost of Work Performed
- PV or BCWS — Planned Value or Budget Cost of Work Scheduled
- BAC — Budget At Completion
- C/SCSC — Cost/Schedule Control Systems Criteria (CS^2)
- CV — Cost Variance to date, BCWP – ACWP
- EAC — Estimate At Completion
- ETC Time — Estimate To Complete expressed in Time
- ETC — Estimate To Complete
- FAC $ — Forecast at Completion
- FC CV — Forecast Cost Variance at Completion (Budget – Forecast)
- FC SV — Forecast Schedule Variance at Completion (Baseline End Date – Scheduled End Date)
- FTC CT — Forecast To Complete Calendar Time
- SV — Schedule Variance to date, BCWP – BCWS
- VAC — Variance At Completion

The **Physical % Complete** field may be used to calculate the Earned Value (Budget Cost of Work Performed) independently from the value in the task **% Complete** field. The **Physical % Complete** function is useful for measuring the progress of work that is not progressing linearly. This may be set for each individual task in the **General** tab of the **Task Information** form. The default for new tasks may be set with the [Earned Value...] button in the **General** tab of the **Options** form, where the Baseline to be used for the Earned Value calculations may be selected.

The method that Microsoft Project uses to calculate the Earned Value data is documented in the Help file and should be read carefully, as different versions of Microsoft calculate these fields differently. Should different Earned Value calculations be required then Custom Data Fields should be considered as an alternative.

20.9 Workshop 18 - Updating a Resourced Schedule

Background

We need to update the tasks and resources.

Assignment

NOTE: If your settings are not exactly the same as the computer on which this exercise was undertaken or you enter data in a different order you may end up with different results.

Close the Leveling workshop and open your OzBuild with Resources project file and complete the following steps:

1. We will initially allow Microsoft Project to calculate costs and hours from the % Complete. Adjust the options using **File**, **Options**, **Schedule** tab, **Calculation options for this project:** to:
   - **CHECK** the **Updating task status updates resource status** option. This will link % Complete and Actual Work. (This option also needs to be checked to allow Summary % Completes to be spread correctly to detail tasks.)
   - **CHECK** the **Actual costs are always calculated by Microsoft Project** option. With this option checked the resource Actual Cost is calculated by Microsoft Project from the resource Work and Rates.
2. Ensure the **Split in-progress tasks** option in the **File**, **Options**, **Schedule** tab, **Scheduling options for this project:** section is **UNCHECKED**.
3. Save the Baseline using **Project**, **Schedule** group, **Set Baseline**.
4. Split the screen. Display the **Gantt Chart** with **Tracking** table in the upper screen and the **Task Details Form** with **Resource Work** details form in the Bottom Pane.
5. Display the **Baseline** bars.
6. Format the Timescale to **Weeks 28 Jan '02** and **Days M,T,W,...** at 100%.
7. Display the **Status Date** as a solid black gridline by selecting **Format**, **Format** group, **Gridlines**.
8. We are recording progress as of the end of the second week in December, so we will set the **Status Date** as Friday 9 Dec 2011. The time will default to the end of the work day:
   - Update the project using **Project**, **Status** group, **Update Project**, as per the picture below:

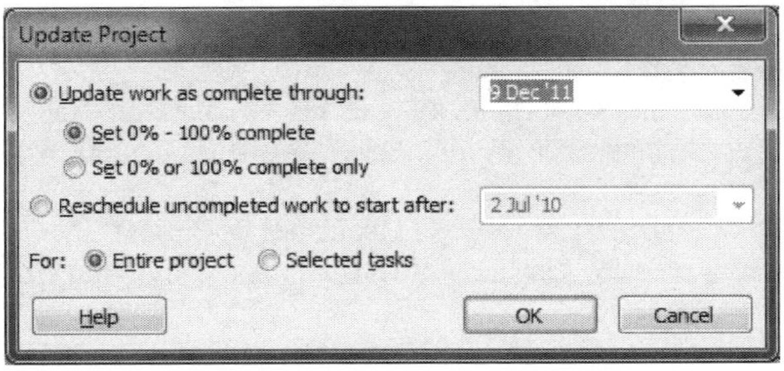

- Check the **Status Date** in the **Project**, **Properties** group, **Project Information** form. It should be 9 Dec 11 and the Status Date should be displayed on the Gantt Chart.
- The **Physical % Complete** has not been updated. This optional field may be used for entering the progress. It is not linked to the durations and may be used for calculating the Earned Value.
- Hide the **Physical % Complete** column if displayed.

9. Update task **4 Determine Installation Requirements**
   - Enter 48 hours in the **Actual Work** cell of task **4 Determine Installation Requirements**.
   - Ensure the Remaining Work remains zero by typing zero against the resources in the Task Details Form.
   - The duration shortens as the task is **Fixed Units** and the cost will change.
   - The Actual Costs have been recalculated, see the **Resource Costs** tab in the bottom pane.
   - Also an Actual Finish has been set without warning.
10. Updating **5 Create Technical Specification**
    - Select task **5 Create Technical Specification** and look at the **Resource Work** and then open the **Resource Cost** forms in the bottom pane. Observe how the Systems Engineer's work and costs have been updated but the Specialists Consultant costs has not been updated. The Specialists Consultant cost could be manually updated if cost had been incurred.
    - Enter an Actual Start Date of 7 Dec 11 and enter 60% Complete against task **5 Create Technical Specification**. Task **6 Identify Supplier Components** should also start earlier as its predecessor is scheduled to finish earlier. Press F9 if required.

	Task Name	Act. Start	Act. Finish	% Comp.	Act. Dur.	Rem. Dur.	Act. Cost	Act. Work
1	**OzBuild Initiation**	**5 Dec '11**	**NA**	**15%**	**5.27d**	**30.73d**	**7,200.00**	**72hrs**
2	**Technical Specific**	**5 Dec '11**	**NA**	**50%**	**5.5d**	**5.5d**	**7,200.00**	**72hrs**
3	Approval to Bic	5 Dec '11	5 Dec '11	100%	0d	0d	0.00	0hrs
4	Determine Inst	5 Dec '11	7 Dec '11	100%	3d	0d	5,040.00	48hrs
5	Create Technic	7 Dec '11	NA	60%	3d	2d	2,160.00	24hrs
6	Identify Suppli	NA	NA	0%	0d	2d	0.00	0hrs
7	Validate Techn	NA	NA	0%	0d	2d	0.00	0hrs

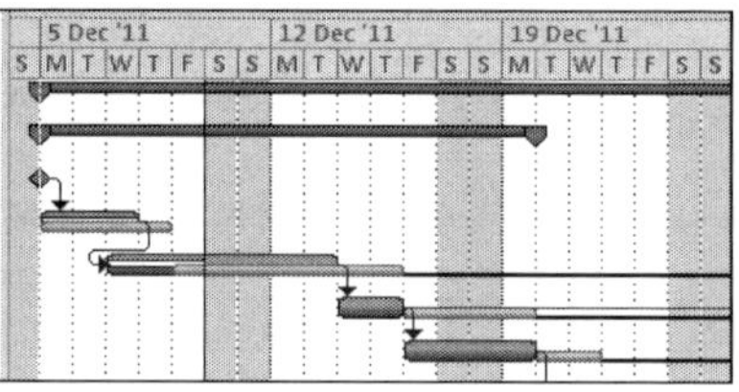

11. Enter 6d Remaining Duration against task **5 Create Technical Specification**, the % Comp should equal 33% and notice in the **Task Details** form that the remaining costs and remaining hours have increased.
    - Press F9 to recalculate and your schedule should look like this:

	Task Name	Act. Start	Act. Finish	% Comp.	Act. Dur.	Rem. Dur.	Act. Cost	Act. Work
1	**OzBuild Initiation**	**5 Dec '11**	**NA**	**13%**	**4.8d**	**31.2d**	**7,200.00**	**72hrs**
2	**Technical Specific**	**5 Dec '11**	**NA**	**38%**	**5.63d**	**9.38d**	**7,200.00**	**72hrs**
3	Approval to Bic	5 Dec '11	5 Dec '11	100%	0d	0d	0.00	0hrs
4	Determine Inst	5 Dec '11	7 Dec '11	100%	3d	0d	5,040.00	48hrs
5	Create Technic	7 Dec '11	NA	33%	3d	6d	2,160.00	24hrs
6	Identify Suppli	NA	NA	0%	0d	2d	0.00	0hrs
7	Validate Techn	NA	NA	0%	0d	2d	0.00	0hrs

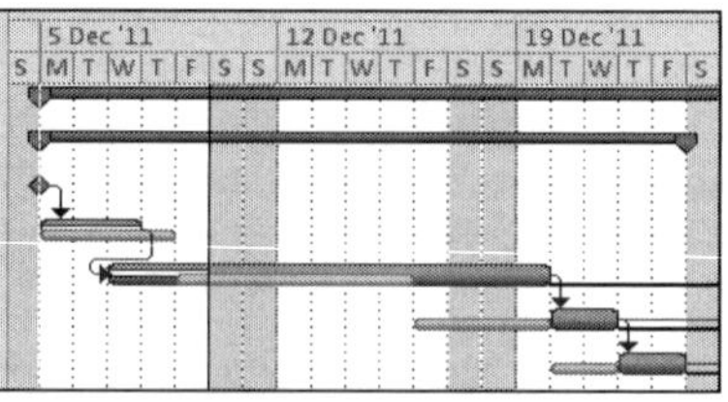

12. Now enter the hours and costs to date and hours to go. To prevent Microsoft Project from calculating the actual costs from the actual hours, open the **File**, **Options** form, **Schedule** tab, **Calculation options for this project** and:
    - **UNCHECK** the **Updating task status updates resource status**. This option is to prevent the updated % Complete from calculating **Actual Work** and **Remaining Work** by unlinking the % Complete from the % Work fields.
    - **UNCHECK** the **Actual costs are always calculated by Project**. This option is to prevent Microsoft Project from calculating the **Actual Costs** from the **Actual Work**.

13. We will now update the tasks:
    - Right-click in the **Task Form** and display the **Work** tab, then
    - Update task **5 Create Technical Specification**, with 72 hours of **Remaining Work** against the **Systems Engineer**,
    - Click the **OK** button to accept the changes.

    NOTE: The task remaining duration extends to 9 days. This is because the task is **Fixed Units**, so the **Units** stayed the same and duration was extended. Your schedule should look like this:

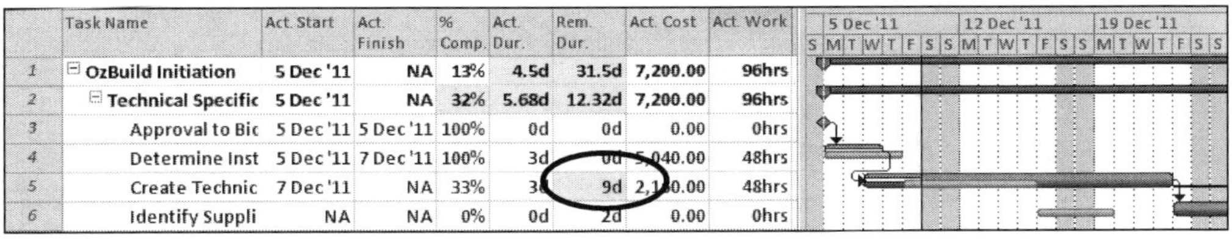

	Task Name	Act. Start	Act. Finish	% Comp.	Act. Dur.	Rem. Dur.	Act. Cost	Act. Work
1	OzBuild Initiation	5 Dec '11	NA	13%	4.5d	31.5d	7,200.00	96hrs
2	Technical Specific	5 Dec '11	NA	32%	5.68d	12.32d	7,200.00	96hrs
3	Approval to Bic	5 Dec '11	5 Dec '11	100%	0d	0d	0.00	0hrs
4	Determine Inst	5 Dec '11	7 Dec '11	100%	3d	0d	5,040.00	48hrs
5	Create Technic	7 Dec '11	NA	33%	3d	9d	2,160.00	48hrs
6	Identify Suppli	NA	NA	0%	0d	2d	0.00	0hrs

14. Apply the **Cost** details form in the bottom pane:
15. Update task **5 Create Technical Specification** with the following information:
    - **Actual Cost** of $3,000.00 against the **Systems Engineer**, and
    - **Actual Cost** of $2,000.00 against the **Specialists Consultant**,
    - Click the **OK** button to accept the changes.
    - The **Remaining Costs** will always be calculated by Microsoft Project and your schedule should look like this:

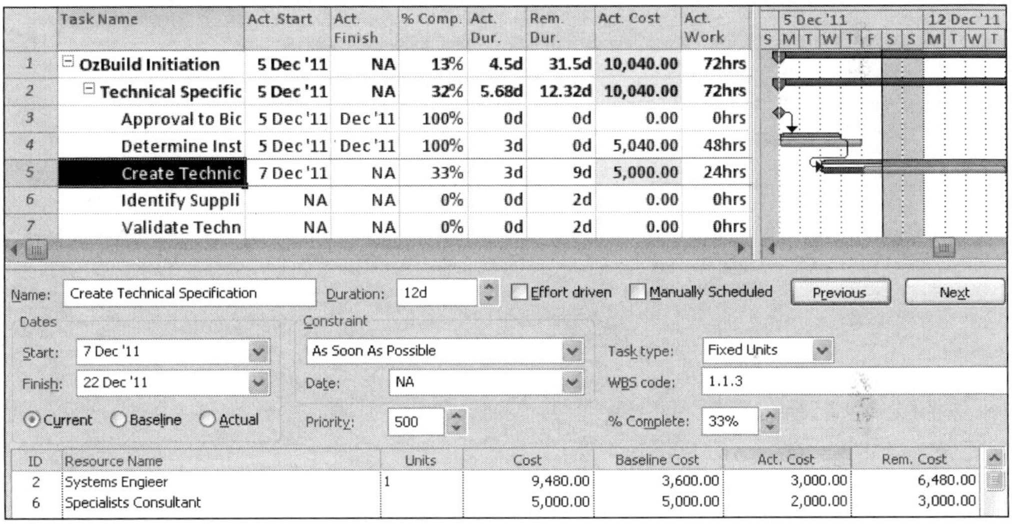

	Task Name	Act. Start	Act. Finish	% Comp.	Act. Dur.	Rem. Dur.	Act. Cost	Act. Work
1	OzBuild Initiation	5 Dec '11	NA	13%	4.5d	31.5d	10,040.00	72hrs
2	Technical Specific	5 Dec '11	NA	32%	5.68d	12.32d	10,040.00	72hrs
3	Approval to Bic	5 Dec '11	Dec '11	100%	0d	0d	0.00	0hrs
4	Determine Inst	5 Dec '11	Dec '11	100%	3d	0d	5,040.00	48hrs
5	Create Technic	7 Dec '11	NA	33%	3d	9d	5,000.00	24hrs
6	Identify Suppli	NA	NA	0%	0d	2d	0.00	0hrs
7	Validate Techn	NA	NA	0%	0d	2d	0.00	0hrs

ID	Resource Name	Units	Cost	Baseline Cost	Act. Cost	Rem. Cost
2	Systems Engieer	1	9,480.00	3,600.00	3,000.00	6,480.00
6	Specialists Consultant		5,000.00	5,000.00	2,000.00	3,000.00

Continued Over...

16. To see what the final forecast costs are you may display the **Costs** table, the fixed costs columns have been hidden in the picture below:

	Task Name	Total Cost	Baseline	Variance	Actual	Remaining
1	⊟ **OzBuild Initiation**	**59,260.00**	**55,060.00**	**4,200.00**	**10,040.00**	**49,220.00**
2	⊟ **Technical Specification**	**24,000.00**	**19,800.00**	**4,200.00**	**10,040.00**	**13,960.00**
3	Approval to Bid	0.00	0.00	0.00	0.00	0.00
4	Determine Installation Requirements	5,040.00	6,720.00	-1,680.00	5,040.00	0.00
5	Create Technical Specification	14,480.00	8,600.00	5,880.00	5,000.00	9,480.00
6	Identify Supplier Components	1,120.00	1,120.00	0.00	0.00	1,120.00
7	Validate Technical Specification	3,360.00	3,360.00	0.00	0.00	3,360.00
8	⊞ **Delivery Plan**	**21,520.00**	**21,520.00**	**0.00**	**0.00**	**21,520.00**
14	⊞ **Bid Document Submitted**	**13,740.00**	**13,740.00**	**0.00**	**0.00**	**13,740.00**

17. To see how the consumption of hours is going you may display to **Work** table:

	Task Name	Work	Baseline	Variance	Actual	Remaining
1	⊟ **OzBuild Initiation**	**560hrs**	**520hrs**	**40hrs**	**72hrs**	**488hrs**
2	⊟ **Technical Specificatio**	**192hrs**	**152hrs**	**40hrs**	**72hrs**	**120hrs**
3	Approval to Bid	0hrs	0hrs	0hrs	0hrs	0hrs
4	Determine Installat	48hrs	64hrs	-16hrs	48hrs	0hrs
5	Create Technical Sp	96hrs	40hrs	56hrs	24hrs	72hrs
6	Identify Supplier Cc	16hrs	16hrs	0hrs	0hrs	16hrs
7	Validate Technical S	32hrs	32hrs	0hrs	0hrs	32hrs
8	⊞ **Delivery Plan**	**224hrs**	**224hrs**	**0hrs**	**0hrs**	**224hrs**
14	⊞ **Bid Document Submitt**	**144hrs**	**144hrs**	**0hrs**	**0hrs**	**144hrs**

18. Now apply the **Earned Value** table. The VAC column does not calculate vertically. Microsoft Project calculates the EAC horizontally using the formula EAC = ACWP + (Baseline cost X - BCWP) / CPI which is not the same value as calculating vertically:

	Task Name	Planned Value - PV (BCWS)	Earned Value - EV (BCWP)	AC (ACWP)	SV	CV	EAC	BAC	VAC
1	⊟ **OzBuild Initiation**	**7,440.00**	**7,908.00**	**8,040.00**	**468.00**	**-132.00**	**55,979.06**	**55,060.00**	**-919.06**
2	⊟ **Technical Specificatio**	**7,440.00**	**7,908.00**	**8,040.00**	**468.00**	**-132.00**	**20,130.50**	**19,800.00**	**-330.50**
3	Approval to Bid	0.00	0.00	0.00	0.00	0.00	0.00	0.00	0.00
4	Determine Installat	6,720.00	6,720.00	5,040.00	0.00	1,680.00	5,040.00	6,720.00	1,680.00
5	Create Technical Sp	720.00	1,188.00	3,000.00	468.00	-1,812.00	21,717.17	8,600.00	13,117.17
6	Identify Supplier Cc	0.00	0.00	0.00	0.00	0.00	1,120.00	1,120.00	0.00
7	Validate Technical S	0.00	0.00	0.00	0.00	0.00	3,360.00	3,360.00	0.00
8	⊞ **Delivery Plan**	**0.00**	**0.00**	**0.00**	**0.00**	**0.00**	**21,520.00**	**21,520.00**	**0.00**
14	⊞ **Bid Document Submitt**	**0.00**	**0.00**	**0.00**	**0.00**	**0.00**	**13,740.00**	**13,740.00**	**0.00**

21 PROJECT OPTIONS

The Options define the rules under which Microsoft project operates.

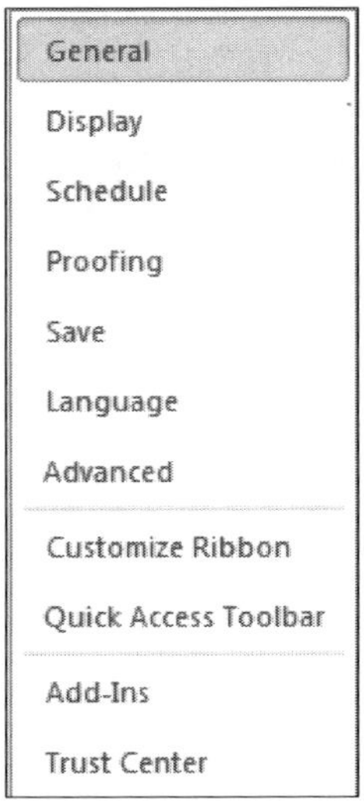

The traditional **Options** form has been revamped in Microsoft Project 2010 and these are now under the **File**, **Options** command which opens the **Project Options** form.

The **Options** forms allow you to decide how Microsoft Project calculates and displays information. Most of the options are self-explanatory.

There are many options that are not essential for scheduling. Unfortunately, it is often difficult for new users to determine which are important and which are not, which can lead to confusion and potentially some scheduling errors. This chapter will explain most of the functions identified on each Options form tab and indicate the important options.

- **General** This is used for editing the Default Date format, Default View and color.
- **Display** Includes the selection of the currency and options for indicators buttons.
- **Schedule** This form has a number of sections controlling how the software calculates and **SHOULD** be understood.
- **Proofing** This form is used to decide how the spell checker works.
- **Language** This is where the language options may be edited.
- **Advanced** This new form has display options that are intended to assist the user but and provide some further advanced scheduling options. These options **SHOULD** be understood.
- **Customize Ribbon** Commands may be added to and removed from the Ribbon.
- **Quick Access Toolbar** Commands may be added to and removed from the Quick Access Toolbar.
- **Add-Ins** This is where Add-Ins may be viewed and managed:
- **Trust Center** Allows the control of privacy and macro security.

Some options apply to the current project only, some to all projects and some to new projects:

- Those that apply to the current project or new project have a drop-down box where this selection may be made.
- Those that apply to all projects do not have any options to select a project.

It is important to understand what the options do and to carefully inspect the options of schedules sent to you.

21.1 General

This is used for editing some global defaults such as the Default Date format, Default View and color scheme:

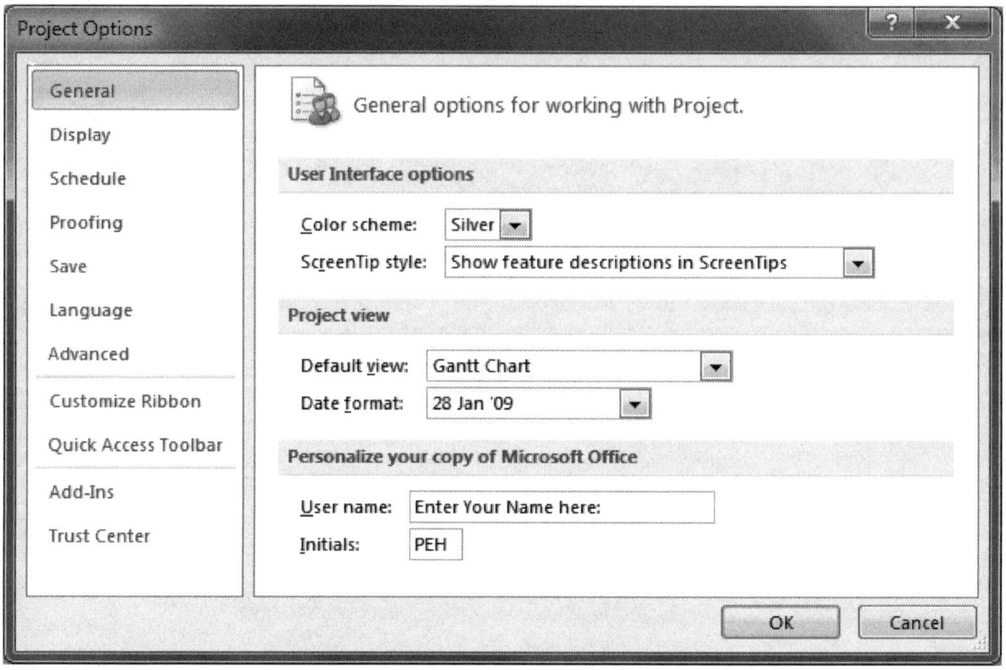

21.1.1 User Interface Options

- **Color scheme:** allows the selection of background colors which mainly affect the print out of Timescale and Column headings.
- **ScreenTip style:** shows the name and a brief description of a command when the mouse is hovered over a button; it is recommended this be left on.

21.1.2 Project view

- **Default view:** selects the View applied when a new project is created.
- **Date format:** provides a selection of date formats from the drop-down box for the display of data in columns. This format is applied to all projects and all views.
  - The date format will be displayed according to a combination of your system default settings and the Microsoft Project Options settings. You may adjust your date format under the system **Control Panel**, **Regional and Language Options**. Changing the Control Panel setting will change the options available in the Microsoft Project **Options** form.
  - The dates on the bars are formatted in the **Format**, **Format** group, **Layout** form.
  - This date format may be over ridden by defining specific dates for each Table in the **Table Definition** form.

Should you wish to display your times in 24-hour format, e.g. 17:00 instead of 5:00pm, which prevents confusion and makes it easier to enter times then:

- Select from the Windows menu **Settings**, **Control Panel**, **Regional Options** tab. Select **Customize**, select the **Time** tab and
- Change the time format from **h:mm:ss tt** to **HH:mm:ss** or **H:mm:ss**.

- **NOTE:** Some versions of Windows may have slightly different commands and this setting will affect many other applications at the same time.

There is often confusion on international projects between the numerical US date style, mmddyy and the numerical European date style, ddmmyy. For example, in the United States 020710 is read as 07 Feb '10 and in many other countries as 02 Jul '10. Consider always adopting either the ddmmmyy style, **06 Jan '07** or mmmddyy style, **Jan 06 '07** for all your plans when multiple countries are involved in a project

21.1.3 Personalize your copy of Microsoft Office

- The **User name:** and **Initials:** may be called up in print headers and footers and sets the default Author in the **Properties** form.

21.2 Display

This form includes the selection of the currency and options for indicators buttons:

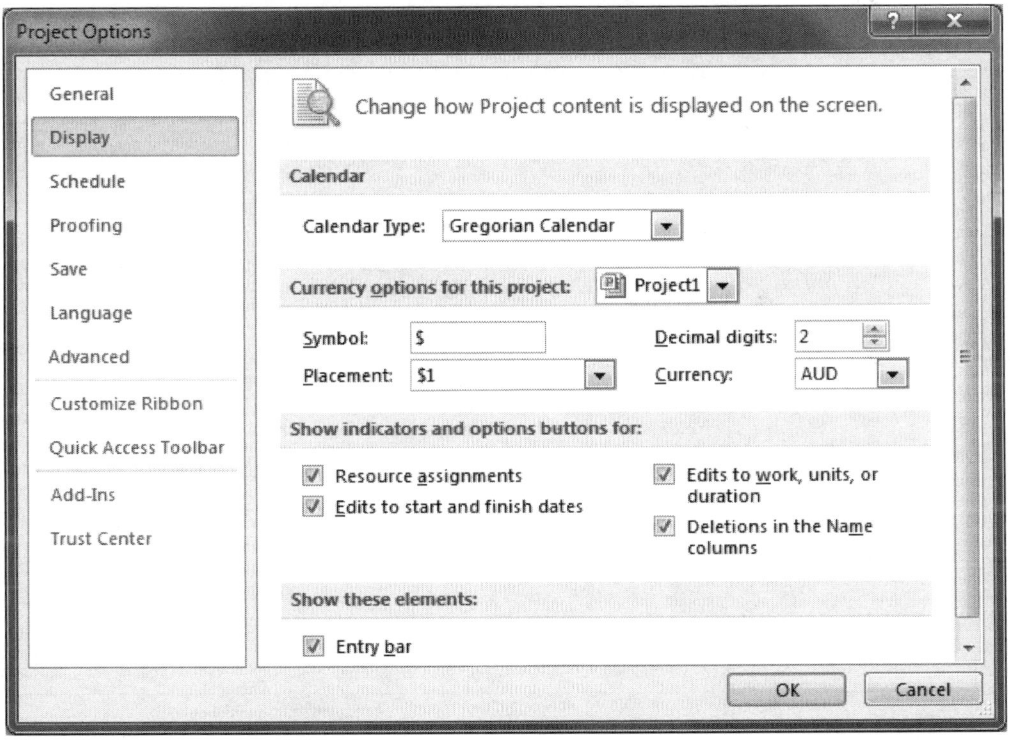

21.2.1 Calendar

Calendar Type: allows the selection of different calendars if the appropriate character set has been installed. This was new to Microsoft Project 2007.

21.2.2 Currency options for this project:

The **Currency:** option was new to Microsoft Project 2007 and allows the specification of the currency used in the schedule.

This option allows you to specify the:

- Currency sign by inserting a sign into the box next to **Symbol:**,
- Placement of the currency sign (before or after the value) as selected from the **Placement:** box, and
- The number of decimal places displayed from the **Decimal digits:** box.

21.2.3 Show indicators and options buttons for:

The Indicator buttons give advice to the scheduler when certain functions are used which have more than one potential outcome.

- Below is an example of how the **Show indicators and Option buttons for:** options work when a task description is deleted:

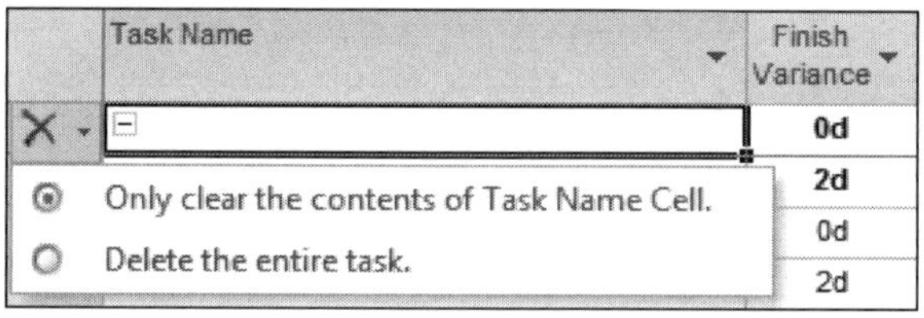

21.2.4 Show these elements

- The **Entry Bar** is at the top of the columns, data may be edited here when it is displayed:

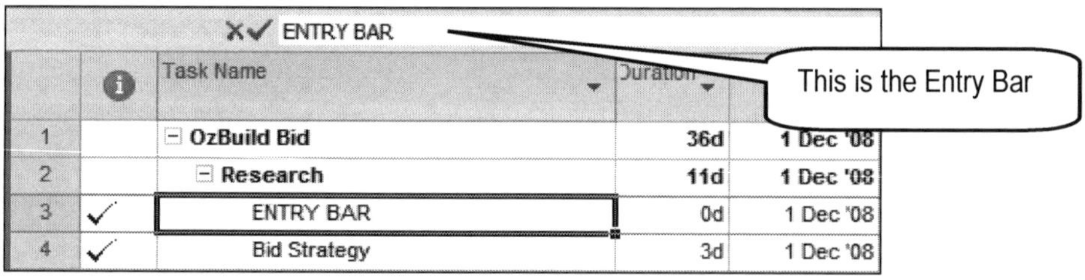

21.3 Schedule

This form has a number of sections controlling how the software calculates and **SHOULD** be understood.

21.3.1 Calendar options for this project:

The title of these options does not clearly indicate their functionality. Options for **Hours per day:**, **Hours per week:** and **Days per month: SHOULD** be understood, especially if multiple Task calendars are used.

- This heading allows the setting of the default for **All New Projects** or for individual projects. This sets the current calendar settings as the default in the Global.mpt project and is used thereafter as the calendar settings in all new projects.

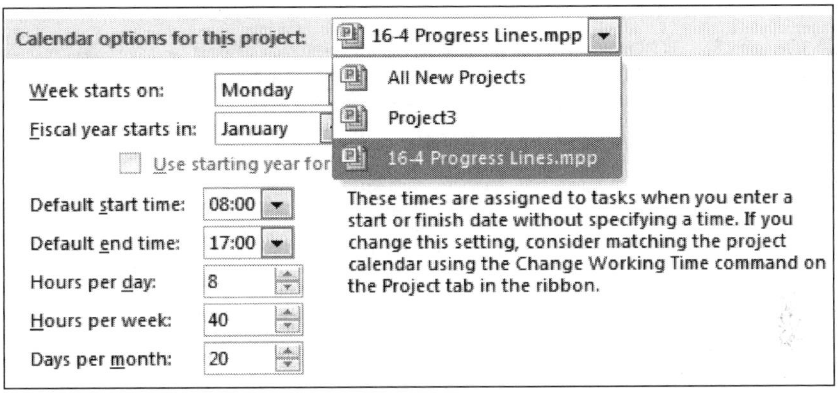

- **Week starts on:** – Sets the first day of the week. This is the day of the week that is displayed in the timescale. This setting affects the display of the calendar in the Change Working Time form. **NOTE:** This is best set to Monday and not Sunday so the date displayed in a weekly timescale is a working day.
- **Fiscal year starts in:** – A month other than January may be selected as the first month of the fiscal year for companies that want to schedule projects using their financial years.
- **Use starting year for FY numbering** – This option becomes available when a month other than January is selected as a **Fiscal year starts in:**. The year in the timescale may be assigned as the year that the fiscal starts or the year that the fiscal year finishes.
- **Default start time:** – This is the time of day that tasks are scheduled to start when a start date constraint (without a time) is applied. It is also the default time for an Actual Start when an Actual Start (without a time) date is entered.
- **Default end time:** – This is the time of day that tasks are scheduled to finish when a finish date constraint (without a time) is entered. It is also the default time for an Actual Finish when an Actual Finish date (without a time) is entered.

It is essential to match both the **Default start time:** and **Default end time:** with your project calendar's normal start and finish times. For example, when the **Default start time:** is set earlier than the calendar normal start time, a task set with a constraint without a time will appear to finish one day later than scheduled. Therefore a one-day task will span two days and a two-day task, three days.

The following options need to be understood as they affect how summary durations are displayed. **NOTE: THESE OPTIONS ARE IMPORTANT**. Microsoft Project effectively calculates in hours. Task durations may be displayed in days, weeks and months. These summarized durations are calculated based on the parameters set in **Options**, **Calendar**. These options work fine when all project calendars are based on the same number of work hours per day. When tasks are scheduled with calendars that do not conform to the **Options**, **Calendar** settings (e.g., when the **Options**, **Calendar** settings are set for 8 hours per day and there are tasks scheduled on a 24-hour per day calendar), the results often create confusion for new users.

- **Hours per day:** – This setting is used to convert the duration in hours to the displayed value of the duration in days. For example, a task entered as a 3-day duration and assigned a 24-hour per day calendar will be displayed in the bar chart as 1-day elapsed duration. This bar chart duration is 1/3 of the duration value since each day is an 8-hour equivalent on a 24-hour calendar and the output is not logical. See Task 1 below.
- **Hours per week:** – This setting is used to convert the calendar hours to the displayed duration in weeks. For example, a task entered as 2 weeks (10 working days) and assigned a 24-hour per day calendar is displayed with a 3-day and 6-hour duration in the bar chart. This is 1/3 of the "normal" duration and again not logical. See Task 2 below.
- **Days per month:** – This option is used to convert the displayed task duration from days to months. For example, a 0.5-month task (10 working days) on a 24-hour per day calendar is displayed as a 3-day and 6-hour duration in the bar chart and again is not logical. See Task 3 below.

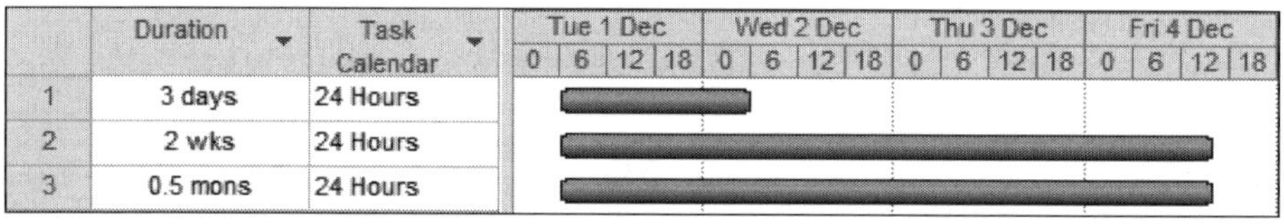

All the durations displayed in the picture are misleading. It is important that this situation be avoided.

Other scheduling software also exhibits the time conversion problem when using multi-calendars. This display can lead to a great deal of confusion. To avoid confusion when using multi-calendars, it is suggested that you only display durations in hours.

This issue is discussed in depth in para 22.1. Refer to this chapter should multiple calendars be considered for a project schedule.

21.3.2 Schedule

- **Show scheduling messages** – Uncheck this box to prevent the software from displaying advice on scheduling.
- **Show assignment unit as a:** – The options are **Percentage** or **Decimal**. You have the option of assigning and displaying resource assignments as either a percentage, such as 50%, or a decimal, such as 0.5. Both these values would assign a person to work half time on that task. When four resources are assigned to a task this would be 400% as **Percentage** or 4 as **Decimal**.

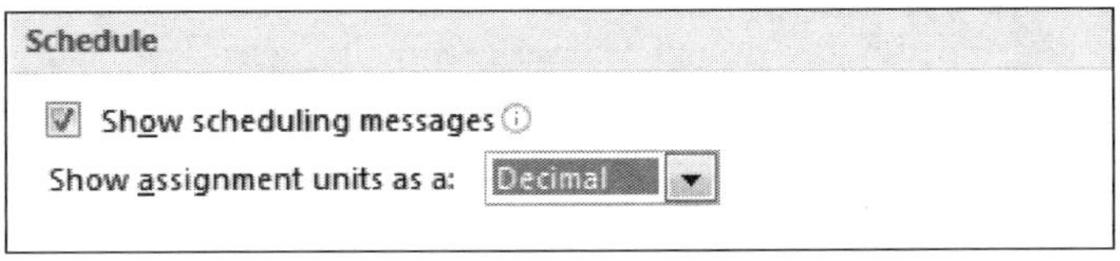

21.3.3 Scheduling options for this project:

The options below affects how your schedules calculate and **SHOULD** be understood. They may be applied to all new projects or to the current project:

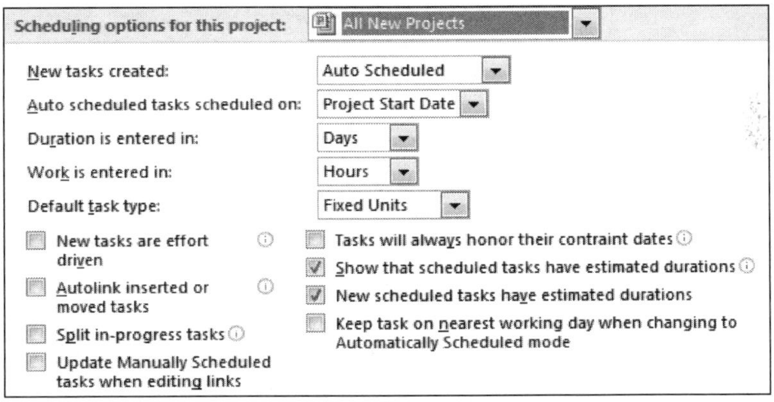

Microsoft has introduced this new task attribute titled **Task Scheduling Mode** in Microsoft Project 2010. In earlier versions of Microsoft Project every task was set to the equivalent of the new **Auto Scheduled** setting in Microsoft Project 2010. In this mode all tasks' Start and Finish dates are calculated with respect to the Project Start (or Finish) date, their Durations, Relationships, Constraints, Calendars and Options. When a task is set to **Manually Scheduled** it does not need a predecessor or constraint to hold the Start date and therefore will not move when the project is scheduled.

- **New tasks created:** When new tasks are created they may be set with the **Task Mode** as either:
  - **Manually Scheduled**, or
  - **Auto Scheduled**.

  The attribute assigned to each task may be changed at a later date and this option only sets the default for new tasks. This topic is covered in detail in para 22.3.1 and will not be covered in detail here.

To produce a Critical Path schedule, tasks have to be set to **Auto Scheduled**.

- **Auto scheduled tasks scheduled on:** – When adding new tasks, you have the option of the new task either:
  - Scheduled to **Start On Project Start Date**, the task will be scheduled **As Soon As Possible**, or
  - **Start on Current Date**, the task will be assigned (without any warning dialog box) a **Start No Earlier Constraint** equal to the current date. **NOTE:** To have a task assigned a constraint without due reason is not considered good scheduling practice and should be avoided, so this option should not be selected.
- **Duration is entered in:** – You should select the units you will most frequently use for your task duration units. When "days" are selected, you will only need to type "**5**" in order to enter a 5-day task duration. You will have to enter "**5w**" for a task that is 5 weeks long or "**5h**" for a task that is 5 hours long.
- **Work is entered in:** – This is similar to the **Durations is entered in:** function, but applies to assigning work to a task. When hours are selected, you will only need to type "**48**" to enter 48 hours of work. If 5 days of work are to be assigned then "**5d**" needs to be entered.

The next two subjects, **Default task type:** and **Effort-Driven**, are **EXTREMELY** important for understanding how resources are used and applied.

- **Default task type:** – There is a relationship between the **Duration** of a task, the **Work** (the number of hours required to complete a task) and the **Units** (per Time Period, the rate of doing the work or the number of people working on the task). The relationship is:

Duration x Units (per time period in Hours or Days) **= Work** (Units)

The three options for the **Default task type:** are:

  - **Fixed Duration** – The **Duration** will stay constant if either **Units** (per time period) or **Work** is changed. If you change the **Duration**, then **Work** changes. This is the **RECOMMENDED** option for new users as the duration will not change as resources are manipulated.
  - **Fixed Units** – The **Units** stay constant if either **Duration** or **Work** is changed. If you change the **Units**, then **Duration** changes.
  - **Fixed Work** – The **Work** stays constant if either **Duration** or **Units per Time Period** is changed. Your estimate will not change when you change **Duration** or **Units**. If you change the **Work**, then **Duration** changes.

Duration type	Change Duration	Change Units/Time	Change Work
Fixed Duration	Work Changes	Work	Units/Time
Fixed Units	Work Changes	Duration	Duration
Fixed Work	Units/Time	Duration	Duration

- **New tasks are effort driven** – An **Effort-Driven** task keeps the total work constant as resources are added and removed from a task. It treats each resource as interchangeable. When a task is not **Effort-Driven** then the addition of resources to a task will increase the total work assigned to a task. This option is not available with a **Fixed Work** task because if it were available then it would not be fixed work. **NOTE:** New users should consider **NOT** checking this option, so resources may be added independently without affecting the other resources work assignment.

- **Autolink inserted or moved tasks** – With this box checked, new or moved tasks are automatically linked to the tasks above and below in the new or inserted location. Moved tasks that had relationships to tasks immediately above and below in the old location are deleted and the original predecessors and successors are now joined with an FS relationship. This function may confuse you since the logic is changed automatically without warning, when you add or move tasks. **NOTE:** It is suggested that the option **NEVER** be switched on as dragging a task to a new location may completely change the logic of a schedule.
- **Split in-progress tasks:** – This option allows the splitting of in-progress tasks. This option **MUST** be checked for the following functions to operate:
  1. **Project**, **Status Group**, **Update Project** form, **Update work as completed through**,
  2. **Project**, **Status Group**, **Update Project** form, **Reschedule uncompleted work to start after:**, and
  3. **File**, **Options**, **Advanced** tab, **Calculation options for this project:** section allowing incomplete or completed parts of tasks to be moved to the **Status Date**.
- **Update Manually Scheduled tasks when editing links**
  When two **Manually Scheduled** tasks are linked they acknowledge the relationship and will reschedule when:
  - The **File**, **Options**, **Schedule** tab, **Scheduling options for this project:** section, **Update Manually Scheduled tasks when editing links** is checked, and
  - A relationship is added or edited.
- **Tasks will always honor their constraint dates**
  This option will make all constraints override relationships. For example, a task with a **Must Start On** constraint, which is prior to a predecessor's Finish Date, will have an Early Start on the constraint date and not the scheduled date. (This is similar to converting all Primavera software **Must Start On** constraints to **Mandatory** constraints.) When checked, the **Total Slack** may not calculate as the difference between Late Start and Early Start. Examine the following two examples with the option box checked and unchecked:

  - **Tasks will always honor their constraint dates** option box checked.

Start	Finish	Late Finish	Total Slack	Constraint Date	Constraint Type
9 Aug	26 Aug	23 Aug	-3 days	NA	As Soon As Possible
27 Aug	27 Aug	24 Aug	-3 days	NA	As Soon As Possible
24 Aug	24 Aug	24 Aug	-3 days	24 Aug	Finish No Later Than

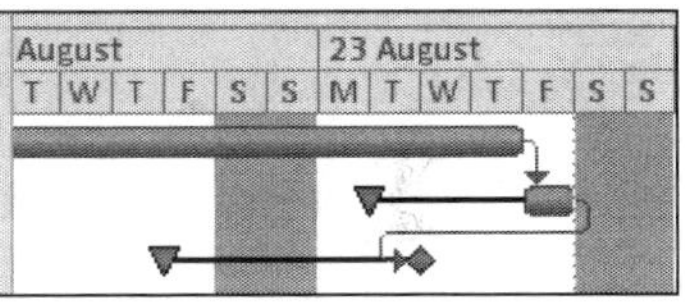

The third task starts before the predecessor finishes and the Total Slack of the second task is calculated at –3 days, which is not the difference between the early and late dates. Thus the Total Float calculation is also incorrect.

  - **Tasks will always honor their constraint dates** option box NOT checked.

Start	Finish	Late Finish	Total Slack	Constraint Date	Constraint Type
9 Aug	26 Aug	23 Aug	-3 days	NA	As Soon As Possible
27 Aug	27 Aug	24 Aug	-3 days	NA	As Soon As Possible
27 Aug	27 Aug	24 Aug	-3 days	24 Aug	Finish No Later Than

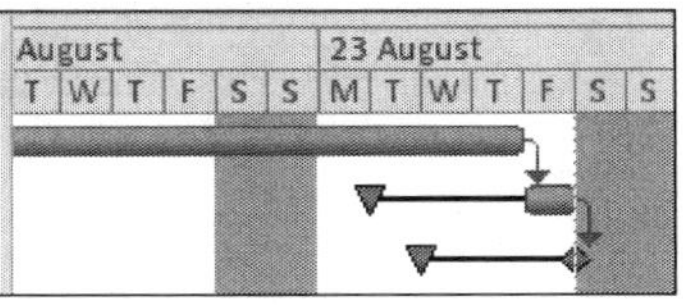

It is suggested that this option is **NEVER** switched on, unless you are very experienced, as the schedule may appear to be achievable when it is not.

- **Estimated Durations** – These two options do not affect the calculation of projects. A new task is assigned an estimated duration. Once a duration is entered by the user, this assignment is removed. The **General** tab on the **Task** form has a check box which establishes when a task has an estimated duration.
  - **Show that scheduled tasks have estimated durations** – A task with an estimated duration is flagged with a "**?**" after the duration in the duration column when this option is checked.
  - **New scheduled tasks have estimated durations** – When a task is added, it will have the estimated check box checked.

Before entering a Duration and after entering a Duration

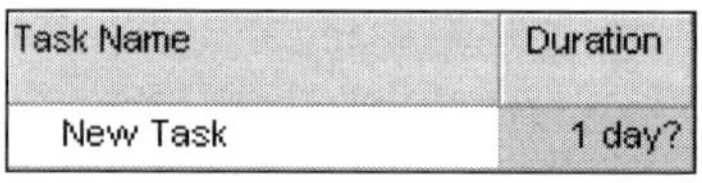

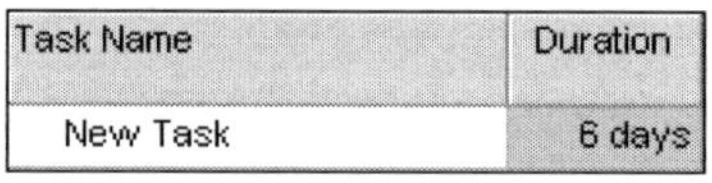

Summary tasks are marked as estimated when one or more **Detailed tasks** associated with it are marked as Estimated.

- **Keep Tasks on nearest working day when changing to Automatically Scheduled mode**
  When a task is **Manually Scheduled** and changed to **Automatically Scheduled** this option with:
  - When checked set a **Start No Earlier** constraint on the task so it does not move forward in time if it has no predecessors, or
  - When unchecked the task will not have a constraint set and will move forward if it has no predecessors.

21.3.4 Schedule Alerts

This allows the turning on or off of advice from Microsoft Project:

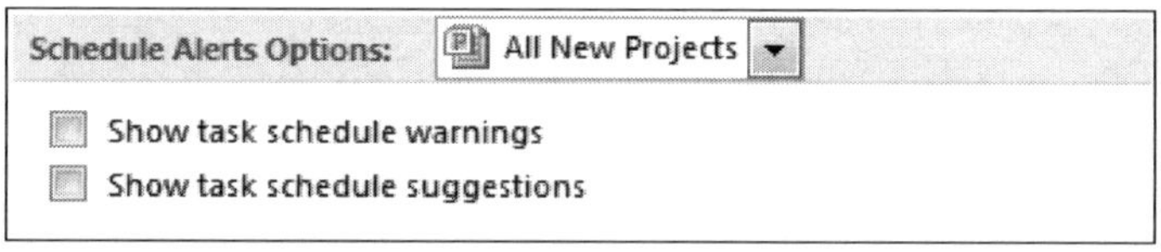

It is suggested that these types of warnings are either read very carefully or disabled as these types of warnings often encourage schedulers to do the wrong thing, such as assign a Finish No Earlier Constraint when the scheduler requires a Finish No Later Constraint to develop Negative Float.

21.3.5 Calculation

Select one of the following two options, which affect the calculation of **Automatically Scheduled** tasks for **ALL** projects that are open:

- **On** – This option recalculates the schedule every time a change is made to data. This is the default option.
- **Off** – This option requires you to press the **F9 Key** to recalculate the schedule.

It is recommended this be left **On**.

21.3.6 Calculation Options for this project:

These options may be assigned to New Projects and selected projects.

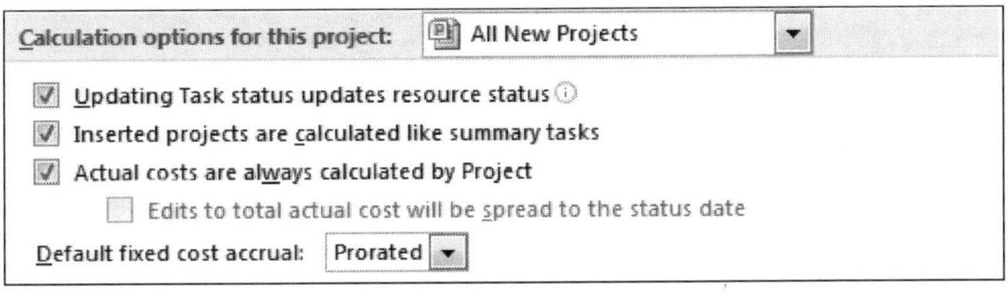

- **Updating task status updates resource status** – This option links **% Complete** to **% Work** and in turn **% Work** is linked to **Actual Work**. Therefore when this option is checked:

  Actual Work = **% Work x Work** and
  Remaining Work = **Work – Actual Work**

  When unchecked the **% Complete** and **% Work** may have different values and **% Work** or **Actual Work** will have to be entered separately from the **% Complete**.

  The example below shows the calculations with this option checked. If you uncheck this option, you may enter Actual Work and Remaining Work independently of the **% Complete**. In the example below the % Work is 50% and % Complete is 20%.

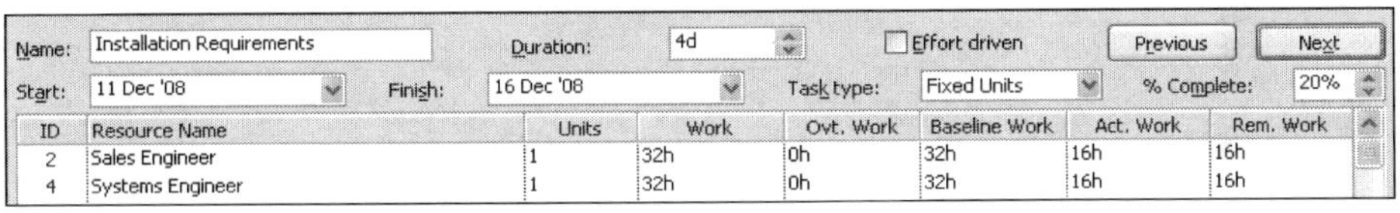

ID	Resource Name	Units	Work	Ovt. Work	Baseline Work	Act. Work	Rem. Work
2	Sales Engineer	1	32h	0h	32h	16h	16h
4	Systems Engineer	1	32h	0h	32h	16h	16h

A summary task **% Work** is calculated based on the sum of **Actual Work** divided by the sum of the **Work** and gives an indication of progress based on hours of effort.

Understanding Summary Duration % Complete

A summary task **% Complete** is calculated from the sum of **Actual Durations** of all the **Detailed Tasks** divided by the sum of the **Durations**.

This option also determines the manner in which a % Complete that is assigned to a Parent Task gets spread to detail tasks. See the following two examples where 60% is applied to the summary task entitled "Research":

- With the **Updating task status updates resource status** CHECKED.

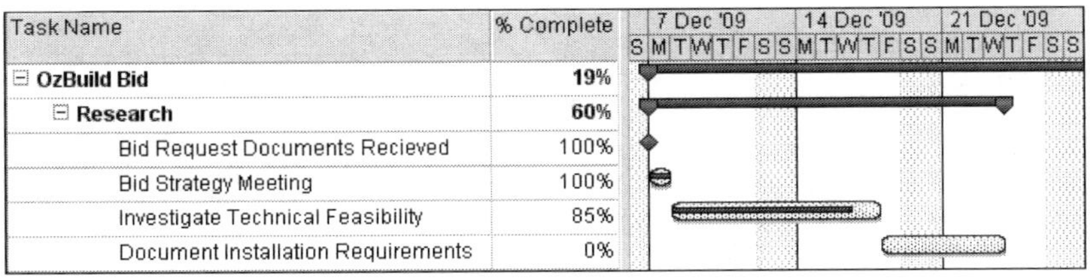

Task Name	% Complete
OzBuild Bid	**19%**
Research	**60%**
Bid Request Documents Recieved	100%
Bid Strategy Meeting	100%
Investigate Technical Feasibility	85%
Document Installation Requirements	0%

- With the **Updating task status updates resource status** UNCHECKED.

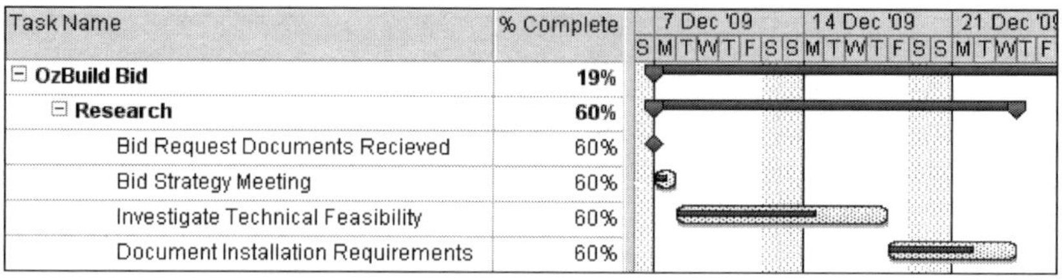

- **Inserted projects are calculated like summary tasks**
  A project may be inserted like a sub-project using the **Project**, **Insert**, **Subproject** command.
  - When checked, an inserted project task's Total Float is calculated to the end of all Projects like a group of related projects.

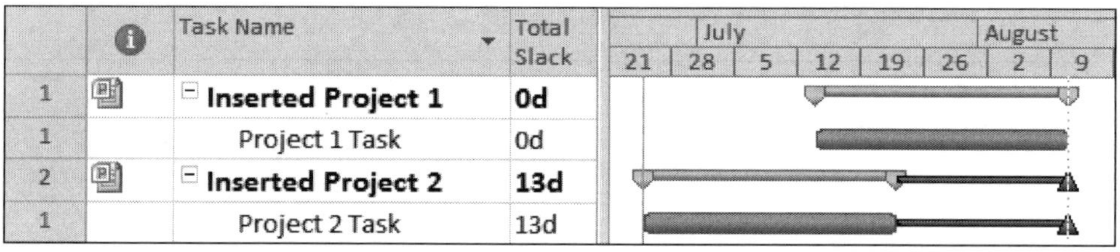

  - When unchecked, each Project's Total Float should be calculated to the end of that Project only.

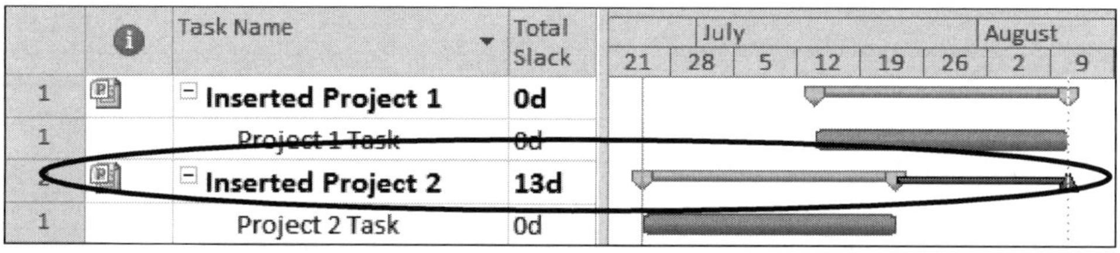

The Inserted Project Tasks calculate correctly but the Inserted Project Summary do not, as per the picture. The float bar on the summary task may be removed manually using the **Bars** form.

When there are several Microsoft Project projects are inserted into a Master project file, they may be treated as:

- Part of the same project with this option checked and the float will be calculated to the end of the last activity of all projects, or
- A group of unrelated projects where the float of each project is calculated independently.

- **Actual costs are always calculated by Project** – With this option checked, the resource **Actual Cost** is calculated by Microsoft Project from the resource **Work** and **Rates**. When unchecked, you have to directly enter the **Actual Cost** and **Actual Work**.

- **Edits to total actual costs will be spread to the status date** – When this option is selected and a **Status Date** is set in the **Project Information** form, then Actual Costs are spread from the Actual Start to the Status Date. Actual Costs should not be entered in a time-phased form such as the Task or Resource Usage forms, but the results may be viewed in these forms. **Actual costs are always calculated by Project** must be unchecked for this option to available.
- **Default fixed cost accrual:** – This option sets the default accrual method for **Fixed Costs** (covered in **ASSIGNING RESOURCES AND COSTS TO TASKS** chapter). Fixed costs may be accrued at the **Start**, **End**, or **Prorated** over the duration of the task.

21.4 Proofing

This form is used to decide how the spell checker works and is similar to other Microsoft products and will not be covered in this book.

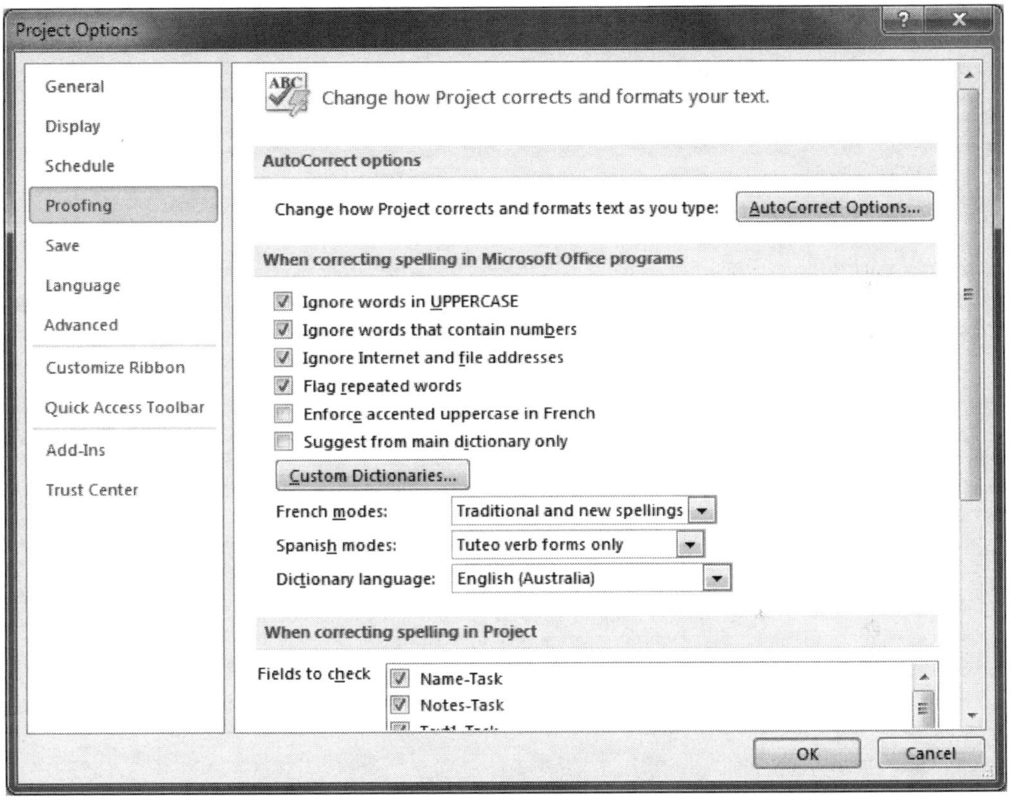

21.5 Save

This form specifies the file format, location and Auto save options.

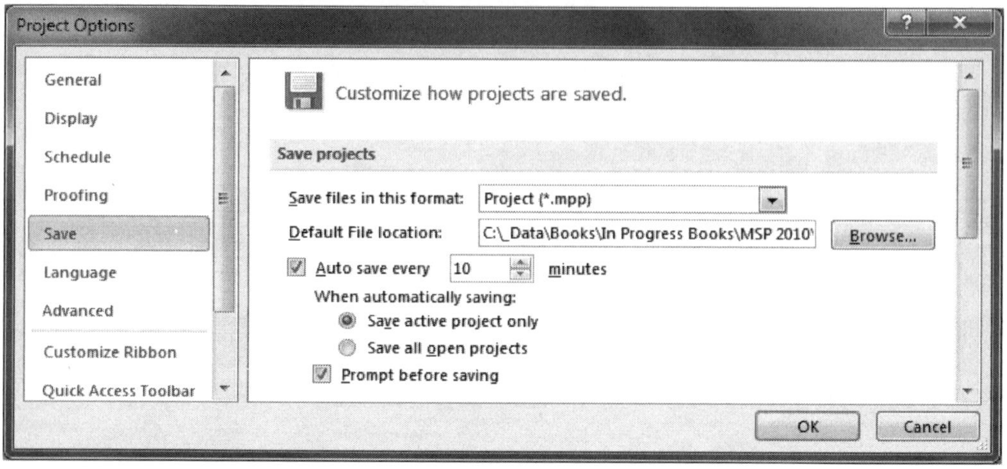

21.5.1 Save projects

- **Save files in this format:**

  There are several formats that your project may be saved in. The default file type may be defined here but the file type may be changed at the time a project file is saved:
  - **Project (*.mpp)** – The normal format to save Microsoft Project 2010 files.
  - **Microsoft Project 2007 (*.mpp)** will save files in this format as a default.
  - **Microsoft Project 2000 – 2003 (*.mpp)** will save files in this format as a default.
  - **Template (*.mpt)** – Use this format to save projects that you want to use as project templates. Save them in the **User templates** directory that is specified below.
  - **Microsoft Project 2007 Templates (*.mpt)**.).
  - **XML format (*.XML) – eXtensive Markup Language** which is increasingly being used by other software packages like Primavera and Asta Powerproject to import and export data
  - A number of other formats are listed but these are mainly for importing and exporting data not saving complete schedules that may then be opened and rescheduled.

  Earlier Microsoft Project versions had some or all of the following options that are no longer available:
  - **Microsoft Project 98 (*.mpp)** – The Microsoft Project 98 format which supported in some Microsoft Project versions released after Microsoft Project 98.
  - **Microsoft Project Exchange (*.mpx)** – If you have Microsoft Project 98, you may save the file in **mpx** format for transfer to other older scheduling programs such as P3 and SureTrak.
  - **Project Database (*.mpd)** – This is a database format, which allows multiple projects to be saved in one database. It may be used for exporting data to other programs.
  - **Microsoft Access Database (*.mdb)** – A part or all of a project may be saved in Microsoft Access format and may be read and modified by Access.
  - **ODBC Database** – Your project may be saved as an ODBC compliant database.

- **Default File location:** – Used to set the default locations for your project data files. **NOTE:** If you are working in the same directory all the time it is well worthwhile setting this directory.

- **Auto save** – These options are self-explanatory.

21.5.2 Save templates

Default user template location: – This is where you set the default locations for your project templates.

21.5.3 Cache

This allows users who are saving their files to a Project Server to speed up response time by saving a copy of the file locally.

21.6 Language

This form specifies the language preferences and will not be covered in this book.

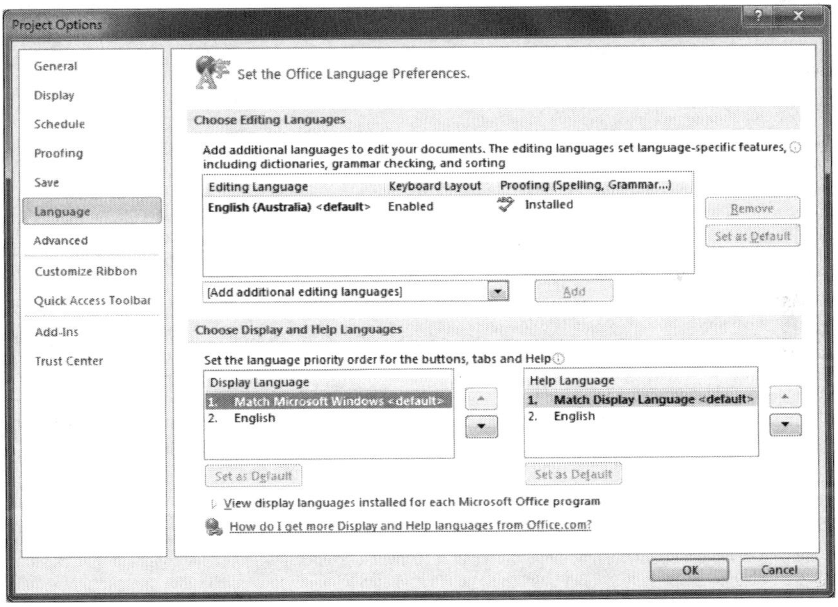

21.7 Advanced

This is where the advanced options may be edited:

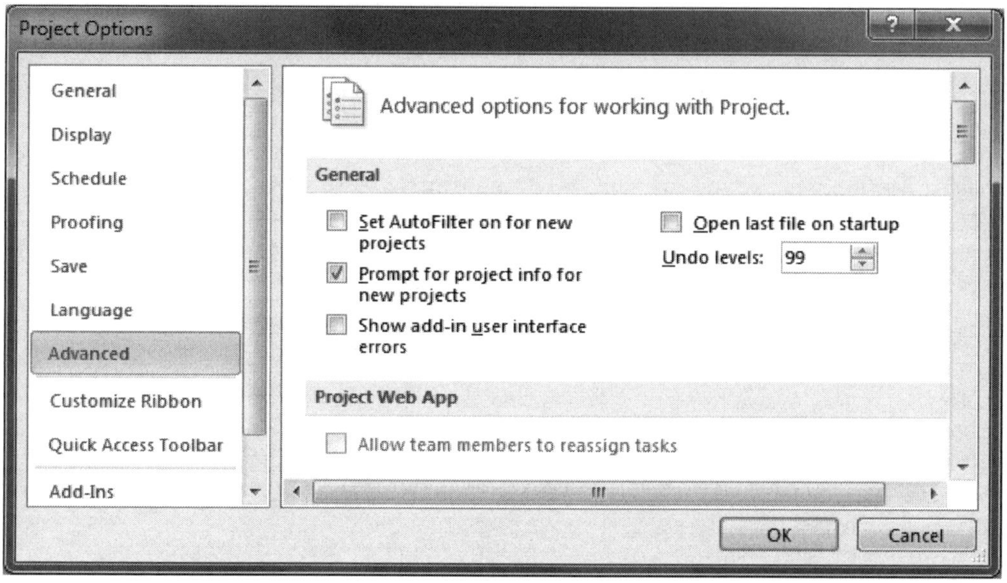

21.7.1 General

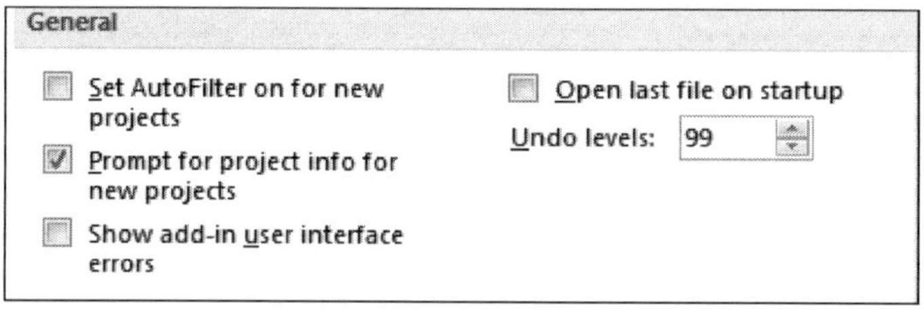

- **Set AutoFilter on for new projects** will display the down arrow by column headings for all new projects which in turn will allow an **AutoFilter** to be used immediately. This function may be turned on or off at any time by clicking on the **Display AutoFilter** button.
- **Prompt for project info for new projects** will open the **Project Information** form when a new project is created from the **Blank Project** template, which uses the **Global.mpt**. **NOTE:** This does not work with other templates.
- **Show add-in user interface errors**. An error will be displayed when this is turned on and add-in software attempts to control the Microsoft Project user interface.
- **Open last file on startup** will open the last file when Microsoft Project is opened which is useful if you only work on one project.
- **Undo levels** may be increased to 99 in Microsoft Project 2007 and this limit remains in 2010. Earlier versions have one undo.

This is a keystroke undo and when you have two files open it will undo changes made in both files. Undos are lost when a project file is saved.

21.7.2 Project Web App

Allows team member to reassign tasks is used with the Microsoft Project Web App as part of Microsoft Project Server and is out of scope of this book.

21.7.3 Planning Wizard

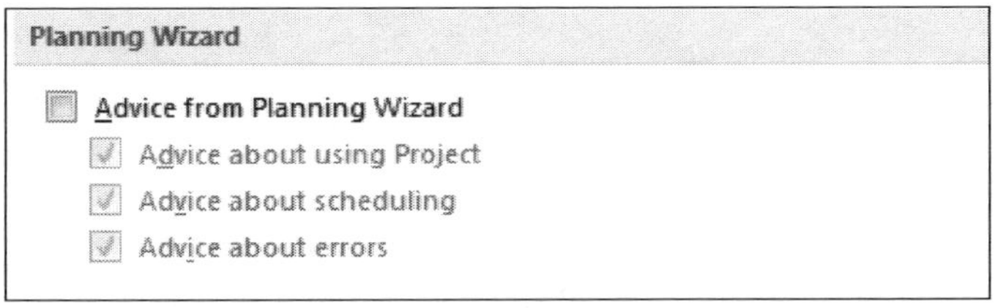

Planning Wizard – These options specify what advice the Planning Wizard will offer you and applies to all projects.

You may find it is better to switch some of the options off once you know how to use the software as they often encourage users to make a change they should not make. Once you know how to use the software it wastes time closing these forms.

21.7.4 General Options

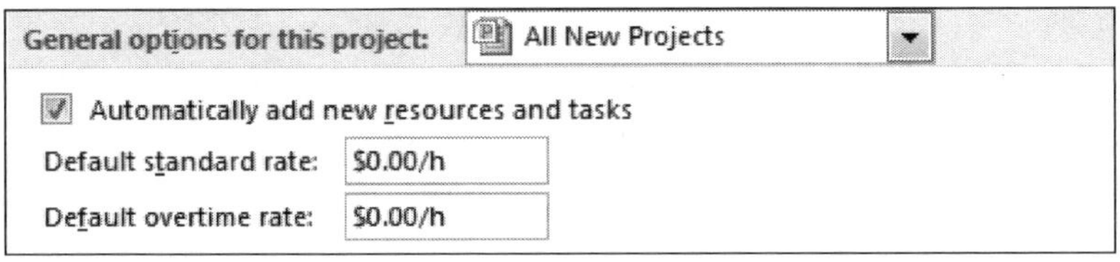

These options may be applied to selected projects or all new projects.

- **Automatically add new resources and tasks** – This option confirms if a resource exists in the resource pool. If the resource does not exist, a form will ask for confirmation to add the Resource to the resource list. This function did not work for the author in Microsoft Project 2010 but did in earlier versions. This may be fixed with the release of software updates.
- **Default standard rate:** is the default standard hourly rate assigned to new resources.
- **Default overtime rate**: is the default overtime rate assigned to new resources.

These rates are not used when work is assigned against a task without a resource being assigned. This is different to the way Oracle Primavera P6 works.

21.7.5 Edit

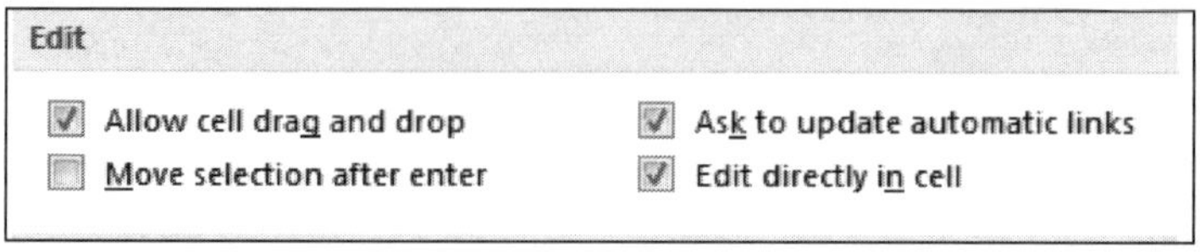

- **Allow cell drag and drop** – Allows you to select a cell and drag the contents to another location.

  This needs to be switched on in order to be able to drag columns.

- **Move selection after enter** – After completing an entry in a cell, pressing the **Enter Key** will result in the cursor moving down a line to the cell below.

  Some users find it a nuisance when the cursor moves down every time the enter key is pressed. If you wish the cursor to stay on the last edited task then uncheck this option.

- **Ask to update automatic links** – On opening a file which has dynamic links to other programs such as Excel, you will be asked if you want to refresh the links to the most recent data. To create a link, copy the selected data from another program. Then, in Microsoft Project, select the **Paste Link command** and the data will be placed in the location of the mouse, which may be in the bar chart area or a cell. See the **ADDING TASKS** chapter for more details.
- **Edit directly in cell** – Allows you to edit the data directly in the cell. Otherwise data has to be edited in the **Edit Bar** near the top of the screen.

21.7.6 Display

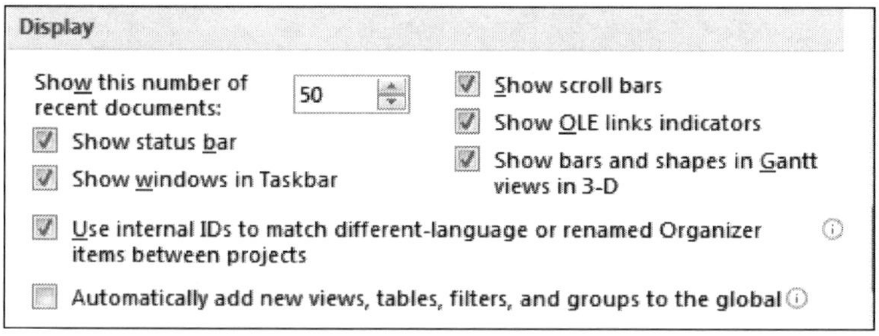

- **Show this number of recent documents:** allows up to 50 recently opened project files to be listed an increase from 9 in Microsoft Project 2007.
- The other "**Show"** options allow each of the display options to be hidden or displayed. The **Bars and shapes in Gantt views in 3-D** is a new function to Microsoft Project 2007.
- **Use internal IDs to match different-language or rename Organizer items between projects** is used in conjunction with Organizer when importing items from another project.
- **Automatically add new views, tables, filters, and groups to the global** is a new function to Microsoft Project 2010 which automatically adds any new views, tables, filters, and groups to the Global.mpt.

Therefore as time progresses with the option **Automatically add new views**, **tables**, **filters**, **and groups to the global** activated, a project that is created from the **Blank Project** will have many Views, Tables and Filters from old projects that may be irrelevant to the current project and it is suggested this be turned off.

21.7.7 Display Options for this Project

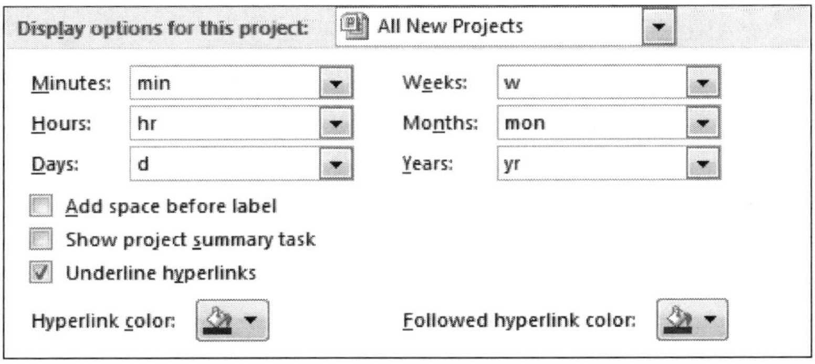

- **Minutes:**, **Hours:**, **Days:**, **Weeks:**, **Months:**, **Years:** – From the drop-down boxes, select your preferred designators for these units.
- **Add space before label** – Places a space between the value and the label; this makes the data column wider.

It is **RECOMMENDED** changing "days" to "d" and "hr" to "h" to make the duration columns narrower and to uncheck **Add space before label** to make duration columns narrower.

- **Show project summary task** will display a virtual Task ID 0, which will summarize all project tasks. A Project Summary Task:
  - May not be assigned resources,
  - Is normally displayed as a gray bar
  - The Task Name is linked to the **File**, **Info**, **Project Information**, **Advanced Properties** form **Summary** tab **Title:** field.

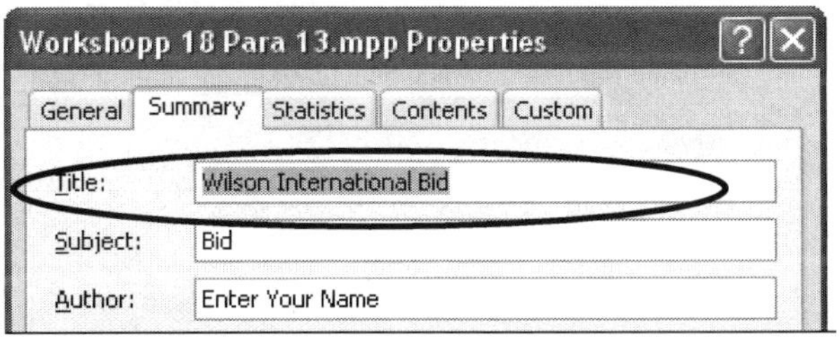

- **Hyperlink appearance in 'Project 1':**
  - **Hyperlink color:** and **Followed hyperlink color:** – Select from the drop-down box the color you require for these data items.
  - **Underline hyperlinks** – Select if you want these data items to be underlined.

21.7.8 Cross project linking options for this project:

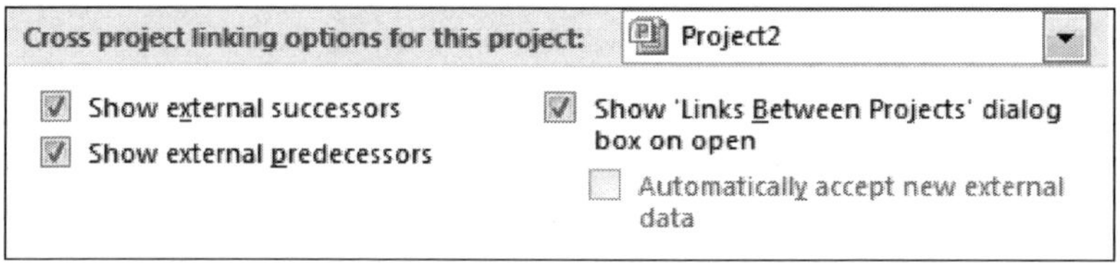

Cross project linking options for 'Selected Project' are options for displaying predecessor and successor task information from other projects. Inter-project relationships are not covered in this book.

It is recommended that inter project links are made from milestone to milestone so they are more visible.

21.7.9 Earned Value options for this project:

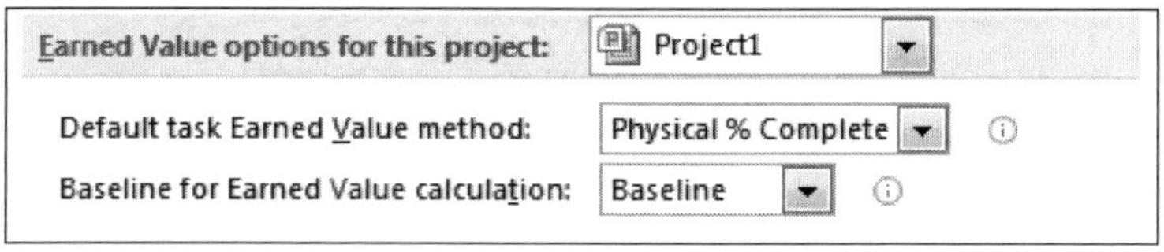

- The **Default task Earned Value method** (a new field in Microsoft Project 2002) may be set to use the task **% Complete** or the **Physical % Complete** to calculate the Earned Value.

  The **Physical % Complete** is useful when the Earned Value is not progressing in proportion to the duration and may be used for recording the actual progress of the deliverables of a task as opposed to % of the Work (recorded in % Work field) or % of Duration (recorded in the % Complete field).

- The **Baseline for Earned Value calculations:** allows the selection of any of the baselines for the calculation of the Earned Value.

  Discipline is required to collect Earned Value data and it is recommended that Custom Fields and Custom Field formulae are used to calculate Earned Value in Microsoft Project as you will be able to set how the summary values are calculated.

21.7.10 Calculation options for this project:

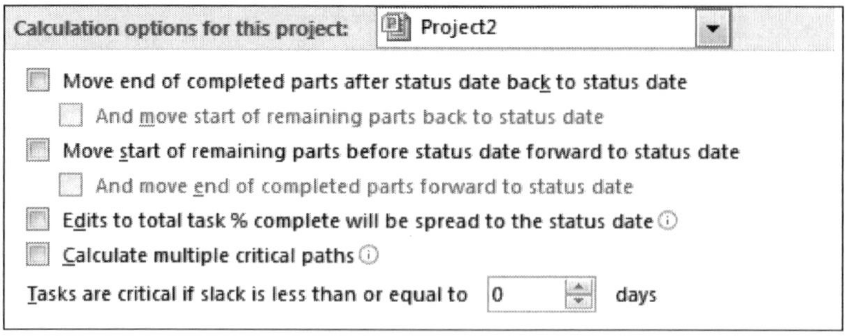

- New functions have been introduced in Microsoft Project 2002, which are intended to assist schedulers to place new tasks in a logical position with respect to the **Status Date**. The following four options were new to Microsoft Project 2002 and are covered in detail in the **Status Date Calculation Options** para 22.9.3.
  - **Move end of completed task parts after status date back to status date**
  - **And move start of remaining parts back to status date**
  - **Move start of remaining parts before status date forward to status date**
  - **And move end of completed parts forward to status date**

These functions do not work intuitively and the instructions in the Microsoft documentation do not describe these functions clearly. Review and understand these options before applying them.

- **Edits to total task % complete will be spread to the status date** – When this option is selected and a **Status Date** is set in the **Project Information** form, and Progress Lines are being viewed then the % Complete is spread from the Actual Start to the Status Date which may be viewed in the **Task** or **Resource Usage** forms.

- **Calculate multiple Critical Paths** – When checked, tasks without successors have their Late Dates set to equal their Early Dates, are calculated with zero Total Slack, are indicated critical in the Critical column and displayed as critical in the bar chart. (This is the same function as the Oracle Primavera software **Open Ends** options.)

  This function is useful if a project has multiple Areas or the Contract has several delivery dates and it is required to create a Critical Path for each Area or Delivery date.

  Calculate multiple Critical Paths – Unchecked, all float is calculated to end of project.

	Task Name	Total Slack
1	**Summary System A**	**0d**
2	Task 1	0d
3	Task 2	5d
4	Task 3	5d
5	Finish System A	5d
6	**Summary System B**	**0d**
7	Task 4	0d
8	Task 5	0d
9	Task 6	0d
10	Finish System B	0d

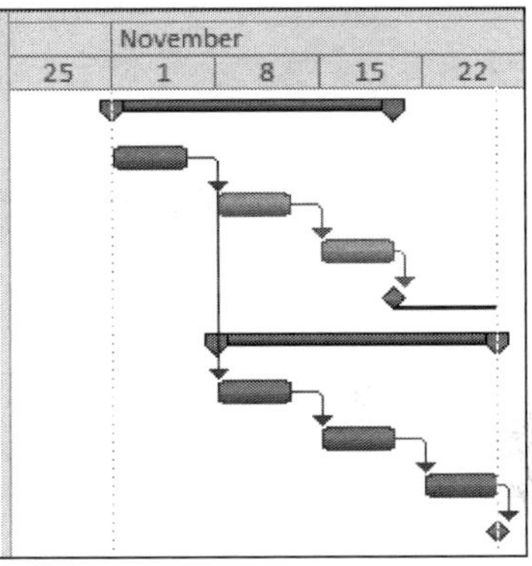

  Calculate multiple Critical Paths – Checked, each network has its own Critical Path.

	Task Name	Total Slack
1	**Summary System A**	**0d**
2	Task 1	0d
3	Task 2	0d
4	Task 3	0d
5	Finish System A	0d
6	**Summary System B**	**0d**
7	Task 4	0d
8	Task 5	0d
9	Task 6	0d
10	Finish System B	0d

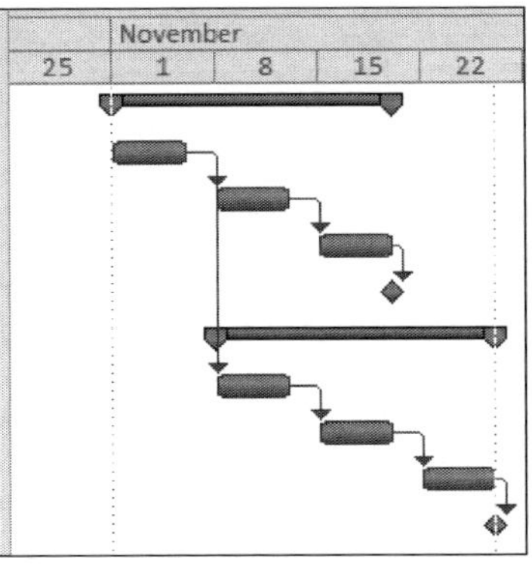

- **Tasks are critical if slack is less than or equal to ? days** – This option will flag tasks as being critical that have **Total Slack** (Total Float) less than or equal to the value entered in this form. Critical tasks may be displayed in the **Critical** column and on bars when the "critical bar" is displayed. This is useful for flagging "near critical" tasks and should be used when multiple calendars are used to identify the critical path.

21.8 Customize Ribbon

This is where commands may be added to and removed from the Ribbon. This works in the same way as other Microsoft products so will not be covered in detail:

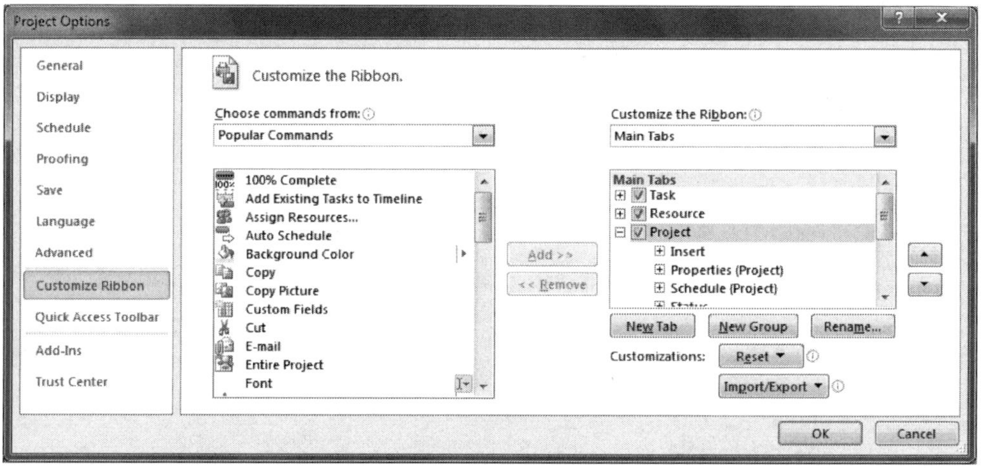

21.9 Quick Access Toolbar

This is where commands may be added to and removed from the Quick Access Toolbar.

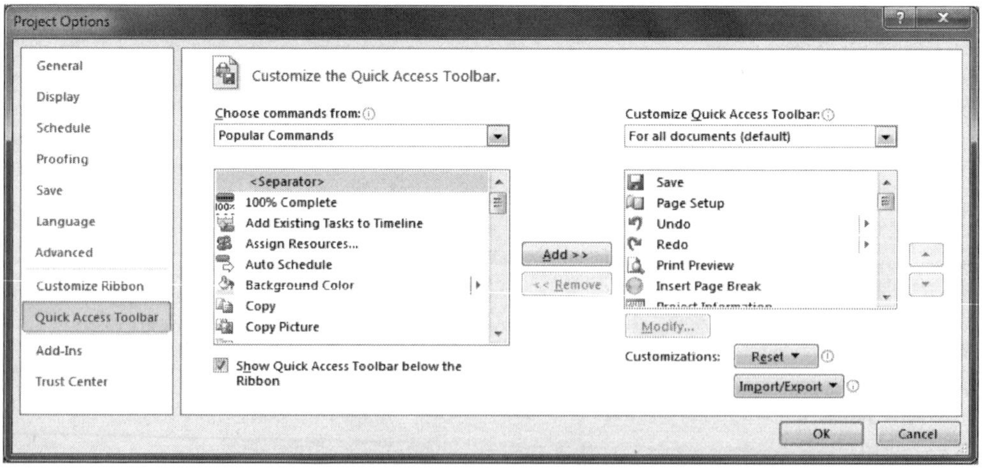

The introduction of the **Ribbon Toolbar** has increased the number of keystrokes required to access commands compared to the traditional toolbars from earlier versions of Microsoft Project. Users may find it simpler to hide the Ribbon using the **Minimize the Ribbon** command, move the **Quick Access Toolbar** below the **Ribbon** and add all the frequently used commands to the Quick Access Toolbar, as they are used, by right-clicking on them. The order may be revised using the **File**, **Options**, **Quick Access Toolbar** tab.

21.10 Add-Ins

This is where Add-ins, additional pieces of software, may be viewed and managed:

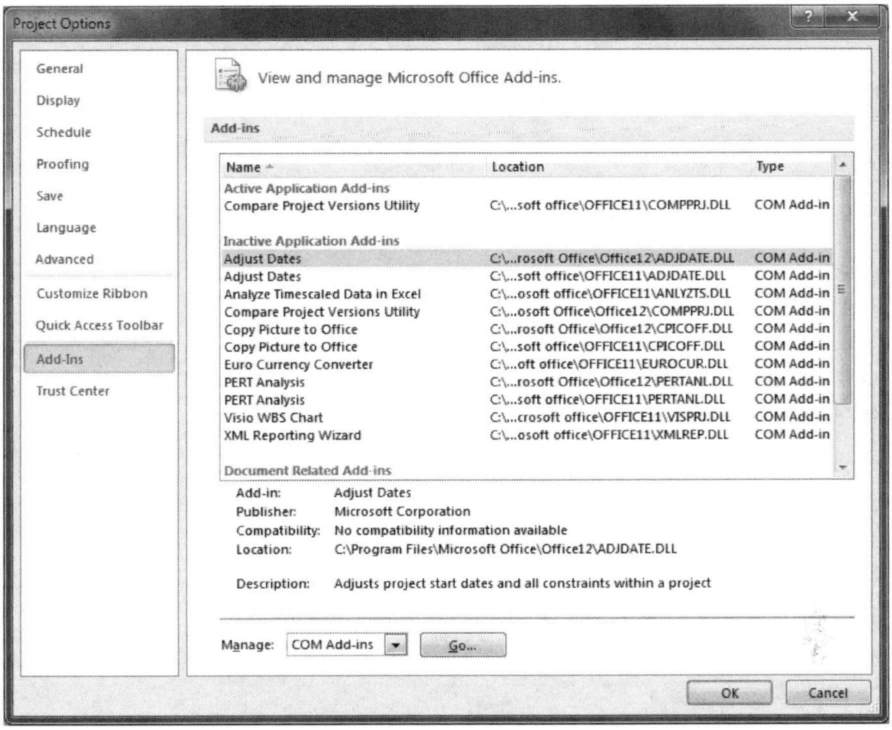

21.11 Trust Center

The **Trust Center** allows the control of privacy and macro security.

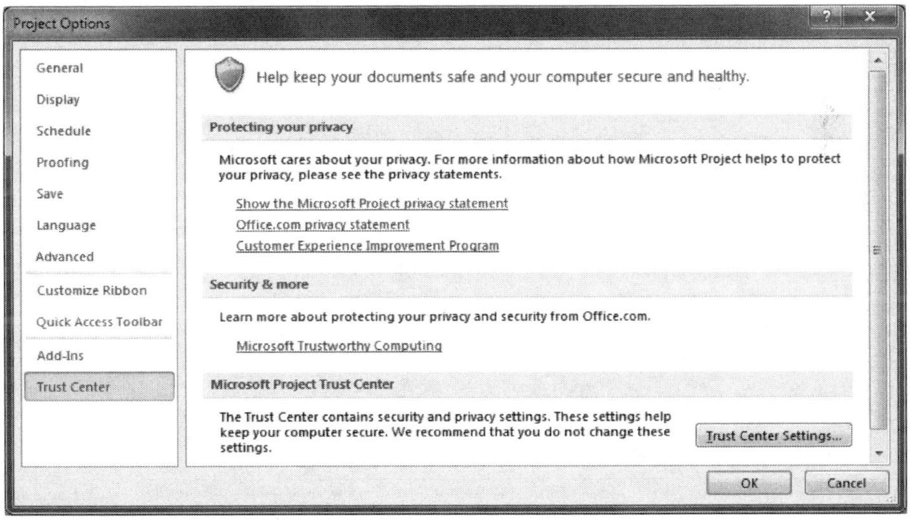

The **Trust Center** may be opened by:

- Clicking on the Trust Center Settings... button, or

- From the **Developer**, **Code** group, ⚠ **Macro Security** button.

21.11.1 Macro Settings

Macro Security was a new feature in Microsoft Project 2003 and these options are set to nominate which macros may or may not be used. This is aimed at preventing macros with a virus being activated.

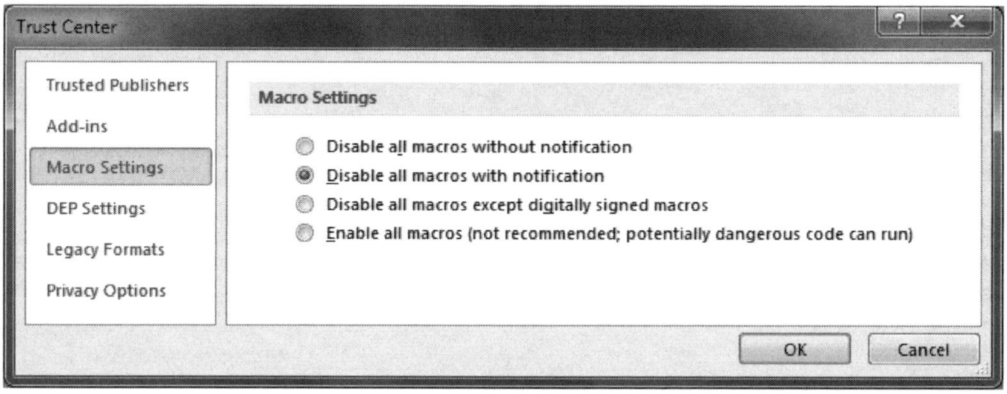

21.11.2 Legacy Formats.

These options, new to Microsoft Project 2007, control the notification and opening of legacy file formats such as Microsoft Project 98 format and Microsoft Project 2000 – 2003 mpp files.

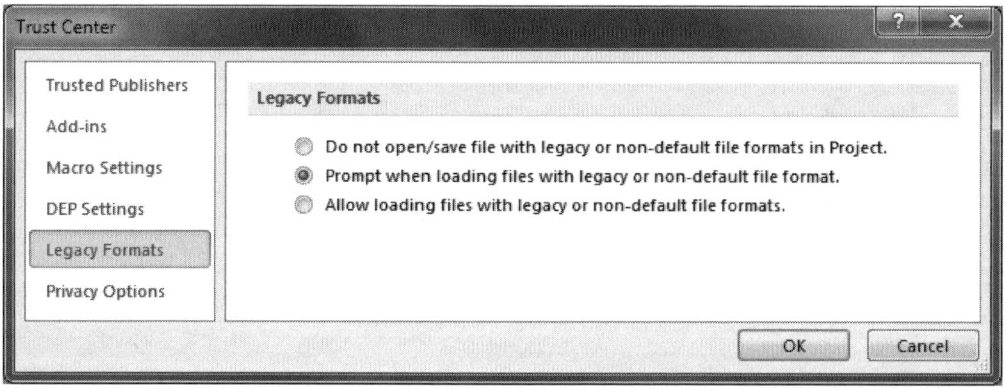

The option in the picture above is recommended as you will not be prevented from opening a file created in an earlier version but will be informed that it is a **Legacy Format**.

It is recommended that you do not operate with files saved in a Legacy Format as this has been associated with file corruption. If a person requires a file in a Legacy Version then you should save the file with a new name indicating it is a Legacy Format, close it and reopen your original file. Avoid going backwards and forwards in versions.

21.11.3 Privacy Options

Privacy Options

The **Privacy Options** section allows you to determine what access Microsoft has to your machine.

Document-specific settings

The properties of Author, Manager, Company and Last Saved By are removed from a file when it is saved. It is recommended that this not b checked if you are taking your page setup header and footer from the **Project Information** form.

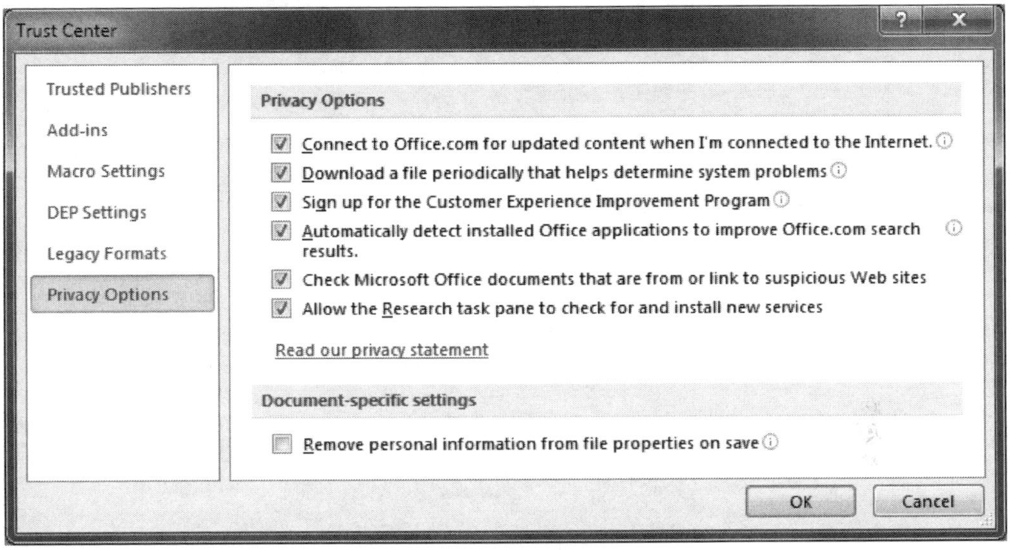

People with projects that have many views often populate the headers and footers with data from the **Project Information** form. This allows all headers and footers to be changed from one place. In this situation you do not want to **Remove personal information from file properties on file save** checked.

21.12 Authors Recommended Setup for New Projects

Many Microsoft Project default options are set for advanced scheduling and should be avoided by inexperienced users.

The screen dumps in this chapter set to the options that the author would suggest are a good defaults for inexperienced and casual users.

The correct setup of options is critical for minimizing the problems that users often experience and time should be spent understanding these options.

21.13 Commands Removed From the Microsoft Project 2007 Options, View Form

The following Outline options have been moved out of the Options form and are now only available as commands which may be added to the **Quick Access Toolbar** or **Ribbon**.

Indent name

- Indents the title for each Outline level to the right or removes the indent. It is useful to remove the indent, as displayed below, when there are a large number of outline levels and small manual indents may be created with a space at the start of each Task Name. This is also a useful function when the summary tasks have been hidden to right align all the tasks descriptions.

	i	Task Name
1		**OzBuild Initiation**
2		Approval to Bid
3		**Technical Specification**
4		Determine Installation Requirements

- The command **Indent Name** may be added to the **Quick Access Toolbar** or **Ribbon**.

Show outline number

- Shows the Outline Number 1, 1.1, 1.1.1, etc; see picture below.

	i	Task Name
1		**1 OzBuild Initiation**
2		1.1 Approval to Bid
3		**1.2 Technical Specification**
4		1.2.1 Determine Installation Requirements

- The command **Outline Number** may be added to the **Quick Access Toolbar** or **Ribbon**.

Show outline symbol

- Displays the [-] and [+] sign by the Task Name, see picture below:

	i	Task Name
1		− **OzBuild Initiation**
2		Approval to Bid
3		− **Technical Specification**
4		Determine Installation Requirements

- The command **Outline Symbol** may be added to the **Quick Access Toolbar** or **Ribbon**.

Show summary tasks

- Uncheck this to hide the summary tasks in the active view.

22 MORE ADVANCED SCHEDULING

The following advanced scheduling options should be considered once a user has some experience in the use of the software.

22.1 Working with Hourly Calendars

Hourly calendars are used for short duration projects such as medical operations, events and plant shutdowns. Hourly calendars add more complexity to a project and this section covers these issues.

22.1.1 Adjusting Calendar Default Working Hours

To adjust the standard working hours of a calendar:

- Select **Project**, **Properties** group, **Change Working Time** to open the **Change Working Time** form:
- Select the calendar to be edited from the **For calendar:** drop-down list,
- Click on the **Work Weeks** tab,

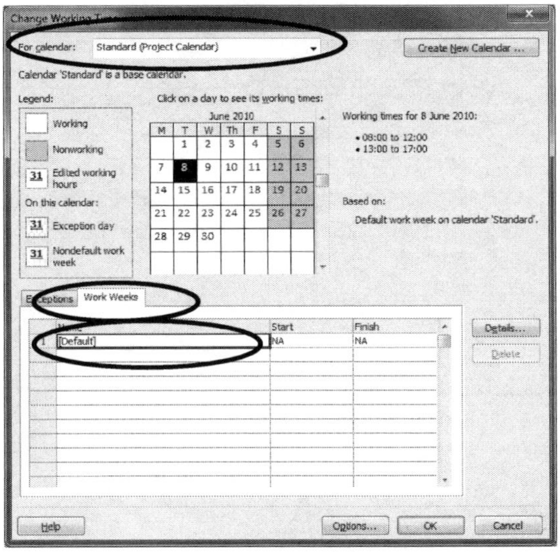

- Select the **[Default]** line in the **Work Weeks** tab,
- Click on the Details... button, or double-click on the **Name** to open the **Details for 'Calendar'** form,
- Days that are to be set the same working hours may be **Ctrl-Clicked** or **Dragged** to select them,
- The working hours for select day/s may be edited in the **From** and **To** cells on the right of the form.

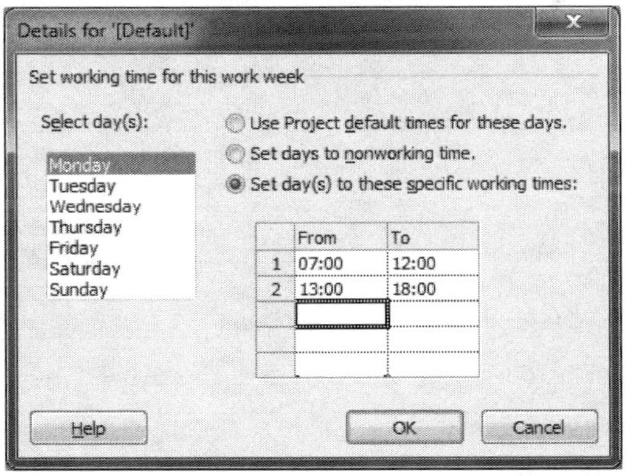

The create a 7-day per week calendar you will need to set up Saturday and Sunday working times the same as Monday to Friday.

22.1.2 Creating Calendar Periods with Alternate Working Hours

This **Work Weeks** tab may be used to create a period of one or more days where the working hours are different from the default working hours. Longer working hours may be required during a system upgrade or shutdown period. To create a period with different working hours from the default:

- Select the calendar that is required to have a special work period. The example below uses the Standard calendar,
- Select the **Work Week** tab,
- Select the first blank line in the **Work Weeks** tab and type in the description for the period. The example below has a unique set of working hours for a February Shutdown,
- Enter the Start and Finish dates of the period in the **Work Weeks** tab,

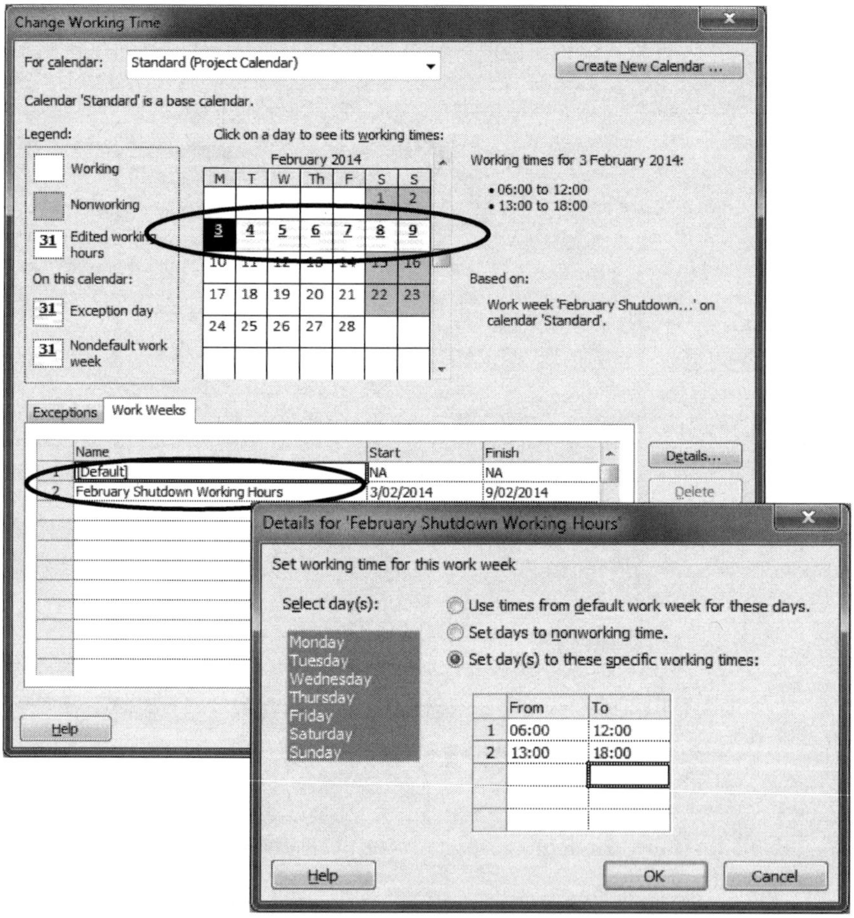

- Click on the Details... tab to open the **Calendar**, **Details for 'Calendar'** form,
- Select the days to be edited by dragging with the mouse pointer or **Ctrl-clicking**,
- Click on the appropriate radio button and edit the hours as required:

i When this option is used and the hours per day are not the same for each day then the durations displayed in days may misleading. Options to manage this issue are discussed later in this chapter

22.1.3 Working with Calendars with Different Hours per Day

There are some workable options to ensure that the durations in days are calculated and/or displayed correctly:

- All the calendars used on a project schedule should have the same number of hours per day for each day. This value is entered in the **Hours per day:** field in the Options form below. Then all durations in days will calculate correctly.
- When there is a requirement to use a different number of hours per day (in either the same calendar or in different calendars) then all durations should only be displayed in hours and the Task Calendar displayed, as per the picture above. Two examples of how this may occur are when:
  - There is an 8-hour working day Monday to Friday and a 4-hour working day on Saturday, or
  - Different calendars are required on a project, for example when some tasks are assigned an 8-hour per day calendar and some a 24-hour per day calendar.

  The **Duration is entered in:** field in the **File**, **Options**, **Schedule** tab, **Scheduling options for this project** section should be set to **Hours**.
- A Customized Field may be used to calculate and display the correct duration by using a formula. The example below uses the **Duration1** field to calculate and display the correct duration in days of a 24-hour per day calendar using a formula.

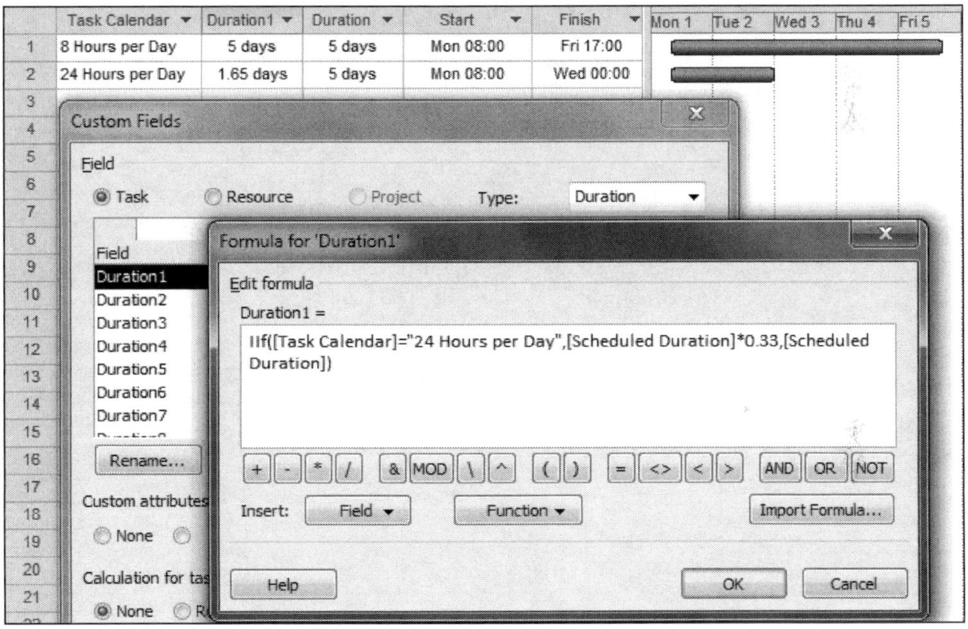

To create the formula displayed above:

- Select **Project**, **Properties**, group, **Custom Fields** to open the **Custom Fields** form,
- Select **Duration 1** from the **Type** drop-down box in the top left-hand side of the form,
- Click on the Formula... button to open the **Formula** form and enter the formula as required.
- The formula in the picture above will work for a schedule that has two calendars in use.
- The formula above is

  IIf([Task Calendar]="24 Hours per Day",[Duration]*0.33,[Duration])

22.1.4 Understanding Default Start and Default End Time

The **Default start time:** and **Default end time:** are the times that the software uses when a date is entered and a time is not entered. These times should be aligned to the **Project** calendar. They are used in Microsoft Project when:

- Constraints are assigned to tasks when a date is typed into a Start or Finish field, and
- Actual Start or Actual Finish dates are assigned.

These times are set in the **Options**, **Calendar** form which may be accessed by:

- Clicking the Options... button from the **Change working time** form, or
- Selecting the **File**, **Options**, **Schedule** tab, **Calendar options for this project:** section:

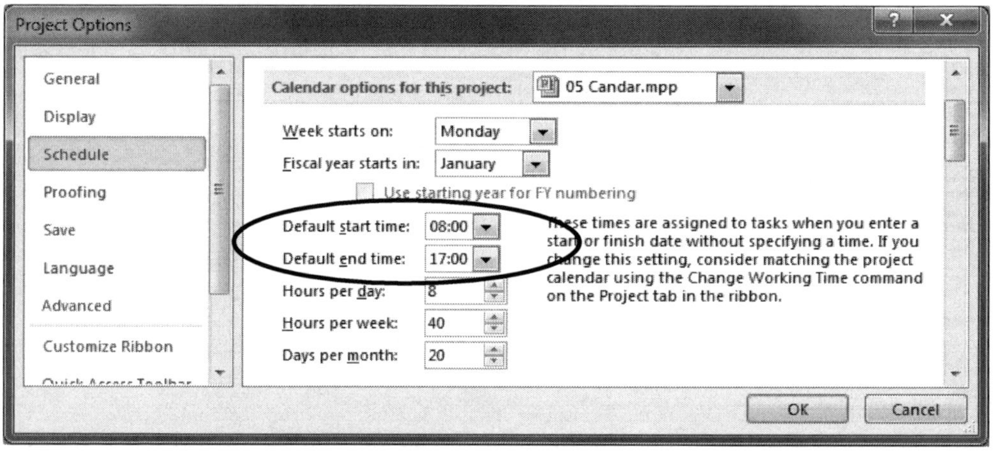

If these times are not aligned then tasks may be displayed one day longer than the duration as per the picture below, where the calendar start time is 8:00am and the Default start time is 9:00am and a 3 -ay task spans 4 days:

22.2 Managing Calendars

22.2.1 Deleting a Calendar

To delete a calendar:

- Select **File**, **Info**, **Organizer**, and select the **Calendars** tab.
- Highlight the calendar you want to delete and click on the [Delete...] button.

22.2.2 Copying Calendars between Projects

To copy a calendar between projects:

- Open both projects,
- Select **File**, **Info**, **Organizer**, and select the **Calendars** tab,
- From the drop-down boxes at the bottom of the tab under **Calendars available in:** select the projects that you want to copy to and from, and
- Select the calendar you want to copy and click on the [Copy >>] button.

22.2.3 Renaming a Calendar

To rename a calendar:

- Select **File**, **Info**, **Organizer**, and select the **Calendars** tab.
- Highlight the calendar you want to rename and click on the [Rename...] button to open the **Rename** form and type in the new name.

22.2.4 Copying a Base Calendar to Global.mpt for Use in Future Projects

Global.mpt is the default project template and all new projects created from a **Blank Project** copy their default settings from the Global.mpt.

Once you have set up a calendar with all the holidays for your location or business, it is suggested that you consider copying it to the Global.mpt to create your own personal template.

- Select **File**, **Info**, **Organizer**, and select the **Calendars** tab.
- Select the **Standard** calendar from your project and click on the [<< Copy] button.

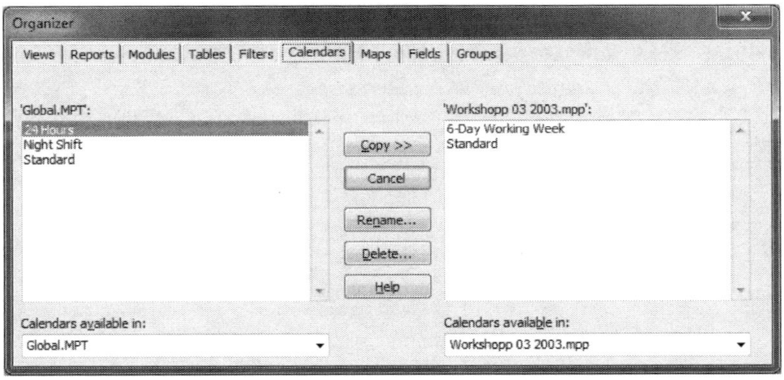

If more than one person needs to use a tailored calendar then a template should be created and made available to all users.

22.2.5 Printing the Calendar

It is always useful to be able to print out the calendar for people to review the working hours and nonwork periods. The options are:

- Print a report using the **Project**, **Reports** group, **Reports**, **Overview...**, **Working Day** report which is preferred by the author, or
- Display the Calendar View by selecting **View**, **Task Views** group, **Calendar** which is discussed in the **TABLES AND GROUPING TASKS** chapter:

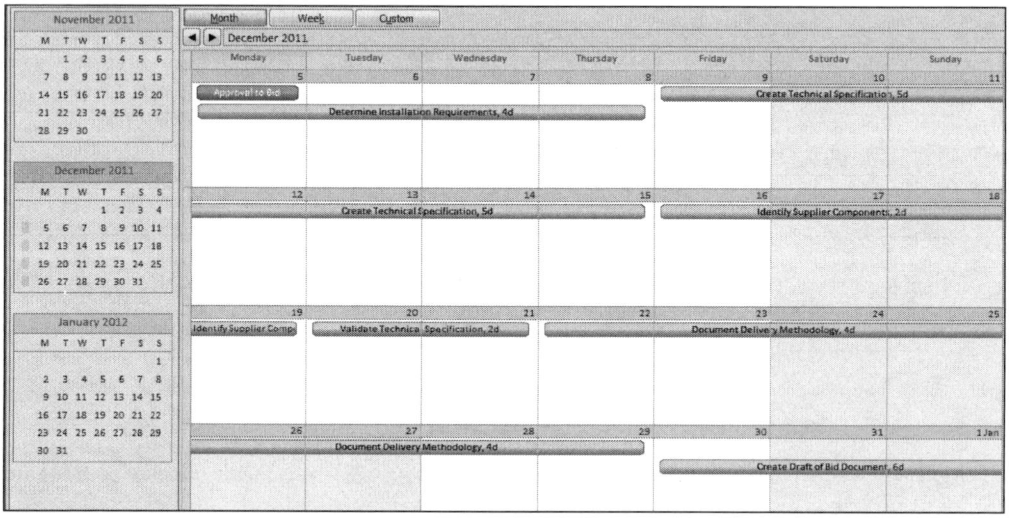

If you open a Microsoft Project 2007 file and this Calendar View is not displayed, select **View**, **Task Views** group, **Rest to default** will display this calendar.

It is useful to print the report to a pdf format so it may be saved and emailed.

22.2.6 Display Times in 24-Hour Clock

Should you wish to display your times in 24-hour format, e.g. 17:00hrs instead of 5:00pm then:

- Select from the windows menu **Setting**, **Control Panel**, **Regional Options** tab, or similar commands if you are not using Windows 7.
- Select **Customize**, select the **Time** tab and
- Change the time format from **h:mm:ss tt** to **HH:mm:ss** or **H:mm:ss**.

This option will affect other programs that use the system settings but makes it simpler to edit times.

22.3 *Adding Tasks*

22.3.1 Task Scheduling Mode - Manually Scheduled or Auto Scheduled

Microsoft has introduced this new task attribute titled **Task Scheduling Mode** in Microsoft Project 2010. In earlier versions of Microsoft Project every task was set to the equivalent of the new **Auto Scheduled** setting in Microsoft Project 2010. In this mode all tasks' Start and Finish dates are calculated with respect to the Project Start (or Finish) Date, their Durations, Relationships, Constraints, Calendars and Options.

When a task is set to **Manually Scheduled** it does not need a predecessor or constraint to hold the Start Date and therefore will not move when the project is scheduled. When a task is **Manually Scheduled** it takes on the following attributes:

- It is clear from the default bar formatting and **Task Scheduling Mode** which tasks are **Manually Scheduled**.
- Tasks may have text entered as the Start Date, Duration and Finish Date, see Task A below.
- As more information is known they may be assigned Dates, Durations and Resources, see Task B below.
- As the tasks are finalized they may be converted to **Auto Scheduled**, see Task C below. This task is acknowledging the Project Start date of 12 July.

		Task Mode	Task Name	Duration	Start	Finish	Work	Resource Names
1			Task A	About 1 week	Early July	Mid July	0 hrs	
2			Task B	5 days	5 Jul 8:00	9 Jul 17:00	40 hrs	Paul Harris
3			Task C	5 days	5 Jul 8:00	9 Jul 17:00	40 hrs	Paul Harris

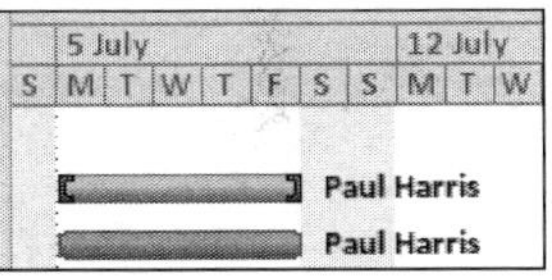

When two **Manually Scheduled** tasks are linked they acknowledge the relationship when:

- The **File**, **Options**, **Schedule** tab, **Scheduling options for this project:** section, **Update Manually Scheduled tasks when editing links** is checked, and
- A relationship is added or edited.
- In the pictures below:
  - ➢ Tasks 20 has been dragged back in time and the Finish-to-Start relationship is not being acknowledged and
  - ➢ The **Task Inspector**, which may be opened by selecting **Task**, **Tasks** group, **Inspect**, has highlighted the Finish Date of Task 20 and the outline of Task 20 is now dotted:

Before change:

	Task Mode	Task Name	Duration	Start	Finish
15		Task 5	4 days	5 Jul '10	8 Jul '10
16		Task 6	5 days	9 Jul '10	15 Jul '10

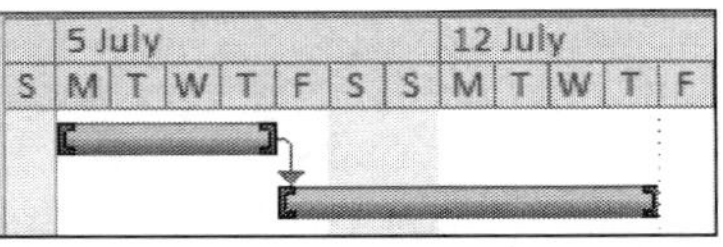

After change:

	Task Mode	Task Name	Duration	Start	Finish
19		Task 5	4 days	5 Jul '10	8 Jul '10
20		Task 6	5 days	6 Jul '10	12 Jul '10

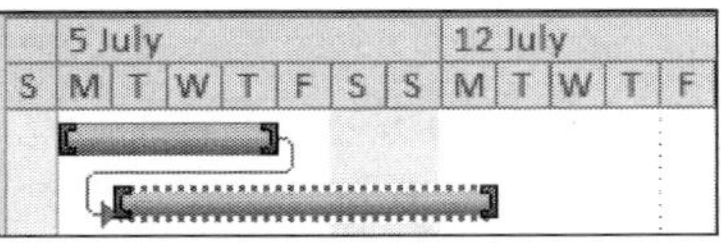

Summary and detail tasks may have different **Task Mode** settings:

- Summary tasks may be made **Manually Scheduled** and detail tasks made **Auto Scheduled**, as per Summary 1 in the picture below.
- The lower bar formatting and Finish date underlining of the Summary 1 is the **Task Inspector** function warning that there is conflict as the summary task duration does not match the detail task durations or dates.
- Summary tasks may be made **Auto Scheduled** and detail tasks made **Manually Scheduled**, as per Summary 2 in the picture below. In this situation the summary task adopts the duration of the detail tasks.

	Task Mode	Task Name	Duration	Start	Finish
1		**Summary 1**	**6 days**	**5 Jul '10**	**12 Jul '10**
2		Task 1	4 days	5 Jul '10	8 Jul '10
3		Task 2	4 days	9 Jul '10	14 Jul '10
4					
5		**Summary 2**	**8 days**	**5 Jul '10**	**14 Jul '10**
6		Task 3	4 days	5 Jul '10	8 Jul '10
7		Task 4	5 days	8 Jul '10	14 Jul '10

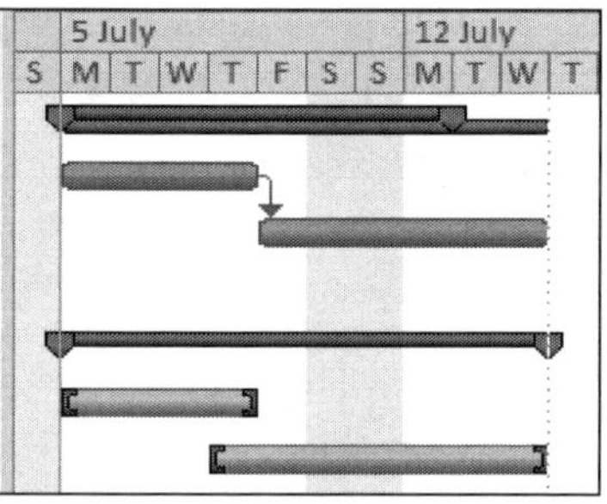

The default setting for new tasks is set in the **File**, **Options**, **Schedule** tab, **Scheduling options for this project:** section, **New tasks created:**:

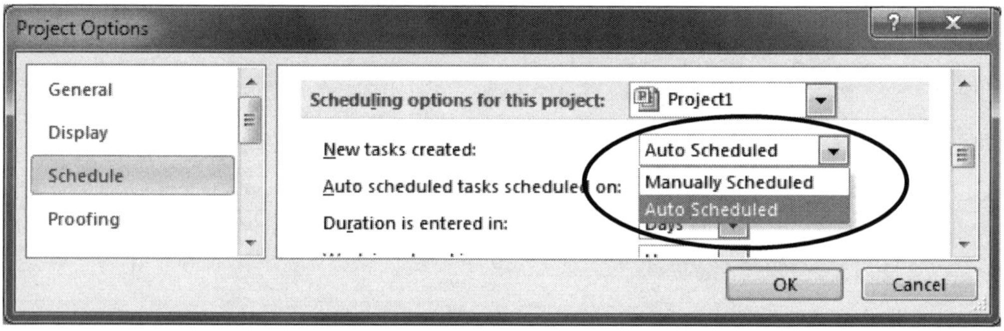

Tasks created as **Manually Scheduled** may be changed to **Auto Scheduled** by selecting the **Task Scheduling Mode** by:

- Displaying the **Task Scheduling Mode** column,
- Clicking on the **Task**, **Task** group, **Mode** button.
- Right-clicking on the task text or bar and selecting the required option from the menu.

When a task is changed from **Manually Scheduled** to **Auto Scheduled** the **File**, **Options**, **Schedule** tab, **Scheduling Options for this project:** section, **Keep Tasks on nearest working day when changing to Automatically Scheduled mode** will:

- When checked it will set a **Start No Earlier** constraint on the task and it will not move forward in time even if it has no predecessors, or
- When unchecked the task will not have a constraint set and will move forward to the **Project Start** date when it has no predecessors.

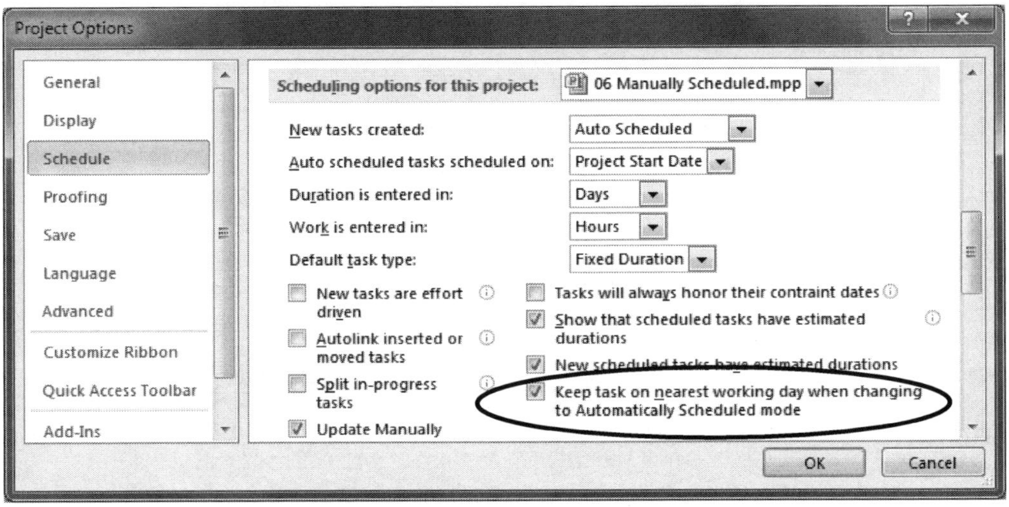

DISCUSSION:

- **Manually Scheduled** tasks would not be considered by many professional schedulers as good practice, as these tasks would not create a Critical Path schedule or meet most contract requirements.
- It could be a useful function during the initial development of a schedule but ultimately it would be considered good practice to have all tasks **Auto Scheduled** before a schedule is submitted for approval or to a customer as part of a submission.

The **Auto Scheduled** option may be turned off so the schedule does not recalculate every time a change is made to the schedule by selecting **File**, **Options**, **Schedule** tab, **Calculation** section **Calculate project after each edit:**. To recalculate the schedule the user presses the **F9** key. This is not the same as setting tasks to **Manually Scheduled** and all tasks set as **Auto Scheduled** will be recalculated and **Manually Scheduled** tasks will not be recalculated when the **F9** key is pressed.

22.3.2 Copying Tasks from Other Programs

Task data may be copied to and from, or updated from other programs such as Excel, by copying and pasting. The columns and rows in your spreadsheet will need to be formatted in the same way as in your schedule before they may be pasted into your schedule.

Microsoft Project 2010 has introduced new functions allowing:

- Copy and Paste to other products to keep the column header, formatting and indenting.
- Copy and Paste from other products to allow the option of keeping the source formatting:

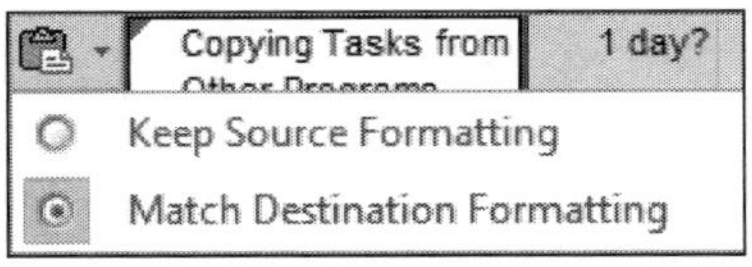

It is often best in Microsoft Project to make all Task Names unique, so for example when you have a building with many floors and trades each Task Name should include the trade and floor. This makes it easier to understand the schedule when a filter has been applied and to find predecessors and successors in a large schedule. These descriptions may be created in a spreadsheet by using the **Concatenate** function, the picture below demonstrates how. Text may be added by including it in double quotation marks:

	A	B	C
1	Floor 1	Concrete Works	=A1&" - "&B1
2	Floor 1	Frame Walls	Floor 1 - Frame Walls
3	Floor 1	Hang Wall Sheeting	Floor 1 - Hang Wall Sheeting
4	Floor 2	Concrete Works	Floor 2 - Concrete Works
5	Floor 2	Frame Walls	Floor 2 - Frame Walls
6	Floor 2	Hang Wall Sheeting	Floor 2 - Hang Wall Sheeting
7	Floor 3	Concrete Works	Floor 3 - Concrete Works

i When you copy and paste dates into the schedule, you may find that tasks are assigned constraints, which you may not desire. It is recommended that you display the **Indicators** column, which will show a button if a constraint has been applied. Avoid copying dates.

22.3.3 Dynamically Linking Cells to Other Programs

It is also possible to dynamically link data to other programs such as an Excel spreadsheet:

- Copy the data from the spreadsheet,
- Select the cell position in the table where the data is to be pasted in Microsoft Project,
- Select **Task**, **Clipboard** group, **Paste Special**, **Paste Link**, **Text Data** option,
- The data will be pasted into the cell(s) and changes to linked cells in the spreadsheet or other program will be reflected in the Microsoft Project schedule.
- The linked cell will have a little triangle in the bottom right-hand side indicating that the cell is linked. The Task Name and Duration cells in the picture below are linked.

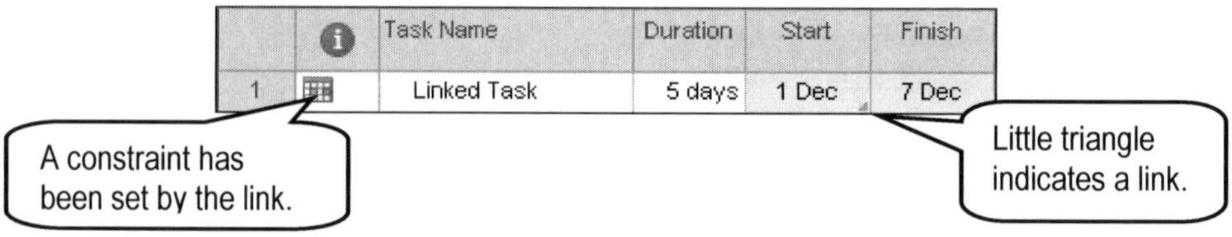

- Be careful when linking dates as this sets constraints. Because the Start date is linked in the picture above this task also has a constraint which is indicated by the **Constraint** icon in the indicator column.
- When reopening the project schedule at a later date you will be asked if you wish to refresh the data from the other application.
- To remove a link delete or change the data in the cell.
- To open the linked document, double-click on the little triangle in the bottom right-hand side of the cell.

It is also possible to link one or more cells in a schedule with another cell in the same schedule so a change in one cell will change all the other linked cell(s) using the **Paste Link** option.

i When a field has been linked to another file you must be careful when changing the file names so you do not sever the link.

22.3.4 Milestones with a Duration

Microsoft Project also has the ability to display a Milestone with a non-zero duration. The Milestone duration may be elapsed, 24-hour per day 7-days per week which is created by typing an "e" before the duration units, or a calendar calculated duration. To create a task with a non-zero duration:

- Highlight the task with a duration that you want to mark as a milestone,
- Open the **Task Information** form by double-clicking on the task,
- Select the **Advanced** tab, and
- Click the **Mark task as milestone** check box.

Task Name	Duration	Start	Finish
Milestone	0 days	1 Sep 08:00	1 Sep 08:00
Task 1	4 days	1 Sep 08:00	4 Sep 17:00
Milestone with a duration	4 days	5 Sep 08:00	10 Sep 17:00
Task 2	2 days	11 Sep 08:00	12 Sep 17:00
Milestone with an elapsed duration	4 edays	4 Sep 17:00	8 Sep 17:00
Task 3	2 days	9 Sep 08:00	10 Sep 17:00

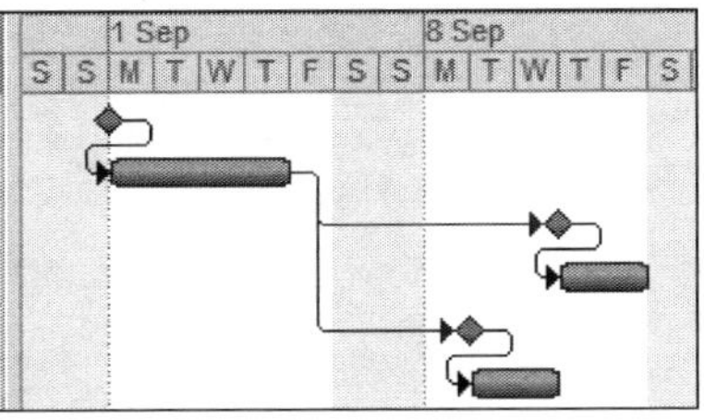

The picture above shows that the Milestone point is displayed at the end of the task duration.

The use of this is not recommended as it makes the schedule difficult to read.

22.3.5 Splitting a In-progress Task

A task may be manually split by clicking on the **Task**, **Schedule** group button, moving your cursor over the point on the task bar where you want a split, and dragging the remaining part of the task. Splitting a task effectively increases the duration of the task but work associated with a split task is scheduled intermittently.

The **File**, **Options**, **Schedule** tab, **Scheduling options for this project:**, **Split in-progress tasks** option does not need to be checked for manual splitting of a task. It must be checked to allow the splitting of a task by Out Of Sequence Progress when a task starts before a predecessor is complete.

An in-progress task may also be split by:

- Dragging the incomplete portion of a task in the bar chart, or
- Using the **Reschedule uncompleted work to start after:** function, or
- Commencing a task before its predecessor finishes as shown by the second task in the diagram below:

	Start	Stop	Resume	Finish
1	30 May	31 May	7 Jun	12 Jun
2	29 May	31 May	12 Jun	17 Jun

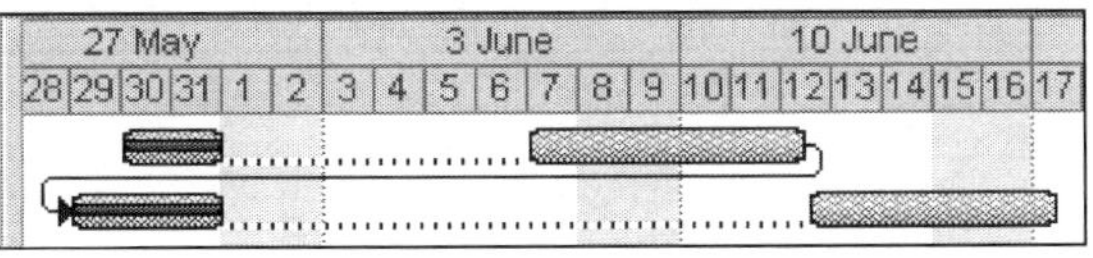

- Task 2 has been split by the relationship with Task 1.
- The Stop and Resume dates, shown in the picture above, may be also manually edited.

22.4 Formatting Bars

22.4.1 Format One or More Specific Task Bars

One or more individual bars may be formatted to make them look different from other bars. To format one or more bars:

- Select:
  - One task bar by clicking on it, or
  - Multiple bars by Ctrl-clicking each bar or left-clicking and dragging with the mouse, then
- Open the **Format Bar** form by:
  - Selecting **Format**, **Bar Styles** group **Format**, **Bar**, or
  - Moving the mouse over a bar in the bar chart until the mouse changes to a  and double-clicking. When more than one bar has been selected you will need to hold the **Ctrl Key** down when double-clicking on a bar.
- Then select the required bar formatting options from the **Format Bar** form:

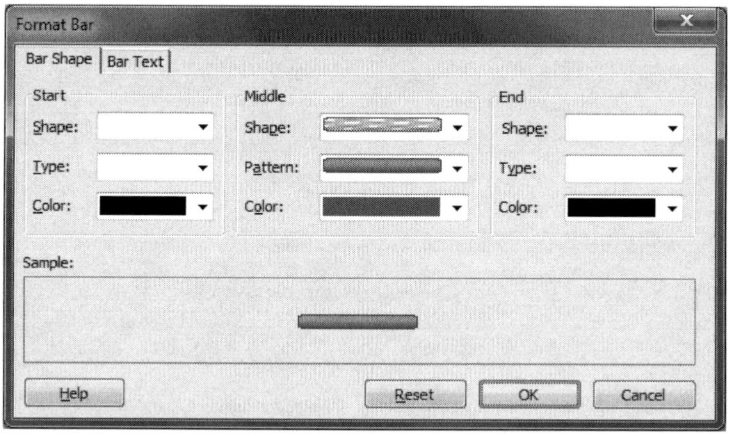

- The  button is used to restore the default bar formatting to selected bars.

The bar shape may be formatted and text information added in the same way as formatting all the bars described earlier in this chapter.

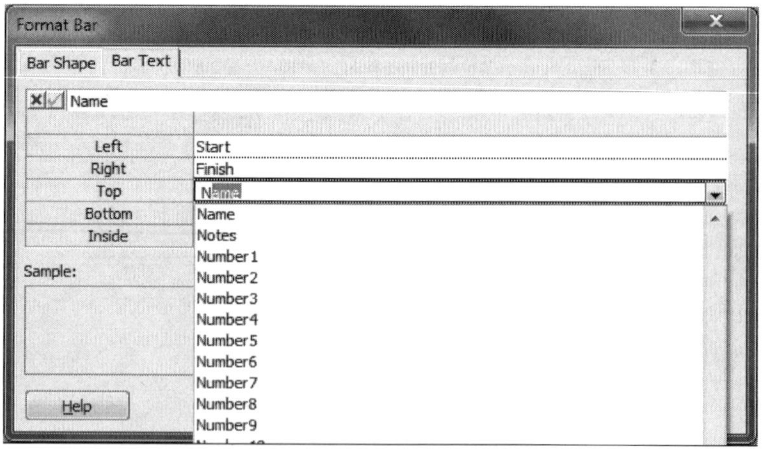

- Select **Format**, **Format** group, **Text styles** to format the text font.

22.4.2 Hiding the Task Bar

A Tasks Bar may be hidden by checking the **Hide bar** option in the **Task Information** form, **General** tab which is opened by double clicking on the Task Name.

22.4.3 Layout Form – Format Bars Options (Date, Height and Rollup)

Select **Format**, **Format** group, **Layout** to open the **Layout** form. This form has some additional bar formatting options for users to customize the appearance of the Gantt Chart.

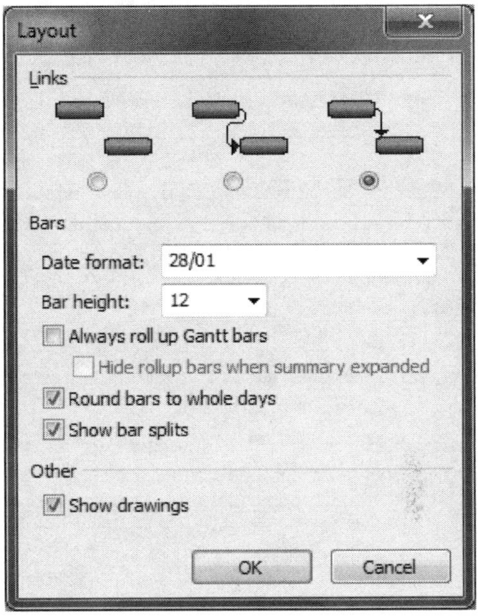

- **Date format:** sets the format for dates displayed on bars only. Dates are displayed on bars using **Format**, **Bar Styles** group, **Format** button and selecting either the **Bar** or **Bar Styles** buttons.
- **Bar height:** sets the height of all the bars. Individual bars may be assigned different heights by selecting a bar shape in the styles form.
- **Always roll up Gantt bars** and **Hide rollup bars when summary expanded** works as follows:

  - Tasks before roll up:

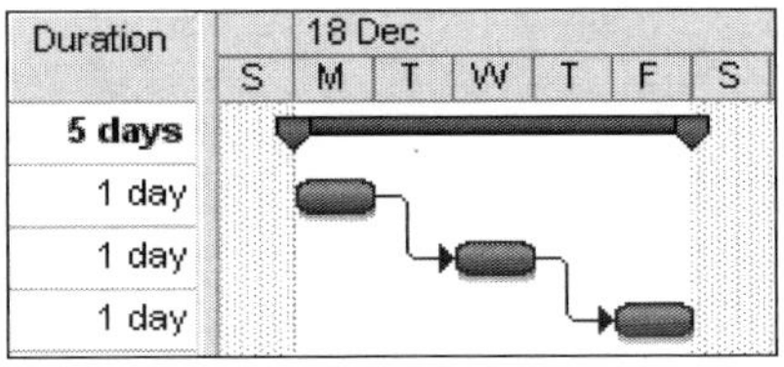

  - With **Always roll up Gantt bars** checked and **Hide rollup bars when summary expanded** unchecked:

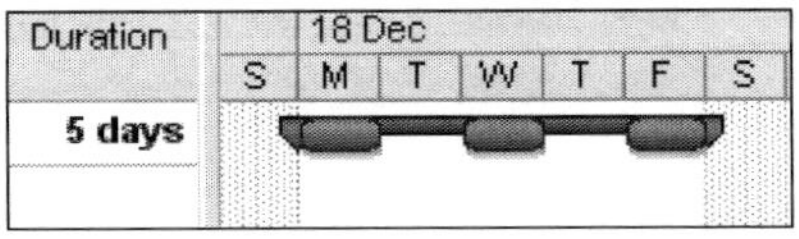

  - With **Always roll up Gantt bars** and **Hide rollup bars when summary expanded** checked:

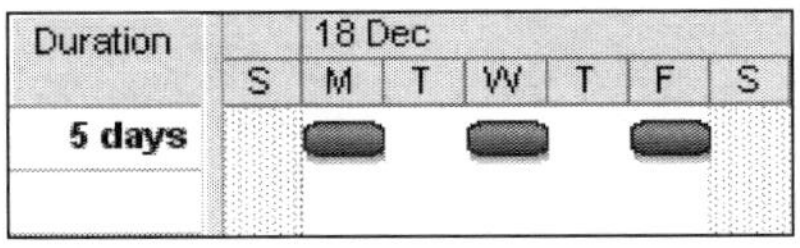

- An individual bar may could be rolled up to a summary task in earlier versions of Microsoft Project using the **Roll up Gantt bar to summary** option in the **Task Information** form when **Always roll up Gantt bars** options are unchecked. This command has been renamed to **Rollup** in Microsoft Project 2010 and the picture below taken from Microsoft Project 2007 was not achieved in the author's version of Microsoft Project 2010. This issue could be fixed with an update.

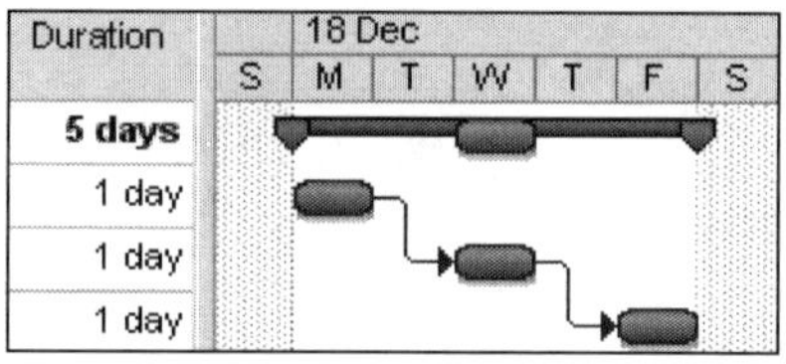

- **Round bars to whole days:**
  - When this option is unchecked, the length of the task will be shown in proportion to the total number of hours worked per day over the 24-hour time span. For example, an 8-hour working duration bar is shown below:

  - When this option is checked, the task bar will be displayed and spanned over the whole day irrespective of working time:

This function is useful as it make short duration tasks more visible on long schedules.

22.5 *Task Splitting*

22.5.1 Splitting Tasks

An un-started task may be split using the **Split Task** button on the **Task**, **Schedule** group, then highlighting the bar to be split and dragging the section of the bar with the mouse to the location where it is planned to conduct the work. The picture below shows the Create Technical Specifications task being split. Splits may be removed by dragging the bar back together again.

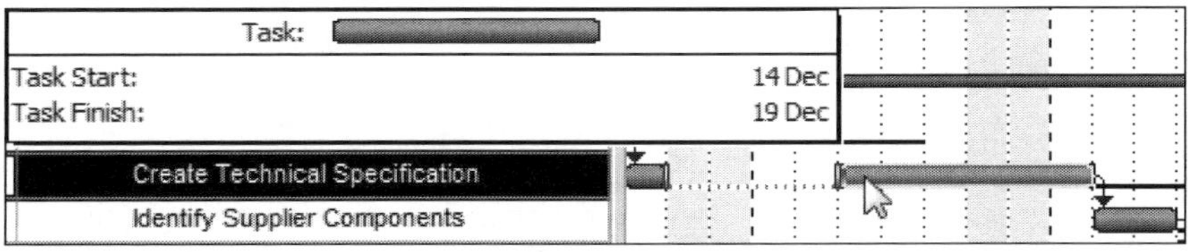

In-progress tasks may be split manually by dragging the incomplete portion to the right or a split may be created automatically by commencing a task before its predecessor is complete. Splitting in-progress tasks is covered in both the **TRACKING PROGRESS** and **OPTIONS** chapters.

22.5.2 Show bars splits

The two pictures below are of the same task, first with the option checked and then unchecked:

- When checked, the task bar will display splits:

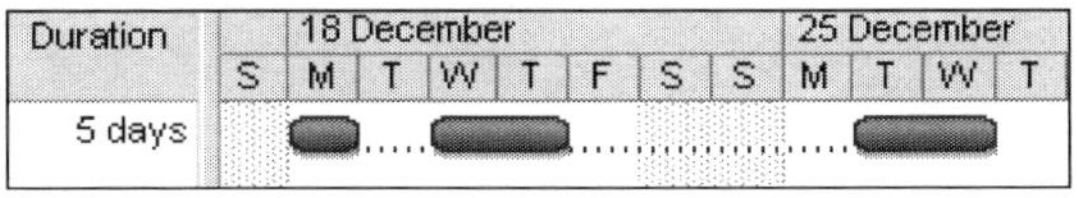

- When unchecked, the task bar will **NOT** display splits:

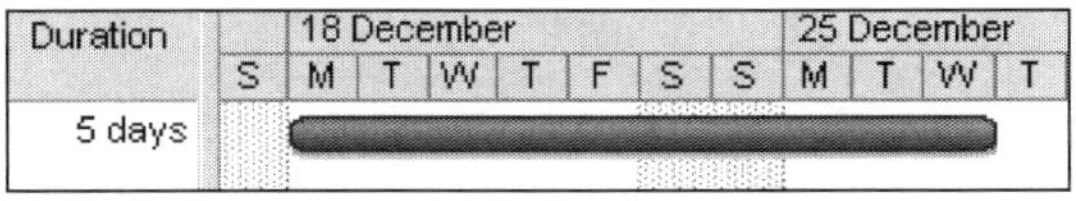

22.5.3 Bar Split Dates.

- The start and finish dates of splits of un-started tasks are not available through the user interface, only the start and finish of the task is available. When an in-progress task is split then the **Stop** date and **Resume** date may be seen in columns, see para 22.9.5.

22.5.4 Split Task Duration

The **Duration Type**, which may be displayed in a column or the **Task Information**, **Advanced** tab etc, determines if a split task displays the working duration or the elapsed duration:

- **Fixed Units** and **Fixed Work** show the worked duration of 10 days, and
- **Fixed Duration** shows the duration of 15 days from the start to finish of a task.

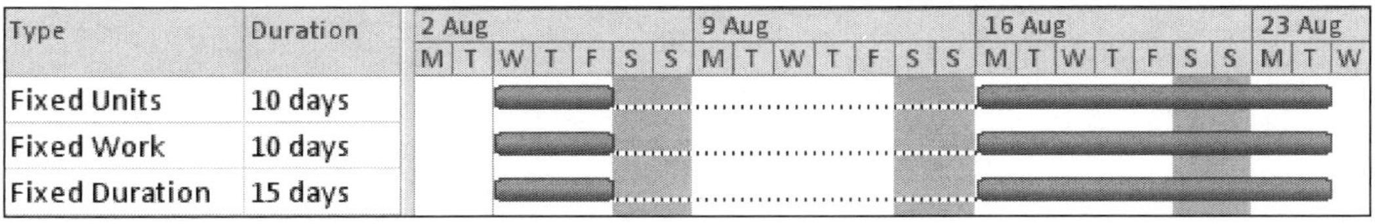

22.6 *Logic*

22.6.1 Unique ID Predecessor or Unique ID Successor Columns

Each task is assigned a Unique ID when it is created and this number is not used again in the schedule, even if the task is deleted. The Unique ID is changed for all new tasks, even when they are created by copy and pasting existing tasks.

There are two other columns that may be used to edit and display relationships using the Unique ID:

- The **Unique ID Predecessor**, and
- The **Unique ID Successor**.

The Task **Unique ID** will allow users to identify easily which tasks have been added or deleted when a revised schedule has been submitted. On the other hand if one wants to reset the unique ID, or hide the addition or deletion of tasks then a new schedule may be created, the calendars transferred with Organizer and all the tasks copied and pasted into the new schedule. There is also a unique **Resource ID** and a Resource Assignment **Unique ID**.

22.6.2 Reviewing Relationships Using WBS Predecessor or Successor Columns

There are two other columns that may be used only to display (and not edit) the **Predecessors** and **Successors**:

- The **WBS Predecessor**, and
- **WBS Successor**.

22.6.3 Task Drivers

A task may not be on the Critical Path and may have more than one predecessor. A **Driving Relationship** is the predecessor that determines the Early Start of a task.

- Microsoft Project 2000 – 2003 does not identify the difference between **Driving** and **Non-driving Relationships**, which often makes analyzing a schedule difficult. With earlier versions of Microsoft Project often the simplest way to determine the driving relationship for tasks not on the Critical Path and with more than one predecessor, was to delete the relationships until the task moved.
- Oracle Primavera products have always displayed the driving predecessors and successors in the Predecessor and Successors form.
- Microsoft Project 2007 introduced a **Task Drivers** form that indicates which is the driving predecessor and whether the schedule has been Resource Leveled. It also displays the effects of leveling.

In Microsoft Project 2010 the **Task Drivers** form has been renamed **Inspect Task** and additional functionality has been added. Select **Task**, **Tasks** group, **Inspect**, **Inspect Tasks** button open the **Task Inspector** pane:

- The picture below shows that Task 10 is the driving predecessor of Task 11.

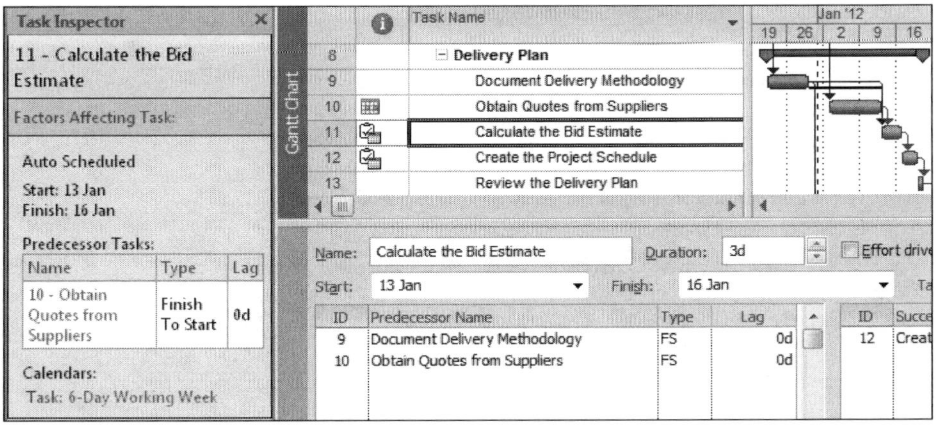

- The picture below shows that Task 15 has issues with resource overloading and makes some suggestions for resolving the issues:

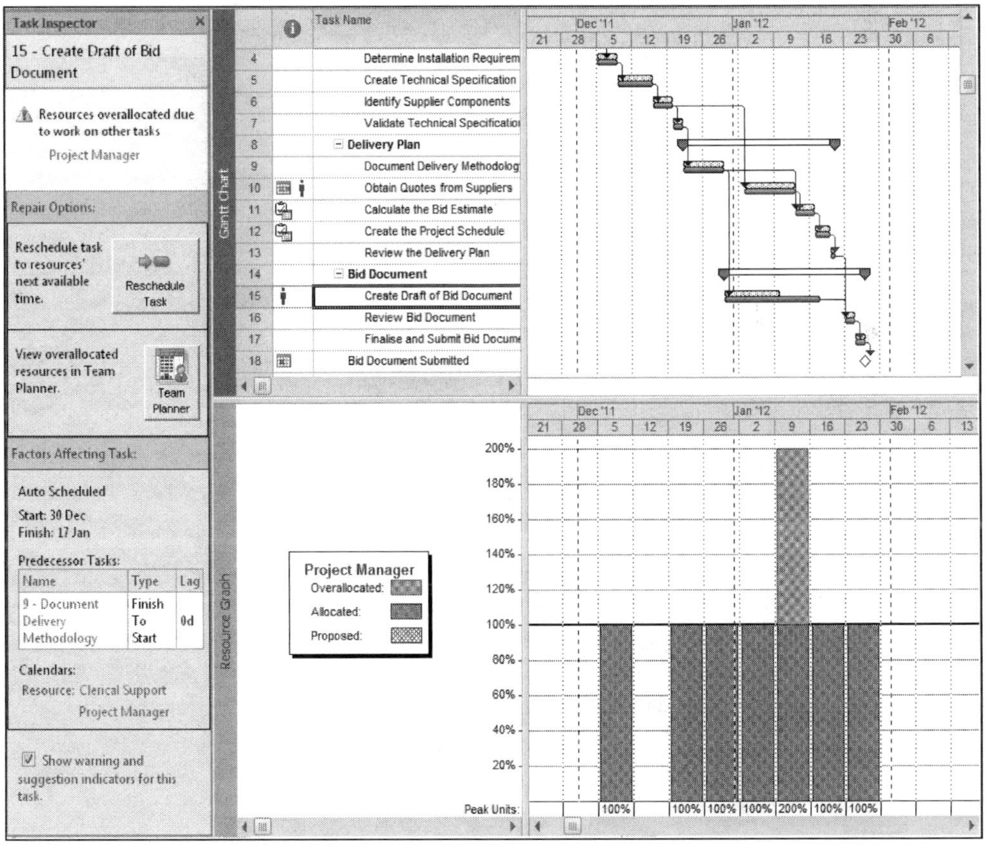

22.6.4 Manually Scheduled Relationships

When two **Manually Scheduled** tasks are linked they acknowledge the relationship when:

- The **File**, **Options**, **Schedule** tab, **Scheduling options for this project:** section, **Update Manually Scheduled tasks when editing links** is checked, and
- A relationship is added or edited.

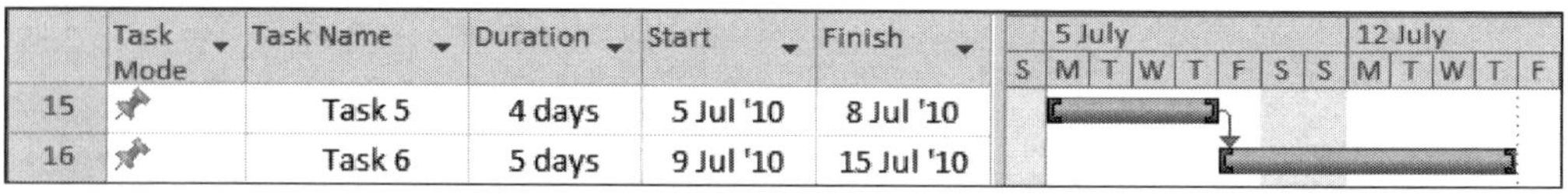

In the picture below:

- Tasks 6 has been dragged forward in time and the Finish-to-Start relationship is not being acknowledged and
- The **Task Inspector** has highlighted the Finish Date of Task 6 and the outline of Task 6 is now dotted:

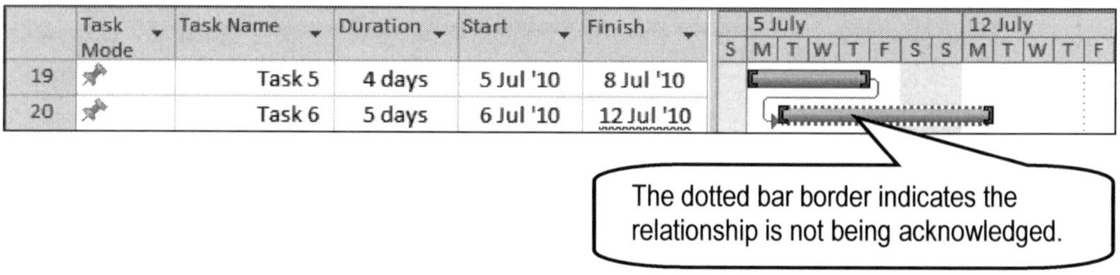

22.6.5 Schedule From Project Finish Date

You are able to impose an absolute project finish date by setting the **Schedule from:** option to **Project Finish Date** in the **Project Information** form.

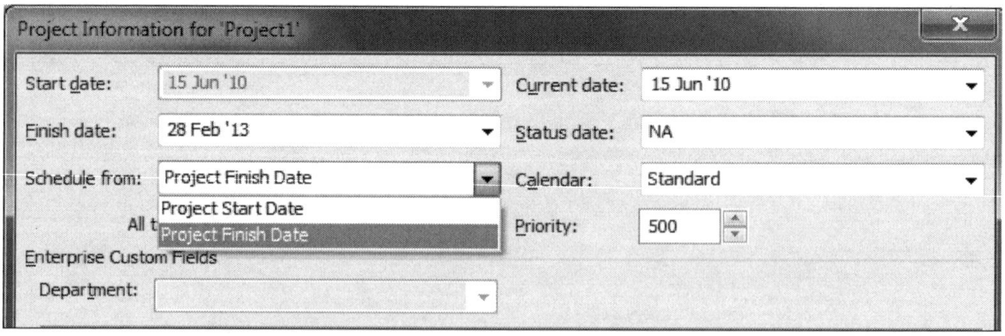

This option may be set after tasks have been added to the schedule. From the point in time that the project is set to schedule from the Project Finish date all new tasks will be assigned with an **As Late As Possible** (ALAP) constraint as they are created.

Any original tasks which may be set as **As Soon As Possible** (ASAP) may either be:

- Reset as ALAP, and calculated with all new tasks as ALAP, or
- Left as ASAP.

When the original tasks are left as ASAP, the tasks will be scheduled as ASAP with a Start No Earlier constraint which is calculated either:

- With no float when their combined durations are greater than the ALAP tasks, and the Total Float extends beyond the **Project Finish Date**, identified by the vertical line in the pictures below:

Constraint Type	Total Slack
As Soon As Possible	0 days
As Soon As Possible	0 days
As Late As Possible	4 days
As Late As Possible	4 days

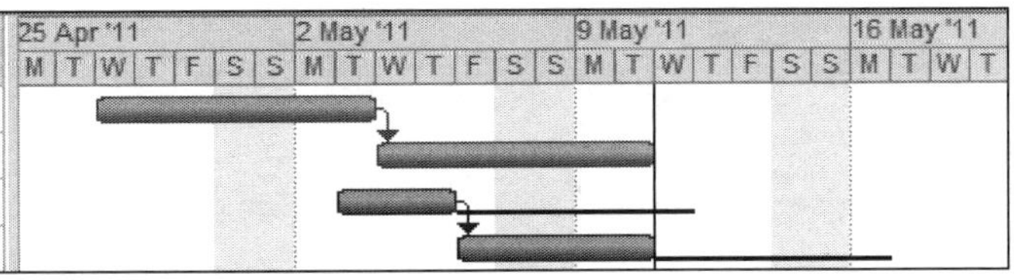

- Will not start earlier than the earliest Early Start of the ALAP tasks when their combined durations are greater than the ALAP tasks.

Constraint Type	Total Slack
As Soon As Possible	2 days
As Soon As Possible	2 days
As Late As Possible	0 days
As Late As Possible	0 days

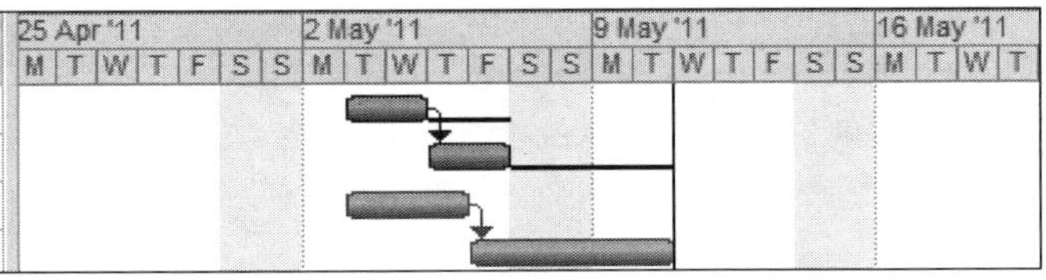

Unlike in Oracle Primavera software it is not possible in Microsoft Project to set both a start and finish date on a project. These dates are often called project constraints.

22.6.6 Move Project

The **Move Project**, **Schedule** group, **Move Project** function opens the Move Project form which allows the resetting of the **Project Start** date:

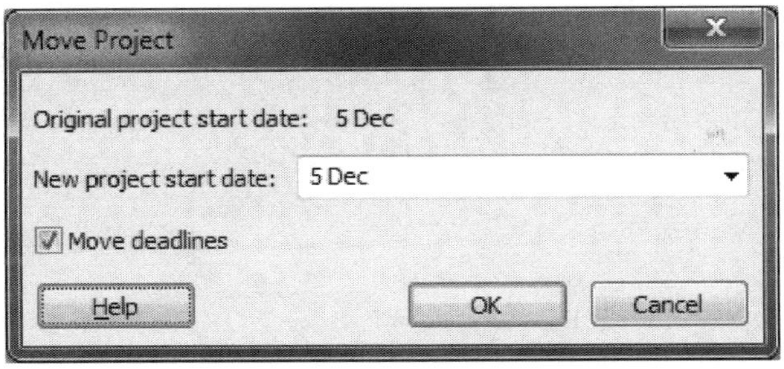

This option will change Actual Dates and should be used with caution if used with a progressed schedule.

22.7 Custom Outline Codes and WBS

22.7.1 Custom Outline Codes

There are **Task Custom Outline Codes** and **Resource Outline Codes** that may be renamed to suit the project requirements.

- Task Custom Outline Codes may be used for any hierarchical project breakdown structure, such as a PRINCE2 Product Breakdown Structure, Contract Breakdown Structure, and
- Resource Custom Outline Codes may be used for organizational breakdown structures such as the hierarchy of authority, locations and departments.

The process to use this function has three steps:

- Define the new Custom Outline Code structure,
- Assign the codes to the tasks, and
- Create a Group to organize the tasks under the new Custom Outline Code structure.

There is no **Ribbon** menu button for opening the **Custom Fields** form therefore you should consider adding the **Custom Fields** button to your **Quick Access Toolbar** or **Ribbon**.

22.7.2 Define a Custom Outline Code

Click on the **Custom Fields** button to open the form:

- An Outline Code may be created for either Task or Resource or Project in an Enterprise version data by clicking on the appropriate radio button under the title **Field**.
- Select **Outline Code** from the **Type:** drop-down box,
- The Rename... button opens a form to edit the name of the Outline Code. Two codes in the picture have been renamed Stage and System.

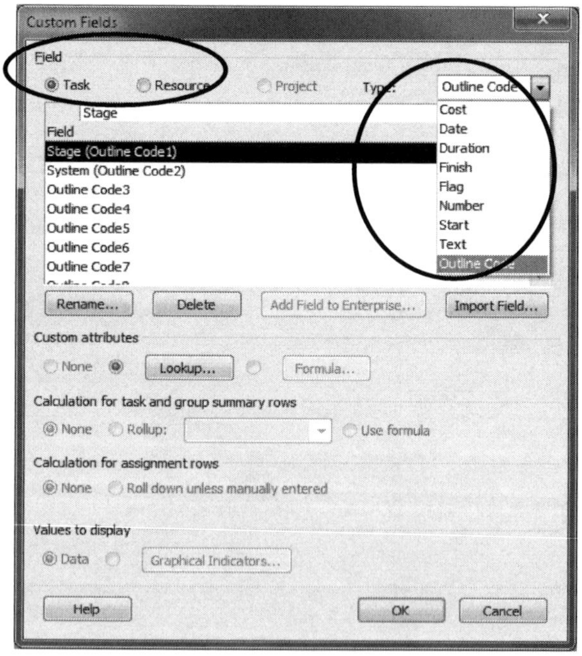

- The Import Field... opens the **Import Custom Field** form allowing a code structure from another project to be imported in a similar method to Organizer.
- **NOTE:** Text from another product such as Excel may be simply cut and pasted into most Microsoft Project lists and does not have to be manually typed in.

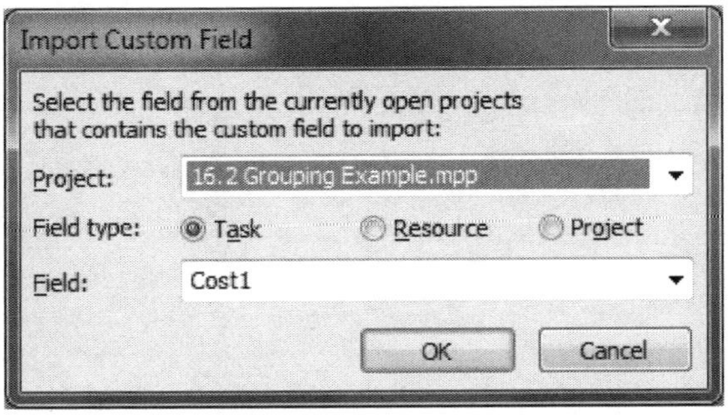

- The Lookup... opens **Edit Lookup Table** form for the selected Outline Code.

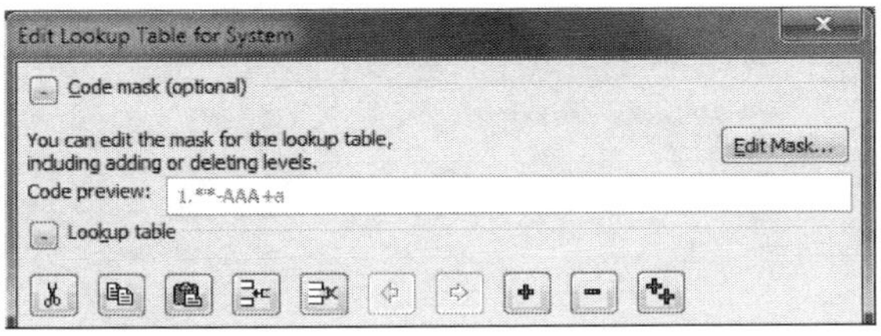

- Before codes are entered the **Mask** or code structure may be defined by clicking on the Edit Mask... button at the top right-hand side. This will open the **Outline Code Definition** form where the code structure is defined.
  - As each **Level** is created it is assigned a number.
  - The **Sequence** defines the type of text that may be entered for the code: Numbers, Uppercase, Lowercase or Characters (text).
  - The **Length** specifies how many characters the Code Level may have: any number of characters, or a number between 1 and 10.
  - The **Separator** defines the character that separates each level in the structure.

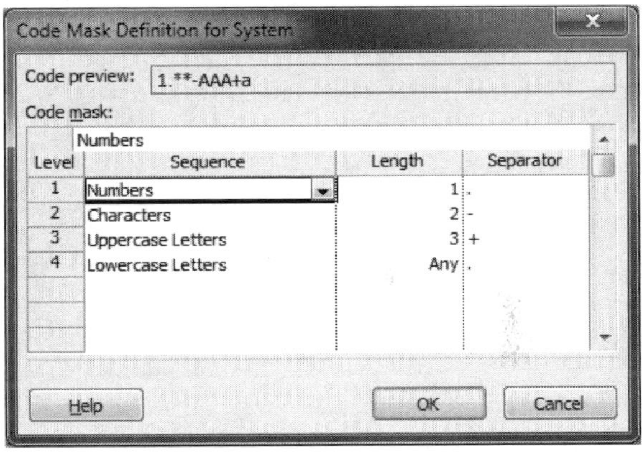

- Click the OK button to return to the **Edit Lookup Table** form where the Code Values and Descriptions are entered:
  - The picture shows two "Units" at level 1 and each Unit's Subsystem at level 2.
  - The buttons along the top of the form have a similar function to their use in Outlining and may be used to indent and outdent codes and copy and paste code groups.
  - The other options in the form are self-explanatory.

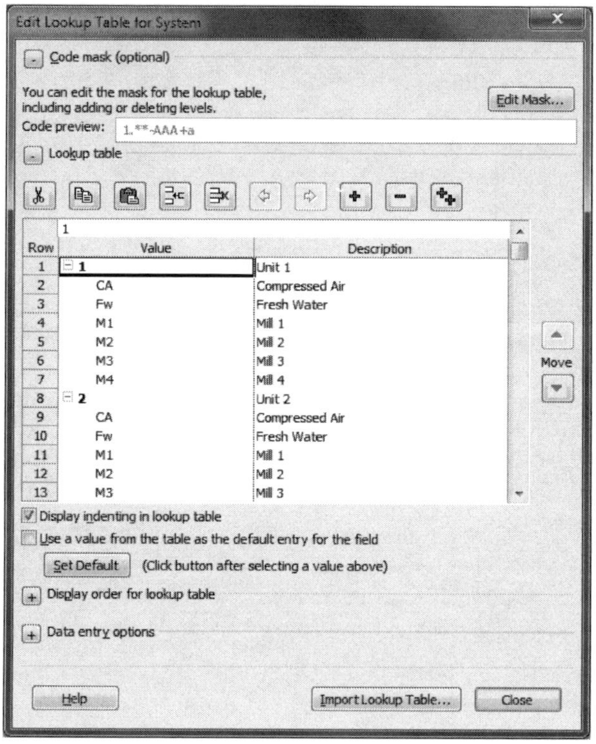

Assigning Custom Codes to Tasks

The codes are assigned by:

- Displaying the appropriate column:

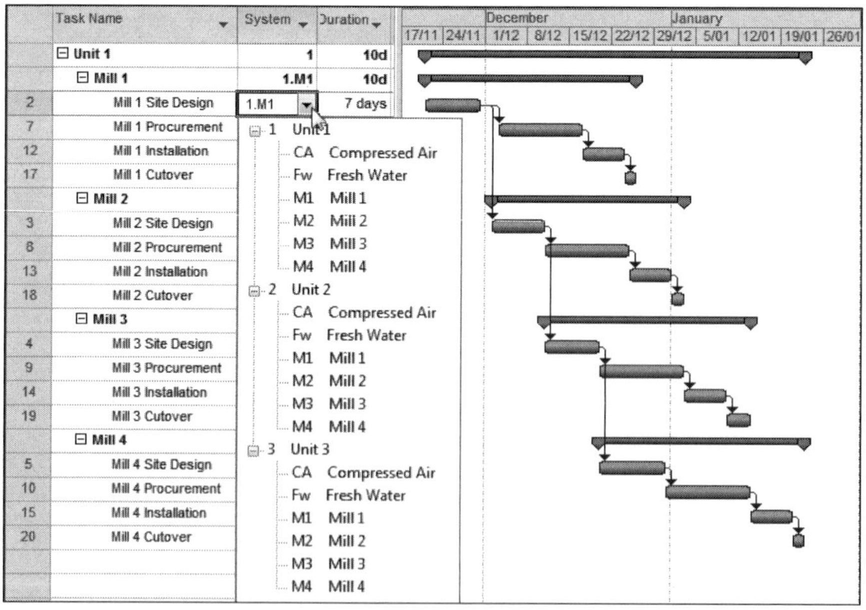

- Or by opening the **Task Information** or **Resource Information** form:

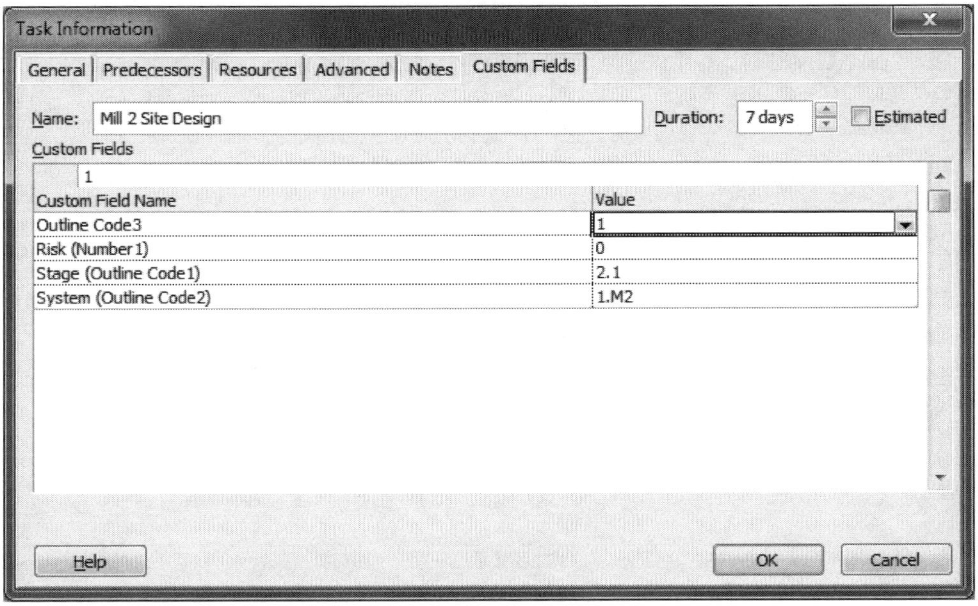

Organize Tasks Under a Custom Outline Code Structure

Select the **View**, **Data** group, **Group by:**, **More Groups...** option to create a grouping to display the tasks under the Custom Outline Code. The same process is used as outlined in the previous section to create a grouping:

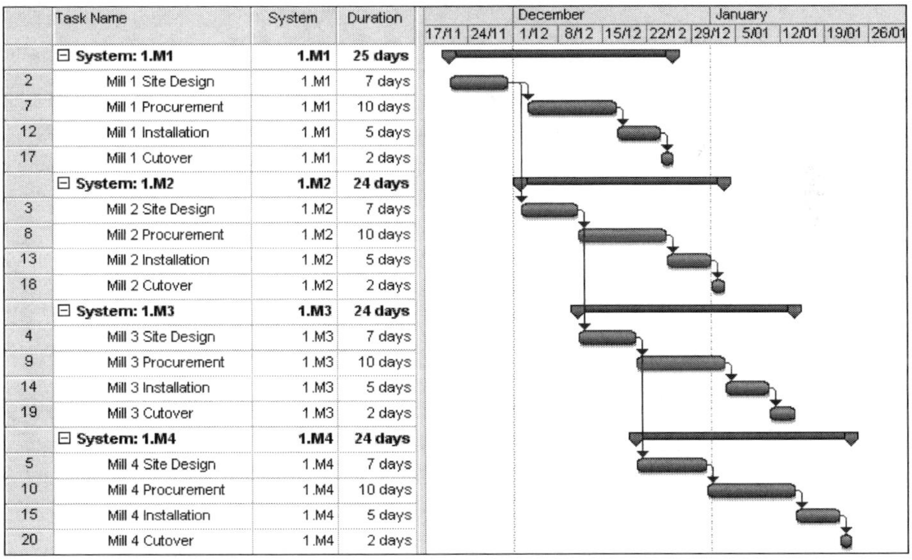

The Summary tasks are virtual tasks and may **NOT** have resources and costs assigned to them.

There are some restrictions with the use of Custom Outline Codes as the code **Value** is only shown in columns and the code **Description** only in the banding.

22.7.3 Outline Codes

The Microsoft Project **Outlining** function may be used to code the Project Breakdown Structure.

- Display the Outline Code against each task in the schedule by displaying the **Outline Code** column.
- An **Outline Level** displays how many levels down in the Outline Code structure the Task lays.
- The **Outline Number** may be displayed against the task Name by adding the Outline Number button to the Quick Access Toolbar.

	Outline Number	Outline Level	Task Name
1	**1**	**1**	**OzBuild Initiation**
2	1.1	2	Approval to Bid
3	**1.2**	**2**	**Technical Specification**
4	1.2.1	3	Determine Installation Requirements
5	1.2.2	3	Create Technical Specification
6	1.2.3	3	Identify Supplier Components
7	1.2.4	3	Validate Technical Specification
8	**1.3**	**2**	**Delivery Plan**
9	1.3.1	3	Document Delivery Methodology
10	1.3.2	3	Obtain Quotes from Suppliers
11	1.3.3	3	Calculate the Bid Estimate
12	1.3.4	3	Create the Project Schedule
13	1.3.5	3	Review the Delivery Plan
14	**1.4**	**2**	**Bid Document**
15	1.4.1	3	Create Draft of Bid Document
16	1.4.2	3	Review Bid Document
17	1.4.3	3	Finalise and Submit Bid Document
18	1.5	2	Bid Document Submitted

22.7.4 User Defined WBS Function

There are occasions when information must be presented under a predefined WBS Code structure. This structure could be a company standard, project-specific need, or defined by a client. The **WBS Code Definition** function is a method of tailoring the display of the **Outline Code** in a column titled **WBS**. This does not provide an additional set of codes to organize your project tasks; it only allows an alternate display of the Outline Code.

In a new project, the default WBS code is identical to the Outline Code. The example below displays both the WBS and Outline codes of the OzBuild schedule before doing any tailoring of the WBS code:

	WBS	Outline Number	Outline Level	Task Name
1	**1**	**1**	**1**	**1 OzBuild Bid**
2	**1.1**	**1.1**	**2**	**1.1 Research**
3	1.1.1	1.1.1	3	1.1.1 Bid Request Documents Received
4	1.1.2	1.1.2	3	1.1.2 Bid Strategy Meeting
5	1.1.3	1.1.3	3	1.1.3 Investigate Technical Feasibility
6	1.1.4	1.1.4	3	1.1.4 Document Installation Requirements
7	**1.2**	**1.2**	**2**	**1.2 Estimation**
8	1.2.1	1.2.1	3	1.2.1 Request Component Bids
9	1.2.2	1.2.2	3	1.2.2 Develop Project Schedule
10	1.2.3	1.2.3	3	1.2.3 Draft Technical Details Schedule
11	1.2.4	1.2.4	3	1.2.4 Compile Costs from Component Bids

The WBS Codes structure may be tailored to suit your own requirements. Below is an example of a WBS code that has been tailored using the WBS code function. The Outline sequential numbers may be replaced by user defined sequences of numbers or letters.

	WBS	Outline Number	Task Name
1	**OzBuild1**	**1**	⊟ **Ozbuild Bid**
2	**OzBuild1.AA**	**1.1**	⊟ **Research**
3	OzBuild1.AA-001	1.1.1	Bid Document Received
4	OzBuild1.AA-002	1.1.2	Bid Strategy Meeting
5	OzBuild1.AA-003	1.1.3	Investigate Technical Feasibility
6	OzBuild1.AA-004	1.1.4	Document Installation Requirements
7	**OzBuild1.AB**	**1.2**	⊟ **Estimation**
8	OzBuild1.AB-001	1.2.1	Request Component Bids
9	OzBuild1.AB-002	1.2.2	Develop Project Schedule
10	OzBuild1.AB-003	1.2.3	Draft Technical Details Schedule
11	OzBuild1.AB-004	1.2.4	Compile Costs from Bids
12	**OzBuild1.AC**	**1.3**	⊟ **Proposal**
13	OzBuild1.AC-001	1.3.1	Draft Bid Documents
14	OzBuild1.AC-002	1.3.2	Draft Bid Meeting
15	OzBuild1.AC-003	1.3.3	Design Presentation
16	OzBuild1.AC-004	1.3.4	Edit Proposal Draft
17	OzBuild1.AC-005	1.3.5	Finalise Bid Package
18	OzBuild1.AC-006	1.3.6	Final Bid Meeting
19	OzBuild1.AC-007	1.3.7	Submit Bid

To create your own user defined WBS codes, you will need to:

- Add the **WBS** button on your **Ribbon** or **Quick Access Toolbar**,
- Click on the **WBS** button,
- Click on the **Define Code** button to open the **WBS Code Definition** form:

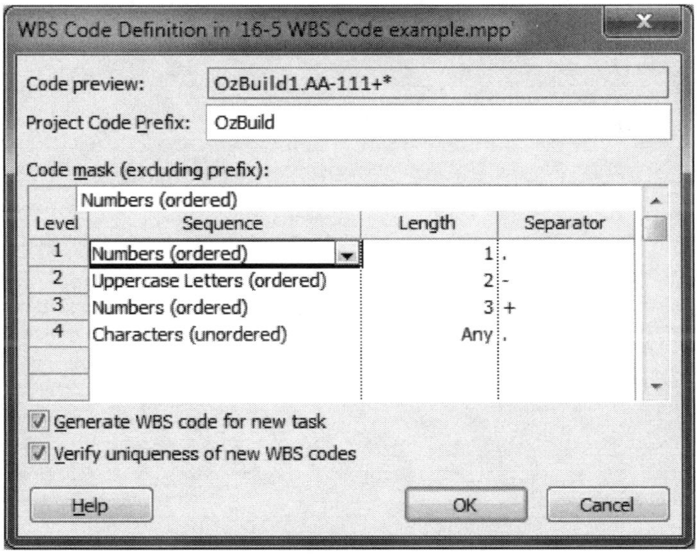

- The **Project Code Prefix:** is where you enter a text string that will precede all **WBS** codes. See the example above.

- Each code level is defined in the **Sequence** column. There are four code types. Each is displayed in the picture above:
  - Numbers (ordered)
  - Uppercase Letters (ordered)
  - Lowercase Letters (ordered)
  - Characters (unordered)

  The **Numbers**, **Uppercase Letters** and **Lowercase Letters** are numbered automatically.

  The **Characters** option will initially define all WBS codes at this level as an * and these may be overwritten with text. Microsoft Project will not renumber them.

- A **Length** of 1 to 10 or "Any" may be selected as the length of the code.
- Check **Generate WBS code for new task** and each new task will be automatically coded when created. When left unchecked, no WBS code is assigned to new tasks.
- Check **Verify uniqueness of new WBS codes** to prevent the creation of duplicate WBS codes.

You may renumber the WBS codes y selecting **All** or **Selected Tasks**, Select **Project**, **Properties** group, **WBS**, **Renumber...** from the menu.

22.8 Sharing Resources with Other Projects

Microsoft Project allows resources to be shared with multiple projects. This feature is not covered in detail in this book. Select **Resource**, **Assignments** group, **Resource Pool**, **Share Resources...** to open the **Share Resources** form, select the project to share resources from and set calculation options for leveling.

22.9 *Tracking Progress*

22.9.1 Setting an Interim Baseline

It may be necessary to save an interim baseline. This may occur when the scope of a project has changed and a new baseline is required to measure progress against, but at the same time you may also want to keep a copy of the original baseline. This process may also be used to display the effect of scope changes on an original project plan by comparing one baseline with another.

There are two types of data fields to save interim baselines:

- Using one of the 10 additional baselines titled **Baselines 1** to **10**. These Baselines will save start date, finish date, work and cost information.
- Using one of the 10 sets of **Start Date**, **Finish Date** and **Duration** fields. This function will only save the start and finish date information. This is termed an **Interim Plan** by Microsoft Project.
- **Set baseline** to save the current schedule to one of the 11 Baselines, or
- **Set interim plan** then:
  - ➢ Select the dates you want to copy from using the **Copy:** drop-down box, and then
  - ➢ Select where you want to copy the dates to using the **Into:** drop-down box.

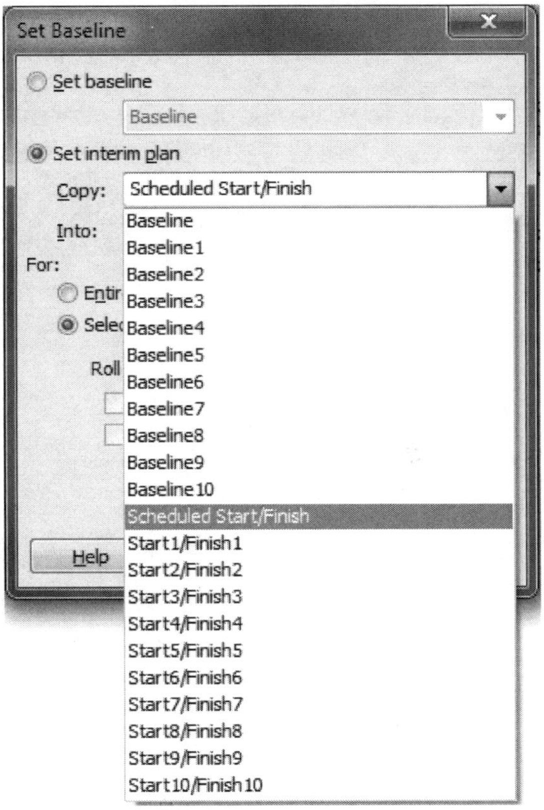

The **Baseline** data may be reviewed in some Views such as the **Task Details Form** and in columns. You will be able to display the **Baseline 1** to **10** and **Interim Plan** dates and durations in columns and as a bar on the Gantt Chart but not in the forms. Therefore, it is recommended that the current baseline be saved as **Baseline** since the data is more accessible that way. Previous baselines should be copied to **Baselines 1** to **10**.

Custom Date fields may be renamed with the **Customize Fields** form. Select **Project**, **Properties** group, **Customize Fields** to open the **Customize Fields** form. This may be useful to record the reason why a baseline has been saved.

22.9.2 Resetting the Baseline Using "Roll Up Baselines"

When a detail task is moved from one Summary task to another, the Baseline dates are moved with the detail task. The Summary task Baseline dates are not recalculated so they may not be valid. Likewise, the original Summary Baseline dates are not recalculated when new tasks are added to a schedule so they may not be valid.

When a task has costs or work assigned to it, then any movement of a detail task from one Summary task to another Summary task should result in a change to the baseline value of the Summary tasks, but these new values are not automatically recalculated by Microsoft Project. Costs and Work Baseline calculations are covered in the **UPDATING PROJECT WITH RESOURCES** chapter.

In the pictures below, the task Detailed 2.3 was moved from below Parent 2 to below Parent 1 so the baseline of tasks Parent 1 and Parent 2 (the lower bar on each task) are no longer an accurately reflect a summary of the detail task Baseline dates.

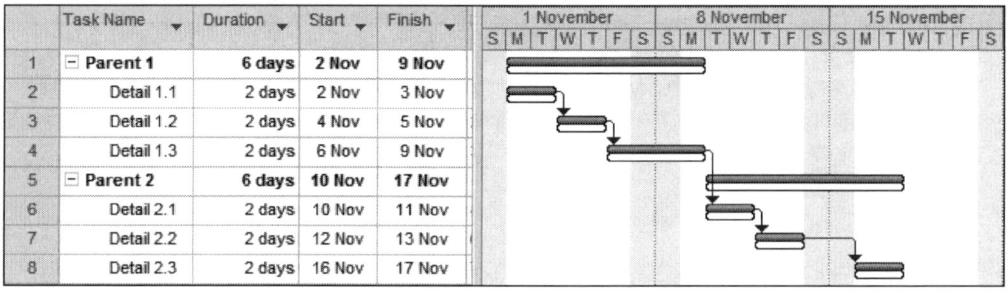

	Task Name	Duration	Start	Finish
1	**Parent 1**	**6 days**	**2 Nov**	**9 Nov**
2	Detail 1.1	2 days	2 Nov	3 Nov
3	Detail 1.2	2 days	4 Nov	5 Nov
4	Detail 1.3	2 days	6 Nov	9 Nov
5	**Parent 2**	**6 days**	**10 Nov**	**17 Nov**
6	Detail 2.1	2 days	10 Nov	11 Nov
7	Detail 2.2	2 days	12 Nov	13 Nov
8	Detail 2.3	2 days	16 Nov	17 Nov

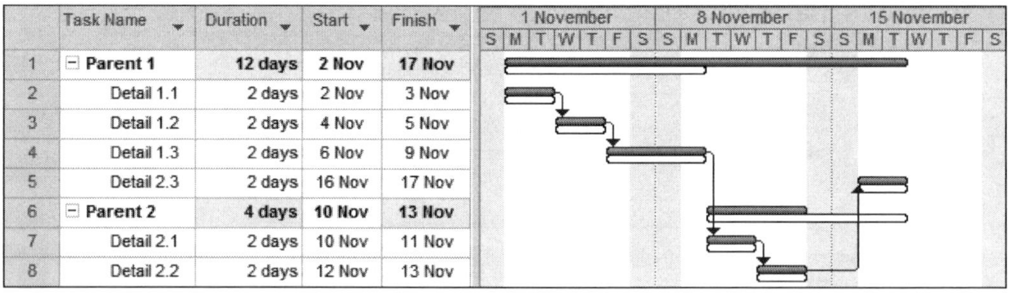

	Task Name	Duration	Start	Finish
1	**Parent 1**	**12 days**	**2 Nov**	**17 Nov**
2	Detail 1.1	2 days	2 Nov	3 Nov
3	Detail 1.2	2 days	4 Nov	5 Nov
4	Detail 1.3	2 days	6 Nov	9 Nov
5	Detail 2.3	2 days	16 Nov	17 Nov
6	**Parent 2**	**4 days**	**10 Nov**	**13 Nov**
7	Detail 2.1	2 days	10 Nov	11 Nov
8	Detail 2.2	2 days	12 Nov	13 Nov

In the example above, when the task was moved the option **Autolink inserted or moved tasks** found under the **File**, **Options**, **Schedule** tab is unchecked, otherwise the logic would have been changed. The formatting of these bars has been achieved using the Gantt Chart Wizard which results in clearer screen shots.

The **Roll up baselines** option in the **Set Baseline** form will recalculate the summary task Baseline data when a detail task is moved to a different Summary task or a new task is added to the schedule. There are three options when **Selected tasks: - Roll up Baselines:** is selected:

- Check only **To all summary tasks**,
- Check only **From subtasks to selected summary task(s)**, or
- Check both of the above options.

The options function differently when a Summary task or when a detail task is selected. These options are difficult to understand and the author prefers to reset Baselines of Summary tasks manually.

In the example below two new tasks have been added, thus the old Baseline is no longer the same as the current schedule. In addition the start date has been delayed:

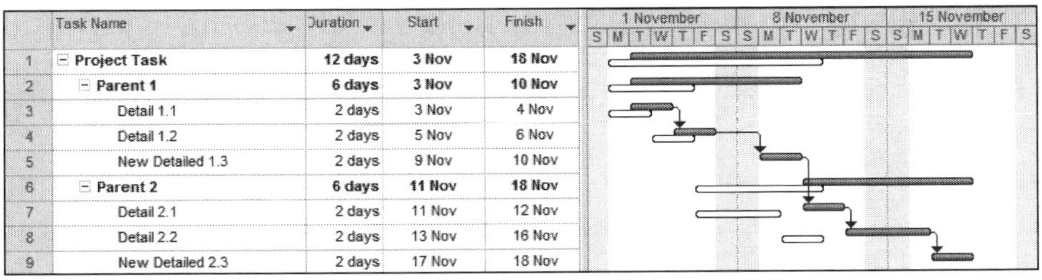

	Task Name	Duration	Start	Finish
1	Project Task	**12 days**	**3 Nov**	**18 Nov**
2	Parent 1	**6 days**	**3 Nov**	**10 Nov**
3	Detail 1.1	2 days	3 Nov	4 Nov
4	Detail 1.2	2 days	5 Nov	6 Nov
5	New Detailed 1.3	2 days	9 Nov	10 Nov
6	Parent 2	**6 days**	**11 Nov**	**18 Nov**
7	Detail 2.1	2 days	11 Nov	12 Nov
8	Detail 2.2	2 days	13 Nov	16 Nov
9	New Detailed 2.3	2 days	17 Nov	18 Nov

To all summary tasks

- When the **To all summary tasks** option is checked and only a **Detailed task** is selected, such as the New Detailed 2.3 task below, then in this option:
  - ➢ The selected detail task has its Baseline set based on the current schedule, see New Detailed 2.3 task, and
  - ➢ Related Summary tasks have their baselines set based on the new detail task Baseline, see Parent Task and Parent 2.

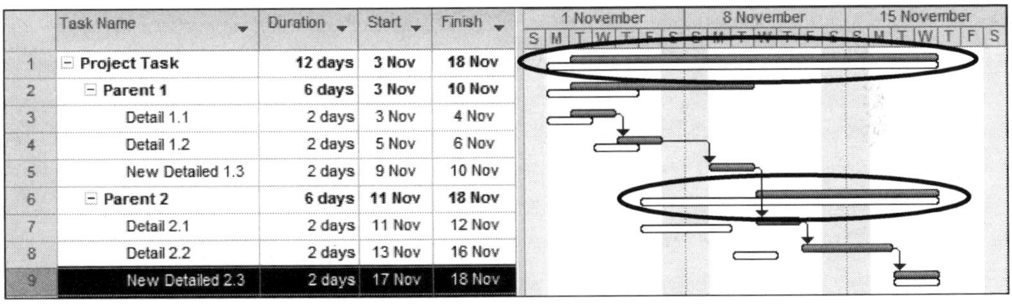

	Task Name	Duration	Start	Finish
1	Project Task	**12 days**	**3 Nov**	**18 Nov**
2	Parent 1	**6 days**	**3 Nov**	**10 Nov**
3	Detail 1.1	2 days	3 Nov	4 Nov
4	Detail 1.2	2 days	5 Nov	6 Nov
5	New Detailed 1.3	2 days	9 Nov	10 Nov
6	Parent 2	**6 days**	**11 Nov**	**18 Nov**
7	Detail 2.1	2 days	11 Nov	12 Nov
8	Detail 2.2	2 days	13 Nov	16 Nov
9	New Detailed 2.3	2 days	17 Nov	18 Nov

- When the **To all summary tasks** option is checked and a **Detailed task** and a **Summary task** is selected, such as the Parent 2 and New Detailed 2.3 task below, then:
  - ➢ The selected detail task and summary task have their Baseline set based on the Current dates, not the Baseline dates, see New Detailed 2.3 task and Parent 2,
  - ➢ Related summary tasks have their baselines set based on the new Baseline dates, see Project Task:

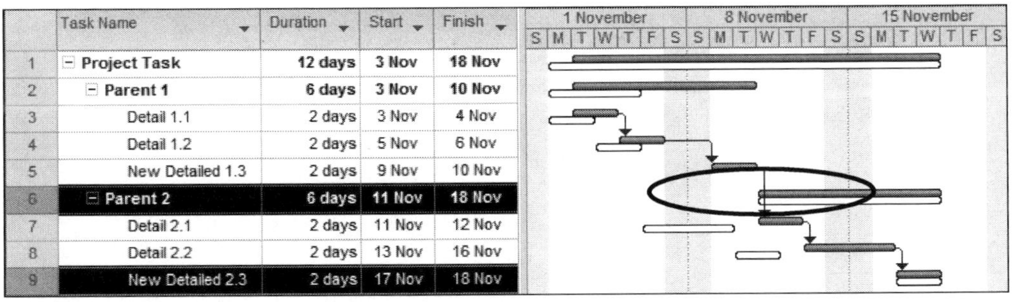

	Task Name	Duration	Start	Finish
1	Project Task	**12 days**	**3 Nov**	**18 Nov**
2	Parent 1	**6 days**	**3 Nov**	**10 Nov**
3	Detail 1.1	2 days	3 Nov	4 Nov
4	Detail 1.2	2 days	5 Nov	6 Nov
5	New Detailed 1.3	2 days	9 Nov	10 Nov
6	Parent 2	**6 days**	**11 Nov**	**18 Nov**
7	Detail 2.1	2 days	11 Nov	12 Nov
8	Detail 2.2	2 days	13 Nov	16 Nov
9	New Detailed 2.3	2 days	17 Nov	18 Nov

Resetting Baseline dates of the summary task may not be intended and in the example above the Parent 2 Baseline dates are no longer summarized on the detail tasks Baseline dates. So when using the **To all summary tasks** option it is recommended that no summary tasks should be selected.

From subtasks to selected summary task(s)

- When the **From subtasks to selected summary task(s)** option is checked and both Summary and detail tasks are selected, such as Parent 2 and New Detailed 2.3 tasks below:
  - The selected detail tasks have their Baseline reset based on the current schedule,
  - Selected summary tasks have their Baseline dates set based on the Baseline dates of their detail tasks,
  - The unselected summary tasks do not have their baselines reset, see task Parent 1 and Parent Task below.

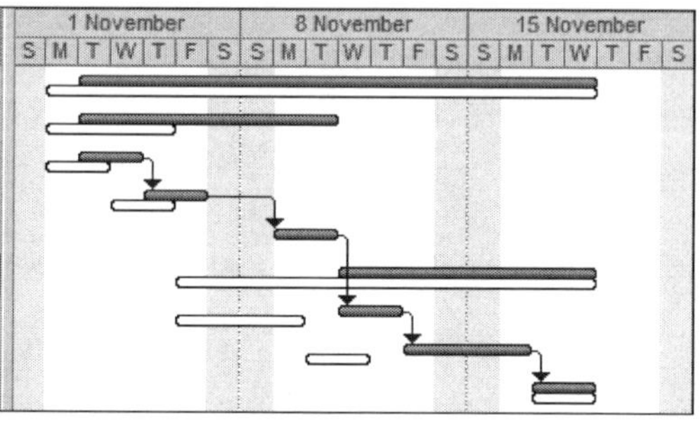

	Task Name	Duration	Start	Finish
1	Project Task	12 days	3 Nov	18 Nov
2	Parent 1	6 days	3 Nov	10 Nov
3	Detail 1.1	2 days	3 Nov	4 Nov
4	Detail 1.2	2 days	5 Nov	6 Nov
5	New Detailed 1.3	2 days	9 Nov	10 Nov
6	Parent 2	6 days	11 Nov	18 Nov
7	Detail 2.1	2 days	11 Nov	12 Nov
8	Detail 2.2	2 days	13 Nov	16 Nov
9	New Detailed 2.3	2 days	17 Nov	18 Nov

From subtasks to selected summary task(s) and **To all summary tasks** option selected

- When the **From subtasks to selected summary task(s)** option and the **To all summary tasks** option is checked then:
  - Any selected detail task has the Baseline set or reset, and
  - All associated summary tasks have their Baselines reset based on the associated Baseline dates.

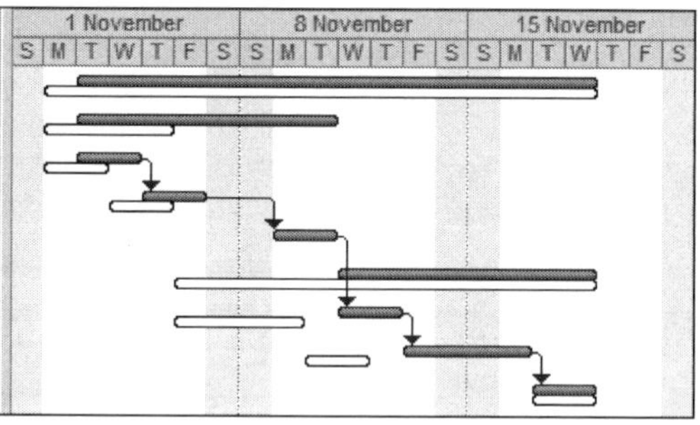

	Task Name	Duration	Start	Finish
1	Project Task	12 days	3 Nov	18 Nov
2	Parent 1	6 days	3 Nov	10 Nov
3	Detail 1.1	2 days	3 Nov	4 Nov
4	Detail 1.2	2 days	5 Nov	6 Nov
5	New Detailed 1.3	2 days	9 Nov	10 Nov
6	Parent 2	6 days	11 Nov	18 Nov
7	Detail 2.1	2 days	11 Nov	12 Nov
8	Detail 2.2	2 days	13 Nov	16 Nov
9	New Detailed 2.3	2 days	17 Nov	18 Nov

i

It is recommended to set a revised baseline when a new detail task has been added. The new task and the associated Parent tasks should be highlighted and the option **From subtasks to selected summary task(s)** applied.

22.9.3 Status Date Calculation Options - New Tasks

New functions were introduced in Microsoft Project 2002 intended to assist schedulers to place the new tasks as they are added to the schedule in a logical position with respect to the **Status Date**. If the **Status Date** has not been set then the **Current Date** is used. In the example below the vertical black line is the **Status Date**:

- Task 1 has completed work in the future, which is not logical,
- Task 2 would normally be considered in the logical position with respect to the **Status Date**, and
- Task 3 has incomplete work in the past, which is also not logical.

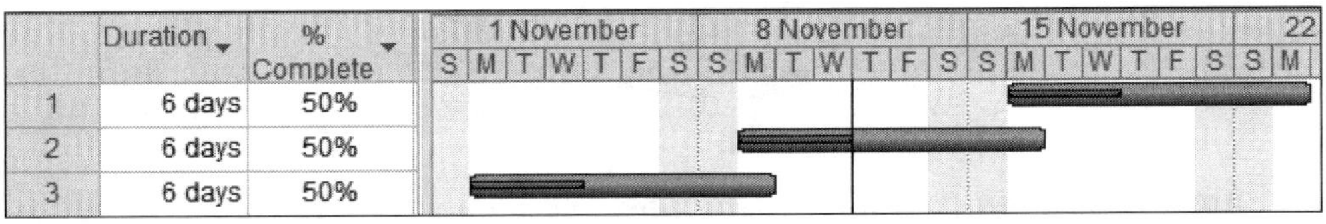

These options are found under **File**, **Options**, **Advanced** tab, **Calculation options for this project:** section:

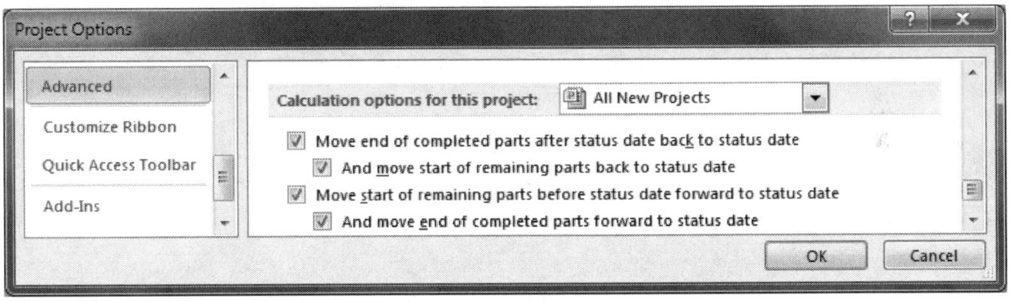

For all these options to operate all four of the following parameters must be met:

- The **Split in-progress tasks** option in the **Schedule** tab must be checked, and
- The required option on the **Calculation** tab must be checked before the task is added or edited, and
- The **Updating task status updates resource status** option on the **Calculation** tab must be checked.
- The Task **MUST NOT BE** assigned **Task Duration Type** of **Fixed Duration**, which is often recommended.

The documentation found in the earlier Microsoft Project Help files is not precise and does not make it clear to the user that these options may NOT be turned on and off to recalculate all tasks. The options only works on new tasks when they are added to a schedule or when a task is updated by changing the % Complete.

The following four options are available:

- Check only **Move end of completed parts after status date back to status date**. This is the effect on Task 1 in the picture on the previous page when the % Complete is increased to 60%:

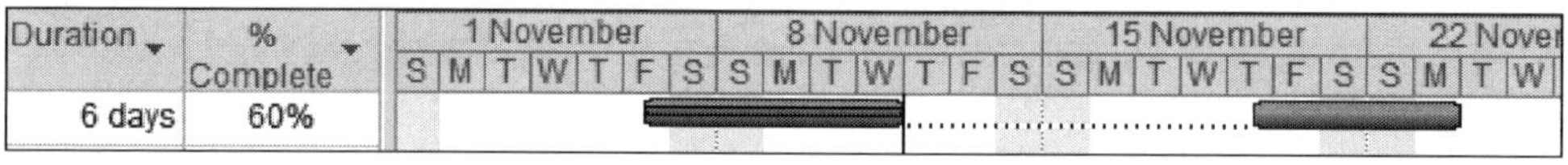

- The **And move start of remaining parts back to status date** option is only available after the option above is checked, if checked the result would be as per the picture below:

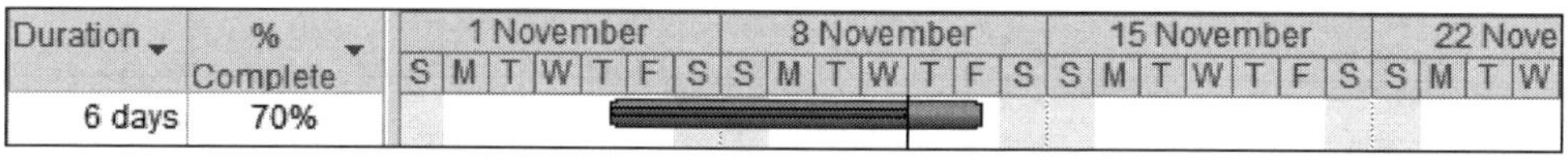

- The **Move start of remaining parts before status date forward to status date** may be checked at any time. The picture below shows the effect on Task 3 from the picture on the previous page when the % Complete is changed to 60%:

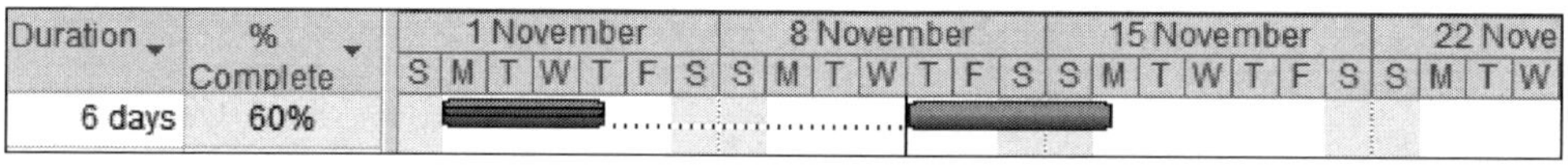

- The **And move end of completed parts forward to status date** may be checked after the option above is checked and before a % Complete is entered, if checked the result would be as per the picture below:

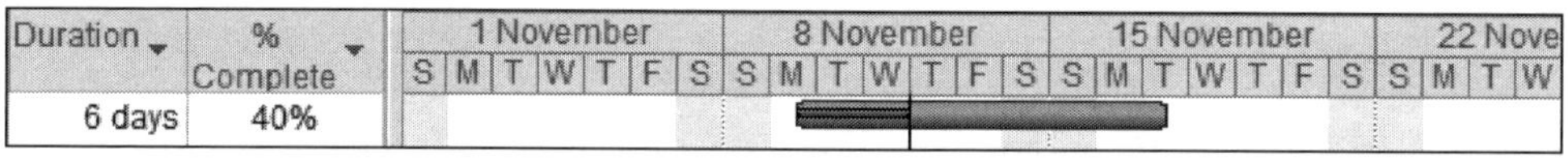

This function will ignore constraints even when the Schedule Option **Tasks will always honor their constraint dates** has been set.

Experimentation by the author indicates that the tasks will adopt the rules that are set in the options form when the task is added or when a task % Complete is changed. Therefore this function may not be applied to existing schedules, but only to new tasks if the options are set before the tasks are added or when a task % Complete is updated.

This function in its current form has some restrictions that schedulers may find unacceptable:

- Existing schedules may not be opened and the function applied.
- When the **Move start of remaining parts before status date forward to status date** is used, it overrides any **Actual Start** date that you have entered prior to entering a % Complete.

This option should be used with caution and users should ensure they fully understand how this function operates by updating a simple schedule multiple times.

22.9.4 Status Date Calculation Options - When Updating a Schedule

The Status Date Calculation Options also operates when a schedule is updated by changing the % Complete of Tasks. The example below shows a task with the Status Date, the dark vertical line, set to the next period:

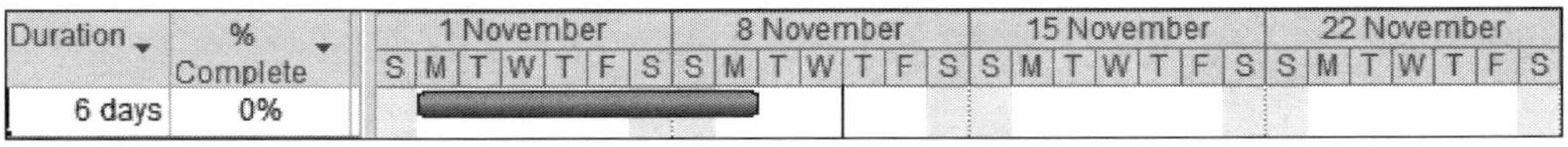

When all the **Status Date Calculation Option** options are checked and the percent complete is changed from 0% to 40% the task is aligned to the new Status Date:

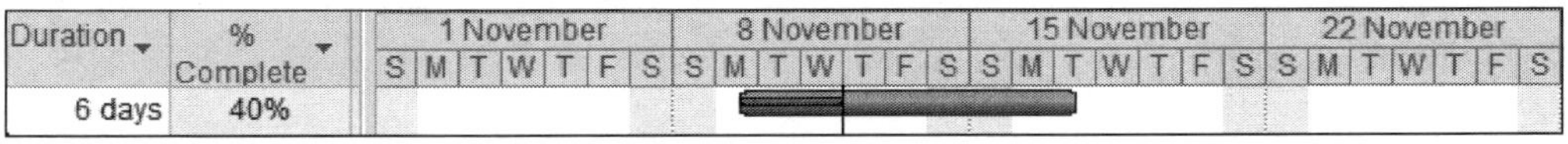

Now the Status Date has been moved to the next week. The tasks have not moved in respect to the Status Date and will not move when the project is recalculated:

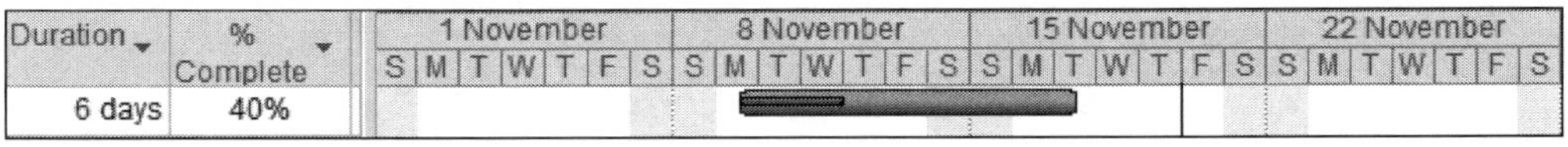

After percent complete is changed to 60%, the task splits and the un-worked portion of the task is set to be completed after the new Status Date:

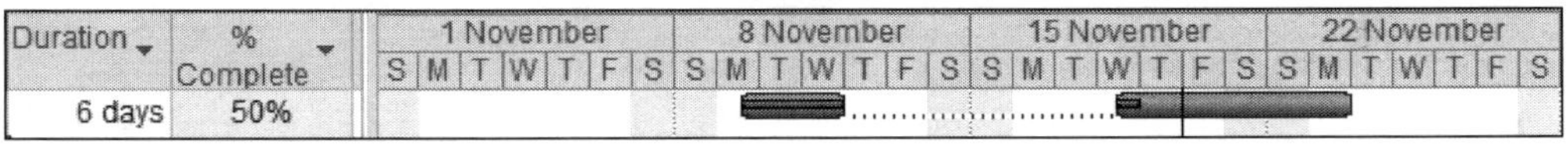

22.9.5 Stop and Resume Dates

The **Stop** date represents the point in time where the completed work finishes. The **Resume** date represents the point in time that the incomplete work is scheduled to restart. These dates may be displayed columns and edited from these columns. Task B Resume date has been manually edited:

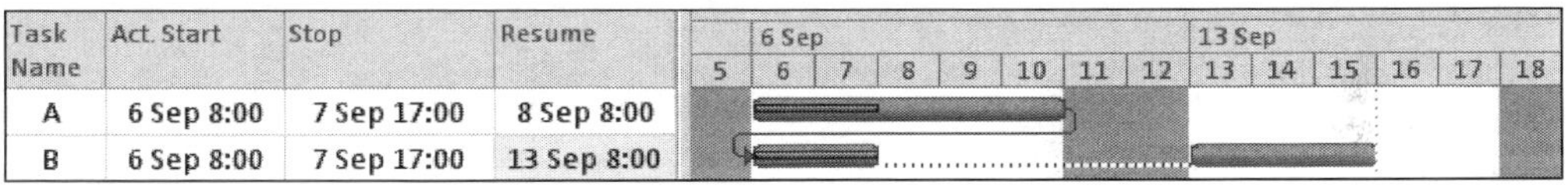

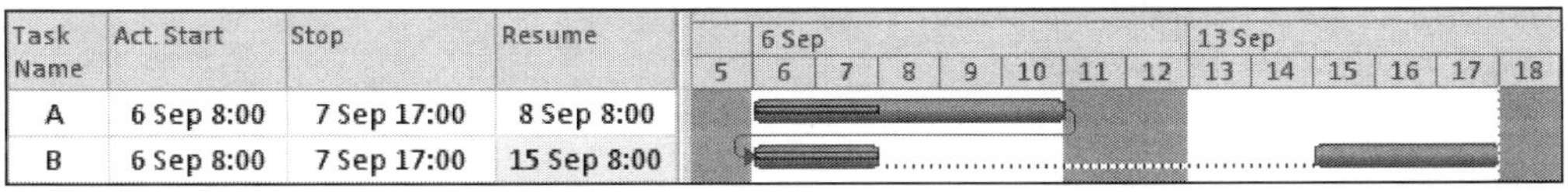

22.9.6 Marking Up Summary Tasks

It is not normal to mark up summary tasks and is not recommended. Actual Dates may not be entered against summary tasks. But a % Complete may be entered against a summary task and all the subordinate tasks will be auto-updated to match the summary % Complete.

When a **% Complete** is entered against a summary task, all subordinate tasks, both Summary and Detail, inherit a value depending upon the setting of the **Updating task status updates resource status** option found in **File**, **Options**, **Schedule** tab, **Calculation options for this project:** section.

To explain this concept further, see the following two examples. Both schedules pictured below had 15% entered against Task 1, the OzBuild Initiation task. All other Actual dates and % Completes were calculated by Microsoft Project.

- With the **Updating task status updates resource status CHECKED** the tasks are updated as if they were completed according to plan:

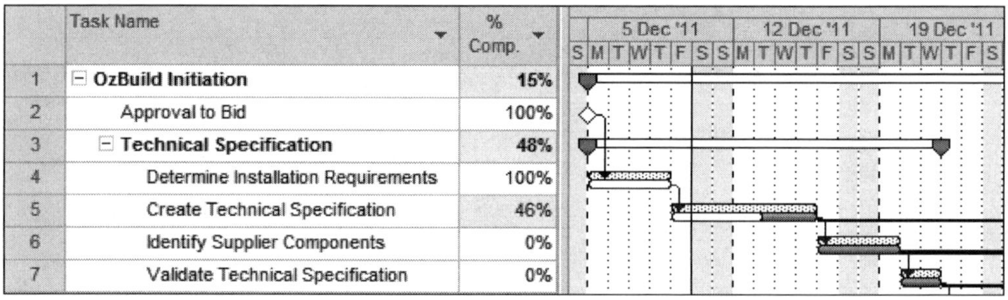

	Task Name	% Comp.
1	**OzBuild Initiation**	**15%**
2	Approval to Bid	100%
3	**Technical Specification**	**48%**
4	Determine Installation Requirements	100%
5	Create Technical Specification	46%
6	Identify Supplier Components	0%
7	Validate Technical Specification	0%

- With the **Updating task status updates resource status UNCHECKED** all tasks are assigned to 15% complete, which is not the logical progression of the project:

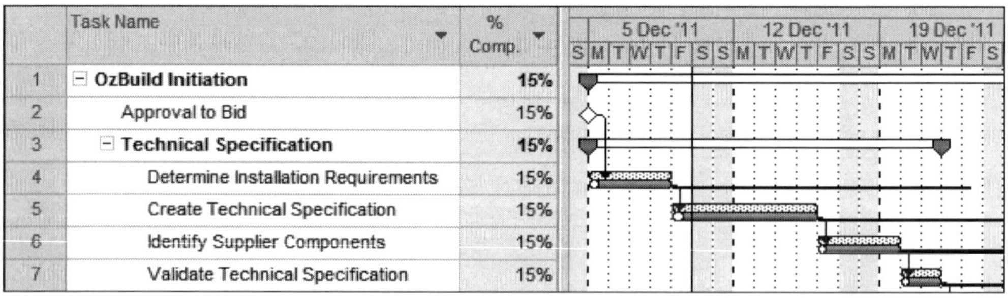

	Task Name	% Comp.
1	**OzBuild Initiation**	**15%**
2	Approval to Bid	15%
3	**Technical Specification**	**15%**
4	Determine Installation Requirements	15%
5	Create Technical Specification	15%
6	Identify Supplier Components	15%
7	Validate Technical Specification	15%

22.9.7 Moving Tasks Using Task, Tasks group Move

The **Task**, **Task** group **Move** functions are new to Microsoft Project 2010. They are able to move a task backward or forward in time:

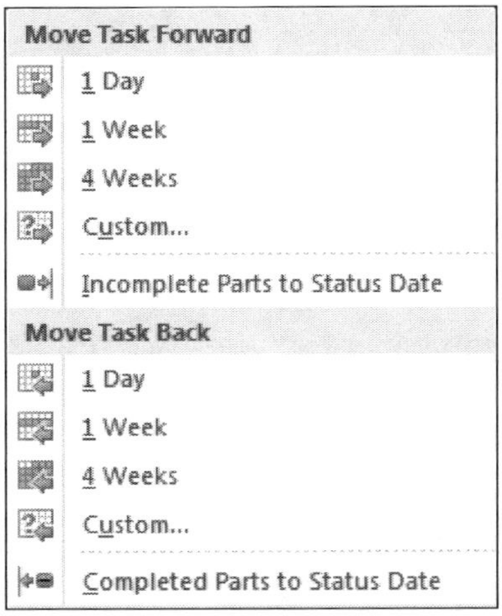

To demonstrate some of the functions of these commands a task has added to a schedule and is positioned on the Project Start Date:

- Moved unprogressed tasks will have a constraint set without warning and this is similar to dragging a task which will also set a constraint:

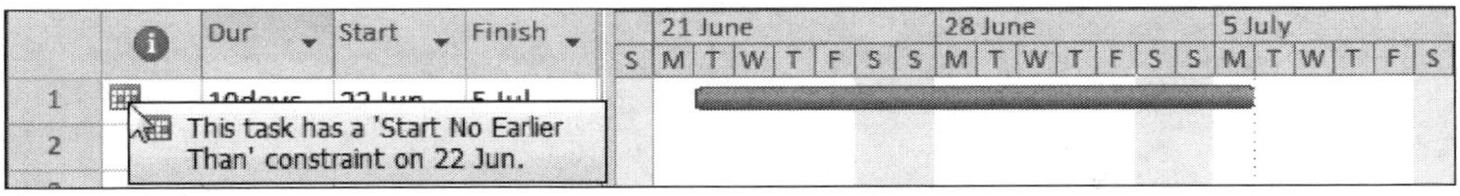

- If it is required to move the incomplete portion of a task then **File**, **Options**, **Schedule** tab, **Scheduling options for this project:** section, **Split in-progress tasks** must be checked otherwise the task will not split. The Task below was moved forward one day after a % Complete had been assigned and once split, it develops an interesting error massage:

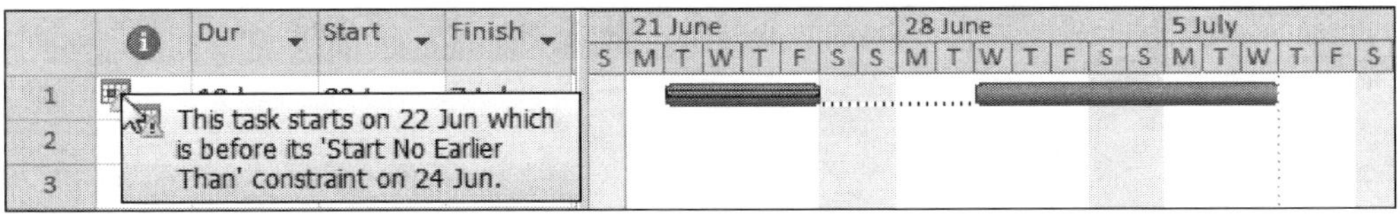

22.9.8 Progress Lines and Variance Columns

Start Variance and **Finish Variance** columns are variances from the Baseline and may be displayed in columns as per the picture below.

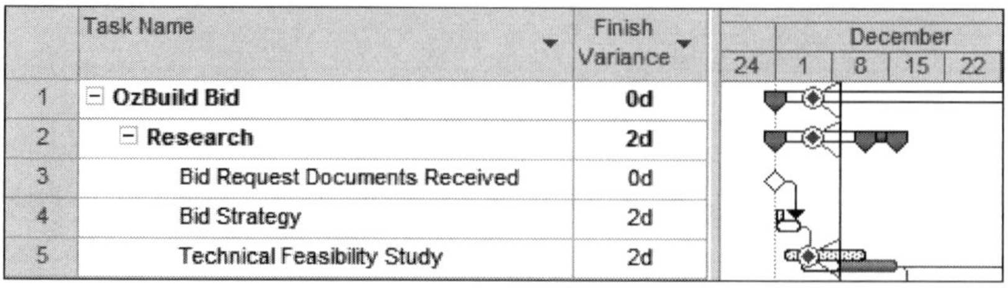

Some users like to display **Progress Lines** which are usually displayed as zigzag lines on the Gantt Chart showing how far ahead or behind the project tasks are:

- The **Progress Lines** button should be added to the **Quick Access Toolbar** or **Ribbon**
- Click on the **Progress Lines** to open the **Progress Line** form where the progress lines may be formatted:

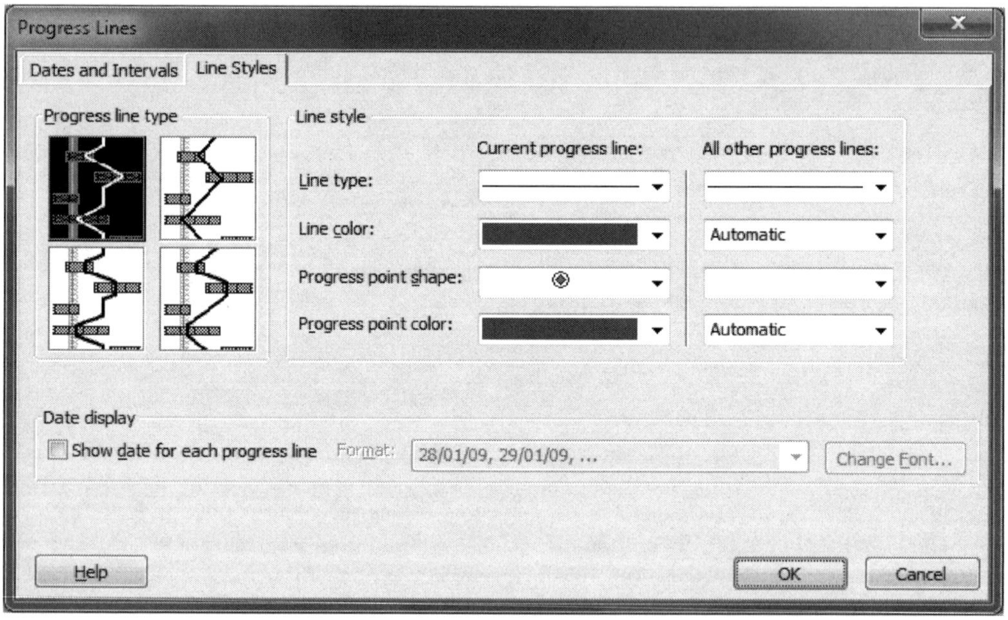

Progress Lines become less relevant when a schedule is updated using Actual dates and remaining durations.

23 TOOLS AND TECHNIQUES FOR SCHEDULING

23.1 Understanding Menu Options

You will find that the menu options change as you select rows, cells, all rows and cells, or views. Therefore, not all menu options are always available and some buttons are grayed out and inoperable. The following topics will be covered in this chapter:

- Menu items sometimes found by right-clicking:
  - **Cut**, **Copy** and **Paste Task**
  - **Cut**, **Copy** and **Paste Cell**
  - **Copy Picture**
  - **Fill**
  - **Clear**
  - **Find** and **Replace**
  - **Go To**
- **Insert**, **Recurring tasks...**
- **Splitting** a Task
- **Copy**, **Cut** and **Paste** from Spreadsheets
- **Unique Task**, **Resource** and **Assignment ID**
- **Organizer** is used to transfer data such as Tables and View from one project to another.
- **File types**

23.2 Cut, Copy and Paste Row

This function allows you to select one or more consecutive or non-consecutive tasks (using Ctrl-click) and either copy them, or cut them and paste as a group to a new location that you select with your mouse. Any inter-task relationships are also copied but external relationships to unselected tasks are not copied. Ensure you select the whole task by highlighting the Task ID.

23.3 Cut, Copy and Paste Cell

You may cut or copy information and then paste into one or more cells from:

- One cell, or
- Adjacent cells by dragging in rows and/or columns, or
- A non-contiguous group of cells by Ctrl-clicking.

This function operates in a similar way to Excel's copy/cut-and-paste operation:

- Highlight the cell(s) you want to copy or cut.
- Select **Copy Cell** or **Ctrl+C** to copy a cell or **Cut Cell** or **Ctrl+X** to cut a cell.
- Position the mouse where you want to paste the data and select **Paste** or **Ctrl+V**.

This is an interesting function since it allows you to copy from one column to another when the format is compatible. This function may also be used for transferring and/or updating your schedule from other software such as Excel which is covered later in this chapter.

23.4 Copy Picture

This allows a section or total screen to be copied to the clipboard and then either pasted into a document or saved as a **gif** file. Select **Task**, **Clipboard** group, select the **Copy** button and select **Copy Picture** to open the **Copy Picture** form:

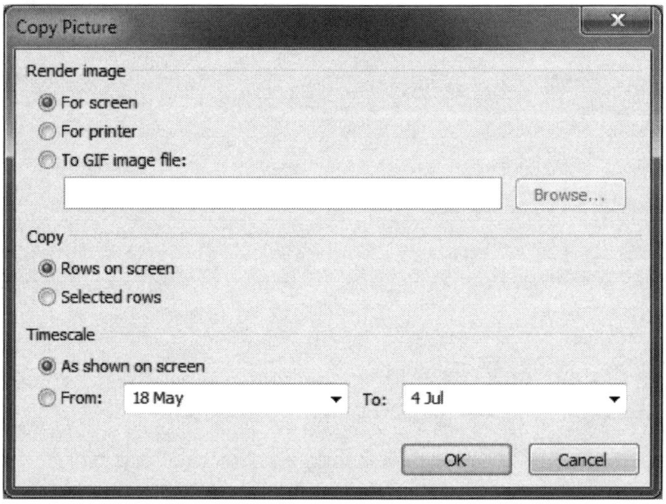

The options are self-explanatory and when pasted into a document the picture looks like the example below:

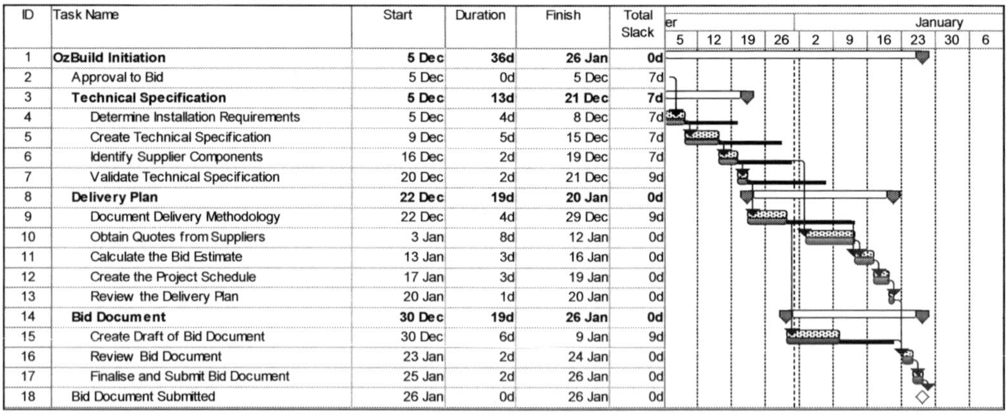

ID	Task Name	Start	Duration	Finish	Total Slack
1	**OzBuild Initiation**	**5 Dec**	**36d**	**26 Jan**	**0d**
2	Approval to Bid	5 Dec	0d	5 Dec	7d
3	**Technical Specification**	**5 Dec**	**13d**	**21 Dec**	**7d**
4	Determine Installation Requirements	5 Dec	4d	8 Dec	7d
5	Create Technical Specification	9 Dec	5d	15 Dec	7d
6	Identify Supplier Components	16 Dec	2d	19 Dec	7d
7	Validate Technical Specification	20 Dec	2d	21 Dec	9d
8	**Delivery Plan**	**22 Dec**	**19d**	**20 Jan**	**0d**
9	Document Delivery Methodology	22 Dec	4d	29 Dec	9d
10	Obtain Quotes from Suppliers	3 Jan	8d	12 Jan	0d
11	Calculate the Bid Estimate	13 Jan	3d	16 Jan	0d
12	Create the Project Schedule	17 Jan	3d	19 Jan	0d
13	Review the Delivery Plan	20 Jan	1d	20 Jan	0d
14	**Bid Document**	**30 Dec**	**19d**	**26 Jan**	**0d**
15	Create Draft of Bid Document	30 Dec	6d	9 Jan	9d
16	Review Bid Document	23 Jan	2d	24 Jan	0d
17	Finalise and Submit Bid Document	25 Jan	2d	26 Jan	0d
18	Bid Document Submitted	26 Jan	0d	26 Jan	0d

23.5 Fill Down

The **Fill Down** command allows you to select one cell or a range of cells and then copy them up, down, left, or right without the need to copy and paste.

23.6 Clear Contents

The **Clear Contents** command allows you to clear the contents from a task.

23.7 Find and Replace

The **Ctrl+F**, **Find** and **Ctrl+H**, **Find** and **Replace** functions allow you to find any task by matching data with your defined criteria. This will also allow you to find the data and then replace it with another piece of information.

23.8 Go To

The **Go To...** function allows you to quickly find a date and move the timescale horizontally to that date or to a task if you know the Task ID number. The command would need to be added to the **Quick Access Toolbar** or **Ribbon** to be used:

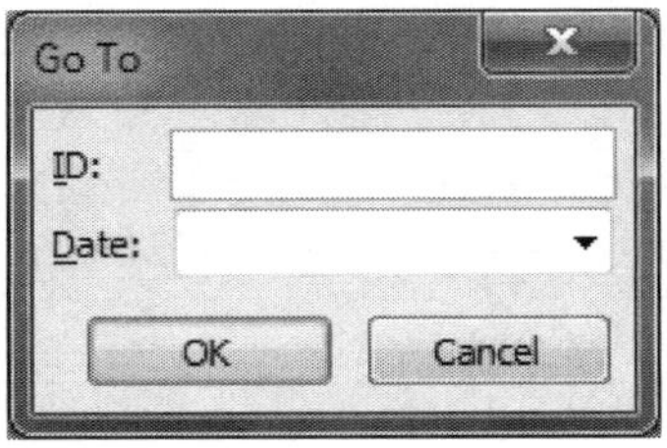

23.9 Insert Recurring Task

The **Task**, **Insert** group, **Recurring tasks...** function allows the insertion of more than one task that occurs on a regular basis. The options are self-explanatory and are very handy for scheduling meetings and other regular tasks. These tasks use the Rollup bars in the **Bars Styles** form.

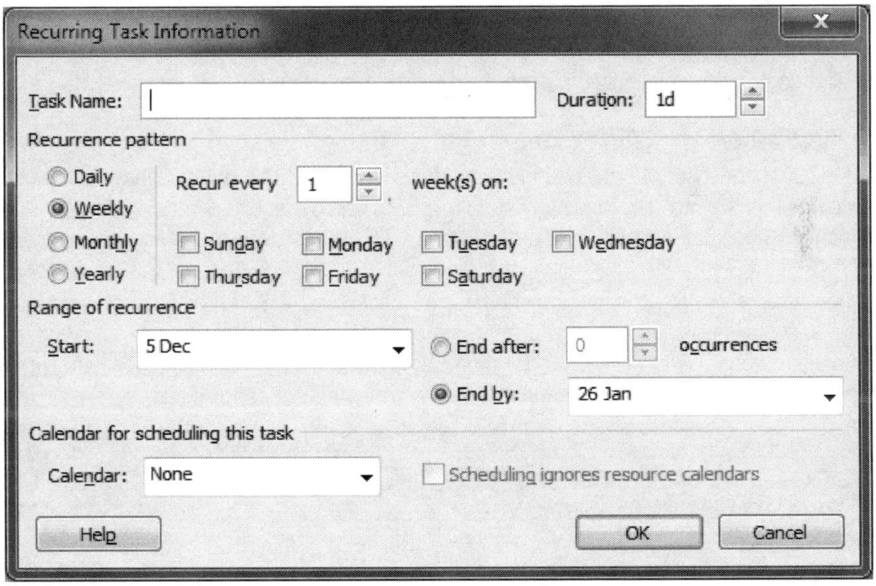

23.10 *Copy or Cut-and-Paste to and from Spreadsheets*

Microsoft Project will allow **Copy** or **Cut**-and-**Paste** to and from spreadsheets and other software packages. Microsoft Project 2010 will now copy the formatting and headers. This may be useful for a number of purposes:

- Importing Tasks from other applications,
- Assigning Codes and Resources to Tasks,
- Updating a schedule, and
- Exporting Data to other packages.

The **Copy** or **Cut** function copies the task data from highlighted columns and rows in the schedule to the Windows clipboard. These may then be pasted into another software package:

- Highlight the data in your schedule that you want to transfer to another software package and cut or copy the data.
- Move to the spreadsheet application and paste the task information. In earlier versions of Microsoft Project the column headers are not pasted into the application; only data from the schedule is pasted. Microsoft Project 2010 now keeps the formatting and headers.
- The data may be edited or updated in the application, as required.
- The tasks may be selected and pasted back into the schedule to update it with the normal copy and paste functions.

23.11 *Paste Link – Cell Values in Columns*

A cell may be copied, and then "Paste Linked" to another cell or an external application. Thus when the copied cell is updated, the linked cell is also updated with the same value. For example this could be used to update a number of tasks that have the same % Complete. A linked cell has a small triangle in the corner, and the linking may be removed by overtyping the cell value.

23.12 *Unique Task, Resource and Assignment ID*

The Task IDs change for all tasks below an inserted task. There are many contractual and management reasons to be able to identify each task by a unique task number.

23.12.1 Task Unique ID

When a new task is added to a blank schedule, it is assigned a **Unique ID** commencing with the number 1. When tasks are deleted these numbers are not re-used and any new task is assigned a new sequential number. This **Unique ID** number may be displayed in a column titled **Unique ID**. It is also possible to display the **Unique Predecessor** and **Unique Successor** columns:

	Unique ID	Task Name	Unique ID Predecessors	Unique ID Successors
1	**15**	**OzBuild Initiation**		
2	1	Approval to Bid		2
3	**16**	**Technical Specification**		
4	2	Determine Installation Requirements	1	3
5	3	Create Technical Specification	2	4
6	4	Identify Supplier Components	3	5,7
7	5	Validate Technical Specification	4	6

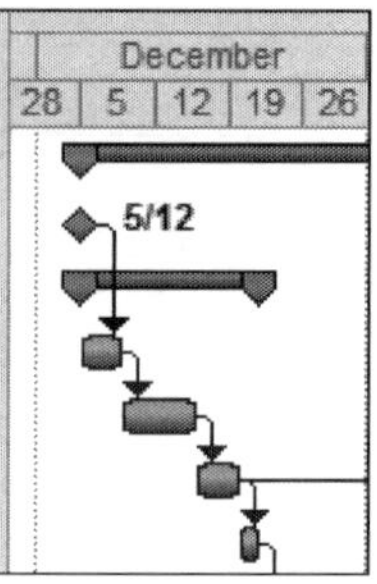

The cutting and pasting of tasks creates new Unique IDs for each task but dragging task to a new position does not. To renumber the Unique IDs just copy all the tasks and paste below the existing tasks and delete the original tasks.

23.12.2 Resource Unique ID

A resource **Unique ID** is created for each resource. Again, when a resource is deleted, the resource **Unique ID** is not re-used. This number may be displayed in the **Resource Sheet** or **Resources Usage** view column titled **Unique ID**.

23.12.3 Resource Assignment Unique ID

When a resource is assigned to a task, the assignment is given a unique **Assignment ID**. This number may be displayed in the **Resource Sheet** or **Resource Usage** view column titled **Unique ID**:

	i	Task Mode	Task Name	Work	Unique ID
3			⊟ **Technical Specification**	**192hrs**	**16**
4	✓		⊟ Determine Installation Requirements	48hrs	2
			Project Manager	*24hrs*	*1048591*
			Systems Engineer	*24hrs*	*1048592*
5			⊟ Create Technical Specification	96hrs	3
			Systems Engineer	*96hrs*	*1048593*
			Specialists Consultant		*1048594*

23.13 *Organizer*

The **Global.mpt** file holds the schedule's default settings such as **Tables** and **Views**, which are inherited by new projects not created from a template. The **Organizer** function is also used to copy information between projects or to update the **Global.mpt**.

The **Organizer** form may be opened from many menus:

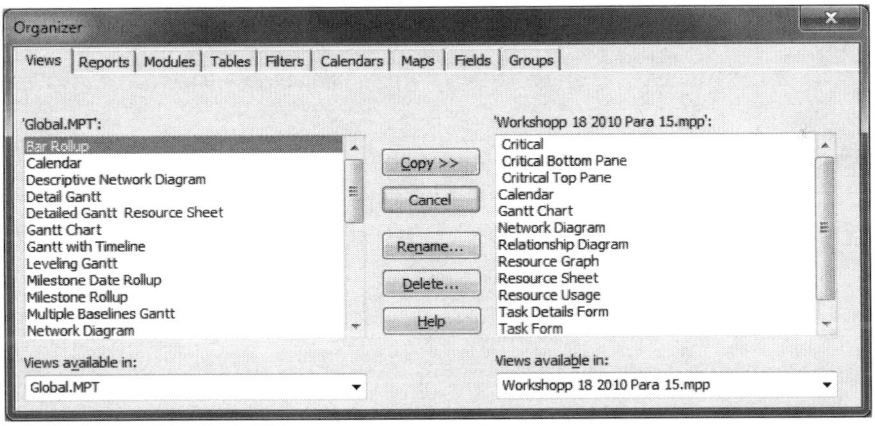

Except for the **Global.mpt**, the projects you want to copy settings to and from will have to be opened in order to copy data.

- The Organizer function is used for copying, renaming and deleting most items such as **Tables**, **Views and Calendars**.
- The two tab titles above that are not self-explanatory are:
  - **Maps** – These are predefined tables for mapping data to be exported or imported, and
  - **Modules** – These are Visual Basic Macros.

23.14 File Types

Microsoft Project is compatible and will operate with the following file types:

- **Microsoft Project (*.mpp)**. This is the default file format for Microsoft Project 2010. All earlier versions will not open or save to a **Project (*.mpp)** file created by Microsoft Project 2010.
- **Microsoft Project 2007 (*.mpp)**. This is the default file format for Microsoft Project 2007. This is a different format than the ***.mpp** file created by Microsoft Project 2000 - 2003 and 98.
- **Microsoft Project 2000 – 2003 (*.mpp**). This is the default file format for Microsoft Project 2000, 2002 and 2003. This is a different format than the ***.mpp** file created by Microsoft Project 2010, 2007 and Microsoft Project 98.
- **Microsoft Project 98 (*.mpp)**. This is the format created by Microsoft Project 98.
  - Microsoft Project 98 will not open or save a **Project (*.mpp)** file created by Microsoft Project 2000 and later versions.
  - Microsoft Project 2000, 2002 and 2003 will open and save to a **Microsoft Project 98 (*.mpp)** file.
  - Microsoft Project 2007 or 2010 will not save to a **Microsoft Project 98 (*.mpp)** file.
- **MPX (*.mpx).** This is a text format data file created by Microsoft Project 98.
  - This format may be opened by all Microsoft Project Versions but cannot be created by Microsoft Project 2000 - 2003, 2007 and 2010.
  - **mpx** is a format that may be imported and exported by many other older project scheduling software packages, but the trend is to move towards using Microsoft XML format for importing Microsoft Project files into other software packages such as Asta Powerproject and Oracle Primavera P6.
  - Some third-party software will convert mpx files to and from Microsoft Project 2000 – 2003 mpp format files. You may search the Internet for the latest available products.
- **Project Template (*.mpt)**. This 2010 format is used for creating project templates.
- **Microsoft Project 2007 Templates (*.mpt)**. This is the 2007 template format.
- **Project Database (*.mpd)**. This is a Microsoft Project database format, but is not available in Microsoft Project 2007 or 2010.
- **Microsoft Access Database (*.mdb)**. This is the Microsoft Access format in Microsoft Project 2000 – 2003 that is not available in Microsoft Project 2007 or 2010.
- Data may be saved to (and imported from) files in the following additional formats using **File**, **Save**, **File**, **Save As** and **File**, **Open**:
  - Portable Document Format read by software such as Adode Acrobat, (*.pdf)
  - XML Paper Specification, a file format developed by Microsoft providing device-independent documents appearance and provides a similar outcome to a pdf file, (*.xps)
  - Excel Workbook (*.xlsx)).
  - Excel Binary Workbook (*.xlsb)
  - Excel 97 - 2003 Workbook (*.xls)
  - Web page (save only) (*.html; *.htm)
  - Text – Tab delimited text files (*.txt)
  - CSV – Comma delimited text files (*.csv)

> ➢ XML format (*.xml). Introduced in Microsoft Project 2002, this enables files to be saved in XML (eXtended Markup Language) format allowing data to be shared with other applications. This is becoming the more popular format for importing Microsoft Project files into other software packages such as Asta Powerproject and Oracle Primavera P6.

- The Excel Pivot Table (save only) format from Microsoft Project 2007 is no longer available.

23.15 Recording a Macro

Macros record keystrokes and are useful for performing functions where there are not inbuilt Microsoft Project functions. A typical example is recording a macro to add a Negative Float or Total Float bar. To record a macro:

- Practice the keystrokes you wish to record
- Select Developer, Record Macro to open the **Record Macro** form:

- Enter the Macro name: without spaces,
- Enter the Shortcut key:, you must not use a letter that has already been assigned such as the letters C, V, Y, B etc
- Click OK,
- Record the macro by typing your keystrokes,
- When complete select Stop Recording from the Developer, Code group.
- Press Ctl+ your short cut key to run the macro.
- Select Developer, Code, View Macros Options... to edit the shortcut key.

24 WHAT IS NEW IN MICROSOFT PROJECT 2010

Microsoft Office Project 2010 introduced many new features including a new **Ribbon** style menu that replaces the traditional menu and toolbars. Some new functions that make the product look and feel very different. This chapter covers the following new functions:

- The Ribbon
- The File Tab
- Task Scheduling Mode - Manually Scheduled or Auto Scheduled
- Task Inspector
- Move Project
- Top-down Summary Tasks
- Renaming Columns
- Add a New Column Using the New Column function
- Zoom Slider
- Zoom Commands on Ribbon Menu
- Marking a Task Inactive
- Multiple Task Linking
- Wrap Text Command
- Insert Summary Task
- Right Mouse Clicking
- Gantt Chart Styles Group Menu
- Format Individual Cells Font Command
- New Timeline and Team Planner Views
- Maintain Hierarchy in Current Group
- AutoFilters
- Assigning Resources from the Resource Column
- Using the Alt Key and Keystrokes to Access Commands
- Copy and Paste Enhancements
- Display Number of Recently Opened Files
- Automatically Add New Views, Tables, Filters, and Groups to the Global Template
- Compatibility with Earlier Project Versions
- Status Bar
- Improvements in Collaboration – SharePoint list synchronization

24.1 The Ribbon

The Ribbon has replaced the traditional menus and toolbars in the same style as other Microsoft Office products. Under each tab you will find commands grouped by a similar theme.

All the tabs are highly customizable allowing a high degree of customization to suit the types of project you work with and how you like to work. The operation of these menus is covered in detail in the **NAVIGATING AROUND THE SCREEN** chapter.

24.2 The File Tab

File tab takes the user to an area also titled **Backstage**.

- This is where you are able to manage your project files with options for saving, opening, and printing files.
- The **Options** form button is also found under this menu.
- If you are using the Professional version connected to a Microsoft Project Server then you are also able to manage your server connections and are able to check out and publish projects.

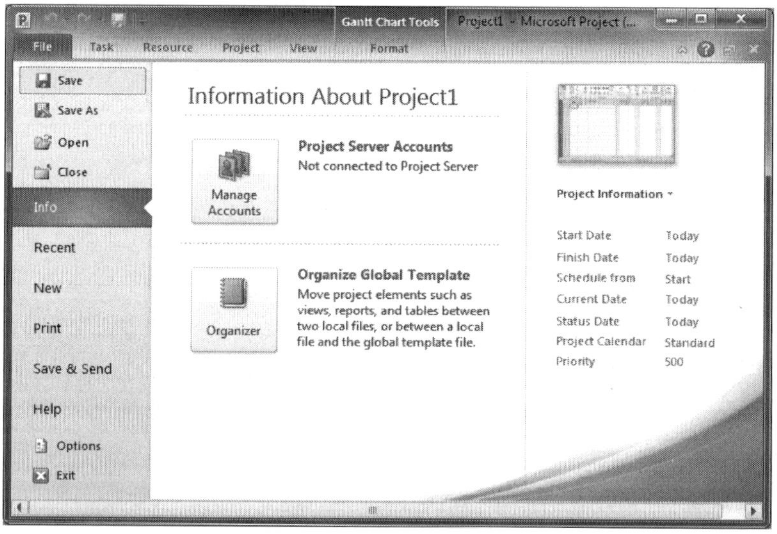

24.3 Task Scheduling Mode - Manually Scheduled or Auto Scheduled

Microsoft has introduced a new Task attribute titled **Task Scheduling Mode**. In earlier versions of Microsoft Project every task was set to the equivalent of the new **Auto Scheduled** setting in Microsoft Project 2010. In this **Auto Scheduled** mode all tasks' Start and Finish dates are calculated with respect to the Project Start (or Finish) Date, their Durations, Relationships, Constraints, Calendars and Options.

This subject is extensively covered in the **MORE ADVANCED SCHEDULING** chapter and will not be printed here.

24.4 Task Inspector

When the successor task is dragged forward in time they adopts a dotted outline bar format and the Finish date is underlined indicating a **Warning**:

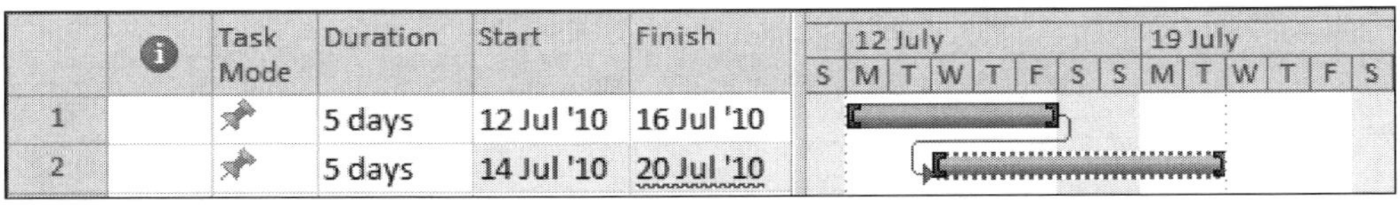

The **Warning** may be read by moving the mouse pointer over the task bar:

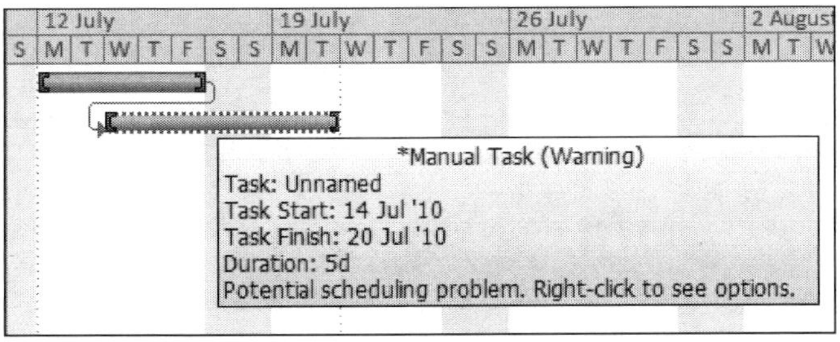

The **Task**, **Task** group, **Inspect Task** option opens the **Task Inspector** form that provides advice on how this **Warning** may be resolved.

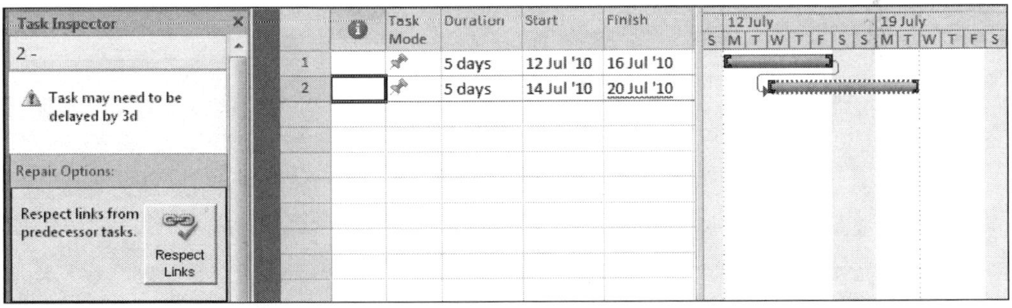

24.5 Move Project

The **Move Project**, **Schedule** group, **Move Project** function opens the Move Project form which allows the resetting of the **Project Start** date:

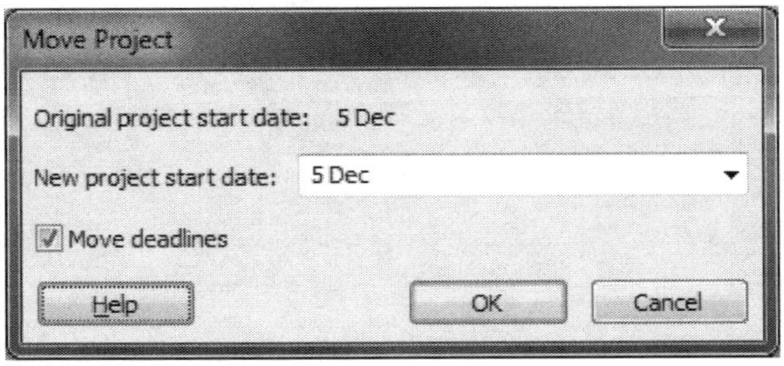

This option will change Actual Dates and should be used with caution if used with a progressed schedule.

24.6 Top-down Summary Tasks

It is also possible to make summary tasks **Manually Scheduled** when the related detail tasks are either **Manually Scheduled** or **Auto Scheduled** and the summary task dates are no longer adopted from the detail tasks.

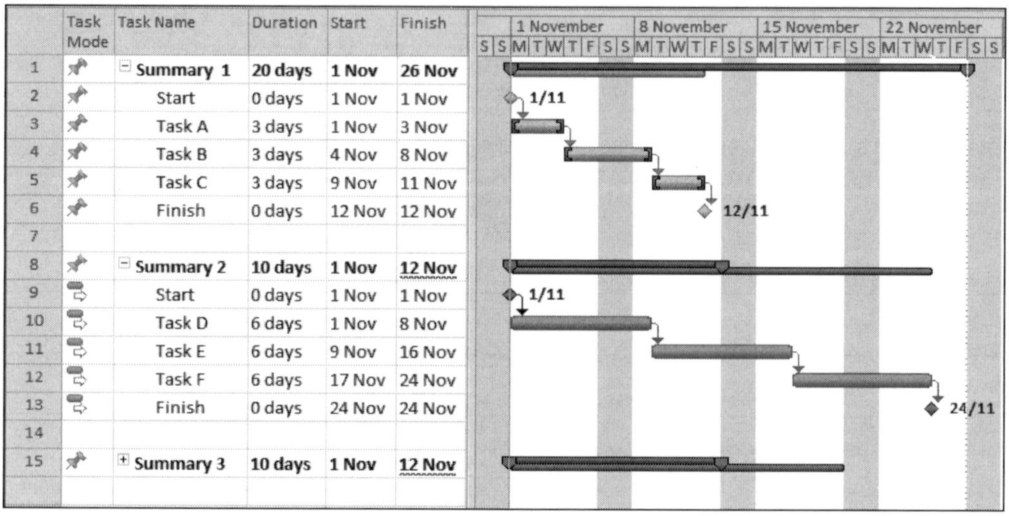

This option prevents the summary task from changing duration as the detail tasks are manipulated during the development of the schedule.

The lower bar displays the duration of the detail tasks.

24.7 Renaming Columns

A column may now be renamed by clicking into the column heading and typing the new name.

24.8 Add a New Column Using the "Add New Column" Column

To add a new column, click on the **Add New Column** heading on the right of the columns and type the name of the column you require in the drop-down box. A column can also be quickly renamed by clicking on its title and typing a different name. Customizing a column has never been so easy.

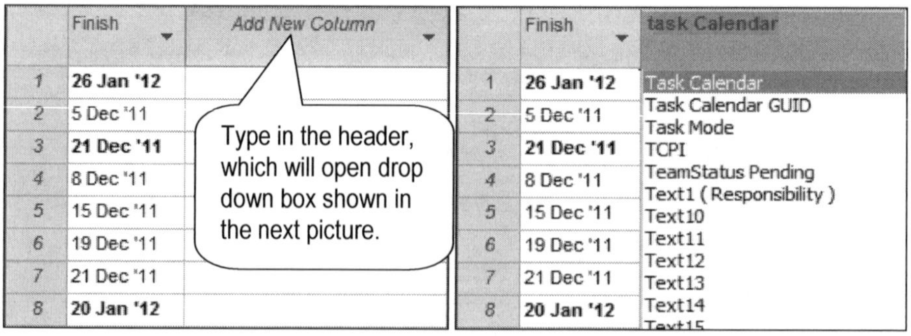

24.9 Zoom Slider

The **Zoom Slider** may be found at the bottom right-hand side of the screen and provides a simple way of scaling the time scale in the Gantt Chart and all other time scaled views such as the Calendar and Network Diagram View.

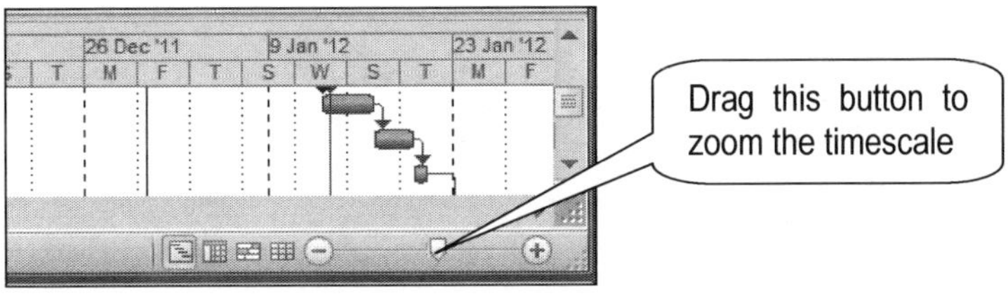

This function works differently than other scheduling software in that it changes the scale and the displayed time units at the same time and may result in some undesirable time units being displayed.

The author has found that better results are achieved by using the traditional  **Zoom In** and **Zoom Out** functions which may be added to the **Quick Access Toolbar**.

24.10 Zoom Command on Ribbon menu

There are some new commands available with Microsoft Project 2010 on the **Ribbon**:

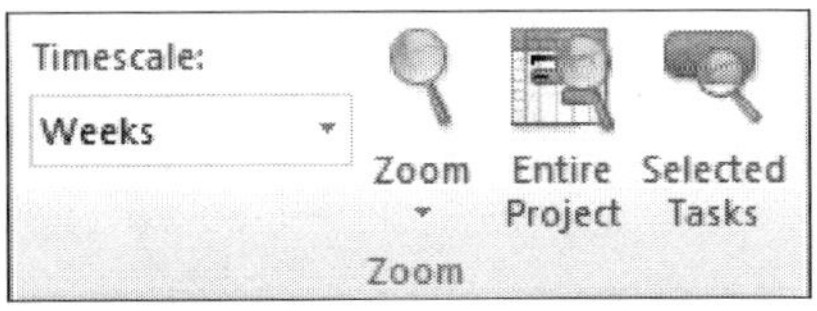

- The **Timescale:** option is a quick method of selecting the **Minor Timescale**, the lower line in the Timescale,
- Zoom opens a self-explanatory menu,
- **Entire Project** zooms the timescale to fit the whole project Gantt Chart to fit in the available space,
- **Selected Tasks** zooms the timescale to fit the bars of selected tasks to fit in the available space.

It has been the author's experience that most of the Microsoft Project timescale functions impose their own date formats and apply strange **Counts** to the timescale, thus the user looses any user timescale formatting permanently. The  Zoom In and Zoom Out buttons appear to give the best results.

24.11 *Marking a Task Inactive*

When a task is marked **Inactive** by checking the option in the **Task Information** form **General** tab then the task is not considered in the scheduling process. Relationships to and from tasks are ignored and Resource Hours and Costs are not included in the summary tasks rolled up values, but Baseline Values are maintained:

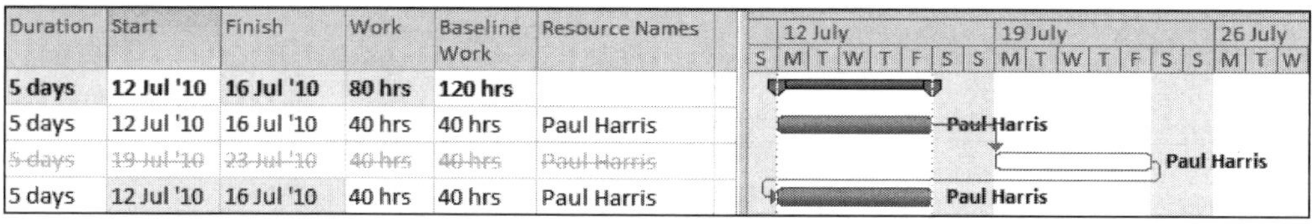

Duration	Start	Finish	Work	Baseline Work	Resource Names
5 days	**12 Jul '10**	**16 Jul '10**	**80 hrs**	**120 hrs**	
5 days	12 Jul '10	16 Jul '10	40 hrs	40 hrs	Paul Harris
~~5 days~~	~~19 Jul '10~~	~~23 Jul '10~~	~~40 hrs~~	~~40 hrs~~	~~Paul Harris~~
5 days	12 Jul '10	16 Jul '10	40 hrs	40 hrs	Paul Harris

24.12 *Multiple Task Linking*

The limit of a maximum of 10 groups of tasks that could be linked by selecting multiple tasks has been removed from Microsoft Project 2010.

24.13 *Wrap Text Command*

Microsoft Project 2010 has introduced a **Wrap Text** command found on the **Format**, **Columns** group, **Column Settings**, **Wrap Text** which automatically adjusts the row height to fit the text into the available column width.

24.14 *Insert Summary Task*

A summary task may be created by using the new **Insert Summary Task** function:

- Selecting the tasks you wish to create a summary task above,

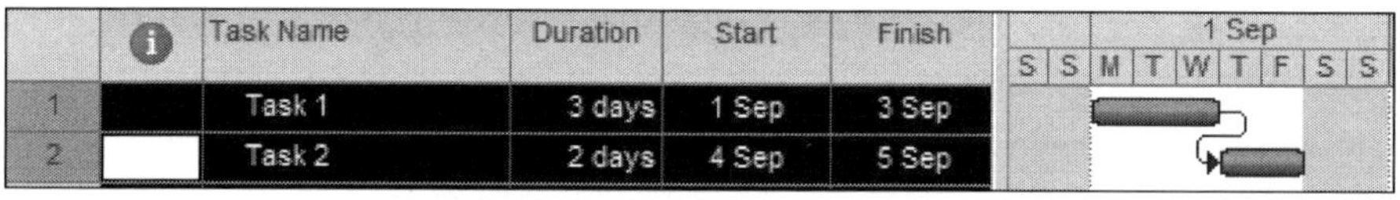

		Task Name	Duration	Start	Finish
1		Task 1	3 days	1 Sep	3 Sep
2		Task 2	2 days	4 Sep	5 Sep

- Click on **Task**, **Insert** group, **Summary** button,
- Rename the newly created summary task:

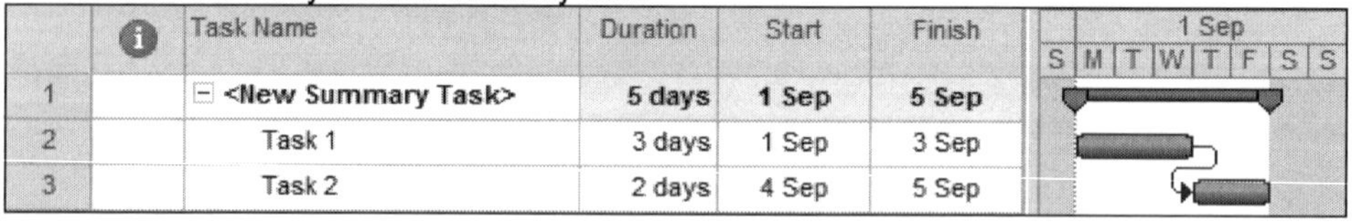

		Task Name	Duration	Start	Finish
1		**<New Summary Task>**	**5 days**	**1 Sep**	**5 Sep**
2		Task 1	3 days	1 Sep	3 Sep
3		Task 2	2 days	4 Sep	5 Sep

24.15 Right Mouse Clicking

The Right Mouse Clicking operation has been enhanced so you may find many of the applicable commands available in a menu when you right-click on any object such as bars, bar chart area, text, etc:

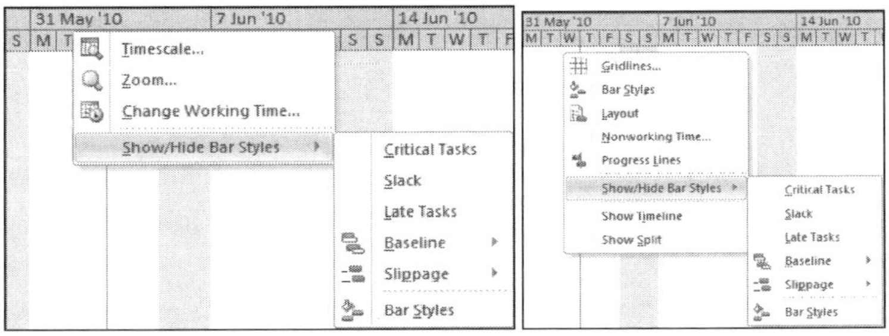

24.16 Gantt Chart Styles Group Menu

Select **Format**, **Gantt Chart Styles** group to see the option for coloring bars. This function is new to Microsoft Project 2010.

The button at the bottom right-hand side opens the **Bar Styles** form.

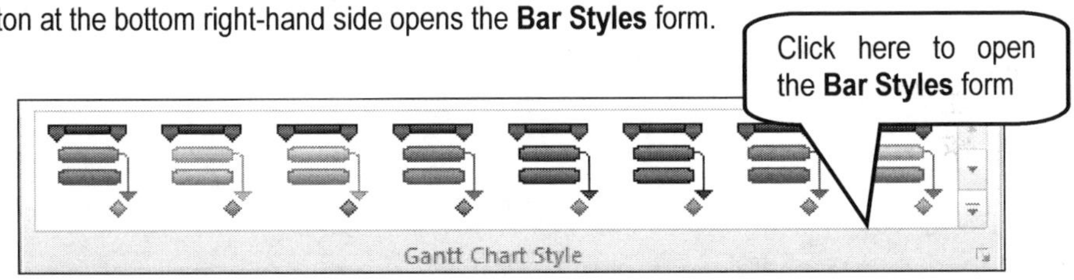

24.17 Format Individual Cells Font Command

The **Format**, **Font...** function from Microsoft 2007 and earlier has been replaced with a right-click option and allows you to format any selected text in selected, cells, rows or columns:

- Select the text to be formatted,
- Right-click and two toolbars are opened The upper toolbar in the picture below has four buttons that may be used for formatting individual cells:

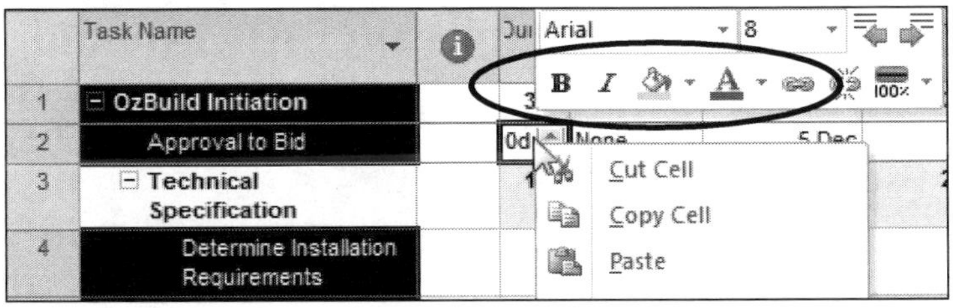

24.18 New Timeline and Team Planner Views

New viewing features have also been added to help you understand with greater clarity how your team is performing and where they are over allocated. These views may also help you and others in your organization see the big picture (and potentially major resource problems) with the Timeline and Team Planner Views.

24.18.1 Timeline View

This view allows you to clearly understand how much of the Gantt Chart is displayed on the screen. The picture below demonstrates that about one-third of the project is displayed in the Gantt Chart.

The **Timescale** view is shown above the Gantt Chart by selecting **View**, **Split View** group and checking the **Timeline** check box.

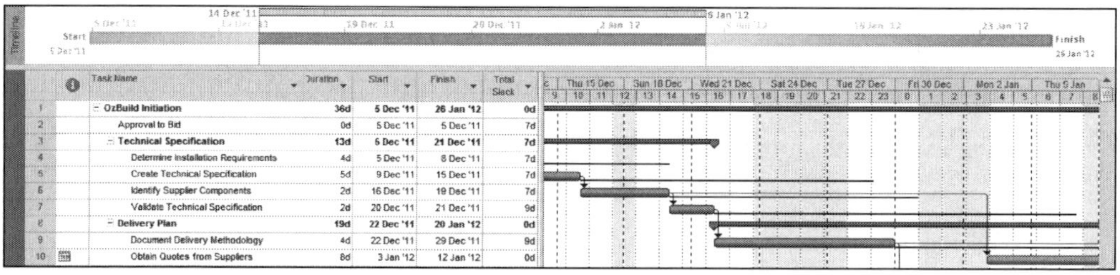

A task may be added to the **Timeline** view by selecting the **Add to Timeline** found in many menus, including right clicking. Important tasks that need to be highlighted should be considered for this type of treatment. In the picture below the Start and Finish Milestones and Obtain Quotes have been added to the Timeline view:

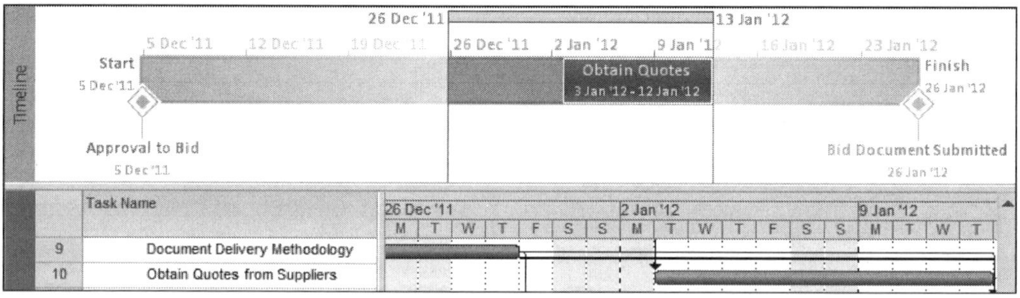

24.18.2 Team Planner View

This view allows a **Production Planning** type view where tasks may be assigned to resources as opposed to **Project Planning** where resources are assigned to tasks. This view allows:

- All task information such as resource allocations to be viewed by highlighting the task with the mouse.
- Identification of overloading with the ability to see what tasks a resource is assigned to at the same time by the highlighting behind the task. See the picture below.
- The assignment or reassignment of resources by dragging tasks from one resource to another. The **Estimate Review** task below could be assigned to a resource by dragging it onto a resource:

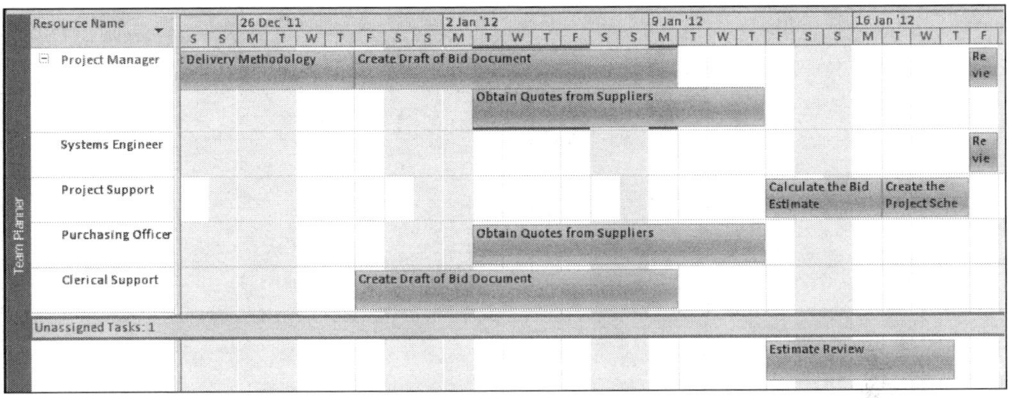

24.19 Maintain Hierarchy in Current Group

Maintain Hierarchy in Current Group is a new feature to Microsoft Project 2010 and allows the user to see the Outline hierarchy when Grouping by Tasks. The picture below displays the effect of grouping by two Custom Text columns, with the lower picture having this option turned one:

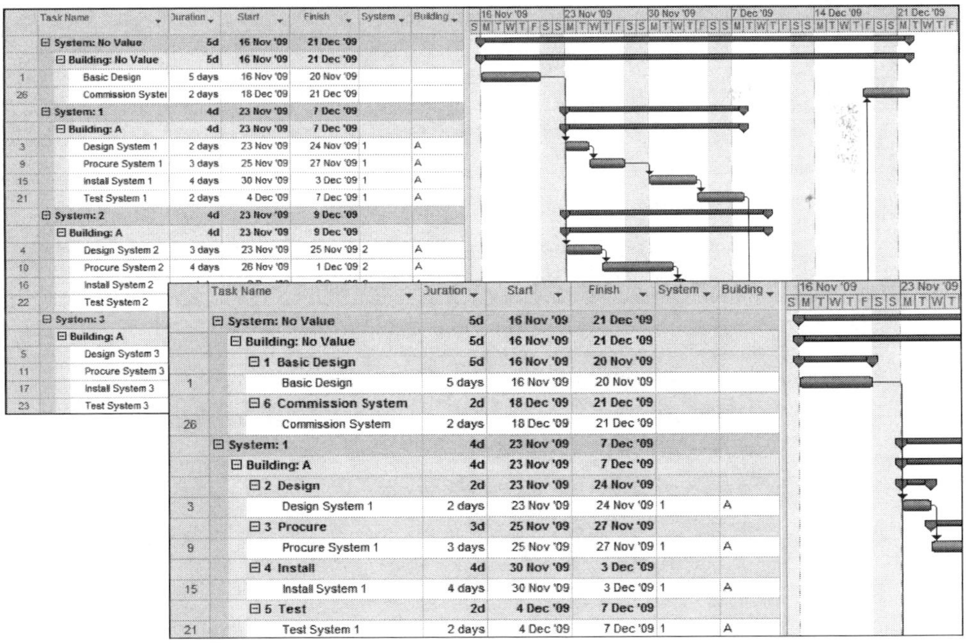

24.20 AutoFilters

This function has been greatly enhanced in Microsoft project 2010. Microsoft Project **AutoFilters** are similar to the Excel **AutoFilter** function and allow you to select the filter criteria from drop-down menus in the column headers. This function allows both **Grouping** and **Sorting** of tasks, which will be covered in the **TABLES AND GROUPING** chapter.

To create an **AutoFilter** based on one parameter:

- Turn on the **AutoFilter** function by selecting **View**, **Data** group, **Filter:** drop-down box, **Display AutoFilter**.
- The column headers will display the button in the column header. Click on this button in one of the columns to display a drop-down box:

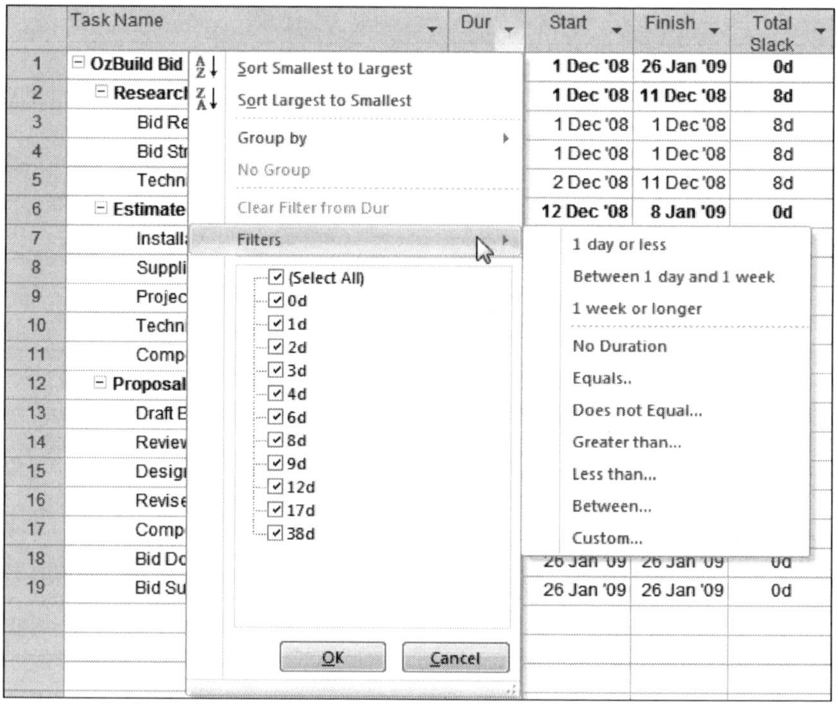

- Select the required criteria from the check box list, or
- Click on the **Filters** heading, as displayed above, to open up a second set of selections, which in turn will provide many more options which will open the **Custom AutoFilter** form:

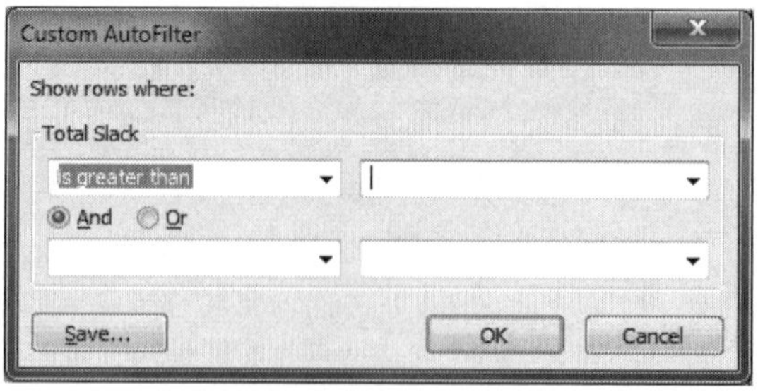

- Select the parameters you want to operate on from the four drop-down boxes and check the **And** or **Or** radio button.
- To save a drop-down filter as a normal filter, click on the 

button, which opens the **Filter Definition** form.
- You may now select another column and create a filter based on two parameters to reduce the number of tasks displayed.
- After an AutoFilter has been applied the indicator in the column heading changes to a 

.

AutoFilters always select the associated summary tasks of any selected detail tasks.

24.21 Using the Alt Key and Keystrokes to Access Commands

Microsoft Project 2010 has introduced a function that displays the keystroke commands when the **Alt** key is pressed. The picture below shows the keystroke commands after pressing the **Alt** key and pressing the **F** key will open the **File** menu:

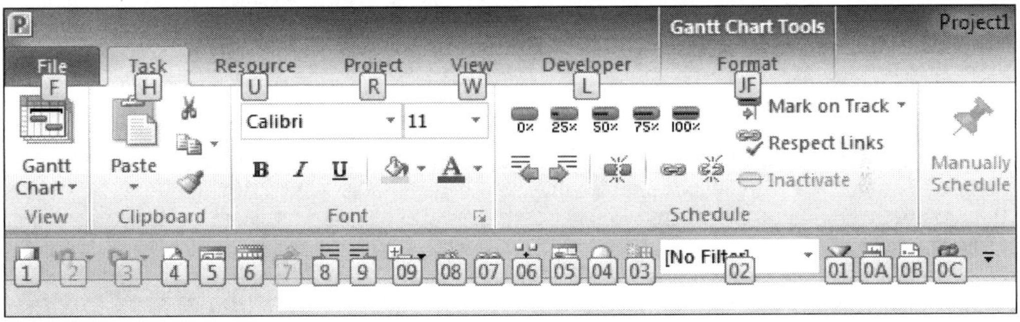

Microsoft Project 2010 has changed many of the traditional keystroke commands.

24.22 Assigning Resources from the Resource Column

Resources may be assigned by displaying the Resource Names column and clicking in the cell which will display the available resources.

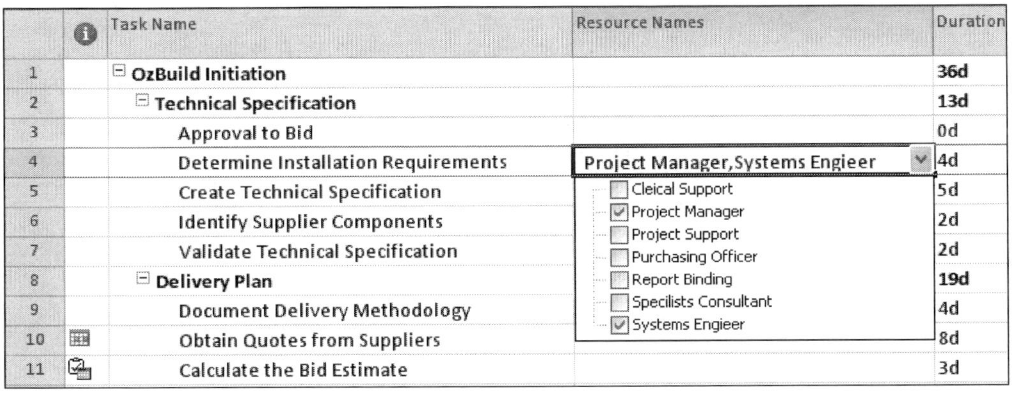

24.23 Copy and Paste Enhancements

Microsoft Project 2010 has introduced new functions allowing:

- Copy and Paste to other products keeps the column header, formatting and indenting.
- Copy and Paste from other products allow the option of keeping the source formatting:

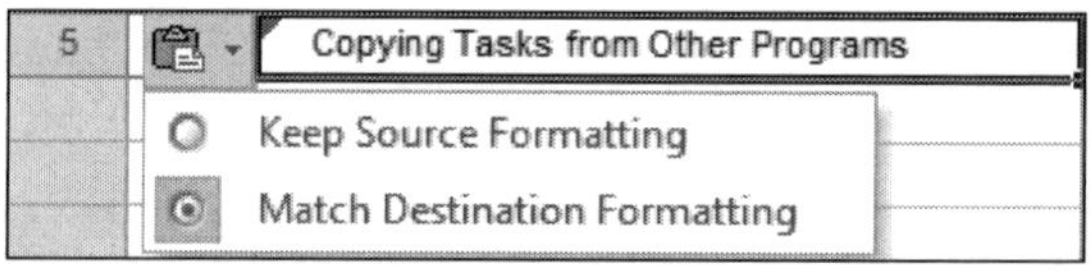

24.24 Display Number of Recently Opened Files

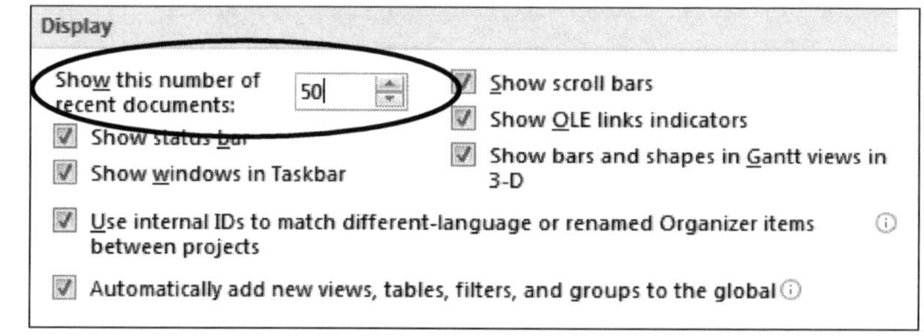

Select **File**, **Options Advanced** tab, **Display** section and the **Show this number of recent documents:** allows up to 50 recently opened project files to be listed, an increase of 9 available in Microsoft Project 2007.

24.25 Automatically Add New Views, Tables, Filters, and Groups to the Global

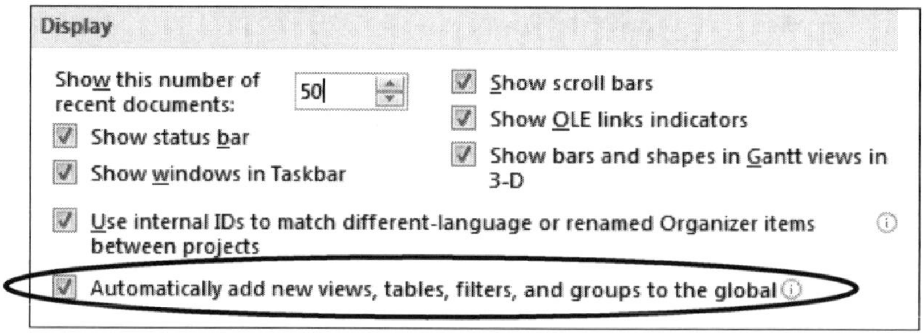

Select **File**, **Options Advanced** tab, **Display** section and the **Automatically add new views**, **tables**, **filters**, **and groups to the global** function will automatically add New Views, Tables, Filters, and Groups to the Global.mpt.

Therefore as time progresses the **Automatically add new views**, **tables**, **filters**, **and groups to the global**, will add more and more views, table and filters to the **Global.mpt**. A project that is created from the **Blank Project** will have many unwanted views table and filters. It is suggested this option is turned off.

24.26 Compatibility with Earlier Project Versions

Microsoft Office Project 2010 files may be saved in the 2007 or 2000 - 2003 formats using **File**, **Save As** and selecting the required format from the **Save as type:** drop-down box. When a file is saved in earlier versions:

- Microsoft Project displays the words **[Compatibility Mode]** after the project name in the top center of the window,
- New Microsoft Project 2010 functions such as **Blank Dates**, **Manually Scheduled** and **Inactive Tasks** are not available when the file is saved and used with in an earlier version.
- Tasks that were created as **Manually Scheduled** are converted to **Auto Scheduled**,
- **Inactive Tasks** are deleted,
- When a project is saved in the 2000 - 2003 format then:
  - Calendar Exceptions information is also lost when a project is saved from Microsoft Office Project 2007 to 2000 - 2003 format,
  - **Cost Resources** are converted to **Material Resources** and values may change,
  - **New Fields** and **Custom Fields** lose their options and formulae.

24.27 Status Bar

The **Status Bar** may be formatted by right-clicking on it:

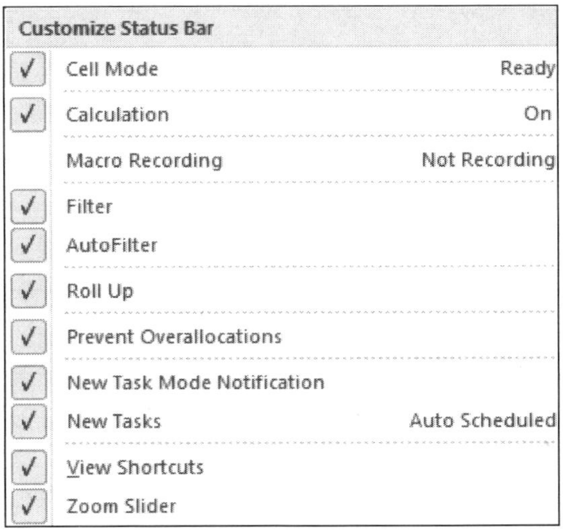

24.28 Improvements in collaboration - SharePoint list Synchronization

Microsoft Office Project Professional 2010 users may synchronize their project files to SharePoint.

25 APPENDIX 1 – SCREENS USED TO CREATE VIEWS

Microsoft Project has the following methods of accessing the data on screen.

- The screen may be split with an **Top** and **Bottom Pane**.
  - The **Top Pane** displays all project information, except when a filter is applied.
  - The **Bottom Pane** displays information about the task or tasks or resources that are highlighted in the Top pane.
- A **View** may be created and edited from the **More Views** form. A **View** is created from a **Screen** in the **View Definition** form by clicking New... in the **More Views** form.
  - A **Single View** may be applied to either the **Primary View (**Top Pane) or **Details Pane** (Bottom Pane) as long as the **Screen** may be displayed in that **Pane**.
  - A **Combination View** selects an existing view for both the **Primary View (**Top Pane) or **Details Pane** (Bottom Pane).
- There are many **Screens**, most of which may be applied to the **Primary View (**Top Pane) or **Details Pane** (Bottom Pane) through **Views**.
  - There are some restrictions. For example, the **Calendar** screen may not be applied to the bottom pane.
  - Some **Screens** are not useful when displayed in the incorrect pane. It is better to display the **Task** form in the **Details Pane** and leave a **Gantt Chart** in the **Primary View (**Top Pane).
  - Some **Screens** are very similar to each other, such as the **Task** screen and the **Task Details** screen.
- Some **Screens** have **Details** forms where the content of a **View** may be changed. An example of this is a **Task Usage** view, which may be formatted to show **Work** or **Costs** and **Cumulative** or **Period**.
- Some Screens are split vertically and have a left-hand side and a right-hand side such as the **Gantt Screen**. Other **Screens** do not split vertically, like the **Task Screen** and the **Task Details Screen**, which are used in the **Task Form** view and the **Task Details Form** view.

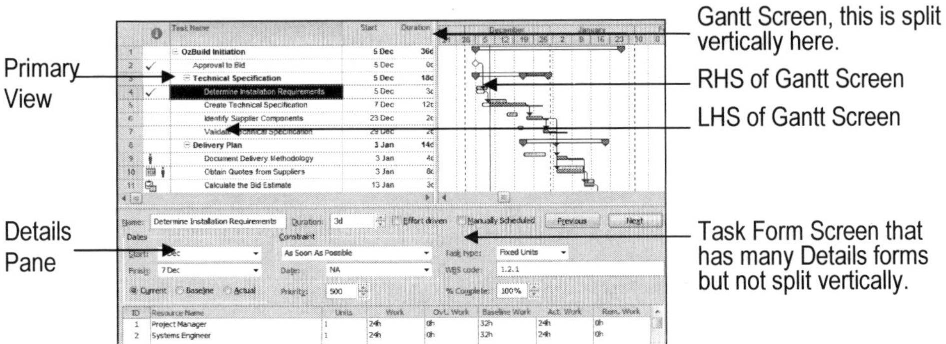

The following table summarizes the **Screen**, **View** and **Details** options:

	Screen Name	**Panes**	**Split Verti-cally**	**Details Options**	**Format Column Options**
1	Calendar	Top Only	No	None	Right-click Format Options 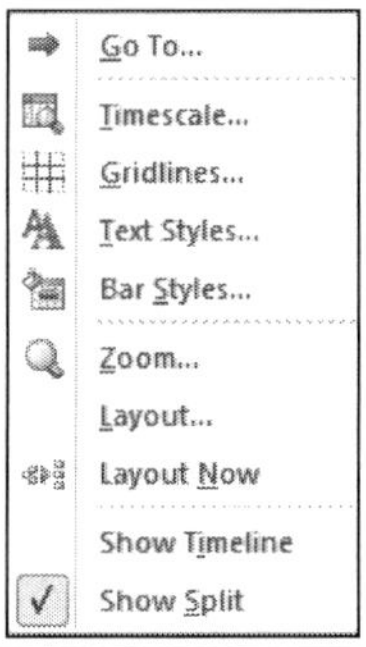
2	Gantt Chart	Best in Top	Yes	Bars and Columns may be formatted	Yes
3	Network Diagram	Best in Top	No	Task Boxes may be edited	No
4	Relationship Diagram	Either	No	None	No
5	Resource Form	Best in Bottom	No	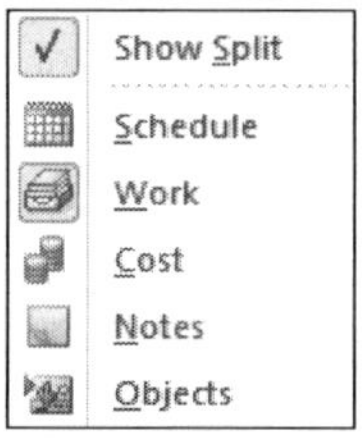	No
6	Resource Graph	Best in Bottom	No	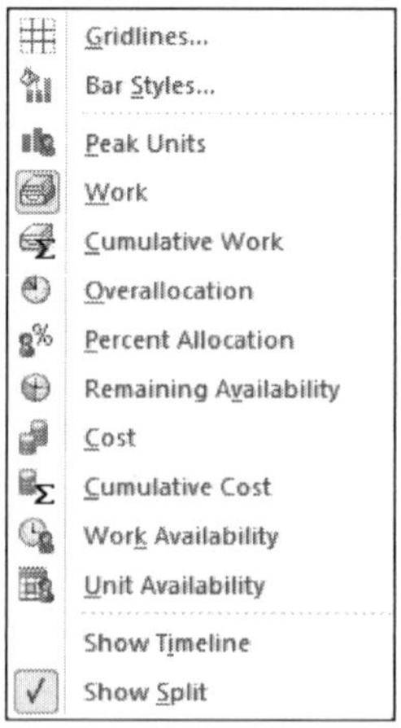	No

	Screen Name	Panes	Split Verti-cally	Details Options	Format Column Options
7	Resource Name Form	Best in Bottom	No		No
8	Resource Sheet	Either	No	None	Yes
9	Resource Usage	Either	Yes	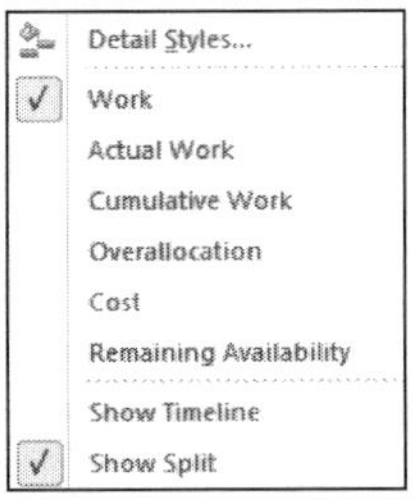	No
10	Task Details Form	Best in Bottom	Yes	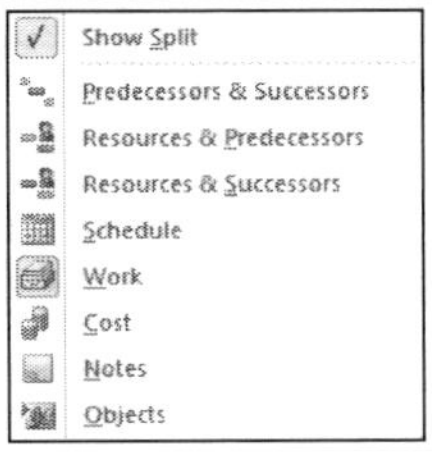	No
11	Task Form	Best in Bottom	No		No
12	Task Name Form	Best in Bottom	No		No
13	Task Sheet	Best In Top	No	None	Yes
14	Task Usage	Best in Bottom	Yes	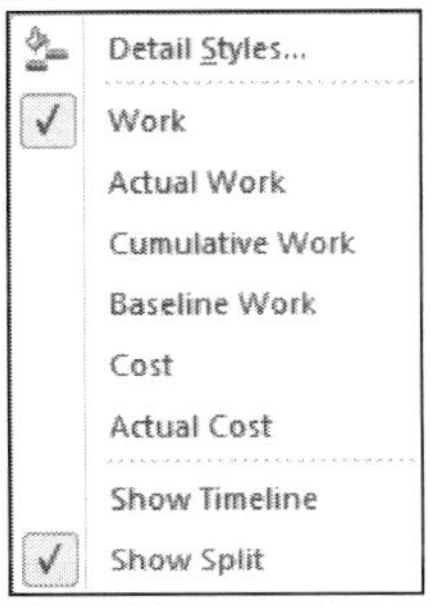	Yes
15	Team Planner	Top Only	No	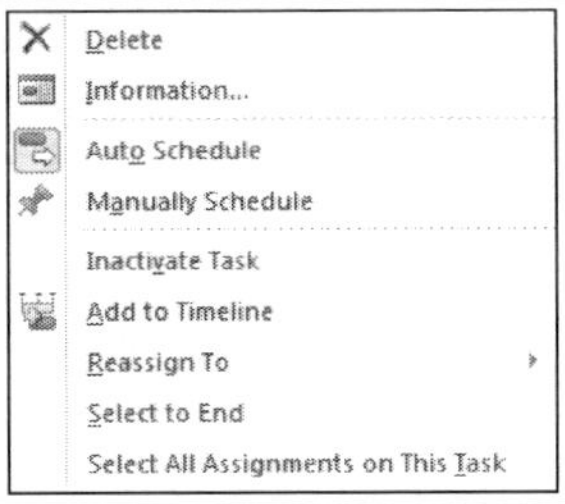	No

<table>
<tr><th></th><th>Screen Name</th><th>Panes</th><th>Split Verti-cally</th><th>Details Options</th><th>Format Column Options</th></tr>
<tr><td>16</td><td>Timeline</td><td>Top Only</td><td>No</td><td>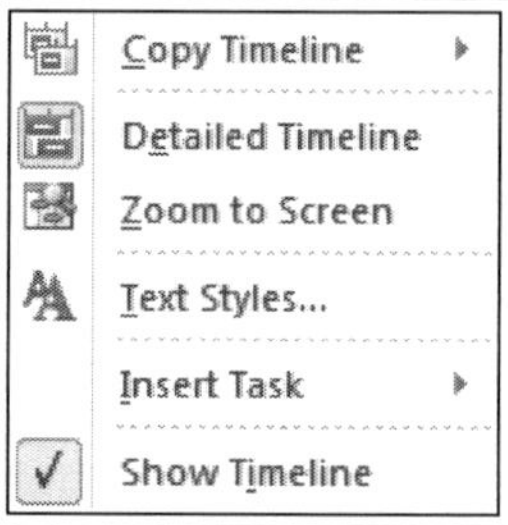
</td><td>No</td></tr>
</table>

The following table displays the Screens and provides some background on each:

<table>
<tr><th>Screen Name</th><th>Note and/or Screen Dumps</th></tr>
<tr><td>1. Calendar</td><td>May be displayed in top pane only.

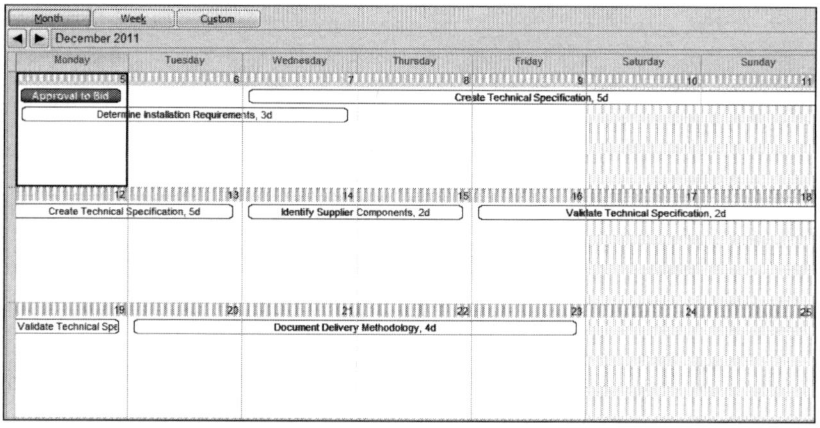

Some formatting is available through right-click, **Layout...**:

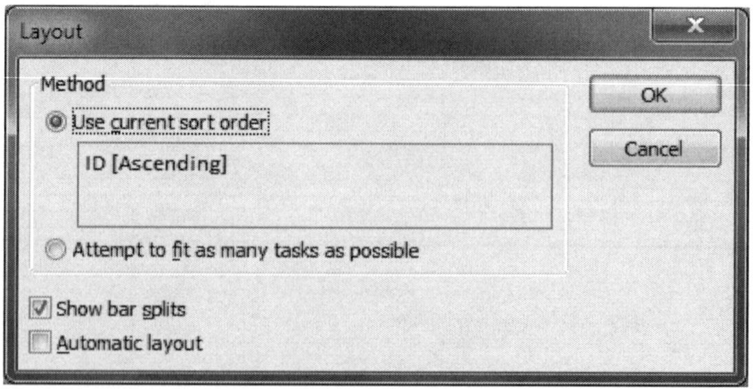
</td></tr>
</table>

<table>
<tr><th>Screen Name</th><th>Note and/or Screen Dumps</th></tr>
<tr><td>2. Gantt Chart</td><td>Designed to be displayed in the top pane:
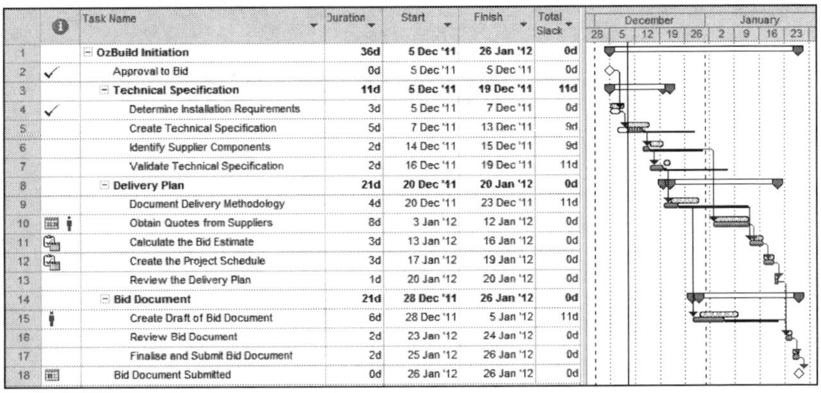
<table>
<tr><th></th><th></th><th>Task Name</th><th>Duration</th><th>Start</th><th>Finish</th><th>Total Slack</th></tr>
<tr><td>1</td><td></td><td>OzBuild Initiation</td><td>36d</td><td>5 Dec '11</td><td>26 Jan '12</td><td>0d</td></tr>
<tr><td>2</td><td>✓</td><td>Approval to Bid</td><td>0d</td><td>5 Dec '11</td><td>5 Dec '11</td><td>0d</td></tr>
<tr><td>3</td><td></td><td>Technical Specification</td><td>11d</td><td>5 Dec '11</td><td>19 Dec '11</td><td>11d</td></tr>
<tr><td>4</td><td>✓</td><td>Determine Installation Requirements</td><td>3d</td><td>5 Dec '11</td><td>7 Dec '11</td><td>0d</td></tr>
<tr><td>5</td><td></td><td>Create Technical Specification</td><td>5d</td><td>7 Dec '11</td><td>13 Dec '11</td><td>9d</td></tr>
<tr><td>6</td><td></td><td>Identify Supplier Components</td><td>2d</td><td>14 Dec '11</td><td>15 Dec '11</td><td>9d</td></tr>
<tr><td>7</td><td></td><td>Validate Technical Specification</td><td>2d</td><td>16 Dec '11</td><td>19 Dec '11</td><td>11d</td></tr>
<tr><td>8</td><td></td><td>Delivery Plan</td><td>21d</td><td>20 Dec '11</td><td>20 Jan '12</td><td>0d</td></tr>
<tr><td>9</td><td></td><td>Document Delivery Methodology</td><td>4d</td><td>20 Dec '11</td><td>23 Dec '11</td><td>11d</td></tr>
<tr><td>10</td><td></td><td>Obtain Quotes from Suppliers</td><td>8d</td><td>3 Jan '12</td><td>12 Jan '12</td><td>0d</td></tr>
<tr><td>11</td><td></td><td>Calculate the Bid Estimate</td><td>3d</td><td>13 Jan '12</td><td>16 Jan '12</td><td>0d</td></tr>
<tr><td>12</td><td></td><td>Create the Project Schedule</td><td>3d</td><td>17 Jan '12</td><td>19 Jan '12</td><td>0d</td></tr>
<tr><td>13</td><td></td><td>Review the Delivery Plan</td><td>1d</td><td>20 Jan '12</td><td>20 Jan '12</td><td>0d</td></tr>
<tr><td>14</td><td></td><td>Bid Document</td><td>21d</td><td>28 Dec '11</td><td>26 Jan '12</td><td>0d</td></tr>
<tr><td>15</td><td></td><td>Create Draft of Bid Document</td><td>6d</td><td>28 Dec '11</td><td>5 Jan '12</td><td>11d</td></tr>
<tr><td>16</td><td></td><td>Review Bid Document</td><td>2d</td><td>23 Jan '12</td><td>24 Jan '12</td><td>0d</td></tr>
<tr><td>17</td><td></td><td>Finalise and Submit Bid Document</td><td>2d</td><td>25 Jan '12</td><td>26 Jan '12</td><td>0d</td></tr>
<tr><td>18</td><td></td><td>Bid Document Submitted</td><td>0d</td><td>26 Jan '12</td><td>26 Jan '12</td><td>0d</td></tr>
</table>

Columns may be added and removed and bars may be formatted.</td></tr>
<tr><td>3. Network Diagram</td><td>Designed to be displayed in the top pane:
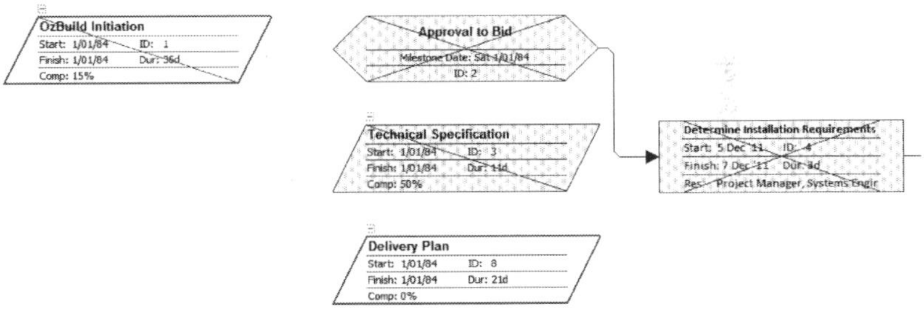
</td></tr>
<tr><td>4. Relationship Diagram</td><td>This displays relationships between tasks and may not be printed or edited. Click on a predecessor or successor check these other task relationships.

</td></tr>
</table>

<table>
<tr><th>Screen Name</th><th>Note and/or Screen Dumps</th></tr>
<tr><td>5. Resource Form</td><td>

Designed for the bottom pane:

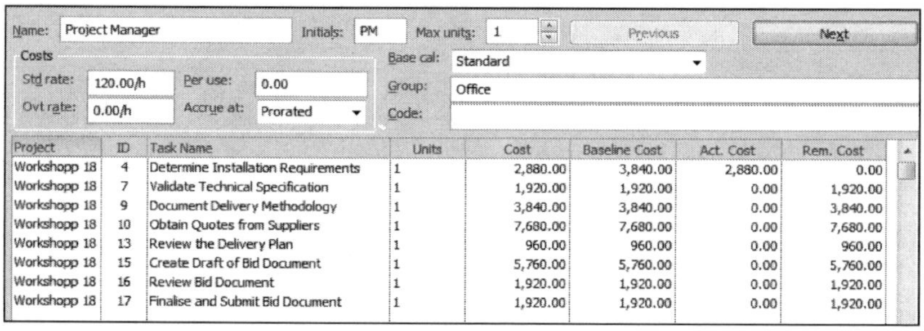

This View has the following options by right-clicking:

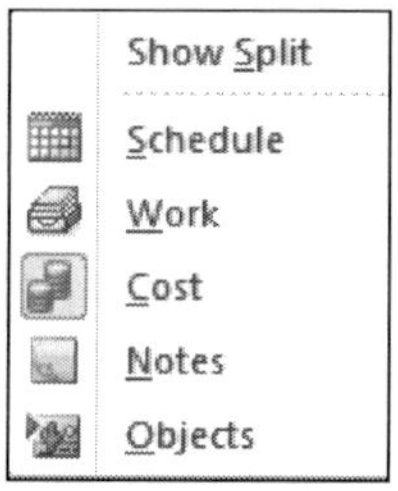

</td></tr>
<tr><td>6. Resource Graph</td><td>

This View is designed to be displayed in the bottom pane:

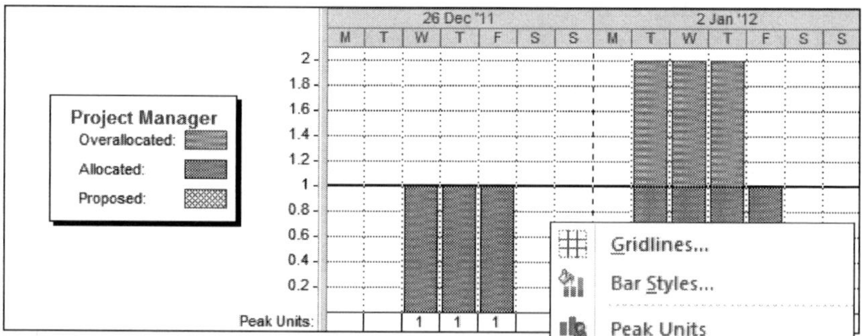

This View has the following options by right-clicking:

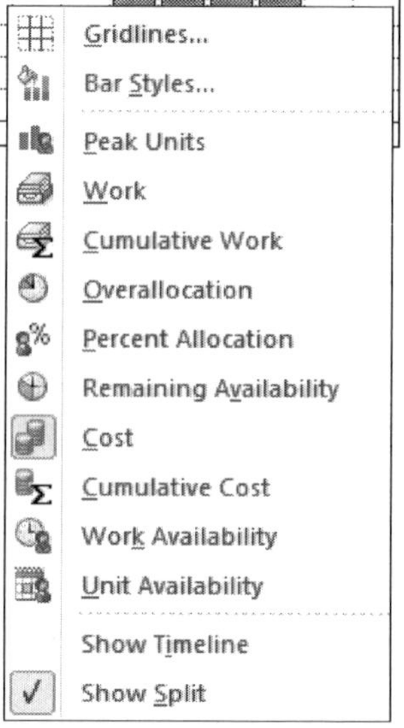

</td></tr>
</table>

<table>
<tr><th>Screen Name</th><th>Note and/or Screen Dumps</th></tr>
<tr><td>7. Resource Name Form</td><td>
This screen is designed for the bottom pane with the Resources Sheet view in the Top pane:
Name: Project Manager | Previous | Next
<table>
<tr><th>Project</th><th>ID</th><th>Task Name</th><th>Units</th><th>Cost</th><th>Baseline Cost</th><th>Act. Cost</th><th>Rem. Cost</th></tr>
<tr><td>Workshopp 18</td><td>4</td><td>Determine Installation Requirements</td><td>1</td><td>2,880.00</td><td>3,840.00</td><td>2,880.00</td><td>0.00</td></tr>
<tr><td>Workshopp 18</td><td>7</td><td>Validate Technical Specification</td><td>1</td><td>1,920.00</td><td>1,920.00</td><td>0.00</td><td>1,920.00</td></tr>
<tr><td>Workshopp 18</td><td>9</td><td>Document Delivery Methodology</td><td>1</td><td>3,840.00</td><td>3,840.00</td><td>0.00</td><td>3,840.00</td></tr>
<tr><td>Workshopp 18</td><td>10</td><td>Obtain Quotes from Suppliers</td><td>1</td><td>7,680.00</td><td>7,680.00</td><td>0.00</td><td>7,680.00</td></tr>
<tr><td>Workshopp 18</td><td>13</td><td>Review the Delivery Plan</td><td>1</td><td>960.00</td><td>960.00</td><td>0.00</td><td>960.00</td></tr>
<tr><td>Workshopp 18</td><td>15</td><td>Create Draft of Bid Document</td><td>1</td><td>5,760.00</td><td>5,760.00</td><td>0.00</td><td>5,760.00</td></tr>
<tr><td>Workshopp 18</td><td>16</td><td>Review Bid Document</td><td>1</td><td>1,920.00</td><td>1,920.00</td><td>0.00</td><td>1,920.00</td></tr>
<tr><td>Workshopp 18</td><td>17</td><td>Finalise and Submit Bid Document</td><td>1</td><td>1,920.00</td><td>1,920.00</td><td>0.00</td><td>1,920.00</td></tr>
</table>
This View has the following options by right-clicking:
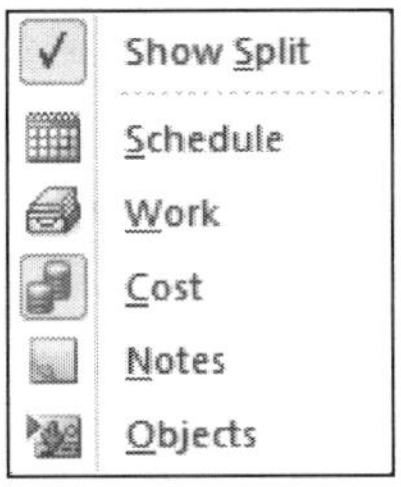

</td></tr>
<tr><td>8. Resource Sheet</td><td>
This screen may be used in the top or bottom pane and the columns may be formatted with the Table and Columns functions:
<table>
<tr><th></th><th>i</th><th>Resource Name</th><th>Type</th><th>Material Label</th><th>Initials</th><th>Group</th><th>Max. Units</th><th>Std. Rate</th><th>Base Calendar</th><th>Cost/Use</th><th>Ovt. Rate</th><th>Accrue At</th></tr>
<tr><td>1</td><td>◈</td><td>Project Manager</td><td>Work</td><td></td><td>PM</td><td>Office</td><td>1</td><td>120.00/hr</td><td>Standard</td><td>0.00</td><td>0.00/hr</td><td>Prorated</td></tr>
<tr><td>2</td><td></td><td>Systems Engineer</td><td>Work</td><td></td><td>SE</td><td>Office</td><td>1</td><td>90.00/hr</td><td>Standard</td><td>0.00</td><td>0.00/hr</td><td>Prorated</td></tr>
<tr><td>3</td><td></td><td>Project Support</td><td>Work</td><td></td><td>PS</td><td>Site</td><td>1</td><td>80.00/hr</td><td>6-Day Working Week</td><td>0.00</td><td>0.00/hr</td><td>Prorated</td></tr>
<tr><td>4</td><td></td><td>Purchasing Officer</td><td>Work</td><td></td><td>PO</td><td>Office</td><td>1</td><td>70.00/hr</td><td>Standard</td><td>0.00</td><td>0.00/hr</td><td>Prorated</td></tr>
<tr><td>5</td><td></td><td>Clerical Support</td><td>Work</td><td></td><td>CS</td><td>Office</td><td>1</td><td>50.00/hr</td><td>Standard</td><td>0.00</td><td>0.00/hr</td><td>Prorated</td></tr>
<tr><td>6</td><td></td><td>Specialists Consultant</td><td>Cost</td><td></td><td>SC</td><td>Contractor</td><td></td><td></td><td></td><td></td><td></td><td>Prorated</td></tr>
<tr><td>7</td><td></td><td>Report Binding</td><td>Material</td><td>each</td><td>RB</td><td></td><td></td><td>100.00</td><td></td><td>0.00</td><td></td><td>Prorated</td></tr>
</table>
</td></tr>
</table>

<table>
<tr><th>Screen Name</th><th>Note and/or Screen Dumps</th></tr>
<tr><td>9. Resource Usage</td><td>

This screen may be used in the top or bottom pane:

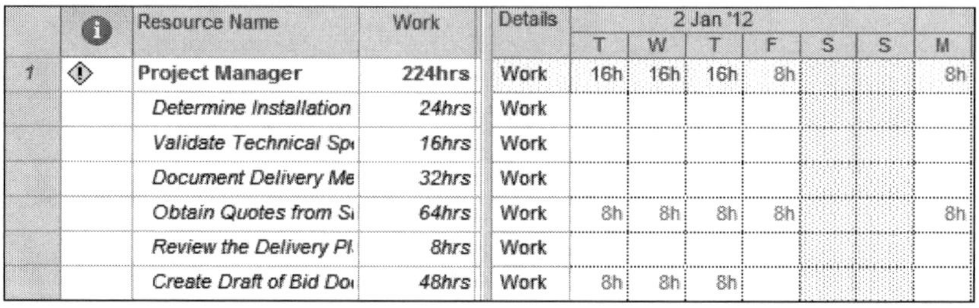

The columns may be formatted with the **Table and Columns** functions and the **Details** area on the right-hand side. It is formatted by right-clicking to open the **Detail Styles** form:

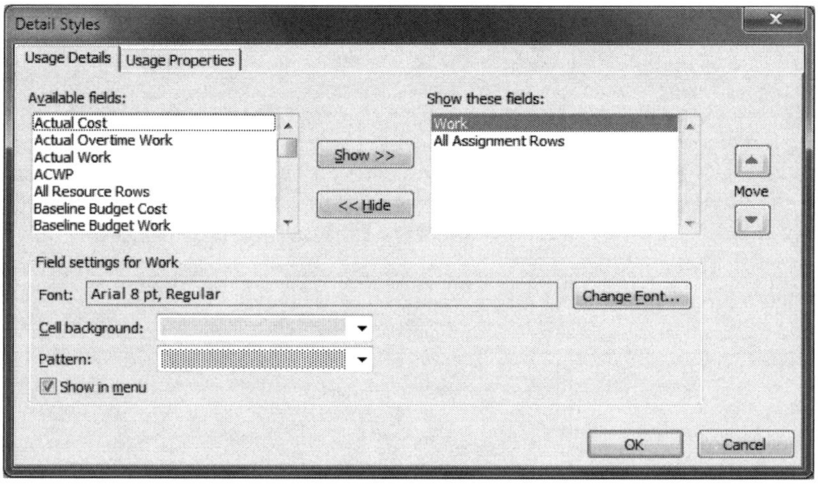

This View has the following options by right-clicking:

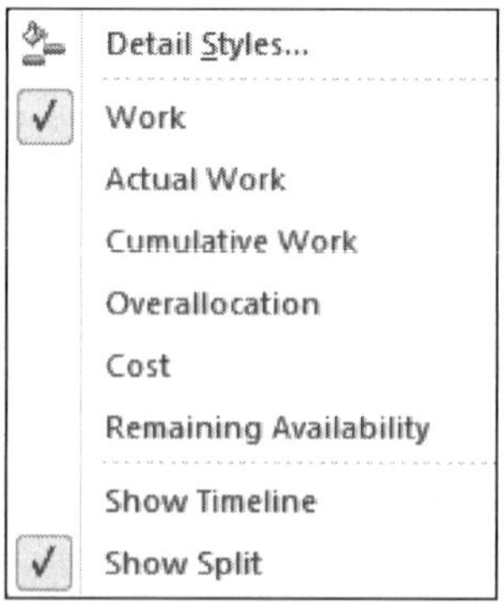

</td></tr>
</table>

<table>
<tr><th>Screen Name</th><th>Note and/or Screen Dumps</th></tr>
<tr><td>10. Task Details Form</td><td>This form is best displayed in the bottom pane and displays information about the task highlighted in the top pane:

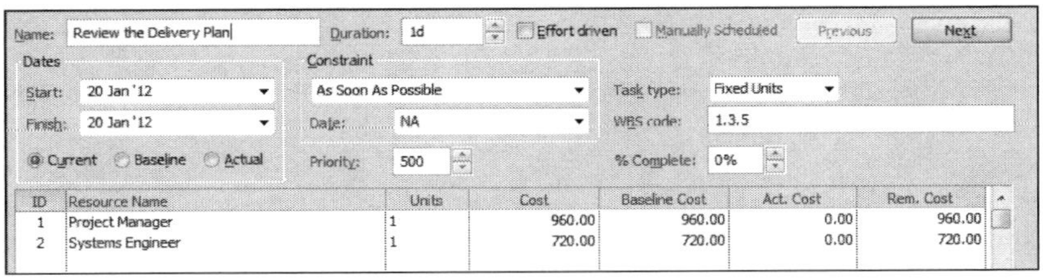

This View has the following options by right-clicking:

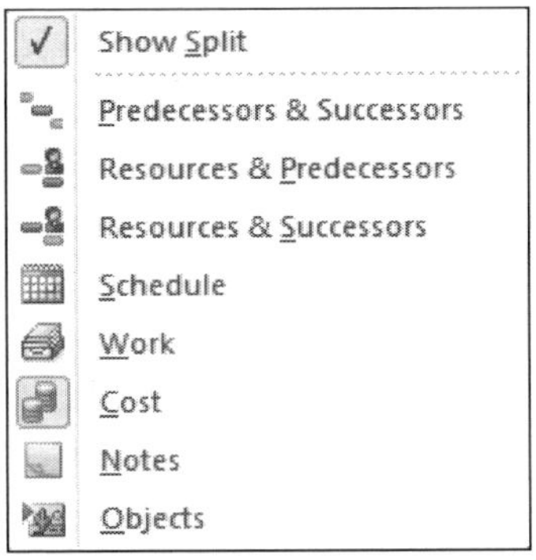
</td></tr>
<tr><td>11. Task Form</td><td>This form is best displayed in the bottom pane.

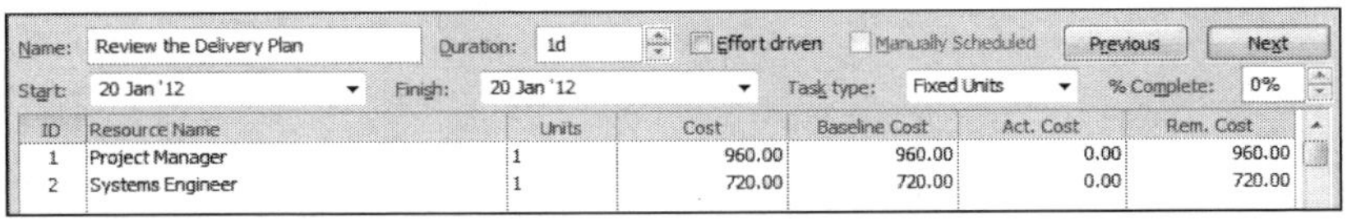

This View has the following options by right-clicking:

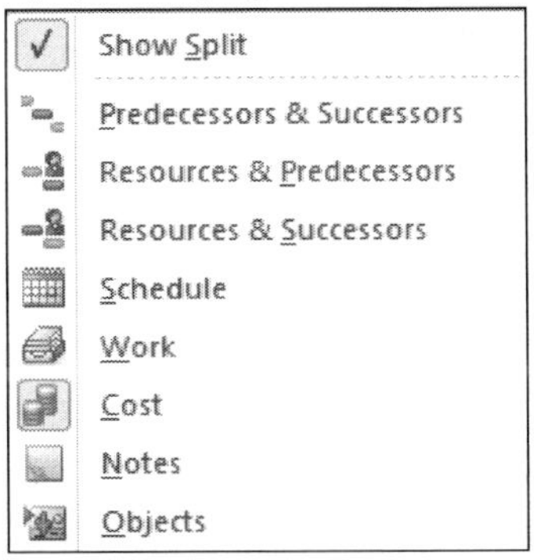
</td></tr>
</table>

Screen Name	Note and/or Screen Dumps
12. Task Name Form	This form is best displayed in the bottom pane.

Name: Review the Delivery Plan | Previous | Next

ID	Resource Name	Units	Cost	Baseline Cost	Act. Cost	Rem. Cost
1	Project Manager	1	960.00	960.00	0.00	960.00
2	Systems Engineer	1	720.00	720.00	0.00	720.00

This View has the following options by right-clicking:

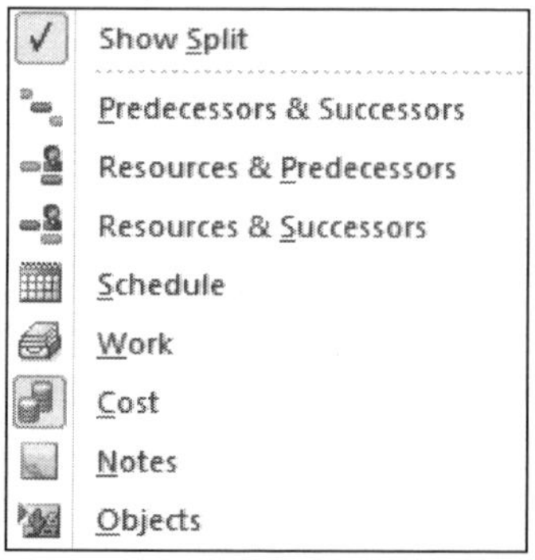

Screen Name	Note and/or Screen Dumps
13. Task Sheet	This View is similar to the Gantt but without displaying the bars. The columns may be formatted using the **Table** and **Columns** functions.

	Task Name	Duration	Start	Finish	Total Slack	Predecessors
1	**OzBuild Initiation**	**36d**	**5 Dec '11**	**26 Jan '12**	**0d**	
2	Approval to Bid	0d	5 Dec '11	5 Dec '11	0d	
3	**Technical Specification**	**11d**	**5 Dec '11**	**19 Dec '11**	**11d**	
4	Determine Installation Requireme	3d	5 Dec '11	7 Dec '11	0d	2
5	Create Technical Specification	5d	7 Dec '11	13 Dec '11	9d	4
6	Identify Supplier Components	2d	14 Dec '11	15 Dec '11	9d	5
7	Validate Technical Specification	2d	16 Dec '11	19 Dec '11	11d	6
8	**Delivery Plan**	**21d**	**20 Dec '11**	**20 Jan '12**	**0d**	

Screen Name	Note and/or Screen Dumps
14. Task Usage	This view displays the tasks and assignments in the columns and the resources and work on the right-hand side:

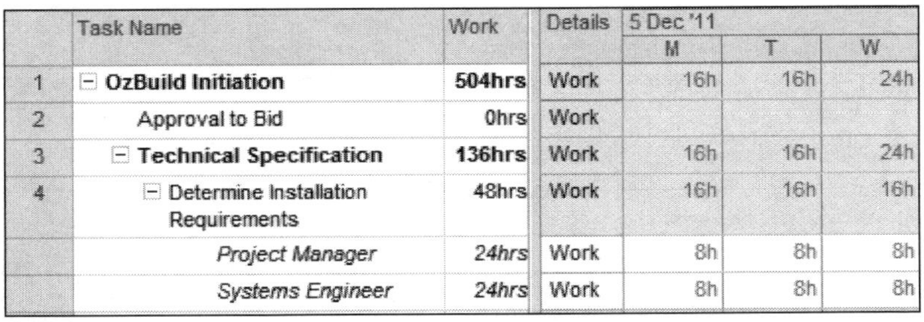

	Task Name	Work	Details	5 Dec '11 M	T	W
1	OzBuild Initiation	504hrs	Work	16h	16h	24h
2	Approval to Bid	0hrs	Work			
3	Technical Specification	136hrs	Work	16h	16h	24h
4	Determine Installation Requirements	48hrs	Work	16h	16h	16h
	Project Manager	*24hrs*	Work	8h	8h	8h
	Systems Engineer	*24hrs*	Work	8h	8h	8h

The columns may be formatted using the **Table** and **Columns** functions.

This View has the following options by right-clicking:

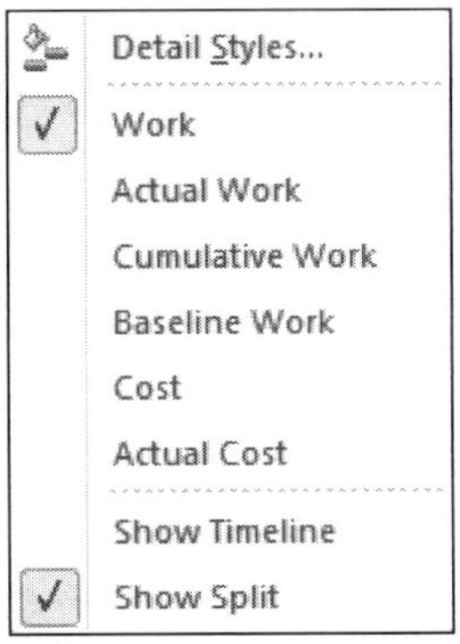

The formatting of the right-hand side of the screen may be changed by right-clicking to open the **Detail Styles** form:

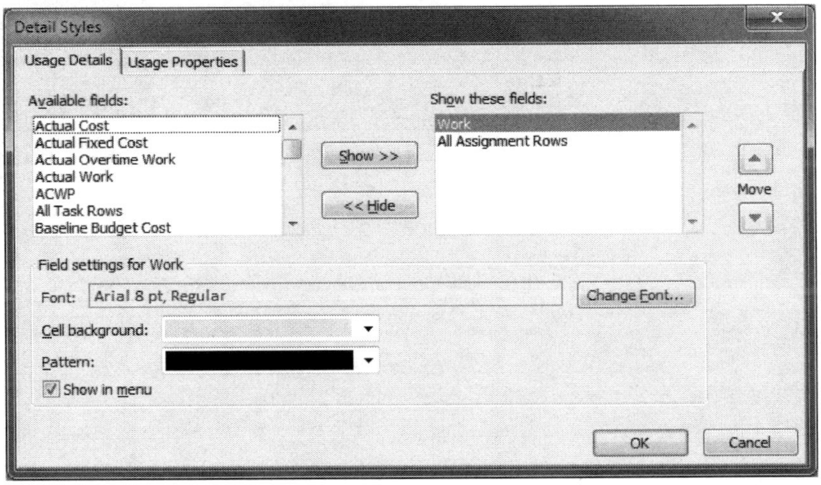

<table>
<tr><th>Screen Name</th><th>Note and/or Screen Dumps</th></tr>
<tr><td>15. Team Planner</td><td>

This view displays the resources on the left-hand side and the tasks assignments on the right:

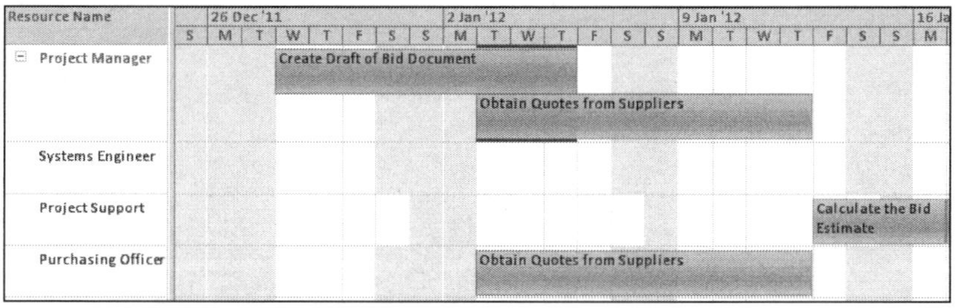

This View has the following options by right-clicking on a task:

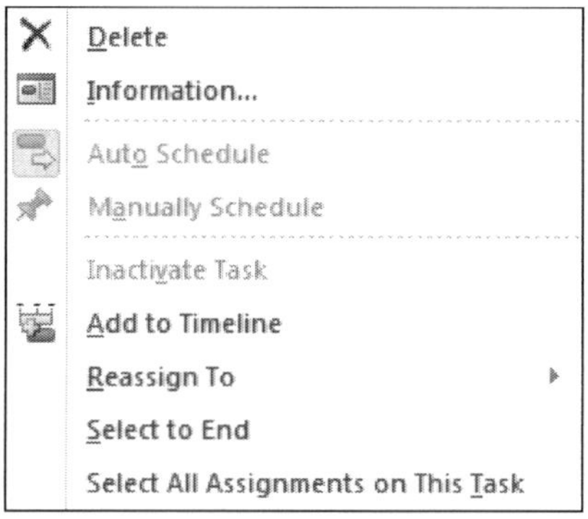

</td></tr>
<tr><td>16. Timeline</td><td>

Must be shown by selecting **View**, **Split View** group and checking **Timeline:**

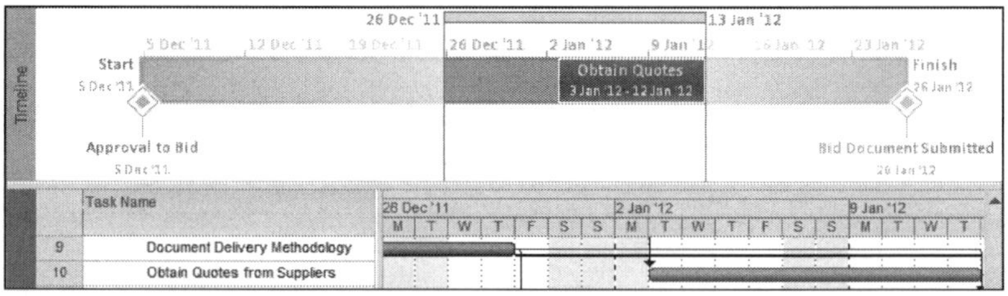

Tasks may be added to the Timeline.

This View has the following options by right-clicking on a task:

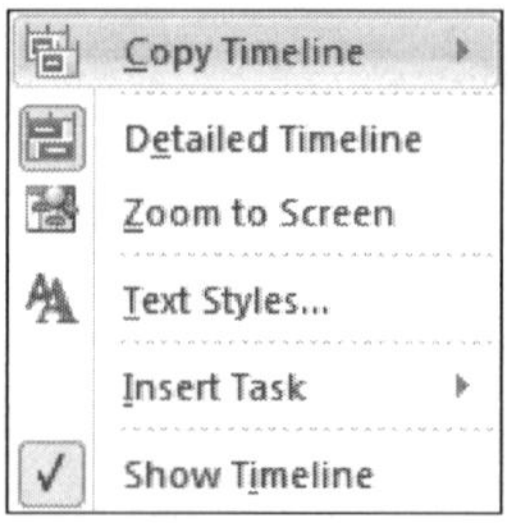

</td></tr>
</table>

26 INDEX

CHANGE Aide

A toolkit for Programme & Project Teams

Features Continued...

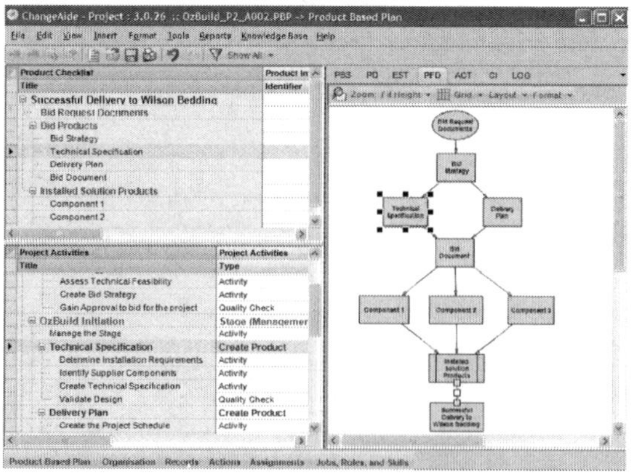

- **Product Flow Diagram (PFD)/ Network Diagram** for all the products identified on the PBS/WBS;
- **Project Tasks** to structure the work needed;
- Project **Daily Log**;
- **Product Description** reports and **Project Task** reports; and
- **Stage PBSs and PFDs** as the project progresses.
- **Status Pictures** to indicate status of the project.

Many potential errors are automatically prevented because these are all consistently merged into a single "PBP container".

Documents can be exported in various formats, including DHTML, PDF, Excel, Word.

Most importantly, ChangeAide will create project plans for instant export into MS Project!

BENEFITS OF ChangeAide

- **Reduces the amount of project manager time** needed to create and maintain consistent Product Based Plans.
- Provides **interactive tracking** of all these project elements and the relationships between them, thus reducing time to find information within the plan.
- Includes **help files and integrated tutorials** to show how to use the toolset.
- Provides **example projects** to demonstrate an integrated view of a Product Based Plan.
- Provides valuable support in **learning and applying the underlying PRINCE2™ methods**.
- Eases the creation of plans for Microsoft Project.
- Provides a **Visual Status** mechanism to highlight incomplete products in ongoing projects.

PRODUCT ENVIRONMENT

ChangeAide can be installed on windows based PCs running Windows 2000 or later as a standalone Microsoft .Net Framework application

AVAILABILITY

ChangeAide is available through Eastwood Harris Pty Ltd at www.eh.com.au, download your trial version now.

Eastwood Harris Pty Ltd Web: www.eh.com.au Email: harrispe@eh.com.au Tel: +61 (0)4 1118 7701 Fax: +61 (0)3 9856 7700

Made in the USA
Monee, IL
01 March 2026

45211016R00205